SIXTH EDITION

REAL ESTATE
An Introduction
to the
Profession

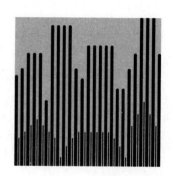

BRUCE M. HARWOOD
CHARLES J. JACOBUS, D.R.E.I.

Regents/Prentice Hall, Englewood Cliffs, New Jersey 07632

Library of Congress Cataloging-in-Publication Data

Harwood, Bruce M.
   Real estate : introduction to the profession / Bruce M. Harwood,
 Charles J. Jacobus. -- 6th ed.
      p.   cm.
   Includes bibliographical references and index.
   ISBN 0-13-765728-5
   1. Real property--United States.   2. Vendors and purchasers-
 -United States.   3. Real estate business--Law and legislation-
 -United States.   I. Jacobus, Charles J.   II. Title.
 KF570.H28 1993
 346.7304'3--dc20
 [347.30643]   92-31971
                                                         CIP

Aquisition Editor: *Jim Boyd, Edward L. Francis*
Editorial/production supervision: *Penelope Linskey*
Interior design: *Peg Kenselaar, Linda Rosa, and Laura Ierardi*
Cover design: *Anne Ricigliano*
Manufacturing buyer: *Ed O'Dougherty*
Prepress buyer: *Ilene Levy*
Editorial Assistant: *Gloria Schaffer*

This book is dedicated
to the memory of Bruce Harwood,
and his commitment to excellence
in real estate education.

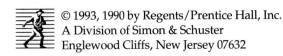 © 1993, 1990 by Regents/Prentice Hall, Inc.
A Division of Simon & Schuster
Englewood Cliffs, New Jersey 07632

Printed in the United States of America

10 9 8 7 6 5 4 3 2 1

0-13-765728-5

Prentice-Hall International (UK) Limited, *London*
Prentice-Hall of Australia Pty. Limited, *Sydney*
Prentice-Hall Canada Inc., *Toronto*
Prentice-Hall Hispanoamericana, S.A., *Mexico*
Prentice-Hall of India Private Limited, *New Delhi*
Prentice-Hall of Japan, Inc., *Tokyo*
Simon & Schuster Asia Pte. Ltd., *Singapore*
Editors Prentice-Hall do Brazil, Ltda., *Rio de Janeiro*

Contents

Preface

Is your goal a full-time or part-time career in real estate? Do you own or plan to own your home or an investment property? Are you a student of real estate desiring to broaden your knowledge of this subject? If you answered "Yes" to one or more of these questions, the contents of this book will be of immense help to you.

In this book you will learn about real estate brokerage, appraisal, financing, contracts, closings, and investing. Additionally, you will learn about land descriptions, rights and interests, fair housing, taxes, leases, condominiums, zoning, careers, and licensing and the use of computers in real estate. You will find particularly valuable the attention given to such timely topics as a real estate agent's liability and professional obligation to buyers and sellers, brokers who represent buyers, advance fee listings, errors and omission insurance, foreclosure, and timesharing. Included throughout the book are numerous examples from actual practice, including important decisions in several recent court cases.

Throughout this book emphasis is placed on an easily readable style of writing that will take and lead you through the chapters in a pleasant and enjoyable experience. You will find emphasis placed on explanations that combine "how" things are done in real estate with "why" they are done. Numerous tables, sketches, and diagrams will help you to visualize real estate rights and interests, financing techniques, appraisal methods, closing statements, and map reading. Simplified, plain English examples of real estate documents are used so their key elements can be easily identified and not lost in a maze of legal language. Warranty deeds, grant deeds, quitclaim deeds, trust deeds, title insurance policies, promissory notes, and mortgages are among the documents so treated.

Starting with Chapter 2, key real estate terms are listed and defined at the beginning of each chapter in addition to being explained in the chapter. Correspondingly, you will find end-of-the-chapter vocabulary reviews plus questions and problems to test your comprehension of the material just read. Also presented at the end of each chapter are additional readings you may wish to use in furthering your real estate education.

The appendices of this book contain easy-to-understand residential construction illustrations plus sample questions typical of those found on real estate license tests. You will also find a real estate math review and answers to the chapter-end vocabulary reviews, questions, and problems. Lastly, there is a combined index and glossary that allows you to simultaneously find a short definition of a word and a page reference for further information.

Charles J. Jacobus received his Bachelor of Science degree from the University of Houston in 1970, and his Doctor of Jurisprudence degree from the University of Houston Law Center in 1973. He is Board Certified by the State Bar of Texas as a Specialist in both Commercial and Residential Real Estate Law. He is a member of the American College of Real Estate Lawyers, has served as President of the Real Estate Educators Association, and Chairman of the Real Estate Section of the Houston Bar Association. He is a frequent lecturer at various educational programs throughout the United States, is currently Editor-in-Chief of the Texas Real Estate Law Reporter, and Chairman of the American Bar Association's Committee on Real Estate Brokers and Brokerage.

Bruce Harwood completed his undergraduate work in real estate at the University of California, Berkeley, in 1963. In 1972 he completed doctoral studies in Business Administration, with a specialization in finance and real estate, at the University of Colorado. He has taught real estate at the college level in Florida, Colorado, California, and Hawaii. Dr. Harwood passed away on February 7, 1987, leaving behind a legacy which will benefit us all for many years to come.

Criticisms of and suggestions for improving this book are welcomed. They should be sent to the Real Estate Editor, College Editorial Department, Prentice Hall, Englewood Cliffs, N.J. 07632.

ACKNOWLEDGMENTS

A personal thanks to the following people who by written correspondence, telephone calls, or personal meeting have helped to shape this book:

Floyd Adashek, Otis T. Amory, David F. Barry, Merlin Bauer, Sandy Berens, A. L. Bocchini, Sandra Bodie, Barry W. Bosiger, Arthur Bowman, Carolyn Bohling, Mark Brothers, Carolyn R. Burdette, Charles P. Cartee, Martin I. Caruso, Sandra Cece, Jerry C. Chaney, Lowell D. Clay, Tom Cook, John Cornelius, Robert Coulthard, Wallace Dean Davis, James O. Desreumaux, Keith Donaldson, Burnell Ellis, Jack Ellis, D. Delos Ellsworth, Bernard DiOrio, Charles E. Fadely II, Barney Fletcher, Al Ganser, Carroll Gentry, Thomas E. Gillett, Helen L. Grant, Glen O. Grimmel, Steven Guice, Jr., Willis F. Gupton, Charles Haley, Ronald W. Halsac, Martin Hass, John W. Hill, Lynn Hoover, Anne Hruby, Joseph W. Isert, Jr., Ed Jutzi, F. Jeffrey Keil, Jack Kessinger, Jay Lamont, Cecil Lawter, David Lawter, Frank Lembo, Bruce Lindeman, Bernard W. Luster, Tom Lynch, Darline Mallick, Ralph K. Manley, Jerlyn L. Mardis, Ben Marilla, John Marshall, Jr., Roger Meade, Don Moseley, Susan Moseley, Narayanaswamy H. Nadig, Alan Natella, W. F. Orth, Gene Padgham, Leonard Palumbo, Linda Phillips, Lee Frew Platt, Hugh Prichard, Judith Rachap, Clyde W. Richey, Phil Sapp, Elaine Schiff, Rudy Schmidt, Malcolm Searle, Terry Selles, Laurence L. Shapiro, Carolyn Shea, Morris Sleight, Marie Spodek, Martie Stegall, Jean Tate, John P. Torbush, Brad Vincent, Hugo Weber, Jr., Wayne Weeks, A. P. Werbner, Dorothy Whetstone, Evonne Whitney, Kathleen Witalisz, and Michael Witt.

There are also those to whom I owe a special debt in preparing this edition: Sherry Weeks and Barbara Appel.

Introduction to Real Estate

Welcome!

Real estate is a unique subject, and because it is unique, real estate has spawned complex legal theories and very unusual fact situations. No two situations are ever exactly alike, and the subject never ceases to be intellectually stimulating. Everyone has a favorite story about real estate, and it has remained a fascinating topic for centuries. This fascination is what makes real estate such a fun, interesting business.

As a new real estate student, one must be prepared to learn a lot of new concepts, and be willing to commit the time and effort to that end. There are some who say that the only way to learn real estate is by experience. Many years ago this was the traditional concept. Real estate was then considered to be a "marketing" or "salesmanship" business, and experience was the best teacher. Recent years, however, have seen the development of extensive academic applications in real estate education. Real estate has come to the academic forefront—undergraduate degrees in real estate are becoming more common, and graduate-level degree programs are proliferating. There is also a resulting emphasis on the professionalism and ethics of these new real estate professionals. Unlike many other academic subjects, however, real estate continues to emphasize experience in the "people oriented" aspects of the business. Experience has a high correlation with success in the real estate business.

With these combinations in mind, this book has been written to provide you with an understanding of the basic principles and business fundamentals of real estate. Emphasis is placed on an easily readable presentation that combines explanations of the basic principles of the subject with the "why" things are done and "how" these principles apply to everyday activities.

HOW TO READ THIS BOOK

At the beginning of each chapter (2 through 23) there is a list of the new Key Terms that you will learn, along with brief definitions. Read these before starting the chapter. In the body of the chapter these terms, as well as other terms important to real estate, are set in **boldface type** and are given a more in-depth discussion. At the end of each chapter is a vocabulary review plus questions and problems. These are designed to help you test yourself on your comprehension of the material in the chapter you've just read. The answers are given in Appendix D in the back of the book.

Also at the back of this book is a combined index and glossary, meant to reinforce your familiarity with the language of real estate. Terms in this index and glossary receive a short definition, followed by a page reference for more detailed discussion.

Another feature of this book is its simplified documents. Deeds, mortgages and title policies, for example, are sometimes written in legal language which may be confusing to anyone except a lawyer. In the chapters ahead, you will find simplified versions of these documents, written in plain English and set in standard size type. The intention is to give you a clearer understanding of these important real estate documents.

Another special feature of this book is the wide margin on each page. Besides its eye appeal, it is helpful for locating subject headings and provides handy space for your study notes.

TRANSACTION OVERVIEW

Figure 1:1 provides a visual summary of the real estate transaction cycle. It is included here to give you an overview of the different steps involved in the sale of real property and to show

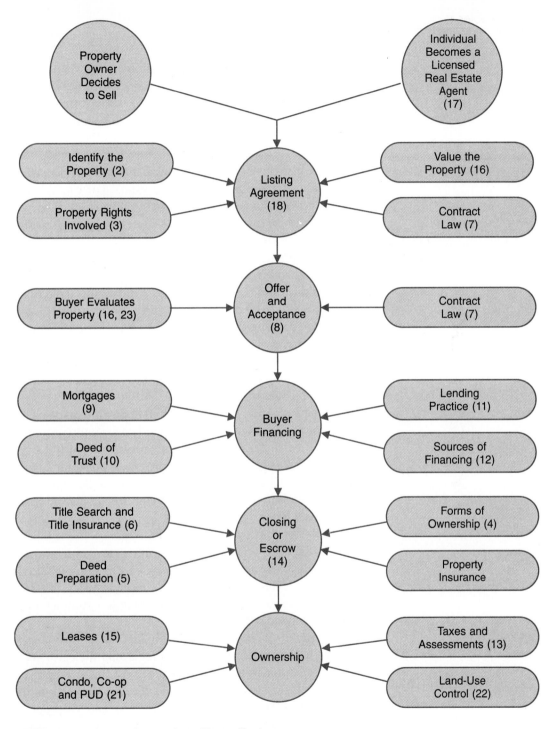

NOTE: Numbers in parentheses refer to Chapter Numbers.

Figure 1:1. An Overview of a Real Estate Transaction

how these steps are related to one another. The chapter where each step is discussed is shown in parentheses. Whether your point of view is that of a real estate agent, owner, buyer, or seller, you will find the chapters which follow to be informative and valuable.

Chapter Organization   Great care has been taken to organize this text in a manner that will build your knowledge of real estate. For example, land description methods and rights and interests in land are necessary to sales contracts, abstracts, deeds, mortgages, and listings and therefore are discussed early in the text.

In Chapter 2 you will find such topics as metes and bounds and tract maps. You will also find a discussion of what is real estate and what is not, and how land is physically and economically different from other commodities. Having described real estate, the next logical step is to look at the various rights and interests that exist in a given parcel of land. In Chapter 3 you will see that there is much more to ownership of land than meets the eye! In Chapter 4 we look at how a given right or interest in land can be held by an individual, by two or more persons, or by a business entity. Included in this chapter are discussions of joint tenancy, tenancy in common, and community property.

Chapters 5 and 6 deal with the process by which the ownership of real estate is transferred from one person to another. In particular, Chapter 5 discusses deeds and wills, and Chapter 6 deals with how a person gives evidence to the world that he possesses a given right or interest in land. Abstracts and title insurance are among the topics included.

In Chapters 7 and 8 we turn to contract law and its application to offers and acceptances. Because so much of what takes place in real estate is in the form of contracts, you will want to have a solid understanding of what makes a contract legally binding, and what doesn't.

Chapters 9 through 12 are devoted to real estate finance. In Chapter 9 mortgages and the laws regarding their use are explained. Chapter 10 covers the deed of trust and is intended for readers in those states where the deed of trust is used in place of a mortgage. Amortized loans, points, FHA and VA programs, loan application, and mortgage insurance are discussed in Chapter 11. Mortgage lenders, the secondary mortgage market, due-on-sale clauses, adjustable rate mortgages, and financing alternatives are covered in Chapter 12.

In Chapter 13 we see how property taxes and assessments are calculated, and Chapter 14 explains title closing and escrow. Chapter 15 deals with leasing real estate and includes a sample lease document with discussion. Chapter 16 explores the language, principles, and techniques of real estate appraisal.

Chapter 17 deals with real estate license law requirements, how a salesperson chooses a broker, and professional ethics. In Chapter 18 we examine the relationship between real estate agents and buyers and sellers. Chapter 19 concentrates on the law of agency. Special emphasis is placed on the duties and obligations of brokers to their clients and on fair housing laws in Chapter 20.

The remaining chapters of this book deal with a number of individual and specialized real estate topics. Chapter 21 explores the condominium, cooperative, and planned unit development forms of real estate ownership. Included is a look at how they are created and the various rights and interests in land that are created by them including timesharing.

Zoning, land planning, and deed restrictions are covered in Chapter 22. These are important topics because any limitation on a landowner's right to develop and use land can have a substantial effect on its value. The final chapter, Chapter 23, is an introduction to the opportunities available to you as a real estate investor. Topics include tax shelter, equity build-up, what to buy, and when to buy.

Following the final chapter are several appendices which you will find useful. There are compound interest, present value, and measurement conversion tables. (Amortization and loan balance tables are located in Chapter 11.) There is also an appendix containing construction illustrations to help acquaint you with construction terminology. Additionally, you will find a short real estate math review section plus the answers to the quizzes and problems found at the end of Chapters 2 through 23.

CAREER OPPORTUNITIES

The contents and organization of this book are designed for people who are interested in real estate because they now own or plan to own real estate, and for people who are interested in real estate as a career. It is to those who are considering real estate as a profession that the balance of this chapter is devoted.

Most people who are considering a career in real estate think of becoming a real estate agent who specializes in selling homes. This is quite natural because home selling is the most visible segment of the real estate industry. It is the area of the business most people enter, and the one in which most practicing real estate licensees make their living. Selling residential property is a good experience. Entry level positions are more available, and it can help you to decide whether or not real estate sales appeals to you.

Residential Brokerage

Residential brokerage requires a broad knowledge of the community and its neighborhoods, an understanding of real estate principles, law and practice, and an ability to work well with people. Working hours will often include nights and weekends as these times are usually most convenient to buyers and sellers. A residential agent must also supply an automobile that is suitable for taking clients to see property.

In only a few real estate offices are new residential salespersons given a minimum guaranteed salary or a draw against future commissions. Therefore, a newcomer should have enough capital to survive until the first commissions are earned—and that can take four to six months. Additionally, the salesperson must be capable of developing and handling a personal budget that will withstand the feast and famine cycles that can occur in real estate selling.

A person who is adept at interpersonal relations, who can identify clients' buying motives and find the property to fit, will probably be quite successful in this business.

Commercial Brokerage

Commercial brokers, also called income property brokers, specialize in income-producing properties such as apartment and office buildings, retail stores, and warehouses. In this specialty, the salesperson is primarily selling monetary benefits. These benefits are the income, appreciation, mortgage reduction, and tax shelter that a property can reasonably be expected to produce.

To be successful in income property brokerage, one must be very competent in mathematics, know how to finance transactions, and keep abreast of current tax laws. One must also have a sense for what makes a good investment, what makes an investment salable, and what the growth possibilities are in the neighborhood where a property is located.

Commission income from commercial brokerage is likely to be less frequent, but in larger amounts than from residential brokerage. The time required to break into the business is longer, but once in the business, agent turnover is low. The working hours of a commercial broker are much closer to regular business hours than for those in residential selling.

Industrial brokers specialize in finding suitable land and buildings for industrial concerns. This includes leasing and developing industrial property as well as listing and selling it. An industrial broker must be familiar with industry requirements such as proximity to raw materials, water and power, labor supplies, and transportation. An industrial broker must also know about local building, zoning, and tax laws as they pertain to possible sites, and about the schools, housing, cultural, and recreational facilities that would be used by future employees of the plant.

Industrial Brokerage

Commissions are irregular, but usually substantial. Working hours are regular business hours and sales efforts are primarily aimed at locating facts and figures and presenting them to clients in an orderly fashion. Industrial clients are usually sophisticated business people. Gaining entry to industrial brokerage and acquiring a client list can be slow.

With the rapid disappearance of the family farm, the farm broker's role is changing. Today a farm broker must be equally capable of handling the 160-acre spread of farmer Jones and the 10,000-acre operation owned by an agribusiness corporation. College training in agriculture is an advantage and on-the-job training is a must. Knowledge of soils, seeds, plants, fertilizers, production methods, new machinery, government subsidies, and tax laws is vital to success. Farm brokerage offers as many opportunities to earn commissions and fees from leasing and property management as from listing and selling property.

Farm Brokerage

For an investment property, the property manager's job is to supervise every aspect of a property's operation so as to produce the highest possible financial return over the longest

Property Management

period of time. The manager's tasks include renting, tenant relations, building repair and maintenance, accounting, advertising, and supervision of personnel and tradesmen.

The current boom in condominiums has resulted in a growing demand for property managers to maintain them. In addition, large businesses that own property for their own use hire property managers. Property managers are usually paid a salary, and if the property is a rental, a bonus for keeping the building fully occupied. To be successful, a property manager should be not only a public relations expert and a good bookkeeper, but also at ease with tenants, handy with tools, and knowledgeable about laws applicable to rental units.

Rental Listing Services

In some cities there are rental listing services that help tenants find rental units and landlords find tenants. Most compile lists of available rentals and sell this information to persons looking for rentals. A few also charge the landlord for listing the property. The objective is to save a person time and gasoline by providing pertinent information on a large number of rentals. Each property on the list is accompanied by information regarding location, size, rent, security deposit, pet policy, etc.

Especially popular in cities with substantial numbers of single persons are roommate listing services. These maintain files on persons with space to share (such as the second bedroom in a two-bedroom apartment) and those looking for space. The files contain such information as location, rent, gender, smoking preference, etc. Most roommate and rental listing services have been started by individual entrepreneurs and are not affiliated with real estate offices. Depending on the state, a real estate license may or may not be required.

Real Estate Appraising

The job of the real estate appraiser is to gather and evaluate all available facts affecting a property's value. Appraisal is a real estate career opportunity that does not require property selling; however, it does demand a special set of skills of its own. The job requires practical experience, technical education, and good judgment. If you have an analytical mind and like to collect and interpret data, you might consider becoming a real estate appraiser. The job combines office work and field work, and the income of an expert appraiser can match that of a top real estate salesperson. One can be an independent appraiser, or there are numerous opportunities to work as a salaried appraiser for local tax authorities or lending institutions. The appraisal process is now becoming more complex, however. Most lenders and taxing authorities require that their appraisers have some advanced credential designation to assure an adequate level of competence.

Approximately one-third of the land in the United States is government owned. This includes vacant and forested lands, office buildings, museums, parks, zoos, schools, hospitals, public housing, libraries, fire and police stations, roads and highways, subways, airports, and courthouses. All of these are real estate and all of these require government employees who can negotiate purchases and sales, appraise, finance, manage, plan, and develop. Cities, counties, and state governments all have extensive real estate holdings. At the federal level, the Forest Service, Park Service, Department of Agriculture, Army Corps of Engineers, Bureau of Land Management, and General Services Administration are all major landholders. In addition to outright real estate ownership, government agencies such as the Federal Housing Administration, VA, and Federal Home Loan Bank employ thousands of real estate specialists to operate their real estate lending programs.

Government Service

Most new homes in the United States are built by developers who in turn sell them to homeowners and investors. Some homes are built by small-scale developers who produce only a few a year. Others are part of 400-home subdivisions and 40-story condominiums that are developed and constructed by large corporations that have their own planning, appraising, financing, construction, and marketing personnel. There is equal opportunity for success in development whether you build 4 houses a year or work for a firm that builds 400 a year.

Land Development

Urban planners work with local governments and civic groups for the purpose of anticipating future growth and land-use changes. The urban planner makes recommendations for new streets, highways, sewer and water lines, schools, parks, and libraries. Emphasis on environmental protection and controlled growth has made urban planning one of real estate's most rapidly expanding specialties. An urban planning job is usually a salaried position and does not emphasize sales ability.

Urban Planning

Mortgage Financing

Specialists in mortgage financing have a dual role: (1) to find economically sound properties for lenders, and (2) to locate money for borrowers. A mortgage specialist can work independently, receiving a fee from the borrower for locating a lender, or as a salaried employee of a lending institution. The ease with which mortgages can be bought and sold has encouraged many individuals to open their own mortgage companies in competition with established lending institutions. Some mortgage specialists also offer real estate loan consulting for a fee. They will help a borrower choose from among the numerous mortgage loan formats available today, find the best loan for the client, and assist in filling out and processing the loan application.

Securities and Syndications

Limited partnerships and other forms of real estate syndications that combine the investment capital of a number of investors to buy large properties number in the thousands. The investment opportunities and professional management offered by syndications are eagerly sought after by people with money to invest in real estate. As a result, there are job opportunities in creating, promoting, and managing real estate syndications.

Consulting

Real estate consulting involves giving others advice about real estate for a fee. A consultant must have a very broad knowledge about real estate including financing, appraising, brokerage, management, development, construction, investing, leasing, zoning, taxes, title, economics, and law. To remain in business as a consultant, one must develop a good track record of successful suggestions and advice.

Research and Education

A person interested in real estate research can concentrate on such matters as improved construction materials and management methods, or on finding answers to economic questions such as "What is the demand for homes going to be next year in this community (state, country)?"

Opportunities abound in real estate education. Nearly all states require the completion of specified real estate courses before a real estate license can be issued. A growing number of states also require continued education for license renewal. As a result, persons with experience in the industry and an ability to effectively teach the subject are much sought after as instructors.

One of the advantages of the free enterprise system is that you can choose to become a full-time investor solely for yourself. A substantial number of people have quit their jobs to work full time with their investment properties and have done quite well at it. A popular and successful route for many has been to purchase, inexpensively and with a low down payment, a small apartment building that has not been maintained, but is in a good neighborhood. The property is then thoroughly reconditioned and rents are raised. This process increases the value of the property. The increase is parlayed into a larger building—often through a tax-deferred exchange, and the process is repeated. Alternatively, the investor can increase the mortgage loan on the building and take the cash he receives as a "salary" for himself or use it as a down payment on another not-too-well maintained apartment building in a good neighborhood. This can also be done with single-family houses. It is not unusual for an investor to acquire several dozen rental houses over a period of years.

Full-time Investor

Other individual investors have done well financially by searching newspaper ads and regularly visiting real estate brokerage offices looking for underpriced properties that can be sold at a mark-up. A variation of this is to write to out-of-town property owners in a given neighborhood to see if any wish to sell at a bargain price. Another approach is to become a small-scale developer and contractor. (No license is needed if you work with your own property.) Through your own personal efforts you create value in your projects and then hold them as investments.

Property owners who deal only with their own property are not required to hold a real estate license. However, any person who for compensation or the promise of compensation lists or offers to list, sells or offers to sell, buys or offers to buy, negotiates or offers to negotiate either directly or indirectly for the purpose of bringing about a sale, purchase, or option to purchase, exchange, auction, lease, or rental of real estate, or any interest in real estate, is required to hold a valid real estate license. Some states also require persons offering their services as real estate appraisers, property managers, syndicators, counselors, mortgage bankers, or rent collectors to hold real estate licenses.

LICENSE REQUIREMENTS

If your real estate plans are such that you may need a license, you should skip ahead to Chapter 18 and read the material there regarding real estate licensing.

Nature and Description of Real Estate

In this chapter you will be introduced to the terminology used to define and describe real estate. Real estate is defined, and rights in land are also described. Other topics include fixtures, appurtenances, water rights, and land descriptions. The metes and bounds description of land and the rectangular survey system of describing land is also covered as well as other land descriptive survey systems. The chapter is concluded with coverage of the physical and economic characteristics of land. Key terms, such as scarcity, homogeneity, immobility, fixity, and situs are also defined. These and other defined terms within this second chapter should be studied thoroughly and be remembered to enhance your understanding of material in subsequent chapters.

OVERVIEW OF CHAPTER 2

LEARNING OBJECTIVES

After successful completion of this chapter, you should be able to:
1. Define real estate, land, improvements, fixtures, and water rights.
2. Apply the tests of a fixture.
3. Define such terms as the water table, riparian rights, littoral rights, and other such terms dealing with water rights.
4. Describe land by using the metes and bounds method, the rectangular survey system, or by a recorded plat.
5. Explain the use of assessor's parcel numbers.
6. Describe the land in terms of vertical measurements.
7. Explain the physical characteristics of land.
8. Explain the economic characteristics of land.
9. Understand the significance of "location, location, location."

KEY • TERMS

Fixture: an object that has been attached to land so as to become real estate

Improvements: any form of land development, such as buildings, roads, fences, pipelines, etc.

Meridians: imaginary lines running north and south, used as references in mapping land

Metes and bounds: a detailed method of land description that identifies a parcel by specifying its shape and boundaries

Monument: an iron pipe, stone, tree, or other fixed point used in making a survey

Personal property: a right or interest in things of a temporary or movable nature; anything not classed as real property

Real estate: land and improvements in a physical sense as well as the rights to own or use them

Recorded plat: a subdivision map filed in the county recorder's office that shows the location and boundaries of individual parcels of land

Riparian right: the right of a landowner whose land borders a river or stream to use and enjoy that water

What is real estate? **Real estate** or **real property** is land and the improvements made to land, and the rights to use them. Let us begin in this chapter by looking more closely at what is meant by land and improvements. Then in the next chapter we shall focus our attention on the various rights one may possess in land and improvements.

LAND

Often we think of land as only the surface of the earth. But, it is substantially more than that. As Figure 2:1 illustrates, land starts at the center of the earth, passes through the earth's surface, and continues on into space. An understanding of this concept is important because, given a particular parcel of land, it is possible for one person to own the rights to use its surface **(surface rights)**, another to own the rights to drill or dig below its surface **(subsurface rights)**, and still another to own the rights to use the airspace above it **(air rights)**.

IMPROVEMENTS

Anything affixed to land with the intent of being permanent is considered to be part of the land and therefore real estate. Thus houses, schools, factories, barns, fences, roads, pipelines, and landscaping are real estate. As a group, these are referred to as **improvements** because they improve or develop land.

Being able to identify what is real estate and what is not is important. For example, in conveying ownership to a house,

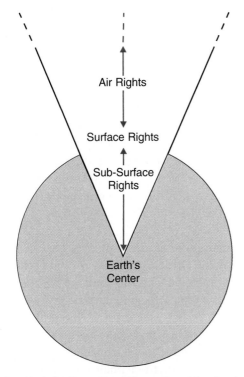

Land includes the surface of the earth and the sky above and everything to the center of the earth.

Figure 2:1.

only the lot is described in the deed. It is not necessary to describe the dwelling unit itself, or the landscaping, driveways, sidewalks, wiring, or plumbing. Items that are not a part of the land, such as tables, chairs, beds, desks, automobiles, farm machinery, and the like, are classified as **personal property**; if the right to use them is to be transferred to the buyer, there must be a separate **bill of sale** in addition to the deed. Broadly speaking, personal property is everything that is not real property and vice versa.

When an object that was once personal property is attached to land (or a building thereon) so as to become real estate, it is called a **fixture**. As a rule, a fixture is the property of the landowner and when the land is conveyed to a new owner, it is automatically included with the land. The question of whether an item is a fixture also arises with regard to property taxes, mortgages,

FIXTURES

lease terminations, and hazard insurance policies. Specifically, real estate taxes are based on real property valuation. Real estate mortgages are secured by real property. Objects attached to a building by a tenant may become real property and hence belong to the building's owner. Hazard insurance policies treat real property differently than personal property.

Whether or not an object becomes real estate depends on whether the object was affixed or installed with the **intention** of permanently improving the land. Intention is evidenced by four tests: (1) the manner of attachment, (2) the adaptation of the object, (3) the existence of an agreement, and (4) the relationship of the parties involved.

Manner of Attachment

The first test, **manner of attachment**, refers to how the object is attached to the land. Ordinarily, when an object which was once personal property is attached to land by virtue of its being imbedded in the land or affixed to the land by means of cement, nails, bolts, etc., it becomes a fixture. To illustrate, when asphalt and concrete for driveways and sidewalks are still on the delivery truck, they are movable and therefore personal property. But once they are poured into place, the asphalt and concrete become part of the land. Similarly, lumber, wiring, pipes, doors, toilets, sinks, water heaters, furnaces, and other construction materials change from personal property to real estate when they become part of a building. Items brought into the house that do not become permanently affixed to the land remain personal property; for example, furniture, clothing, cooking utensils, radios, and television sets.

Adaptation of the Object

Historically, the manner of attachment was the only method of classifying an object as personal property or real estate, but as time progressed this test alone was no longer adequate. For example, how would you classify custom-made drapes, made for an unusual window? For the answer, we must apply a second test: **How is the article adapted** to the building? If the drapes are specifically made for the window, they are automatically included in the purchase or rental of the building. Another example is the key to a house. Although it spends most of its useful life in a pocket or purse, it is nonetheless quite specifically adapted to the house and therefore a part of it.

The third test is the **existence of an agreement** between the parties involved. For example, a seller can clarify in advance and in writing to the broker what he considers personal property and thus will be removed, and what he does not consider personal property and thus will transfer to the buyer. Likewise, a tenant may obtain an agreement from his landlord stating that items installed by the tenant will not be considered fixtures by the landlord. When it is not readily clear if an item is real or personal property, the use of a well-written agreement can avoid a subsequent controversy.

Existence of an Agreement

The fourth test in determining whether an item of personal property has become a fixture is to look at the **relationship of the parties**. For example, a supermarket moves into a rented building, then buys and bolts to the floor various **trade fixtures** such as display shelves, meat and dairy coolers, frozen-food counters, and checkout stands. When the supermarket later moves out, do these items, by virtue of their attachment, become the property of the building owner? Modern courts rule that tenant-owned trade fixtures do not become the property of the landlord. However, they must be removed before the expiration of the lease and without seriously damaging the building.

Relationship of the Parties

Trees, cultivated perennial plants, and uncultivated vegetation of any sort are considered part of the land. For example, landscaping is included in the sale or rental of a house. If a tenant plants a tree or plant in the ground while renting, the tree or plant stays when the lease expires unless both landlord and tenant agree otherwise. Plants and trees in movable pots are personal property and are not generally included in a sale or lease.

Ownership of Plants, Trees, and Crops

Annual cultivated crops are called **emblements** and most courts of law regard them as personal property even though they are attached to the soil. For example, a tenant farmer is entitled to the fruits of his labor even though the landlord terminates the lease part way through the growing season. When property with harvestable plants, trees, or crops is offered for sale or lease, it is good practice to make clear in any listing, sale, or lease agreement who will have the right to harvest the crop that season. This is particularly true of farm property where the value of the crop can be quite substantial.

APPURTENANCES   The conveyance of land carries with it any appurtenances to the land. An **appurtenance** is a right or privilege or improvement that belongs to and passes with land but is not necessarily a part of the land. Examples of appurtenances are easements and rights-of-way (discussed in Chapter 3), condominium parking stalls, and shares of stock in a mutual water company that services the land.

WATER RIGHTS   The ownership of land that borders on a river or stream carries with it the right to use that water in common with the other landowners whose lands border the same watercourse. This is known as a **riparian right**. The landowner does not have absolute ownership of the water that flows past his land but may use it in a reasonable manner. In some states, riparian rights have been modified by the **doctrine of prior appropriation**: the first owner to divert water for his own use may continue to do so, even though it is not equitable to the other landowners along the watercourse. Where land borders on a lake or sea, it is said to carry **littoral rights** rather than riparian rights. Littoral rights allow a landowner to use and enjoy the water touching his land provided he does not alter the water's position by artificial means. A lakefront lot owner would be an example of this.

Ownership of land normally includes the right to drill for and remove water found below the surface. Where water is not confined to a defined underground waterway, it is known as **percolating water**. In some states a landowner has the right, in conjunction with neighboring owners, to draw his share of percolating water. Other states subscribe to the doctrine of prior appropriation. When speaking of underground water, the term **water table** refers to the upper limit of percolating water below the earth's surface. It is also called the **groundwater level**. This may be only a few feet below the surface or hundreds of feet down.

LAND DESCRIPTIONS   There are six commonly used methods of describing the location of land: (1) informal reference, (2) metes and bounds, (3) rectangular survey system, (4) recorded plat, (5) assessor parcel number, and (6) reference to documents other than maps. We shall look at each in detail.

Street numbers and place names are informal references: the house located at 7216 Maple Street; the apartment identified as Apartment 101, 875 First Street; the office identified as Suite 222, 3570 Oakview Boulevard; or the ranch known as the Rocking K Ranch—in each case followed by the city (or county) and state where it is located—are informal references. The advantage of an informal reference is that it is easily understood. The disadvantage from a real estate standpoint is that it is not a precise method of land description: a street number or place name does not provide the boundaries of the land at that location, and these numbers and names change over the years. Consequently, in real estate the use of informal references is limited to situations in which convenience is more important than precision. Thus, in a rental contract, Apartment 101, 875 First Street, city and state, is sufficient for a tenant to find the apartment unit. However, if you were buying the apartment building, you would want a more precise land description.

Informal References

Early land descriptions in America depended heavily on convenient natural or man-made objects called **monuments**. A stream might serve to mark one side of a parcel, an old oak tree to mark a corner, a road another side, a pile of rocks a second corner, a fence another side, and so forth. This survey method was handy, but it had two major drawbacks: there might not be a convenient corner or boundary marker where one was needed, and over time, oak trees died, stone heaps were moved, streams and rivers changed course, stumps rotted, fences were removed, and unused roads became overgrown with vegetation. The following description excerpted from the Hartford, Connecticut probate court records for 1812 illustrates just how difficult it can be to try to precisely locate a parcel's boundaries using only convenient natural or man-made objects:

Metes and Bounds

> Commencing at a heap of stone about a stone's throw from a certain small clump of alders, near a brook running down off from a rather high part of said ridge; thence, by a straight line to a certain marked white birch tree, about two or three times as far from a jog in a fence going around a ledge nearby; thence by another straight line in a different direction,

around said ledge, and the Great Swamp, so called; thence... to the "Horn," so called, and passing around the same as aforesaid, as far as the "Great Bend," so called, and... to a stake and stone not far off from the old Indian trail; thence, by another straight line ... to the stump of the big hemlock tree where Philo Blake killed the bear; thence, to the corner begun at by two straight lines of about equal length, which are to be run by some skilled and competent surveyor, so as to include the area and acreage as herein before set forth.[*]

Permanent Monuments

The drawbacks of the above outmoded method of land description are resolved by setting a permanent man-made **monument** at one corner of the parcel. This monument will typically be an iron pin or pipe one to two inches in diameter driven several feet into the ground. Sometimes concrete or stone monuments are used. To guard against the possibility that the monument might later be destroyed or removed, it is referenced by means of a connection line to a nearby permanent reference mark established by a government survey agency. Other parcels in the vicinity will also be referenced to the same permanent reference mark.

The surveyor then describes the parcel in terms of distance and direction from that point. This is called **metes and bounds** surveying, which means distance (metes) and direction (bounds). From the monument, the surveyor runs the parcel's outside lines by compass and distance so as to take in the land area being described. Distances are measured in feet, usually to the nearest one-tenth or one-hundredth of a foot. Direction is shown in degrees, minutes, and seconds. There are 360 degrees (°) in a circle, 60 minutes (') in each degree, and 60 seconds (") in each minute. The abbreviation 29°14'52" would be read as 29 degrees, 14 minutes, and 52 seconds. Figure 2:2 illustrates a simple modern metes and bounds land description.

Note in Figure 2:2 that with a metes and bounds description you start from a permanent reference mark and travel to the nearest corner of the property. This is where the parcel survey begins and is called the **point of beginning** or **point of**

[*] F. H. Moffit and Harry Bouchard, *Surveying*, 6th ed. (New York: Harper and Row, 1975). By permission.

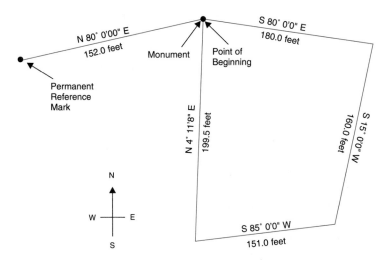

Figure 2:2. Describing Land by Metes and Bounds

commencement. From this point in Figure 2:2, we travel clockwise along the parcel's perimeter, reaching the next corner by going in the direction 80 degrees east of south for a distance of 180 feet. We then travel in a direction 15 degrees west of south for 160 feet, thence 85 degrees west of south for 151 feet, and thence 4 degrees, 11 minutes, and 18 seconds east of north for 199.5 feet back to the point of beginning. In mapping shorthand, this parcel would be described by first identifying the monument, then the county and state within which it lies, and "thence S80°0'0"E, 180.0'; thence S15°0'0"W, 160.0'; thence S85°0'0"W, 151.0'; thence N4°11'18"E, 199.5' back to the p.o.b." Although one can successfully describe a parcel by traveling around it either clockwise or counterclockwise, it is customary to travel clockwise.

The job of taking a written land description (such as the one just described) and locating it on the ground is done by a two-person survey team. The survey team drives a wooden or metal stake into the ground at each corner of the parcel. If a corner lies on a sidewalk, a nail through a brass disc about one-half inch wide is used. (Look closely for these next time you are out walking. At construction sites you will see that corner stakes often have colored streamers on them.) The basic equipment of a survey team includes a compass, a transit, a sight pole or rod, a steel tape, and a computation book. A transit

Survey Team

consists of a very accurate compass plus a telescope with cross hairs that can be rotated horizontally and vertically. It will measure angles accurately to one second of a degree. The sight pole is about 8 feet high and held by the rodman, the second member of the survey team. Marks on the sight pole are aligned by the surveyor with the cross hairs in the telescope. A 100-foot steel tape of special alloy to resist expansion on hot days is used to measure distances. For longer distances, and especially distances across water, canyons, heavy brush, etc., surveyors use laser beam equipment. The beam is aimed at a mirror on the sight pole, bounced back, and electronically converted to a digital readout that shows the distance to the pole. Handheld computers now perform many of the angle and distance computations necessary to a survey.

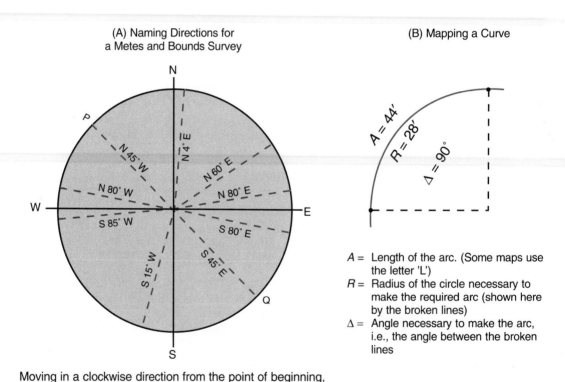

(A) Naming Directions for a Metes and Bounds Survey

(B) Mapping a Curve

$A =$ Length of the arc. (Some maps use the letter 'L')
$R =$ Radius of the circle necessary to make the required arc (shown here by the broken lines)
$\Delta =$ Angle necessary to make the arc, i.e., the angle between the broken lines

Moving in a clockwise direction from the point of beginning, set the center of a circle compass (like the one shown above) on each corner of the parcel to find the direction of travel to the next corner.

Figure 2:3. Metes and Bounds Mapping

The compass illustrated in Figure 2:3A shows how the direction of travel along each side of the parcel in Figure 2:2 is determined. Note that the same line can be labeled two ways, depending on which direction you are traveling. To illustrate, look at the line from *P* to *Q*. If you are traveling toward *P* on the line, you are going N45°W. But, if you are traveling toward point *Q* on the line, you are going S45°E.

Compass Directions

Curved boundary lines are produced by using arcs of a circle. The length of the arc is labeled *L* or *A*; the radius of the circle producing the arc is labeled *R*. The symbol Δ (delta) indicates the angle used to produce the arc (see Figure 2:3B). Where an arc connects to a straight boundary or another arc, the connection is indicated by a small circle or by a dot as shown in Figure 2:3B.

Bench marks are commonly used as permanent reference marks. A bench mark is a fixed mark of known location and elevation. It may be as simple as an iron post or as elaborate as an engraved 3 ¾" brass disc set into concrete. The mark is usually set in place by a government survey team from the United States Geological Survey (USGS) or the United States Coast and Geodetic Survey (USCGS). Bench marks are referenced to each other by distance and direction. The advantages of this type of reference point, compared to stumps, trees, rocks, and the like, are permanence and accuracy to within a fraction of an inch. Additionally, even though it is possible to destroy a reference point or monument, it can be replaced in its exact former position because the location of each is related to other reference points. In states using the rectangular survey system or a grid system (discussed shortly), a section corner or a grid intersection is often used as a permanent reference mark. As a convenience to surveyors, it will be physically marked with an iron post or a brass disc set in concrete.

The **rectangular survey system** was authorized by Congress in May 1785. It was designed to provide a faster and simpler method than metes and bounds for describing land in newly annexed territories and states. Rather than using available physical monuments, the rectangular survey system, also known as the **government survey** or **U.S. public land survey**, is based on imaginary lines. These lines are the east-west **latitude** lines and the north-south **longitude** lines that encircle

Rectangular Survey System

the earth, as illustrated in Figure 2:4. A helpful way to remember this is that longitude lines run the long way around the earth.

Certain longitude lines were selected as **principal meridians**. For each of these an intercepting latitude line was selected as a **base line**. Every 24 miles north and south of a base line, **correction lines** or **standard parallels** were established. Every 24 miles east and west of a principal meridian, **guide meridians** were established to run from one standard parallel to the next. These are needed because the earth is a sphere, not a flat surface. As one travels north in the United States, longitude (meridian) lines come closer together, that is, they converge. Figure 2:4 shows how guide meridians and correction lines adjust for this problem. Each 24-by-24-mile area created by the guide meridians and correction lines is called a **check** or **quadrangle**.

There are 36 principal meridians and their intersecting base lines in the U.S. public land survey system. Figure 2:5 shows the states in which this system is used and the land area for which each principal meridian and base line act as a reference. For example, the Sixth Principal Meridian is the reference point for land surveys in Kansas, Nebraska, and portions of Colorado,

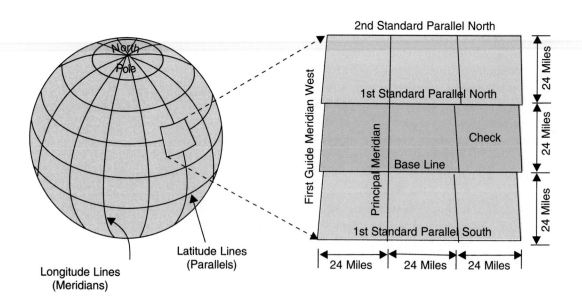

Figure 2:4. Selected Latitude and Longitude Lines Serve as Base Lines and Meridians

Figure 2:5. The Public Land Survey Systems of the United States

Wyoming, and South Dakota. In addition to the U.S. public land survey system, a portion of western Kentucky was surveyed into townships by a special state survey. Also, the state of Ohio contains eight public land surveys that are rectangular in design, but which use state boundaries and major rivers rather than latitude and longitude as reference lines.

Figure 2:6 shows how land is referenced to a principal meridian and a base line. Every 6 miles east and west of each principal meridian, parallel imaginary lines are drawn. The resulting 6-mile-wide columns are called **ranges** and are numbered consecutively east and west of the principal meridian. For example, the first range west is called Range 1 West and abbreviated R1W. The next range west is R2W, and so forth. The fourth range east is R4E.

Range

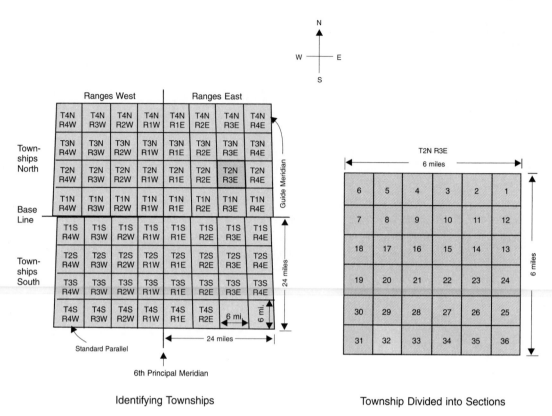

Identifying Townships

Township Divided into Sections

Figure 2:6. Identifying Townships and Sections

Township

Every six miles north and south of a base line, township lines are drawn. They intersect with the range lines and produce 6-by-6-mile imaginary squares called **townships** (not to be confused with the word *township* as applied to political subdivisions). Each tier or row of townships thus created is numbered with respect to the base line. Townships lying in the first tier north of a base line all carry the designation Township 1 North, abbreviated T1N. Townships lying in the first tier south of the base line are all designated T1S, and in the second tier south, T2S. By adding a range reference, an individual township can be identified. Thus, T2S, R2W would identify the township lying in the second tier south of the base line and the second range west of the principal meridian. T14N, R52W would be a township 14 tiers north of the base line and 52 ranges west of the principal meridian.

Each 36-square-mile township is divided into 36 one-square-mile units called **sections**. When one flies over farming areas, particularly in the Midwest, the checkerboard pattern of farms and roads that follow section boundaries can be seen. Sections are numbered 1 through 36, starting in the upper-right corner of the township. With this numbering system, any two sections with consecutive numbers share a common boundary. The section numbering system is illustrated in the right half of Figure 2:6 where the shaded section is described as Section 32, T2N, R3E, 6th Principal Meridian.

Section

Each square-mile **section** contains 640 acres, and each **acre** contains 43,560 square feet. Any parcel of land smaller than a full 640-acre section is identified by its position in the section. This is done by dividing the section into quarters and halves as shown in Figure 2:7. For example, the shaded parcel shown at A is described as the NW¼ of the SW¼ of Section 32, T2N, R3E,

Acre

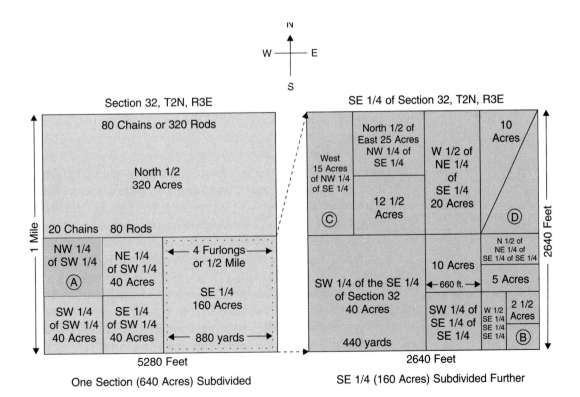

Figure 2:7. Subdividing a Section

6th P.M. Additionally, it is customary to name the county and state in which the land lies. How much land does the NW¼ of the SW¼ of a section contain? A section contains 640 acres; therefore, a quarter-section contains 160 acres. Dividing a quarter-section again into quarters results in four 40-acre parcels. Thus, the northwest quarter of the southwest quarter contains 40 acres.

The rectangular survey system is not limited to parcels of 40 or more acres. To demonstrate this point, the SE¼ of section 32 is exploded in the right half of Figure 2:7. Parcel B is described as the SE¼ of the SE¼ of the SE¼ of the SE¼ of section 32 and contains 2½ acres. Parcel C is described as the west 15 acres of the NW¼ of the SE¼ of section 32. Parcel D would be described in metes and bounds using the northeast corner of the SE¼ of section 32 as the starting point. When locating or sketching a rectangular survey on paper, many people find it helpful to start at the end of the description and work to the beginning, i.e., work backwards. Try it.

Not all sections contain exactly 640 acres. Some are smaller because the earth's longitude lines converge toward the North Pole. Also, a section may be larger or smaller than 640 acres due to historical accommodations or survey errors dating back a hundred years or more. For the same reason, not all townships contain exactly 36 square miles. Between 1785 and 1910, the U.S. government paid independent surveyors by the mile. The job was often accomplished by tying a rag to one spoke of the wheel of a buckboard wagon. A team of horses was hitched to the wagon and the surveyor, compass in hand, headed out across the prairie. Distance was measured by counting the number of wheel turns and multiplying by the circumference of the wheel. Today, large area surveys are made with the aid of aerial photographs, sophisticated electronic equipment, and earth satellites.

In terms of surface area, more land in the United States is described by the rectangular survey system than by any other survey method. But in terms of number of properties, the recorded plat is the most important survey method.

Recorded Plat   When a tract of land is ready for subdividing into lots for homes and businesses, reference by **recorded plat** provides the simplest and most convenient method of land description. A

plat is a map that shows the location and boundaries of individual properties. Also known as the **lot-block-tract system, recorded map**, or **recorded survey**, this method of land description is based on the filing of a surveyor's plat in the public recorder's office of the county where the land is located. Figure 2:8 illustrates a plat. Notice that a metes and bounds survey has been made and a map prepared to show in detail the boundaries of each parcel of land. Each parcel is then assigned a lot number. Each block in the tract is given a block number, and the tract itself is given a name or number. A plat showing all the blocks in the tract is delivered to the county recorder's office, where it is placed in **map books** or **survey books**, along with plats of other subdivisions in the county.

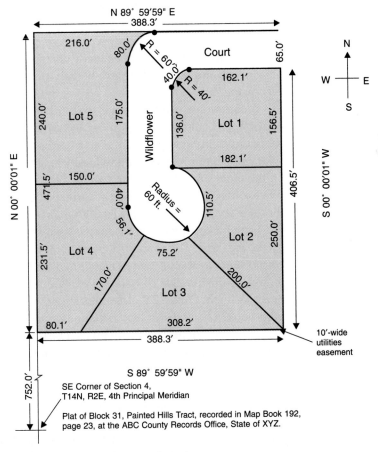

Figure 2:8. Land Description by Recorded Plat

Each plat is given a book and page reference number, and all map books are available for public inspection. From that point on, it is no longer necessary to give a lengthy metes and bounds description to describe a parcel. Instead, one need only provide the lot and block number, tract name, map book reference, county, and state. To find the location and dimensions of a recorded lot, one simply looks in the map book at the county recorder's office.

Note that the plat in Figure 2:8 combines both of the land descriptions just discussed. The boundaries of the numbered lots are in metes and bounds. These, in turn, are referenced to a section corner in the rectangular survey system.

Assessor's Parcel Numbers

In many counties in the United States, the tax assessor assigns an **assessor's parcel number** to each parcel of land in the county. The primary purpose is to aid in the assessment of property for tax collection purposes. However, these parcel numbers are public information and real estate brokers, appraisers, and investors can and do use them extensively to assist in identifying real properties.

A commonly used system is to divide the county into map books. Each book is given a number and covers a given portion of the county. On every page of the map book are parcel maps, each with its own number. For subdivided lots, these maps are based on the plats submitted by the subdivider to the county records office when the subdivision was made. For unsubdivided land, the assessor's office prepares its own maps.

Each parcel of land on the map is assigned a parcel number by the assessor. The assessor's parcel number may or may not be the same as the lot number assigned by the subdivider. To reduce confusion, the assessor's parcel number is either circled or underlined. Figure 2:9 illustrates a page out of an assessor's map book. The assessor also produces an assessment roll that lists every parcel in the county by its assessor's parcel number. Stored and printed by computer now, this roll shows the current owner's name and address and the assessed value of the land and buildings.

The assessor's maps are open to viewing by the public at the assessor's office. In many counties, private firms reproduce the maps and the accompanying list of property owners and make

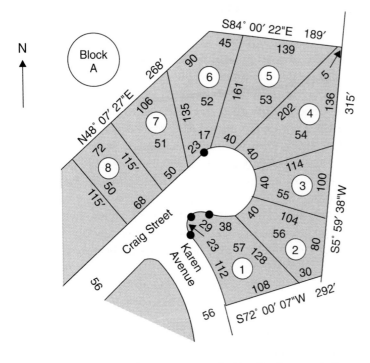

The tax assessor assigns every parcel of land in the county its own parcel number. For example, the westernmost parcel (Lot 50) in the map would carry the number 34-18-8, meaning Book 34, Page 18, Parcel 8.

Figure 2:9. Assessor's Map

them available to real estate brokers, appraisers, and lenders for a fee.

Before leaving the topic of assessor's maps, a word of caution is in order. These maps should not be relied upon as the final authority for the legal description of a parcel. That can come only from a title search that includes looking at the current deed to the property and the recorded copy of the subdivider's plat. Note also that an assessor's parcel number is never used as a legal description in a deed.

Land can also be described by referring to another publicly recorded document, such as a deed or a mortgage, that contains a full legal description of the parcel in question. For example,

Reference to Documents
Other Than Maps

suppose that several years ago Baker received a deed from Adams which contained a long and complicated metes and bounds description. Baker recorded the deed in the public records office, where a photocopy was placed in Book 1089, page 456. If Baker later wants to deed the same land to Cooper, Baker can describe the parcel in his deed to Cooper by saying, "all the land described in the deed from Adams to Baker recorded in Book 1089, page 456, county of ABC, state of XYZ, at the public recorder's office for said county and state." Since these books are open to the public, Cooper (or anyone else) could go to Book 1089, page 456 and find a detailed description of the parcel's boundaries.

The key test of a land description is: "Can another person, reading what I have written or drawn, understand my description and go out and locate the boundaries of the parcel?"

GRID SYSTEMS

Several states, such as North Carolina and Connecticut, have developed their own statewide systems of reference points for land surveying. The North Carolina system, for example, divides that state into a grid of 84 blocks, each side of which corresponds to 30 minutes (one-half of one degree) of latitude or longitude. This establishes a **grid system** of intersecting points throughout the state to which metes and bounds surveys can be referenced. State-sponsored grid systems (also called coordinate systems) are especially helpful for surveying large parcels of remote area land.

VERTICAL LAND
DESCRIPTION

In addition to surface land descriptions, land may also be described in terms of vertical measurements. This type of measurement is necessary when air rights or subsurface rights need to be described—as for multistory condominiums or oil and mineral rights.

A point, line, or surface from which a vertical height or depth is measured is called a **datum**. The most commonly used datum plane in the United States is mean sea level, although a number of cities have established other data surfaces for use in local surveys. Starting from a datum, **bench marks** are set at calculated intervals by government survey teams; thus, a surveyor need not travel to the original datum to determine an elevation. These same bench marks are used as reference points for metes and bounds surveys.

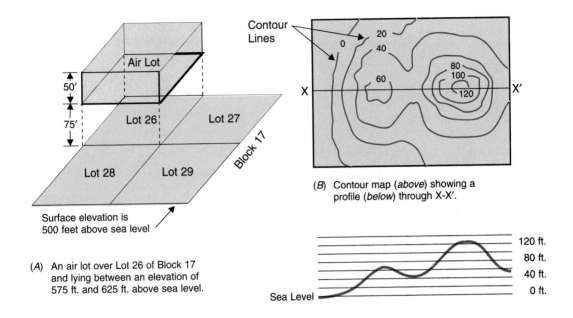

(A) An air lot over Lot 26 of Block 17
and lying between an elevation of
575 ft. and 625 ft. above sea level.

(B) Contour map (*above*) showing a
profile (*below*) through X-X'.

Figure 2:10. Air Lot and Contour Lines

In selling or leasing subsurface drilling or mineral rights,
the chosen datum is often the surface of the parcel. For
example, an oil lease may permit the extraction of oil and gas
from a depth greater than 500 feet beneath the surface of a
parcel of land. (Subsurface rights are discussed in Chapter 3.)

An **air lot** (a space over a given parcel of land) is described
by identifying both the parcel of land beneath the air lot and the
elevation of the air lot above the parcel (see Figure 2:10A).
Multistory condominiums use this system of land description.

Contour maps (topographic maps) indicate elevations. On
these maps, **contour lines** connect all points having the same
elevation. The purpose is to show hills and valleys, slopes, and
water runoff. If the land is to be developed, the map shows
where soil will have to be moved to provide level building lots.
Figure 2:10B illustrates how vertical distances are shown using
contour lines.

In talking about subdivisions there are several terms with   *LOT TYPES*
which you should be familiar. All of these are illustrated in

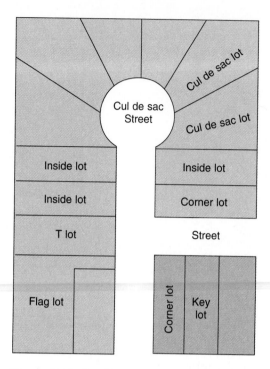

Figure 2:11. Lot Types

Figure 2:11. A **cul de sac** is a street that is closed at one end with a circular turnaround. The pie-shaped lots fronting on the turn-around are called **cul de sac lots**. A **flag lot** is a lot shaped like a flag on a flagpole. It's a popular method of creating a buildable lot out of the land at the back of a larger lot. A **corner lot** is a lot that fronts on two or more streets. Because of added light and access, a corner lot is usually worth more than an **inside lot**, i.e., a lot with only one side on a street. A **key lot** is a lot that adjoins the side or rear property line of a corner lot. The key lot has added value if it is needed by the corner lot for expansion. A **T lot** is a lot at the end of a **T intersection** as shown in Figure 2:11.

REVIEW QUESTIONS

1. In determining whether an article of personal property has become a fixture, which of the following tests would NOT be applied?
   A. The manner of attachment.
   B. The cost of the article.
   C. The adaptation of the article to the land.
   D. The existence of an agreement between the parties.

2. The term "real estate" includes
   A. the right to use land.
   B. anything affixed to land with the intent of being permanent.
   C. rights to the air above the land.
   D. rights to subsurface minerals.
   E. All of the above

3. Determining what is a fixture and what is not is important when
   A. property taxes are calculated.
   B. real estate is mortgaged.
   C. a tenant attaches an object to a rented building.
   D. hazard insurance is purchased.
   E. All of the above

4. In remodeling their home, the Wades put the items described below in the home. Once in place all would be fixtures EXCEPT:
   A. an oriental throw rug in the front entry hall.
   B. the built-in kitchen range.
   C. the built-in dishwasher.
   D. custom fitted wall-to-wall carpet installed over plywood sub-flooring.

5. Which of the following are NOT classified as real property?
   A. Fixtures.
   B. Emblements.
   C. A shrub planted in the ground.
   D. Air rights.

6. The right of an owner to use water from a stream for his own use is called
   A. an emblement right.
   B. a riparian right.
   C. a littoral right.
   D. a percolated right.

7. Which of the following land description methods identifies a parcel of land by specifying its shape and boundaries?
   A. Metes and bounds.
   B. Government survey.
   C. Recorded plat.
   D. Assessor's parcel number.
   E. All of the above

8. Which of the following have been utilized as monuments to designate the corner of a parcel of land in the metes and bounds description of the land?
   A. An iron pipe driven in the ground.
   B. A tree.
   C. A fence corner
   D. All of the above.
   E. None of the above.

9. The term "point of beginning" refers to
   A. a permanent reference marker.
   B. the first corner of the parcel to be surveyed.
   C. a benchmark.
   D. the intersection of a principal meridian with its base line.

10. 1/60th of 1/60th of 1/360th of a circle is known as a
    A. degree.
    B. minute.
    C. second.
    D. None of the above.

11. In the rectangular survey system of land descriptions, which of the following run in an east-west direction?
    A. Principal meridians.
    B. Guide meridians.
    C. Longitude lines.
    D. Standard parallels.

12. East-west lines in the government rectangular survey system are known as
    A. Base lines.
    B. Guide meridians.
    C. meridians.
    D. quadrangles.

13. In a diagram of a township, section 10 lies directly south of section
    A. 3.
    B. 4.
    C. 16.
    D. 15.

14. A township is
    A. six miles square.
    B. one mile square.
    C. six square miles.
    D. one square mile.

15. Forty-three thousand, five hundred and sixty is the number of square feet in
    A. an acre.
    B. a section.
    C. a township.
    D. a tier.

16. The NW 1/4 of the NW 1/4 of the NW 1/4 of a section of land contains
    A. 80 acres.
    B. 10 acres.
    C. 20 acres.
    D. 40 acres.

17. An assessor's parcel number
    A. is the final authority for the legal description of a parcel of land.
    B. is often used as a legal description in a deed.
    C. Both A and B.
    D. Neither A nor B.

18. Which of the following is NOT a physical characteristic of land?
    A. Immobility.
    B. Indestructibility.
    C. Nonhomogeneity.
    D. Fungibility.

19. Because one parcel of land cannot be precisely substituted for another, it is said to be
    A. nonfungible.
    B. immobile.
    C. fungible.
    D. mobile.

20. Area preference in the location of land is described as
    A. fixity.
    B. situs.
    C. sunk costs.
    D. surface rights.

Rights and Interests in Land

The purpose of this chapter is to provide the student with general and legal information concerning rights and interests in land. The chapter begins with a brief discussion of government rights in land, individual rights, easements, encroachments, deed restrictions, and types of liens. Other topics covered in this chapter include various types of estates, homestead rights and limitation, chattels, and subsurface rights.

OVERVIEW OF
CHAPTER 3

LEARNING OBJECTIVES

At the conclusion of this chapter, you should be able to:
1. Distinguish between the feudal and allodial systems of land ownership.
2. Explain the rights that government has in land.
3. Explain the fee simple bundle of rights.
4. Understand such terms as fee simple, encumbrances, easements, encroachments, deed restrictions, and liens.
5. Define and explain the various types of liens.
6. Explain the various types of estates and understand their usage.
7. Distinguish between freehold and leasehold estates.
8. Define such terms as license and chattels.
9. Understand and explain subsurface rights.

KEY • TERMS

Chattel: an article of personal property

Easement: the right or privilege one party has to use land belonging to another for a special purpose not inconsistent with the owner's use of the land

Eminent domain: the right of government to take privately held land for public use provided fair compensation is paid

Encroachment: the unauthorized intrusion of a building or other improvement onto another person's land

Encumbrance: any impediment to a clear title, such as a lien, lease or easement

Estate: one's legal interest or rights in land

Fee simple: the largest, most complete bundle of rights one can hold in land; land ownership

Lien: a hold or claim which one person has on the property of another to secure payment of a debt or other obligation

Title: the right to or ownership of something; also the evidence of ownership, such as a deed or bill of sale

GOVERNMENT RIGHTS IN LAND

Under the feudal system, the king was responsible for organizing defense against invaders, making decisions on land use, providing services such as roads and bridges, and the general administration of the land and his subjects. An important aspect of the transition from feudal to allodial ownership was that the need for these services did not end. Consequently, even though ownership could now be held by private citizens, it became necessary for the government to retain the rights of taxation, eminent domain, police power and escheat. Let us look at each of these more closely.

Property Taxes

Under the feudal system, governments financed themselves by requiring lords and vassals to share a portion of the benefits they received from the use of the king's lands. With the change to private ownership, the need to finance governments did not end. Thus, the government retained the right to collect **property taxes** from landowners. Before the advent of income taxes, the taxes levied against land were the main source of government revenues. Taxing land was a logical method of raising revenue for two reasons: (1) until the Industrial Revolution, which started in the mid-eighteenth century, land and agriculture were the primary sources of income; the more land one owned, the wealthier one was considered to be and therefore the better able to pay taxes to support the government; (2) land is impossible to hide, making it easily identifiable for taxation. This is not true of other valuables such as gold or money.

The real property tax has endured over the centuries, and today it is still a major source of government revenue. The major change in real estate taxation is that initially it was used to support all levels of government, including defense. Today, defense is supported by the income tax, and real estate taxes are sources of city, county, and, in some places, state revenues. At state and local government levels, the real property tax provides money for such things as schools, fire and police protection, parks, and libraries. To encourage property owners to pay their taxes in full and on time, the right of taxation also enables the government to seize ownership of real estate upon which taxes are delinquent and to sell the property to recover the unpaid taxes.

The right of government to take ownership of privately held real estate regardless of the owner's wishes is called **eminent domain.** Land for schools, freeways, streets, parks, urban renewal, public housing, public parking, and other social and public purposes is obtained this way. Quasi-public organizations, such as utility companies and railroads, are also permitted to obtain land needed for utility lines, pipes, and tracks by state law. The legal proceeding involved in eminent domain is a **condemnation proceeding,** and the property owner must be paid the fair market value of the property taken from him. The actual condemnation is usually preceded by negotiations between the property owner and an agent of the public body wanting to acquire ownership. If the agent and the property owner can arrive at a mutually acceptable price, the property is purchased outright. If an agreement cannot be reached, a formal proceeding in eminent domain is filed against the property owner in a court of law. The court hears expert opinions from appraisers brought by both parties, and then sets the price the property owner must accept in return for the loss of ownership.

Eminent Domain

When only a portion of a parcel of land is being taken, **severance damages** may be awarded in addition to payment for land actually being taken. For example, if a new highway requires a 40-acre strip of land through the middle of a 160-acre farm, the farm owner will not only be paid for the 40 acres, but will also receive severance damages to compensate for the fact that the farm will be more difficult to work because it is no longer in one piece.

An **inverse condemnation** is a proceeding brought about by a property owner demanding that his land be purchased from him. In a number of cities, homeowners at the end of airport runways have forced airport authorities to buy their homes because of the deafening noise of jet aircraft during takeoffs. Damage awards may also be made when land itself is not taken but its usefulness is reduced because of a nearby condemnation. These are **consequential damages,** and might be awarded, for instance, when land is taken for a sewage treatment plant, and privately owned land downwind from the plant suffers a loss in value owing to foul odors.

Police Power   The right of government to enact laws and enforce them for the order, safety, health, morals and general welfare of the public is called **police power.** Examples of police power applied to real estate are zoning laws, planning laws, building, health and fire codes, and rent control. A key difference between police power and eminent domain is that, although police power restricts how real estate may be used, there is no legally recognized "taking" of property. Consequently, there is no payment to an owner who suffers a loss of value through the exercise of police power. A government may not utilize police power in an offhand or capricious manner; any law that restricts how an owner may use his real estate must be deemed in the public interest and applied evenhandedly to be valid. The breaking of a law based upon police power results in either a civil or criminal penalty rather than in the seizing of real estate, as in the case of unpaid property taxes. Of the various rights government holds in land, police power has the most impact on land value.

Escheat   When a person dies and leaves no heirs and no instructions as to how to dispose of his real and personal property, or when property is abandoned, the ownership of that property reverts to the state. This reversion to the state is called **escheat** from the Anglo-French word meaning to *fall back.* Escheat solves the problem of property becoming ownerless.

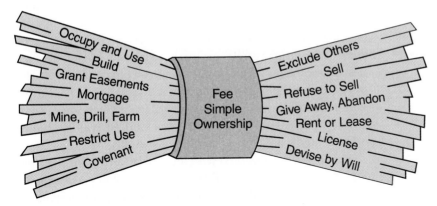

Real estate ownership is, in actuality, the ownership of rights to land. The largest bundle available for private ownership is called "fee simple."

Figure 3:1. The Fee Simple Bundle of Rights

It cannot be overemphasized that, to have real estate, there must be a system or means of protecting rightful claims to the use of land and the improvements thereon. In the United States, the federal government is given the task of organizing a defense system to prevent confiscation of those rights by a foreign power. The federal government, in combination with state and local governments, also establishes laws and courts within the country to protect the ownership rights of one citizen in relation to another citizen. Whereas the armed forces protect against a foreign takeover, within a country deeds, public records, contracts, and other documents have replaced the need for brute force to prove and protect ownership of real estate.

PROTECTING OWNERSHIP

The concept of real estate ownership can be more easily understood when viewed as a collection or bundle of rights. Under the allodial system, the rights of taxation, eminent domain, police power, and escheat are retained by the government. The remaining bundle of rights, called **fee simple,** is available for private ownership. The fee simple bundle of rights can be held by a person and his heirs forever, or until his government can no longer protect those rights. Figure 3:1 illustrates the fee simple bundle of rights concept.

FEE SIMPLE

The word **estate** is synonymous with bundle of rights. Stated another way, *estate* refers to one's legal interest or rights in land, not the physical quantity of land as shown on a map. A fee simple is the largest estate one can hold in land. Most real estate sales are for the fee simple estate. When a person says he or she "owns" or has "title" to real estate, it is usually the fee simple estate that is being discussed. The word *title* refers to the ownership of something. All other lesser estates in land, such as life estates and leaseholds, are created from the fee estate.

Real estate is concerned with the "sticks" in the bundle: how many there are, how useful they are, and who possesses the sticks not in the bundle. With that in mind, let us describe what happens when sticks are removed from the bundle.

ENCUMBRANCES

Whenever a stick is removed from the fee simple bundle, it creates an impediment to the free and clear ownership and use of that property. These impediments to title are called encumbrances. An **encumbrance** is defined as any claim, right, lien, estate, or liability that limits the fee simple title to property. An encumbrance is, in effect, a stick that has been removed from the bundle. Commonly found encumbrances are easements, encroachments, deed restrictions, liens, leases, and air and subsurface rights. In addition, qualified fee estates are encumbered estates, as are life estates.

The party holding a stick from someone else's fee simple bundle is said to hold a claim to or a right or interest in that land. In other words, what is one person's encumbrance is another person's right or interest or claim. For example, a lease is an encumbrance from the standpoint of the fee simple owner. But from the tenant's standpoint, it is an interest in land that gives the tenant the right to the exclusive use of land and buildings. A mortgage is an encumbrance from the fee owner's viewpoint but a right to foreclose from the lender's viewpoint. A property that is encumbered with a lease and a mortgage is called "a fee simple subject to a lease and a mortgage." Figure 3:2 illustrates how a fee simple bundle shrinks as rights are removed from it. Meanwhile, let us turn our attention to a discussion of individual sticks found in the fee simple bundle.

Easements

An **easement** is a right or privilege one party has to the use of land of another for a special purpose consistent with the general

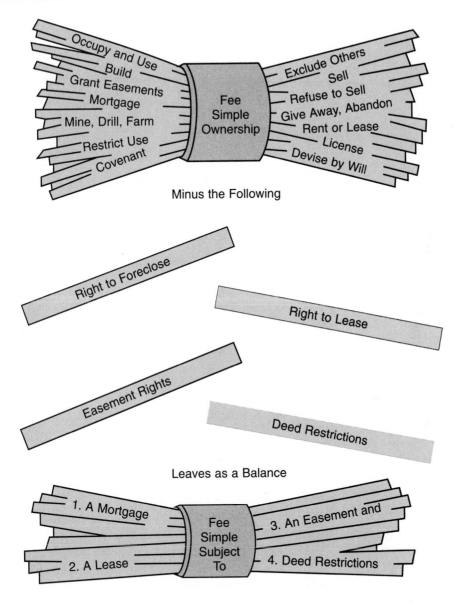

Minus the Following

Leaves as a Balance

Note that the fee simple bundle shrinks as an owner voluntarily removes rights from it.

Figure 3:2. Removing Sticks from the Fee Simple Bundle

use of the land. The landowner is not dispossessed from his land, but rather coexists side by side with the holder of the easement. Examples of easements are those given to telephone and electric companies to erect poles and run lines over private property,

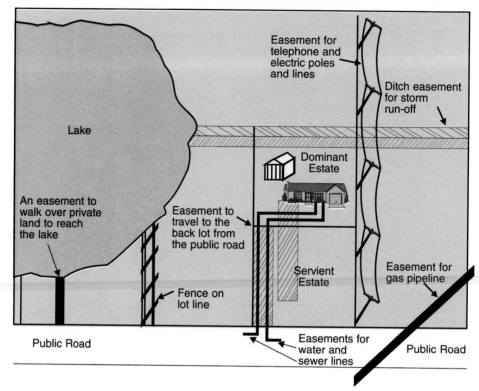

Figure 3:3. Commonly Found Easements

easements given to people to drive or walk across someone else's land, and easements given to gas and water companies to run pipelines to serve their customers. Figure 3:3 illustrates several examples of easements.

There are several different ways an easement can come into being. One is for the landowner to use a written document to specifically **grant** an easement to another party. A second way is for an owner to reserve (withhold) an easement in the deed when granting the property to another party. For example, a land developer may reserve easements for utility lines when selling the lots and then grant the easements to the utility companies that will service the lots. Another way for an easement to be created is by government condemnation, such as when a government flood control district purchases an easement to run a drainage pipe under someone's land.

It is also possible for an easement to arise without a written document. For example, a parcel of land fronts on a road and the owner sells the back half of the parcel. If the only access to the back half is by crossing over the front half, even if the seller did not expressly grant an easement, the law will generally protect the buyer's right to travel over the front half to get to his land. The buyer cannot be landlocked by the seller. This is known as an **easement by necessity.** Another method of acquiring an easement without a written document is by constant use, or **easement by prescription:** if a person acts as though he owns an easement long enough, he will have a legally recognized easement. Persons using a private road without permission for a long enough period of time can acquire a legally recognized easement by this method.

In Figure 3:3, the driveway from the road to the back lot is called an **easement appurtenant.** This driveway is automatically included with the back lot whenever the back lot is sold or otherwise conveyed. This is so because this easement is legally connected (appurtenant) to the back lot. Please note that just as the back lot benefits from this easement, the front lot is burdened by it. Whenever the front lot is sold or otherwise conveyed, the new owners must continue to respect the easement to the back lot. The owner of the front lot owns all the front lot, but cannot put a fence across the easement, or plant trees on it, or grow a garden on it, or otherwise hamper access to the back lot. Because the front lot serves the back lot the front lot is called the **servient estate** and the back lot is called the **dominant estate.** When one party has the right or privilege, by usage or contract, to travel over a designated portion of another person's land, it is called a **right-of-way.**

Although the law generally protects the first purchaser through the doctrine of easement by necessity, it is nonetheless critical that any subsequent purchaser of back lots and back acreage carefully inspect the public records and the property to make certain there is both legal and actual means of access from a public road to the parcel. It is also important for anyone purchasing land to inspect the public records and the property for evidence of the rights of others to pass over that land, for example, a driveway or private road to a back lot or a pathway used by the public to get from a road to a beach.

An **easement in gross** differs from an easement appurtenant because there is a servient estate but no dominant estate. Some examples will illustrate this: telephone, electricity, and gas line

Easement Appurtenant

Easement in Gross

easements are all easements in gross. These easements belong to the telephone, electric, and gas companies, respectively, not to a parcel of land. The servient estate is the parcel on which the telephone, electric, and gas companies have the right to run their lines. All future owners of the parcel are bound by these easements.

Although utility easements are the most common examples of easements in gross, the ditch easement for storm runoff in Figure 3:3 is also one. It will most likely be owned by a flood control district. Note that utility and drainage easements, although legally a burden on a parcel, are consistent with the use of a parcel if the purpose of the easement is to provide utility service or flood control for the parcel. In fact, without these services, a parcel would be less useful and hence less valuable.

It is also possible to grant an easement to an individual for personal use. In Figure 3:3, a landowner has given a friend a personal easement in gross to walk over his land to reach a choice fishing area on the lakeshore. An easement in gross for personal use is not transferable and terminates with the death of the person holding the easement. In contrast, the holder of a commercial easement, such as a utility or flood control easement, usually has the right to sell, assign, or devise that easement.

Party Wall Easement

Party wall easements exist when a single wall is located on the lot line that separates two parcels of land. The wall may be either a fence or the wall of a building. In either case, each lot owner owns that portion of the wall on his land, plus an easement in the other half of the wall for physical support. Party walls are common where stores and office buildings are built right up to the lot line. Such a wall can present an interesting problem when the owner of one lot wants to demolish his building. Since the wall provides support for the building next door, he must leave the wall, and provide special supports for the adjacent building during demolition and until another building is constructed on the lot. A party wall is an easement appurtenant.

Easement Termination

Easements may be terminated when the necessity for the easement no longer exists (for example, a public road is built adjacent to the back half of the lot mentioned earlier), or when the dominant and servient estates are combined (merged) with the intent of extinguishing the easement, or by release from the easement holder to the servient estate, or by lack of use (abandonment).

The unauthorized intrusion of a building or other form of real property onto another person's land is called an **encroachment.** A tree that overhangs into a neighbor's yard, or a building or eave of a roof that crosses a property line are examples of encroachments. The owner of the property being encroached upon has the right to force the removal of the encroachment. Failure to do so may eventually injure his title and make his land more difficult to sell. Ultimately, inaction may result in the encroaching neighbor claiming a legal right to continue his use. Figure 3:4 illustrates several commonly found encroachments.

Encroachments

Private agreements that govern the use of land are known as **deed restrictions** or **deed covenants.** For example, a land subdivider can require that persons who purchase lots from him build only single-family homes containing 1,200 square feet or

Deed Restrictions

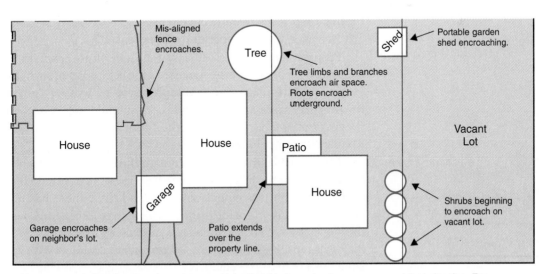

Most commonly found encroachments are not intentional but are due to poor or nonexistent planning. For example, a weekend garden shed, fence, or patio project is built without surveying to find the lot line, or a tree or bush grows so large it encroaches upon a neighbor's land.

Figure 3:4. Commonly Found Encroachments

more. The purpose would be to protect those who have already built houses from an erosion in property value due to the construction of nearby buildings not compatible with the neighborhood. Where scenic views are important, deed restrictions may limit the height of buildings and trees to 15 feet. A buyer would still obtain fee simple ownership, but at the same time would voluntarily give up some of his rights to do as he pleases. As a buyer, he is said to receive a fee simple title subject to deed restrictions. The right to enforce the restrictions is usually given by the developer to the subdivision's homeowner association. Violation of a deed restriction can result in a civil court action brought by other property owners who are bound by the same deed restriction.

Liens

A hold or claim that one person has on the property of another to secure payment of a debt or other obligation is called a **lien.** Common examples are property tax liens, mechanic's liens, judgment liens, and mortgage liens. From the standpoint of the property owner, a lien is an encumbrance on his title. Note that a lien does not transfer title to property. The debtor retains title until the lien is foreclosed. When there is more than one lien against a property, the lien that was recorded first usually has the highest priority in the event of foreclosure. Property tax liens are, however, always superior to other liens.

Property Tax Liens

Property tax liens result from the right of government to collect taxes from property owners. At the beginning of each tax year, a tax lien is placed on taxable property. It is removed when the property taxes are paid. If they are not paid, the lien gives the government the right to force the sale of the property in order to collect the unpaid taxes.

Mechanic's Lien

Mechanic's lien laws give anyone who has furnished labor or materials for the improvement of land the right to place a lien against those improvements and the land if payment has not been received. A sale of the property can then be forced to recover the money owed. To be entitled to a mechanic's lien, the work or materials must have been provided pursuant to contract with the landowner or his representative. For example, if a landowner hires a contractor to build a house or add a room to his existing house, and then fails to pay the contractor, the contractor may file a mechanic's lien against the land and its improvements. Furthermore, if the landowner pays the contractor, but the contractor does not pay his subcontractors, the subcontractors are entitled to file a mechanic's lien against the property. In this situation, the owner may have to pay twice.

The legal theory behind mechanic's lien rights is that the labor and materials supplied enhance the value of the property. Therefore the property should be security for payment. If the property owner does not pay voluntarily, the lien can be enforced with a court supervised foreclosure sale.

Mechanics (contractors), materialmen, architects, surveyors, and engineers are among those who may be entitled to the protection of mechanic's lien laws. All mechanic's liens attach and take effect at the time the first item of labor or material is furnished, even though no document has been filed with the county recorder. To preserve the lien, a lien statement must be filed in the county where the property is located and within 20 to 120 days (depending on the state) after labor or material has been furnished. This is called **perfecting the lien.**

Whenever improvements are made to the land, all persons (including sellers under a contract for deed and landlords) may be held to have authorized the improvements. As protection, an owner can serve or post notice that the improvements are being made without the owner's authority.

A lender planning to finance a property will be particularly alert for the possibility of mechanic's liens. If work has commenced or material has been delivered before the mortgage is recorded, the mechanic's lien may be superior to the mortgage in the event of foreclosure.

Judgment liens arise from lawsuits for which money damages are awarded. The law permits a hold to be placed against the real and personal property of the debtor until the judgment is paid. Usually the lien created by the judgment covers only property in the county where the judgment was awarded. However, the creditor can extend the lien to property in other counties by filing a **notice of lien** in each of those counties. If the debtor does not repay the lien voluntarily, the creditor can ask the court to issue a **writ of execution** that directs the county sheriff to seize and sell a sufficient amount of the debtor's property to pay the debt and expenses of the sale.

Judgment Lien

A **mortgage lien** is created when property is offered by its owner as security for the repayment of a debt. If the debt secured by the mortgage lien is not repaid, the creditor can foreclose and

Mortgage Lien

sell the property. If this is insufficient to repay the debt, some states allow the creditor to petition the court for a judgment lien for the balance due. (Mortgage law is covered in more detail in Chapter 9.)

Voluntary and Involuntary Liens

A **voluntary lien** is a lien created by the property owner. A mortgage lien is an example of a voluntary lien; the owner voluntarily creates a lien against his/her property in order to borrow money. An **involuntary lien** is created by operation of law. Examples are property tax liens, judgment liens, and mechanic's liens.

Special and General Liens

A **special lien** is a lien on a specific property. A property tax lien is a special lien because it is a lien against a specific property and no other. Thus, if a person owns five parcels of land scattered throughout a given county and fails to pay the taxes on one of those parcels, the county can force the sale of just that one parcel; the others cannot be touched. Mortgages and mechanic's liens are also special liens in that they apply to only the property receiving the materials or labor. In contrast, a **general lien** is a lien on all the property of a person in a given jurisdiction. For example, a judgment lien is a lien on all the debtor's property in the county or counties where the judgment has been filed. Federal and state tax liens are also general liens.

QUALIFIED FEE ESTATES

A **qualified fee estate** is a fee estate that is subject to certain limitations imposed by the person creating the estate. Qualified fee estates fall into three categories: determinable, condition subsequent, and condition precedent. They will be discussed only briefly as they are rather uncommon.

A **fee simple determinable estate** indicates that the duration of the estate can be determined from the deed itself. For example, Mr. Smith donates a parcel of land to a church so long as the land is used for religious purposes. The key words are *so long as*. So long as the land is used for religious purposes, the church has all the rights of fee simple ownership. But, if some other use is made of the land, it reverts back to the grantor (Mr. Smith) or someone else named by Mr. Smith (called a **remainderman**). Note that the termination of the estate is automatic if the land is used contrary to the limitation stated in the deed.

A **fee simple subject to condition subsequent** gives the grantor the *right* to terminate the estate. Continuing the above example, Mr. Smith would have the right to reenter the property and take it back if it was no longer being used for religious purposes.

With a **fee simple upon condition precedent,** title will not take effect until a condition is performed. For example, Mr. Smith could deed his land to a church with the condition that the deed will not take effect until a religious sanctuary is built.

Occasionally, qualified fees have been used by land developers in lieu of deed restrictions or zoning. For example, the buyer has fee title so long as he uses the land for a single-family residence. In another example, a land developer might use a condition precedent to encourage lot purchasers to build promptly. This would enhance the value of his unsold lots. From the standpoint of the property owner, a qualification is an encumbrance to his title.

A **life estate** conveys an estate for the duration of someone's life. The duration of the estate can be tied to the life of the **life tenant** (the person holding the life estate) or to a third party. In addition, someone must be named to acquire the estate upon its termination. The following example will illustrate the life estate concept. Suppose you have an aunt who needs financial assistance and you have decided to grant her, for the rest of her life, a house to live in. When you create the life estate, she becomes the life tenant. Additionally, you must decide who gets the house upon her death. If you want it back, you would want a **reversion** for yourself. This way the house reverts back to you, or if you predecease her, to your heirs. If you want the house to go to someone else, your son or daughter for example, you could name him or her as the remainderman. Alternatively, you could name a friend, relative, or charity as the **remainderman.** Sometimes a life estate is used to avoid the time and expense of probating a will and to reduce estate taxes. For example, an aging father could deed his real estate to his children but retain a life estate for himself.

LIFE ESTATES

Since a life estate arrangement is temporary, the life tenant must not commit **waste** by destroying or harming the property. Furthermore, the life tenant is required to keep the property in reasonable repair and to pay any property taxes, assessments, and interest on debt secured by the property. The life tenant is

Prohibition of Waste

entitled to income generated by the property, and may sell, lease, rent, or mortgage his or her interest.

Although the life estate concept offers intriguing gift and estate planning possibilities, the uncertainty of the duration of the estate makes it rather unmarketable. Thus, you will rarely see a life estate advertised for sale in a newspaper or listed for sale at a real estate brokerage office.

STATUTORY ESTATES   Statutory estates are created by state law. They include **dower,** which gives a wife rights in her husband's real property; **curtesy**, which gives a husband rights in his wife's real property; and **community property,** which gives each spouse a one-half interest in marital property. Additionally there is **homestead protection,** which is designed to protect the family's home from certain debts and, upon the death of one spouse, provide the other with a home for life.

Dower   Historically **dower** came from old English common law in which the marriage ceremony was viewed as merging the wife's legal existence into that of her husband's. From this viewpoint, property bought during marriage belongs to the husband, with both husband and wife sharing the use of it. As a counterbalance, the dower right recognizes the wife's efforts in marriage and grants her legal ownership to one-third (in some states one-half) of the family's real property for the rest of her life. This prevents the husband from conveying ownership of the family's real estate without the wife's permission and protects her even if she is left out of her husband's will.

In real estate sales, the effect of dower laws is that when a husband and wife sell their property, the wife must relinquish her dower rights. This is usually accomplished by the wife signing the deed with her husband or by signing a separate quitclaim deed. If she does not relinquish her dower rights, the buyer (or even a future buyer) may find that, upon the husband's death, the wife may return to legally claim an undivided ownership in the property. This is important if you buy real estate. Have the property's ownership researched by an abstracter and the title insured by a title insurance company.

Curtesy   Roughly the opposite of dower, **curtesy** gives the husband benefits in his deceased wife's property as long as he lives.

However, unlike dower, the wife can defeat those rights in her will. Furthermore, state law may require the couple to have had a child in order for the husband to qualify for curtesy.

Because dower and curtesy rights originally were unequal, some states interpret dower and curtesy so as to give equal rights while other states have enacted additional legislation to protect spousal rights. To summarize, the basic purpose of dower and curtesy (and community property laws) is to require both spouses to sign any deed or mortgage or other document affecting title to their lands, and to provide legal protection for the property rights of a surviving spouse.

Community Property

Eight states (Arizona, California, Idaho, Louisiana, Nevada, New Mexico, Texas, and Washington) subscribe to the legal theory that each spouse has an equal interest in all property acquired by their joint efforts during the marriage. This jointly produced property is called **community property.** Upon the death of one spouse, one-half of the community property passes to the heirs. The other one-half is retained by the surviving spouse. When community property is sold or mortgaged, both spouses must sign the document. Community property rights arise upon marriage (either formal or common law) and terminate upon divorce or death. Community property is discussed at greater length in Chapter 4.

Homestead Protection

Nearly all states have passed **homestead protection laws,** usually with two purposes in mind: (1) to provide some legal protection for the homestead claimants from debts and judgments against them that might result in the forced sale and loss of the home, and (2) to provide a home for a widow, and sometimes a widower, for life. Homestead laws also restrict one spouse from acting without the other when conveying the homestead or using it as collateral for a loan. Although dower, curtesy, and community property rights are automatic in those states that have them, the homestead right may require that a written declaration be recorded in the public records. As referred to here, homestead is not the acquiring of title to state or federally owned lands by filing and establishing a residence (see Chapter 5). Additionally, *homestead protection* should not be confused with the *homestead exemption* some states grant to homeowners in order to reduce their property taxes (see Chapter 13).

A homeowner is also protected by the Federal Bankruptcy Reform Act of 1979. A person who seeks protection under this act is entitled to an exemption of up to $7,500 of the equity in his/her residence. Also exempt is any household item that does not exceed $200 in value.

FREEHOLD ESTATES

In a carryover from the old English court system, estates in land are classified as either **freehold estates** or **leasehold estates.** The main difference is that freehold estate cases are tried under real property laws whereas leasehold (also called nonfreehold or less-than-freehold) estates are tried under personal property laws.

The two distinguishing features of a freehold estate are (1) there must be actual ownership of the land, and (2) the estate must be of unpredictable duration. Fee estates, life estates, and estates created by statute are freehold estates. The distinguishing features of a leasehold estate are (1) although there is possession of the land, there is no ownership, and (2) the estate is of definite duration. Stated another way, freehold means ownership and less-than-freehold means rental.

LEASEHOLD ESTATES

As previously noted, the user of a property need not be its owner. Under a leasehold estate, the user is called the **lessee** or **tenant,** and the person from whom he leases is the **lessor** or **landlord.** As long as the tenant has a valid lease, abides by it, and pays the rent on time, the owner, even though he owns the property, cannot occupy it until the lease has expired. During the lease period, the freehold estate owner is said to hold a **reversion.** This is his right to recover possession at the end of the lease period. Meanwhile, the lease is an encumbrance against the property.

There are four categories of leasehold estates: estate for years, periodic estate, estate at will, and tenancy at sufferance. Note that in this chapter we will be examining leases primarily from the standpoint of estates in land. Leases as financing tools are discussed in Chapter 12 and lease contracts are covered in Chapter 15.

Estate for Years

Also called a tenancy for years, the **estate for years** is somewhat misleadingly named as it implies that a lease for a number of years has been created. Actually, the key criterion is that the lease have a specific starting time and a specific ending time. It can be for any length of time, ranging from less than a day to many years. An estate for years does not automatically renew itself. Neither the landlord nor the tenant must act to terminate it, as the lease agreement itself specifies a termination date.

Usually the lessor is the freehold estate owner. However, the lessor could also be a lessee. To illustrate, a fee owner leases to a lessee who in turn leases to another person. By doing this, this first lessee has become a **sublessor.** The person who leases from him is a **sublessee.** It is important to realize that in no case can a sublessee acquire from the lessee any more rights than the lessee has. Thus, if a lessee has a 5-year lease with 3 years remaining, he can assign to a sublessee only the remaining 3 years or a portion of it.

Periodic Estate

Also called an estate from year-to-year or a periodic tenancy, a **periodic estate** has an original lease period with fixed length; when it runs out, unless the tenant or the landlord acts to terminate it, renewal is automatic for another like period of time. A month-to-month apartment rental is an example of this arrangement. To avoid last minute confusion, rental agreements usually require that advance notice be given if either the landlord or the tenant wishes to terminate the tenancy.

Estate at Will

Also called a tenancy at will, an **estate at will** is a landlord-tenant relationship with all the normal rights and duties of a lessor-lessee relationship, except that the estate may be terminated by either the lessor or the lessee at anytime. However, most states recognize the inconvenience a literal interpretation of *anytime* can cause, and require that reasonable advance notice be given. What is considered "reasonable" notice is often specified by state law.

Tenancy at Sufferance

A **tenancy at sufferance** occurs when a tenant stays beyond his legal tenancy without the consent of the landlord. In other words, the tenant wrongfully holds the property against the owner's wishes. In a tenancy at sufferance, the tenant is commonly called a **holdover tenant,** although once the stay exceeds the terms of the lease or rental agreement he is not actually a tenant in the normal landlord-tenant sense. The landlord is entitled to evict him and recover possession of the property, provided the landlord does so in a timely manner. A tenant at sufferance differs from a trespasser only in that the original entry was rightful. If during the holdover period the tenant pays and the landlord accepts rent, the tenancy at sufferance changes to a periodic estate.

OVERVIEW   Figure 3:5 provides an overview of the various rights and interests in land that are discussed in this chapter and the previous chapter. This chart is designed to give you an overall perspective of what real estate includes.

License   A **license** is not a right or an estate in land, but a personal privilege given to someone to use land. It is nonassignable and can be canceled by the person who issues it. A license to park is typically what an automobile parking lot operator provides for persons parking in his lot. The contract creating the license is usually written on the stub that the lot attendant gives the driver, or it is posted on a sign on the lot. Tickets to theaters and sporting events also fall into this category. Because it is a personal privilege, a license is not an encumbrance against land.

Chattels   A **chattel** is an article of personal property. The word comes from the old English word for cattle, which, of course, were (and still are) personal property. Chattel is a word more often heard in a law office than in a real estate office. Occasionally you will see it used in legal documents, such as in the case of a **chattel mortgage,** which is a mortgage against personal property.

Law Sources   You will better understand real estate law when you understand its roots. Most American law originally came from early English law through English colonization of America. Additionally, Spanish law, via Spain's colonization of Mexico, can be found in Arizona, California, Idaho, Nevada, New Mexico, Texas, and Washington. Lastly, old French civil law, by way of the French ownership of Louisiana, is the basis for that state's law. In all three of these, the law that took root in America originated in predominantly agricultural economies. Consequently, there has been a great deal of legal modification over the years by legislatures and courts.

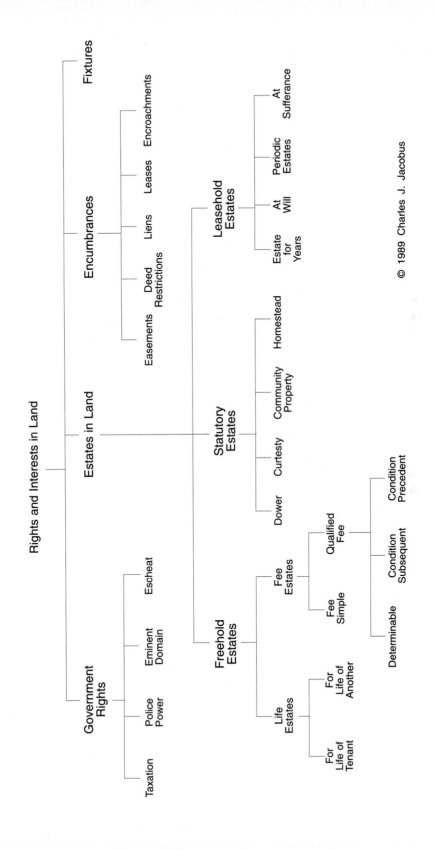

© 1989 Charles J. Jacobus

Figure 3:5. Rights and Interests in Land

Common Law   You will also find it helpful to understand the difference between common law and statutory law. **Common law** derives its authority from usage and custom over long periods of time. Thus the concepts of fee simple estates, qualified fee estates, life estates, leasehold estates, mortgages, air rights and subsurface rights, for example, grew out of usage over hundreds of years. Individual court decisions (called **case law**) also contributed to the development of common law in England and the United States.

Statutory Law   **Statutory law** is created by the enactment of legislation. Examples of statutory laws are laws enacted by state legislatures that require the licensing of real estate agents. Zoning laws and building codes are also statutory laws as they have their source in legislative enactment. Federal and state income tax and local property tax laws are statutory laws.

Sometimes common law concepts are enacted into statutory law. For example, many statutory laws pertaining to leasehold estates and the rights and obligations of landlords and tenants have come directly from common law. Additionally, statutory laws have been passed where common law was held to be unclear or unreasonable. For example, old English law did not provide equality in property rights for both spouses. Modern statutory laws do provide equality.

REVIEW QUESTIONS

1. The system under which individuals are given the right to own land is known as the
   A. feudal system.
   B. allodial system.
   C. chattel system.
   D. fee system.

2. By which of the following processes may a government acquire ownership of privately held land?
   A. Condemnation.
   B. Taxation.
   C. Police power.
   D. Escheat.
   E. Both A and D.

3. The right of the government to place reasonable restrictions on the use of privately held land is known as
   A. a restrictive covenant.
   B. police power.
   C. escheat.
   D. estate.

4. Which of the following is NOT an example of a government's exercise of its police powers?
   A. Rent controls.
   B. Building codes.
   C. Zoning laws.
   D. Restrictive covenants.

5. Property owned by a person who dies intestate and without heirs will escheat to the
   A. city.
   B. city or county.
   C. state or county.
   D. federal government.

6. A property owner who holds fee simple title to land will have all of the following "sticks" in his bundle of rights EXCEPT the right to:
   A. occupy and use it.
   B. restrict the use of the land.
   C. devise it by will.
   D. violate building, health, and safety codes.

7. The term "estate" refers to
   A. the quantity of land as shown on a plat of the property.
   B. one's legal rights in the land.
   C. both A and B.
   D. Neither A nor B.

8. All of the following constitute an encumbrance on the fee simple title to real property EXCEPT
   A. a will conveying the property to the owner's heirs upon death of the owner.
   B. a restrictive covenant in the deed to the property.
   C. a mortgage.
   D. a lease.

9. Which of the following easements could be created without a written document?
   A. An easement by necessity.
   B. An easement by prescription.
   C. Both A and B.
   D. Neither A nor B.

10. An easement is
    A. an appurtenance to the holder of the dominant tenement.
    B. an encumbrance to the holder of the servient tenement.
    C. Both A and B.
    D. Neither A nor B.

11. Morris sold the back half of his lot to Katz, and gave Katz a permanent easement across his land in order for Katz to have access to the road. Which of the following statements is true?
    A. The easement is an easement in gross.
    B. The easement is an easement appurtenant.
    C. The servient estate is held by Katz.
    D. The dominant estate is held by Morris.

12. An easement appurtenant may NOT be terminated
    A. by combination of the dominant and servient tenements.
    B. when the purpose for the easement no longer exists.
    C. by lack of use.
    D. unilaterally by the holder of the servient tenement.

13. All of the following may constitute a lien on real property EXCEPT:
   A. a mortgage.
   B. unpaid real property taxes.
   C. a restrictive covenant in a deed.
   D. a judgment against the owner.

14. Which of the following are examples of special liens?
   A. Mechanic's liens.
   B. Judgment liens.
   C. Ad valorem tax liens.
   D. Federal income tax liens.
   E. Both A and C.

15. Which of the following is NOT classified as a freehold estate?
   A. An estate created by statute.
   B. A life estate.
   C. A fee simple estate.
   D. A leasehold estate.

16. Real estate held as a leasehold
   A. is used by the owner rather than the tenant.
   B. reverts to the tenant upon termination of the lease.
   C. Both A and B.
   D. Neither A nor B.

17. Unless the landlord or tenant acts to terminate it, an estate from period-to-period
   A. automatically renews itself.
   B. continues for an indefinite time.
   C. Both A and B.
   D. Neither A nor B.

18. The lessor holds a reversion in which of the following situations?
   A. Estate for years.   D. Tenancy at sufferance.
   B. Periodic estate.   E. All of the above.
   C. Estate at will.

19. A tenant at sufferance is
   A. a legal tenant.   C. a licensee.
   B. a trespasser.   D. a guest.

20. A chattel is
   A. an item of personal property.
   B. an item of real property such as a building.
   C. a freehold estate in land.
   D. a term that refers to land used for cattle ranching.

Forms of Ownership

This chapter will look at how a given right or interest in land is held by one or more individuals. It covers such topics as sole ownership, tenants in common, joint tenancy, tenancy by the entirety, and community property.

OVERVIEW OF
CHAPTER 4

LEARNING OBJECTIVES

After completion of this chapter, you should be able to:

1. Explain the characteristics and benefits of sole ownership.
2. Understand the advantages and disadvantages of community property.
3. Describe the various types of partnerships.
4. Define a joint venture and explain the benefits of such a venture.
5. Explain the types of corporation.
6. Describe real estate associations and trusts.
7. Understand the advantages of a limited partnership or S corporation.
8. Define and explain the significance of the four unities.
9. Explain the different aspects of community and separate property.

KEY • TERMS

Community property: spouses are treated as equal partners with each owning a one-half interest

Concurrent ownership: ownership by two or more persons at the same time

Estate in severalty: owned by one person; sole ownership

Joint tenancy: a form of property co-ownership that features the right of survivorship

Limited Liability Company: organization of members or managers with little formal organization and limited liability

Limited partnership: composed of general partners who mainly organize and operate the partnership and limited partners who provide the capital

Right of survivorship: a feature of joint tenancy whereby the surviving joint tenants automatically acquire all the rights, title, and interest of the deceased joint tenant

Tenancy by the entirety: a form of joint ownership reserved for married persons; right of survivorship exists and neither spouse has a disposable interest during the lifetime of the other

Tenants in common: shared ownership of a single property among two or more persons; interests need not be equal and no right of survivorship exists

Undivided interest: ownership by two or more persons that gives each the right to use the entire property

In Chapter 2 we looked at land from a physical standpoint: the size and shape of a parcel, where it is located, and what was affixed to it. In Chapter 3 we explored various legal rights and interests that can be held in land. In this chapter we shall look at how a given right or interest in land can be held by one or more individuals.

SOLE OWNERSHIP

When title to property is held by one person, it is called an **estate in severalty** or **sole ownership.** Although the word *severalty* seems to imply that several persons own a single property, the correct meaning can be easily remembered by thinking of "severed" ownership. Sole ownership is available to single and married persons. As a general rule, property acquired by a person before marriage continues to be the sole property of that person during marriage. Property acquired during marriage may be sole property if it can be proved it was bought with separate funds or there is a written waiver of marital property rights by one spouse. Businesses usually hold title to property in severalty. It is from the estate in severalty that all other tenancies are created.

The major advantage of sole ownership for an individual is flexibility. As a sole owner you can make all the decisions regarding a property without having to get the agreement of co-owners. You can decide what property or properties to buy, when to buy, and how much to offer. You can decide whether to pay all cash or to seek a loan by using the property as collateral. Once bought, you control (within the bounds of the law) how the property will be used, how much will be charged if it is rented, and how it will be managed. If you decide to sell, you alone decide when to offer the property for sale and at what price and terms.

But freedom and responsibility go together. For example, if you purchase a rental property you must determine the prevailing rents, find tenants, prepare contracts, collect the rent, and keep the property in repair; or, you must hire and pay someone else to manage the property. Another deterrent to sole ownership is the high entry cost. This form of real estate ownership is usually not possible for someone with only a few hundred dollars to invest.

Let us now turn to methods of **concurrent ownership,** i.e., ownership by two or more persons at the same time.

When two or more persons wish to share the ownership of a single property, they may do so as **tenants in common.** As tenants in common, each owns an **undivided interest** in the whole property. This means that each owner has a right to possession of the entire property. None can exclude the others nor claim any specific portion for himself. In a tenancy in common, these interests need not be the same size, and each owner can independently sell, mortgage, give away, or devise his individual interest. This independence is possible because each tenant in common has a separate legal title to his undivided interest.

TENANTS IN COMMON

Suppose that you invest $20,000 along with two of your friends, who invest $30,000 and $50,000, respectively; together you buy 100 acres of land as tenants in common. Presuming that everyone's ownership interest is proportional to his or her cash investment, you will hold a 20% interest in the entire 100 acres and your two friends will hold 30% and 50%. You cannot pick out 20 acres and exclude the other co-owners from them, nor can you pick out 20 acres and say, "These are mine and I'm going to sell them;" nor can they do that to you. You do, however, have the legal right to sell or otherwise dispose of your 20% interest (or a portion of it) without the permission of your two friends. Your friends have the same right. If one of you sells, the purchaser becomes a new tenant in common with the remaining co-owners.

Wording of Conveyance

As a rule, a tenancy in common is indicated by naming the co-owners in the conveyance and adding the words *as tenants in common*. For example, a deed might read, "Samuel Smith, John Jones, and Robert Miller, as tenants in common." If nothing is said regarding the size of each co-owner's interest in the property, the law presumes that all interests are equal. Therefore, if the co-owners intend their interests to be unequal, the size of each co-owner's undivided interest must be stated as a percent or a fraction, such as 60% and 40% or one-third and two-thirds.

In nearly all states, if two or more persons are named as owners, and there is no specific indication as to how they are taking title, they are presumed to be tenants in common. Thus, if a deed is made out to "Donna Adams and Barbara Kelly," the law would consider them to be tenants in common, each holding an undivided one-half interest in the property. An important exception to this presumption is when the co-owners are married to each other. In this case, they may be automatically considered to be taking ownership as joint tenants, tenants by the entirety, or community property depending on state law.

No Right of Survivorship

When a tenancy in common exists, if a co-owner dies his interest passes to his heirs or devisees, who then become tenants in common with the remaining co-owners. There is no **right of survivorship;** that is, the remaining co-owners do not acquire the deceased's interest unless they are named in the **deceased's last will and testament** to do so. When a creditor has a claim on a co-owner's interest and forces its sale to satisfy the debt, the new buyer becomes a tenant in common with the remaining co-owners. If one co-owner wants to sell (or give away) only a portion of his undivided interest, he may; the new owner becomes a tenant in common with the other co-owners.

Co-owner Responsibilities

Any income generated by the property belongs to the tenants in common in proportion to the size of their interests. Similarly, each co-owner is responsible for paying his proportionate share of property taxes, repairs, upkeep, and so on, plus interest and debt repayment, if any. If any co-owner fails to contribute his proportionate share, the other co-owners can pay on his behalf and then sue him for that amount. If co-owners find that they cannot agree as to how the property is to be run and cannot agree on a plan for dividing or selling it, it is possible to request a court-ordered partition. A **partition** divides the property into distinct portions so that each person can hold his proportionate interest in severalty. If this is physically impossible, such as when three co-owners each have a one-third interest in a house, the court will order the property sold and the proceeds divided among the co-owners.

"What Ifs"

The major advantage of tenancy in common is that it allows two or more persons to achieve goals that one person could not accomplish alone. However, prospective co-owners should give advance thought to what they will do (short of going to court) (1) if a co-owner fails to pay his share of ownership expenses, (2) if differences arise regarding how the property is to be operated, (3) if agreement cannot be reached as to when to sell, for how much, and on what terms, and (4) if a co-owner dies and those who inherit his interest have little in common with the surviving co-owners. The counsel of an attorney experienced in property ownership can be very helpful when considering the co-ownership of property.

JOINT TENANCY

Another form of concurrent ownership is **joint tenancy.** The most distinguishing characteristic of joint tenancy is the right of survivorship. Upon the death of a joint tenant, his interest does not descend to his heirs or pass by his will. Rather, the entire ownership remains in the surviving joint tenant(s). In other words, there is simply one less owner.

Four Unities

To create a joint tenancy, **four unities** must be present. They are the unities of time, title, interest, and possession.

Unity of time means that each joint tenant must acquire his or her ownership interest at the same moment. Once a joint tenancy is formed, it is not possible to add new joint tenants later unless an entirely new joint tenancy is formed among the existing co-owners and the new co-owner. To illustrate, suppose that *A,*

B, and *C* own a parcel of land as joint tenants. If *A* sells his interest to *D*, then *B*, *C*, and *D* must sign documents to create a new joint tenancy among them. If this is not done, *D* automatically becomes a tenant in common with *B* and *C* who, between themselves, remain joint tenants. *D* will then own an undivided one-third interest in common with *B* and *C* who will own an undivided two-thirds interest as joint tenants.

Unity of title means that the joint tenants acquire their interests from the same source, i.e., the same deed or will. (Some states allow a property owner to create a valid joint tenancy by conveying to himself, or herself, and another without going through a third party.)

Unity of interest means that the joint tenants own one interest together and each joint tenant has exactly the same right in that interest. (This, by the way, is the foundation upon which the survivorship feature rests.) If the joint tenants list individual interests, they lack unity of interest and will be treated as tenants in common. Unity of interest also means that, if one joint tenant holds a fee simple interest in the property, the others cannot hold anything but a fee simple interest.

Unity of possession means that the joint tenants must enjoy the same undivided possession of the whole property. All joint tenants have the use of the entire property, and no individual owns a particular portion of it. By way of contrast, unity of possession is the only unity essential to a tenancy in common.

Right of Survivorship

The feature of joint tenancy ownership that is most widely recognized is its **right of survivorship.** Upon the death of a joint tenant, that interest in the property is extinguished. In a two-person joint tenancy, when one person dies, the other immediately becomes the sole owner. With more than two persons as joint tenants, when one dies, the remaining joint tenants are automatically left as owners. Ultimately, the last survivor becomes the sole owner. The legal philosophy is that the joint tenants constitute a single owning unit. The death of one joint tenant does not destroy that unit—it only reduces the number of persons owning the unit. For the public record, a copy of the death certificate and an affidavit of death of the joint tenant is recorded in the county where the property is located. The property must also be released from any estate tax liens.

It is the right of survivorship that has made joint tenancy a popular form of ownership among married couples. Married couples often want the surviving spouse to have sole ownership of the marital property. Any property held in joint tenancy goes to the surviving spouse without the delay of probate and usually with less legal expense.

Because of the survivorship feature, joint tenancy has loosely been labeled a "poor man's will." However, it cannot replace a properly drawn will as it affects only that property held in joint tenancy. Moreover, a will can be changed if the persons named therein are no longer in one's favor. But once a joint tenancy is formed, title is permanently conveyed and there is no further opportunity for change. As a joint tenant, you cannot will your joint tenancy interest to someone because your interest ends upon your death. Also, be aware that ownership in joint tenancy may result in additional estate taxes.

"Poor Man's Will"

Another important aspect of joint tenancy ownership is that it can be used to defeat dower or curtesy rights. If a married man forms a joint tenancy with someone other than his wife (such as a business partner) and then dies, his wife has no dower rights in that joint tenancy. As a result, courts have begun to look with disfavor upon the right of survivorship. Louisiana, Ohio, and Oregon either do not recognize joint tenancy or have abolished it.[*] Of the remaining states that recognize joint tenancy ownership (see Table 4:1), 14 have abolished the automatic presumption of survivorship. In these states, if the right of survivorship is desired in a joint tenancy, it must be clearly stated in the conveyance. For example, a deed might read, "Karen Carson and Judith Johnson, as joint tenants with the right of survivorship and not as tenants in common." Even in those states not requiring it, this wording is often used to ensure that the right of survivorship is intended. In community property states, one spouse cannot take

---

[*] In Ohio and Oregon other means are available to achieve rights of survivorship between nonmarried persons. When two or more persons own property together in Louisiana, it is termed an "ownership in indivision" or a "joint ownership." Louisiana law is based on old French civil law.

Table 4:1. Concurrent Ownership By States

	Tenancy in Common	Joint Tenancy	Tenancy by the Entirety	Community Property		Tenancy in Common	Joint Tenancy	Tenancy by the Entirety	Community Property
Alabama	X	X			Missouri	X	X	X	
Alaska	X	X	X		Montana	X	X		
Arizona	X	X		X					
Arkansas	X	X	X		Nebraska	X	X		
					Nevada	X	X		X
California	X	X		X	New Hampshire	X	X		
Colorado	X	X			New Jersey	X	X	X	
Connecticut	X	X			New Mexico	X	X		X
					New York	X	X	X	
Delaware	X	X	X		North Carolina	X	X	X	
District of Columbia	X	X	X		North Dakota	X	X		
					Ohio	X		X	
Florida	X	X	X		Oklahoma	X	X	X	
					Oregon	X		X	
Georgia	X	X			Pennsylvania	X	X	X	
Hawaii	X	X	X		Rhode Island	X	X	X	
Idaho	X	X		X					
Illinois	X	X			South Carolina	X	X		
Indiana	X	X	X		South Dakota	X	X		
Iowa	X	X							
					Tennessee	X	X	X	
Kansas	X	X			Texas	X	X		X
Kentucky	X	X	X		Utah	X	X	X	
Louisiana				X					
					Vermont	X	X	X	
Maine	X	X			Virginia	X	X	X	
Maryland	X	X	X						
Massachusetts	X	X	X		Washington	X	X		X
Michigan	X	X	X		West Virginia	X	X	X	
Minnesota	X	X			Wisconsin	X	X		
Mississippi	X	X	X		Wyoming	X	X	X	

community funds and establish a valid joint tenancy with a third party.

There is a popular misconception that a debtor can protect himself from creditors' claims by taking title to property as a joint tenant. It is true that in a joint tenancy the surviving joint tenant(s) acquire(s) the property free and clear of any liens against the deceased. However, this can happen only if the debtor dies before the creditor seizes the debtor's interest.

Only a human being can be a joint tenant. A corporation cannot be a joint tenant. This is because a corporation is an artificial legal being and can exist in perpetuity, i.e., never die. Joint tenancy ownership is not limited to the ownership of land; any estate in land and any chattel interest may be held in joint tenancy.

Tenancy by the entirety (also called tenancy by the entireties) is a form of joint tenancy specifically for married persons. To the four unities of a joint tenancy is added a fifth: **unity of person.** The basis for this is the legal premise that a husband and wife are an indivisible legal unit. Two key characteristics of a tenancy by the entirety are (1) the surviving spouse becomes the sole owner of the property upon the death of the other, and (2) neither spouse has a disposable interest in the property during the lifetime of the other. Thus, while both are alive and married to each other, both signatures are necessary to convey title to the property. With respect to the first characteristic, tenancy by the entirety is similar to joint tenancy because both feature the right of survivorship. They are quite different, however, with respect to the second characteristic. Whereas a joint tenant can convey to another party without approval of the other joint tenant(s), a tenancy by the entirety can be terminated only by joint action of husband and wife.

States that recognize tenancy by the entirety are listed in Table 4:1. Some of these states automatically assume that a tenancy by the entirety is created when married persons buy real estate. However, it is best to use a phrase such as "John and Mary Smith, husband and wife as tenants by the entirety with the right of survivorship" on deeds and other conveyances. This avoids later questions as to whether their intention might have been to create a joint tenancy or a tenancy in common.

There are several important advantages to tenancy by the entirety ownership: (1) it protects against one spouse conveying or mortgaging the couple's property without the consent of the other, (2) it provides in many states some protection from the forced

TENANCY BY THE ENTIRETY

Advantages and Disadvantages

sale of jointly held property to satisfy a debt judgment against one of the spouses, and (3) it features automatic survivorship. Disadvantages are that (1) tenancy by the entirety provides for no one except the surviving spouse, (2) it may create estate tax problems, and (3) it does not replace the need for a will to direct how the couple's personal property shall be disposed.

Effect of Divorce

In the event of divorce, the parting spouses become tenants in common. This change is automatic, as tenancy by the entirety can exist only when the co-owners are husband and wife. If the ex-spouses do not wish to continue co-ownership, either can sell his or her individual interest. If a buyer cannot be found for a partial interest nor an amicable agreement reached for selling the interests of both ex-spouses simultaneously, either may seek a court action to partition the property.

Note that severalty, tenancy in common, joint tenancy, and tenancy by the entirety are called English common law estates because of their historical roots in English common law.

COMMUNITY PROPERTY

Laws and customs acquired from Spain and France when vast areas of the United States were under their control are the basis for the **community property** system of ownership for married persons. Table 4:1 identifies the eight community property states. The laws of each community property state vary slightly, but the underlying concept is that the husband and wife contribute jointly and equally to their marriage and thus should share equally in any property purchased during marriage. Whereas English law is based on the merging of husband and wife upon marriage, community property law treats husband and wife as equal partners, with each owning a one-half interest.

Separate Property

Property owned before marriage, and property acquired after marriage by gift, inheritance, or purchase with separate funds, can be exempted from the couple's community property. Such property is called **separate property** and can be conveyed or mortgaged without the signature of the owner's spouse. The owner of a separate property also has full control over naming someone in his or her will to receive the property. All other property acquired by the husband or wife during marriage is considered community property and requires the signature of both spouses before it can be conveyed or mortgaged. Each spouse can name in his or her will the person to receive his or her one-half interest. It does not have to go to the surviving spouse. If death occurs without a will, in five states (California, Idaho, Nevada, New Mexico and Washington) the deceased spouse's interest goes to the surviving spouse. In Arizona, Louisiana, and Texas, the descendants of the deceased spouse are the prime recipients. Texas also allows community property to be held with a right of survivorship. Neither dower nor curtesy exists in community property states.

Philosophy

The major advantage of the community property system is found in its philosophy: it treats the spouses as equal partners in property acquired through their mutual efforts during marriage. Even if the wife elects to be a full-time homemaker and all the money brought into the household is the result of her husband's job (or vice versa), the law treats them as equal co-owners in any property bought with that money. This is true even if only one spouse is named as the owner.

In the event of divorce, if the parting couple cannot amicably decide how to divide their community property, the courts will usually do so. If the courts do not, the ex-spouses will become tenants in common with each other. If it later becomes necessary, either can file suit for partition.

Caveat to Agents

Often, while preparing a real estate purchase contract, the buyers will ask the real estate agent how to take title. This is an especially common question posed by married couples purchasing a home. If the agent attempts to answer with a specific recommendation, the agent is practicing law, and that requires a license to practice law. The agent can describe the ownership methods available in the state, but should then refer the buyers to their lawyer for a specific recommendation. This is important because the choice of ownership method cannot be made in the vacuum of a single purchase. It must be made in the light of the buyers' total financial picture and estate plans, by someone well-versed in federal and state estate and tax laws. Meanwhile, on the purchase contract the agent can enter the names of the purchasers and add the words, *vesting to be supplied before closing.* This gives the buyers time to decide how to hold title without delaying preparation of the purchase contract. The buyers can then seek legal counsel and advise the closing agent how they want to take title on the deed.

1. Able, Baker, and Charles are going to purchase an investment property as co-owners, and will take title as joint tenants. Which of the following statements are incorrect?
   A. All will acquire their interests at the same moment in time.
   B. Each will receive a separate deed for his share.
   C. All will have equal interest in the property.
   D. All will enjoy equal rights of possession.

2. A married person can hold as separate property
   A. property bought by that person before marriage.
   B. property inherited by that person after marriage.
   C. Both A and B.
   D. Neither A nor B.

3. A tenant in common may NOT
   A. claim a portion of the property for his own use.
   B. convey his interest by will.
   C. use his share of the property as collateral for a mortgage loan.
   D. sell his share without the agreement of the other tenants.

4. All of the following are true of joint tenancy EXCEPT:
   A. Unities of time, title, interest, and possession must be present.
   B. New joint tenants may be added without forming a new joint tenancy.
   C. Survivorship exists among joint tenants.
   D. A husband and wife may hold title as joint tenants.

5. Joint tenants must acquire their interests in jointly held property
   A. at the same time.
   B. from the same source.
   C. in the same instrument.
   D. All of the above.

6. If any unity of joint tenancy is broken, the law will regard the estate as
   A. a tenancy by the entireties.
   B. community property.
   C. a tenancy in common.
   D. an estate in severalty.

7. If tenants by the entireties divorce, barring any other agreement
   A. they become tenants in common with each other.
   B. divorce does not affect the status of the title to the property.
   C. the ex-wife takes title in severalty.
   D. the ex-husband takes title in severalty.

8. Community property laws are derived from legal concepts which have their origin in
   A. Spanish and French law.
   B. English common law.
   C. American statutory law.
   D. English parliamentary law.

9. Mr. and Mrs. Marvin live in a community property state. Which of the following would most likely be considered their community property?
   A. Property which is inherited by either spouse.
   B. Property conveyed as a gift to either spouse.
   C. Property purchased after they were married.
   D. Property owned by either spouse prior to their marriage.

10. In community property states, which of the following exists?
   A. Dower.
   B. Curtesy.
   C. Both A and B.
   D. Neither A nor B.

11. Smith, Duncan and Robbins formed a partnership to purchase real estate. Robbins and Smith want to restrict their liability, naming Smith as the general partner. What type of ownership did they create?
   A. A syndicate.
   B. General partnership.
   C. Joint venture.
   D. Limited partnership.

12. In order to hold property in the name of the partnership, a list of the partners must be published in each county and state
   A. where the partnership does business.
   B. where the partnership owns property.
   C. Both A and B.
   D. Neither A nor B.

13. In a general partnership,
   A. each partner has unlimited financial liability.
   B. each partner pays individual taxes on his/her share of the partnership's earnings.
   C. Both A and B.
   D. Neither A nor B.

14. An advantage of the partnership form of ownership is
   A. the aggregation of capital and individual expertise.
   B. individual taxation of profits and/or losses.
   C. Both A and B.
   D. Neither A nor B.

15. The limited partnership has become popular as a means of owning real estate because of
   A. limited liability.
   B. minimum management responsibility.
   C. direct pass-through of profits.
   D. All of the above.

16. A joint venture differs from a partnership in that
   A. a joint venture is formed to carry out a single project.
   B. a joint venturer cannot bind the other joint venturers to a contract.
   C. Both A and B.
   D. Neither A nor B.

17. Which of the following usually offers the most liquid form of property ownership?
   A. Limited partnership.
   B. Joint tenancy.
   C. Sole ownership.
   D. General partnership.

18. The possibility of double taxation on income is a negative factor in
    A. the corporate form of ownership.
    B. the limited partnership form of ownership.
    C. major corporations only.
    D. All of the above.

19. Protection from personal liability is an advantage of
    A. corporate ownership.
    B. general partnership ownership.
    C. Both A and B.
    D. Neither A nor B.

20. Mr. Rose wants to set up a trust to provide income for his minor children, to take effect after his death. What form of trust would this be?
    A. Inter vivos trust.   C. General trust.
    B. Testamentary trust.   D. Corporate trust.

Transferring Title

In this chapter you will learn how the ownership of real estate is conveyed from one owner to another. Voluntary conveyance of real estate by deed, conveyance after death and conveyance by occupancy, accession, public grant, dedication, and forfeiture are covered. An important part of this chapter and a part that you should review very carefully is the coverage of the essential elements of a deed. Likewise, the various covenants and warranties should be reviewed.

*OVERVIEW OF
CHAPTER 5*

LEARNING OBJECTIVES

After completion of this chapter, you should be able to:

1. Understand the essential elements of a deed.
2. Describe the various covenants and warranties.
3. Explain the different types of deeds, such as the general warranty deed, the special warranty deed, the bargain and sale deed, and the quitclaim deed.
4. Explain how real estate is conveyed after death.
5. Define codicil, adverse possession, tacking on, easement by prescription, and ownership by accession.
6. Explain how property is transferred by public grant, dedication, reversion, and alienation.
7. Define a gift deed, guardian deed, and other types of deeds.

KEY • TERMS

Adverse possession: acquisition of land through prolonged and unauthorized occupation

Bargain and sale deed: a deed that contains no covenants, but does imply that the grantor owns the property being conveyed

Cloud on the title: any claim, lien, or encumbrance that impairs title to property

Color of title: some plausible, but not completely clear-cut indication of ownership rights

Consideration: anything of value given to induce another to enter into a contract

Covenant: a written agreement or promise

Deed: a written document that when properly executed and delivered conveys title to land.

Grantee: the person named in a deed who acquires ownership

Grantor: the person named in a deed who conveys ownership

Quitclaim deed: a legal instrument used to convey whatever title the grantor has; it contains no covenants, warranties nor implication of the grantor's ownership

Special warranty deed: grantor warrants title only against defects occurring during the grantor's ownership

Warranty: an assurance or guarantee that something is true as stated

The previous three chapters emphasized how real estate is described, the rights and interests available for ownership, and how title can be held. In this chapter we shall discuss how ownership of real estate is conveyed from one owner to another. We begin with the voluntary conveyance of real estate by deed, and then continue with conveyance after death, and conveyance by occupancy, accession, public grant, dedication, and forfeiture.

DEEDS A **deed** is a written legal document by which ownership of real property is conveyed from one party to another. Deeds were not always used to transfer real estate. In early England, when land was sold, its title was conveyed by inviting the purchaser onto the land. In the presence of witnesses, the seller picked up a clod of earth and handed it to the purchaser. Simultaneously, the seller stated that he was delivering ownership of the land to the purchaser. In times when land sales were rare, because ownership usually passed from generation to generation, and when witnesses seldom moved from the towns or farms where they were born, this method worked well. However, as transactions became more common and people more mobile, this method of title transfer became less reliable. Furthermore, it was susceptible to fraud if enough people could be bribed or forced to make false statements. In 1677, England passed a law known as the **Statute of Frauds.** This law, subsequently adopted by each of the American states, requires that transfers of real estate ownership be in writing and signed in order to be enforceable in a court of law. Thus, the need for a deed was created.

What makes a written document a deed? What special phrases, statements, and actions are necessary to convey the ownership rights one has in land and buildings? First, a deed must identify the **grantor,** who is the person giving up ownership, and the **grantee,** the person who is acquiring that ownership. The actual act of conveying ownership is known as a **grant.** To be legally enforceable, the grantor must be of legal age (18 years in most states) and of sound mind.

Essential Elements of a Deed

Second, the deed must state that **consideration** was given by the grantee to the grantor. It is common to see the phrase, *For ten dollars ($10.00) and other good and valuable consideration,* or the phrase, *For valuable consideration.* These meet the legal requirement that consideration be shown, but retain privacy regarding the exact amount paid.

If the conveyance is a gift, the phrase *For natural love and affection* may be used, provided the gift is not for the purpose of defrauding the grantor's creditors. In these situations, consideration is not required in a deed, and the conveyance is still valid.

Third, the deed must contain **words of conveyance.** With these words the grantor (1) clearly states that he is making a grant of real property to the grantee, and (2) identifies the quantity of the estate being granted. Usually the estate is fee simple, but it may also be a lesser estate (such as a life estate) or an easement.

Words of Conveyance

A **land description** that cannot possibly be misunderstood is the fourth requirement. Acceptable legal descriptions are made by the metes and bounds method, by the government survey system, by recorded plat, or by reference to another recorded document that in turn uses one of these methods. Street names and numbers are not used because they do not identify the exact boundaries of the land and because street names and numbers can and do change over time. Assessor parcel numbers are not used either. They are subject to change

Figure 5:1.

> *Witnesseth,* __John Stanley__ *, grantor, for valuable consideration given by* __Robert Brenner__ *, grantee, does hereby grant and release unto the grantee, his heirs and assigns to have and to hold forever, the following described land: [insert legal description here].*
>
> __John Stanley__
> Grantor's signature

by the assessor, and the maps they refer to are for the purpose of collecting taxes. If the deed conveys only an easement or air right, the deed states that fact along with the legal description of the land. The key point is that a deed must clearly specify what the grantor is granting to the grantee.

Signature

Fifth, the grantor executes the deed by signing it. Eight states require that the grantor's signature be witnessed and that the witnesses sign the deed. If the grantor is unable to write his name, he may make a mark, usually an *X*, in the presence of witnesses. They in turn print his name next to the *X* and sign as witnesses. If the grantor is a corporation, the corporation's seal is affixed to the deed and two of the corporation's officers sign it.

Figure 5:1 illustrates the essential elements that combine to form a deed. Notice that the example includes an identification of the grantor and grantee, fulfills the requirement for consideration, has words of conveyance, a legal description of the land involved, and the grantor's signature. The words of conveyance are *grant and release* and the phrase *to have and to hold forever* says that the grantor is conveying all future benefits, not just a life estate or a tenancy for years. Ordinarily, the grantee does not sign the deed.

Delivery and Acceptance

For a deed to convey ownership, there must also be **delivery and acceptance.** Although a deed may be completed and signed, it does not transfer title to the grantee until the grantor voluntarily delivers it to the grantee and the grantee willingly accepts it. At that moment title passes. As a practical matter, the grantee is presumed to have accepted the deed if the grantee retains the deed, records the deed, encumbers the title, or performs any other act of ownership. This includes the grantee's appointment of someone else to accept and/or record the deed on the grantee's behalf. Once delivery and acceptance have occurred, the deed is evidence that the title transfer has taken place.

Although legally adequate, a deed meeting the preceding requirements can still leave a very important question unanswered in the grantee's mind: "Does the grantor possess all the right, title, and interest he is purporting to convey by this deed?" As a protective measure, the grantee can ask the grantor to include certain covenants and warranties in the deed. These are written promises by the grantor that the condition of title is as stated in the deed together with the grantor's guarantee that if title is not as stated he will compensate the grantee for any loss suffered. Five covenants and warranties have evolved over the centuries for use in deeds, and a deed may contain none, some, or all of them, in addition to the essential elements already discussed. They are seizin, quiet enjoyment, against encumbrances, further assurance, and warranty forever.

Under the **covenant of seizin** (sometimes spelled seisin), the grantor warrants (guarantees) that he is the owner and possessor of the property being conveyed and that he has the right to convey it. Under the **covenant of quiet enjoyment,** the grantor warrants to the grantee that the grantee will not be disturbed, after he takes possession, by someone else claiming an interest in the property.

In the **covenant against encumbrances,** the grantor guarantees to the grantee that the title is not encumbered with any easements, restrictions, unpaid property taxes, assessments, mortgages, judgments, etc., except as stated in the deed. If the grantee later discovers an undisclosed encumbrance, he can sue the grantor for the cost of removing it. The **covenant of further assurance** requires the grantor to procure and deliver to the grantee any subsequent documents that might be necessary to make good the grantee's title. **Warranty forever** is a guarantee to the grantee that the grantor will bear the expense of defending the grantee's title. If at any time in the future someone else can prove that he is the rightful owner, the grantee can sue the grantor for damages up to the value of the property at the time of the sale. Because these warranties and covenants are a formidable

Covenants and Warranties

Figure 5:2.

WARRANTY DEED ①

② *THIS DEED, made in the city of* ③ <u>Exeter</u> , *state of* <u>XY</u> *on the* ④ <u>4th</u> *day of* <u>April</u> , *19 <u>xx</u> , between* ⑤ <u>Henry Odom, a single man</u> , *residing at* ⑥ <u>1234 Pleasant Rd., Exeter, XY</u> , *herein called the GRANTOR,* ⑦ *and* ⑧ <u>Peter Letz and Julie Letz, husband and wife as tenants by the entirety</u> , *residing at* ⑨ <u>567 Friendly Lane, Exeter, XY,</u> *herein called the GRANTEE.* ⑩

WITNESSETH that in consideration ⑪ *of ten dollars ($10.00) and other valuable consideration, paid by the Grantee to the Grantor, the Grantor does hereby grant* ⑫ *and convey unto the Grantee, the Grantee's* ⑬ *heirs and assigns forever, the following described parcel of land:*

[legal description of land] ⑭

together with the buildings ⑮ *and improvements thereon and all the estate* ⑯ *and rights pertaining thereto,*

⑰ *TO HAVE AND TO HOLD the premises herein granted unto the Grantee, the Grantee's heirs* ⑱ *and assigns forever.*

The premises are free from encumbrances except as stated herein: ⑲

[note exceptions here]

The Grantee shall not: ⑳

[list restrictions imposed by Grantor on the Grantee]

The Grantor is lawfully seized ㉑ *of a good, absolute, and indefeasible estate in fee simple and has good right, full power, and lawful authority to convey the same by this deed.*

The Grantee, the Grantee's heirs and assigns, shall peaceably ㉒ *and quietly have, hold, use, occupy, possess, and enjoy the said premises.*

Figure 5:2. continued

> The Grantor shall execute or procure any further ㉓ necessary assurance of the title to said premises, and the Grantor will forever ㉔ warrant and defend the title to said premises.
>
> IN WITNESS WHEREOF, the Grantor has duly executed this deed the day and year first written above. ㉕

[location of the acknowledgment: see Chapter 6] ㉘

㉖ Henry Odom

(Grantor's signature)

㉗ (SEAL)

set of promises, grantors often back them up with title insurance (see Chapter 6). The grantee is also more comfortable if the deed is backed by title insurance.

Although it is customary to show on the deed the **date** it is executed by the grantor, it is not essential to the deed's validity. Remember that title passes upon **delivery** of the deed to the grantee, and that this may not necessarily be the date it is signed.

Date and Acknowledgment

It is standard practice to have the grantor appear before a notary public or other public officer and formally declare that he signed the deed as a voluntary act. This is known as an **acknowledgment.** Most states consider a deed to be valid even though it is not witnessed or acknowledged, but very few states will allow such a deed to be recorded in the public records. Acknowledgments and the importance of recording deeds will be covered in more detail in Chapter 6. Meanwhile, let us turn our attention to examples of the most commonly used deeds in the United States.

The **full covenant and warranty deed,** also known as the **general warranty deed** or **warranty deed,** contains all five covenants and warranties. It is thus considered to be the best deed a grantee can receive, and is used extensively in most states.

Full Covenant and Warranty Deed

Figure 5:2 illustrates in plain language the essential parts of a warranty deed. Beginning at ① , it is customary to identify at the top of the document that it is a warranty deed. At ② the wording begins with *This deed ....* These words are introductory in purpose. The fact that this is a deed depends on what it contains, not on what it is labeled. A commonly found variation starts with *This indenture* (meaning this agreement or contract) and is equally acceptable. The place the deed was made ③ and the date it was signed ④ are customarily included, but are not necessary to make the deed valid.

At ⑤ and ⑥ the grantor is identified by name and, to avoid confusion with other persons having the same name, by address. Marital status is also stated: husband and wife, single man, single woman, widow, widower, divorced and not remarried. To avoid the inconvenience of repeating the grantor's name each time it is needed, the wording at ⑦ states that in the balance of the deed the word *Grantor* will be used instead. A common variation of this is to call the first party named *the party of the first part*. Next appears the name and marital status of the *Grantee* ⑧ and the method by which title is being taken (severalty, tenants in common, joint tenants, etc.). The grantee's address appears at ⑨, and the wording at ⑩ states that the word *Grantee* will now be used instead of the grantee's name. The alternative method is to call the grantee *the party of the second part*.

Granting Clause

The legal requirement that consideration be shown is fulfilled at ⑪. Next we come to the **granting clause** at ⑫. Here the grantor states that the intent of this document is to pass ownership to the grantee; and at ⑬ the grantor describes the extent of the estate being granted. The phrase *The grantee's heirs and assigns forever* indicates a fee simple estate. The word **assigns** refers to anyone the grantee may later convey the property to, such as by sale or gift.

The legal description of the land involved is then shown at ⑭. When a grantor is unable or does not wish to convey certain rights of ownership, he can list the exceptions here. For example, a grantor either not having or wishing to hold back oil and gas rights may convey to the grantee the land described, "except for the right to explore and recover oil and gas at a depth below 500 feet beneath the surface." The separate mention at numbers ⑮ and ⑯ of buildings, estate, and rights is not an essential requirement as the definition of land already includes these items. Some deed forms add the word **appurtenances** at ⑯. Again, this is not essential wording as appurtenances by definition belong to and pass with the conveyance of the land unless specifically withheld by the grantor. Examples of real estate appurtenances are rights-of-way and other easements, water rights, condominium parking stalls, and improvements to land.

The **habendum clause,** sometimes called the "To have and to hold clause," begins at ⑰ and continues through ⑱. This clause, together with the statements at ⑫ and ⑬, forms the deed's words of conveyance. For this reason, the words at ⑱ must match those at ⑬. Number ⑲ identifies the covenant against encumbrances. The grantor warrants that there are no encumbrances on the property except as listed here. The most common exceptions are property taxes, mortgages, and assessment (improvement district) bonds. For instance, a deed may recite, "Subject to an existing mortgage ...," and name the mortgage holder and the original amount of the loan, or "Subject to a city sewer improvement district bond in the amount of $1,500."

At ⑳ the grantor may impose restrictions as to how the grantee may use the property. For example, "The grantee shall not build upon this land a home with less than 1,500 square feet of living space."

The covenants of seizin and quiet enjoyment are located at ㉑ and ㉒, respectively. Number ㉓ identifies the covenant of further assurance, and at ㉔ the grantor agrees to warrant and defend forever the title he is granting. The order of grouping of the five covenants is not critical, and in some states there are laws that permit the use of two or three special words to imply the presence of all five covenants. For example, in Alaska, Illinois, Kansas, Michigan, Minnesota, and Wisconsin, if the grantor uses the words *convey and warrant* he implies the five covenants even though he does not list them in the deed. The words *warrant generally* accomplish the same purpose in Pennsylvania, Vermont, Virginia, and West Virginia, as do *grant, bargain, and sell* in the states of Arkansas, Florida, Idaho, Missouri, and Nevada.

At ㉕ the grantor states that he signed this deed on the date noted at ④. This is the **testimony clause;** although customarily included in deeds, it is redundant and could be left out as long as the grantor signs the deed at ㉖. Historically, a seal made with hot wax was essential to the validity of a deed. Today, those few states that require a seal ㉗ accept a hot wax seal, a glued paper seal, an embossed seal, the word *seal* or *L.S.* The letters *L.S.* are an abbreviation for the Latin words *locus sigilli* (place of the seal). The acknowledgment is placed at ㉘, the full wording of which

Habendum Clause

Special Wording

is given in Chapter 6. If an acknowledgment is not used, this space is used for the signatures of witnesses to the grantor's signature. Their names would be preceded by the words *In the presence of, ...*

Deed Preparation

The exact style or form of a deed is not critical as long as it contains all the essentials clearly stated and in conformity with state law. For example, one commonly used warranty deed format begins with the words *Know all men by these presents*, is written in the first person, and has the date at the end. Although a person may prepare his own deed, the writing of deeds should be left to experts in the field. In fact, some states permit only attorneys to write deeds for other persons. Even the preparation of preprinted deeds from stationery stores and title companies should be left to knowledgeable persons. Preprinted deeds contain several pitfalls for the unwary. First, the form may have been prepared and printed in another state and, as a result, may not meet the laws of your state. Second, if the blanks are incorrectly filled in, the deed may not accomplish its intended purpose. This is a particularly difficult problem when neither the grantor nor grantee realizes it until several years after the deed's delivery. Third, the use of a form deed presumes that the grantor's situation can be fitted to the form and that the grantor will be knowledgeable enough to select the correct form.

Grant Deed

Some states, notably California, Idaho, and North Dakota, use a grant deed instead of a warranty deed. In a **grant deed** the grantor covenants and warrants that (1) he has not previously conveyed the estate being granted to another party, (2) he has not encumbered the property except as noted in the deed, and (3) he will convey to the grantee any title to the property he may later acquire. These covenants are fewer in number and narrower in coverage than those found in a warranty deed, particularly the covenant regarding encumbrances. In the warranty deed, the grantor makes himself responsible for the encumbrances of prior owners as well as his own. The grant deed limits the grantor's responsibility to the period of time he owned the property. Figure 5:3 summarizes the key elements of a California grant deed.

Referring to the circled numbers in Figure 5:3, ① labels the document, ② fulfills the requirement that consideration be shown and ③ is for the name and marital status of the grantor.

Figure 5:3

GRANT DEED (1)

For a valuable (2) *consideration, receipt of which is hereby ac-knowledged,* _____(3)_____ *hereby*
(name of grantor)

GRANT(S) (4) *to* _____(5)_____ *the following*
(name of the grantee)

described real property in the _____(6)_____ ,
(city, town, etc.)

County of _____ , *State of California:*

[legal description of land here] (7)

Subject to:

[note exceptions and restrictions here] (8)

Dated __(9)_____ _____(10)_____
(Grantor's signature)

(11) [location of the acknowledgment]

By California statutory law, the single word *GRANT(S)* at (4) is both the granting clause *and* habendum, *and* it implies the covenants and warranties of possession, prior encumbrances, and further title. Thus, they need not be individually listed.

Number (5) is for the name and marital status of the grantee and the method by which title is being taken. Numbers (6) and (7) identify the property being conveyed. Easements, property taxes, conditions, reservations, restrictions, etc., are noted at (8). The deed is dated at (9), signed at (10) and acknowledged at (11).

Why have grantees, in states with more than one-tenth of the total U.S. population, been willing to accept a deed with fewer covenants than a warranty deed? The primary reason is the early development and extensive use of title insurance in these states, whereby the grantor and grantee acquire an insurance policy to protect themselves if a flaw in ownership is later discovered. Title insurance is now available in all parts of the United States and is explained in Chapter 6.

Special Warranty Deed

In a **special warranty deed,** the grantor warrants the property's title only against defects occurring during the grantor's ownership and not against defects existing before that time. The special warranty deed is typically used by executors and trustees who convey on behalf of an estate or principal because the executor or trustee has no authority to warrant and defend the acts of previous holders of title. The grantee can protect against this gap in warranty by purchasing title insurance. The special warranty deed is also known in some states as a bargain and sale deed with a covenant against only the grantor's acts.

Figure 5:4

BARGAIN AND SALE DEED

THIS DEED made _____ , between _____
            (date)

residing at _____ , herein called the Grantor, and _____ residing at _____ , herein called the Grantee.
    WITNESSETH, that the Grantor, in consideration of _____ , does hereby grant and release unto the Grantee, the Grantee's heirs, successors, and assigns forever, all that parcel of land described as

[legal description of land]

    TOGETHER WITH the appurtenances and all the estate and rights of the Grantor in and to said property.
    TO HAVE AND TO HOLD the premises herein granted together with the appurtenances unto the Grantee. This conveyance is made, however, without any warranties, express, implied, or statutory.
    IN WITNESS WHEREOF, the Grantor sets his hand and seal the day and year first written above.

_____ *L.S.*
            (Grantor)

[location of the acknowledgment]

The basic **bargain and sale deed** contains no covenants and only the minimum essentials of a deed (see Figure 5:4). It has a date, identifies the grantor and grantee, recites consideration, describes the property, contains words of conveyance, and has the grantor's signature. But lacking covenants, what assurance does the grantee have that he is acquiring title to anything? Actually, none. In this deed the grantor only *implies* that he owns the property described in the deed, and that he is granting it to the grantee. Logically, then, a grantee will much prefer a warranty deed over a bargain and sale deed, or require title insurance.

Bargain and Sale Deed

Figure 5:5

QUITCLAIM DEED

THIS DEED, made the _____ day of _____ , 19 _____ , BETWEEN _____ of _____ , party of the first part, and _____ of _____ , party of the second part.

WITNESSETH, that the party of the first part, in consideration of ten dollars ($10.00) and other valuable consideration, paid by the party of the second part, does hereby remise, release, and quitclaim unto the party of the second part, the heirs, successors, and assigns of the party of the second part forever.

ALL that certain parcel of land, with the buildings and improvements thereon, described as follows,
[legal description of land]

TOGETHER WITH the appurtenances and all the estate and rights of the Grantor in and to said property.

TO HAVE AND TO HOLD the premises herein granted unto the party of the second part, the heirs or successors and assigns of the party of the second part, forever.

IN WITNESS WHEREOF, the party of the first part has duly executed this deed the day and year first above written.

_____
(Grantor)

[location of the acknowledgment]

Quitclaim Deed

A **quitclaim deed** has no covenants or warranties (see Figure 5:5). Moreover, the grantor makes no statement, nor does he even imply that he owns the property he is quitclaiming to the grantee. Whatever rights the grantor possesses at the time the deed is delivered are conveyed to the grantee. If the grantor has no interest, right or title to the property described in the deed, none is conveyed to the grantee. However, if the grantor possesses fee simple title, fee simple title will be conveyed to the grantee.

The critical wording in a quitclaim deed is the grantor's statement that he *does hereby remise, release, and quitclaim forever.* **Quitclaim** means to renounce all possession, right, or interest. **Remise** means to give up any existing claim one may have, as does the word **release** in this usage. If the grantor subsequently acquires any right or interest in the property, he is not obligated to convey it to the grantee.

At first glance it may seem strange that such a deed should even exist, but it does serve a very useful purpose. Situations often arise in real estate transactions when a person claims to have a partial or incomplete right or interest in a parcel of land. Such a right or interest, known as a **title defect** or **cloud on the title,** may have been due to an inheritance, a dower, curtesy, or community property right, or to a mortgage or right of redemption due to a court-ordered foreclosure sale. By releasing that claim to the fee simple owner through the use of a quitclaim deed, the cloud on the fee owner's title is removed. A quitclaim deed can also be used to create an easement as well as release (extinguish) an easement. It can also be used to release remainder and reversion interests.

Other Types of Deeds

A **gift deed** is created by simply replacing the recitation of money and other valuable consideration with the statement, *in consideration of his [her, their] natural love and affection.* This phrase may be used in a warranty, special warranty, or grant deed. However, it is most often used in quitclaim or bargain and sale deeds, as these permit the grantor to avoid being committed to any warranties regarding the property.

A **guardian's deed** is used to convey a minor's interest in real property. It contains only one covenant, that the guardian and minor have not encumbered the property. The deed must state the legal authority (usually a court order) that permits the guardian to convey the minor's property.

Sheriff's deeds and **referee's deeds in foreclosure** are issued to the new buyer when a person's real estate is sold as the result of a mortgage or other court-ordered foreclosure sale. The deed should state the source of the sheriff's or referee's authority and the amount of consideration paid. Such a deed conveys only the foreclosed party's title, and, at the most, carries only one covenant: that the sheriff or referee has not damaged the property's title.

A **correction deed,** also called a deed of confirmation, is used to correct an error in a previously executed and delivered deed. For example, a name may have been misspelled or an error found in the property description. A quitclaim deed containing a statement regarding the error is used for this purpose. A **cession deed** is a form of a quitclaim deed wherein a property owner conveys street rights to a county or municipality. An **interspousal deed** is used in some states to transfer real property between spouses. A **tax deed** is used to convey title to real estate that has been sold by the government because of the nonpayment of taxes. A **deed of trust** may be used to convey real estate to a third party as security for a loan, and is discussed in Chapter 10.

CONVEYANCE AFTER DEATH

If a person dies without leaving a last will and testament (or leaves one that is subsequently ruled void by the courts because it was improperly prepared), he is said to have died **intestate,** which means without a testament. When this happens, state law directs how the deceased's assets shall be distributed. This is known as a **title by descent** or **intestate succession.** The surviving spouse and children are the dominant recipients of the deceased's assets. The deceased's grandchildren receive the next largest share, followed by the deceased's parents, brothers and sisters, and their children. These are known as the deceased's **heirs** or, in some states, **distributees.** The amount each heir receives, if anything, depends on individual state law and on how many persons with superior positions in the succession are alive. If no heirs can be found, the deceased's property escheats (reverts) to the state.

Testate, Intestate

A person who dies and leaves a valid will is said to have died **testate,** which means that a testament with instructions for property disposal was left behind. The person who made the will is the **testator** (masculine) or **testatrix** (feminine). In the will, the testator names the persons or organizations who are to receive the testator's real and personal property. Real property that is willed is known as a **devise** and the recipient, a **devisee.** Personal property that is willed is known as a **bequest** or **legacy,** and the recipient, a **legatee.** In the will, the testator usually names an **executor** (masculine) or **executrix** (feminine) to carry out the instructions. If one is not named, the court appoints an **administrator.** In some states the person named in the will or appointed by the court to settle the estate is called a **personal representative.**

Notice an important difference between the transfer of real estate ownership by deed and by will: once a deed is made and delivered, the ownership transfer is permanent, the grantor cannot have a change of mind and take back the property. With respect to a will, the devisees, although named, have no rights to the testator's property until the testator dies. Until that time the testator is free to have a change of mind, revoke the old will, and write a new one.

Probate or Surrogate Court

Upon death, the deceased's will must be filed with a court having power to admit and certify wills, usually called a **probate** or **surrogate court.** This court determines whether or not the will meets all the requirements of law: in particular, that it is genuine, properly signed and witnessed, and that the testator was of sound mind when the will was made. At this time anyone may step forward and contest the validity of the will. If the court finds the will to be valid, the executor is permitted to carry out its terms. If the testator owned real property, its ownership is conveyed using an **executor's deed** prepared and signed by the executor. The executor's deed is used both to transfer title to a devisee and to sell real property to raise cash. It contains only one covenant, a covenant that the executor has not encumbered the property. An executor's deed is a special warranty deed.

Protecting the Deceased's Intentions

Because the deceased is not present, state laws attempt to ensure that fair market value is received for the deceased's real estate by requiring court approval of proposed sales, and in some cases by sponsoring open bidding in the courtroom. As protection, a purchaser should ascertain that the executor has the authority to convey title.

For a will to be valid it must meet specific legal requirements. All states recognize the **formal** or **witnessed** will, a written document prepared in most cases by an attorney. The testator must declare it to be his/her will and sign it in the presence of two to four witnesses (depending on the state), who, at the testator's request and in the presence of each other, sign the will as witnesses. A formal will prepared by an attorney is the preferred method, as the will then conforms explicitly to the law. This greatly reduces the likelihood of its being contested after the testator's death. Additionally, an attorney may offer valuable advice on how to word the will to reduce estate and inheritance taxes.

A **holographic will** is a will that is entirely handwritten, with no typed or preprinted words. The will is dated and signed by the testator, but there are no witnesses. Nineteen states recognize holographic wills as legally binding. Persons selecting this form of will generally do so because it saves the time and expense of seeking professional legal aid, and because it is entirely private. Besides the fact that holographic wills are considered to have no effect in 31 states, they often result in much legal argument in states that do accept them. This can occur when the testator is not fully aware of the law as it pertains to the making of wills. Many otherwise happy families have been torn apart by dissension when a relative dies and they read the will, only to find that there is a question as to whether or not it was properly prepared, and hence valid. Unfortunately, what follows is not what the deceased intended; those who would receive more from intestate succession will request that the will be declared void and of no effect. Those with more to gain if the will stands as written will muster legal forces to argue for its acceptance by the probate court.

Holographic Will

An **oral will,** more properly known as a **nuncupative will,** is a will spoken by a person who is very near death. The witness must promptly put in writing what was heard and submit it to probate. An oral will can only be used to dispose of personal property. Any real estate belonging to the deceased is disposed

Oral Will

of by intestate succession. Some states limit the use of oral wills to those serving in the armed forces.

Codicil

A **codicil** is a written supplement or amendment made to a previously existing will. It is used to change some aspect of the will or to add a new instruction, without the work of rewriting the entire will. The codicil must be dated, signed, and witnessed in the same manner as the original will. The only way to change a will is with a codicil or by writing a completely new will. The law will not recognize cross-outs, notations, or other alterations made on the will itself.

ADVERSE POSSESSION

Through the unauthorized occupation of another person's land for a long enough period of time, it is possible under certain conditions to acquire ownership by **adverse possession.** The historical roots of adverse possession go back many centuries to a time before written deeds were used as evidence of ownership. At that time, in the absence of any claims to the contrary, a person who occupied a parcel of land was presumed to be its owner. Today, adverse possession is, in effect, a statute of limitations that bars a legal owner from claiming title to land when he has done nothing to oust an adverse occupant during the statutory period. From the adverse occupant's standpoint, adverse possession is a method of acquiring title by possessing land for a specified period of time under certain conditions.

Courts of law are quite demanding of proof before they will issue a decree in favor of a person claiming title by virtue of adverse possession. The claimant must have maintained actual, visible, continuous, hostile, exclusive, and notorious possession and be publicly claiming ownership to the property. These requirements mean that the claimant's use must have been visible and obvious to the legal owner, continuous and not just occasional, and exclusive enough to give notice of the claimant's individual claim. Furthermore, the use must have been without permission (hostile), and the claimant must have acted as though he were the owner, even in the presence of the actual owner. Finally, the adverse claimant must be able to prove that he has met these requirements for a period ranging from 3 to 30 years, as shown in Table 5:1.

The required occupancy period is shortened and the claimant's chances of obtaining legal ownership are enhanced in many states if he has been paying the property taxes and the possession has been under "color of title." **Color of title** suggests some plausible appearance of ownership interest, such as an improperly prepared deed that purports to transfer title to the claimant or a claim of ownership by inheritance. In accumulating the required number of years, an adverse claimant may **tack on** his period of possession to that of a prior adverse occupant. This could be done through the purchase of that right. The current adverse occupant could in turn sell his claim to a still later adverse occupant until enough years were accumulated to present a claim in court.

Although the concept of adverse possession often creates the mental picture of a trespasser moving onto someone else's land and living there long enough to acquire title in fee, this is not the usual application. More often, adverse possession is used to extinguish weak or questionable claims to title. For example, if a person buys property at a tax sale, takes possession, and pays the property taxes each year afterward, adverse possession laws act to cut off claims to title by the previous owner. Another source of successful adverse possession claims arises from encroachments. If a building extends over a property line and nothing is said about it for a long enough period of time, the building will be permitted to stay.

An easement can also be acquired by prolonged adverse use. This is known as acquiring an **easement by prescription.** As with adverse possession, the laws are strict: the usage must be openly visible, continuous and exclusive, as well as hostile and adverse to the owner. Additionally, the use must have occurred over a period of 5 to 20 years, depending on the state. All these facts must be proved in a court of law before the court will issue the claimant a document legally recognizing his ownership of the easement. As an easement is a right to use land for a specific purpose, and not ownership of the land itself, courts rarely require the payment of property taxes to acquire a prescriptive easement.

As may be seen from the foregoing discussion, a landowner must be given obvious notification *at the location* of his land that someone is attempting to claim ownership or an easement. Since

Table 5:1. Adverse Possession: Number of Years of Occupancy Required to Claim Title*

State	Adverse Occupant Lacks Color of Title & Does Not Pay the Property Taxes	Adverse Occupant Has Color of Title &/or Pays the Property Taxes	State	Adverse Occupant Lacks Color of Title & Does Not Pay the Property Taxes	Adverse Occupant Has Color of Title &/or Pays the Property Taxes
Alabama	20	3-10	Missouri	10	10
Alaska	10	7	Montana		5
Arizona	10	3	Nebraska	10	10
Arkansas	15	2-7	Nevada		5
California		5	New Hampshire	20	20
Colorado	18	7	New Jersey	30-60	20-30
Connecticut	15	15	New Mexico	10	10
Delaware	20	20	New York	10	10
District of Columbia	15	15	North Carolina	20-30	7-21
			North Dakota	20	10
Florida		7	Ohio	21	21
Georgia	20	7	Oklahoma	15	15
Hawaii	20	20	Oregon	10	10
Idaho	5	5	Pennsylvania	21	21
Illinois	20	7	Rhode Island	10	10
Indiana		10	South Carolina	10-20	10
Iowa	10	10	South Dakota	20	10
Kansas	15	15	Tennessee	20	7
Kentucky	15	7	Texas	10-25	3-5
Louisiana	30	10	Utah		7
Maine	20	20	Vermont	15	15
Maryland	20	20	Virginia	15	15
Massachusetts	20	20	Washington	10	7
Michigan	15	5-10	West Virginia	10	10
Minnesota	15	15	Wisconsin	20	10
Mississippi	10	10	Wyoming	10	10

*As may be seen, in a substantial number of states, the waiting period for title by adverse possession is shortened if the adverse occupant has color of title and/or pays the property taxes. In California, Florida, Indiana, Montana, Nevada and Utah, the property taxes must be paid to obtain the title. Generally speaking, adverse possession does not work against minors and other legal incompetents. However, when the owner becomes legally competent, the adverse possession must be broken within the time limit set by each state's law (the range is 1 to 10 years). In the states of Louisiana, Oklahoma, and Tennessee, adverse possession is referred to as title by prescription.

an adverse claim must be continuous and hostile, an owner can break it by ejecting the trespassers or by preventing them from trespassing, or by simply giving them permission to be there. Any of these actions would demonstrate the landowner's superior title. Owners of stores and office buildings with private sidewalks or streets used by the public can take action to break claims to a public easement by either periodically barricading the sidewalk or street or by posting signs giving permission to pass. These signs are often seen in the form of brass plaques embedded in the sidewalk or street. In certain states, a landowner may record with the public records office a **notice of consent.** This is evidence that subsequent uses of his land for the purposes stated in the notice are permissive and not adverse. The notice may later be revoked by recording a **notice of revocation.** Federal, state, and local governments protect themselves against adverse claims to their lands by passing laws making themselves immune.

OWNERSHIP BY ACCESSION

The extent of one's ownership of land can be altered by **accession.** This can result from natural or man-made causes. With regard to natural causes, the owner of land fronting on a lake, river, or ocean may acquire additional land because of the gradual accumulation of rock, sand, and soil. This process is called **accretion** and the results are referred to as *alluvion* and *reliction.* **Alluvion** is the increase of land that results when waterborne soil is gradually deposited to produce firm dry ground. **Reliction** (or dereliction) results when a lake, sea, or river permanently recedes, exposing dry land. When land is rapidly washed away by the action of water, it is known as **avulsion.** Man-made accession occurs through **annexation** of personal property to real estate. For example, when lumber, nails, and cement are used to build a house, they alter the extent of one's land ownership.

PUBLIC GRANT

A transfer of land by a government body to a private party is called a **public grant.** Since 1776, the federal government has granted millions of acres of land to settlers, land companies, railroads, state colleges, mining and logging promoters, and any war veteran from the American Revolution through the Mexican War. Most famous was the Homestead Act passed by the U.S. Congress in 1862. That act permitted persons wishing to settle on otherwise unappropriated federal land to acquire fee simple ownership by paying a small filing charge and occupying and cultivating the land for 5 years. Similarly, for only a few dollars, a person may file a mining claim to public land for the purpose of extracting whatever valuable minerals can be found. To retain the claim, a certain amount of work must be performed on the land each year. Otherwise, the government will consider the claim abandoned and another person may claim it. If the claim is worked long enough, a public grant can be sought and fee simple title obtained. In the case of both the homestead settler and the mining claim, the conveyance document that passes fee title from the government to the grantee is known as a **land patent.** In 1976, the U.S. government ended the homesteading program in all states except Alaska.

DEDICATION

When an owner makes a voluntary gift of his land to the public, it is known as **dedication.** To illustrate, a land developer buys a large parcel of vacant land and develops it into streets and lots. The lots are sold to private buyers, but what about the streets? In all probability they will be dedicated to the town, city, or county. By doing this, the developer, and later the lot buyers, will not have to pay taxes on the streets, and the public will be responsible for maintaining them. The fastest way to accomplish the transfer is by either statutory dedication or dedication by deed. In **statutory dedication** the developer prepares a map showing the streets, has the map approved by local government officials, and then records it as a public document. In **dedication by deed** the developer prepares a deed that identifies the streets and grants them to the city.

Common law dedication takes place when a landowner, by his acts or words, shows that he intends part of his land to be dedicated even though he has never officially made a written dedication. For example, a landowner may encourage the public to travel on his roads in an attempt to convince a local road department to take over maintenance.

FORFEITURE

Forfeiture can occur when a deed contains a condition or limitation. For example, a grantor states in the deed that the land conveyed may be used for residential purposes only. If the grantee constructs commercial buildings, the grantor can reacquire title on the grounds that the grantee did not use the land for the required purpose.

A change in ownership of any kind is known as an **alienation.** In addition to the forms of alienation discussed in this chapter, alienation can result from court action in connection with escheat, eminent domain, partition, foreclosure, execution sales, quiet title suits, and marriage. These topics are discussed in other chapters.

ALIENATION

REVIEW QUESTIONS

1. A written legal document by which ownership of real property is transferred from one party to another is
   A. a bill of sale.
   B. a lease.
   C. a contract of sale.
   D. a deed.

2. Which of the following is essential to the validity of a deed?
   A. The grantor must be of legal age.
   B. The grantor must be of sound mind.
   C. Both A and B.
   D. Neither A nor B.

3. Which of the following may not be conveyed by deed?
   A. Fee simple estate.
   B. Life estate.
   C. Easements.
   D. Leasehold estate.

4. With the words conveyance in a deed, the grantor
   A. States that he is making a grant of the property to the grantee.
   B. Warrants that he has the right to convey title to the property.
   C. Both A and B.
   D. Neither A nor B.

5. In order to convey title to real property, a deed must be signed by the
   A. grantee.
   B. grantor.
   C. agent.
   D. buyer.

6. In order to convey title, a deed must be
   A. delivered by the grantor to the grantee.
   B. accepted by the grantee.
   C. Both A and B.
   D. Neither A nor B.

7. A grantee is assured that he will not be disturbed by someone else claiming an interest in the property by the covenant of
   A. seizin.
   B. quiet enjoyment.
   C. further assurance.
   D. warranty forever.

8. Should additional documents be necessary to perfect the grantee's title, this would be required by the
   A. covenant of seizin.
   B. covenant of further assurance.
   C. covenant against encumbrances.
   D. covenant of warranty forever.

9. The deed considered to be the best deed a grantee can receive is a
   A. general warranty deed.   C. bargain and sale deed.
   B. special warranty deed.   D. quitclaim deed.

10. Which of the following are the same?
    A. Grantor–Party conveying title.
    B. Grantee–Party acquiring title.
    C. Both A and B.
    D. Neither A nor B.

11. The phrase "the grantee's heirs and assigns forever" indicates the conveyance of a
    A. fee simple estate.   C. leasehold estate.
    B. life estate.   D. less than freehold estate.

12. The description of the land in a deed may be by
    A. metes and bounds.   C. recorded plat.
    B. government survey.   D. Any of the above.

13. Quitclaim deeds are often used
    A. to remove a cloud from the title.
    B. to convey the grantor's interest without imposing any future obligations to defend the title upon the grantor.
    C. Both A and B.
    D. Neither A nor B.

14. You would expect to find the words "remise" and "release" in a
    A. warranty deed.   C. grant deed.
    B. special warranty deed.   D. quitclaim deed.

15. A court of law with the power to admit and certify wills is called a
    A. probate court.   C. Both A and B.
    B. surrogate court.   D. Neither A nor B.

16. Title acquired as the result of inheritance from a person who dies intestate is know as
    A. title by descent.   D. Both A and C.
    B. a devise.   E. Both B and C.
    C. title by intestate succession.

17. A handwritten will signed by the testator but not witnessed is known as a
    A. nuncupative will.   C. oral will.
    B. holographic will.   D. formal will.

18. An easement acquired by prolonged adverse use is acquired by
    A. implied grant.   C. prescription.
    B. necessity.   D. condemnation.

19. An owner can break a claim of adverse possession by
    A. ejecting the trespasser.
    B. giving the trespasser permission to trespass.
    C. Both A and B.
    D. Neither A nor B.

20. The process of increasing land due to the gradual deposition of waterborne soil is known as
    A. reliction.   C. accretion.
    B. avulsion.   D. alluvion.

Recordation, Abstracts, and Title Insurance

This chapter is focused on "(1) the need for a method of determining real property ownership, (2) the process by which current and past ownership is determined from public records, (3) the availability of insurance against errors made in determining ownership, (4) the Torrens System of land title registration, and (5) the Uniform Marketable Title Act." The chapter covers the need for public records, requirements for recording, public records organization, chain of title, abstract, title insurance, quiet title suits, Torrens System, and marketable title acts.

OVERVIEW OF CHAPTER 6

LEARNING OBJECTIVES

After completion of this chapter, you should be able to:
1. Understand the need for public records.
2. Delineate and explain the requirements for recording.
3. Describe the typical public records organization.
4. Define an abstract and a chain of title.
5. Explain the purpose and application of title insurance.
6. Describe a quiet title suit.
7. Describe the Torrens System.
8. Explain the purpose and application of marketable title acts.

KEY • TERMS

Abstract: a summary of all recorded documents affecting title to a given parcel of land

Acknowledgment: a formal declaration by a person signing a document that he or she, in fact, did sign the document

Actual notice: knowledge gained from what one has actually seen, heard, read, or observed

Chain of title: the linkage of property ownership that connects the present owner to the original source of title

Constructive notice: notice given by the public records and by visible possession, coupled with the legal presumption that all persons are thereby notified

Marketable title: title that is free from reasonable doubt as to who is the owner

Public recorder's office: a government-operated facility wherein documents are entered in the public records

Quiet title suit: court-ordered hearings held to determine land ownership

Title insurance: an insurance policy against defects in title not listed in the title report or abstract

Torrens System: a state-sponsored method of registering land titles

In this chapter we shall focus on (1) the need for a method of determining real property ownership, (2) the process by which current and past ownership is determined from public records, (3) the availability of insurance against errors made in determining ownership, (4) the Torrens system of land title registration, and (5) the Uniform Marketable Title Act.

NEED FOR PUBLIC RECORDS

Until the enactment of the Statute of Frauds in England in 1677, determining who owned a parcel of land was primarily a matter of observing who was in physical possession. A landowner gave notice to the world of his claim to ownership by visibly occupying his land. When land changed hands, the old owner moved off the land and the new owner moved onto the land. After 1677 written deeds were required to show transfers of ownership. The problem then became one of finding the person holding the most current deed to the land. This was easy if the deedholder also occupied the land, but more difficult if he did not. The solution was to create a government-sponsored public recording service where a person could record his deed. These records would then be open free of charge to anyone. In this fashion, an owner could post notice to all that he claimed ownership of a parcel of land.

There are two ways a person can give notice of a claim or right to land. One is by recording documents in the public records that give written notice to that effect. The other is by visibly occupying or otherwise visibly making use of the land. At the same time, the law holds interested parties responsible for examining the public records and looking at the land for this notice of right or claim. This is called **constructive notice.** Constructive notice (also sometimes referred to as **legal notice**) charges the public with the responsibility of looking in the public records and at the property itself to obtain knowledge of all who are claiming a right or interest. In other words, our legal system provides an avenue by which a person can give notice (recording and occupancy) and makes the presumption that anyone interested in the property has inspected the records *and* the property.

Constructive Notice

A person interested in a property is also held by law to be responsible for making further inquiry of anyone giving visible or recorded notice. This is referred to as **inquiry notice** and is notice that the law presumes a reasonably diligent person would obtain by making further inquiry. For example, suppose you are considering the purchase of vacant acreage and, upon inspecting it, see a dirt road cutting across the land that is not mentioned in the public records. The law expects you to make further inquiry. The road may be a legal easement across the property. Another example is that any time you buy rental property, you are expected to make inquiry as to the rights of the occupants. They may hold substantial rights you would not know about without asking them.

Inquiry Notice

Actual notice is knowledge that one has actually gained based on what one has seen, heard, read, or observed. For example, if you read a deed from Jones to Smith, you have actual notice of the deed and Smith's claim to the property. If you go to the property and you see someone in possession, you have actual notice of that person's claim to be there.

Actual Notice

Remember that anyone claiming an interest or right is expected to make it known either by recorded claim or visible use of the property. Anyone acquiring a right or interest is expected to look in the public records and go to the property to make a visual inspection for claims and inquire as to the extent of those claims.

Recording Acts   All states have passed **recording acts** to provide for the recording of every instrument (i.e., document) by which an estate, interest, or right in land is created, transferred, or encumbered. Within each state, each county has a **public recorder's office,** known variously as the County Recorder's Office, County Clerk's Office, Circuit Court Clerk's Office, County Registrar's Office, or Bureau of Conveyances. The person in charge is called the recorder, clerk, or registrar. Located at the seat of county government, each public recorder's office will record documents submitted to it that pertain to real property in that county. Thus a deed to property in XYZ County is recorded with the public recorder in XYZ County. Similarly, anyone seeking information regarding ownership of land in XYZ County would go to the recorder's office in XYZ County. Some cities also maintain record rooms where deeds are recorded. The recording process itself involves photocopying the documents and filing them for future reference.

To encourage people to use public recording facilities, laws in each state decree that (1) a deed, mortgage, or other instrument affecting real estate is not effective as far as subsequent purchasers and lenders are concerned if it is not recorded, and (2) prospective purchasers, mortgage lenders, and the public at

The public recorder's office serves as a central information station for changes in rights, estates, and interests in land.

Figure 6:1.

large are presumed notified when a document is recorded. Figure 6:1 illustrates the concept of public recording.

Unrecorded Leases

Although recording acts permit the recording of any estate, right, or interest in land, many lesser rights are rarely recorded because of the cost and effort involved. Month-to-month rentals and leases for a year or less fall into this category. Consequently, only an on-site inspection would reveal their existence, or the existence of any developing adverse possession or prescriptive easement claim.

Summary

To summarize, if you are a prospective purchaser (or lessee or lender), you are presumed by law to have inspected both the land itself and the public records to determine the present rights and interests of others. If you receive a deed, mortgage, or other document relating to an estate, right, or interest in land, have it *immediately* recorded in the county in which the land is located. If you hold an unrecorded rental or lease, you should visibly occupy the property.

REQUIREMENTS FOR RECORDING

Nearly all states require that a document be **acknowledged** before it is eligible to be recorded. A few states will permit proper witnessing as a substitute. Some states require both. The objective of these requirements is to make certain that the person who signs the document is the same person named in the document and that the signing was a free and voluntary act. This is done to reduce the possibility that forged or fraudulently induced documents will enter the public records.

Figure 6:2.

IN WITNESS whereof, the grantor has duly executed this deed in the presence of:

____________________ ____________________

Witness Grantor

____

Witness

Witnesses   In states that accept witnesses, the person executing the document signs in the presence of at least two witnesses, who in turn sign the document indicating that they are witnesses. To protect themselves, witnesses should not sign unless they know that the person named in the document is the person signing. In the event the witnessed signature is contested, the witnesses would be summoned to a court of law and under oath testify to the authenticity of the signature. An example of a witness statement is shown in Figure 6:2.

Acknowledgment   An **acknowledgment** is a formal declaration by a person signing a document that he or she, in fact, did sign the document. Persons authorized to take acknowledgments include notaries public, recording office clerks, commissioners of deeds, judges of courts of record, justices of the peace, and certain others as authorized by state law. Commissioned military officers are authorized to take the acknowledgments of persons in the military; foreign ministers and consular agents can take acknowledgments abroad. If an acknowledgment is taken outside the

Figure 6:3.

ACKNOWLEDGMENT FOR AN INDIVIDUAL

STATE OF _____
COUNTY OF _____ *ss*

On this _____ *day of* _____ *, 19* _____ *, before me, the undersigned, a Notary Public in and for said State, personally appeared* [name of person executing document] *known to me to be the person whose name is subscribed to the within instrument and acknowledged that he (she) executed the same [in some states, the words "by his (her) free act and deed" are added here]. Witness my hand and official seal.*

[space for seal or
stamp of the notary   _____
public]   Signature of notary public

My commission expires _____
                                               Date

state where the document will be recorded, either the recording county must already recognize the out-of-state official's authority or the out-of-state official must provide certification that he or she is qualified to take acknowledgments. The official seal or stamp of the notary on the acknowledgment normally fulfills this requirement.

An acknowledgment is illustrated in Figure 6:3. Notice the words; the person signing the document must personally appear before the notary *and* the notary states that he or she knows that person to be the person described in the document. If they are strangers, the notary will require proof of identity. The person acknowledging the document does so by voluntarily signing it in the presence of the notary. Note that it is the signer who does the acknowledging, not the notary. At the completion of the signing, a notation of the event is made in a permanent record book kept by the notary. This record is later given to the state government for safekeeping.

Each document brought to a public recorder's office for recordation is photocopied and then returned to its owner. The photocopy is placed in chronological order with photocopies of other documents. These are stamped with consecutive **page numbers** and bound into a **book.** These books are placed in chronological order on shelves that are open to the public for inspection. Before modern-day photocopy machines, public recorders' offices used large cameras with light-sensitive paper (roughly 1920 to 1955). Before that, documents were copied by hand using typewriters (roughly 1900 to 1920), and before that, copying was done in longhand. The current trend is toward entirely paperless systems wherein documents are recorded directly onto microfilm and then returned to their owners. Each document is assigned a book and page number or a reel and frame number. Microfilm readers are made available to anyone wanting to read the microfilms.

Filing incoming documents in chronological order is necessary to establish the chronological priority of documents; however, it does not provide an easy means for a person to locate all the documents relevant to a given parcel of land. Suppose that you are planning to purchase a parcel of land and want to make certain that the person selling it is the legally recognized owner. Without an index to guide you, you might have to inspect every

PUBLIC RECORDS ORGANIZATION

document in every volume. Consequently, recording offices have developed systems of indexing. The two most commonly used are the grantor and grantee indexes, used by all states, and the tract index, used by nine states.

Tract Indexes

Of the two indexing systems, the **tract index** is the simplest to use. In it, one page is allocated to either a single parcel of land or to a group of parcels, called a tract. On that page you will find listed all the recorded deeds, mortgages, and other documents at the recorder's office that relate to that parcel. A few words describing each document are given, together with the book and page where a photocopy of the document can be found.

Grantor and Grantee Indexes

Grantor and grantee indexes are alphabetical indexes and are usually bound in book form. There are several variations in use in the United States, but the basic principle is the same. For each calendar year, the **grantor index** lists in alphabetical order all grantors named in the documents recorded that year. Next to each grantor's name is the name of the grantee named in the document, the book and page where a photocopy of the document can be found, and a few words describing the document. The **grantee index** is arranged by grantee names and gives the name of the grantor and the location and description of the document.

CHAIN OF TITLE

By looking for Miller's name in the 1989 grantee index and then working backward in time through the yearly indexes, you will eventually find his name and a reference to Lot 2, Block 2 in the Hilldale Tract. Next to Miller's name you will find the name of the grantor and a reference to the book and page where the deed was recorded.

By looking for that name in the grantee index, you will locate the next previous deed. By continuing this process you can construct a chain of title. A **chain of title** shows the linkage of property ownership that connects the present owner to the original source of title. In most cases the chain starts with the original sale or grant of the land from the government to a private citizen. It is used to prove how title came to be **vested** in (i.e., possessed by) the current owner. Figure 6:4 illustrates the chain-of-title concept.

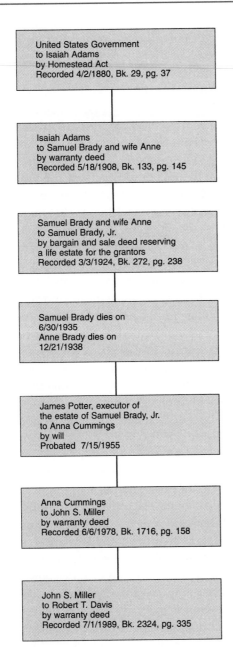

Figure 6:4. Chain of Title

Sometimes, while tracing (running) a chain of title back through time, an apparent break or dead end will occur. This can happen because the grantor is an administrator, executor, sheriff, or judge, or because the owner died, or because a mortgage against the land was foreclosed. To regain the title sequence, one must search outside the recorder's office by checking probate court records in the case of a death, or by checking civil court actions in the case of a foreclosure. The chain must be complete from the original source of title to the present owner. If there is a missing link the current "owner" does not have valid title to the property.

In addition to looking for grantors and grantees, a search must be made for any outstanding mortgages, judgments, actions pending, liens, and unpaid taxes that may affect the title. With regard to searching for mortgages, states again differ slightly. Some place mortgages in the general grantor and grantee indexes, listing the borrower (mortgagor) as the grantor and the lender (mortgagee) as the grantee. Other states have separate index books for mortgagors and mortgagees. The process involves looking for the name of each owner in each annual **mortgagor index** published while that owner owned the land. If a mortgage is found, a further check will reveal whether or not it has been satisfied and released. If it has been released, the recorder's office will have noted on the margin of the recorded mortgage the book and page where the release is located. When one knows the lender's name, the mortgage location and its subsequent release can also be found by searching the **mortgagee index.**

Title may be clouded by judgments against recent owners, or there may be lawsuits pending that might later affect title. This information is found, respectively, on the **judgment rolls** and in the **lis pendens index** at the office of the county clerk. The term *lis pendens* is Latin for pending lawsuits. A separate search is made for **mechanic's liens** against the property by workmen and material suppliers. This step includes both a search of the public records and an on-site inspection of the land for any recent construction activity or material deliveries. A visit is made to the local tax assessor's office to check the tax rolls for unpaid property taxes, and to county map records to determine changes in deed restriction or subdivision plats. This does not exhaust all possible places that must be visited to do a thorough title search. A title searcher may also be found researching birth, marriage, divorce, and adoption records, probate records, military files, and federal tax liens in an effort to identify all the parties with an interest or potential interest in a given parcel of land and its improvements.

Although it is useful for the real estate practitioner to be able to find a name or document in the public records, full-scale title searching should be left to professionals. In a sparsely populated county, title searching is usually done on a part-time basis by an attorney. In more heavily populated counties a full-time **abstracter** will search the records. These persons are experts in the field of title search and for a fee will prepare an abstract of title for a parcel of land.

An **abstract of title** (or abstract) is a complete historical summary of all recorded documents affecting the title of a property. It recites in chronological order all recorded grants and conveyances and recorded easements, mortgages, wills, tax liens, judgments, pending lawsuits, marriages, divorces, etc., that might affect title. The abstracter will summarize each document, note the book and page (or other source) where it was found and give the date it was recorded or entered. In the case of a deed, for example, the abstracter identifies the grantor and grantee and type of deed, and gives a brief description of the property, any conditions or restrictions found in the deed, the date on the deed, the recording date, and the book and page. For a mortgage, the abstracter identifies the borrower and lender, gives a brief description of the mortgage contents, and if repaid, the book and page location of the mortgage release document and its date of recordation. The abstract also includes a list of the public records searched, and not searched, in preparing the abstract.

The abstract is next sent to an attorney. On the basis of the attorney's knowledge of law and the legal history presented in the abstract, the attorney renders an **opinion** as to who the fee owner is and names anyone else with a legitimate right or interest in the property. This opinion, when written, signed by the attorney, and attached to the abstract, is known in many states as a **certificate of title.** In some parts of the United States, this certified abstract is so valuable that it is brought up to date each time the property is sold and passed from seller to buyer. Generally speaking, the seller pays the cost of updating the abstract and getting a current attorney's opinion and certificate.

ABSTRACT OF TITLE

"What Ifs"   Despite the diligent efforts of abstracters and attorneys to give as accurate a picture of land ownership as possible, there is no guarantee that the finished abstract, or its certification, is completely accurate. Persons preparing abstracts and opinions are liable for mistakes due to their own negligence, and they can be sued if that negligence results in a loss to a client. But what if a recorded deed in the title chain is a forgery? Or what if a married person represented himself on a deed as a single person, thus resulting in unextinguished dower rights? Or what if a deed was executed by a minor or an otherwise legally incompetent person? Or, what if a deed contained an erroneous land description? Or what if a document was misfiled, or there were undisclosed heirs, or a missing will later came to light, or there was confusion because of similar names on documents? These situations can result in substantial losses to a property owner; yet the fault may not lie with the abstracter or attorney. Nor is the recorder's office responsible for verifying the contents of a deed, just that it shows an acceptable acknowledgment. The solution has been the organization of private companies to sell insurance against losses arising from title defects such as these as well as from errors in title examination.

TITLE INSURANCE   Efforts to insure titles date back to the last century were primarily organized by and for the benefit of attorneys who wanted protection from errors that they might make in the interpretation of abstracts. As time passed, **title insurance** (also called **title guarantee**) became available to anyone wishing to purchase it. The basic principle of title insurance is similar to any form of insurance: many persons pay a small amount into an insurance pool that is then available if any one of them should suffer a loss. In some parts of the United States, it is customary to purchase the title insurance policy through the attorney who reads and certifies the abstract. Elsewhere it is the custom to purchase it from a title company that combines the search and policy in one fee.

Title Report   When a title company receives a request for a title insurance policy, the first step is an examination of the public records. This is usually done by an abstracter or **title searcher** employed by the title company. A company attorney then reviews the findings and renders an opinion as to who the fee owner is and lists anyone

Figure 6:5.

TITLE REPORT

The following is a report of the title to the land described in your application for a policy of title insurance.

LAND DESCRIPTION: Lot 17, Block M, Atwater's Addition, Jefferson County, State of _____ .

DATE AND TIME OF SEARCH: March 3, 19xx at 9:00 am

VESTEE: Barbara Baker, a single woman

ESTATE OR INTEREST: Fee simple

EXCEPTIONS:

PART I:

1. *A lien in favor of Jefferson County for property taxes, in the amount of $645.00, due on or before April 30, 19xx.*

2. *A mortgage in favor of the First National Bank in the amount of $30,000.00, recorded June 2, 1974, in Book 2975, Page 245 of the Official County Records.*

3. *An easement in favor of the Southern Telephone Company along the eastern five feet of said land for telephone poles and conduits. Recorded on June 15, 1946, in Book 1210, Page 113 of the Official County Records.*

4. *An easement in favor of Coastal States Gas and Electric Company along the north ten feet of said land for underground pipes. Recorded on June 16, 1946, in Book 1210, Page 137 of the Official County Records.*

PART II:

1. *Taxes or assessments not shown by the records of any taxing authority or by the public records.*

2. *Any facts, rights, interests, or claims that, although not shown by the public records, could be determined by inspection of the land and inquiry of persons in possession.*

3. *Discrepancies or conflicts in boundary lines or area or encroachments that would be shown by a survey, but which are not shown by the public records.*

4. *Easements, liens, or encumbrances not shown by the public records.*

5. *Zoning and governmental restrictions.*

6. *Unpatented mining claims and water rights or claims.*

else with a legitimate right or interest in the property such as a mortgage lender or easement holder. This information is typed up and becomes the **title report.** An example of a title report is illustrated in plain language in Figure 6:5. Sometimes called a **preliminary title report,** a title report does not commit the title company to insure the property nor is it an insurance policy. It does serve as the basis for a commitment to insure (also called a **binder**) and for the actual title insurance policy.

Notice how a title report differs from an abstract. Whereas an abstract is a chronologically arranged summary of all recorded events that have affected the title to a given parcel of land, a title report is more like a snapshot that shows the condition of title at a specific moment in time. A title report does not tell who the previous owners were; it only tells who the current owner is. A title report does not list all mortgage loans ever made against the land, but only those that have not been removed. The title report in Figure 6:5 states that a search of the public records shows Barbara Baker to be the fee owner of Lot 17, Block M, at the time the search was conducted.

In Part I, the report lists all recorded objections that could be found to Baker's fee estate, in this case, county property taxes, a mortgage, and two easements. In Part II, the title company states that there may be certain unrecorded matters that either could not be or were not researched in preparing the report. Note in particular that the title company does not make a visual inspection of the land nor does it make a boundary survey. The buyer is responsible for making the on-site inspection and for hiring a surveyor if uncertain as to the land's boundaries. It is also the buyer's responsibility to check the zoning of the land and any other governmental restrictions on the land.

Although an owner may purchase a title insurance policy on his property at any time, it is most often purchased when real estate is sold. In connection with a sale, the title report is used to verify that the seller is indeed the owner. Additionally, the title report alerts the buyer and seller as to what needs to be done to bring title to the condition called for in the sales contract. For example, referring to Figure 6:5, the present owner (Barbara Baker) may have agreed to remove the existing mortgage so that the buyer can get a new and larger loan. Once this is done and the seller has delivered her deed to the buyer, the title company issues a title policy that deletes the old mortgage, adds the new mortgage, and shows the buyer as the owner. Note that title policies are often required by long-term lessees (10 years or more). They too want to know who has property rights superior to theirs.

In some parts of the United States it is customary for the seller to pay the cost of both the title search and the insurance. In other parts, the seller pays for the search and the buyer for the insurance. In a relatively few instances, the buyer pays for both. Customarily, when a property is sold, it is insured for an amount equal to the purchase price. This insurance remains effective as long as the buyer (owner) or his heirs have an interest in the property.

Policy Premium

The insurance premium consists of a single payment. On the average-priced home, the combined charge for a title report and title insurance amounts to about of 1% of the amount of insurance purchased. Each time the property is sold, a new policy must be purchased. The old policy cannot be assigned to the new owner. Some title insurance companies offer reduced **reissue rates** if the previous owner's policy is available for updating.

Thus far our discussion of title insurance has centered on what is called an **owner's policy.** In addition, title insurance companies also offer what is called a **lender's policy.** This gives title protection to a lender who has taken real estate as collateral for a loan. There are three significant differences between an owner's title policy and a lender's title policy. First, the owner's policy is good for the full amount of coverage stated on the policy for as long as the insured or the insured's heirs have an interest in the property. In contrast, the lender's policy protects only for the amount owed on the mortgage loan. Thus, the coverage on a lender's policy declines and finally terminates when the loan is fully repaid. The second difference is that the lender's policy does not make exceptions for claims to ownership that could have been determined by physically inspecting the property. The third difference is that the lender's policy is assignable to subsequent holders of that same loan; an owner's policy is not.

Owner's and Lender's Policies

The cost of a lender's policy (also known as a mortgagee's title policy or a loan policy) is similar to an owner's policy. Although the insurance company takes added risks by eliminating some exceptions found in the owner's policy, this is balanced by the fact that the liability decreases as the loan is repaid. When an owner's and a lender's policy are purchased at the same time, as in the case of a sale with new financing, the combined cost is only a few dollars more than the cost of the owner's policy alone. Note that the lender's policy covers only title problems. It does not insure that the loan will be repaid by the borrower.

Claims for Losses The last item in a title policy is a statement as to how the company will handle claims. Although this "Conditions and Stipulations Section" is too lengthy to reproduce here, its key aspects can be summarized as follows. When an insured defect arises, the title insurance company reserves the right to either pay the loss or fight the claim in court. If it elects to fight, any legal costs the company incurs are in addition to the amount of coverage stated in the policy. If a loss is paid, the amount of coverage is reduced by that amount and any unused coverage is still in effect. If the company pays a loss, it acquires the right to collect from the party who caused the loss.

In comparing title insurance to other forms of insurance (e.g., life, fire, automobile), note that title insurance protects against something that has already happened but has not been discovered. A forged deed may result in a disagreement over ownership: the forgery is a fact of history, the insurance is in the event of its discovery. But in some cases the problem will never be discovered. For example, a married couple may be totally unaware of dower and curtesy rights and fail to extinguish them when they sell their property. If neither later claims them, when they die, the rights extinguish themselves, and the intervening property owners will have been unaffected.

Only a small part of the premiums collected by title insurance companies are used to pay claims. This is largely because title companies take great pains to maintain on their own premises complete photographic copies (often computer indexed) of the public records for each county in which they do business. These are called **title plants.** In many cases they are actually more complete and better organized than those available at the public recorder's office. The philosophy is that the better the quality of the title search, the fewer the claims that must be paid.

The Growth of Title Insurance

The title insurance business has mushroomed due to four important reasons. First, in a warranty deed the grantor makes several strongly worded covenants. As you will recall, the grantor covenants that he is the owner, that the grantee will not be disturbed in his possession, that there are no encumbrances except as stated in the deed, that the grantor will procure any necessary further assurance of title for the grantee, and that the grantor will bear the expense of defending the grantee's title and possession. Thus, signing a warranty deed places a great obligation on the grantor. By purchasing title insurance, the grantor can transfer that obligation to an insurance company.

Second, a grantee is also motivated to have title insurance. Even with a warranty deed, there is always the lingering question of whether or not the seller would be financially capable of making good on his covenants and warranties. They are useless if one cannot enforce them. Moreover, title insurance typically provides a grantee broader assurance than a warranty deed. For example, an outsider's claim must produce physical dispossession of the grantee before the covenant of quiet enjoyment is considered broken. Yet the same claim would be covered by title insurance before dispossession took place.

Third, the broad use of title insurance has made mortgage lending more attractive and borrowing a little easier and cheaper for real property owners. This is because title insurance has removed the risk of loss due to defective titles. As a result, lenders can charge a lower rate of interest. Secondary market purchasers of loans such as FNMA and FHLMC (Chapter 12) require title insurance on every loan they buy.

Marketable Title

Fourth, title insurance has made titles to land much more marketable. In nearly all real estate transactions the seller agrees to deliver **marketable title** to the buyer. Marketable title is title that is free from reasonable doubt as to who the owner is. Even when the seller makes no mention of the quality of the title, courts ordinarily require that marketable title be conveyed. To illustrate, a seller orders an abstract prepared, and it is read by an attorney who certifies it as showing marketable title. The buyer's attorney feels that certain technical defects in the title chain contradict certification as marketable. He advises the buyer to refuse to complete the sale. The line between what is and what is not marketable title can be exceedingly thin, and differences of legal opinion are quite possible. One means of breaking the stalemate is to locate a title insurance company that will insure the title as being marketable. If the defect is not serious, the insurance company will accept the risk. If it is a serious risk, the company may either accept the risk and increase the insurance fee or recommend a quiet title suit.

QUIET TITLE SUIT

When a title defect (also called a **cloud on the title** or a **title cloud**) must be removed, it is logical to remove it by using the path of least resistance. For example, if an abstract or title report shows unpaid property taxes, the buyer may require the seller to pay them in full before the deal is completed. A cloud on the title due to pending foreclosure proceedings can be halted by either bringing the loan payments up to date or negotiating with the lender for a new loan repayment schedule. Similarly, a distant relative with ownership rights might be willing, upon negotiation, to quitclaim them for a price.

Sometimes a stronger means is necessary to remove title defects. For example, the distant relative may refuse to negotiate, or the lender may refuse to remove a mortgage lien despite pleas from the borrower that it has been paid, or there is a missing link in a chain of title. The solution is a **quiet title suit** (also called a quiet title action). Forty-seven states have enacted legislation that permits a property owner to ask the courts to hold hearings on the ownership of his land. At these hearings anyone claiming to have an interest or right to the land in question may present verbal or written evidence of that claim. A judge, acting on the evidence presented and the laws of his state, rules on the validity of each claim. The result is to legally recognize those with a genuine right or interest and to "quiet" those without a genuine interest.

THE TORRENS SYSTEM

Over a century ago, Sir Robert Torrens, a British administrator in Australia, devised an improved system of identifying land ownership. He was impressed by the relative simplicity of the British system of sailing-ship registration. The government maintained an official ships' registry that listed on a single page a ship's name, its owner, and any liens or encumbrances against it. Torrens felt land titles might be registered in a similar manner. The system he designed, known as the **Torrens system** of land title registration, starts with a landowner's application for registration and the preparation of an abstract. This is followed by a quiet title suit at which all parties named in the abstract and anyone else claiming a right or interest to the land in question may attend and be heard.

Based on the outcome of the suit, a government-appointed **registrar of titles** prepares a **certificate of title.** This certificate names the legally recognized fee owner and lists any legally recognized exceptions to that ownership, such as mortgages, easements, long-term leases, or life estates. The registrar keeps the original certificate of title and issues a duplicate to the fee owner. (Although they sound similar, a Torrens certificate of title is not the same as an attorney's certificate of title. The former shows ownership and claims against that ownership as established by a court of law. The latter is strictly an opinion of the condition of title.)

Torrens Certificate of Title

    Once a title is registered, any subsequent liens or encumbrances against it must be entered on the registrar's copy of the certificate of title in order to give constructive notice. When a lien or encumbrance is removed, its notation on the certificate is canceled. In this manner, the entire concept of constructive notice for a given parcel of land is reduced to a single-page document open to public view at the registrar's office. This, Torrens argued, would make the whole process of title transfer much simpler and cheaper.

    When registered land is conveyed, the grantor gives the grantee a deed. The grantee takes the deed to the registrar of titles, who transfers the title by canceling the grantor's certificate and issuing a new certificate in the name of the grantee. With a Torrens property this is the point in time when title is conveyed, not when the deed is delivered by the grantor to the grantee. Any liens or other encumbrances not removed at the same time are carried over from the old to the new certificate. The deed and certificate are kept by the registrar; the grantee receives a duplicate of the certificate. If the conveyance is accompanied by a new mortgage, it is noted on the new certificate, and a copy of the mortgage is retained by the registrar. Except for the quiet title suit aspect, the concept of land title registration is quite similar to that used in the United States for registering ownership of motor vehicles.

Adoption

In the United States, the first state to have a land registration act was Illinois in 1895. Other states slowly followed, but often their laws were vague and cumbersome to the point of being useless. At one point, 20 states had land title registration acts, but since then 9 states have repealed their acts and only 11 remain. They are Hawaii, Illinois, Massachusetts, Minnesota, New York, Colorado, Georgia, North Carolina, Ohio, Virginia, and Washington.

In all 11 states Torrens co-exists with the regular recording procedures described earlier in this chapter. Thus it is possible for a house on one side of a street to be Torrens registered and a house across the street to be recorded the regular way. Also, it may be customary to use Torrens in just certain areas of the state. In Illinois, use has been concentrated in Cook County (the Chicago area); in Minnesota, in the Minneapolis area; in Massachusetts, the Boston area; and in New York, Suffolk County (eastern Long Island). In Hawaii, Torrens is used statewide, but primarily by large landowners and subdivision developers who want to clear up complex title problems. In the remaining 6 states the public has made relatively little use of land title registration. This limited adoption of Torrens is due, among other things, to the promotion, widespread availability, and lower short-run cost of title insurance. (The quiet title suit can be costly.) Note too that although a state-run insurance fund is usually available to cover registration errors, some lenders feel this is not adequate protection and require title insurance.

MARKETABLE TITLE ACTS

At least 10 states have a **Marketable Title Act.** This is *not* a system of title registration. Rather, it is legislation aimed at making abstracts easier to prepare and less prone to error. This is done by cutting off claims to rights or interests in land that have been inactive for longer than the act's statutory period. In Connecticut, Michigan, Utah, Vermont, and Wisconsin, this is 40 years. Thus, in these states, a person who has an unbroken chain of title with no defects for at least 40 years is regarded by the law as having marketable title. Any defects more than 40 years old are outlawed. The result is to concentrate the title search process on the immediate past 40 years. Thus, abstracts can be produced with less effort and expense, and the chance for an error either by the abstracter or in the documents themselves is greatly reduced. This is particularly true in view of the fact that record-keeping procedures in the past were not as sophisticated as they are today.

The philosophy of a marketable title act is that a person has 40 years to come forward and make his claim known; if he does not, then he apparently does not consider it worth pursuing. As protection for a person actively pursuing a claim that is about to become more than 40 years old, the claim can be renewed for another 40 years by again recording notice of the claim in the public records. In certain situations, a title must be searched back more than 40 years (e.g., when there is a lease of more than 40-year duration or when no document affecting ownership has been recorded in over 40 years). In Nebraska the statutory period is 22 years; in Florida, North Carolina, and Oklahoma it is 30 years; in Indiana, 50 years.

Marketable title acts do not eliminate the need for legal notice nor do they eliminate the role of adverse possession.

REVIEW QUESTIONS

1. Once a person is aware of another's rights or interest in property, that person is said to have
   A. constructive notice.
   B. legal notice.
   C. inquiry notice.
   D. actual notice.

2. Constructive notice requires that
   A. a landowner give public notice of his/her claim of ownership.
   B. anyone interested in the property inspect the property and the public records.
   C. Both A and B.
   D. Neither A nor B.

3. The public recorder's office
   A. serves as a central information station for documents pertaining to interests in land.
   B. is an agency of the federal government.
   C. Both A and B.
   D. Neither A nor B.

4. Farmer Sorensen leases 320 acres adjacent to his ranch. Sorensen can give notice to the world at large by
   A. plowing the land.
   B. storing his equipment on it.
   C. putting a fence around it.
   D. All of the above.
   E. None of the above.

5. Priority of a recorded instrument is determined by the date of
   A. acknowledgment.   C. the instrument.
   B. delivery to the grantee. D. recordation.

6. Deed and other instruments which affect land titles should be recorded
   A. immediately after delivery or execution.
   B. in order to provide constructive notice.
   C. Both A an B.
   D. Neither A nor B.

7. The purpose of having a person's signature acknowledged is to
   A. make certain the person signing the document is the same person named in the document, and that the signing was voluntary.
   B. make the document admissible to the public records.
   C. Both A and B.
   D. Neither A nor B.

8. In a jurisdiction which indexes recorded instruments by grantee and grantor, if one knew the name of the current owner of a property, and wished to search the records to verify that ownership, one would look in the
   A. grantee index.   C. Both A and B.
   B. grantor index.   D. Neither A nor B.

9. Instruments are recorded in the public records in what order?
   A. Alphabetical order, based on the grantee's last name.
   B. Chronological order, as received for recordation.
   C. According to the date of the instrument.
   D. Alphabetical order, based on the grantor's last name.

10. The name of the borrower would be filed alphabetically in the
    A. mortgagee index.   C. Lis Pendens.
    B. grantor index.   D. Lender's index.

11. Which of the following would not ordinarily be checked in searching a title to a parcel of land?
    A. Judgment records.
    B. Lien records.
    C. Chattel mortgage records.
    D. Lis pendens index.

12. A lis pendens index is
    A. an index of existing leases on property.
    B. an index of pending lawsuits.
    C. a tract index.
    D. a chain of title.

13. It is conceivable that in some circumstances a title searcher may find it necessary to check
    A. birth, death, and marriage records.
    B. divorce, adoption, military, and tax records.
    C. Both A and B.
    D. Neither A nor B.

14. A summary of all recorded documents affecting title to a given parcel of land is called
   A. a chain of title.
   B. an abstract of title.
   C. a title report
   D. All of the above.

15. Protection against a loss occasioned by which of the following would not be covered by title insurance?
   A. Forged deeds, or deeds by incompetents.
   B. Unextinguished dower or curtesy rights.
   C. Claims by undisclosed or missing heirs.
   D. Destruction of improvements by a tornado.

16. Should a title insurance company elect to fight a claim in court, the legal expenses incurred will be
   A. deducted from the coverage under the policy.
   B. assumed by the title insurance company without affecting the policy coverage.
   C. shared by the insured and the insurance company.
   D. paid by the insured.

17. The purchase of title insurance eliminates the need for
   A. casualty insurance.
   B. a survey of the property.
   C. constructive notice.
   D. None of the above.
   E. All of the above.

18. All of the following are true of a quiet title suit EXCEPT that it
   A. is a judicial proceeding.
   B. removes all claims to title other than the owner's.
   C. quiets those without a genuine interest in the property.
   D. can be used to clear up a disputed title.

19. A Torrens certificate of title does which of the following?
   A. Recognizes legitimate claims against the title at the time the certificate is issued.
   B. Eliminates the need to search back further in time than the quiet title suit.
   C. Both A and B.
   D. Neither A nor B.

20. Marketable title acts
   A. are a system of title registration.
   B. make abstracts easier to prepare.
   C. cut off inactive claims.
   D. Both B and C.
   E. Both A and C.

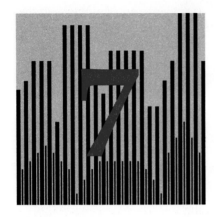

Contract Law

OVERVIEW OF
CHAPTER 7

This chapter will introduce you to contract law and how a contract is created. The essentials of a valid contract are also covered in detail. Other topics covered include offer and acceptance, fraud, mistake, lawful objective, consideration, performance, and breach of contract. Although this is a short chapter, its importance should not be underestimated.

LEARNING OBJECTIVES

After completion of this chapter, you should be able to:

1. Explain how a contract is created and its legal effect.
2. Describe the essentials of a valid contract.
3. Understand the use of the power of attorney.
4. Explain the factors involved in mutual agreement including the offer and acceptance, counteroffers, fraud, misrepresentation, mistake, and duress.
5. Explain the parol evidence rule.
6. Describe breach of contract and unilateral or mutual rescission.
7. Explain the purpose and application of the Statute of Limitations.
8. Describe an implied obligation.

KEY • TERMS

Breach of contract: failure, without legal excuse, to perform as required by a contract

Competent parties: persons considered legally capable of entering into a binding contract

Consideration: an act or promise given in exchange for something

Contract: a legally enforceable agreement to do (or not to do) a particular thing

Duress: the application of force to obtain an agreement

Fraud: an act intended to deceive for the purpose of inducing another to give up something of value

Liquidated damages: an amount of money specified in a contract as compensation to be paid if the contract is not satisfactorily completed

Power of attorney: a document by which one person authorizes another to act on his behalf

Specific performance: contract performance according to the precise terms agreed upon

Void contract: a contract that has no binding effect on the parties who made it

Voidable contract: a contract that is able to be voided by one of its parties

A **contract** is a legally enforceable agreement to do (or not to do) a specific thing. In this chapter we shall see how a contract is created and what makes it legally binding. Topics covered include offer and acceptance, fraud, mistake, lawful objective, consideration, performance, and breach of contract. In Chapter 8 we will turn our attention to the purchase contract, installment contract, lease with option to buy, first right of refusal, and trade agreement.

A contract may be either expressed or implied. An **expressed contract** occurs when the parties to the contract declare their intentions either orally or in writing. (The word **party** [plural, **parties**] is a legal term that refers to a person or group involved in a legal proceeding.) A lease or rental agreement, for example, is an expressed contract. The lessor (landlord) expresses the intent to permit the lessee (tenant) to use the premises, and the lessee agrees to pay rent in return. A contract to purchase real estate is also an expressed contract.

An **implied contract** is created by neither words nor writing but rather by actions of the parties indicating that they intend to create a contract. For example, when you step into a taxicab, you imply that you will pay the fare. The cab driver, by allowing you in the cab, implies that you will be taken where you want to go. The same thing occurs at a restaurant. The presence of tables,

HOW A CONTRACT IS CREATED

silverware, menus, waiters, and waitresses implies that you will be served food. When you order, you imply that you are going to pay when the bill is presented.

Bilateral Contract

A contract may be either bilateral or unilateral. A **bilateral contract** results when a promise is exchanged for a promise. For example, in a typical real estate sale, the buyer promises to pay the agreed price, and the seller promises to deliver title to the buyer. In a lease contract the lessor promises the use of the premises to the lessee, and the lessee promises to pay rent in return. A bilateral contract is basically an "I will do this *and* you will do that" arrangement. Depending on its wording, a listing can be a bilateral contract with the broker promising his/her best efforts to locate a buyer and the seller promising to pay a commission when a buyer is found. Or, a listing can be a unilateral contract, discussed next.

Unilateral Contract

A **unilateral contract** results when a promise is exchanged for performance. For instance, during a campaign to get more listings, a real estate office manager announces to the firm's sales staff that an extra $100 bonus will be paid for each saleable new listing. No promises or agreements are necessary from the salespersons. However, each time a salesperson performs by bringing in a saleable listing, he or she is entitled to the promised $100 bonus. An option to purchase is a unilateral contract until it is exercised, at which time it becomes a bilateral contract. A listing can be structured as a unilateral contract wherein the seller agrees to pay a commission if the broker finds a buyer. When the broker produces a buyer for the property the contract becomes bilateral. A unilateral contract is basically an "I will do this *if* you will do that" arrangement.

Forbearance

Most contract agreements are based on promises by the parties involved to act in some manner (pay money, provide services, or deliver title). However, a contract can contain a promise to **forbear** (not to act) by one or more of its parties. For example, a lender may agree not to foreclose on a delinquent mortgage loan if the borrower agrees to a new payment schedule.

Valid, Void, Voidable

A **valid contract** is one that meets all the requirements of law. It is binding upon its parties and legally enforceable in a court of law. A **void contract** has no legal effect and, in fact, is not a contract at all. Even though the parties may have gone through the motions of attempting to make a contract, no legal rights are created and any party thereto may ignore it at his pleasure. A **voidable contract** is a contract that is able to be voided by one of its parties. In effect, it is a contract that is not binding on one of its parties. Examples of valid, void, and voidable contracts are included throughout this chapter. Let us turn our attention to the requirements of a valid contract.

For a contract to be **legally valid,** and hence binding and enforceable, the following five requirements must be met:

1. Legally competent parties.
2. Mutual agreement.
3. Lawful objective.
4. Consideration or cause.
5. Contract in writing when required by law.

If these conditions are met, any party to the contract may, if the need arises, call upon a court of law to either enforce the contract as written or award money damages for nonperformance. In reality, a properly written contract seldom ends up in court because each party knows it will be enforced as written. It is the poorly written contract or the contract that borders between enforceable and unenforceable that ends up in court. A judge must then decide if a contract actually exists and the obligations of each party. Using the courts, however, is an expensive and time-consuming method of interpreting an agreement. It is much better to have a correctly prepared contract in the first place. Let's look more closely at the five requirements of an enforceable contract.

ESSENTIALS OF A VALID CONTRACT

For a contract to be legally enforceable, all parties entering into it must be legally competent. In deciding competency, the law provides a mixture of objective and subjective standards. The most objective standard is that of age. A person must reach the age of **majority** to be legally capable of entering into a contract. **Minors** do not have contractual capability. In most states the age for entering into legally binding contracts is 18 years. The purpose of majority laws is to protect minors (also known as "infants" in legal terminology) from entering into contracts that they may not be old enough to understand. Most contracts made

Competent Parties

with minors, except those for necessities, such as food and clothing, are voidable by the minor at the minor's option. For example, a deed by a minor is voidable, although a minor can be a grantee. A minor wishing to disaffirm a contract must do so while still a minor or within a reasonable time after reaching majority. If not, the contract becomes valid. In some cases a contract with a minor is void. For example, a minor does not have the capacity to appoint someone to sell his property. Any contract to do so (called a power of attorney) is void from the outset. If a contract with a minor is required, it is still possible to obtain a binding contract by working through the minor's legal guardian.

Regarding intoxicated persons, if there was a deliberate attempt to intoxicate a person for the purpose of approving a contract, the intoxicated person, upon sobering up, can call upon the courts to cancel the contract. If the contracting party was voluntarily drunk to the point of incompetence, when he is sober he may ratify or deny the contract if he does so promptly. However, some courts look at the matter strictly from the standpoint of whether or not the intoxicated person had the capability of formulating the intent to enter into a contract. Obviously, there are some fine and subjective distinctions here, and a judge may interpret them differently than the parties to the contract. The points made in this paragraph also apply to a person who contracts while under the influence of other legal or illegal drugs.

Persons of unsound mind who have been declared incompetent by a judge may not make a valid contract, and any attempt to do so results in a void contract. The solution is to contract through the person appointed to act on behalf of the incompetent. If a person has not been judged legally incompetent but nonetheless appears incapable of understanding the transaction in question, he has no legal power to contract. Illegal aliens also lack legal competency. In some states persons convicted of felonies may not enter into valid contracts without the prior approval of the parole board.

Power of Attorney   An individual can give another person the power to act on his behalf: for example, to buy or sell land or sign a lease. The document that accomplishes this is called a **power of attorney.** The person holding the power of attorney is called an **attorney-in-fact.** With regard to real estate, a power of attorney must be in writing because the real estate documents to be signed must be in writing. Any document signed with a power of attorney should be executed as follows: "Paul Jones, principal, by Samuel Smith, agent, his attorney-in-fact." If the attorney-in-fact is to convey title to land, then the power of attorney must be acknowledged by the principal and recorded. The attorney-in-fact is legally competent to the extent of the powers granted to him by the principal as long as the principal remains legally competent, and as long as both of them are alive. The power of attorney can, of course, be terminated by the principal at any time. A recorded notice of revocation is needed to revoke a recorded power of attorney.

Corporations are considered legally competent parties. However, the individual contracting on behalf of the corporation must have authority from the board of directors. Some states also require that the corporate seal be affixed to contracts. A partnership can contract either in the name of the partnership or in the name of any of its general partners. Executors and administrators with court authorization can contract on behalf of estates, and trustees on behalf of trusts.

Corporations, etc.

The requirement of **mutual agreement** (also called **mutual consent,** or **mutual assent,** or **meeting of the minds**) means that there must be agreement to the provisions of the contract by the parties involved. In other words, there must be a mutual willingness to enter into a contract. The existence of mutual agreement is evidenced by the words and acts of the parties indicating that there is a valid offer and an unqualified acceptance. In addition, there must be no fraud, misrepresentation, or mistake, and the agreement must be genuine and freely given. Let us consider each of these points in more detail.

Mutual Agreement

Offer and acceptance requires that one party (the **offeror**) makes an offer to another party (the **offeree**). If the offer is acceptable, the offeree must then communicate the acceptance to the offeror. The means of communication may be spoken or written or an action that implies acceptance. To illustrate, suppose that you own a house and want to sell it. You tell your listing broker that you will accept $100,000 and that you would deliver a general warranty deed and pay the normal closing costs for the area. Within a few days, the broker submits a signed document from a prospective buyer. This constitutes an offer, and the buyer (the offeror) has just communicated it to you (the

Offer and Acceptance

offeree). One requirement of a valid offer is that the offer be specific in its terms. Mutual agreement cannot exist if the terms of the offer are vague or undisclosed and/or the offer does not clearly state the obligations of each party involved. If the seller were to say to a prospective purchaser, "Do you want to buy this house?" without stating the price, and the prospective purchaser said yes, the law would not consider this to be a valid offer.

Counter-offer

Upon receiving the offer, the offeree has three options: to agree to it, to reject it, or to make a counteroffer. If the offeree agrees, he must agree to every item of the offer. An offer is considered by law to be rejected not only if the offeree rejects it outright but also if any change is made in the terms. *Any* change in the terms is considered a counteroffer. Although it may appear that the offeree is only amending the offer before he accepts it, the offeree has actually rejected it, and is making a new offer. This now makes the seller the offeror. To illustrate, suppose the prospective purchaser submits an offer to the listing broker to purchase the property for $95,000, but instead of accepting the $95,000 offer, the seller amends the contract to reflect a selling price of $100,000. This is a rejection of the original offer and creates a counteroffer to the purchaser. The purchaser now has the right to accept or reject this counteroffer. If, however, the original $95,000 offer is agreeable to the offeree (seller) he must communicate the acceptance to the purchaser. While a spoken "Yes, I'll take it," would be legally adequate, prudent real estate brokers should obtain the signature of the seller on a contract, without any further changes.

It should also be pointed out that an offer can be revoked by the offeror at any time prior to the offeror hearing of its acceptance. For example, if you tell a prospective tenant that he can rent the property for $495 per month and, while waiting for his response you find another prospective tenant who is willing to pay more, you can revoke your first offer at any time prior to hearing of its acceptance, then make your contract with the second prospective tenant. An offeror should be strongly advised, however, not to initiate more than one offer at a time, since considerable confusion can be caused by multiple offers, revocations, and acceptances in one transaction.

Fraud

Mutual agreement requires that there be no fraud, misrepresentation or mistake in the contract if it is to be valid. A **fraud** is an act intended ... cing another to part with somet... knowingly telling a lie or ma... of perform- ance. For exampl... nent and a prospective tenant ... ice nearby. There isn't, but you ... ortant and want to rent the a ... rents the apartment, relying ... moves in. The next day he call... sportation and he wants to br... ately. Be- cause mutual agree... rescind (cancel) the contract...

Fraud can also ... nportant information, thereby ... ffer. For example, the day you ... spective tenant the weather is ... every rainstorm the tenant's ... a lake of water 6 inches dee... if the prospective tenant was ... before agreeing to the rental c... permit the aggrieved party to re... tenant does not have to rescind ... atures of the apartment enough ... oded parking stall.

If a real estate agent ... the deceived party later resci... the commission lost, but expla... ther parties of the contract. Mo... for suspension or revocation ... ent acts.

Innocent misrepresent... nal misrepresentation) in that the ... ation is not doing so to de... of reaching an agreement. To il... st year you have observed that ... nt building. If you tell a prospec... only to learn the day after the te... last week, this is innocent misr... no dishonesty involved, the ten... contract. If performance has r... case the tenant has not moved

Innocent
Misrepresentation

notice that he **disaffirms** (revokes) the contract. However, if the tenant wants to break the contract, he must do so in a timely manner; otherwise the law will presume that the situation is satisfactory to the tenant.

Mistake

Mistake as applied in contract law has a very narrow meaning. It does not include innocent misrepresentation nor does it include ignorance, inability, or poor judgment. If a person enters into a contract that he later regrets because he did not investigate it thoroughly enough, or because it did not turn out to be beneficial, the law will not grant relief to him on the grounds of mistake, even though he may now consider it was a "mistake" to have made the contract in the first place. Mistake as used in contract law arises from ambiguity in negotiations and mistake of material fact. For example, you offer to sell your mountain cabin to an acquaintance. He has never seen your cabin, and you give him instructions on how to get there to look at it. He returns and accepts your offer. However, he made a wrong turn and the cabin he looked at was not your cabin. A week later he discovers his error. The law considers this ambiguity in negotiations. In this case the buyer, in his mind, was purchasing a different cabin from the one the seller was selling; therefore, there is no mutual agreement and any contract signed is void.

To illustrate a mistake of fact, suppose that you show your apartment to a prospective tenant and tell him that he must let you know by tomorrow if he wants to rent it. The next day he visits you and together you enter into a rental contract. Although neither of you is aware of it, there has just been a serious fire in the apartment. Since a fire-gutted apartment is not what the two of you had in mind when the rental contract was signed, there is no mutual agreement.

Occasionally, "mistake of law" will be claimed as grounds for relief from a contract. However, mistake as to one's legal rights in a contract is not generally accepted by courts of law unless it is coupled with a mistake of fact. Ignorance of the law is not considered a mistake.

Contractual Intent

Mutual agreement also requires that the parties express **contractual intent.** This means that their intention is to be bound by the agreement, thus precluding jokes or jests from becoming valid contracts.

Duress

The last requirement of mutual agreement is that the offer and acceptance be genuine and freely given. **Duress** (use of force), **menace** (threat of violence) or **undue influence** (unfair advantage) cannot be used to obtain agreement. The law permits a contract made under any of these conditions to be revoked by the aggrieved party.

Lawful Objective

To be enforceable, a contract cannot call for the breaking of laws. This is because a court of law cannot be called upon to enforce a contract that requires that a law be broken. Such a contract is void, or if already in operation, it is unenforceable in a court of law. For example, a debt contract requiring an interest rate in excess of that allowed by state law would be void. If the borrower had started repaying the debt and then later stopped, the lender would not be able to look to the courts to enforce collection of the balance. Contracts contrary to good morals and general public policy are also unenforceable.

Consideration

For an agreement to be enforceable it must be supported by **consideration.** The purpose of requiring consideration is to demonstrate that a bargain has been struck between the parties to the contract. The size, quantity, nature, or amount of what is being exchanged is irrelevant as long as it is present. Consideration is usually something of value such as a promise to do something, money, property, or personal services. For example, there can be an exchange of a promise for a promise, money for a promise, money for property, goods for services, etc. Forbearance also qualifies as consideration.

Exchange of Promises

In a typical offer to purchase a home, the consideration is the mutual exchange of promises by the buyer and seller to obligate themselves to do something they were not previously required to do. In other words, the seller agrees to sell on the terms agreed and the buyer agrees to buy the property on those same terms. The earnest money the buyer may put down is not the consideration necessary to make the contract valid. Rather, earnest money is a tangible indication of the buyer's intent and may become a source of compensation (damages) to the seller in the event the buyer does not carry out his promises.

In a deed the consideration requirement is usually met with a statement such as "For ten dollars and other good and valuable consideration." Also, the purchase contract is part of the consideration and is legally merged into the deed. In a lease, the periodic payment of rent is the consideration for the use of the premises.

Valuable Consideration

A contract fails to be legally binding if consideration is lacking from any party to the contract. The legal philosophy is that a person cannot promise to do something of value for someone else without receiving in turn some form of consideration. Stated another way, each party must give up something, i.e., each must suffer a detriment. For example, if I promise to give you my car, the consideration requirement is not met since you promise nothing in return. But if I promise to give you my car when you take me to Hawaii, the consideration requirement is met. As a group, money, plus promises, property, legal rights, services, and forbearance, if they are worth money, are classified as **valuable consideration.**

Good Consideration

What about outright gifts such as the gift of real property from a parent to a child based solely on love and affection? Although this is not valuable consideration, it is nonetheless **good consideration** and as such fulfills the legal requirement that consideration be present. The law generally will not inquire as to the adequacy of the consideration unless there is evidence of fraud, mistake, duress, threat, or undue influence. For instance, if a man gave away his property or sold it very cheaply to keep it from his creditors, the creditors could ask the courts to set aside those transfers.

Multiple Meanings of the Word *Consideration*

If the word *consideration* continues to be confusing to you, it is because the word has three meanings in real estate. The first is consideration from the standpoint of a legal requirement for a valid contract. You may wish to think of this form of consideration as **legal consideration** or **cause.** The second meaning is money. For example, the consideration upon which conveyance taxes are charged is the amount of money exchanged in the transaction. The third meaning is acknowledgment. Thus the phrase "in consideration of ten dollars" means "in acknowledgment of" or "in receipt of."

Contract in Writing

In each state there is a law that is commonly known as a **statute of frauds.** Its purpose is to prevent frauds by requiring that all contracts for the sale of land, or an interest in land, be in writing and signed to be enforceable in a court of law. This includes such things as offers, acceptances, binders, land contracts, deeds, escrows, and options to purchase. Mortgages and trust deeds (and their accompanying bonds and notes) and leases for more than one year must also be in writing to be enforceable. In addition, most states have adopted the **Uniform Commercial Code** that requires, among other things, that the sale of personal property with value in excess of $500 be in writing. Most states also require that real estate listing contracts be expressed in writing.

The purpose of requiring that a contract be written and signed is to prevent perjury and fraudulent attempts to seek legal enforcement of a contract that never existed. It is not necessary that a contract be a single formal document. It can consist of a series of signed letters or memoranda as long as the essentials of a valid contract are present. Note that the requirement for a written contract relates only to the enforceability of the contract. Thus if Mr. Colby orally agrees to sell his land to Mr. Conan and they carry out the deal, neither can come back after the contract was performed and ask a court to rescind the deal because the agreement to sell was oral.

Purpose

The most common real estate contract that does not need to be in writing to be enforceable is a month-to-month rental agreement that can be terminated by either landlord or tenant on one month's notice. Nonetheless, most are in writing because people tend to forget oral promises. While the unhappy party can go to court, the judge may have a difficult time determining what oral promises were made, particularly if there were no witnesses other than the parties to the agreement. Hence, it is advisable to put all important contracts in writing and for each party to recognize the agreement by signing it. If a party is a corporation, most states require the signatures of two corporate officers plus the corporate seal. It is also customary to date written contracts, although most can be enforced without showing the date the agreement was reached.

A written contract will supersede an oral one. Thus, if two parties orally promise one thing and then write and sign something else, the written contract will prevail. This has been the basis for many complaints against overzealous real estate agents who make oral promises that do not appear anywhere in the written sales contract.

Under certain circumstances the **parol evidence rule** permits oral evidence to complete an otherwise incomplete or ambiguous written contract. However, the application of this

Parol Evidence Rule

rule is quite narrow. If a contract is complete and clear in its intent, the courts presume that what the parties put into writing is what they agreed upon.

Executory, Executed, Execute

A contract that is in the process of being carried out is said to be **executory,** i.e., in the process of being performed. Once completed, it is said to be **executed,** i.e., performance has taken place. This may refer to the signing of the contract or to its completed performance depending on what the contract requires. The word **execute,** a much more frequently used term, refers to the process of completing, performing, or carrying out something. Thus, you execute a document when you sign it, and this is the most common use of the term. Once signed, you execute the terms of the contract by carrying out its terms.

PERFORMANCE AND DISCHARGE OF CONTRACTS

Most contracts are discharged by being fully performed by the contracting parties in accordance with the contract terms. However, alternatives are open to the parties of the contract. One is to sell or otherwise **assign** the contract to another party. Unless prohibited by the contract, rights, benefits, and obligations under a contract can be assigned to someone else. The original party to the contract, however, still remains ultimately liable for its performance. Note, too, that an assignment is a contract in itself and must meet all the essential contract requirements to be enforceable. A common example of an assignment occurs when a lessee wants to move out and sells his lease to another party. When a contract creates a personal obligation, such as a listing agreement with a broker, an assignment may not be made.

Novation

A contract can also be performed by **novation.** Novation is the substitution of a new contract between the same or new parties. For example, novation occurs when a buyer assumes a seller's loan, *and* the lender releases the seller from the loan contract. With novation the departing party is released from the obligation to complete the contract.

If the objective of a contract becomes legally impossible to accomplish, the law will consider the contract discharged. For example, a new legislative statute may forbid what the contract originally intended. If the parties mutually agree to cancel their contract before it is executed, this too is a form of discharge. For instance, you sign a 5-year lease to pay $900 per month for an office. Three years later you find a better location and want to move. Meanwhile, rents for similar offices in your building have increased to $1,000 per month. Under these conditions the landlord might be happy to agree to cancel your lease.

If one of the contracting parties dies, a contract is considered discharged if it calls for some specific act that only the dead person could have performed. For example, if you hired a free-lance gardener to tend your landscaping and he died, the contract would be discharged. However, if your contract is with a firm that employs other gardeners who can do the job, the contract would still be valid.

Deceased Party

If there is a valid purchase contract and one party dies, the contract is usually enforceable against the estate because the estate has the authority to carry out the deceased's affairs. Similarly, if a person mortgages his or her property and dies, the estate must continue the payments or lose the property.

Under the **Uniform Vendor and Purchaser Risk Act,** if neither possession nor title has passed and there is material destruction to the property, the seller cannot enforce the contract and the purchaser is entitled to his money back. If damage is minor and promptly repaired by the seller, the contract would still be enforceable. If either title or possession has passed and destruction occurs, the purchaser is not relieved of his duty to pay the price, nor is he entitled to a refund of money already paid.

Property Damage

When one party fails to perform as required by a contract and the law does not recognize the reason for failure to be a valid excuse, there is a **breach of contract.** The wronged or innocent party has six alternatives: (1) to accept partial performance, (2) to rescind the contract unilaterally, (3) to sue for specific performance, (4) to sue for money damages, (5) to accept liquidated money damages, or (6) to mutually rescind the contract. Let us consider each of these.

BREACH OF CONTRACT

Partial performance may be acceptable to the innocent party because there may not be a great deal at stake or because the innocent party feels that the time and effort to sue would not be worth the rewards. Suppose that you contracted with a roofing repairman to fix your roof for $400. When he was finished you

Partial Performance

paid him. A week later you discover a spot that he had agreed to fix, but missed. After many futile phone calls, you accept the breach and consider the contract discharged because it is easier to fix the spot yourself than to keep pursuing the repairman.

Unilateral Rescission

Under certain circumstances, the innocent party can **unilaterally rescind** a contract. That is, the innocent party can take the position that if the other party is not going to perform his obligations, then the innocent party will not either. An example would be a rent strike in retaliation to a landlord who fails to keep the premises habitable. Unilateral rescission should be resorted to only after consulting an attorney.

Lawsuit for Money Damages

If the damages to the innocent party can be reasonably expressed in terms of money, the innocent party can sue for **money damages.** For example, you rent an apartment to a tenant. As part of the rental contract you furnish the refrigerator and freezer unit. While the tenant is on vacation, the unit breaks down and $200 worth of frozen meat and other perishables spoil. Since your obligation under the contract is to provide the tenant with a working refrigerator-freezer, the tenant can sue you for $200 in money damages. He can also recover interest on the money awarded to him from the day of the loss to the day you reimburse him.

Lawsuit for Specific Performance

A lawsuit for **specific performance** is an action in court by the innocent party to force the breaching party to carry out the remainder of the contract according to the precise terms, price, and conditions agreed upon. For example, you make an offer to purchase a parcel of land and the seller accepts. A written contract is prepared and signed by both of you. If you carry out all your obligations under the contract, but the seller has a change of mind and refuses to deliver title to you, you may bring a lawsuit against the seller for specific performance. In reviewing your suit, the court will determine whether or not the contract is valid and legal, whether or not you have carried out your duties under the contract, and whether or not the contract is just and reasonable. If you win your lawsuit, the court will force the seller to deliver title to you as specified in the contract.

Note the difference between suing for money damages and
suing for specific performance. When money can be used to
restore one's position (as in the case of the tenant who can buy
$200 worth of fresh food), a suit for money damages is appro-
priate. In situations where money cannot provide an adequate
remedy, and this is often the case in real estate because no two
properties are exactly alike, specific performance is appropriate.
Notice, too, that the mere existence of the legal rights of the
wronged party is often enough to gain cooperation. In the case
of the spoiled food, you would give the tenant the value of the
lost food before spending time and money in court to hear a
judge tell you to do the same thing. A threat of a lawsuit will
often bring the desired results if the defendant knows that the
law will side with the wronged party. The cases that do go to
court are usually those in which the identity of the wronged
party and/or the extent of the damages is not clear.

Comparison

The parties to a contract may decide in advance the amount of
damages to be paid in the event either party breaches the contract. An example is an offer to purchase real estate that includes
a statement to the effect that, once the seller accepts the offer, if
the buyer fails to complete the purchase, the seller may keep the
buyer's deposit (the earnest money) as **liquidated damages.** If
a broker is involved, seller and broker usually agree to divide
the damages, thus compensating the seller for damages and the
broker for time and effort. Another case of liquidated damages
occurs when a builder promises to finish a building by a certain
date or pay the party that hired him a certain number of dollars
per day until it is completed. This impresses upon the builder
the need for prompt completion and compensates the property
owner for losses due to the delay.

Liquidated Damages

Specific performance, money damages, and liquidated damages
are all designed to aid the innocent party in the event of a breach
of contract. However, as a practical matter, the time and cost of
pursuing a remedy in a court of law may sometimes exceed the
benefits to be derived. Moreover, there is the possibility the
judge for your case may not agree with your point of view.
Therefore, even though you are the innocent party and you feel
you have a legitimate case that can be pursued in the courts, you
may find it more practical to agree with the other party (or

Mutual Rescission

parties) to simply rescind (i.e., cancel or annul) the contract. To properly protect everyone involved, the agreement to cancel must be in writing and signed by the parties to the original contract. Properly executed, **mutual rescission** relieves the parties to the contract from their obligations to each other.

An alternative to mutual rescission is novation. As noted earlier, this is the substitution of a new contract for an existing one. Novation provides a middle ground between suing and rescinding. Thus the breaching party may be willing to complete the contract provided the innocent party will voluntarily make certain changes in it. If this is acceptable, the changes should be put into writing (or the contract redrafted) and then signed by the parties involved.

STATUTE OF LIMITATIONS

The **statute of limitations** limits by law the amount of time a wronged party has to seek the aid of a court in obtaining justice. The aggrieved party must start legal proceedings within a certain period of time or the courts will not help him. The amount of time varies from state to state and by type of legal action involved. However, time limits of 3 to 7 years are typical for breach of contract.

IMPLIED OBLIGATIONS

As was pointed out at the beginning of this chapter, one can incur contractual obligations by implication as well as by oral or written contracts. Home builders and real estate agents provide two timely examples. For many years, if a homeowner discovered poor design or workmanship after he had bought a new home, it was his problem. The philosophy was **caveat emptor,** let the buyer beware *before* he buys. Today, courts of law find that in building a home and offering it for sale, the builder simultaneously implies that it is fit for living. Thus, if a builder installs a toilet in a bathroom, the implication is that it will work. In fact, many states have now passed legislation that makes builders liable for their work for one year.

Similarly, real estate agent trade organizations, such as the National Association of Realtors and state and local realtor associations, are constantly working to elevate the status of real estate brokers and salespersons to that of a competent professional in the public's mind. But as professional status is gained, there is an implied obligation to dispense professional-quality service. Thus, an individual agent is not only responsible for acting in accordance with written laws, but will also be held responsible for being competent and knowledgeable. Once recognized as a professional by the public, the real estate agent will not be able to plead ignorance.

In view of the present trend toward consumer protection, the concept of "Let the buyer beware" is being replaced with "Let the seller beware" and "Let the agent beware."

1. Which of the following would be defined as a party to a contract?
   A. Buyer.
   B. Seller.
   C. Landlord.
   D. Tenant.
   E. All of the above.

2. A contract based upon a promise exchanged for a promise is a
   A. semilateral contract.
   B. dilateral contract.
   C. binary contract.
   D. bilateral contract.

3. A contract based upon one party's promise in exchange for an act from the other party is classified as
   A. a bilateral contract.
   B. an unenforceable contract.
   C. an executed contract.
   D. a unilateral contract.

4. A unilateral contract is enforceable against
   A. either party.
   B. the offeror.
   C. the offeree.
   D. neither party.

5. A contract which binds one party but not the other is
   A. unenforceable.
   B. void.
   C. voidable.
   D. illegal.

6. A person who has not reached the age of majority is also known as
   A. a minor.
   B. an infant.
   C. Both A and B.
   D. Neither A nor B.

7. As a rule, a contract between an adult and a minor is NOT
   A. voidable by the minor.
   B. enforceable against the adult.
   C. enforceable against either party.
   D. enforceable against the minor.

8. An attorney-in-fact derives his powers from
   A. the state bar association.
   B. a power of attorney.
   C. judicial appointment.
   D. popular election.

9. A partnership may contract in the name of
   A. its general partners.
   B. the partnership.
   C. Both A and B.
   D. Neither A nor B.

10. When an offeror makes a valid offer and communicates it to the offeree, the offeree may
    A. reject the offer.
    B. accept the offer.
    C. make a counteroffer.
    D. All of the above.

REVIEW QUESTIONS

11. An offer may be terminated by
A. withdrawal of the offer.   C. the lapse of time.
B. refusal from the offeree.   D. All of the above.

12. Mutual agreement is missing when a contract is made under
A. menace.   C. duress.
B. undue influence.   D. All of the above.

13. An act intended to deceive the other party in a contract is
A. duress.   C. mistake.
B. menace.   D. fraud.

14. A contract made as a joke or in jest is precluded from becoming a valid contract because it lacks
A. contractual intent.   C. Both A and B.
B. mutual agreement.   D. Neither A nor B.

15. A contract which is in the process of being carried out is
A. executed.   C. executory.
B. executing.   D. executrix.

16. When a lessee in a rented property assigns his lease to another party, he assumes the role of
A. assignor.   C. sublessee.
B. assignee.   D. None of the above.

17. Substitution of a new contract and a new party for a previous one is known as
A. innovation.   C. subrogation.
B. assignment.   D. novation.

18. Legal action to force the breaching party to carry out the remainder of a contract is called a suit for
A. liquidated damages.   C. partial performance.
B. specific performance.   D. breach of contract.

19. The law which limits the time in which a wronged party may file legal action for obtaining justice is the statue of
A. frauds.   C. novation.
B. limitations.   D. performance.

20. In view of current trends toward consumer protection, the watchwords for real estate salespersons and brokers might well be
A. caveat emptor.   C. Both A and B.
B. caveat agent.   D. Neither A nor B.

Real Estate Sales Contracts

Chapter 8 focuses on real estate contracts, especially the purchase contract. Other contracts covered include the installment contract and a lease with the option to buy. The right of first refusal and tax deferred exchange are also discussed. The Earnest Money Contract will be covered in detail along with the property addendum.

OVERVIEW OF
CHAPTER 8

LEARNING OBJECTIVES

After successful completion of this chapter, you should be able to:

1. Explain the provisions of a typical purchaser contract.
2. Describe the purpose and features of the property condition addendum.
3. Explain the use of an installment contract and lease with the option to buy.
4. Define and explain the right of first refusal.
5. Describe the exchange agreement and delayed exchanges.
6. Distinguish between real estate practice and practicing law.

KEY • TERMS

Binder: a short purchase contract used to secure a real estate transaction until a more formal contract can be signed

Counteroffer: an offer made in response to an offer

Default: failure to perform a legal duty, such as failure to carry out the terms of a contract

Earnest money deposit: money that accompanies an offer to purchase as evidence of good faith

Equitable title: the right to demand that title be conveyed upon payment of the purchase price

Installment contract: a method of selling and financing property whereby the seller retains title but the buyer takes possession while making the payments

"Lease-option": allows the tenant to buy the property at preset price and terms for a given period of time

Right of first refusal: the right to match or better an offer before the property is sold to someone else

Tax deferred exchange: a sale of real property in exchange for another parcel of real estate, to affect a non-taxable gain.

"Time is of the essence": a phrase that means that the time limits of a contract must be faithfully observed or the contract is voidable

The present chapter focuses on contracts used to initiate the sale of real estate. Chiefly we will look at the purchase contract, the installment contract, and the lease with option to buy. There will also be brief discussions of a real estate binder, letter of intent, first right of refusal, and real estate exchange.

PURPOSE OF SALES CONTRACTS

What is the purpose of a real estate sales contract? If a buyer and a seller agree on a price, why can't the buyer hand the seller the necessary money and the seller simultaneously hand the buyer a deed? The main reason is that the buyer needs time to ascertain that the seller is, in fact, legally capable of conveying title. For protection, the buyer enters into a written and signed contract with the seller, promising that the purchase price will be paid only after title has been searched and found to be in satisfactory condition. The seller, in turn, promises to deliver a deed to the buyer when the buyer has paid his money. This exchange of promises forms the legal consideration of the contract. A contract also gives the buyer time to arrange financing and to specify how such matters as taxes, existing debts, leases, and property inspections will be handled.

REAL ESTATE PURCHASE CONTRACT

① *City of* __Riverdale__ *, State of* _____ ,
__October 10, 19 xx__ ② .

③ Samson Byers *(herein called the Buyer) agrees to
purchase and* ④ William Ohner and Sarah Ohner *(herein
called the Seller) agree to sell the following described real property located in the City of* ⑤ Riverdale *, County of* Lakeside ,
State of _____ , __a single-family dwelling__ commonly
known as 1704 Main Street *, and legally described as* __Lot
21, Block C of Madison's Subdivision as per map in Survey
Book 10, page 51, in the Office of the County Recorder of
said County_____ .

⑥ *The total purchase price is* __ninety thousand__ *dollars*
__($90,000.00),__ *payable as follows:* __Three thousand dollars
($3,000.00) is given today as an earnest money deposit,
receipt of which is hereby acknowledged. An additional
$15,000.00 is to be placed into escrow by the Buyer before
the closing date. The remaining $72,000.00 is to be by way
of a new mortgage on said property_____ .

⑦ *Seller will deliver to the Buyer a* __warranty__ *deed to said
property. Seller will furnish to the Buyer at the* __Seller's__ *expense a standard American Land Title Association title insurance policy issued by* __First Security Title Company__ *showing
title vested in the Buyer and that the Seller is conveying title free
of liens, encumbrances, easements, rights, and conditions except
as follows:* __People's Gas and Electric Company utility easement
along eastern five feet of said lot__ .

⑧ *The escrow agent shall be* __First Security Title Company__
*and escrow instructions shall be signed by the Buyer and Seller
and delivered to escrow within five days upon receipt thereof. The
close of escrow shall be* __45__ *days after the date of mutual
agreement to this contract.*

⑨ *Property taxes, property insurance, mortgage interest,
income and expense items shall be prorated as of* __the close of
escrow__ .

Figure 8:1. continued

(10) *Any outstanding bonds or assessments on the property shall be* __paid by the Seller__ .

(11) *Any existing mortgage indebtedness against the property is to be* __paid by the Seller__ .

(12) *Seller will provide Buyer with a report from a licensed pest control inspector that the property is free of termites and wood rot. The cost of the report and any corrective work deemed necessary by the report are to be paid for by the* __Seller__.

(13) *Possession of the property is to be delivered to the Buyer* __upon close of escrow__ .

(14) *Escrow expenses shall be* __shared equally by the Buyer and Seller__ .

(15) *Conveyance tax to be paid by* __Seller__ .

(16) *The earnest money deposit to be held* __in escrow__ .

(17) *All attached floor coverings, attached television antenna, window screens, screen doors, storm windows, storm doors, plumbing and lighting fixtures (except floor, standing and swag lamp), curtain rods, shades, venetian blinds, bathroom fixtures, trees, plants, shrubbery, water heaters, awnings, built-in heating, ventilating, and cooling systems, built-in stoves and ranges, and fences now on the premises shall be included unless otherwise noted. Any leased fixtures on the premises are not included unless specifically stated.*

(18) *Other provisions:* __the purchase of this property is contingent upon the Buyer obtaining a mortgage loan on this property in the amount of $72,000.00 or more, with a maturity date of at least 25 years, at an interest rate no higher than 11½% per year and loan fees not to exceed two points. Purchase price to include the refrigerator currently on the premises. Purchase is subject to buyer's approval of a qualified building inspector's report. Said report to be obtained within 7 days at Buyer's expense__.

(19) *If the improvements on the property are destroyed or materially damaged prior to the close of escrow, or if the Buyer is unable to obtain financing as stated herein, or if the Seller is unable to deliver title as promised, then the Buyer, at his option, may terminate this agreement and the deposit made by him shall*

Figure 8:1. continued

be returned to him in full. If the Seller fails to fulfill any of the other agreements made herein, the Buyer may terminate this agreement with full refund of deposit, accept lesser performance, or sue for specific performance.

(20) If this purchase is not completed by reason of the Buyer's default, the Seller is released from his obligation sell to the Buyer and shall retain the deposit money as his sole right to damages.

(21) Upon the signature of the Buyer, this document becomes an offer to the Seller to purchase the property described herein. The Seller has until 11:00 p.m., October 13, 19xx to indicate acceptance of this offer by signing and delivering it to the Buyer. If acceptance is not received by that time, this offer shall be deemed revoked and the deposit shall be returned in full to the Buyer.

(22) Time is of the essence in this contract.

Real Estate Broker Riverdale Realty Company .

By (23)Shirley Newhouse .

Address 1234 Riverdale Blvd. Telephone 333-1234 .

(24) The undersigned offers and agrees to buy the above described property on the terms and conditions stated herein and acknowledges receipt of a copy hereof.

> Buyer Samson Byers
> Address 2323 Cedar Ave., Riverdale
> Telephone 666-2468

Acceptance

(25) The undersigned accepts the foregoing offer and agrees to sell the property described above on the terms and conditions set forth.

(26) The undersigned has employed Lakeside Realty Company as Broker and for Broker's services agrees to pay said Broker as commission the sum of fifty-four hundred———— dollars ($5,400.00) payable upon recordation of the deed or if completion of this sale is prevented by the Seller. If completion of this contract is prevented by the Buyer, Broker shall share equally in any damages collected by the Seller, not to exceed the above stated commission.

Figure 8:1. continued

㉗ *The undersigned acknowledges receipt of a copy hereof.*
  Seller __Sarah Ohner__
  Seller __William Ohner__
  Address __1704 Tenth St., Riverdale__
  Telephone __333-3579__ *Date* __10/10/xx__

Notification of Acceptance
㉘ *Receipt of a copy of the foregoing agreement is hereby acknowledged.*

  Buyer __Samson Byers__ *Date* __10/10/xx__

A properly prepared contract commits each party to its terms. Once a sales contract is in writing and signed, the seller cannot change his mind and sell to another person. The seller is obligated to convey title to the buyer when the buyer has performed as required by the contract. Likewise, the buyer must carry out his promises, including paying for the property, provided the seller has done everything required by the contract.

PURCHASE CONTRACTS

Variously known as a purchase contract, deposit receipt, offer and acceptance, purchase offer, or purchase and sales agreement, these preprinted forms contain four key parts: (1) provision for the buyer's earnest money deposit, (2) the buyer's offer to purchase, (3) the acceptance of the offer by the seller, and (4) provisions for the payment of a brokerage commission.

Figure 8:1 illustrates in simplified language the highlights of a real estate purchase contract.[*] The purchase contract begins at ① and ② by identifying the location and date of the deposit and offer. At ③, the name of the buyer is written, and at ④, the name of the property owner (seller). At ⑤, the property for which the buyer is making his offer is described. Although the street address and type of property (in this case a house) are not necessary to the validity of the contract, this information is often included for convenience in locating the property. The legal

---

[*] This illustration has been prepared for discussion purposes only and not as a form to copy and use in a real estate sale. For that purpose, you must use a contract specifically legal in your state.

description that follows is crucial. Care must be taken to make certain that it is correct.

The price that the buyer is willing to pay, along with the manner in which he proposes to pay it, is inserted at ⑥. Of particular importance in this paragraph is the **earnest money deposit** that the buyer submits with his offer. With the exception of court-ordered sales, no laws govern the size of the deposit or even the need for one. Generally speaking though, the seller and his agent will want a reasonably substantial deposit to show the buyer's earnest intentions and to have something for their trouble if the seller accepts and the buyer fails to follow through. The buyer will prefer to make as small a deposit as possible, as a deposit ties up his capital and there is the possibility of losing it. However, the buyer also recognizes that the seller may refuse even to consider the offer unless accompanied by a reasonable deposit. In most parts of the country, a deposit of $2,000 to $5,000 on a $90,000 offer would be considered acceptable. In court-ordered sales, the required deposit is usually 10% of the offering price.

Earnest Money Deposit

At ⑦, the buyer requests that the seller convey title by means of a warranty deed and provide and pay for a policy of title insurance showing the condition of title to be as described here. Before the offer is made, the broker and seller will have told the buyer about the condition of title. However, the buyer has no way of verifying that information until the title is actually searched. To protect himself, the buyer states at ⑦ the condition of title that he is willing to accept. If title to the property is not presently in this condition, the seller is required by the contract to take whatever steps are necessary to place title in this condition before title is conveyed. If, for example, there is an existing mortgage or judgment lien against the property, the seller must have it removed. If there are other owners, their interests must be extinguished. If anyone has a right to use the property (such as a tenant under a lease), or controls the use of the property (such as a deed restriction), or has an easement, other than what is specifically mentioned, the seller must remove these before conveying title to the buyer.

Deed and Condition of Title

Closing Agent In a growing number of states, escrow agents (described in more detail in Chapter 14) handle the closing. Number ⑧ names the escrow agent, states that the escrow instructions must be signed promptly, and sets the closing date for the transaction. It is on that date that the seller will receive his money and the buyer his deed. The selection of a closing date is based on the estimated length of time necessary to carry out the conditions of the purchase contract. Normally, the most time-consuming item is finding a lender to make the necessary mortgage loan. Typically, this takes from 30 to 60 days, depending on the lender and the availability of loan money. The other conditions of the contract, such as the title search and arrangements to pay off any existing liens, take less time and can be done while arranging for a new mortgage loan. Once a satisfactory loan source is found, the lender makes a commitment to the buyer that the needed loan money will be placed into escrow on the closing date.

In regions of the United States where the custom is to use a closing meeting rather than an escrow, this section of the contract would name the attorney, broker, or other person responsible for carrying out the paperwork and details of the purchase agreement. A date would also be set for the closing meeting at which the buyer and seller and their attorneys, the lender, and the title company representative would be present to conclude the transaction.

Prorating Number ⑨ deals with the question of how certain ongoing expenses, such as property taxes, insurance, and mortgage interest, will be divided between the buyer and the seller. For example, if the seller pays $220 in advance for a one-year fire insurance policy and then sells his house halfway through the policy year, what happens to the remaining six months of coverage that the seller paid for but will not use? One solution is to transfer the remaining six months of coverage to the buyer for $110. Income items are also prorated. Suppose that the seller has been renting the basement of his house to a college student for $90 per month. The student pays the $90 rent in advance on the first of each month. If the property is sold part way through the month, the buyer is entitled to the portion of the month's rent that is earned while he owns the property. This process of dividing ongoing expenses and income items is known as **prorating.** More information and examples regarding the prorating process are included in Chapter 14.

At ⑩, the buyer states that, if there are any unpaid assessments or bonds currently against the property, the seller shall pay them as a condition of the sale. Alternatively, the buyer could agree to assume responsibility for paying them off. Since the buyer wants the property free of mortgages so that he can arrange for his own loan, at ⑪ he asks the seller to remove any existing indebtedness. On the closing date, part of the money received from the buyer is used to clear the seller's debts against the property. Alternatively, the buyer could agree to assume responsibility for paying off the existing debt against the property as part of the purchase price.

Termite Inspection

At ⑫, the buyer asks that the property be inspected at the seller's expense for signs of termites and rotted wood (dry rot), and that the seller pay for extermination and repairs. If the property is offered for sale as being in sound condition, a termite and wood rot clause is reasonable. If the property is being offered for sale on an **"as is"** basis in its present condition with no guarantee or warranty of quality and if it has a price to match, then the clause is not reasonable. If the seller is quite sure that there are no termites or wood rot, this condition would not be a major negotiating point, as the cost of an inspection without corrective work is a minor cost in a real estate transaction.

Possession

The day on which possession of the property will be turned over to the buyer is inserted at ⑬. As a rule, this is the same day as the closing date. If the buyer needs possession sooner or the seller wants possession after the closing date, the usual procedure is to arrange for a separate rental agreement between the buyer and seller. Such an agreement produces fewer problems if the closing date is later changed or if the transaction falls through and the closing never occurs.

At ⑭, the purchase contract calls for the buyer and seller to share escrow expenses equally. The buyer and seller could divide them differently if they mutually agreed. Most states charge a conveyance tax when a deed is recorded. At ⑮ the seller agrees to pay this tax. This is in addition to the fee the buyer pays to have the deed recorded in the public records. At ⑯, the buyer and seller agree as to where the buyer's deposit money is to be held pending the close of the transaction. It could be held by the escrow agent, the broker, the seller, or an attorney.

The paragraph at 17 is not absolutely essential to a valid real estate purchase contract, since what is considered real estate (and is therefore included in the price) and what is personal property (and is not included in the price) is a matter of law. However, because the buyer and seller may not be familiar with the differences between real property and personal property, this statement is often included to avoid misunderstandings. Moreover, such a statement can clarify whether or not an item like a storm window or trash compactor, which may or may not be real property depending on its design, is included in the purchase price. If it is the intention of the buyer and seller that an item mentioned here not be included, that item is crossed out and initialed by all of them.

Loan Conditions   At (18), space is left to add conditions and agreements not provided for elsewhere in the preprinted contract. To complete his purchase of this property the buyer must obtain a $72,000 loan. However, what if he agrees to the purchase but cannot get a loan? Rather than risk losing his deposit money, the buyer makes his offer subject to obtaining a $72,000 loan on the property. To further protect himself against having to accept a loan "at any price," he states the terms on which he must be able to borrow. The seller, of course, takes certain risks in accepting an offer subject to obtaining financing. If the buyer is unable to obtain financing on these terms, the seller will have to return the buyer's deposit and begin searching for another buyer. Meanwhile, the seller may have lost anywhere from a few days to a few weeks of selling time. But without such a condition a buyer may hesitate to make an offer at all. The solution is for the seller to accept only those loan conditions that are reasonable in the light of current loan availability. For example, if lenders are currently quoting 12½% interest for loans on similar properties, the seller would not want to accept an offer subject to the buyer obtaining a 10% loan. The possibility is too remote. If the buyer's offer is subject to obtaining a loan at current interest rates, the probability of the transaction collapsing on this condition is greatly reduced. The same principle applies to the amount of loan needed, the number of years to maturity, and loan fees: they must be reasonable in light of current market conditions.

In Figure 8:1, the buyer has until the closing date to find the required loan, a period of 45 days. However, to move things along and release the property sooner if the required loan is unavailable, the contract could contain wording that calls for the buyer to obtain within 30 days a letter from a lender stating that the lender will make the required loan at the closing. If this **loan commitment** letter is not obtained, the seller is released from the deal.

Additional Conditions

In the paragraph at ⑱, we also find that the buyer is asking the seller to include an item of personal property in the selling price. While technically a bill of sale is used for the sale of personal property, such items are often included in the real estate purchase contract if the list is not long. If the refrigerator were real property rather than personal, no mention would be required, as all real property falling within the descriptions at ⑤ and ⑰ is automatically included in the price. The third item in the paragraph at ⑱ gives the buyer an opportunity to have the property inspected by a professional building inspector. Most home buyers do not know what to look for in the way of structural deterioration or defects that may soon require expensive repairs. Consequently, in the past several years property inspection clauses in purchase contracts have become more common. The cost of this inspection is borne by the buyer. The inspector's report should be completed as soon as possible so that the property can be returned to the market if the buyer does not approve of the findings.

Property Damage

The paragraph at ⑲ sets forth conditions under which the buyer can free himself of his obligations under this contract and recover his deposit in full. It begins by addressing the question of property destruction between the contract signing and the closing date. Fire, wind, rain, earthquake, or other damage does occasionally occur during that period of time. Whose responsibility would it be to repair the damage, and could the buyer point to the damage as a legitimate reason for breaking the contract? It is reasonable for the buyer to expect that the property will be delivered to him in as good a condition as when he offered to buy it. Consequently, if there is major damage or destruction, the wording here gives the buyer the option of rescinding the contract and recovering his deposit in full. Note, however, that this clause does not prevent the buyer from accepting the damaged property or the seller from negotiating with the buyer to repair any damage in order to preserve the transaction.

Paragraph ⑲ also states that, if the buyer is unable to obtain financing as outlined at ⑱ or the seller is unable to convey title as stated at ⑦, the buyer can rescind the contract and have his deposit refunded. However, if the buyer is ready to close the transaction and the seller decides he does not want to sell, perhaps because the value of the property has increased between the signing of the contract and the closing date, the buyer can force the seller to convey title through use of a lawsuit for specific performance.

Buyer Default   Once the contract is signed by all parties involved, if the buyer fails to carry out his obligations, the standard choices for the seller are (1) release the buyer and return his deposit in full, (2) sue the buyer for specific performance, or (3) sue the buyer for damages suffered. Returning the deposit does not compensate for the time and effort the seller and his broker spent with the buyer, nor for the possibility that, while the seller was committed to the buyer, the real estate market turned sour. Yet the time, effort, and cost of suing for specific performance or damages may be uneconomical. Consequently, it has become common practice in many parts of the country to insert a clause in the purchase contract whereby the buyer agrees in advance to forfeit his deposit if he defaults on the contract, and the seller agrees to accept the deposit as his sole right to damages. Thus, the seller gives up the right to sue the buyer and accepts instead the buyer's deposit. The buyer knows in advance how much it will cost if he defaults, and the cost of default is limited to that amount. This is the purpose of paragraph ⑳.

Time Limits   At ㉑, the buyer clearly states that he is making an offer to buy and gives the seller a certain amount of time to accept. If the seller does not accept the offer within the time allotted, the offer is void. This feature is automatic: the buyer does not have to contact the seller to tell him that the offer is no longer open. The offer must be open long enough for the seller to physically receive it, make a decision, sign it, and return it to the buyer. If the seller lives nearby, the transaction is not complicated, and the offer can be delivered in person, 3 days is reasonable. If the offer must be mailed to an out-of-town seller, 7 to 10 days is appropriate.

If the buyer wants to offer on another property should the first offer not be accepted, the offer can be made valid for only a day, or even a few hours. A short offer life also limits the amount of time the seller has to hold out for a better offer. If a property is highly marketable, a buyer will want his offer accepted before someone else makes a better offer. Some experienced real estate buyers argue that a purposely short offer life has a psychological value. It motivates the seller to accept before the offer expires. Note too, a buyer can withdraw and cancel his offer at any time before the seller has accepted and the buyer is aware of that acceptance.

"Time is of the essence" at ㉒ means that the time limits set by the contract must be faithfully observed or the contract is voidable by the nondefaulting party. Moreover, lateness may give cause for an action for damages. Neither buyer nor seller should expect extensions of time to complete their obligations. This clause does not prohibit the buyer or seller from voluntarily giving the other an extension. But, extensions are neither automatic nor mandatory.

"Time is of the Essence"

"Time is of the essence" is a very difficult issue to litigate in court, and courts interpret it inconsistently. Generally speaking, courts disfavor automatic cancellation and forfeiture of valuable contract rights after "slight" or "reasonable" delays in performance. This is because unexpected delays are commonplace, and buyers and sellers customarily overlook delays in order to allow a deal to close. As a practical matter, the phrase, when used without additional supporting language, seems to be a firm reminder to all parties to keep things moving toward completion. If time is truly an important issue (as in an option contract, for example), the parties must be very explicit in the contract regarding their intentions.

The real estate agency and salesperson responsible for producing this offer to buy are identified at ㉓. At ㉔, the buyer clearly states that this is an offer to purchase. If the buyer has any doubts

Signatures

or questions regarding the legal effect of the offer, he should take it to an attorney for counsel before signing it. After he signs, the buyer retains one copy and the rest are delivered to the seller for his decision. By retaining one copy, the buyer has a written record to remind him of his obligations under the offer. Equally important, the seller cannot forge a change on the offer, as he does not have all the copies. Regarding delivery, the standard procedure is for the salesperson who obtained the offer to make an appointment with the agent who obtained the listing, and together they call upon the seller and present the offer.

Acceptance   For an offer to become binding, the seller must accept everything in it. The rejection of even the smallest portion of the offer is a rejection of the entire offer. If the seller wishes to reject the offer but keep negotiations alive, the seller can make a counteroffer. This is a written offer to sell to the buyer at a new price and with terms that are closer to the buyer's offer than the seller's original asking price and terms. The agent prepares the counteroffer by either filling out a fresh purchase contract identical in all ways to the buyer's offer except for these changes, or by writing on the back of the offer (or on another sheet of paper) that the seller offers to sell at the terms the buyer had offered except for the stated changes. The counteroffer is then dated and signed by the seller, and a time limit is given to the buyer to accept. The seller keeps a copy, and the counteroffer is delivered to the buyer for his decision. If the counteroffer is acceptable to the buyer, he signs and dates it, and the contract is complete. Another commonly used but less desirable practice is to take the buyer's offer, cross out each item unacceptable to the seller, and write above or below it what the seller will accept. Each change is then initialed by the seller and buyer.

Notification   Returning to Figure 8:1, suppose that the sellers accept the offer as presented to them. At ㉕, they indicate acceptance; at ㉖, they state that they employed the Lakeside Realty Company and agree on a commission of $5,400 for brokerage services, to be paid upon closing and recordation of the deed. Provisions are also included as to the amount of the commission if the sale is not completed. At ㉗, the sellers sign and date the contract and acknowledge receipt of a copy. The last step is to notify the buyer that his offer has been accepted, give him a copy of the completed agreement, and at ㉘ have him acknowledge receipt of it. If a party to a purchase contract dies after it has been signed, the deceased's heirs are, as a rule, required to fulfill the agreement. Thus, if a husband and wife sign a purchase contract and one of them dies, the sellers can look to the deceased's estate and the survivor to carry out the terms of the contract. Similarly, if a seller dies, the buyer is still entitled to receive the property as called for in the contract.

If an offer is rejected, it is good practice to have the sellers write the word *rejected* on the offer, followed by their signatures.

Federal Clauses

In two instances the government requires that specific clauses be included in real estate sales contracts. First, an **amendatory language** clause must be included whenever a sales contract is signed by a purchaser prior to the receipt of an FHA Appraised Value or a VA Certificate of Reasonable Value on the property. The purpose is to assure that the purchaser may terminate the contract without loss when it appears that the agreed purchase price may be significantly above the appraised value. The specific clauses, which must be used verbatim, are available from FHA and VA approved lenders. Second, the Federal Trade Commission (FTC) requires that builders and sellers of new homes include **insulation disclosures** in all purchase contracts. Disclosures, which may be based upon manufacturer claims, must cite the type, thickness, and R-value of the insulation installed in the home. The exact clause will be provided by the builder or seller of the home based on model clauses provided by the National Association of Homebuilders as modified by local laws.

Preprinted Clauses

The purchase contract in Figure 8:1 is designed to present and explain the basic elements of a purchase contract for a house. One popular preprinted purchase contract presently for sale to real estate agents consists of four legal-size pages that contain dozens of preprinted clauses. The buyer, seller, and agent select and fill in those clauses pertinent to their transaction. For example, if the home is a condominium, there are clauses that pertain to the condominium documents and maintenance reserves. If the home is in a flood zone, there is a clause for disclosing that fact to the buyer and the requirement of flood insurance by lenders.

There are four different pest inspection and repair clauses from which the buyer and seller can choose. There are smoke detector clauses and roof inspection clauses as well as detailed contingency and default clauses. There are clauses for personal property included in the sale and guarantees by the seller that electrical, heating, cooling, sewer, plumbing, built-in appliances, etc., are all in normal working order at the closing. Additionally, there may be state-mandated clauses. For example, some states require specific, due-on-sale balloon payment and insulation disclosures. The benefit of preprinted clauses is that much of the language of the contract has already been written for the buyer, seller, and agent. But, the buyer, seller, and agent must read all the clauses and choose those appropriate to the transaction.

Riders

A **rider** is any addition annexed to a document and made a part of the document by reference. A rider is usually written, typed, or printed on a separate piece of paper and stapled to the document. There will be a reference in the document that the rider is a part of the document and a statement in the rider that it is a part of the document. It is good practice to have the parties to the document place their initials on the rider. Riders are also known as **addendums** or **attachments.**

Negotiation

One of the most important principles of purchase contracts (and real estate contracts in general) is that nearly everything is negotiable and nearly everything has a price. In preparing or analyzing any contract, consider what the advantages and disadvantages of each condition are to each party to the contract. A solid contract results when the buyer and seller each feel that they have gained more than they have given up. The prime example is the sale price of the property itself. The seller prefers the money over the property, while the buyer prefers the property over the money. Each small negotiable item in the purchase contract has its price too. For example, the seller may agree to include the refrigerator for $200 more. Equally important in negotiating is the relative bargaining power of the buyer and seller. If the seller is confident of having plenty of buyers at the asking price, he can elect to refuse offers for less money, and reject those with numerous conditions or insufficient earnest money. However, if the owner is anxious to sell and has received only one offer in several months, he may be quite willing to accept a lower price and numerous conditions.

THE BINDER

Throughout most of the United States, the real estate agent prepares the purchase contract as soon as the agent is about to (or has) put a deal together. Using preprinted forms available from real estate trade associations, title companies, and stationary stores, the agent fills in the purchase price, down payment, and other details of the transaction and has the buyer and seller sign it as soon as they reach agreement.

In a few communities, particularly in the northeastern United States, the practice is for the real estate agent to prepare a short-form contract called a **binder.** The purpose of a binder is to hold a deal together until a more formal purchase contract can be drawn by an attorney and signed by the buyer and seller. In the binder, the buyer and seller agree to the purchase price, the down payment, and how the balance will be financed. The brokerage commission (to whom and how much) is stated along with an agreement to meet again to draw up a more formal contract that will contain all the remaining details of the sale. The agent then arranges a meeting at the office of the seller's attorney. In attendance are the seller and his attorney, the buyer and his attorney, and the real estate agents responsible for bringing about the sale. Together they prepare a written contract which the buyer and seller sign. Note that when the seller's attorney writes the formal contract, the contract will favor the seller. This is because the seller's attorney is expected to protect the seller's best interests at all times. The purchaser, to protect his interests, should not rely on the seller's attorney for advice, but should bring his own attorney.

What the Binder Does Not Say

While it is easy to minimize the importance of a binder because it is replaced by another contract, it does nonetheless meet all the requirements of a legally binding contract. In the absence of another contract, it can be used to enforce completion of a sale by a buyer or seller. The major weakness of a binder is in what it *does not say.* For example, the binder will probably make no mention of a termite inspection, the type of deed the seller is expected to use, or the closing date. Unless the buyer and seller can agree on these matters at the formal contract meeting, a dilemma results. Certainly, the buyer will wonder if his refusal to meet all the seller's demands at the contract meeting will result in the loss of his deposit money. If a stalemate develops, the courts may be asked to decide the termite question, deed type, closing date, and any other unresolved points. However, because this is costly and time consuming for all involved, there is give-and-take negotiation at the contract meeting. If a completely unnegotiable impasse is reached, as a practical matter the binder is usually rescinded by the buyer and seller and the buyer's deposit returned.

LETTER OF INTENT

If two or more parties want to express their mutual intention to buy, sell, lease, develop, or invest, and wish to do so without creating any firm, legal obligation, they may use a **letter of intent.** Generally, such a letter contains an outline of the proposal and concludes with language to the effect that the letter is only an expression of mutual intent and that no liability or obligation is created by it. In other words, a letter of intent is neither a contract nor an agreement to enter into a contract. However, it is expected, and usually stipulated in the letter, that the parties signing the letter will proceed promptly and in good faith to conclude the deal proposed in the letter. The letter of intent is usually found in connection with commercial leases, real estate development, and construction projects, and with multimillion-dollar real estate sales.

PRACTICING LAW

Historically in the United States, the sale of real estate was primarily a legal service. Lawyers matched buyers with sellers, wrote the sales contract, and prepared the mortgage and deed. When persons other than lawyers began to specialize in real estate brokerage, the question of who should write the sales contract became important. The lawyer was more qualified in matters of contract law, but the broker wanted something that could be signed the moment the buyer and seller were in agreement. For many years the solution was a compromise. The broker had the buyer and seller sign a binder, and they agreed to meet again in the presence of a lawyer to draw up and sign a more formal contract. The trend today however, is for the real estate agent to prepare a complete purchase contract as soon as there is a meeting of the minds.

The preparation of contracts by real estate agents for their clients has not gone unnoticed by lawyers. The legal profession maintains that preparing contracts for clients is practicing law, and state laws restrict the practice of law to lawyers. This has been, and continues to be, a controversial issue between brokers and lawyers. Resolution of the matter has come in the form of **accords** between the real estate brokerage industry and the legal profession. In nearly all states courts have ruled that a real estate agent is permitted to prepare purchase, installment, and rental contracts provided the agent uses a preprinted form approved by a lawyer and provided the agent is limited to filling in only the blank spaces on the form. (Figure 8:1 illustrates this concept.) If the preprinted form requires extensive crossouts, changes, and riders, the contract should be drafted by a lawyer. A real estate license is *not* a permit to practice law.

INSTALLMENT CONTRACTS

An installment contract (also known as a **land contract, conditional sales contract, contract for deed** or **agreement of sale**) combines features from a sales contract, a deed, and a mortgage. An installment contract contains most of the provisions of the purchase contract described in Figure 8:1, plus wording familiar to the warranty deed described in Chapter 5, plus many of the provisions of the mortgage described in the next chapter.

The most important feature of an **installment contract** is that the seller does not deliver a deed to the buyer at the closing. Rather, the seller promises to deliver the deed at some future date. Meanwhile, the purchaser is given the right to occupy the property and have for all practical purposes the rights, obligations and privileges of ownership.

The widest use of the installment contract occurs when the buyer does not have the full purchase price in cash or is unable to borrow it from a lender. To sell under these conditions, the seller must accept a down payment plus monthly payments. To carry this out the seller can choose to either (1) deliver a deed to the buyer at the closing and at the same moment take back from the buyer a promissory note and a mortgage secured by the property (a mortgage carryback), or (2) enter into an installment contract wherein the buyer makes the required payments to the seller before the seller delivers a deed to the buyer.

Vendor, Vendee

Historically, installment contracts were most commonly used to sell vacant land where the buyer put only a modest amount of money down and the seller agreed to receive the balance as installment payments. When all the installments were made, the seller delivered a deed to the purchaser. The terms of these contracts were usually weighted in favor of the seller. For example, if the buyer (called the **vendee**) failed to make all the payments on time, the seller (called the **vendor**) could rescind the contract, retain payments already made as rent, and retake possession of the land. Additionally, the seller might insert a clause in the installment contract prohibiting the buyer from recording it. The public records would continue to show the seller as owner and the seller could use the land as collateral for loans. That such a one-sided contract would even exist may seem surprising. But, if a buyer did not have all cash, or enough cash down to obtain financing from another source, the buyer was stuck with accepting what the seller offered, or not buying the property. Sellers took the position that if they were selling to buyers who were unwilling or unable to find their own sources of financing, then sellers wanted a quick and easy way of recovering the property if the payments were not made. By selling on an installment contract and not allowing it to be recorded, the seller could save the time and expense of regular foreclosure proceedings. The seller would simply notify the buyer in writing that the contract was in default, and thereby rescind it. Meanwhile, as far as the public records were concerned, title was still in the seller's name.

Public Criticism   Such strongly worded agreements received much criticism, as did the possibility that even if the buyer made all the payments, the seller might not be capable of delivering good title. For example, the buyer could make all payments, yet find that the seller had encumbered the property with debt, had gone bankrupt, had become legally incapacitated, or had died.

Then, in the late 1970s interest rates rose sharply. In order to sell their properties, sellers looked for ways of passing along the benefits of their fixed-rate, low-interest loans to buyers. The installment contract was rediscovered, and it moved from being used primarily to sell land to being used to sell houses and apartment buildings and even office buildings and industrial property. Basically, the seller kept the property and mortgage in the seller's name and made the mortgage payments out of the buyer's monthly payments. This continued until the buyer found alternative financing, at which time the seller delivered the deed.

With its increased popularity, the need for more sophisticated and more protective installment contracts was created. Simultaneously, courts and legislatures in various states were listening to consumer complaints and finding existing installment contract provisions too harsh. One by one, states began requiring that a buyer be given a specified period to cure any default before the seller could rescind. Some states began requiring that installment contracts be foreclosed like regular mortgages. And most states now require that installment contracts be recorded and/or prohibit a seller from enforcing nonrecording clauses.

Protections

Buyers have become much more sophisticated also. For example, it is common practice today to require the seller to place the deed (usually a warranty deed) in an escrow at the time the installment contract is made. This relieves a number of the problems noted above regarding the unwillingness or inability of the seller to prepare and deliver the deed later. Additionally, the astute buyer will require that a collection account be used to collect the buyer's payments and make the payments on the underlying mortgage. This is done using a neutral third party such as the escrowholder of the deed, a bank, or a trust company. The seller will probably insist that the buyer place one-twelfth of the annual property taxes and hazard insurance in the escrow account each month to pay for these items. The buyer will want to record the contract to establish the buyer's rights to the property. The buyer may also want to include provisions whereby the seller delivers a deed to the buyer and takes back a mortgage from the buyer once the buyer has paid, say, 30% or 40% of the purchase price.

Other provisions found in an installment contract include the names of the buyer and seller, the sale price, the terms of payment, a full legal description of the property, any restrictions on the use of the property, who is to maintain the property and take the risk of loss due to property damage, how the taxes and insurance will be paid, what encumbrances exist and who is responsible, and any prepayment or due-on-sale provisions.

Other Provisions

The installment contract can be the original purchase contract, i.e., a one-step process that combines the offer, acceptance, agreement to finance, and provision for delivery of the deed. More likely, especially for improved property, the purchase contract will call for the preparation of a separate installment contract. The buyer and seller sign and acknowledge duplicate copies of the installment contract and each receives a copy at the closing. The buyer then records his copy, or has the person in charge of the closing record it on his behalf.

If an installment contract is used for the purchase of real estate, it should be done with the help of legal counsel to make certain that it provides adequate safeguards for the buyer as well as the seller. In Chapter 11, the installment contract is discussed as a tool to finance the sale of improved property when other sources of financing are not available.

EQUITABLE TITLE
Between the moment that a buyer and seller sign a valid purchase contract and the moment the seller delivers a deed to the buyer, who holds title to the property? Similarly, under an installment contract, until the seller delivers a deed to the buyer, who holds title to the property? The answer in both cases is the seller. But this is only technically true because the buyer is entitled to receive a deed (and thereby title) once the buyer has completed the terms of the purchase or installment contract. During the period beginning with the buyer and seller signing the contract and the seller delivering the deed, the buyer is said to hold **equitable title** to the property. The concept of equitable title stems from the fact that a buyer can enforce specific performance of the contract in a court of equity to get title. Meanwhile, the seller holds bare or naked title, i.e., title in name only and without full ownership rights.

The equitable title that a purchaser holds under a purchase or installment contract is transferable by subcontract, assignment, or deed. Equitable title can be sold, given away, or mortgaged, and it passes to the purchaser's heirs and devisees upon the purchaser's death.

It is not unusual to see a property offered for sale wherein the vendee under an installment contract is offering those rights for sale. Barring any due-on-sale clause in the installment contract, this can be done. The buyer receives from the vendee an assignment of the contract and with it the vendee's equitable title. The buyer then takes possession and continues to make the payments called for by the contract. When the payments are completed, the deed and title transfer can be handled in one of two ways. One way is for the original seller to agree to deliver a deed to the new buyer. The other, and the most common way, is for the vendee to place a deed to the new buyer in escrow. When the last payment is made, the deed from the original seller to the vendee is recorded, and immediately after it, the deed from the vendee to the new buyer.

An option is an agreement to keep an offer open for a fixed period of time. One of the most popular option contracts in real estate is the **lease with option to buy.** Often simply referred to as a **lease-option,** it allows the tenant to buy the property at preset price and terms during the option period. For a residential property, the lease is typically for one year, and the option to buy must be exercised during that time. Let's look more closely.

LEASE WITH OPTION TO BUY

In a lease-option contract all the normal provisions of a lease are present, such as those shown in Figure 15:1. All the normal provisions of a purchase contract are present such as those shown in Figure 8:1. In addition, there will be wording stating that the tenant has the option of exercising the purchase contract provided the tenant notifies the landlord in writing of that intent during the option period. All terms of the purchase contract must be negotiated and in writing when the lease is signed. Both the tenant and the landlord must sign the lease. Only the landlord must sign the purchase contract and option agreement, although both parties often do so. If the tenant wants to buy during the option period, the tenant notifies the landlord in writing that the tenant wishes to exercise the purchase contract. Together they proceed to carry out the purchase contract as in a normal sale.

If the tenant does not exercise the option within the option period, the option expires and the purchase contract is null and void. If the lease also expires at the end of the option period, the tenant must either arrange with the landlord to continue renting or move out. Alternatively, they can negotiate a new purchase contract or a new lease-option contract.

Lease-options are particularly popular in soft real estate markets where a home seller is having difficulty finding a buyer. One solution is to lower the asking price and/or make the financing terms more attractive. However, the seller may wish to hold out

Popularity

in hopes that prices will rise within a year. In the meantime the seller needs someone to occupy the property and provide some income.

The lease-option is attractive to a tenant because the tenant has a place to rent plus the option of buying any time during the option period for the price in the purchase contract. In other words, the tenant can wait a year and see if he/she likes the property and if values rise to or above the price in the purchase contract. If the tenant does not like the property and/or the property does not rise in value, the tenant is under no obligation to buy. Once the lease expires, the tenant is also under no obligation to continue renting.

Examples   To encourage a tenant to exercise the option to buy, the contract may allow the tenant to apply part or all of the rent paid to the purchase price. In fact, quite a bit of flexibility and negotiation can take place in creating a lease-option. For example, take a home that would rent for $750 per month and sell for $100,000 on the open market. Suppose the owner wants $110,000 and won't come down to the market price. Meanwhile the home is vacant and there are mortgage payments to be made. The owner could offer a one-year lease-option with a rental charge of $750 each month and an exercise price of $110,000. Within a year, $110,000 may look good to the tenant, especially if the market value of the property has risen significantly above $110,000. The tenant can exercise the option or, if not prohibited by the contract, sell it to someone who intends to exercise it. The owner receives $10,000 more for the property than he could have gotten last year, and the tenant has the benefit of any value increase above that.

Continuing the above example, what if the property rises to $105,000 in value? There is no economic incentive for the tenant to exercise the option at $110,000. The tenant can simply disregard the option and make an offer of $105,000 to the owner. The owner's choice is to sell at that price or continue renting the home, perhaps with another one-year lease-option.

Option Fee   The owner can also charge the tenant extra for the privilege of having the option, but it must make economic sense to the tenant. Suppose in the above example the purchase price is set equal to the current market value, i.e., $100,000. This would be a valuable benefit to the tenant, and the owner could charge an up-front cash fee for the option and/or charge above-market rent. The amounts would depend on the market's expectations regarding the value of this home a year from now. There is nothing special about a one-year option period, although it is a very popular length of time. The owner and tenant can agree to a three-month, six-month, or nine-month option if it fits their needs, and the lease can run longer than the option period. Options for longer than one year are generally reserved for commercial properties. For example, a businessperson just starting out, or perhaps expanding, wants to buy a building but needs a year or two to see how successful the business will be and how much space it will need.

Caveats

Be aware that lease-options may create income tax consequences that require professional tax counseling. Legal advice is also very helpful in preparing and reviewing the lease-option papers. This is because the entire deal (lease, option, and purchase contract) must be water-tight from the beginning. One cannot wait until the option is exercised to write the purchase contract or even a material part of it. If a real estate agent puts a lease-option together, the agent is entitled to a leasing commission at the time the lease is signed. If the option is exercised, the agent is due a sales commission on the purchase contract.

Evidence that the option to buy exists should be recorded to establish not only the tenant's rights to purchase the property, but also to establish those rights back to the date the option was recorded. An option is an example of a unilateral contract. When it is exercised, it becomes bilateral. The lease portion of a lease-option is a bilateral contract. The party giving the option is called the **optionor** (owner in a lease-option). The party receiving the option is the **optionee** (tenant in a lease-option). Sometimes an option to buy is referred to as a **call.** You will see how an option can be used by a home builder to buy land in Chapter 12 and how options can be used to renew leases in Chapter 15.

RIGHT OF FIRST REFUSAL

Sometimes a tenant will agree to rent a property only if given an opportunity to purchase it before someone else does. In other words, the tenant is saying, "Mr. Owner, if you get a valid offer from someone else to purchase this property, show it to me and give me an opportunity to match the offer." This is called a **right**

of first refusal. If someone presents the owner with a valid offer, the owner must show it to the tenant before accepting it. If the tenant decides not to match it, the owner is free to accept it.

A right of first refusal protects a tenant from having the property sold out from under him when, in fact, if the tenant knew about the offer he would have been willing to match it. The owner usually does not care who buys, as long as the price and terms are the same. Therefore, an owner may agree to include a right of first refusal clause in a rental contract for little or no additional charge if the tenant requests it. The right of first refusal concept is not limited to just landlord-tenant situations, but that is as deep as we will go here.

REVIEW QUESTIONS

1. A formal real estate sales contract, prepared at the outset by an agent using prepared forms, may be identified as any of the following EXCEPT:
   A. a purchase contract.
   B. an option contract.
   C. an offer and acceptance.
   D. a purchase offer.

2. Martin purchased real estate from Stevens under an agreement which called for him to pay for the property in installments, and to receive a deed upon payment of the entire purchase price. This agreement could properly be identified as a
   A. land contract.
   B. contract for deed.
   C. conditional sales contract.
   D. installment contract.
   E. All of the above.

3. In normal real estate brokerage practice, the amount of earnest money deposit paid by the purchaser is
   A. determined by negotiation.
   B. set by state law.
   C. equal to the agent's commission.
   D. the minimum required to make the contract valid.

4. Property taxes, insurance, loan interest, etc. may be divided between the buyer and seller by the process of
   A. allocation.
   B. appropriation.
   C. proration.
   D. proportioning.

5. Typically, physical possession of the property is given to the buyer
   A. upon signing of the sale contract.
   B. before close of escrow (settlement).
   C. the day of close of escrow (settlement).
   D. 30 days following close of escrow (settlement).

6. Martin is going to purchase a newly built home from the builder. He will finance the purchase by means of a VA-guaranteed loan. The builder must include in the purchase contract
   A. an amendatory clause.   C. Both A and B.
   B. insulation disclosures.   D. Neither A nor B.

7. Mr. and Mrs. Silver entered into a real estate contract with Mr. and Mrs. Gold. If Mr. Gold dies before settlement takes place,
   A. Mr. and Mrs. Silver are obligated to carry out the contract.
   B. Mrs. Gold is obligated to carry out the contract.
   C. Mr. Gold's estate is obligated to carry out the contract.
   D. All of the above.

8. The major weakness of a binder lies in
   A. its unenforceability.
   B. what it does not say.

9. A letter of intent is
   A. one which created no liability.
   B. an agreement to enter into a contract.
   C. binding on the seller.
   D. binding on the buyer.
   E. binding on both buyer and seller.

10. When property is sold by means of an installment contract, the
   A. seller delivers a deed at closing.
   B. buyer is NOT given the right to occupy the property until the contract terms have been fulfilled.
   C. Both A and B.
   D. Neither A nor B.

11. Installment contracts may be used when
   A. the buyer does not have the full purchase price in cash.
   B. the buyer is unable to borrow part of the purchase price from a lender.
   C. Both A and B.
   D. Neither A nor B.

12. The purchaser under an installment contract may protect his interests by requiring that the
   A. seller place a deed in escrow at settlement.
   B. contract be recorded in the land records.
   C. Both A and B.
   D. Neither A nor B.

13. Equitable title can be
   A. transferred by sale.   D. transferred by deed.
   B. inherited.   E. All of the above.
   C. mortgaged.

14. The option portion of a lease-option contract can be attached to the lease as
   A. a rider.   C. a binder.
   B. an accord.   D. a purchase agreement.

15. Lease-option contracts tend to increase in popularity during a
    A. seller's market.
    B. buyer's market.

16. An option to buy is an example of
    A. an executory contract.   D. Both A and B.
    B. a bilateral contract.   E. Both A and C.
    C. a unilateral contract.

17. Under the terms of a right of first refusal, the tenant is given the right to
    A. match an offer to purchase the property.
    B. purchase the property at a previously agreed price.
    C. Both A and B.
    D. Neither A nor B.

18. The party with the least amount of flexibility in a lease-option agreement is the
    A. optionor.
    B. optionee.

19. Real estate exchanges are possible only when
    A. all properties are of equal value.
    B. no more than two properties are involved.
    C. Both A and B.
    D. Neither A nor B.

20. A broker who arranges a four-way trade of real properties will normally expect to receive
    A. one commission.
    B. four commissions.
    C. a commission based on the amount of cash involved.
    D. no commission if no cash is involved in the trades.

Mortgage and Note

In this chapter we will take a brief look at mortgage theory and law. A mortgage is basically a pledge of property to secure the repayment of a debt. The chapter includes coverage of lien theory and title theory, pledge methods, promissory notes, the mortgage instrument, the "subject to" clause, loan assumption, and debt priorities. The last part of the chapter deals with the foreclosure process dividing the discussion between judicial and non-judicial foreclosure.

OVERVIEW OF CHAPTER 9

LEARNING OBJECTIVES

After successful completion of this chapter, you should be able to:
1. Distinguish between lien theory and title theory.
2. Explain early mortgage application and the various pledge methods.
3. Describe the parts of the promissory note and the mortgage instrument.
4. Explain hypothecation, mortgage satisfaction, and the "subject to" clause.
5. List in order, debt priorities.
6. Explain the foreclosure process.
7. Describe both judicial and non-judicial foreclosure.
8. Explain the purpose of a deed in lieu for foreclosure.

KEY • TERMS

Acceleration clause: allows the lender to demand immediate payment of entire loan if the borrower defaults

Deficiency judgment: a judgment against a borrower if the foreclosure sale does not bring enough to pay the balance owed

First mortgage: the mortgage loan with highest priority for repayment in the event of foreclosure

Foreclosure: the procedure by which a person's property can be taken and sold to satisfy an unpaid debt

Junior mortgage: any mortgage on a property that is subordinate to the first mortgage in priority

Mortgage: a document which makes property security for the repayment of a debt

Mortgagee: the party receiving the mortgage; the lender

Mortgagor: the party who gives a mortgage; the borrower

Power of sale: allows a mortgagee to conduct a foreclosure sale without first going to court

Promissory note: a written promise to repay a debt

Subordination: voluntary acceptance of a lower mortgage priority than one would otherwise be entitled to

There are two documents involved in a mortgage loan. The first is the promissory note and the second is the mortgage. In 16 states it is customary to use a deed of trust in preference to a mortgage. We begin by describing the promissory note because it is common to both the mortgage and deed of trust. Then we shall discuss the mortgage document at length. This will be followed by an explanation of foreclosure and brief descriptions of the deed of trust, equitable mortgage, security deed, and chattel mortgage. (If you either live in or deal with property in a state where the deed of trust is the customary security instrument, you will also want to read Chapter 10 as it deals exclusively with the deed of trust.) Meanwhile, let's begin with the promissory note.

PROMISSORY NOTE

The **promissory note** is a contract between a borrower and a lender. It establishes the amount of the debt, the terms of repayment, and the interest rate. A sample promissory note, usually referred to simply as a **note,** is shown in Figure 9:1. Some states use a **bond** to accomplish the same purpose as the promissory note. What is said here regarding promissory notes also applies to bonds.

Figure 9:1.

**PROMISSORY NOTE SECURED
BY MORTGAGE** (1)

(2) <u>City, State</u>   <u>March 31, 19xx</u>

(3) *For value received, I promise to pay to* (4) <u>Pennywise Mortgage Company</u> , (5) *or order, at* <u>2242 National Blvd.,</u> <u>[City, State]</u> *, the sum of* (6) <u>Sixty thousand and no/100——</u> <u>————————</u> *dollars, with interest from* <u>March 31,</u> <u>19xx</u> *, on unpaid principal at the rate of* (7) <u>twelve</u> *percent per annum; principal and interest payable in installments of* (8) <u>six hundred seventeen and 40/100</u>————— *dollars on the* <u>first</u> *day of each month beginning* (9) <u>May 1, 19xx</u> *, and continuing until said principal and interest have been paid.*

(10) *This note may be prepaid in whole or in part at any time without penalty.*

(11) *There shall be a ten-day grace period for each monthly payment. A late of of $12.50 will be added to each payment made after its grace period.*

(12) *Each payment shall be credited first on interest then due and the remainder on principal. Unpaid interest shall bear interest like the principal.*

(13) *Should default be made in payment of any installment when due, the entire principal plus accrued interest shall immediately become due at the option of the holder of the note.*

(14) *If legal action is necessary to collect this note, I promise to pay such sum as the court may fix.*

(15) *This note is secured by a mortgage bearing the same date as this note and made in favor of* <u>Pennywise Mortgage Company.</u>

(16) <u>Mort Gage</u>
Borrower

(17) [this space for witnesses
and/or acknowledgement
if required by state law]

To be valid as evidence of debt, a note must (1) be in writing, (2) be between a borrower and lender both of whom have contractual capacity, (3) state the borrower's promise to pay a certain sum of money, (4) show the terms of payment, (5) be signed by the borrower, and (6) be voluntarily delivered by the borrower and accepted by the lender. If the note is secured by a mortgage or trust deed, it must say so. Otherwise, it is solely a personal obligation of the borrower. Although interest is not required to make the note valid, most loans do carry an interest charge; when they do, the rate of interest must be stated in the note. Finally, in some states it is necessary for the borrower's signature on the note to be acknowledged and/or witnessed.

Obligor, Obligee   Referring to Figure 9:1, number ① identifies the document as a promissory note and ② gives the location and date of the note's execution (signing). As with any contract, the location stated in the contract establishes the applicable state laws. For example, a note that says it was executed in Virginia will be governed by the laws of the state of Virginia. At ③, the borrower states that he has received something of value and in turn promises to pay the debt described in the note. Typically, the "value received" is a loan of money in the amount described in the note; it could, however, be services or goods or anything else of value.

The section of the note at ④ identifies to whom the obligation is owed, sometimes referred to as the **obligee,** and where the payments are to be sent. The words *or order* at ⑤ mean that the lender can direct the borrower (the **obligor**) to make payments to someone else if the lender sells the note.

The Principal   The **principal** or amount of the obligation, $60,000, is shown at ⑥. The rate of interest on the debt and the date from which it will be charged are given at ⑦. The amount of the periodic payment at ⑧ is calculated from the loan tables discussed in Chapter 11. In this case, $617.40 each month for 30 years will return the lender's $60,000 plus interest at the rate of 12% per year on the unpaid portion of the principal. When payments will begin and when subsequent payments will be due are outlined at ⑨. In this example, they are due on the first day of each month until the full $60,000 and interest have been paid. The clause at ⑩ is a **prepayment privilege** for the borrower. It allows the borrower to pay more than the required $617.40 per month and to pay the loan off early without penalty. Without this very important privilege, the note requires the borrower to pay $617.40 per month, no more and no less, until the $60,000 plus interest has been paid. On some note forms, the prepayment privilege is created by inserting the words *or more* after the word *dollars* where it appears between ⑧ and ⑨. The note would then read "six hundred seventeen and 40/100 dollars or more..." The "or more" can be any amount from $617.41 up to and including the entire balance remaining.

At ⑪, the lender gives the borrower a 10-day grace period to accommodate late payments. For payments made after that, the borrower agrees to pay a late charge of $12.50. The clause at ⑫ states that, whenever a payment is made, any interest due on the loan is first deducted, and then the remainder is applied to reducing the loan balance. Also, if interest is not paid, it too will earn interest at the same rate as the principal, in this example 12% per year. The provision at ⑬ allows the lender to demand immediate payment of the entire balance remaining on the note if the borrower misses any of the individual payments. This is called an **acceleration clause,** as it "speeds up" the remaining payments due on the note. Without this clause, the lender can only foreclose on the payments that have come due and have not been paid. In this example, that could take as long as 30 years. This clause also has a certain psychological value: knowing that the lender has the option of calling the entire loan balance due upon default makes the borrower think twice about being late with the payments.

Acceleration Clause

At ⑭, the borrower agrees to pay any collection costs incurred by the lender if the borrower falls behind in his payments. At ⑮, the promissory note is tied to the mortgage that secures it, making it a mortgage loan. Without this reference, it would be a personal loan. At ⑯, the borrower signs the note. A person who signs a note is sometimes referred to as a **maker** of the note. If two or more persons sign the note, it is common to include a statement in the note that the borrowers are "jointly and severally liable" for all provisions in the note. This means that the terms of the note and the obligations it creates are enforceable upon the makers as a group and upon each maker individually. If the

Signature

Figure 9:2.

MORTGAGE

① *THIS MORTGAGE is made this* __31st__ *day of* __March,__ __19xx__ , *between* __Mort Gage__ *hereinafter called the Mortgagor, and* __Pennywise Mortgage Company__ *hereinafter called the Mortgagee.*

② *WHEREAS, the Mortgagor is indebted to the Mortgagee in the principal sum of* __sixty thousand and no/100__ ―― ―― *dollars, payable* __$617.40, including 12% interest per__ __annum, on the first day of each month starting May 1, 19xx,__ __and continuing until paid__ , *as evidenced by the Mortgagor's note of the same date as this mortgage, hereinafter called the Note.*

③ *TO SECURE the Mortgagee the repayment of the indebtedness evidenced by said Note, with interest thereon, the Mortgagor does hereby mortgage, grant, and convey to the Mortgagee the following described property in the County of* __Evans__ *, State of* _____ *;*

④ *Lot 39, Block 17, Harrison's Subdivision, as shown on Page 19 of May Book 25, filed with the County Recorder of said County and State.*

⑤ *FURTHERMORE, the Mortgagor fully warrants the title to said land and will defend the same against the lawful claims of all persons.*

⑥ *IF THE MORTGAGOR, his heirs, legal representatives, or assigns pay unto the Mortgagee, his legal representatives or assigns, all sums due by said Note, then this mortgage and the estate created hereby SHALL CEASE AND BE NULL AND VOID.*

⑦ *UNTIL SAID NOTE is fully paid:*

⑧ *A. The Mortgagor agrees to pay all taxes on said land.*

⑨ *B. The Mortgagor agrees not to remove or demolish buildings or other improvements on the mortgaged land without the approval of the lender.*

⑩ *C. The Mortgagor agrees to carry adequate insurance to protect the lender in the event of damage or destruction of the mortgaged property.*

⑪ *D. The Mortgagor agrees to keep the mortgaged property in good repair and not permit waste or deterioration.*

Figure 9:2. continued

IT IS FURTHER AGREED THAT:

(12) *E.   The Mortgagee shall have the right to inspect the mortgaged property as may be necessary for the security of the Note.*

(13) *F. If the Mortgagor does not abide by this mortgage or the accompanying Note, the Mortgagee may declare the entire unpaid balance on the Note immediately due and payable.*

(14) *G. If the Mortgagor sells or otherwise conveys title to the mortgaged property, the Mortgagee may declare the entire unpaid balance on the Note immediately due and payable.*

(15) *H.   If all or part of the mortgaged property is taken by action of eminent domain, any sums of money received shall be applied to the Note.*

(16) *IN WITNESS WHEREOF, the Mortgagor has executed this mortgage.*

(17) [this space for witnesses   <u>Mort Gage</u>   (SEAL)
and/or acknowledgement   Mortgagor
if required by state law]

borrower is married, lenders generally require both husband and wife to sign. Finally, if state law requires the signatures of witnesses or an acknowledgment, this would appear at (17). Usually this is not required as it is the mortgage rather than the note that is recorded in public records.

The mortgage is a separate agreement from the promissory note. Whereas the note is evidence of a debt and a promise to pay, the **mortgage** provides security (collateral) that the lender can sell if the note is not paid. The technical term for this is hypothecation. **Hypothecation** means the borrower retains the right to possess and use the property while it serves as collateral. In contrast, **pledging** means to give up possession of the property to the lender while it serves as collateral. An example of pledging is the loan made by a pawn shop. The shop holds the collateral until the loan is repaid. The sample mortgage in Figure 9:2 illustrates in simplified language the key provisions most com-

THE MORTGAGE INSTRUMENT

monly found in real estate mortgages used in the United States. Let us look at these provisions.

The mortgage begins at ① with the date of its making and the names of the parties involved. In mortgage agreements, the person or party who hypothecates his property and gives the mortgage is the **mortgagor.** The person or party who receives the mortgage (the lender) is the **mortgagee.** For the reader's convenience, we shall refer to the mortgagor as the borrower and the mortgagee as the lender.

At ②, the debt for which this mortgage provides security is identified. Only property named in the mortgage is security for that mortgage. At ③, the borrower conveys to the lender the property described at ④. This will most often be the property that the borrower purchased with the loan money, but this is not a requirement. The mortgaged property need only be something of sufficient value in the eyes of the lender; it could just as easily be some other real estate the borrower owns. At ⑤, the borrower states that the property is his and that he will defend its ownership. The lender will, of course, verify this with a title search before making the loan.

Provisions for the defeat of the mortgage are given at ⑥. The key words here state that the "mortgage and the estate created hereby shall cease and be null and void" when the note is paid in full. This is the **defeasance clause.**

As you may have already noticed, the wording of ③, ④, and ⑤ is strikingly similar to that found in a warranty deed. In states taking the **title theory** position toward mortgages, the wording at ③ is interpreted to mean that the borrower is deeding his property to the lender. Sometimes you will see the words *Mortgage Deed* printed at the top of a mortgage for, in fact, a mortgage does technically deed the property to the lender, at least in title theory states. In **lien theory** states, the wording at ③ gives only a lien right to the lender, and the borrower (mortgagor) retains title. In **intermediate theory** states, a mortgage is a lien unless the borrower defaults, at which time it conveys title to the lender. No matter which legal philosophy prevails, the borrower retains possession of the mortgaged property, and when the loan is repaid in full the mortgage is defeated as stated in the defeasance clause.

After ⑦, there is a list of covenants (promises) that the borrower makes to the lender. They are the covenants of taxes, removal, insurance, and repair. These covenants protect the security for the loan.

Covenants

In the **covenant to pay taxes** at ⑧, the borrower agrees to pay the taxes on the mortgaged property even though the title may be technically with the lender. This is important to the lender, because if the taxes are not paid they become a lien on the property that is superior to the lender's mortgage.

In the **covenant against removal** at ⑨, the borrower promises not to remove or demolish any buildings or improvements. To do so may reduce the value of the property as security for the lender.

The **covenant of insurance** at ⑩ requires the borrower to carry adequate insurance against damage or destruction of the mortgaged property. This protects the value of the collateral for the loan, for without insurance, if buildings or other improvements on the mortgaged property are damaged or destroyed, the value of the property might fall below the amount owed on the debt. With insurance, the buildings can be repaired or replaced, thus restoring the value of the collateral.

The **covenant of good repair** at ⑪, also referred to as the covenant of preservation and maintenance, requires the borrower to keep the mortgaged property in good condition. The clause at ⑫ gives the lender permission to inspect the property to make sure that it is being kept in good repair and has not been damaged or demolished.

If the borrower breaks any of the mortgage covenants or note agreements, the lender wants the right to terminate the loan. Thus, an **acceleration clause** at ⑬ is included to permit the lender to demand the balance be paid in full immediately. If the borrower cannot pay, foreclosure takes place and the property is sold.

When used in a mortgage, an **alienation clause** (also called a **due-on-sale clause**) gives the lender the right to call the entire loan balance due if the mortgaged property is sold or otherwise conveyed (alienated) by the borrower. An example is shown at ⑭. The purpose of an alienation clause is twofold. If the mortgaged property is put up for sale and a buyer proposes to assume the existing loan, the lender can refuse to accept that

Alienation Clause

buyer as a substitute borrower if the buyer's credit is not good. But, more importantly, lenders have been using it as an opportunity to eliminate old loans with low rates of interest. This issue, from both borrower and lender perspectives, is discussed in Chapter 12.

Condemnation Clause

Number ⑮ is a **condemnation clause.** If all or part of the property is taken by action of eminent domain, any money so received is used to reduce the balance owing on the note.

At ⑯, the mortgagor states that he has made this mortgage. Actually, the execution statement is more a formality than a requirement; the mortgagor's signature alone indicates his execution of the mortgage and agreement to its provisions. At ⑰, the mortgage is acknowledged and/or witnessed as required by state law for placement in the public records. Like deeds, mortgages must be recorded if they are to be effective against any subsequent purchaser, mortgagee, or lessee. The reason the mortgage is recorded, but not the promissory note, is that the mortgage deals with rights and interests in real property, whereas the note represents a personal obligation. Moreover, most people do not want the details of their promissory note in the public records.

MORTGAGE SATISFACTION

By far, most mortgage loans are paid in full either on or ahead of schedule. When the loan is paid, the standard practice is for the lender to return the promissory note to the borrower along with a document called a **satisfaction of mortgage** (or a **release of mortgage**). Issued by the lender, this document states that the promissory note or bond has been paid in full and the accompanying mortgage may be discharged from the public records. It is extremely important that this document be promptly recorded by the public recorder in the same county where the mortgage is recorded. Otherwise, the records will continue to indicate that the property is mortgaged. When a satisfaction or release is recorded, a recording office employee makes a note of its book and page location on the margin of the recorded mortgage. This is done to assist title searchers and is called a **marginal release.**

Partial Release

Occasionally, the situation arises where the borrower wants the lender to release a portion of the mortgaged property from the mortgage after part of the loan has been repaid. This is known as asking for a **partial release.** For example, a land developer purchases 40 acres of land for a total price of $500,000 and finances his purchase with $100,000 in cash plus a mortgage and note for $400,000 to the seller. In the mortgage agreement he might ask that the seller release 10 acres free and clear of the mortgage encumbrance for each $100,000 paid against the loan. This would allow the subdivider to develop and sell those 10 acres without first paying the entire $400,000 remaining balance.

If an existing mortgage on a property does not contain a due-on-sale clause, the seller can pass the benefits of that financing along to the buyer. (This can occur when the existing loan carries a lower rate of interest than currently available on new loans.) One method of doing this is for the buyer to purchase the property **subject to the existing loan.** In the purchase contract the buyer states that he is aware of the existence of the loan and the mortgage that secures it, but takes no personal liability for it. Although the buyer pays the remaining loan payments as they come due, the seller continues to be personally liable to the lender for the loan. As long as the buyer faithfully continues to make the loan payments, which he would normally do as long as the property is worth more than the debts against it, this arrangement presents no problem to the seller. However, if the buyer stops making payments before the loan is fully paid, even though it may be years later, in most states the lender can require the seller to pay the balance due plus interest. This is true even though the seller thought he was free of the loan because he sold the property.

"SUBJECT TO"

The seller is on safer ground if he requires the buyer to **assume the loan.** Under this arrangement the buyer promises in writing to the seller that he will pay the loan, thus personally obligating himself to the seller. In the event of default on the loan the lender will look to both the buyer and the seller because the seller's name is still on the original promissory note. The seller may have to make the payments, but can file suit against the buyer for the money.

ASSUMPTION

NOVATION   The safest arrangement for the seller is to ask the lender to **substitute** the buyer's liability for his. This releases the seller from the personal obligation created by his promissory note, and the lender can now require only the buyer to repay the loan. The lender will require the buyer to prove financial capability to repay by having the buyer fill out a loan application and by running a credit check on the buyer. The lender may also adjust the rate of interest on the loan to reflect current market interest rates. The seller is also on safe ground if the mortgage agreement or state law prohibits deficiency judgments, a topic that will be explained shortly.

ESTOPPEL   When a buyer is to continue making payments on an existing loan, he will want to know exactly how much is still owing. A **certificate of reduction** is prepared by the lender to show how much of the loan remains to be paid. If a recorded mortgage states that it secures a loan for $35,000, but the borrower has reduced the amount owed to $25,000, the certificate of reduction will show that $25,000 remains to be paid. Roughly the mirror image of a certificate of reduction is the **estoppel certificate.** In it, the borrower is asked to verify the amount still owed and the rate of interest. The most common application of an estoppel certificate is when the holder of a loan sells the loan to another investor. It avoids future confusion and litigation over misunderstandings as to how much is still owed on a loan. The word *estoppel* comes from the Latin, "to stop up."

DEBT PRIORITIES   The same property can usually be used as collateral for more than one mortgage. This presents no problems to the lenders involved as long as the borrower makes the required payments on each note secured by the property. The difficulty arises when a default occurs on one or more of the loans, and the price the property brings at its foreclosure sale does not cover all the loans against it. As a result, a priority system is necessary. The debt with the highest priority is satisfied first from the foreclosure sale proceeds, then the next highest priority debt is satisfied, then the next, and so on until either the foreclosure sale proceeds are exhausted or all debts secured by the property are satisfied.

First Mortgage   In the vast majority of foreclosures, the sale proceeds are not sufficient to pay all the outstanding debt against the property;

thus, it becomes extremely important that a lender know his priority position before making a loan. Unless there is a compelling reason otherwise, a lender will want to be in the most senior position possible. This is normally accomplished by being the first lender to record a mortgage against a property that is otherwise free and clear of mortgage debt; this lender is said to hold a **first mortgage** on the property. If the same property is later used to secure another note before the first is fully satisfied, the new mortgage is a **second mortgage,** and so on. The first mortgage is also known as the **senior mortgage.** Any mortgage with a lower priority is known as a **junior mortgage.** As time passes and higher priority mortgages are satisfied, the lower priority mortgages move up in priority. Thus, if a property is secured by a first and a second mortgage and the first is paid off, the second becomes a first mortgage. Note that nothing is stamped or written on a mortgage document to indicate if it is a first or second or third, etc. That can only be determined by searching the public records for mortgages recorded against the property that have not been released.

Subordination

Sometimes a lender will voluntarily take a lower priority position than the lender would otherwise be entitled to by virtue of recording date. This is known as **subordination** and it allows a junior loan to move up in priority. For example, the holder of a first mortgage can volunteer to become a second mortgagee and allow the second mortgage to move into the first position. Although it seems irrational that a lender would actually volunteer to lower his priority position, it is sometimes done by landowners to encourage developers to buy their land.

Chattel Liens

An interesting situation regarding priority occurs when chattels are bought on credit and then affixed to land that is already mortgaged. If the chattels are not paid for, can the chattel lienholder come onto the land and remove them? If there is default on the mortgage loan against the land, are the chattels sold as fixtures? The solution is for the chattel lienholder to record a **chattel mortgage** or a **financing statement.** This protects the lienholder even though the chattel becomes a fixture when it is affixed to land. A chattel mortgage is a mortgage secured by personal property. If the borrower defaults, the lender is permitted to take possession and sell the mortgaged goods. A more streamlined approach, and one used by most states today, is to file a financing statement as provided by the Uniform Commercial Code to establish lien priority regarding personal property.

THE FORECLOSURE
PROCESS

Although relatively few mortgages are foreclosed, it is important to have a basic understanding of what happens when foreclosure takes place. First, knowledge of what causes foreclosure can help in avoiding it; and, second, if foreclosure does occur, one should know the rights of the parties involved. As you read the material below, keep in mind that to **foreclose** simply means to cut off. What the lender is saying is, "Mr. Borrower, you are not keeping your end of the bargain. We want you out so the property can be put into the hands of someone who will keep the agreements." (What is often unsaid is that the lender has commitments to its savers that must be met. Can you imagine going to your bank or savings and loan and asking for the interest on your savings account and hearing the teller say they don't have it because their borrowers have not been making payments?)

Delinquent Loan

Although noncompliance with any part of the mortgage agreement by the borrower can result in the lender calling the entire balance immediately due, in most cases foreclosure occurs because the note is not being repaid on time. When a borrower runs behind in his payments, the loan is said to be **delinquent.** At this stage, rather than presume that foreclosure is automatically next, the borrower and lender usually meet and attempt to work out an alternative payment program. Contrary to early motion picture plots in which lenders seemed anxious to foreclose their mortgages, today's lender considers foreclosure to be the last resort. This is because the foreclosure process is time-consuming, expensive, and unprofitable. The lender would much rather have the borrower make regular payments. Consequently, if a borrower is behind in loan payments, the lender prefers to arrange a new, stretched-out, payment schedule rather than immediately declare the acceleration clause in effect and move toward foreclosing the borrower's rights to the property.

If a borrower realizes that stretching out payments is not going to solve his financial problem, instead of presuming foreclosure to be inevitable, he can seek a buyer for the property who can make the payments. This, more than any other reason, is why relatively few real estate mortgages are foreclosed. The borrower, realizing the financial trouble, sells his property. It is only when the borrower cannot find a buyer and when the lender sees no further sense in stretching the payments that the acceleration clause is invoked and the path toward foreclosure taken.

Basically there are two foreclosure routes: judicial and nonjudicial. **Judicial foreclosure** means taking the matter to a court of law in the form of a lawsuit that asks the judge to foreclose (cut off) the borrower. A **nonjudicial foreclosure** does not go to court and is not heard by a judge. It is conducted by the lender (or by a trustee) in accordance with provisions in the mortgage and in accordance with state law pertaining to nonjudicial foreclosures. Comparing the two, a judicial foreclosure is more costly and more time-consuming, but it does carry the approval of a court of law and it may give the lender rights to collect the full amount of the loan if the property sells for less than the amount owed. It is also the preferred method when the foreclosure case is complicated and involves many parties and interests. The nonjudicial route is usually faster, simpler, and cheaper, and it is preferred by lenders when the case is simple and straightforward. Let us now look at foreclosure methods for standard mortgages. (Deed of trust foreclosure will be discussed in Chapter 10.)

Foreclosure Routes

The judicial foreclosure process begins with a title search. Next, the lender files a lawsuit naming as defendants the borrower and anyone who acquired a right or interest in the property after the lender recorded his mortgage. In the lawsuit the lender identifies the debt and the mortgage securing it, and states that it is in default. The lender then asks the court for a judgment directing that (1) the defendants' interests in the property be cut off in order to return the condition of title to what it was when the loan was made, (2) the property to be sold at a public auction, and (3) the lender's claim to be paid from the sale proceeds.

JUDICIAL FORECLOSURE

A copy of the complaint along with a summons is delivered to the defendants. This officially notifies them of the pending legal

Surplus Money Action

action against their interests. A junior mortgage holder who has been named as a defendant has basically two choices. One choice is to allow the foreclosure to proceed and file a **surplus money action.** By doing this, the junior mortgage holder hopes that the property will sell at the foreclosure sale for enough money to pay all senior claims as well as his own claim against the borrower. The other choice is to halt the foreclosure process by making the delinquent payments on behalf of the borrower and then adding them to the amount the borrower owes the junior mortgage holder. To do this, the junior mortgage holder must use cash out of his own pocket and decide whether this is a case of "good money chasing bad." In making this decision the junior mortgage holder must consider whether or not he will have any better luck being paid than did the holder of the senior mortgage.

Notice of Lis Pendens   At the same time that the lawsuit to foreclose is filed with the court, a **notice of lis pendens** is filed with the county recorder's office where the property is located. This notice informs the public that a legal action is pending against the property. If the borrower attempts to sell the property at this time, the prospective buyer, upon making a title search, will learn of the pending litigation. The buyer can still proceed to purchase the property but is now informed of the unsettled lawsuit.

Public Auction   The borrower, or any other defendant named in the lawsuit, may now reply to the suit by presenting his side of the issue to the court judge. If no reply is made, or if the issues raised by the reply are found in favor of the lender, the judge wil! order that the interests of the borrower and other defendants in the property be foreclosed and the property sold. The sale is usually a **public auction.** The objective is to obtain the best possible price for the property by inviting competitive bidding and conducting the sale in full view of the public. To announce the sale, the judge orders a notice to be posted on the courthouse door and advertised in local newspapers.

Equity of Redemption   The sale is conducted by the **county sheriff** or by a **referee** or **master** appointed by the judge. At the sale, which is held at either the property or at the courthouse, the lender and all parties interested in purchasing the property are present. If the borrower should suddenly locate sufficient funds to pay the judgment, the borrower can, up to the minute the property goes on sale, step forward and redeem the property. This privilege to redeem property anytime between the first sign of delinquency and the moment of foreclosure sale is the borrower's **equity of redemption.** If no redemption is made, the bidding begins. Anyone with adequate funds can bid. Typically, a cash deposit of 10% of the successful bid must be made at the sale, with the balance of the bid price due upon closing, usually 30 days later.

While the lender and borrower hope that someone at the auction will bid more than the amount owed on the defaulted loan, the probability is not high. If the borrower was unable to find a buyer at a price equal to or higher than the loan balance, the best cash bid will probably be less than the balance owed. If this happens, the lender usually enters a bid of his own. The lender is in the unique position of being able to "bid the loan," that is, the lender can bid up to the amount owed without having to pay cash. All other bidders must pay cash, as the purpose of the sale is to obtain cash to pay the defaulted loan. In the event the borrower bids at the sale and is successful in buying back the property, the junior liens against the property are not eliminated. Note, however, no matter who is the successful bidder, the foreclosure does not cut off property tax liens against the property. They remain.

Deficiency Judgment

If the property sells for more than the claims against it, including any junior mortgage holders, the borrower receives the excess. For example, if a property with $50,000 in claims against it sells for $55,000, the borrower will receive the $5,000 difference, less unpaid property taxes and expenses of the sale. However, if the highest bid is only $40,000, how is the $10,000 deficiency treated? The laws of the various states differ on this question. Forty states allow the lender to pursue a **deficiency judgment** for the $10,000, with which the lender can proceed against the borrower's other unsecured assets. In other words, the borrower is still personally obligated to the lender for $10,000, and the lender is entitled to collect it. This may require the borrower to sell other assets.

Only a judge can award a lender a deficiency judgment. If the property sells for an obviously depressed price at its foreclosure sale, a deficiency judgment may be allowed only for the difference between the court's estimate of the property's fair market value and the amount still owing against it. Note that if a borrower is in a strong enough bargaining position, it is possible to add wording in the promissory note that the note is *without recourse.* This generally prohibits the lender from seeking a deficiency judgment. But this must be done before the note is signed.

The purchaser at the foreclosure sale receives either a **referee's deed in foreclosure** or a **sheriff's deed.** These are usually special warranty deeds that convey the title the borrower had at the time the foreclosed mortgage was originally made. The purchaser may take immediate possession, and the court will assist him in removing anyone in possession who was cut off in the foreclosure proceedings.

Statutory Redemption

In states with **statutory redemption laws,** the foreclosed borrower has, depending on the state, from one month to one year or more after the foreclosure sale to pay in full the judgment and retake title. This leaves the high bidder at the foreclosure auction in the dilemma of not knowing if he will get the property for certain until the statutory redemption period has run out. Meanwhile, the high bidder receives a **certificate of sale** entitling him to a referee's or sheriff's deed if no redemption is made. Depending on the state, the purchaser may or may not get possession until then. If not, the foreclosed borrower may allow the property to deteriorate and lose value. Knowing this, bidders tend to offer less than what the property would be worth if title and possession could be delivered immediately after the foreclosure sale. In this respect, statutory redemption works against the borrower as well as the lender. This problem can be made less severe if the court appoints a **receiver** (manager) to take charge of the property during the redemption period. Judicial foreclosure with public auction is the predominant method in 21 states, and 9 of them allow a statutory redemption period.

STRICT FORECLOSURE

Strict foreclosure is a judicial foreclosure without a judicial sale and usually without a statutory redemption period. Basically, the lender files a lawsuit requesting that the borrower be given a period of time to exercise the equitable right of redemption or lose all rights to the property with title vesting irrevocably in the lender. Although this conjures up visions of a greedy lender foreclosing on a borrower who has nearly paid for the property and misses a payment or two, the court will give the borrower time to make up the back payments or sell the property on the open market. Much more likely is the situation where the debt owed clearly exceeds the property's value. In this case there is little to be gained by conducting a judicial sale. Strict foreclosure is the predominant method of foreclosure in two states and is occasionally used in others. Where the debt exceeds the property's value and the foreclosure prohibits a deficiency judgment, this method may be advantageous to the borrower.

In 27 states the predominant method of foreclosure is by **power of sale,** also known as **sale by advertisement.** This clause, which must be placed in the mortgage before it is signed, gives the lender the power to conduct the foreclosure and sell the mortgaged property without taking the issue to court. The procedure begins when a lender files a **notice of default** with the public recorder. Next is a waiting period that is the borrower's equity of redemption. The property is then advertised and sold at an auction held by the lender and open to the public. The precise procedures the lender must follow are set by state statutes. After the auction, the borrower can still redeem the property if his state offers statutory redemption. The deed the purchaser receives is prepared and signed by the lender or trustee.

POWER OF SALE

A lender foreclosing under power of sale cannot award himself a deficiency judgment. If there is a deficiency as a result of the sale, and the lender wants a deficiency judgment, the lender must go to court for it. Because power of sale foreclosures take place outside the jurisdiction of a courtroom, it is said that courts watch them with a jealous eye. If a borrower feels mistreated by power of sale proceedings, the borrower can appeal the issue to a court. Wise lenders know this and keep scrupulous records and follow foreclosure rules carefully. The wise junior mortgage holder will have already filed a **request for notice of default** with the public records office when the junior mortgage was recorded. This requires anyone holding a more senior lien to notify the junior mortgagee if a default notice has been filed. (Usually the junior mortgagee is aware of the problem because if the borrower is not making payments to the holder of the first mortgage, the borrower probably is not making payments to any junior mortgage holders.)

ENTRY AND POSSESSION

Used as the predominant method of foreclosure in one state and to a lesser degree in three others, **entry and possession** is based on the lender giving notice to the borrower that the lender wants possession of the property. The borrower moves out and the lender takes possession, and this is witnessed and recorded in the public records. If the borrower does not peacefully agree to relinquish possession, the lender will have to use a judicial method of foreclosure.

DEED IN LIEU OF FORECLOSURE

To avoid the hassle of foreclosure proceedings and possible deficiency judgment, a borrower may want to voluntarily deed the mortgaged property to the lender. In turn, the borrower should demand cancellation of the unpaid debt and a letter to that effect from the lender. This method relieves the lender of foreclosing and waiting out any required redemption periods, but it also presents the lender with a sensitive situation. With the borrower in financial distress and about to be foreclosed, it is quite easy for the lender to take advantage of the borrower. As a result, a court of law will usually side with the borrower if he complains of any unfair dealings. Therefore, the lender must be prepared to prove conclusively that the borrower received a fair deal by deeding the property voluntarily to the lender in return for cancellation of the debt. If the property is worth more than the balance due on the debt, the lender must pay the borrower the difference in cash. A **deed in lieu of foreclosure** is a voluntary act by both borrower and lender and hence is sometimes called a "friendly foreclosure." Nonetheless, if either feels he will fare better in regular foreclosure proceedings, he need not agree to it. Note also that a deed in lieu of foreclosure will not cut off the rights of junior mortgage holders. This means the lender will have to make those payments or be foreclosed by the junior mortgage holder(s). Figure 9:3 summarizes through illustration the five methods of mortgage foreclosure that have just been discussed.

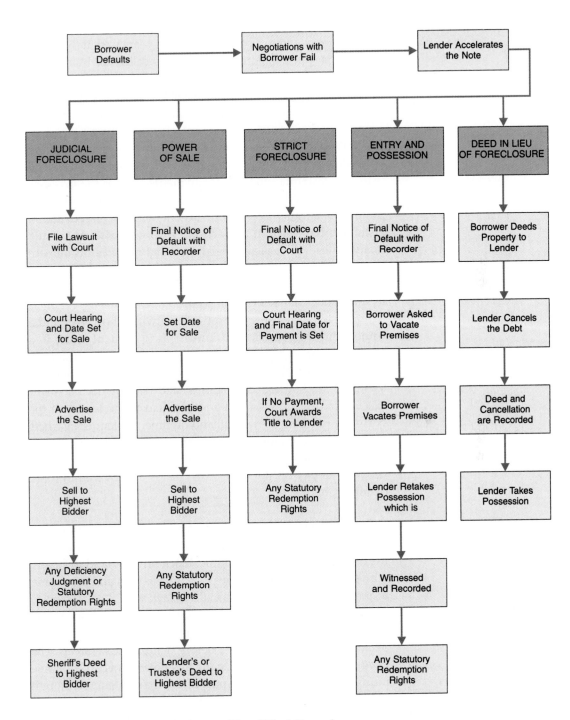

Figure 9:3. Mortgage Foreclosure Simplified Overview

INSTALLMENT CONTRACT FORECLOSURE

An installment contract (discussed in Chapter 8) is both a purchase contract and a debt instrument. In years past, if the buyer (vendee) stopped making the payments called for by the contract, the seller (vendor) simply rescinded the contract. The buyer gave up possession; the seller kept all the payments to date; and there was no deficiency judgment. (This effectively is a strict foreclosure without the protection of a court.)

State legislatures found installment contracts too often one-sided in favor of the seller, especially where the buyer had made a substantial number of payments and/or the property had appreciated in value. The need for added consumer protection became even more urgent with increased use of installment contracts in connection with house sales. As a result, many states have enacted legislation that requires installment contracts to be foreclosed like regular mortgages.

DEED OF TRUST

In some states debts are often secured by trust deeds. Whereas a mortgage is a two-party arrangement with a borrower and a lender, the **trust deed,** also known as a **deed of trust,** is a three-party arrangement consisting of the borrower (the trustor), the lender (the beneficiary), and a neutral third party (a trustee). The key aspect of this system is that the borrower executes a deed to the trustee rather than to the lender. If the borrower pays the debt in full and on time, the lender instructs the trustee to reconvey title back to the borrower. If the borrower defaults on the loan, the lender instructs the trustee to sell the property to pay off the debt. Trust deeds are covered in more detail in Chapter 10.

EQUITABLE MORTGAGE

An **equitable mortgage** is a written agreement that, although it does not follow the form of a regular mortgage, is considered by the courts to be one. For example, Black sells his land to Green, with Green paying part of the price now in cash and promising to pay the balance later. Normally, Black would ask Green to execute a regular mortgage as security for the balance due. However, instead of doing this, Black makes a note of the balance due him on the deed before handing it to Green. The laws of most states would regard this notation as an equitable mortgage. For all intents and purposes it is a mortgage, although not specifically called one. Another example of an equitable mortgage can arise from the deposit money accompanying an offer to purchase property. If the seller refuses the offer and refuses to return the deposit, the courts will hold that the purchaser has an equitable mortgage in the amount of the deposit against the seller's property.

Occasionally, a borrower will give a bargain and sale or warranty **deed as security** for a loan. On the face of it, the lender (grantee) would appear to own the property. However, if the borrower can prove that the deed was, in fact, security for a loan, the lender must foreclose like a regular mortgage if the borrower fails to repay. If the loan is repaid in full and on time, the lender is obligated to convey the land back to the borrower. Like the equitable mortgage, a deed used as security is treated according to its intent, not its label.

In one state, Georgia, the standard mortgage instrument is the **security deed.** This is a warranty deed with a reconveyance clause. The security deed transfers title to the lender and when all payments have been made on the accompanying note, the lender executes the reconveyance (or cancellation) clause on the reverse of the deed, and it is recorded. If the borrower defaults, a power of sale clause in the deed allows the lender to advertise and sell the property without going through judicial foreclosure.

Generally speaking, a lender will choose, and ask the borrower to sign, whatever security instrument provides the smoothest foreclosure in that state. To illustrate, some states require a statutory redemption period for a mortgage foreclosure but not for a deed of trust foreclosure. Some will allow power of sale for a deed of trust but not for a mortgage. All states allow the use of a deed of trust, but some require that it be foreclosed like a mortgage. More and more states require installment contracts to be foreclosed like mortgages. An analogy for the development of security instrument law is that of a plant growing up through a pile of rocks. Its path up may be twisted and curved, but it reaches its goal—the sunlight. Security instruments follow many paths, but always with one goal in mind—to get money to the borrower who uses it and then returns it to the lender.

Lastly, take a look at Figures 10:1 and 10:5 in the next chapter. These illustrations will help you visualize the differences between a mortgage, deed of trust, and land contract at the time of creation, repayment, and foreclosure.

1. Evidence of the amount and terms of a borrower's debt to a lender is provided by means of a
   A. mortgage.
   B. promissory note.
   C. Deed of Trust.
   D. First Mortgage.

2. A promissory note which fails to state that it is to be secured by a mortgage or deed of trust is
   A. a personal obligation of the borrower.
   B. an unsecured obligation of the borrower.
   C. Both A and B.
   D. Neither A nor B.

3. Should a borrower fail to make payments when due, the lender may demand immediate payment of the entire balance under the terms of the
   A. prepayment clause.
   B. defeasance clause.
   C. acceleration clause.
   D. hypothecation clause.

4. Which of the following statements is/are correct?
   A. A promissory note is evidence of a borrower's debt to a lender.
   B. A mortgage hypothecates property as collateral for a loan.
   C. Both A and B.
   D. Neither A nor B.

5. At the time of origination, a mortgage creates a lien on the mortgaged property in states which subscribe to the
   A. lien theory.
   B. title theory.
   C. intermediate theory.
   D. Both A and B.
   E. Both A and C.

6. Which of the following covenants will NOT appear in a mortgage?
   A. Covenants to pay taxes and insurance.
   B. Covenant against removal.
   C. Covenant against encumbrances.
   D. Covenant of good repair.

7. The clause which gives the lender the right to call in the note if the mortgaged property is sold or otherwise conveyed by the borrower is known as the
   A. due-on-sale clause.
   B. alienation clause.
   C. Both A and B.
   D. Neither A nor B.

8. Who may be held responsible for mortgage loan repayment when a loan is assumed as part of a real estate sale?
   A. The purchaser.
   B. The seller.
   C. Both A and B.
   D. Neither A nor B.

9. When a loan is assumed, the
   A. seller can be relieved of liability by novation.
   B. the buyer should verify the loan balance with the lender.
   C. Both A and B.
   D. Neither A nor B.

10. The rights of a creditor who is owed for chattels which have been affixed to real property may be protected by recording a
   A. chattel mortgage.
   B. financing statement.
   C. Both A and B.
   D. Neither A nor B.

11. The period of equitable redemption given to a borrower
   A. begins when the loan goes into default.
   B. ends when the property is sold at foreclosure.
   C. Both A and B.
   D. Neither A nor B.

12. When the amount received from a foreclosure sale is insufficient to pay off the mortgage loan and the other expenses of the sale, the lender may sometimes secure
   A. a deficiency judgment.
   B. a mechanic's lien.
   C. an estoppel lien.
   D. a statutory lien.

13. The deed given to the purchaser at foreclosure by the sheriff or other officer of the court usually takes the form of a
   A. general warranty deed.
   B. quitclaim deed.
   C. special warranty deed.
   D. bargain and sale deed.

14. The period of time set by state law after a foreclosure sale, during which the mortgagor may redeem the property is known as the period of
   A. equitable redemption.
   B. legal redemption.
   C. voluntary redemption.
   D. statutory redemption.

15. A borrower who feels mistreated by a power of sale foreclosure can
   A. obtain a judicial foreclosure.
   B. appeal the issue to the courts.
   C. obtain a judgment.
   D. obtain a lien.

16. By voluntarily giving the lender a deed in lieu of foreclosure, a delinquent borrower can avoid
   A. foreclosure proceedings.
   B. possible deficiency judgments.
   C. Both A and B.
   D. Neither A nor B.

17. Generally, lenders ask borrowers to sign whatever security instrument
   A. is permitted by state law.
   B. permits the smoothest foreclosure proceedings in that state.
   C. Both A and B.
   D. Neither A nor B.

18. A document that for all intents and purposes is a mortgage, although not labeled one, would most likely be
   A. an installment contract.
   B. a deed of trust.
   C. an equitable mortgage.
   D. a deed as security.

19. The borrower under a deed of trust is the
   A. beneficiary.
   B. trustee.
   C. trustor.
   D. assignor.

20. The lender under a deed of trust is the
   A. beneficiary.
   B. trustee.
   C. trustor.
   D. assignee.

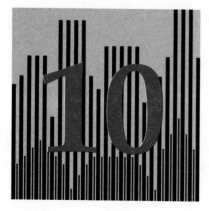

Deed of Trust

OVERVIEW OF
CHAPTER 10

The basic purpose of the deed of trust, also called a trust deed, is the same as a mortgage. However, the deed of trust involves a neutral third party called the trustee. More on that subject is discussed in chapter 10, which also covers the foreclosure process in regard to the deed of trust, redemption, jurisdictions using the deeds of trust, and advantages of a deed of trust.

LEARNING OBJECTIVES

After successful completion of this chapter, you should be able to:
1. Distinguish between a deed of trust and a mortgage.
2. Explain the various paragraphs in a deed of trust.
3. Describe the foreclosure process wherein a deed of trust is used.
4. Explain the redemption process.
5. Have a general knowledge of jurisdictions which use the deed of trust.
6. List the advantages of a deed of trust.

KEY • TERMS

Assignment of rents: establishes the lender's right to take possession and collect rents in the event of loan default

Beneficiary: one for whose benefit a trust is created; the lender in a deed of trust arrangement

Deed of trust: a document that conveys legal title to a neutral third party (a trustee) as security for a debt

Naked title: title that lacks the rights and privileges usually associated with ownership

Reconveyance or release deed: a document used to reconvey title from the trustee back to the property owner once the debt has been paid

Trustee: one who holds property in trust for another

Trustor: one who creates a trust; the borrower in a deed of trust arrangement

The basic purpose of a **deed of trust,** also referred to as a **trust deed,** is the same as a mortgage. Real property is used as security for a debt; if the debt is not repaid, the property is sold and the proceeds are applied to the balance owed. The main legal difference between a deed of trust and a mortgage is diagrammed in Figure 10:1.

PARTIES TO A DEED OF TRUST

Figure 10:1A shows that when a debt is secured by a mortgage the borrower delivers his promissory note and mortgage to the lender, who keeps them until the debt is paid. But when a note is secured by a deed of trust, three parties are involved: the borrower (the **trustor**), the lender (the **beneficiary**), and a neutral third party (the **trustee**). The lender makes a loan to the borrower, and the borrower gives the lender a promissory note (like the one shown in Chapter 9) and a deed of trust. In the deed of trust document, the borrower conveys title to the trustee, to be held in trust until the note is paid in full. (This is the distinguishing feature of a deed of trust.)

The deed of trust is recorded in the county where the property is located and then is given to either the lender or the trustee for safekeeping. Anyone searching the title records would find the deed of trust conveying title to the trustee. This would alert the title searcher to the existence of a debt against the property.

The title that the borrower grants to the trustee is sometimes referred to as a **naked title** or **bare title.** This is because the borrower still retains the usual rights of an owner such as the right to occupy and use the property and the right to sell it. The title held by the trustee is limited only to what is necessary to carry out the terms of the trust. In fact, as long as the note is not in default, the trustee's title lies dormant. The lender does not receive title, but only a right that allows the lender to request the trustee to act. Before continuing, take a moment to reread this chapter thus far.

RECONVEYANCE   Referring to Figure 10:1B, we see that when the note is repaid in full under a regular mortgage, the lender cancels the note and returns it to the borrower together with a mortgage satisfaction or release. Upon recordation, the mortgage satisfaction or release informs the world at large that the mortgage is nullified and no longer encumbers the property. Under the deed of trust arrangement, the lender sends to the trustee the note, the deed of trust, and a **request for reconveyance.** The trustee cancels the note and issues to the borrower a **reconveyance** or a **release deed** that reconveys title back to the borrower. The borrower

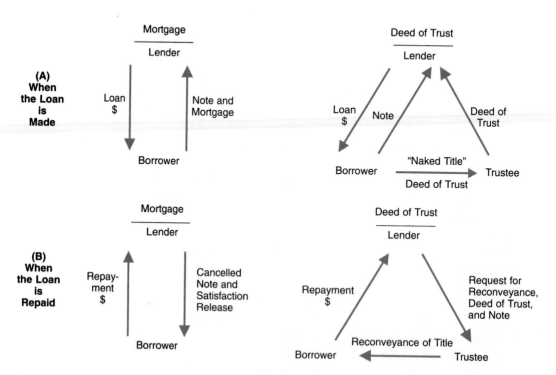

Figure 10:1: Comparing a Mortgage with Deed of Trust

records this document to inform the world that the trustee no longer has title. At the recorder's office, a marginal note is made on the record copy of the original deed of trust to show that it has been discharged.

Default

If a borrower defaults under a deed of trust, the lender delivers the deed of trust to the trustee with instructions to sell the property and pay the balance due on the note. The trustee can do this because of two important features found in the deed of trust. First, by virtue of signing the deed of trust, the borrower has already conveyed title to the trustee. Second, the power of sale clause found in a deed of trust is designed to give the trustee the authority to sell the property without having to go through a court-ordered foreclosure proceeding.

Trustee

In nearly all states, a title, trust, or escrow company or the trust department of a bank may act as a **trustee.** An individual can be named as a trustee in most jurisdictions. However, this can present a problem if the person dies before reconveyance is made. Therefore, a corporate trustee is preferred because its life span is not limited by the human life span. In a few jurisdictions, Colorado for example, the role of trustee is performed by a government official known as a **public trustee.** Whether public or private, the trustee is expected to be neutral and fair to both the borrower and the lender. To accomplish this, the trustee carefully abides by the agreements found in the deed of trust.

DEED OF TRUST DOCUMENT

Figure 10:2 is a simplified example of a deed of trust that shows the agreements between the borrower and lender and states the responsibilities of the trustee. Beginning at ①, the document is identified as a deed of trust. This is followed by the date of its execution and the names of the trustor, beneficiary, and trustee. For discussion purposes, this chapter will continue to refer to them as the borrower, lender, and trustee, respectively.

At ②, the **promissory note** that accompanies this deed of trust is identified, and it is clearly stated that the purpose of this deed is to provide security for that note. In other words, although this deed grants and conveys title to the trustee at ③, it is understood that the quantity of title the trustee receives is only that which is necessary to protect the note. This permits the borrower to continue to possess and enjoy the use of the property as long as the promissory note is not in default.

Power of Sale   Under the **power of sale** clause at ④, if the borrower defaults, the trustee has the right to foreclose and sell the property and convey ownership to the purchaser. If the borrower does not default, this power lies dormant. The presence of a power of sale right does not prohibit the trustee from using a court-ordered foreclosure. If the rights of the parties involved, including junior debt holders and other claimants, are not clear, the trustee can request a court-ordered foreclosure.

Figure 10:2.

DEED OF TRUST WITH POWER OF SALE

① *This Deed of Trust, made this* __15th__ *day of* __April__ *, 19* __xx__ *, between* __Victor Raffaelli and Mary Raffaelli, Husband and Wife__ *, herein called the Trustor, and* __District Mortgage Company__ *, herein called the Beneficiary, and* __Safety Title and Trust Co., Inc.__ *, herein called the Trustee.*

② *WITNESSETH: To secure the repayment of one promissory note in the principal sum of* __$ 70,000__ *executed by the Trustor in favor of the Beneficiary and bearing the same date as this Deed, and to secure the agreements shown below, the Trustor irrevocably* ③ *grants and conveys to the Trustee, in trust with* ④ *power of sale, the following described real property in the County of* __Graham__ *, State of* __Confusion__ *:*

⑤ *Lot 21, Block "A," of Tract 2468, as shown in Map Book 29, Page 17, filed in the Public Records Office of the above County and State.*

⑥ *FURTHERMORE: The trustor warrants the title to said property and will defend the same against all claims.*

⑦ *UPON WRITTEN REQUEST by the Beneficiary to the Trustee stating that all sums secured hereby have been paid, and upon surrender of this Deed and said Note to the Trustee for cancellation, the Trustee shall reconvey the above described property to the Trustor.*

⑧ *THIS DEED BINDS all parties hereto, their successors, assigns, heirs, devises, administrators, and executors.*

Figure 10:2. continued

⑨ *UNTIL SAID NOTE IS PAID IN FULL:*

A. The Trustor agrees to pay all taxes on said property.

B. The Trustor agrees not to remove or demolish any buildings or other improvements on said property without the approval of the Beneficiary

C. The Trustor agrees to carry adequate insurance to protect the Beneficiary in the event of damage or destruction of said property.

D. The Trustor agrees to keep the mortgaged property in good repair and not permit waste or deterioration.

E. The Beneficiary shall have the right to inspect the property as may be necessary for the security of the Note.

F. If all or part of said property is taken by eminent domain, any money received shall be applied to the Note.

UPON DEFAULT BY THE TRUSTOR in payment of the debt secured hereby, or the nonperformance of any agreement hereby made, the Beneficiary:

G. May declare all sums secured hereby immediately due and payable.

⑩ *H. May enter and take possession of said property and collect the rents and profits thereof.*

⑪ *I. May demand the Trustee sell said property in accordance with state law, apply the proceeds to the unpaid portion of the Note, and deliver to the purchaser a Trustee's Deed conveying title to said property.*

⑫ *THE TRUSTEE ACCEPTS THIS TRUST when this Deed, properly executed and acknowledged, is made a public record. The Beneficiary may substitute a successor to the Trustee named herein by recording such change in the public records of the county where said property is located.*

[acknowledgement of trustor's signature is placed here.]

⑬ _Victor Raffaelli_
Trustor

Mary Raffaelli
Trustor

At ⑤, the property being conveyed to the trustee is described, and at ⑥ the borrower states that he has title to the property and he will defend that title against the claims of others. At ⑦, the procedure that must be followed to reconvey the title is described. State laws require that when the note is paid the lender must deliver a request for reconveyance to the trustee. The lender must also deliver the promissory note and deed of trust to the trustee. Upon receiving these three items, the trustee reconveys title to the borrower and the trust arrangement is terminated. (A simplified request for reconveyance is illustrated in Figure 10:3 and a simplified full reconveyance in Figure 10:4.)

Continuing in Figure 10:2, the sections identified at ⑧ and⑨ (paragraphs A through G) are similar to those found in a regular mortgage. They were discussed in Chapter 9 and will not be repeated here.

Assignment of Rents

At ⑩, the lender reserves the right to take physical possession of the pledged property, operate it, and collect any rents or income generated by it. The right to collect rents in the event of default is called an **assignment of rents** clause. The lender would only exercise this right if the borrower continued to collect rental income from the property without paying on the note. The right to take physical possession in the event of default is important because it gives the lender the opportunity to preserve the value of the property until the foreclosure sale takes place. Very likely, if the borrower has defaulted on the note, his financial condition is such that he is no longer maintaining the property. If this continues, the property will be less valuable by the time the foreclosure sale occurs.

Foreclosure

At ⑪ is the lender's right to instruct the trustee to sell the property in the event of the borrower's default on the note or nonperformance of the agreements in the deed of trust. This section also sets forth the rules which the trustee is to follow if there is a foreclosure sale. Either appropriate state laws are referred to or each step of the process is listed in the deed of trust. Generally, state laws regarding power of sale foreclosure require that (1) the lender demonstrate to the trustee that there is reason to cut off the borrower's interest in the property, (2) a notice of default be filed with the public recorder, (3) the notice of default be followed by a 90- to 120-day waiting period before sale advertising begins, (4) advertising of the proposed foreclosure sale occur for at least 3 weeks in public places and a local newspaper, (5) the sale itself be a public auction held in the county where the property is located, and (6) the purchaser at the sale be given a **trustee's deed** conveying all title held by the trustee. This is all the right, title, and interest the borrower had at the time he deeded the property to the trustee.

Proceeds from the sale are used to pay (1) the expenses of the sale, (2) the lender, (3) any junior claims, and (4) the borrower, in that order. Once the sale is held, the borrower's equitable right of redemption ends. In some states, statutory redemption may still exist. Anyone can bid at the sale, including the borrower. However, junior claims that would normally be cut off by the sale are not extinguished if the borrower is the successful bidder.

Proceeds

The wording at ⑫ reflects what is called the **automatic form** of trusteeship. The trustee is named in the deed of trust, but is not personally notified of the appointment. In fact, the trustee is not usually aware of the appointment until called upon to either reconvey or proceed under the power of sale provision. The alternative method is called the **accepted form:** the trustee is notified in advance and either accepts or rejects the appointment. Its primary advantage is that it provides positive acceptance of appointment. The main advantage of the automatic form is that it is faster and easier. In the event the trustee cannot

Trustee Appointment

Figure 10:3.

REQUEST FOR FULL RECONVEYANCE

To: <u>Safety Title and Trust Company, Inc.,</u> *trustee.*
The undersigned is the owner of the debt secured by the above Deed of Trust. This debt has been fully paid and you are requested to reconvey to the parties designated in the Deed of Trust, the estate now held by you under same.

Date _____   <u>District Mortgage</u>
                                                Beneficiary

[As a matter of convenience, this form is often printed at the bottom or on the reverse of the trust deed itself.]

or will not perform when called upon by the lender, the wording at (12) permits the lender to name a substitute trustee. This would be necessary if an individual appointed as a trustee had died, or a corporate trustee was dissolved or an appointed trustee refused to perform. Finally, the borrowers sign at (13), their signatures are acknowledged at (14), and the deed of trust is recorded in the county where the property is located. Figure 10:5 is a summary comparison of a deed of trust, regular mortgage, and land contract at creation, repayment, and foreclosure.

JURISDICTIONS USING DEEDS OF TRUST

The deed of trust is the customary security instrument in Alaska, Arizona, California, Colorado, the District of Columbia, Idaho, Maryland, Mississippi, Missouri, North Carolina, Oregon, Tennessee, Texas, Virginia, and West Virginia. The deed of trust is also used to a certain extent in Alabama, Delaware, Hawaii, Illinois, Montana, Nevada, New Mexico,

Figure 10:4.

FULL RECONVEYANCE

  Safety Title and Trust Company, Inc. , *the Trustee under a deed of trust executed by* Victor Raffaelli and Mary Raffaelli, husband and wife , *Trustors, dated* April 15, 19xx , *and recorded as instrument number* 12345 *in Book* 876 , *Page* 345 , *in the Official Records of* Graham *County, State of* Confusion , *having been requested in writing by the holder of the obligation secured by said deed of trust DOES HEREBY RECONVEY WITHOUT WARRANTY to the person(s) legally entitled thereto the estate held by it under said deed of trust.*

(*Brief property description*)

[Acknowledgment of trustee's signature is placed here.]

  Safety Title
Trustee

[This document must be recorded to give public notice that the debt has been paid.]

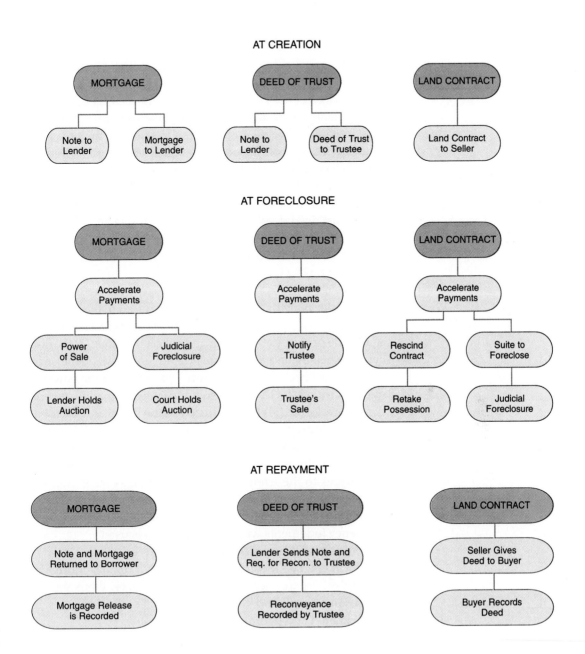

Figure 10:5. Comparing a Mortgage, Deed of Trust, and Land Contract

Utah, Washington, and a few other states. The extent of use in a state is governed by the state's attitude toward conveyance of title to the trustee, power of sale, assignment of rents, and statutory redemption privileges. Many states not listed here allow the use of a deed of trust, but require that it be foreclosed just like a regular mortgage.

The deed of trust may be the customary security instrument because state law recognizes a power of sale clause in a deed of trust, but not in a regular mortgage. Or, state law may require a statutory redemption period for mortgages but not for deeds of trust. In those states that allow all the provisions of a deed of trust to function without hindrance, the deed of trust has flourished. In California, for example, where it is legally well established that a trust deed does convey title to the trustee, that the trustee has the power of sale, and that there is no statutory redemption on trust deeds, trust deed recordings outnumber regular mortgages by a ratio of more than 500 to 1.

ADVANTAGES OF THE DEED OF TRUST

The popularity of the deed of trust can be traced to the following attributes: (1) if a borrower defaults, the lender can take possession of the property to protect it and collect the rents; (2) the time between default and foreclosure is relatively short, on the order of 90 to 180 days; (3) the foreclosure process under the power of sale provision is far less expensive and complex than a court-ordered foreclosure; (4) title is already in the name of the trustee, thus permitting the trustee to grant title to the purchaser after the foreclosure sale; and (5) once the foreclosure sale takes place, there is usually no statutory redemption. These are primarily advantages to the lender, but such advantages have attracted lenders and made real estate loans easier and less expensive for borrowers to obtain. Some states prohibit or restrict the use of deficiency judgments when a deed of trust is used.

Property can be purchased "subject to" an existing deed of trust or it can be "assumed," just as with a regular mortgage. Debt priorities are established as for mortgages: there are first and second, senior and junior trust deeds. Deeds of trust can be subordinated and partial releases are possible.

1. Stevens obtained a loan on real estate by means of an instrument which conveyed title to the property to a trustee. This instrument is a
   A. deed of trust.
   B. trust deed.
   C. mortgage.
   D. Both A and B.
   E. Both A and C.

2. The quantity of title conveyed to a trustee by means of a deed of trust is
   A. fee simple absolute.
   B. fee simple conditional.
   C. naked title.
   D. None of the above.

3. When a deed of trust is recorded, bare title is conveyed by the
   A. lender to the borrower.
   B. borrower to the lender.
   C. borrower to the trustee.
   D. trustee to the lender.

4. When a deed of trust is foreclosed, title is conveyed by the
   A. borrower to the lender.
   B. trustee to the borrower.
   C. borrower to the trustee.
   D. trustee to the purchaser at foreclosure.

5. Which of the following clauses would be found in a deed of trust but not in a mortgage?
   A. A reconveyance clause.
   B. A power of sale clause.
   C. An acceleration clause.
   D. A defeasance clause.

6. Which of the following documents would be recorded in the public records in order to clear an existing deed of trust?
   A. The promissory note.
   B. A reconveyance.
   C. Both A and B.
   D. Neither A nor B.

7. Which of the following would a lender like to have in a deed of trust or mortgage?
   A. Power of sale.
   B. Assignment of rents.
   C. Both A and B.
   D. Neither A nor B.

8. Where trust deeds are used, their popularity may be attributed to which of the following reasons?
   A. The time between default and foreclosure is shortened.
   B. There is usually no statutory redemption period.
   C. The provisions of the assignment of rents clause.
   D. Title is already in the name of the trustee.
   E. All of the above.

9. If the trustee should die or be dissolved before the debt secured by a deed of trust is paid off, a successor may be named by the
   A. trustor.
   B. beneficiary.
   C. judge.
   D. A and B.

10. Comparing a deed of trust to a mortgage, which of the following would be unique to the deed of trust?
    A. Reconveyance.
    B. Power of Sale.
    C. Statutory redemption.
    D. None of the above.

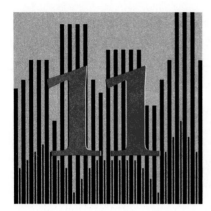

Lending
Practices

OVERVIEW OF
CHAPTER 11

This chapter will introduce you to various loan practices and give you a brief description of current lending practices. Topics covered include term loans, amortized loans, balloon loans, early payoff, refinancing, loan to value ratio, points, equity, FHA and VA programs, and loan application and approval. Under loan application procedures, the chapter goes into detail in a discussion of redlining, settlement funds, borrower analysis, references, and the credit report.

LEARNING OBJECTIVES

After successful completion of this chapter, you should be able to:

1. Explain the features of an amortized loan and respective lending process.
2. Describe a budget mortgage, a term loan, and balloon loans.
3. Explain the type of early payoff and the refinancing process.
4. Describe loan-to-value ratio, equity, origination, and discount points.
5. Describe the FHA and VA programs and lending procedures.
6. Explain the function of the Farmer's Home Administration.
7. Understand the approval procedure for private mortgage insurance.
8. Explain the purpose and features of the Truth in Lending Act.
9. Describe the loan application and approval process.
10. Define redlining, annual percentage rate, and trigger terms.

KEY • TERMS

Amortized loan: a loan requiring periodic payments that include both interest and partial repayment of principal

Balloon loan: any loan in which the final payment is larger than the preceding payments

Conventional loans: real estate loans that are not insured by the FHA or guaranteed by the VA

Equity: the market value of a property less the debt against it

Impound or reserve account: an account into which the lender places monthly tax and insurance payments

Loan-to-value ratio: a percentage reflecting what a lender will lend divided by the market value of the property

Maturity: the end of the life of a loan

OBRA: Omnibus Budget Reconciliation Act

PITI payment: a loan payment that combines principal, interest, taxes, and insurance

Point: one percent of the loan amount

Principal: the balance owing on a loan

Section 203(b): FHA's popular mortgage insurance program for houses

Truth in Lending Act: a federal law that requires certain disclosures when extending or advertising credit

Whereas Chapters 9 and 10 dealt with the legal aspects of notes, mortgages, and trust deeds, Chapters 11 and 12 will deal with the money aspects of these instruments. We will begin in Chapter 11 with term loans, amortized loans, balloon loans, partially amortized loans, loan-to-value, and equity. This will be followed by the functions and importance of the FHA and VA, private mortgage insurance, loan points, and Truth in Lending. The last topic in Chapter 11 will be a helpful and informative description of the loan application and approval process you (or your buyer) will experience when applying for a real estate loan. In Chapter 12, we will look at sources and types of financing. This will include where to find mortgage loan money, where mortgage lenders obtain their money, and various types of financing instruments such as the adjustable rate mortgage, equity mortgage, seller financing, wrap-around mortgage, and so forth. Note that from here on whatever is said about mortgages applies equally to trust deeds.

TERM LOANS

A loan that requires only interest payments until the last day of its life, at which time the full amount borrowed is due, is called a **term loan** (or straight loan). Until 1930, the term loan was the standard method of financing real estate in the United States. These loans were typically made for a period of 3 to 5 years. The borrower signed a note or bond agreeing (1) to pay the lender interest on the loan every 6 months, and (2) to repay the entire amount of the loan upon **maturity;** that is, at the end of the life of the loan. As security, the borrower mortgaged his property to the lender.

Loan Renewal

In practice, most real estate term loans were not paid off when they matured. Instead, the borrower asked the lender, typically a bank, to renew the loan for another 3 to 5 years. The major flaw in this approach to lending was that the borrower might never own the property free and clear of debt. This left the borrower continuously at the mercy of the lender for renewals. As long as the lender was not pressed for funds, the borrower's renewal request was granted. However, if the lender was short of funds, no renewal was granted and the borrower was expected to pay in full.

The inability to renew term loans caused hardship to hundreds of thousands of property owners during the Great Depression that began in 1930 and lasted most of the decade. A similar fate fell to many of the oil-producing states in the 1980s. Banks were unable to accommodate requests for loan renewals and at the same time satisfy unemployed depositors who needed to withdraw their savings to live. As a result, owners of homes, farms, office buildings, factories, and vacant land lost their property as foreclosures reached into the millions. The market was so glutted with properties being offered for sale to satisfy unpaid mortgage loans that real estate prices fell at a sickening pace.

AMORTIZED LOANS

An amortized loan requires regular equal payments during the life of the loan, of sufficient size and number to pay all interest due on the loan and reduce the amount owed to zero by the loan's maturity date. Figure 11:1 illustrates the contrast between an amortized and a term loan. Figure 11:1A shows a 6-year, $1,000 term loan with interest of $90 due each year of its life. At the end of the sixth year the entire **principal** (the amount owed) is due in one lump sum payment along with the final interest payment. In Figure 11:1B, the same $1,000 loan is fully amortized by making six equal annual payments of $222.92. From the

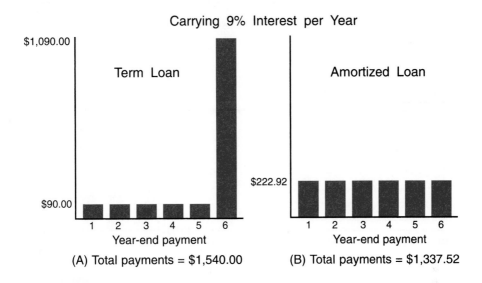

Figure 11:1. Repaying a 6-year $1,000 Loan

borrower's standpoint, $222.92 once each year is easier to budget than $90 for 5 years and $1,090 in the sixth year.

Furthermore, the amortized loan shown in Figure 11:1 actually costs the borrower less than the term loan. The total payments made under the term loan are $90 + $90 + $90 + $90 + $90 + $1,090 = $1,540. Amortizing the same loan requires total payments of 6 × $222.92 = $1,337.52. The difference is due to the fact that under the amortized loan the borrower begins to pay back part of the $1,000 principal with his first payment. In the first year, $90 of the $222.92 payment goes to interest and the remaining $132.92 reduces the principal owed. Thus, the borrower starts the second year owing only $867.08. At 9% interest per year, the interest on $867.08 is $78.04; therefore, when the borrower makes his second payment of $222.92, only $78.04 goes to interest. The remaining $144.88 is applied to reduce the loan balance, and the borrower starts the third year owing $722.20. Figure 11:2 charts this repayment program. Notice that the balance owed drops faster as the loan becomes older, that is, as it matures.

As you have just seen, calculating the payments on a term loan is relatively simple compared to calculating amortized loan payments. The widespread use of computers has greatly simplified

Monthly Payments

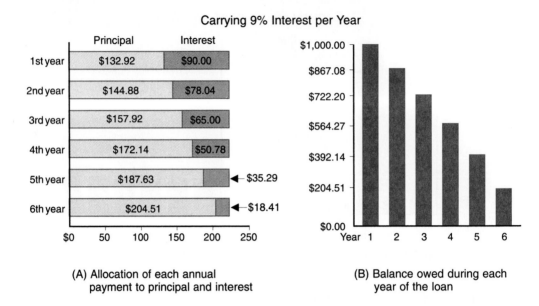

(A) Allocation of each annual
payment to principal and interest

(B) Balance owed during each
year of the loan

Figure 11:2. Repaying a 6-year $1,000 Amortized Loan

the calculations, however. To illustrate how the amortization works, though, we should note that **amortization tables** are published and used throughout the real estate industry. Table 11:1 shows the monthly payments per $1,000 of loan for interest rates from 5% to 25% for periods ranging from 5 to 40 years. (Amortization tables are also published for quarterly, semiannual, and annual payments.) When you use an amortization table, notice that there are five variables: (1) frequency of payment, (2) interest rate, (3) maturity, (4) amount of the loan, and (5) amount of the periodic payment. If you know any four of these, you can obtain the fifth variable from the tables. For example, suppose that you want to know the monthly payment necessary to amortize a $60,000 loan over 30 years at 10½% interest. The first step is to look in Table 11:1 for the 10½% line. Then locate the 30-year column. Where they cross, you will find the necessary monthly payment per $1,000: $9.15. Next, multiply $9.15 by 60 to get the monthly payment for a $60,000 loan: $549. If the loan is to be $67,500, then multiply $9.15 by 67.5 to get the monthly payment: $617.63.

Continuing the above example, suppose we reduce the repayment period to 15 years. First look for the 10½% line, then go over to the 15-year column. The number there is $11.06. Next, multiply $11.06 by 60 to get the monthly payment for a $60,000 loan: $663.60. If the loan is to be $67,500, then multiply $11.06 by 67.5 to get the monthly payment: $746.55.

Amortization tables are also used to determine the amount of loan a borrower can support if you know how much the borrower has available to spend each month on loan payments. Suppose that a prospective home buyer can afford monthly principal and interest payments of $650 and lenders are making 30-year loans at 10%. How large a loan can this buyer afford? In Table 11:1 find where the 10% line and the 30-year column meet. You will see 8.78 there. This means that every $8.78 of monthly payment will support $1,000 of loan. To find how many thousands of dollars $650 per month will support, just divide $650 by $8.78. The answer is 74.031 thousands or $74,031. By adding the buyer's down payment, you know what price property the buyer can afford to purchase. If interest rates are 7½%, the number from the table is 7.00 and the loan amount is $92,857. (You can begin to see why the level of interest rates is so important to real estate prices.)

Loan Size

As you have noticed, everything in Table 11:1 is on a monthly payment per thousand basis. With a full book of amortization tables rather than one page, it is possible to look up monthly payments for loans from $100 to $100,000, to determine loan maturities for each year from 1 to 40 years, and to calculate many more interest rates. Amortization books are available from most local bookstores.

An amortization table also shows the impact on the size of the monthly payment when the life of a loan is extended. For example, at 11% interest, a 10-year loan requires a monthly payment of $13.78 per thousand of loan. Increasing the life of the loan to 20 years drops the monthly payment to $10.33 per $1,000. Extending the loan payback to 30 years reduces the monthly payment to $9.53 per thousand. The smaller monthly payment is why 30 years is a popular loan with borrowers. Note, however, that going beyond 30 years does not significantly reduce the monthly payment. Going from 30 to 35 years reduces the monthly payment by only 16¢ per thousand but adds 5 years of monthly payments. Extending the payback period from 35 to 40 years reduces the monthly payment by just 8¢ per $1,000 ($4

Change in Maturity Date

Table 11:1. Amortization Table Monthly Payment per $1,000 of Loan

Interest Rate per Year	Life of the Loan							
	5 years	10 years	15 years	20 years	25 years	30 years	35 years	40 years
5%	$18.88	$10.61	$ 7.91	$6.60	$5.85	$5.37	$5.05	$4.83
5½	19.11	10.86	8.18	6.88	6.15	5.68	5.38	5.16
6	19.34	11.11	8.44	7.17	6.45	6.00	5.71	5.51
6½	19.57	11.36	8.72	7.46	6.76	6.32	6.05	5.86
7	19.81	11.62	8.99	7.76	7.07	6.66	6.39	6.22
7½	20.04	11.88	9.28	8.06	7.39	7.00	6.75	6.59
8	20.28	12.14	9.56	8.37	7.72	7.34	7.11	6.96
8½	20.52	12.40	9.85	8.68	8.06	7.69	7.47	7.34
9	20.76	12.67	10.15	9.00	8.40	8.05	7.84	7.72
9½	21.01	12.94	10.45	9.33	8.74	8.41	8.22	8.11
10	21.25	13.22	10.75	9.66	9.09	8.78	8.60	8.50
10½	21.50	13.50	11.06	9.99	9.45	9.15	8.99	8.89
11	21.75	13.78	11.37	10.33	9.81	9.53	9.37	9.29
11½	22.00	14.06	11.69	10.67	10.17	9.91	9.77	9.69
12	22.25	14.35	12.01	11.02	10.54	10.29	10.16	10.09
12½	22.50	14.64	12.33	11.37	10.91	10.68	10.56	10.49
13	22.76	14.94	12.66	11.72	11.28	11.07	10.96	10.90
13½	23.01	15.23	12.99	12.08	11.66	11.46	11.36	11.31
14	23.27	15.53	13.32	12.44	12.04	11.85	11.76	11.72
14½	23.53	15.83	13.66	12.80	12.43	12.25	12.17	12.13
15	23.79	16.14	14.00	13.17	12.81	12.65	12.57	12.54
15½	24.06	16.45	14.34	13.54	13.20	13.05	12.98	12.95
16	24.32	16.76	14.69	13.92	13.59	13.45	13.39	13.36
16½	24.59	17.07	15.04	14.29	13.99	13.85	13.80	13.77
17	24.86	17.38	15.39	14.67	14.38	14.26	14.21	14.19
17½	25.13	17.70	15.75	15.05	14.78	14.67	14.62	14.60
18	25.40	18.02	16.11	15.44	15.18	15.08	15.03	15.02
18½	25.67	18.35	16.47	15.82	15.58	15.48	15.45	15.43
19	25.95	18.67	16.83	16.21	15.98	15.89	15.86	15.85
19½	26.22	19.00	17.20	16.60	16.38	16.30	16.27	16.26
20	26.50	19.33	17.57	16.99	16.79	16.72	16.69	16.68
20½	26.78	19.66	17.94	17.39	17.19	17.13	17.10	17.09
21	27.06	20.00	18.31	17.78	17.60	17.54	17.52	17.51
21½	27.34	20.34	18.69	18.18	18.01	17.95	17.93	17.92
22	27.62	20.67	19.06	18.57	18.42	18.36	18.35	18.34
22½	27.91	21.02	19.44	18.97	18.83	18.78	18.76	18.75
23	28.20	21.36	19.82	19.37	19.24	19.19	19.18	19.17
23½	28.48	21.70	20.20	19.78	19.65	19.61	19.59	19.59
24	28.77	22.05	20.59	20.18	20.06	20.02	20.01	20.01
24½	29.06	22.40	20.97	20.58	20.47	20.43	20.42	20.42
25	29.36	22.75	21.36	20.99	20.88	20.85	20.84	20.84

per month on a $50,000 loan) and adds another 60 months of payments at $464.50 per month. As a practical matter, amortized real estate loans are seldom made for more than 30 years.

The **budget mortgage** takes the amortized loan one step further. In addition to collecting the monthly principal and interest payment (often called P + I), the lender collects one-twelfth of the estimated cost of the annual property taxes and hazard insurance on the mortgaged property. The money for tax and insurance payments is placed in an **impound account** (also called an **escrow** or **reserve account**). When taxes and insurance payments are due, the lender pays them. Thus, the lender makes certain that the value of the mortgaged property will not be undermined by unpaid property taxes or by uninsured fire or weather damage. This form of mortgage also helps the borrower to budget for property taxes and insurance on a monthly basis. To illustrate, if insurance is $240 per year and property taxes are $1,800 per year, the lender collects an additional $20 and $150 each month along with the regular principal and interest payments. This combined principal, interest, taxes, and insurance payment is often referred to as a **PITI payment.**

BUDGET MORTGAGE

A **balloon loan** is any loan which has a final payment larger than any of the previous payments on the loan. The final payment is called a **balloon payment.** The term loan described at the beginning of this chapter is a type of balloon loan. Partially amortized loans, discussed next, are also a type of balloon loan. In tight money markets, the use of balloon loans increased considerably. Balloon loans with maturities as short as 3 to 5 years were commonplace. This arrangement gives the buyer (borrower) 3 to 5 years to find cheaper and longer-term financing elsewhere. If such financing does not materialize and the loan is not repaid on time, the lender has the right to foreclose. The alternative is for the lender and borrower to agree to an extension of the loan, usually at prevailing interest rates.

BALLOON LOAN

When the repayment schedule of a loan calls for a series of amortized payments followed by a balloon payment at maturity, it is called a **partially amortized loan.** For example, a lender might agree to a 30-year amortization schedule with a provision that at the end of the tenth year all the remaining principal be

PARTIALLY AMORTIZED LOAN

paid in a single balloon payment. The advantage to the borrower is that for 10 years the monthly payments will be smaller than if the loan was completely amortized in 10 years. (You can verify this in Table 11:1.) However, the disadvantage is that the balloon payment due at the end of the tenth year might be the borrower's financial downfall. Just how large that balloon payment will be can be determined in advance by using a **loan balance table** (also called a **remaining balance table**). Presuming an interest rate of 11½% and a 30-year loan, at the end of 10 years the loan balance table in Table 11:2 shows that for each $1,000 originally loaned, $929 would still be owed. If the original loan was for $100,000, at the end of 10 years 100 × $929 = $92,900 would be due as one payment. This qualifies it as a balloon loan.

As you can see from this example, when an amortized loan has a long maturity, relatively little of the debt is paid off during the initial years of the loan's life. Nearly all the early payments go for interest, so that little remains for principal reduction. For example, Table 11:2 shows that even after 16 years of payments on a 30-year, 11½% loan, 82½% of the loan is still unpaid. Not until this loan is about 6 years from maturity will half of it have been repaid.

EARLIER PAYOFF

During the late 1970s when inflation rates exceeded interest rates, the popular philosophy was to borrow as much as possible for as long as possible. Then in the early 1980s inflation rates dropped below interest rates and the opposite philosophy became attractive to many borrowers. This was especially true for those who had borrowed (or were contemplating borrowing) at double-digit interest rates. Let us use as an example an $80,000 loan at 11½% interest. If the loan has a maturity of 30 years, from Table 11:1 we can determine the monthly payments to be $792.80. (Follow this example on your own.)

15-Year Loan

Suppose the maturity of the above loan is changed from 30 to 15 years. Looking at Table 11:1, the monthly payments will now be $935.20. This is $142.40 more per month, but the loan is fully paid in 15 years, not 30 years. The total amount of interest paid on the 15-year loan is (15 × 12 × $935.20) – $80,000 = $88,336. The total amount of interest paid on the 30-year loan is (30 × 12 × $792.80) – $80,000 = $205,408. Thus, for an extra $142.40 per month

Table 11:2. Balance Owing on a $1,000 Amortized Loan

9½% Annual Interest							11½% Annual Interest						
Age of Loan	**Original Life** (years)						**Age of Loan**	**Original Life** (years)					
(years)	**10**	**15**	**20**	**25**	**30**	**35**	*(years)*	**10**	**15**	**20**	**25**	**30**	**35**
2	$868	$934	$963	$978	$987	$992	2	$880	$944	$971	$984	$991	$995
4	708	853	918	952	971	983	4	729	873	935	965	981	989
6	515	756	864	921	953	971	6	539	784	889	940	967	982
8	282	639	799	883	930	957	8	300	672	831	909	950	972
10		497	720	837	902	940	10		531	759	870	929	960
12		326	625	781	869	920	12		354	667	821	902	945
14		119	510	714	828	896	14		132	553	759	868	926
16			371	633	780	866	16			409	682	825	903
18			203	535	721	830	18			228	585	772	873
20				416	650	787	20				462	704	836
22				273	564	735	22				308	620	789
24				100	460	671	24				115	513	729
26					335	595	26					380	655
28					183	503	28					211	561
30						391	30						444
32						256	32						296
34						94	34						110

for 180 months (which amounts to $25,632) the borrower saves the difference between $205,408 and $88,336 (which is $117,072). Many borrowers consider this a very good return on their money. (It is, in fact, an 11½% compounded rate of return.) Lenders are more receptive to making fixed-rate loans for 15 years than for 30 years. This is because the lender is locked into the loan for 15 years, not 30 years. As a result, a lender is usually willing to offer a 15-year loan at a lower rate of interest than a 30-year loan. In view of these benefits to borrower and lender alike, the 15-year loan is becoming a popular home financing tool.

Biweekly Payments

A small but growing number of lenders offer a biweekly repayment plan. The loan is amortized as if it were going to last 30 years. But instead of paying once a month, the borrower makes one-half the monthly payment every two weeks. This may not sound like much of a difference but the results are eye-opening. Assume you borrow $100,000 at 13% interest, paying (see Table

11:1) $1,107 per month. You will retire the loan in 30 years at a cost of $298,520 in interest. If you decide to pay half of $1,107 every two weeks, the loan will be fully paid in just 18 years and will have cost you $160,023 in interest. This happens because biweekly compounding works in your favor and because you make 26 half-size payments a year, not 24.

Existing Loans   Borrowers with existing loans who want to celebrate with an early mortgage burning, can simply add a few dollars each month to the required monthly payment. This can be particularly beneficial for people who borrowed at rates of 13%, 14%, and 15% or more. In effect, whatever extra amount is added to the monthly payment will "earn" interest at the loan's interest rate. Thus, if a loan has a 14% rate, early payments "earn" at 14%. If the borrower has no alternative places to invest that will yield 14%, then a few additional dollars each month will work miracles. For example, a 30-year, $100,000 loan at 14% interest requires monthly payments (see Table 11:1) of $1,185. Voluntarily adding an extra $19 per month will reduce the maturity (payoff) date from 30 years to 25 years (see Table 11:1 again). If an extra $40 is added to the $19, the maturity date shrinks to 20 years. In other words, an extra $59 per month eliminates 10 years of payments.

You may be wondering why this has not been a popular idea with borrowers. There are two key reasons. First, there was a time in 1979 when inflation was 18% per year and 14% to borrow looked cheap by comparison. Second, when interest rates are around 6% and 7% (as they were in the 1960 decade), the mathematics of early payoff are not as impressive.

LOAN-TO-VALUE
RATIO   The relationship between the amount of money a lender is willing to loan and the lender's estimate of the market value of the property that will serve as security is called the **loan-to-value ratio** (often abbreviated **L/V ratio**). For example, a prospective home buyer wants to purchase a house priced at $80,000. A local lender appraises the house, finds it has a market value of $80,000, and agrees to make an 80% L/V loan. This means that the lender will loan up to 80% of the $80,000 and the buyer must provide at least 20% in cash. In dollars, the lender will loan up to $64,000 and the buyer must make a cash down payment of at least $16,000. If the lender appraises the home for

more than $80,000 the loan will still be $64,000. If the appraisal is for less than $80,000 the loan will be 80% of the appraised value, and the buyer must pay the balance in cash. The rule is that price or value, whichever is lower, is applied to the L/V ratio. This rule exists to prevent the lender from overlending on a property just because the borrower overpaid for it.

EQUITY

The difference between the market value of a property and the debt owed against it is called the owner's **equity.** On a newly purchased $80,000 home with a $16,000 cash down payment, the buyer's equity is $16,000. As the value of the property rises or falls and as the mortgage loan is paid down, the equity changes. For example, if the value of the home rises to $90,000 and the loan is paid down to $62,000, the owner's equity will be $28,000. If the owner completely repays the loan so that there is no debt against the home, the owner's equity is equal to the market value of the property.

LOAN POINTS

Probably no single term in real estate finance causes as much confusion and consternation as the word **points.** In finance, the word **point** means one percent of the loan amount. Thus, on a $60,000 loan, one point is $600. On a $40,000 loan, three points is $1,200. On a $100,000 loan, eight points is $8,000.

The use of points in real estate mortgage finance can be split into two categories: (1) loan origination fees expressed in terms of points, and (2) the use of points to change the effective yield of a mortgage loan to a lender. Let us look at these two uses in more detail.

Origination Fee

When a borrower asks for a mortgage loan, the lender incurs a number of expenses, including such things as the time its loan officer spends interviewing the borrower, office overhead, the purchase and review of credit reports on the borrower, an on-site appraisal of the property to be mortgaged, title searches and review, legal and recording fees, and so on. For these, some lenders make an itemized billing, charging so many dollars for the appraisal, credit report, title search, and so on. The total becomes the **loan origination fee,** which the borrower pays to get his loan. Other lenders do not make an itemized bill, but instead simply state the origination fee in terms of a percentage of the loan amount, for example, one point. Thus, a lender quoting a loan origination fee of one point is saying that, for a $65,000 loan, its fee to originate the loan will be $650.

Discount Points   Points charged to raise the lender's monetary return on a loan are known as **discount points.** A simplified example will illustrate their use and effect. If you are a lender and agree to make a term loan of $100 to a borrower for 1 year at 10% interest, you would normally expect to give the borrower $100 now (disregard loan origination fees for a moment), and 1 year later the borrower would give you $110. In percentage terms, the **effective yield** on your loan is 10% per annum (year) because you received $10 for your 1-year, $100 loan. Now suppose that instead of handing the borrower $100, you handed him $99 but still required him to repay $100 plus $10 in interest at the end of the year. This is a discount of one point ($1 in this case), and the borrower paid it out of his loan funds. The effect of this financial maneuver is to raise the effective yield (yield to maturity) to you without raising the interest rate itself. Therefore, if you loan out $99 and receive $110 at the end of the year, you effectively have a return of $11 for a $99 loan. This gives you an effective yield of $11 ÷ $99 or 11.1%, rather than 10%.

Calculating the effective yield on a discounted 20- or 30-year mortgage loan is more difficult because the amount owed drops over the life of the loan, and because the majority are paid in full ahead of schedule due to refinancing. Computers and calculators usually make these calculations; however, a useful rule of thumb states that on the typical home loan each point of discount raises the effective yield by ⅛ of 1%. Thus, four discount points would raise the effective yield by approximately ½ of 1% and eight points would raise it by 1%. Discount points are most often charged during periods of **tight money,** that is, when mortgage money is in short supply. During periods of **loose money**, when lenders have adequate funds to lend and are actively seeking borrowers, discount points disappear.

FHA INSURANCE   The Great Depression caused a major change in the attitude of
PROGRAMS   the federal government toward home financing in the United States. In 1934, one year after the Home Owners Loan Corporation was established, Congress passed the National Housing Act. The act's most far-reaching provision was to establish the Federal Housing Administration (FHA) for the purpose of en-

couraging new construction as a means of creating jobs. To accomplish this goal, the FHA offered to insure lenders against losses due to nonrepayment when they made loans on both new and existing homes. In turn, the lender had to grant 20-year fully amortized loans with loan-to-value ratios of 80% rather than the 3- to 5-year, 50% to 60% term loans common up to that time.

The FHA did its best to keep from becoming a burden to the American taxpayer. When a prospective borrower approached a lender for an FHA-secured home loan, the FHA reviewed the borrower's income, expenses, assets, and debts. The objective was to determine if there was adequate room in the borrower's budget for the proposed loan payments. The FHA also sent inspectors to the property to make certain that it was of acceptable construction quality and to determine its fair market value. To offset losses that would still inevitably occur, the FHA charged the borrower an annual insurance fee of approximately ½ of 1% of the balance owed on his loan. The FHA was immensely successful in its task. Not only did it create construction jobs, but it raised the level of housing quality in the nation and, in a pleasant surprise to taxpayers, actually returned annual profits to the U.S. Treasury. In response to its success, in 1946 Congress changed its status from temporary to permanent.

The FHA has had a marked influence on lending policies in the real estate industry. Foremost among these is the widespread acceptance of the high loan-to-value, fully amortized loan. In the 1930s, lenders required FHA insurance before making 80% L/V loans. By the 1960s, lenders were readily making 80% L/V loans without FHA insurance. Meanwhile, the FHA insurance program was working so well that the FHA raised the portion it was willing to insure. In 1990, Congress established a new maximum loan-to-value ratio by passing the **Omnibus Budget Reconciliation Act** (OBRA). The OBRA calculation does not include closing costs, but the maximum L/V ratio is 98.75% for houses with a sales price of less than $50,000, and 97.75% for houses with a sales price in excess of $50,000. FHA now insures a lender for the lesser of: (1) the OBRA value or (2) the "old rule," which is 97% of the appraised value up to an appraised value of $50,000. If the property's appraised value exceeds $50,000, FHA insures 97% of the first $25,000 plus 95% of the balance of its appraised value. Utilizing the new OBRA calculations, 57% of

Current FHA Coverage

the good faith estimate of closing costs can be included in calculating the loan amount. To illustrate, on a $60,000 home the FHA would insure 97% of the first $25,000 and 95% of the remaining $35,000, for a total of $57,500. This means a cash down payment of only $2,500 for the buyer. The borrower is not permitted to use a second mortgage to raise this $2,500. The FHA requires some down payment; otherwise, it would be too easy for the borrower to walk away from the debt and leave the FHA to pay the lender's insurance claim. Please be aware that the maximum amount the FHA will insure varies from city to city and is changed from time to time by the FHA. As of 1992, the maximum loan amount in high cost areas is $124,895.

After December 15, 1989, private investors were banned from the FHA single-family program. In addition, no single-family loans originating on or after December 15, 1989 can be assumed by investors. Any loan made before December 15, 1989 may be assumed by an investor, but additional restrictions have to be met: (i) the balance due must be no more than 75% of the cost of the property; and (ii) if the monthly mortgage payment exceeds the net rental income, the mortgage amount must be reduced so that its payment does not exceed the amount amortized by the net rental income.

Assumability

Traditionally, FHA loans were popular because the 30-year fixed-rate loans could be assumed without any increase in interest. This is still true for loans which were originated prior to December 1, 1986. The assumption procedure can be one of two types, a simple assumption or a formal assumption. In the **simple assumption** procedure, the property is sold and the loan is assumed by the buyer without notification to the FHA or its agent. The seller remains fully liable to the FHA for full repayment. In the **formal assumption,** the property is not conveyed to a new buyer until the new buyer's credit worthiness has been approved by the FHA or its agent. When the credit worthy buyer assumes the loan, the seller may obtain a full release of liability from the FHA.

If the FHA loan was originated between December 1, 1986 and December 15, 1989, the owner-occupant cannot sell the property with a loan assumption during the first 12 months after execution of the mortgage without credit worthiness approval for each person who assumes the loan. If the seller is an investor, the assumption cannot be made without prior approval during the first 24 months after execution of the mortgage. Failure to comply with either requirement results in an acceleration of the loan balance. After the one- or two-year loan period, the loan can be assumed without approval. If the assumption is a simple assumption, the seller remains fully liable for five years after the new mortgage is executed. If the loan is not in default after the five years, the seller is automatically released from liability.

If the loan was originated after December 15, 1989, the FHA requires the credit worthiness approval prior to the conveyance of title on all assumption loans. If the borrower assumes a mortgage loan, the lender cannot refuse to release the original borrower from liability on the loan.

The major disadvantage of an FHA loan is the relatively low loan limit. The FHA's mission is to serve buyers with limited funds who are looking for modestly priced housing. It is possible to get an FHA loan on a more expensive home, but the buyer must make such a large down payment that an FHA loan becomes impractical. You will, however, find existing FHA loans on more expensive homes in the resale market. This is because the loan was written 10 or 20 years ago and the value of the home has risen from modest to expensive since then. Nonetheless, these homes are often eagerly sought by buyers because the existing FHA loan is assumable and may carry an interest rate several percentage points below current market rates. Furthermore, a second mortgage can be used to finance the difference between the existing FHA loan and the buyer's down payment.

Mortgage Insurance

The FHA charges a one-time **Up Front Mortgage Insurance Premium (UFMIP)** that is paid when the loan is made. The amount of the UFMIP is 3.8% of the loan amount (for fiscal years 1991 and 1992, it declines to 3% for fiscal years 1993 and 1994) and can be paid in cash or added to the amount borrowed. If borrowed, it can be over and above the FHA ceiling. Thus, if the ceiling is $90,000 and the loan requested is $90,000, the UFMIP will be $3,420 and the total amount financed will be $93,420. The $93,420 becomes the principal amount of the loan and an amortization table is used to find the monthly payment. If the loan is fully repaid within 11 years, the borrower is entitled to a refund of part of the UFMIP. After 11 years, there may be a partial refund depending on loan loss experience for the pool of loans that contains the borrower's particular loan.

The FHA now also charges a new annual premium amounting to ½ of 1% of the annual loan balance. One-twelfth of the annual premium is added to the monthly payment and must be included in the proposed monthly housing expense to qualify for the borrower's income. The amount is calculated each year on the unpaid principal balance without UFMIP and excluding closing costs. Annual premiums are nonrefundable.

Interest Rate Ceilings

Another major change in the way the FHA has done business occurred on November 30, 1983. Effective that date, interest rates on FHA loans were freed from government control. Prior to that date the FHA attempted to hold down interest rates by setting ceilings on how much a lender could charge. Whereas this might be a reasonably workable approach in times of stable interest rates, it created nightmares for buyers, sellers, lenders, and real estate agents when interest rates spurted upward in the 1970s and early 1980s. What happened was that a seller would put his (or her) home on the market. A buyer would see it and make an acceptable offer subject to obtaining an FHA loan. The FHA would appraise the property, evaluate the borrower, and agree to insure a loan. The FHA limited the number of points a borrower could pay to 1 point for existing homes and 2½ points for homes under construction. These were usually consumed by loan origination costs. The FHA required the seller to pay any additional points.

With only two exceptions since 1950, the FHA ceiling was below the prevailing rates on **conventional loans,** i.e., loans not insured by the FHA or guaranteed by the Department of Veterans Affairs (VA). When the FHA ceiling was below the market rate on conventional loans, lenders would not make FHA loans unless they were paid discount points. For example, if the open market rate was 12½% and the FHA ceiling was 12%, it was necessary to offer the lender enough discount points to raise the effective yield of the 12% FHA loan to 12½%. This amounted to 4 points. But since the buyer was limited to 1 point and that was used for origination costs, the 4 points came from the seller's pocket. Suppose the loan amount was $60,000. This amounted to $2,400 in points the seller would have to pay so the buyer could enjoy the privilege of obtaining a loan with an interest rate ½ of 1% below the market.

Seller's Position

By placing yourself in the seller's position, you can see the situation this creates. A buyer making an offer under the above conditions is in effect asking you to take a $2,400 cut in price. If you were planning on reducing your price $2,400 anyway, you would accept the offer. However, if you felt you could readily sell at your price to a buyer not requiring seller's points, you would refuse the offer. The alternative is to price the property high enough to allow for anticipated points. However, this is an effective solution only if your price does not exceed the FHA appraisal or VA certificate of reasonable value. If it does, the FHA or VA buyer is either prohibited from buying or must make a larger cash down payment.

Buyers, sellers, lenders, and real estate agents can learn to live with the above conditions if interest rates remain fairly stable. But such a system is difficult at best when interest rates change rapidly and/or FHA ceilings change between the date the purchase contract was signed and the day the deed is delivered. Horror stories abound of times when a seller agreed to an FHA sale when the number of points required of the seller was 4 at the time the purchase contract was signed and 8 to 12 by the time the deed was to be delivered. (This would be caused by a market rise without a ceiling increase.) Buyers, meanwhile, would secretly hope the ceiling would not be raised before the closing day.

Floating Interest Rates

Fixed-rate FHA loans are now negotiable and float with the market, and the seller now has a choice in how many points to contribute toward the borrower's loan. This can be none, some, or all the points, and the seller can even pay the borrower's MIP. Typical purchase contract language is, "The seller will pay X points and the buyer will pay not more than Y points and the agreed upon interest rate is Z%." Thus, "X" is the contribution the seller will make, and the seller is protected from having to pay more. The buyer will pay any additional points, but not more than "Y" points. Beyond that, the buyer can cancel the purchase contract. That would happen if the market rates rose quickly while the rate at "Z" is fixed.

Other FHA Programs

Thus far, we have been concentrating on the FHA's most popular program—mortgage insurance on single-family houses. The FHA's authority to offer this is found in **Section 203(b)** of Title II of the National Housing Act. These loans are commonly referred to as "Section 203b" loans. However, the FHA administers a number of other real estate mortgage insurance programs and several of the better known will be mentioned now.

Under **Section 203(k)** the FHA insures mortgage loans made to finance home improvements. Under **Section 234** the FHA insures loans on condominium units in a manner similar to Section 203(b). **Section 213** insures loans for cooperative housing projects. **Section 235** offers a single-family residence loan subsidy program.

Under **Section 245** the FHA will insure a graduated payment mortgage (GPM). This loan format allows the borrower to make smaller payments initially and to increase payment size gradually over time. The idea is to parallel the borrower's rising earning capacity. (GPMs will receive more coverage in Chapter 12.) The FHA also insures adjustable rate mortgage loans with a program started in mid-1984. These are available to owner-occupants under Section 203(b) and 203(k) and carry an interest rate tied to one-year U.S. Treasury securities. The rate can be adjusted up or down by not more than 1% annually or 5% over the life of the loan. Negative amortization—the addition of unpaid interest to the principal balance is prohibited. (Adjustable loans will also receive more attention in Chapter 12.)

Loan Qualification

Before leaving the topic of the FHA it is interesting to note that much of what we take for granted as standard loan practice today was the result of FHA innovation years ago. As already noted, standard real estate loan practice called for short-term renewable loans before 1934. Then the FHA boldly offered 20-year amortized loans. Once these were shown to be successful investments for lenders, loans without FHA insurance were made for 20 years. Later, when the FHA successfully went to 30 years, non-FHA-insured loans followed. The FHA also established loan application review techniques that have been widely accepted and copied throughout the real estate industry. The biggest step in this direction was to analyze a borrower's loan application in terms of his earning power. Prior to 1934, emphasis had been placed on how large the borrower's assets were, a measurement that tended to exclude all but the already financially well-to-do from home ownership. Since 1934, the emphasis has shifted primarily to the borrower's ability to meet monthly PITI payments. The rule of thumb today is that no more than 38% of a person's before-tax monthly income should go to the repayment of fixed monthly obligations, including monthly PITI payments.

Since its inception, the FHA has imposed its own minimum construction requirements. Often this was essential where local building codes did not exist or were weaker than the FHA wanted. Before issuing a loan, particularly on new construction, the FHA would impose minimum requirements as to the quantity and quality of building materials to be used. Lot size, street access, landscaping, siting, and general house design also were required to fit within broad FHA guidelines. During construction, an FHA inspector would come to the property several times to check on whether or not work was being done correctly.

Construction Regulations

The reason for such care in building standards was that the FHA recognized that if a building is defective either from a design or construction standpoint, the borrower is more likely to default on the loan and create an insurance claim against the FHA. Furthermore, the same defects will lower the price the property will bring at its foreclosure sale, thus increasing losses to the FHA. Because building codes are now becoming stricter and more standardized in states, counties, and cities, the FHA anticipates eliminating its own minimum property standards.

As we leave the FHA and go to the Department of Veterans Affairs, keep in mind that the FHA is not a lender. The FHA is an insurance agency. The loan itself is obtained from a savings and loan, bank, mortgage company, or similar lender. In addition to principal and interest payments, the lender collects an insurance premium from the borrower which is forwarded to the FHA. The FHA, in turn, guarantees repayment of the loan to the lender. This arrangement makes lenders much more willing to loan to buyers who are putting only 3% to 5% cash down. Thus, when you hear the phrase "FHA loan" in real estate circles, know that it is an FHA-*insured* loan, not a loan from the FHA.

DEPARTMENT OF VETERANS AFFAIRS

In 1944, to show its appreciation to servicemen returning from World War II, Congress passed far-reaching legislation to aid veterans in education, hospitalization, employment training, and housing. In housing, the popularly named G.I. Bill of Rights empowered the comptroller general of the United States to guarantee the repayment of a portion of first mortgage real estate loans made to veterans. For this guarantee, no fee would be charged to the veteran. Rather, the government itself would stand the losses. On March 15, 1989 the Veterans Administration was elevated to Cabinet level and now is officially called the Department of Veterans Affairs ("VA").

No Down Payment

The original 1944 law provided that lenders would be guaranteed against losses up to 50% of the amount of the loan, but in no case more than $2,000. The objective was to make it possible for a veteran to buy a home with no cash down payment. Thus, on a house offered for sale at $5,000 (houses were much cheaper in 1944) this guarantee enabled a veteran to borrow the entire $5,000. From the lender's standpoint, having the top $2,000 of the loan guaranteed by the U.S. government offered the same asset protection as a $2,000 cash down payment. If the veteran defaulted and the property went into foreclosure, the lender had to net less than $3,000 before suffering a loss.

In 1945, Congress increased the guarantee amount to $4,000 and 60% of the loan and turned the entire operation over to the Veterans Administration (predecessor in interest to the VA). The VA was quick to honor claims, and the program rapidly became popular with lenders. Furthermore, the veterans turned out to be excellent credit risks, bettering, in fact, the good record of FHA-insured homeowners. The FHA recognizes this and gives higher insurance limits to FHA borrowers who have served in the Armed Forces.

To keep up with the increased cost of homes, the guarantee has been increased several times. Since February 1, 1988 the VA has used the sliding scale system for calculating the applicable guarantee amounts. The guarantee increases with the amount of the loan using fixed dollar amounts and percentages of loan amounts. These current limits have been in effect since December of 1989:

Loan Amount	Guarantee
Up to $45,000	50% of the Loan Amount
$45,001 to $56,250	$22,500
$56,251 to $90,000	40% of the Loan Amount
$90,001 to $144,000	$36,000
$144,001 to $184,000	25% of the Loan Amount
$184,001 and higher	$46,000

Some lenders will go higher if the borrower makes a down payment.

In the original G.I. Bill of 1944, eligibility was limited to World War II veterans. However, subsequent legislation has broadened eligibility to include any veteran who served for a period of at least 90 days in the armed forces of the United States, or an ally, between September 16, 1940, and July 25, 1947, or between June 27, 1950, and January 31, 1955. Any veteran of the United States who has served at least 181 days of continuous active duty since January 31, 1955 to the present is also eligible. If service was during the Viet Nam conflict period (August 5, 1964 to May 7, 1975) or the Persian Gulf War, 90 days is sufficient to qualify. The veteran's discharge must be on conditions other than dishonorable and the guarantee entitlement is good until used. If not remarried, the spouse of a veteran who died as a result of service can also obtain a housing guarantee. Active duty personnel can also qualify. Shorter active duty periods are allowed for service-connected disabilities.

To determine benefits, a veteran should make application to the Department of Veterans Affairs for a **certificate of eligibility.** This shows whether or not the veteran is qualified and the amount of guarantee available. It is also one of the documents necessary to obtain a VA-guaranteed loan.

VA Certificates

The VA works diligently to protect veterans and reduce foreclosure losses. When a veteran applies for a VA guarantee, the property is appraised and the VA issues a **certificate of reasonable value.** Often abbreviated **CRV,** it reflects the estimated value of the property as determined by the VA staff appraiser. Similarly, the VA establishes income guidelines to make certain that the veteran can comfortably meet the proposed loan payments. Also, the veteran must agree to occupy the property. Pursuant to the newly enacted Safe Drinking Water Act, if the building was constructed after June 19, 1988, the CRV must now reflect a certification that any solders or fluxes used in construction did not contain more than 0.2% lead in any pipes, or that pipe fittings used did not contain more than 8% lead.

The VA will guarantee fixed-rate loans for as long as 30 years on homes, and there is no prepayment penalty if the borrower wishes to pay sooner. Moreover, there is no due-on-sale clause that requires the loan to be repaid if the property is sold. The VA will guarantee loans for the purchase of town-houses and condominiums, to build or improve a home and to buy a mobile home as a residence. A veteran wishing to refinance his existing home or farm can obtain a VA-guaranteed loan provided there is existing debt that will be repaid. The VA will also make direct loans to veterans if there are no private lending institutions nearby.

Financial Liability   No matter what loan guarantee program is elected, the veteran should know that in the event of default and subsequent fore-closure he is required to eventually make good any losses suffered by the VA on his loan. (This is not the case with FHA-insured loans. There the borrower pays for protection against foreclosure losses that may result from his loan.) Even if the veteran sells the property and the buyer assumes the VA loan, the veteran is still financially responsible if the buyer later defaults. To avoid this, the veteran must arrange with the VA to be released from liability. If the VA loan was underwritten after March 1, 1988, Congress created a new Guarantee and Indemnity Fund which allows a release from liability to the VA in the event of foreclosure provided that it meets the following requirements:

1. The loan payments must be current;
2. The prospective purchasers must meet credit worthiness standards as required by the VA; and
3. The prospective purchaser must assume full liability for repayment of the loan, including indemnity liability to the VA.

In the event borrowers are unable to make their mortgage payments, the VA offers an assistance procedure which may be helpful in declining markets. If the borrower can obtain a purchase offer that is insufficient to sell his property and to pay off the existing loan balance, a **compromise agreement** may allow the VA to pay the difference between the sales proceeds and the mortgage balance. To effect the compromise agreement, the borrower must be willing to find a purchaser who will pay fair market value of the house and the original borrower must agree to remain liable to the government for the amount that the VA pays to the noteholder.

A veteran is permitted a full new guarantee entitlement if complete repayment of a previous VA-guaranteed loan has been made. If a veteran has sold and let the buyer assume his VA loan, the balance of the entitlement is still available. For example, if a veteran has used $15,000 of his (her) entitlement to date, the difference between $15,000 and the current VA guarantee amount is still available for use.

Funding Fee

From its inception until October 1, 1982, the VA made loan guarantees on behalf of veterans without a charge. Starting on that date a ½ of 1% fee was charged at the time of loan funding. In 1991, a **funding fee** was increased to 1⅞% of the loan amount for loans with less than 5% down; 1⅜% of the loan amount for loans with at least 5% down but less than 10% down; and 1⅛% of the loan amount for loans with 10% or more down. A major reason has been loan losses. Until the beginning of the 1980s, increasing real estate prices coupled with good repayment records of veterans enabled the VA to avoid any sizable losses. But the situation has changed, and by 1988 the VA had thousands of homes that it had to take from lenders because veterans had stopped making payments. The VA has been selling these through price reductions and attractive financing to anyone willing to buy who can make the payments. (The FHA also offers foreclosed properties for sale.)

As of 1991, the VA still sets interest rate ceilings on the loans it will guarantee. This is nearly the same system that the FHA used until November 30, 1983 at which time the FHA switched to floating rates. If floating rates work well for the FHA, the VA will probably adopt the idea.

Assumption Requirements

On VA loans assumed prior to March 1, 1988, there was no requirement for approval prior to loan assumption. Therefore, the seller could sell their property on assumption without obtaining any approval from the VA, but the seller remained fully liable for its repayment. As stated previously, they could be released from liability if the VA approved the credit worthiness of the new purchaser. After March 1, 1988, the VA required prior approval by the VA for transfer of the property. Federal law now requires that the mortgage or deed of trust and note for loans carry on the first page in type two and one-half times larger than the regular type the following statement:

> THIS LOAN IS NOT ASSUMABLE WITH-OUT THE PRIOR APPROVAL OF THE DEPARTMENT OF VETERANS AFFAIRS OR AUTHORIZED AGENT.

Since Congress frequently changes eligibility and benefits, a person contemplating a VA or FHA loan should make inquiry to the field offices of these two agencies and to mortgage lenders to ascertain the current status and details of the law, as well as the availability of loan money. Field offices also have information on foreclosed properties that are for sale. Additionally, one should query lenders as to the availability of state veteran benefits. A number of states offer special advantages, including mortgage loan assistance, to residents who have served in the armed forces.

PRIVATE MORTGAGE INSURANCE

In 1957, the Mortgage Guaranty Insurance Corporation (MGIC) was formed in Milwaukee, Wisconsin, as a privately owned business venture to insure home mortgage loans. Demand was slow but steady for the first 10 years but then grew rapidly and today there are over a dozen private mortgage insurance companies. Like FHA insurance, the object of **private mortgage insurance (PMI)** is to insure lenders against foreclosure losses. But unlike the FHA, PMI insures only the top 20% to 25% of a loan, not the whole loan. This allows a lender to make 90% and 95% L/V loans with about the same exposure to foreclosure losses as a 70% to 75% L/V loan. The borrower, meanwhile, can purchase a home with a cash down payment of either 10% or 5% rather than the 20% to 30% down required by lenders when mortgage insurance is not purchased. For this privilege the borrower pays a PMI fee of 1% or less when the loan is made plus an annual fee of a fraction of 1%. When the loan is partially repaid (for example, to a 70% L/V), the premiums and coverage can be terminated. PMI is also available on apartment buildings, offices, stores, warehouses, and leaseholds but at higher rates than on homes.

The **Farmer's Home Administration (FmHA)** is a federal agency under the U.S. Department of Agriculture. Like the FHA, it came into existence due to the financial crises of the 1930s. The FmHA offers programs to help purchase or operate farms. The FmHA will either guarantee a portion of a loan made by a private lender or it will make the loan itself. FmHA loans can also be used to help finance the purchase of homes in rural areas.

FARMER'S HOME ADMINISTRATION

The **Federal Consumer Credit Protection Act,** popularly known as the **Truth in Lending Act,** went into effect in 1969. The Act, implemented by Federal Reserve Board **Regulation Z,** requires that a borrower be clearly shown how much he is paying for credit in both dollar terms and percentage terms before committing to the loan. The borrower is also given the right to rescind (cancel) the transaction in certain instances. The act came into being because it was not uncommon to see loans advertised for rates lower than the borrower actually wound up paying. Once the Act took effect, several weaknesses and ambiguities of the Act and Regulation Z became apparent. Thus, the **Truth in Lending Simplification and Reform Act** (TILSRA) was passed by Congress and became effective October 1, 1982. Concurrently, the Federal Reserve Board issued a **Revised Regulation Z** (RRZ) which details rules and regulations for TILSRA. For purposes of discussion we will refer to all of this as the Truth in Lending Act, or TIL.

TRUTH IN LENDING ACT

Whether you are a real estate agent or a property owner acting on your own behalf, TIL rules affect you when you advertise just about anything (including real estate) and include financing terms in the ad. If an advertisement contains any one of the TIL list of financing terms (called **trigger terms** and explained below), the ad must also include other required information. For example, an advertisement that reads: "Bargain! Bargain! Bargain! New 3-bedroom townhouses only $499 per month" may or may not be a bargain depending on other financing information missing from the ad.

Advertising

Trigger Terms   If an ad contains any of the following trigger terms, five specific disclosures must be included in the ad. Here are the trigger terms: the amount of down payment (for example, only 5% down, 10% down, $4,995 down, 95% financing); the amount of any payment (for example, monthly payments only $499, buy for less than $650 a month, payments only 1% per month); the number of payments (for example, only 36 monthly payments and you own it, all paid up in 10 annual payments); the period of repayment (for example, 30-year financing, owner will carry for five years, 10-year second available); and the dollar amount of any finance charge (finance this for only $999) or the statement that there is no charge for credit (pay no interest for three years).

If any of the above trigger terms is used, then the following five disclosures must appear in the ad. They are (1) the cash price or the amount of the loan; (2) the amount of down payment or a statement that none is required; (3) the number, amount, and frequency of repayments; (4) the annual percentage rate; and (5) the deferred payment price or total payments. Item 5 is not a requirement in the case of the sale of a dwelling or a loan secured by a first lien on the dwelling that is being purchased.

Annual Percentage Rate   The **annual percentage rate** (APR) combines the interest rate with the other costs of the loan into a single figure that shows the true annual cost of borrowing. This is one of the most helpful features of the law as it gives the prospective borrower a standardized yardstick by which to compare financing from different sources.

If the annual percentage rate being offered is subject to increase after the transaction takes place (such as with an adjustable rate mortgage), that fact must be stated. For example, "12% annual percentage rate subject to increase after settlement." If the loan has interest rate changes that will follow a predetermined schedule, those terms must be stated. For example, "8% first year, 10% second year, 12% third year, 14% remainder of loan, 13.5% annual percentage rate."

If you wish to say something about financing and avoid triggering full disclosure, you may use general statements. The following would be acceptable: "assumable loan," "financing available," "owner will carry," "terms to fit your budget," "easy monthly payments," or "FHA and VA financing available."

If you are in the business of making loans, the Truth in Lending Act requires you to make 18 disclosures to your borrower. Of these, the four that must be most prominently displayed on the papers the borrower signs are (1) the amount financed, (2) the finance charge, (3) the annual percentage rate and (4) the total payments.

The **amount financed** is the amount of credit provided to the borrower. The **finance charge** is the total dollar amount the credit will cost the borrower over the life of the loan. This includes such things as interest, borrower-paid discount points, loan fees, loan finder's fees, loan service fees, required life insurance, and mortgage guarantee premiums. On a long-term mortgage loan, the total finance charge can easily exceed the amount of money being borrowed. For example, the total amount of interest on an 11%, 30-year, $60,000 loan is just over $145,000.

The annual percentage rate was just described. The **total payments** is the amount in dollars the borrower will have paid after making all the payments as scheduled. In the previous 11%, 30-year loan it would be the interest of $145,000 plus the principal of $60,000 for a total of $205,000.

The other 14 disclosures that a lender must make are as follows: (1) the identity of the lender; (2) the payment schedule; (3) prepayment penalties and rebates; (4) late payment charges; (5) any insurance required; (6) any filing fees; (7) any collateral required; (8) any required deposits; (9) whether or not the loan can be assumed; (10) the demand feature, if the note has one; (11) the total sales price of the item being purchased if the seller is also the creditor; (12) any adjustable rate features of the loan; (13) an itemization of the amount financed; and (14) a reference to any terms not shown on the disclosure statement but which are shown on the loan contract.

These disclosures must be delivered or mailed to the credit applicant within three business days after the creditor receives the applicant's written request for credit. The applicant must have this information before the transaction can take place, e.g., before the closing.

Any person or firm that regularly extends consumer credit subject to a finance charge (such as interest) or payable by written agreement in more than four installments must comply with the lending disclosures. This includes banks, savings and loans, credit unions, finance companies, etc., as well as private individuals who extend credit more than five times a year.

Whoever is named on the note as the creditor must make the lending disclosures even if the note is to be resold. A key difference between the old and the new TIL acts is that the new TIL act does not include mortgage brokers or real estate agents as creditors just because they brokered a deal containing financing. This is because they do not appear as creditors on the note. But if a broker takes back a note for part of the commission on a deal, that is the extension of credit and the lending disclosures must be made.

Exempt Transactions   Certain transactions are exempt from the lending disclosure requirement. The first exemption is for credit extended primarily for business, commercial, or agricultural purposes. This exemption includes dwelling units purchased for rental purposes (unless the property contains four or less units and the owner occupies one of them, in which case special rules apply).

The second exemption applies to credit over $25,000 secured by personal property unless the property is the principal residence of the borrower. For example, a mobile home that secures a loan over $25,000 qualifies under this exemption if it is used as a vacation home. But it is not exempt if it is used as a principal residence.

Failure to Disclose   If the Federal Trade Commission (FTC) determines that an advertiser has broken the law, the FTC can order the advertiser to cease from further violations. Each violation of that order can result in a $10,000 civil penalty each day the violation continues.

Failure to properly disclose when credit is extended can result in a penalty of twice the amount of the finance charge with a minimum of $100 and a maximum of $1,000 plus court costs, attorney fees, and actual damages. In addition, the FTC can add a fine of up to $5,000 and/or one year imprisonment. If the required disclosures are not made or the borrower is not given the required 3 days to cancel (see below), the borrower can cancel the transaction at any time within 3 years following the date of the transaction. In that event the creditor must return all money paid by the borrower, and the borrower returns the property to the creditor.

Figure 11:3.   Uniform Residential Loan Application

This application is designed to be completed by the Borrower(s) with the Lender's assistance. The Co-Borrower Section and all other Co-Borrower questions must be completed and the appropriate box(es) checked if ☐ another person will be jointly obligated with the Borrower on the loan, or ☐ the Borrower is relying on income from alimony, child support or separate maintenance or on the income or assets of another person as a basis for repayment of the loan, or ☐ the Borrower is married and resides in, or the property is located in, a community property state.

I.   TYPE OF MORTGAGE AND TERMS OF LOAN

Mortgage Applied for:	☐ VA ☐ Conventional ☐ Other:		Agency Case Number		Lender Case No.	
	☐ FHA ☐ FmHA					

Amount	Interest Rate	No. of Months	Amortization Type:	☐ Fixed Rate ☐ GPM	☐ Other (explain): ☐ ARM (type):
$	%				

II.   PROPERTY INFORMATION AND PURPOSE OF LOAN

Subject Property Address (street, city, state, & zip code)	No. of Units

Legal Description of Subject Property (attach description if necessary)	Year Built

Purpose of Loan	☐ Purchase ☐ Construction ☐ Other (explain):	Property will be: ☐ Primary Residence ☐ Secondary Residence ☐ Investment
	☐ Refinance ☐ Construction-Permanent	

Complete this line if construction or construction-permanent loan.

Year Lot Acquired	Original Cost	Amount Existing Liens	(a) Present Value of Lot	(b) Cost of Improvements	Total (a + b)
	$	$	$	$	$

Complete this line if this is a refinance loan.

Year Acquired	Original Cost	Amount Existing Liens	Purpose of Refinance	Describe Improvements ☐ made ☐ to be made
	$	$		Cost: $

Title will be held in what Name(s)	Manner in which Title will be held	Estate will be held in: ☐ Fee Simple ☐ Leasehold (show expiration date)

Source of Down Payment, Settlement Charges and/or Subordinate Financing (explain)

III.   BORROWER INFORMATION

Borrower | Co-Borrower

Borrower's Name (include Jr. or Sr. if applicable)	Co-Borrower's Name (include Jr. or Sr. if applicable)

Social Security Number	Home Phone (incl. area code)	Age	Yrs. School	Social Security Number	Home Phone (incl. area code)	Age	Yrs. School

☐ Married ☐ Separated ☐ Unmarried (include single, divorced, widowed)	Dependents (not listed by Co-Borrower) no. ___ ages ___	☐ Married ☐ Separated ☐ Unmarried (include single, divorced, widowed)	Dependents (not listed by Borrower) no. ___ ages ___

Present Address (street, city, state, zip code) ☐ Own ☐ Rent ___ No. Yrs.	Present Address (street, city, state, zip code) ☐ Own ☐ Rent ___ No. Yrs.

If residing at present address for less than seven years, complete the following:

Former Address (street, city, state, zip code) ☐ Own ☐ Rent ___ No. Yrs.	Former Address (street, city, state, zip code) ☐ Own ☐ Rent ___ No. Yrs.

Former Address (street, city, state, zip code) ☐ Own ☐ Rent ___ No. Yrs.	Former Address (street, city, state, zip code) ☐ Own ☐ Rent ___ No. Yrs.

IV.   EMPLOYMENT INFORMATION

Borrower | Co-Borrower

Name & Address of Employer ☐ Self Employed	Yrs. on this job	Name & Address of Employer ☐ Self Employed	Yrs. on this job
	Yrs. employed in this line of work/profession		Yrs. employed in this line of work/profession

Position/Title/Type of Business	Business Phone (incl. area code)	Position/Title/Type of Business	Business Phone (incl. area code)

If employed in current position for less than two years or if currently employed in more than one position, complete the following:

Name & Address of Employer ☐ Self Employed	Dates (from - to)	Name & Address of Employer ☐ Self Employed	Dates (from - to)
	Monthly Income $		Monthly Income $

Position/Title/Type of Business	Business Phone (incl. area code)	Position/Title/Type of Business	Business Phone (incl. area code)

Name & Address of Employer ☐ Self Employed	Dates (from - to)	Name & Address of Employer ☐ Self Employed	Dates (from - to)
	Monthly Income $		Monthly Income $

Position/Title/Type of Business	Business Phone (incl. area code)	Position/Title/Type of Business	Business Phone (incl. area code)

V. MONTHLY INCOME AND COMBINED HOUSING EXPENSE INFORMATION

Gross Monthly Income	Borrower	Co-Borrower	Total	Combined Monthly Housing Expense	Present	Proposed
Base Empl. Income *	$	$	$	Rent	$	▓▓▓▓▓▓▓▓
Overtime				First Mortgage (P&I)		$
Bonuses				Other Financing (P&I)		
Commissions				Hazard Insurance		
Dividends/Interest				Real Estate Taxes		
Net Rental Income				Mortgage Insurance		
Other (before completing, see the notice in "describe other income," below)				Homeowner Assn. Dues		
				Other:		
Total	$	$	$	Total	$	$

* Self Employed Borrower(s) may be required to provide additional documentation such as tax returns and financial statements.

Describe Other Income *Notice:* Alimony, child support, or separate maintenance income need not be revealed if the Borrower (B) or Co-Borrower (C) does not choose to have it considered for repaying this loan.

B/C		Monthly Amount
		$

VI. ASSETS AND LIABILITIES

This Statement and any applicable supporting schedules may be completed jointly by both married and unmarried Co-Borrowers if their assets and liabilities are sufficiently joined so that the Statement can be meaningfully and fairly presented on a combined basis; otherwise separate Statements and Schedules are required. If the Co-Borrower section was completed about a spouse, this Statement and supporting schedules must be completed about that spouse also.

Completed ☐ Jointly ☐ Not Jointly

ASSETS Description	Cash or Market Value	Liabilities and Pledged Assets. List the creditor's name, address and account number for all outstanding debts, including automobile loans, revolving charge accounts, real estate loans, alimony, child support, stock pledges, etc. Use continuation sheet, if necessary. Indicate by (*) those liabilities which will be satisfied upon sale of real estate owned or upon refinancing of the subject property.		
		LIABILITIES	**Monthly Payt. & Mos. Left to Pay**	**Unpaid Balance**
Cash deposit toward purchase held by:	$	Name and address of Company	$ Payt./Mos.	$
List checking and savings accounts below				
Name and address of Bank, S&L, or Credit Union				
		Acct. no.		
		Name and address of Company	$ Payt./Mos.	$
Acct. no.	$			
Name and address of Bank, S&L, or Credit Union				
		Acct. no.		
		Name and address of Company	$ Payt./Mos.	$
Acct. no.	$			
Name and address of Bank, S&L, or Credit Union				
		Acct. no.		
		Name and address of Company	$ Payt./Mos.	$
Acct. no.	$			
Name and address of Bank, S&L, or Credit Union				
		Acct. no.		
		Name and address of Company	$ Payt./Mos.	$
Acct. no.	$			
Stocks & Bonds (Company name/number & description)	$			
		Acct. no.		
		Name and address of Company	$ Payt./Mos.	$
Life insurance net cash value	$			
Face amount: $				
Subtotal Liquid Assets	$			
Real estate owned (enter market value from schedule of real estate owned)	$	Acct. no.		
Vested interest in retirement fund	$	Name and address of Company	$ Payt./Mos.	$
Net worth of business(es) owned (attach financial statement)	$			
Automobiles owned (make and year)	$			
		Acct. no.		
		Alimony/Child Support/Separate Maintenance Payments Owed to:	$	▓▓▓▓▓
Other Assets (itemize)	$	Job Related Expense (child care, union dues, etc.)	$	▓▓▓▓▓
		Total Monthly Payments	$	
Total Assets a.	$	Net Worth (a minus b) ▶	$	Total Liabilities b.	$

Schedule of Real Estate Owned (If additional properties are owned, use continuation sheet.)

Property Address (enter S if sold, PS if pending sale or R if rental being held for income)	Type of Property	Present Market Value	Amount of Mortgages & Liens	Gross Rental Income	Mortgage Payments	Insurance, Maintenance, Taxes & Misc.	Net Rental Income
		$	$	$	$	$	$
	Totals $	$	$	$	$	$	$

List any additional names under which credit has previously been received and indicate appropriate creditor name(s) and account number(s):

Alternate Name	Creditor Name	Account Number

VII. DETAILS OF TRANSACTION		VIII. DECLARATIONS	Borrower		Co-Borrower	
			Yes	No	Yes	No
a. Purchase price	$	If you answer "yes" to any questions a through I, please use continuation sheet for explanation.				
b. Alterations, improvements, repairs						
c. Land (if acquired separately)		a. Are there any outstanding judgments against you?	☐	☐	☐	☐
d. Refinance (incl. debts to be paid off)		b. Have you been declared bankrupt within the past 7 years?	☐	☐	☐	☐
e. Estimated prepaid items		c. Have you had property foreclosed upon or given title or deed in lieu thereof in the last 7 years?	☐	☐	☐	☐
f. Estimated closing costs		d. Are you a party to a law suit?	☐	☐	☐	☐
g. PMI, MIP, Funding Fee paid in cash		e. Have you directly or indirectly been obligated on any loan which resulted in foreclosure, transfer of title in lieu of foreclosure, or judgment? (This would include such loans as home mortgage loans, SBA loans, home improvement loans, educational loans, manufactured (mobile) home loans, any mortgage, financial obligation, bond, or loan guarantee. If "Yes," provide details, including date, name and address of Lender, FHA or VA case number, if any, and reasons for the action.)	☐	☐	☐	☐
h. Discount (if Borrower will pay)						
I. Total costs (add items a through h)						
j. Subordinate financing						
k. Borrower's closing costs paid by Seller						
l. Other Credits (explain)		f. Are you presently delinquent or in default on any Federal debt or any other loan, mortgage, financial obligation, bond, or loan guarantee? If "Yes," give details as described in the preceding question.	☐	☐	☐	☐
		g. Are you obligated to pay alimony, child support, or separate maintenance?	☐	☐	☐	☐
m. Loan amount (subtract j, k & l from i) (exclude PMI, MIP, Funding Fee financed)		h. Is any part of the down payment borrowed?	☐	☐	☐	☐
		i. Are you a co-maker or endorser on a note?	☐	☐	☐	☐
n. PMI, MIP, Funding Fee financed		j. Are you a U.S. citizen?	☐	☐	☐	☐
o. Loan amount (add m & n)		k. Are you a permanent resident alien?	☐	☐	☐	☐
p. Cash from/to Borrower (subtract o from i)		l. Do you intend to occupy the property as your primary residence?	☐	☐	☐	☐

IX. ACKNOWLEDGMENT AND AGREEMENT

The undersigned specifically acknowledge(s) and agree(s) that: (1) the loan requested by this application will be secured by a first mortgage or deed of trust on the property described herein; (2) the property will not be used for any illegal or prohibited purpose or use; (3) all statements made in this application are made for the purpose of obtaining the loan indicated herein; (4) occupation of the property will be as indicated above; (5) verification or reverification of any information contained in the application may be made at any time by the Lender, its agents, successors and assigns, either directly or through a credit reporting agency, from any source named in this application, and the original copy of this application will be retained by the Lender, even if the loan is not approved; (6) the Lender, its agents, successors and assigns will rely on the information contained in the application and I/we have a continuing obligation to amend and/or supplement the information provided in this application if any of the material facts which I/we have represented herein should change prior to closing; (7) in the event my/our payments on the loan indicated in this application become delinquent, the Lender, its agents, successors and assigns, may, in addition to all their other rights and remedies, report my/our name(s) and account information to a credit reporting agency; (8) ownership of the loan may be transferred to successor or assign of the Lender without notice to me and/or the administration of the loan account may be transferred to an agent, successor or assign of the Lender with prior notice to me; (9) the Lender, its agents, successors and assigns make no representations or warranties, express or implied, to the Borrower(s) regarding the property, the condition of the property, or the value of the property.

Certification: I/We certify that the information provided in this application is true and correct as of the date set forth opposite my/our signature(s) on this application and acknowledge my/our understanding that any intentional or negligent misrepresentation(s) of the information contained in this application may result in civil liability and/or criminal penalties including, but not limited to, fine or imprisonment or both under the provisions of Title 18, United States Code, Section 1001, et seq. and liability for monetary damages to the Lender, its agents, successors and assigns, insurers and any other person who may suffer any loss due to reliance upon any misrepresentation which I/we have made on this application.

Borrower's Signature	Date	Co-Borrower's Signature	Date
X		X	

X. INFORMATION FOR GOVERNMENT MONITORING PURPOSES

The following information is requested by the Federal Government for certain types of loans related to a dwelling, in order to monitor the Lender's compliance with equal credit opportunity, fair housing and home mortgage disclosure laws. You are not required to furnish this information, but are encouraged to do so. The law provides that a Lender may neither discriminate on the basis of this information, nor on whether you choose to furnish it. However, if you choose not to furnish it, under Federal regulations this Lender is required to note race and sex on the basis of visual observation or surname. If you do not wish to furnish the above information, please check the box below. (Lender must review the above material to assure that the disclosures satisfy all requirements to which the Lender is subject under applicable state law for the particular type of loan applied for.)

BORROWER

☐ I do not wish to furnish this information

Race/National Origin: ☐ American Indian or Alaskan Native ☐ Asian or Pacific Islander ☐ Black, not of Hispanic origin ☐ White, not of Hispanic origin ☐ Hispanic

Sex: ☐ Female ☐ Male

CO-BORROWER

☐ I do not wish to furnish this information

Race/National Origin: ☐ American Indian or Alaskan Native ☐ Asian or Pacific Islander ☐ Black, not of Hispanic origin ☐ White, not of Hispanic origin ☐ Hispanic

Sex: ☐ Female ☐ Male

To be Completed by Interviewer	Interviewer's Name (print or type)	Name and Address of Interviewer's Employer
This application was taken by: ☐ face-to-face interview ☐ by mail ☐ by telephone	Interviewer's Signature ___ Date	
	Interviewer's Phone Number (incl. area code)	

Continuation Sheet/Residential Loan Application

Use this continuation sheet if you need more space to complete the Residential Loan Application. Mark B for Borrower or C for Co-Borrower.	Borrower:	Agency Case Number:
	Co-Borrower:	Lender Case Number:

/We fully understand that it is a Federal crime punishable by fine or imprisonment, or both, to knowingly make any false statements concerning any of the above facts as applicable under the provisions of Title 18, United States Code, Section 1001, et seq.

Borrower's Signature:	Date	Co-Borrower's Signature:	Date
X		X	

STATEMENT OF ASSETS AND LIABILITIES

(Supplement to Residential Loan Application)

Name

The following information is provided to complete and become a part of the application for a mortgage in the amount of $

with interest at _____ %, for a term of _____ months and to be secured by property known as:

Subject Property Address (street, city, state, & zip code)

Legal Description of Subject Property (attach description if necessary)

ASSETS AND LIABILITIES

This Statement and any applicable supporting schedules may be completed jointly by both married and unmarried Co-Borrowers if their assets and liabilities are sufficiently joined so that the Statement can be meaningfully and fairly presented on a combined basis; otherwise separate Statements and Schedules are required. If the Co-Borrower section was completed about a spouse, this Statement and supporting schedules must be completed about that spouse also.

Completed [ ] Jointly [ ] Not Jointly

ASSETS Description	Cash or Market Value	Liabilities and Pledged Assets. List the creditor's name, address and account number for all outstanding debts, including automobile loans, revolving charge accounts, real estate loans, alimony, child support, stock pledges, etc. Use continuation sheet, if necessary. Indicate by (*) those liabilities which will be satisfied upon sale of real estate owned or upon refinancing of the subject property.	Monthly Payt. & Mos. Left to Pay	Unpaid Balance
Cash deposit toward purchase held by:	$	LIABILITIES		
		Name and address of Company	$ Payt./Mos.	$
List checking and savings accounts below				
Name and address of Bank, S&L, or Credit Union				
		Acct. no.		
		Name and address of Company	$ Payt./Mos.	$
Acct. no.	$			
Name and address of Bank, S&L, or Credit Union				
		Acct. no.		
		Name and address of Company	$ Payt./Mos.	$
Acct. no.	$			
Name and address of Bank, S&L, or Credit Union				
		Acct. no.		
		Name and address of Company	$ Payt./Mos.	$
Acct. no.	$			
Name and address of Bank, S&L, or Credit Union				
		Acct. no.		
		Name and address of Company	$ Payt./Mos.	$
Acct. no.	$			
Stocks & Bonds (Company name/number & description)	$			
		Acct. no.		
		Name and address of Company	$ Payt./Mos.	$
Life insurance net cash value	$			
Face amount: $				
Subtotal Liquid Assets	$			
Real estate owned (enter market value from schedule of real estate owned)	$	Acct. no.		
Vested interest in retirement fund	$	Name and address of Company	$ Payt./Mos.	$
Net worth of business(es) owned (attach financial statement)	$			
Automobiles owned (make and year)	$			
		Acct. no.		
		Alimony/Child Support/Separate Maintenance Payments Owed to:	$	
Other Assets (itemize)	$	Job Related Expense (child care, union dues, etc.)	$	
		Total Monthly Payments	$	
Total Assets a.	$	Net Worth (a minus b) ➤ $	**Total Liabilities b.**	$

ASSETS AND LIABILITIES (cont.)

Schedule of Real Estate Owned (If additional properties are owned, use continuation sheet.)

Property Address (enter S if sold, PS if pending sale or R if rental being held for income)	Type of Property	Present Market Value	Amount of Mortgages & Liens	Gross Rental Income	Mortgage Payments	Insurance, Maintenance, Taxes & Misc.	Net Rental Income
		$	$	$	$	$	$
	Totals	$	$	$	$	$	$

List any additional names under which credit has previously been received and indicate appropriate creditor name(s) and account number(s):

Alternate Name	Creditor Name	Account Number

ACKNOWLEDGMENT AND AGREEMENT

The undersigned specifically acknowledge(s) and agree(s) that: (1) the loan requested by this application will be secured by a first mortgage or deed of trust on the property described herein; (2) the property will not be used for any illegal or prohibited purpose or use; (3) all statements made in this application are made for the purpose of obtaining the loan indicated herein; (4) occupation of the property will be as indicated above; (5) verification or reverification of any information contained in the application may be made at any time by the Lender, its agents, successors and assigns, either directly or through a credit reporting agency, from any source named in this application, and the original copy of this application will be retained by the Lender, even if the loan is not approved; (6) the Lender, its agents, successors and assigns will rely on the information contained in the application and I/we have a continuing obligation to amend and/or supplement the information provided in this application if any of the material facts which I/we have represented herein should change prior to closing; (7) in the event my/our payments on the loan indicated in this application become delinquent, the Lender, its agents, successors and assigns, may, in addition to all their other rights and remedies, report my/our name(s) and account information to a credit reporting agency; (8) ownership of the loan may be transferred to successor or assign of the Lender without notice to me and/or the administration of the loan account may be transferred to an agent, successor or assign of the Lender with prior notice to me; (9) the Lender, its agents, successors and assigns make no representations or warranties, express or implied, to the Borrower(s) regarding the property, the condition of the property, or the value of the property.

Certification: I/We certify that the information provided in this application is true and correct as of the date set forth opposite my/our signature(s) on this application and acknowledge my/our understanding that any intentional or negligent misrepresentation(s) of the information contained in this application may result in civil liability and/or criminal penalties including, but not limited to, fine or imprisonment or both under the provisions of Title 18, United States Code, Section 1001, et seq. and liability for monetary damages to the Lender, its agents, successors and assigns, insurers and any other person who may suffer any loss due to reliance upon any misrepresentation which I/we have made on this application.

Borrower's Signature	Date	Co-Borrower's Signature	Date
X		X	

TO BE COMPLETED BY INTERVIEWER

This application was taken by:	Interviewer's Name (print or type)	Name and Address of Interviewer's Employer
☐ face-to-face interview	Interviewer's Signature Date	
☐ by mail		
☐ by telephone	Interviewer's Phone Number (incl. area code)	

"I'VE <u>GOT</u> TO HAVE A LOAN — I'M UP TO MY NECK IN DEBT"

A borrower has a limited right to rescind (cancel) a credit transaction. The borrower has 3 business days (counting Saturdays) to back out after signing the loan papers. This aspect of the law was inserted primarily to protect a homeowner from unscrupulous sellers of home improvements and appliances where the credit to purchase is secured by a lien on the home. Vacant lots for sale on credit to buyers who expect to use them for principal residences are also subject to cancellation privileges.

The right to rescind does not apply to credit used for the acquisition or initial construction of one's principal dwelling.

Right to Cancel

Truth In Lending regulations are complex and only the highlights have been presented here. If you are involved in transactions that require disclosure, you should seek more information from your local real estate board, lender, attorney, or the FTC. Note that the whole topic of truth in lending deals only with disclosure—who must disclose, in what types of situations, what must be disclosed, etc. Truth in Lending legislation does not set the price a lender can charge for a loan. That is determined by supply and demand for funds in the marketplace and, to a lesser degree, by usury laws.

Summary

When a mortgage lender reviews a real estate loan application, the primary concern for both applicant and lender is to approve loan requests that show a high probability of being repaid in full and on time, and to disapprove requests that are likely to result in default and eventual foreclosure. How is this decision made? Loan analysis varies. However, the five major federal agencies have recently combined their requirements for credit reports. After July 1, 1991 all loans intended for underwriting by Fannie Mae, Freddie Mac, HUD/FHA, VA, or Farmer's Home Administration must comply with the new standards. Figure 11:3 is the new Uniform Residential Loan Application (a requirement for standardized loan application) and summarizes the key terms that a loan officer considers when making a decision regarding a loan request. Let's review these items and observe how they affect the acceptance of a loan to a lender.

Note that in section ① the borrower is requested to specify the type of mortgage and terms of loan he is seeking. This greatly facilitates the lender's ability to determine the loan availability of the loan that the borrower may be seeking.

LOAN APPLICATION AND APPROVAL

In section ②, the lender begins the loan analysis procedure by looking at the property and the proposed financing. Using the property address and legal description, an appraiser is assigned to prepare an appraisal of the property and a title search is ordered. These steps are taken to determine the fair market value of the property and the condition of title. In the event of default, this is the collateral the lender must fall back upon to recover the loan. If the loan request is in connection with a purchase, rather than the refinancing of an existing property, the lender will know the purchase price. As a rule, loans are made on the basis of the appraised value or purchase price, whichever is lower. If the appraised value is lower than the purchase price, the usual procedure is to require the buyer to make a larger cash down payment. The lender does not want to overloan simply because the buyer overpaid for the property.

Settlement Funds   Next in section ②, the lender wants to know if the borrower has adequate funds for settlement. Are these funds presently in a checking or savings account, or are they coming from the sale of the borrower's present property? In the latter case, the lender knows the present loan is contingent on closing that escrow. If the down payment and settlement funds are to be borrowed, then the lender will want to be extra cautious as experience has shown that the less money a borrower personally puts into a purchase, the higher the probability of default and foreclosure.

Purpose of Loan   The lender is also interested in the proposed use of the property. Lenders feel most comfortable when a loan is for the purchase or improvement of a property the loan applicant will actually occupy. This is because owner-occupants usually have pride-of-ownership in maintaining their property and even during bad economic conditions will continue to make the monthly payments. An owner-occupant also realizes that losing the home still means paying for shelter elsewhere. It is standard practice for lenders to ask loan applicants to sign a statement stating whether or not they intend to occupy the property.

If the loan applicant intends to purchase a dwelling to rent out as an investment, the lender will be more cautious. This is because during periods of high vacancy, the property may not generate enough income to meet the loan payments. At that point, a strapped-for-cash borrower is likely to default. Note, too, that lenders generally avoid loans secured by purely speculative real estate. If the value of the property drops below the amount owed, the borrower may see no further logic in making the loan payments.

Lastly in this section, the lender assesses the borrower's attitude toward the proposed loan. A casual attitude, such as "I'm buying because real estate always goes up," or an applicant who does not appear to understand the obligation being undertaken would bring a low rating here. Much more welcome is the applicant who shows a mature attitude and understanding of the loan obligation and who exhibits a strong and logical desire for ownership.

In sections ③ and ④ the lender begins an analysis of the borrower, and if there is one, the co-borrower. At one time age, sex, and marital status played an important role in the lender's decision to lend or not to lend. Often the young and the old had trouble getting loans, as did women and persons who were single, divorced, or widowed. Today, the Federal Equal Credit Opportunity Act prohibits discrimination based on age, sex, race, and marital status. Lenders are no longer permitted to discount income earned by women from part-time jobs or because the woman is of child-bearing age. If the applicant chooses to disclose it, alimony, separate maintenance, and child support must be counted in full. Young adults and single persons cannot be turned down because the lender feels they have not "put down roots." Seniors cannot be turned down as long as life expectancy exceeds the early risk period of the loan and collateral is adequate. In other words, the emphasis in borrower analysis is now focused on job stability, income adequacy, net worth, and credit rating.

Borrower Analysis

Thus in sections ⑤ and ⑥ we see questions directed at how long the applicants have held their present jobs and the stability of those jobs themselves. An applicant who possesses marketable job skills and has been regularly employed with a stable employer is considered the ideal risk. Persons whose income can rise and fall erratically, such as commissioned salespersons, present greater risks. Persons whose skills (or lack of skills) or lack of job seniority result in frequent unemployment are more likely to have difficulty repaying a loan. In these sections the lender also inquires as to the number of dependents the applicant must support out of his or her income. This information provides some insight as to how much will be left for monthly house payments.

Monthly Income   In section ⑦ the lender looks at the amount and sources of the applicants' income. Quantity alone is not enough for loan approval since the income sources must be stable too. Thus a lender will look carefully at overtime, bonus, and commission income in order to estimate the levels at which these may be expected to continue. Interest, dividend, and rental income is considered in light of the stability of their sources also. Income from social security and retirement pensions is entered and added to the totals for the applicants. Alimony, child support, and separate maintenance payments received need not be revealed. However, such sums must be listed in order to be considered as a basis for repaying the loan.

In section ⑧ the lender compares what the applicants have been paying for housing with what they will be paying if the loan is approved. Included in the proposed housing expense total are principal, interest, taxes, and insurance along with any assessments or homeowner association dues (such as in a condominium). Some lenders add the monthly cost of utilities to this list.

At ⑨, proposed monthly housing expense is compared to gross monthly income. A general rule of thumb is that monthly housing expense (PITI) should not exceed 25% to 30% of gross monthly income. A second guideline is that total fixed monthly expenses should not exceed 33% to 38% of income. This includes housing payments plus automobile payments, installment loan payments, alimony, child support, and investments with negative cash flows. These are general guidelines, but lenders recognize that food, health care, clothing, transportation, entertainment, and income taxes must also come from the applicants' income.

Assets and Liabilities   In section ⑩ the lender is interested in the applicants' sources of funds for closing and whether, once the loan is granted, the applicants have assets to fall back upon in the event of an income decrease (a job lay-off) or unexpected expenses (hospital bills). Of particular interest is the portion of those assets that are in cash or are readily convertible into cash in a few days. These are called **liquid assets.** If income drops, they are much more useful in meeting living expenses and loan payments than assets that may require months to sell and convert to cash, that is, assets which are **illiquid.**

Note in section ⑩ that two values are shown for life insurance. **Cash value** is the amount of money the policyholder would receive if the policy were surrendered to the insurance company or, alternatively, the amount the policyholder could borrow against the policy. **Face amount** is the amount that would be paid in the event of the insured's death. Lenders feel most comfortable if the face amount of the policy equals or exceeds the amount of the proposed loan. Obviously a borrower's death is not anticipated before the loan is repaid, but lenders recognize that its possibility increases the probability of default. The likelihood of foreclosure is lessened considerably if the survivors receive life insurance benefits.

In section ⑪, the lender is interested in the applicants' existing debts and liabilities for two reasons. First, these items will compete each month against housing expenses for available monthly income. Thus high monthly payments in this section may reduce the size of the loan the lender calculates that the applicants will be able to repay. The presence of monthly liabilities is not all negative: it can also show the lender that the applicants are capable of repaying their debts. Second, the applicants' total debts are subtracted from their total assets to obtain their **net worth,** reported at ⑫. If the result is negative (more owed than owned) the loan request will probably be turned down as too risky. In contrast, a substantial net worth can often offset weaknesses elsewhere in the application, such as too little monthly income in relation to monthly housing expense or an income that can rise and fall erratically.

At number ⑬, lenders ask for credit references as an indicator of the future. Applicants with no previous credit experience will have more weight placed on income and employment history. Applicants with a history of collections, adverse judgments, foreclosure, or bankruptcy will have to convince the lender that this loan will be repaid on time. Additionally, the applicants may be considered poorer risks if they have guaranteed the repayment of someone else's debt by acting as a comaker or endorser.

References, etc.

In the past, it was not uncommon for lenders to refuse to make loans in certain neighborhoods regardless of the quality of the structure or the ability of the borrower to repay. This was known

Redlining

as **redlining,** and it effectively shut off mortgage loans in many older or so-called "bad risk" neighborhoods across the country. Today a lender cannot refuse to make a loan simply because of the age or location of a property, or because of neighborhood income level, or because of the racial, ethnic, or religious composition of the neighborhood.

A lender can refuse to lend on a structure intended for demolition, a property in a known geological hazard area, a single-family dwelling in an area devoted to industrial or commercial use, or upon a property that is in violation of zoning laws, deed covenants, conditions or restrictions, or significant health, safety, or building codes.

Loan-to-Value Ratios

The lender next looks at the amount of down payment the borrower proposes to make, the size of the loan being requested and the amount of other financing the borrower plans to use. This information is then converted into loan-to-value ratios. As a rule, the larger the down payment, the safer the loan is for the lender. On an uninsured loan, the ideal loan-to-value (L/V) ratio for a lender on owner-occupied residential property is 70% or less. This means the value of the property would have to fall more than 30% before the debt owed would exceed the property's value, thus encouraging the borrower to stop making loan payments.

Loan-to-value ratios from 70% through 80% are considered acceptable but do expose the lender to more risk. Lenders sometimes compensate by charging slightly higher interest rates. Loan-to-value ratios above 80% present even more risk of default to the lender, and the lender will either increase the interest rate charged on these loans or require that an outside insurer, such as the FHA or a private mortgage insurer, be supplied by the borrower.

Credit Report

As part of the loan application, the lender will order a **credit report** on the applicant(s). The applicant is asked to authorize this and to pay for the report. This provides the lender with an independent means of checking the applicant's credit history. A credit report that shows active use of credit with a good repayment record and no derogatory information is most desirable. The applicant will be asked by the lender to explain any negative information. Because it is possible for inaccurate or untrue information in a credit report to unfairly damage a person's credit reputation, Congress passed the **Fair Credit Reporting Act.** This act gives an individual the right to inspect his or her file at a credit bureau, correct any errors, and make explanatory statements to supplement the file.

As previously discussed, the five major federal agencies have recently combined their requirements for credit reports, and loans intended for underwriting by the federal government agencies must comply with the new credit standards. Under these newly adopted rules the name of the consumer reporting agency must be clearly identified as well as who ordered the report and who is paying for it. The information must be furnished from at least two national repositories for each area in which the borrower resided in the past two years, and it must be verified by the previous two years. An explanation must be provided if the information is unavailable, and all questions must be responded to even if the answer must be "unable to verify." A history must be furnished and all missing information must be verified by the lender. The history must have been checked within 90 days of the credit report and indicate the age of the information that is not considered obsolete by the Fair Credit Reporting Act (seven years general credit date or ten years for bankruptcy). If any credit information is incomplete or disclosed information is discovered, the lender must have a personal interview with the borrower. The lender is additionally required to warrant that the credit report complies with all of the new standards.

OVERVIEW

In this chapter you received a good grounding in the mechanics of term loans, amortized loans, balloon loans, partially amortized loans, loan-to-value, and equity. Also, you learned something about the functions and importance of the FHA, the VA, private mortgage insurance, loan points, and Truth in Lending legislation. Lastly you saw a sample of the type of information a lender requests and considers before granting a real estate loan. In the next chapter you will learn about real estate lenders from whom you can borrow and where those lenders get their money. You will also read about financing techniques that are popular in the United States today.

1. A loan wherein the principal is all repaid in one lump sum payment at the end of the loan's life is known as a (an)
   A. straight or term loan.
   B. amortized loan.
   C. budget mortgage.
   D. balloon note.

2. The last day of a loan's life is known as the
   A. settlement date.
   B. maturity date.
   C. sale date.
   D. contract date.

3. To determine the amount of loan payments by using an amortization table, you must know all the following EXCEPT:
   A. loan-to-value ratio.
   B. frequency of payments.
   C. interest rate.
   D. amount of loan.

4. Amortization tables may be used by real estate agents to determine which of the following?
   A. Frequency of payment.
   B. Interest rate.
   C. Maturity.
   D. Amount of loan.
   E. All of the above.

5. A major negative of balloon loan financing is that the borrower may have difficulty
   A. meeting the final payment when it becomes due.
   B. refinancing when the final payment comes due.
   C. Both A and B.
   D. Neither A nor B.

6. Kevin wants to know what portion of a 30-year, fully amortized loan would be paid off by the fourth year of the loan's life. Kevin would consult
   A. an amortization table.
   B. a loan balance table.
   C. a partial amortization table.
   D. loan-to-value ratio.

7. By the tenth year of an 11 1/2 percent 30-year amortization period, how much of the principal balance will have been repaid under a monthly amortization of equal installments? Use Table 11:2 in the text.
   A. One-half.
   B. One-third.
   C. Two-thirds.
   D. None of the above.

8. The difference between a property's market value and the debts against it is known as the
   A. loan-to-value ratio.
   B. owner's equity.
   C. L/V ratio.
   D. effective yield.

9. When a lender charges discount points to make a loan,
   A. the yield to the lender will decrease.
   B. the yield to the lender will increase.
   C. the yield to the lender will not change.
   D. the cost of the loan to the borrower decreases.

10. Discount points on mortgage loans will tend to
    A. increase during periods of tight money.
    B. increase during periods of loose money.
    C. decrease during periods of tight money.
    D. None of the above.

11. The FHA has been influential in bringing about acceptance of
    A. long-term amortization of loans.
    B. standardized construction techniques.
    C. Both A and B.
    D. Neither A nor B.

12. Which of the following loans can be repaid in full ahead of schedule without penalty?
    A. FHA-insured.   C. Both A and B.
    B. VA-guaranteed.   D. Neither A nor B.

13. Which of the following loans are referred to as "conventional loans?"
    A. FHA-insured.   C. Section 245 Loan.
    B. VA-guaranteed.   D. None of the above.

14. The FHA will insure graduated payment loans under
    A. Section 235.   C. Section 240.
    B. Section 245.   D. Section 244.

15. FHA and VA loans can be obtained from
    A. savings and loans associations.
    B. banks.
    C. mortgage companies.
    D. All of the above.

16. VA-guaranteed loans are available for
    A. single-family and mobile homes.   D. houseboats.
    B. apartment projects.   E. All of the above.
    C. strip centers.

17. Regarding mortgage insurance, which of the following statements are true?
    A. PMI insures only the top 20 or 25 percent of the loan.
    B. FHA insures the entire loan.
    C. Both A and B.
    D. Neither A nor B.

18. Which of the following statements regarding the FmHA are correct?
    A. FmHA guarantees loans on farms and rural homes.
    B. FmHA makes loans on farms and rural homes.
    C. Both A and B.
    D. Neither A nor B.

19. The abbreviation APR stands for
    A. average percentage rate.
    B. allotted percentage rate.
    C. approximate percentage rate.
    D. annual percentage rate.

20. The annual percentage rate is
    A. usually lower than the interest rate.
    B. made up of the interest rate combined with the other costs of the loan.
    C. Both A and B.
    D. Neither A nor B.

Sources and Types of Financing

OVERVIEW OF
CHAPTER 12

Chapter 12 will identify the primary and secondary sources of financing, i.e., identify the various mortgage lenders and describe where the lenders get their money. The mortgage loan instrument will be described in detail. Financing techniques currently in use in the United States will also be explained. In addition, this chapter covers FNMA, FHLMC, and computerization. Other items covered include alienation clauses, prepayment penalties, variable rate and adjustable rate mortgages, GMPs, and other types of mortgages and creative financing.

LEARNING OBJECTIVES

After successful completion of this chapter, you should be able to:

1. Describe the primary and secondary sources of mortgage money.
2. Describe various loan programs, the roles of the lender, and mortgage brokers.
3. Explain the purpose and characteristics of FNMA and FHLMC.
4. Define mortgage terms and concepts such as usuary, alienation clauses, and prepayment penalties.
5. Describe variable rate, adjustable rate, graduated payment, and shared appreciation mortgages.
6. Explain the concepts of equity sharing and "rich uncle" financing.
7. Describe other types of mortgages and loan.
8. Distinguish between creative financing and overly-creative financing.
9. Explain various activities such as investing in mortgages, renting property, and leasing land.

KEY • TERMS

Adjustable rate mortgage: a mortgage on which the interest rate rises and falls with changes in prevailing interest rates

Alienation clause: requires immediate repayment of the loan if ownership transfers; also called a due-on-sale clause

Seller financing: a note accepted by a seller instead of cash

Equity sharing: an arrangement whereby a party providing financing gets a portion of the ownership

Fannie Mae: a real estate industry nickname for the Federal National Mortgage Association

Mortgage company: a firm that makes mortgage loans and then sells them to investors

Option: a right, for a given period of time, to buy, sell, or lease property at specified price and terms

Secondary mortgage market: a market where mortgage loans can be sold to investors

Usury: charging a rate of interest higher than that permitted by law

Wraparound mortgage: a mortgage that encompasses any existing mortgages and is subordinate to them

This chapter will (1) identify various mortgage lenders (the primary market), (2) describe where these lenders get much of their money (the secondary market), and (3) explain mortgage loan instruments and financing techniques currently in use in the United States. Many people consider financing to be the most important of all real estate topics because without financing real estate profits and commissions would be difficult to achieve.

PRIMARY MARKET

The **primary market** (also called the **primary mortgage market**) is where lenders originate loans, i.e., where lenders make funds available to borrowers. Examples are savings and loans (S&Ls), commercial banks, mutual savings banks, and mortgage companies. The primary market is what the borrower sees as the source of mortgage loan money. It's the institution with which the borrower has direct and personal contact. It's the place where the loan application is taken, the place where the loan officer interviews the loan applicant, the place where the loan check comes from, and the place to which loan payments are sent by the borrower.

Most borrowers assume that the loan they receive comes from depositors who visit the same bank or S&L to leave their excess funds. This is partly true. But this by itself would be an inadequate source of loan funds in today's market. Thus, primary lenders often sell their loans in what is called the secondary market. Insurance companies, pension funds, and individual investors as well as other primary lenders with excess deposits buy these loans for cash. This makes more money available to a primary lender that, in turn, can be loaned to borrowers. The secondary market is so huge that it rivals the entire U.S. corporate bond market in size of annual offerings. We will return to the secondary market later in this chapter. Meanwhile, let us discuss the various lenders a borrower will encounter when looking for a real estate loan.

SAVINGS AND LOAN ASSOCIATIONS

Historically, the origin of **savings and loan associations** can be traced to early building societies in England and Germany and to the first American building society, the Oxford Provident Building Association, started in 1831 in Pennsylvania. These early building societies were cooperatives whose savers were also borrowers. As time progressed, savings and loan associations became a primary source of residential real estate loans. To encourage residential lending, the federally chartered savings and loans were required by federal regulation to hold at least 80% of their assets in residential loans. In addition, they were subjected to special tax laws which permitted a savings and loan association to defer payment of income taxes on profits, so long as they were held in surplus accounts and not distributed to the savings and loan association's owners. To qualify for the deferment, commercial loans were limited to no more than 18% of their assets. The remainder of the loans (82% or more) had to be in residential loans, which included apartment projects. During this same period, there were also limits on the interest rate that could be paid on savings accounts. This provided the savings and loan associations with a dependable source of funds at a fixed interest rate, which gave them the potential for making long-term loans at reasonable rates. For instance, if the passbook savings account was limited to 5 1/4% per annum, home loans in the vicinity of 7 1/2% to 8 1/2% would still allow for reasonable profit margins. Unfortunately, the nature of the finance markets began to change in the late 1970s when an inflationary economy caused interest rates to skyrocket. This created problems that were unforeseen by the savings and loan industry.

In addition to passbook accounts, savings and loans also offer **certificates of deposit (CDs)** at rates higher than passbook rates in order to attract depositors. This is necessary to compete with higher yields offered by U.S. Treasury bills, notes, and bonds and to prevent disintermediation. **Disintermediation** results when depositors take money out of their savings accounts and invest directly in government securities, corporate bonds, and money market funds. A major problem, and one that nearly brought the S&L industry to its knees in the late 1970s and early 1980s, was that S&Ls traditionally relied heavily upon short-term deposits from savers and then loaned that money on long-term (often 30-year) loans to borrowers. When interest rates rose sharply in the 1970s, S&Ls either had to raise the interest paid to their depositors or watch depositors withdraw their savings and take the money elsewhere for higher returns. Meanwhile, the S&Ls were holding long-term, fixed-rate mortgage loans, and with interest rates rising, borrowers were not anxious to repay those loans early.

Disintermediation

Disintermediation was only the beginning of the problems. Loan demand at S&Ls was declining. In 1976, 57% of the residential mortgage loans were held by savings and loan institutions. By 1987, only 31% of the residential loans were held in savings and loan institutions, and by 1990 the percentage fell to 26%. There are many reasons for this flow of funds out of the savings and loan industry. One of the primary reasons, however, appears to be the deregulation of the lending industry. In March of 1980, President Carter signed the Depository Institution's Deregulation and Monetary Control Act. It eliminated most of the S&Ls incentives to make residential mortgage loans, and made other lending sources (such as banks) more competitive in those markets. While it raised the limits on insured deposits (up to $100,000 per depositor), it also loosened the restrictions on investments and loans that savings institutions could make. Many of the S&Ls began making higher risk loans on undeveloped land, real estate development loans, and joint venture loans (often to themselves as developers!). Generally, the new law allowed S&Ls to use depositors' money to enter into higher risk business ventures, rather than staying with the low-risk residential loans that had been encouraged in the past. In addition, the proliferation of savings and loans during the '80s resulted in many being

The Crisis of the 1980s

managed by poorly trained administrators and officers. As in many other cases when a business enters a new, uncharted territory, many savings and loans were not prepared for the "down" cycles of real estate investment.

When the federal regulators enforced their reporting requirements, it created still another problem. If the savings and loan had invested and developed large quantities of real estate, it subjected itself to down cycles, previously discussed. When reporting financial status to the federal government, however, the result was that a substantial asset base in real property (for instance, raw land cost of $8 million at acquisition) could be required to be "written down" to a smaller fair market value (for instance, $4 million), because the federal regulatory agencies require a realistic asset reporting value to accurately reflect the solvency of the savings and loan institution. When an institution's asset basis is depleted by 50% it results in an insolvent institution! Insolvent institutions are required by the federal government to be closed to protect depositors and maintain confidence in the system.

Restructuring the System   One of the comforting aspects of governmental regulation of lending institutions is that it provides a solvent recovery fund for the depositors in the event that a lending institution fails. For the savings and loan industry it has traditionally been the Federal Savings and Loan Insurance Corporation. During the late '70s and all of the '80s, disintermediation, coupled with bad lending practices and the complications of deregulation, resulted in a substantial amount of savings and loan institutions being declared insolvent. The FSLIC simply did not have enough funds to adequately insure the deposits. In short, the FSLIC was insolvent, and more urgent steps needed to be taken to resolve the issue.

In August of 1989, President Bush signed into law a sweeping revision of the regulatory authorities governing savings & loans. This law is referred to as The Financial Institutions Reform, Recovery, and Enforcement Act of 1989, commonly called FIRREA. The law redefined or created seven new regulatory authorities, and initiated a system of federally designated real property appraisers, discussed in greater detail in Chapter 16. Over the next several years, as many as two-thirds of the existing

Savings & Loan Associations may be closed or merged as a result of the new FIRREA legislation.

The new regulatory agencies and functions are not always clearly defined, but consist of the following:

(1) The Office of Thrift Supervision (OTS). The Office of Thrift Supervision is a new arm of the Treasury Department. The OTS replaces the abolished Federal Home Loan Bank Board as a regulator of the thrift industry. Its authority is broader than the Federal Home Loan Bank Board's because it covers both federal and state charter lending institutions that carry federal deposit insurance. It also regulates those lender's holding companies.

(2) The Federal Housing Finance Board (FHFB). The Federal Housing Finance Board was created to take over the Federal Home Loan Bank Board role as supervisor of the Mortgage Lending by the twelve regional home loan banks. These twelve banks are back-up sources of funds for the thrift industry, meaning that they make funds available for primary loans and the home loan market. The FHFB is also responsible for handling statistical data for the housing industry.

(3) The Resolution Trust Corporation (RTC). The Resolution Trust Corporation was organized to sell or liquidate failing savings & loans, and other thrift institutions. The RTC also manages troubled institutions under conservatorship, a duty which it shares along with the OTS and FDIC.

(4) The Resolution Trust Corporation Oversight Board. The Resolution Trust Corporation Oversight Board was created to set guidelines and overall supervision of the RTC and FDIC and is responsible for the release of money needed by the RTC for the selling or liquidation of failed institutions.

(5) The Federal Deposit Insurance Corporation (FDIC). The Federal Deposit Insurance Corporation was a previously existing organization which now takes on new supervision and regulatory duties. The

FDIC has been given responsibility for administrating federal deposit insurance funds for savings associations, as well as continuing to oversee the funds for commercial banks and savings banks. In the past, the Federal Savings & Loan Insurance Corporation liquidated failed savings & loan institutions. Now the FDIC administers the FSLIC Resolution Fund. The FDIC is also the receiver to handle disposition of failed institutions, along with the RTC.

All the new federal agencies have been assigned specific responsibilities. There is some overlapping of their duties, and some confusion still remains in the restructuring of the system. There is no doubt that in a few years, the savings & loan business as we know it today will cease to exist.

COMMERCIAL BANKS

The nation's 15,000 **commercial banks** store far more of the country's money than the S&Ls. However, only one bank dollar in six goes to real estate lending. As a result, in total number of dollars, commercial banks still rank second behind S&Ls in importance in real estate lending. Of the loans made by banks on real estate, the tendency is to emphasize short-term maturities, and adjustable rate mortgages, since the bulk of a bank's deposit money comes from demand deposits (checking accounts) and a much smaller portion from savings and time deposits.

Oddly enough, the same factors which seem to have been plaguing the S&Ls seem to have helped the commercial banks. During the Deregulation Acts of 1980 and 1982, banks began making more home loans, but they were short term, with adjustable rates. This prevents the problem of disintermediation, as the loan rates can rise with the rates that are required by the source of funds. Commercial banks, too, have realized that first lien residential loans are also very secure, low risk loans. They have also determined that it is a market advantage to maintain all of a customer's loan accounts, including his home loan, in the bank's portfolio. "One stop banking" has become a very successful marketing tool. The merger of many banks into large multi-state national banks has also created a larger source of funds to lend. To accommodate this higher demand and facilitate the organization of sources of funds for the bank's lending purposes, many banks have now organized their own mortgage departments to assist customers in making home loans, even through sources other than bank deposits.

Important contributors to real estate credit in several states are the nation's 400 **mutual savings banks.** Started in Philadelphia in 1816 and in Boston in 1817, mutual savings banks are found primarily in the northeastern United States, where they compete aggressively for the savings dollar. The states of Massachusetts, New York, and Connecticut account for 75% of the nation's total. As the word *mutual* implies, the depositors are the owners, and the "interest" they receive is the result of the bank's success or failure in lending. Mutual savings banks offer accounts similar to those offered by S&Ls. To protect depositors, laws require mutual savings banks to place deposits in high-quality investments, including sound real estate mortgage loans.

MUTUAL SAVINGS BANKS

As a group, the nation's 2,200 **life insurance companies** have long been active investors in real estate as developers, owners, and long-term lenders. Their source of money is the premiums paid by policyholders. These premiums are invested and ultimately returned to the policyholders. Because premiums are collected in regular amounts on regular dates and because policy payoffs can be calculated from actuarial tables, life insurers are in ideal positions to commit money to long-term investments. Life insurance companies channel their funds primarily into government and corporate bonds and real estate. The dollars allocated to real estate go to buy land and buildings, which are leased to users, and to make loans on commercial, industrial, and residential property. Generally, life insurers specialize in large-scale investments such as shopping centers, office and apartment buildings, and million-dollar blocks of home loans purchased in the secondary mortgage market.

LIFE INSURANCE COMPANIES

Repayment terms on loans made by insurance companies for shopping centers, office buildings, and apartment complexes sometimes call for interest and a percentage of any profits from rentals over a certain level. This **participation** feature, or "piece of the action," is intended to provide the insurance company with more inflation protection than a fixed rate of interest.

MORTGAGE COMPANIES

A **mortgage company** makes a mortgage loan and then sells it to a long-term investor. The process begins with locating borrowers, qualifying them, preparing the necessary loan papers, and finally making the loans. Once a loan is made, it is sold for cash on the secondary market. The mortgage company will usually continue to **service the loan,** that is, collect the monthly payments and handle such matters as insurance and property tax impounds, delinquencies, early payoffs, and mortgage releases.

Mortgage companies, also known as **mortgage bankers,** vary in size from one or two persons to several dozen. As a rule, they are locally oriented, finding and making loans within 25 or 50 miles of their offices. This gives them a feel for their market, greatly aids in identifying sound loans, and makes loan servicing much easier. For their efforts, mortgage bankers typically receive 1% to 3% of the amount of the loan when it is originated, and from ¼ to ½ of 1% of the outstanding balance each year thereafter for servicing. Mortgage banking, as this business is called, is not limited to mortgage companies. Commercial banks, savings and loan associations, and mutual savings banks in active real estate areas often originate more real estate loans than they can hold themselves, and these are sold on the secondary market. Mortgage companies often do a large amount of their business in FHA and VA loans.

MORTGAGE BROKERS

Mortgage brokers, in contrast to mortgage bankers, specialize in bringing together borrowers and lenders, just as real estate brokers bring together buyers and sellers. The mortgage broker does not lend money, and usually does not service loans. The mortgage broker's fee is expressed in points and is usually paid by the borrower. Mortgage brokers are locally oriented and often are small firms of from 1 to 10 persons.

The mortgage brokering businesses actually felt an explosion of mortgage brokers during the late 1980s and early 1990s. The secondary market (discussed later in this chapter) has made investor's funds more readily available, and virtually anyone with some expertise in loan qualifications can originate loans and sell to the secondary market purchasers. As a result, the field has become crowded with new loan originators such as home builders, finance companies, commercial credit companies, insurance agents, attorneys, and real estate brokers. These have generally been considered to be nontraditional lenders, but they can originate mortgage loans with their own resources or through various networks to have the loan funded directly through to the secondary market purchaser. These new loan originators have offered substantial competition to regulated lenders.

There has been a "gray" area of the law as to whether or not a real estate broker may operate as a mortgage broker and collect a fee for placing a loan. The concern expressed by some is that the fee retained by the broker (which is in addition to his real estate broker's fee) may be an undisclosed kickback which violates the Real Estate Settlement Procedures Act (see Chapter 14). There are also agency law concerns because a real estate broker may be "representing" the buyer on his loan while also "representing" the seller in the sale of the home. Lenders also have some concern that the real estate agent may "fudge" mortgage qualification criteria to facilitate a lucrative sale. The law is not very clear in this area, and both HUD and Congress have taken the matter under consideration to establish some guidelines for this function in the future.

Computerized Loan Origination

The growth of the computer networks has enabled many independent loan processors to work under the guidance of the large lending institutions and mortgage companies. Using a Computerized Loan Origination (CLO), a real estate broker, attorney, insurance agent, or mortgage company, can arrange to have a computer link installed in their office, connected to the lender's main frame computers. By utilizing a series of questions, the borrower can obtain preliminary loan approval immediately from the loan originator with a firm acceptance or rejection from the lending instituting within a few days. If a real estate broker anticipates using a CLO network to qualify their potential buyers, they must be sure to do a careful review of the real estate settlement procedures guidelines to determine whether or not a fee for a CLO generated loan could be a violation of RESPA, discussed previously.

MUNICIPAL BONDS

In some cities, **municipal bonds** provide a source of mortgage money for home buyers. The special advantage to borrowers is that municipal bonds pay interest that is tax-free from federal income taxes. Knowing this, bond investors will accept a lower rate of interest than they would if the interest were taxable—as it normally is on mortgage loans. This saving is passed on to the home buyer. Those who qualify will typically pay about 2% less than if they had borrowed through conventional channels.

The objective of such programs is to make home ownership more affordable for low- and middle-income households. Also, a city may stipulate that loans be used in neighborhoods the city wants to revitalize. The loans are made by local lenders who are paid a fee for originating and servicing these loans. Although popular with the real estate industry, the U.S. Treasury has been less than enthusiastic about the concept because it bears the cost in lost tax revenues. As a result, federal legislation has been passed to limit the future use of this source of money.

OTHER LENDERS

Pension funds and **trust funds** traditionally have channeled their money to high-grade government and corporate bonds and stocks. However, the trend now is to place more money into real estate loans. Already active buyers on the secondary market, pension and trust funds will likely become a still larger source of real estate financing in the future. In some localities, pension fund members can tap their own pension funds for home mortgages at very reasonable rates. This is an often overlooked source of primary market financing.

Finance companies that specialize in making business and consumer loans also provide limited financing for real estate. As a rule, finance companies seek second mortgages at interest rates 2% to 5% higher than the rates prevailing on first mortgages. First mortgages are also taken as collateral; however, the lenders already discussed usually charge lower interest rates for these loans and thus are more competitive.

Credit unions normally specialize in consumer loans. However, real estate loans are becoming more and more important as many of the country's 16,000 credit unions have branched out into first and second mortgage loans. Credit unions are an often overlooked but excellent source of home loan money.

Individuals are sometimes a source of cash loans for real estate, with the bulk of these loans made between relatives or friends. Generally, loan maturities are shorter than those obtainable from the institutional lenders already described. In some cities, persons can be found who specialize in making or buying second and third mortgage loans of up to 10-year maturities.

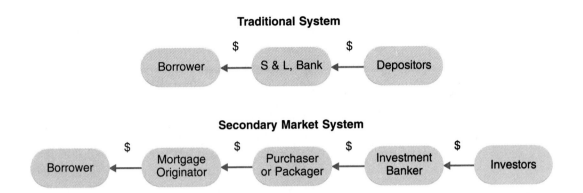

Figure 12:1. Mortgage Loan Delivery Systems

Individuals are beginning to invest substantial amounts of money in secondary mortgage market securities. Ironically, these investments are often made with money that would have otherwise been deposited in a savings and loan.

Individuals are heavily involved in seller financing. This is where the seller agrees to take payments from the buyer rather than cash. Because of its importance, seller financing is discussed under its own heading later in this chapter.

The **secondary market** (also called the **secondary mortgage market**) provides a way for a lender to sell a loan. It also permits investment in real estate loans without the need for loan origination and servicing facilities. Although not directly encountered by real estate buyers, sellers, and agents, the secondary market plays an important role in getting money from those who want to lend to those who want to borrow. In other words, think of the secondary market as a pipeline for loan money. Visualize that pipeline running via the Wall Street financial district in New York City as Wall Street is now a major participant in residential mortgage lending. Figure 12:1 illustrates this pipeline and diagrams key differences between the traditional mortgage delivery system and the secondary market system.

SECONDARY MARKET

Notice in Figure 12:1 that in the traditional system the lender is a local institution gathering deposits from the community and then

Traditional Delivery System

lending that money as real estate loans in the same community. Traditionally, each lender (S&L, mutual savings bank, commercial bank, credit union) was an independent unit that developed its own appraisal technique, loan application form, loan approval criteria, note and mortgage forms, servicing method, and foreclosure policy. Nonetheless, three major problems needed solving. The first was the institution that had an imbalance of depositors and borrowers. Rapidly growing areas of the United States often needed more loan money than their savers were capable of depositing. Stable regions had more depositors than loan opportunities. Thus it was common to see correspondent relationships between lenders where, for example, a lender in Los Angeles would sell some of its mortgage loans to a savings bank in Brooklyn. This provided loans for borrowers and interest for savers. The system worked well, but required individual correspondent relationships.

The second problem occurs when depositors want to withdraw their money from their accounts and invest it in other sources. Lenders have to attract these depositors, raising their interest rates, which results in loan rates increasing. The third problem is timing. Lenders must borrow "short" (from their deposit relationships) and lend long (30-year mortgages). Savers then are encouraged to leave their money on deposit for longer periods of time.

The answer to these three problems is relatively simple: Find a market to sell your loans to investors who will pay cash for them and reimburse you, the primary lender. The result, then, is that there is an investor who is willing to hold the loan long term for its guaranteed rate of return. The primary lender continues to make loans, gambling that he will find another investor in the secondary market to buy that loan for a long term. In effect, the primary lenders can make loans from the secondary market instead of from their deposits.

Secondary Market Delivery Systems

As shown in Figure 12:1, with the secondary market system the borrower obtains a loan from a mortgage originator. This includes mortgage companies, banks, CLOs, and thrifts that originate loans they intend to sell. The mortgage originator packages the loan with other loans and then either sells the package as a whole or keeps the package and sells securities that are backed by the loans in the package. If the originator is not large enough to package its own mortgages, it will sell the loans to someone who can.

There are now two sources for this secondary market. The first is private investors such as commercial banks, savings and loans, pension plans, trust funds, and other investors who were looking for low risk, long-term returns on their investments. The second group of investors, relatively new in the investment business, is the investment "pools" or "poolers" who are looking for more security in their investments. This results in two primary investors in the secondary market: (1) the pure portfolio purchasers who are looking for the initial investments with an attractive return, and (2) the "poolers" who are looking for the longer-term, more stable return.

A major stumbling block to a highly organized and efficient secondary market has been the uniqueness of both lenders and loans. Traditionally, each primary lender developed its own special loan forms and procedures. Moreover, each loan is a unique combination of real estate and borrower. No two are exactly alike. How do you package such diversity into an attractive package for investors? A large part of the answer has come through standardized loan application forms, standardized appraisal forms, standardized credit report forms, standardized closing statements, standardized loan approval criteria, and standardized promissory notes, mortgages, and trust deeds. Loan terms have been standardized into categories, for example, fixed-rate 30-year loans, fixed-rate 15-year loans, and various adjustable rate combinations. Additionally, nearly all loans must be insured. This can take the form of FHA or private mortgage insurance, or a VA guarantee on each loan in the package. Additionally, there will be some form of assurance of timely repayment of the mortgage package as a whole. The net result is a mortgage security that is attractive to investors who in the past have not been interested in investing in mortgages.

Standardized Loan Procedures

Let's now look at some of the key secondary market participants including the giants of the industry: the FNMA, GNMA, FHLMC, and Farmer Mac.

The **Federal National Mortgage Association (FNMA)** was organized by the federal government in 1938 to buy FHA mortgage loans from lenders. This made it possible for lenders to

FNMA

grant more loans to consumers. Ten years later it began purchasing VA loans. FNMA (fondly known in the real estate business and to itself as **"Fannie Mae"**) was successful in its mission.

In 1968 Congress divided the FNMA into two organizations: the Government National Mortgage Association (to be discussed in the next section) and the FNMA, as we know it today. As part of that division, the FNMA changed from a government agency to a private profit-making corporation, chartered by Congress but owned by its shareholders and managed independently of the government. There are some 60 million shares of Fannie Mae stock in existence, and it is one of the most actively traded issues on the New York Stock Exchange. Fannie Mae buys FHA and VA loans and, since 1972, conventional whole loans from lenders across the United States. Money to buy these loans comes from the sale of FNMA stock plus the sale of FNMA bonds and notes. FNMA bond and note holders look to Fannie Mae for timely payment of principal and interest on these bonds and notes, and Fannie Mae looks to its mortgagors for principal and interest payments on the loans it owns. Thus, Fannie Mae stands in the middle and, although it is very careful to match interest rates and maturities between the loans it buys and the bonds and notes it sells, it still takes the risk of the middleman. In this respect, it is like a giant thrift institution.

Commitments

Fannie Mae's method of operation is to sell commitments to lenders pledging to buy specified dollar amounts of mortgage loans within a fixed period of time and usually at a specified yield. Lenders are not obligated to sell loans to Fannie Mae if they can find better terms elsewhere. However, Fannie Mae must purchase all loans delivered to it under the terms of the commitments. Loans must be made using FNMA-approved forms and loan approval criteria. The largest loan Fannie Mae would buy in 1988 was $168,700 for a single family unit. This limit is adjusted each year as housing prices change. Fannie Mae will also buy loans on duplexes, triplexes, and fourplexes all at larger loan limits. Although the FNMA loan limit may seem inadequate for some houses and neighborhoods, the intention of Congress is that Fannie Mae cater to the mid-range of housing prices and leave the upper end of the market to others.

In addition to purchasing first mortgages, Fannie Mae also purchases second mortgages from lenders. FNMA forms and criteria must be followed and the loan-to-value ratio of the combined first and second mortgages cannot exceed 80% if owner-occupied and 70% if not owner-occupied. This is a very helpful program for a person who has watched the value of his or her home increase and wants to borrow against that increase without first having to repay the existing mortgage loan.

FNMA Pooling

The demand for loans in the primary market could not match the demand that investors required in the secondary market, so Fannie Mae began purchasing large blocks of mortgage loans, and then assigned them to specified pools with an "agency guarantee" certificate which guaranteed long-term return to the pool investors. Fannie Mae guarantees to pass through to the certificate holders whatever principal, interest, and prepayments of principal are generated by the loans into the underlying pool of mortgage investors. Fannie Mae's pooling arrangements undertook the issuance of **mortgage-backed securities (MBS)** which began in 1982. Utilizing this system of issuing securities which are backed by mortgages, the securities markets could then be used as a source for investment funds. In the third quarter of 1988, Fannie Mae held $102 billion of loans in portfolio investments. At the same time, however, Fannie Mae had underwritten $167 billion in mortgage pools. This is an incredible shift in loan procedures since 1982. This is also a strong indication that the guaranteed loan pools (whether government or agency guarantees) provide a much better procedure for making funds available in the secondary market. This, in turn, assures funds available for the primary market and long-term mortgage loans for individual home purchasers.

Home Seller Program

Another innovation of Fannie Mae to help real estate is the **home seller program.** This is a secondary market for sellers who carry back mortgages. To qualify, the note and mortgage must be prepared by a FNMA-approved lender using standard FNMA loan qualification procedures. The note and mortgage may be kept by the home seller as an investment or sold to a FNMA-approved lender for possible resale to the FNMA.

In other developments, Fannie Mae has standardized the terms of adjustable rate mortgages it will purchase. This is a major step forward in reducing the proliferation of variety in these loans. Fannie Mae is also test marketing mortgage-backed securities in $1,000 increments to appeal to individuals, particularly for Individual Retirement Accounts. Additionally, Fannie Mae has started a collateralized mortgage obligation program and begun a mortgage pass-through program, both of which will be defined in the near future.

GNMA

The **Government National Mortgage Association (GNMA,** popularly known to the industry and to itself as **"Ginnie Mae")** was created in 1968 when the FNMA was partitioned into two separate corporations. Ginnie Mae is a federal agency entirely within the Department of Housing and Urban Development (HUD). Although Ginnie Mae has some low-income housing functions, it is best known for its mortgage-backed securities (MBS) program. Previously discussed, the MBS program attracts additional sources of credit to FHA, VA, and FmHA mortgages. Ginnie Mae does this by guaranteeing timely repayment of privately issued securities backed by pools of these mortgages. Remember that the FNMA MBS program offers "agency guarantees" for their investors. GNMA offers a government guarantee of repayment, backed by the full faith and credit of the U.S. government.

Ginnie Mae Procedures

Ginnie Mae is limited to underwriting only HUD/FHA, VA, and certain farmer's home administration loans. Ginnie Mae sets its own requirements for loans that can be accepted into their mortgage pool, then it subsequently approves loan poolers who are committed to comply with those requirements. Ginnie Mae examines the loans and the loan poolers before it can determine its ability to guarantee those loans into the loan pooler source of funds.

The result is that Ginnie Mae issues guarantee certificates which are popularly known as "Ginnie Maes." It carries the equivalent of a U.S. government bond guarantee and pays the holder of those certificates, the loan pooler, an interest rate of 1% to 1-½% higher than that of a government bond.

FHLMC

The **Federal Home Loan Mortgage Corporation (FHLMC,** also known to the industry and to itself as **"Freddie Mac"** or the "Mortgage Corporation") was created by Congress in 1970. Its goal, like that of the FNMA and GNMA, is to increase the availability of financing for residential mortgages. Where it differs is that Freddie Mac deals primarily in conventional mortgages.

Freddie Mac was initially established to serve as a secondary market for S&L members of the Federal Home Loan Bank System. The ownership of Freddie Mac was originally held by more than 3,000 savings associations. In 1988 the shares were released and sold publicly by the savings associations. Unlike Ginnie Mae, which guarantees securities issued by others, Freddie Mac issues its own securities against its own mortgage pools. These securities are its participation certificates and collateralized mortgage obligations. By the third quarter of 1988, Freddie Mac held nearly $14 billion in its own loan portfolio, accounting for almost 11% of all outstanding loans in residential lending.

Participation certificates (PCs) allow a mortgage originator to deliver to Freddie Mac either whole mortgages or part interest in a pool of whole mortgages. In return, Freddie Mac gives the mortgage originator a PC representing an undivided interest in a pool of investment-quality conventional mortgages created from mortgages and mortgage interests purchased by Freddie Mac. Freddie Mac guarantees that the interest and principal on these PCs will be repaid in full and on time, even if the underlying mortgages are in default. (Freddie Mac reduces its losses by setting strict loan qualification criteria and requiring mortgage insurance on high loan-to-value loans.) The PCs can be kept as investments, sold for cash, or used as collateral for loans. PCs are popular investments for S&Ls, pension funds, and other institutional investors looking for high-yield investments. Individuals who can meet the $25,000 minimum also find PCs attractive. Freddie Mac also has a collateralized mortgage obligation program and plans to offer a trust for investments in mortgages. These are designed to deal with the unpredictability of mortgage maturities caused by early repayment. This is accomplished by dividing the cash flows from a mortgage pool into separate securities with separate maturities which are then sold to investors.

The newest agency created by Congress to underwrite loan pools is the Federal Agricultural Mortgage Corporation, known

Participation Certificates

FARMER MAC

as Farmer Mac. The Agricultural Credit Act of 1987 established Farmer Mac as a separate agency within the Farm Credit System to establish the secondary market needed for farm real estate loans. It started its actual operations in 1989.

Farmer Mac functions similarly to Ginnie Mae in that it certifies loan poolers rather than purchasing loans. Farmer Mac guarantees timely repayment of principal and interest in the loan pool, but does not guarantee any individual loans within that pool. Similar to the other governmental or quasi-governmental agencies, Farmer Mac charges a fee for its credit enhancement.

One of the peculiar requirements for Farmer Mac is that the loan poolers and loan originators must act as co-insurers, assuming at least the first 10% of any losses. All Farmer Mac securities involved in the loan pooling arrangement must be registered with the Securities and Exchange Commission.

Loan Qualification

To qualify for a pool, a loan must be collateralized by agricultural real estate located in the United States. The real estate can include a home which can cost no more than $100,000 and must be located in a rural community with a population of 2,500 or less. The maximum loan is $2.5 million or the amount secured by no more than 1,000 acres, whichever is larger. The loan-to-value ratio must be less than 80% and the borrower must demonstrate a capability to repay the loan and be a United States citizen engaged in agriculture.

PRIVATE CONDUITS

The financial success of the three giants of the secondary mortgage market (FNMA, GNMA and FHLMC) has brought private mortgage packagers into the marketplace. These are organizations such as MGIC Investment Corporation (a subsidiary of Mortgage Guaranty Investment Corporation); Residential Funding Corporation (a subsidiary of Norwest Mortgage Corp.); financial subsidiaries of such household-name companies as General Electric, Lockheed Aircraft, and Sears, Roebuck; and mortgage packaging subsidiaries of state realtor associations. These organizations both compete with the big three and specialize in markets not served by them. For example, Residential Funding Corp. will package mortgage loans as large as $500,000, well above the limits imposed by FNMA and FHLMC (same as FNMA) and limits on FHA and VA loans. All of these organizations will buy from loan originators who are not large enough to create their own pools. At least one specializes in helping to originate seller carryback loans that can be sold on the secondary market.

Before leaving the topic of the secondary market, it is important to note that without electronic data transmission and computers, the programs just described would be severely handicapped. There are currently thousands of mortgage pools each containing from $1 million to $500 million (and more) in mortgage loans. Each loan in a pool has its own monthly payment schedule, and each payment must be broken down into its principal and interest components and any property tax and insurance impounds. Computers do this work as well as issue receipts and late notices. The pool, in turn, will be owned by several dozen to a hundred or more investors each with a different fractional interest in the pool. Once a month incoming mortgage payments are tallied, a small fee deducted for the operation of the pool, and the balance allotted among the investors, all by computer. A computer will also print and mail checks to investors and provide them with an accounting of the pool's asset level.

COMPUTERIZATION

With advanced computer programs now available, secondary market operators are dispensing with the monthly mailing of checks to large investors. Instead, funds are electronically transmitted directly to the investor's bank account and the investor receives a notice that this has been done. If an investor is in more than one pool, the computer combines all payments due into one statement and one automatic deposit. Keeping track of the numbers is no small matter when a single large investor can be in as many as 1,000 different pools, and Freddie Mac, for example, is issuing 12 to 40 new pools a day. (By comparison, Fannie Mae does about as much business—$20 billion a year, as Freddie Mac. Ginnie Mae does about $50 billion a year.)

Electronic Transfers

Old timers in real estate will remember when a weekly sheet listing mortgage lenders in town with their current loan rates was passed around each real estate office. As interest rates began to fluctuate wildly in the late 1970s, this sheet was updated and circulated more often. In some real estate offices one person was

MORTGAGE NETWORKS

given the job of calling lenders daily for quotes on loan availability and interest rates. Since then, rate changes have become a bit less frequent and, more importantly, the weekly loan sheet is being replaced by a computer terminal. A salesperson simply types in words that request loan information, and the computer screen shows lenders' names plus their current loan offerings and interest rates. A salesperson can shop by computer for the best loan for a buyer and the buyer can watch. The salesperson (or buyer) then makes telephone contact with the lender and arranges for a loan interview.

Some of the more sophisticated mortgage networks go further. The salesperson can touch additional keys, and the computer will prequalify the buyer, match the buyer with a loan and tell the lender to mail loan application papers to that real estate office. If the real estate office has a printer, a loan application and loan agreement can be typed out on the spot.

There are currently a dozen computerized mortgage networks in the United States and more are being formed. Some networks are local and some are national. Some offer information only, and others allow the real estate office to interact with the lender. Some networks will issue a loan commitment by computer in the real estate office. With loan formats becoming more standardized because of the secondary mortgage market, shopping for a mortgage loan by computer is beginning to resemble shopping for generic brands at discount stores. Note that a lender will not be on a computer network unless it chooses to be and pays a fee. Nonmember lenders would still have to be contacted by telephone. The networks also charge real estate offices to be on the network.

AVAILABILITY
AND PRICE OF
MORTGAGE MONEY

Thus far we have been concerned with the money pipelines between lenders and borrowers. Ultimately though, money must have a source. These sources are savings generated by individuals and businesses as a result of their spending less than they earn (**real savings**), and government-created money, called **fiat money** or "printing press money." This second source does not represent unconsumed labor and materials; instead it competes for available goods and services alongside the savings of individuals and businesses.

In the arena of money and capital, real estate borrowers must compete with the needs of government, business, and consumers. Governments, particularly the federal government, compete the hardest when they borrow to finance a deficit. Not to borrow would mean bankruptcy and the inability to pay government employees and provide government programs and services. Strong competition also comes from business and consumer credit sectors. In the face of such strong competition for loan funds, home buyers must either pay higher interest or be outbid.

One "solution" to this problem is for the federal government to create more money, thus making competition for funds easier and interest rates lower. Unfortunately, the net result is often "too much money chasing too few goods," and prices are pulled upward by the demand caused by the newly created money. This is followed by rising interest rates as savers demand higher returns to compensate for losses in purchasing power. Many economists feel that the higher price levels and interest rates of the 1970s resulted from applying too much of this "solution" to the economy since 1965.

The alternative solution, from the standpoint of residential loans, is to increase real savings or decrease competing demands for available money. A number of plans and ideas have been put forth by civic, business, and political leaders. They include proposals to simplify income taxes and balance the federal budget, incentives to increase productive output, and incentives to save money in retirement accounts.

Usury

An old idea that has been tried, but is of dubious value for holding down interest rates, is legislation to impose interest rate ceilings. Known as **usury laws** and found in nearly all states, these laws were originally enacted to prohibit lenders from overcharging interest on loans to individuals. However, since the end of World War II, the ceilings in some states have failed to keep in step with rising interest rates with the result that borrowers are denied loans. Most states have raised usury limits in response to higher interest rates. But the rules and exceptions are so complex that a local attorney must be consulted. Additionally, the U.S. Congress passed legislation in 1980 that exempts from state usury limits most home loans made by institutional lenders.

Price to the Borrower

Ultimately, the rate of interest the borrower must pay to obtain a loan is dependent on the cost of money to the lender, reserves for default, loan servicing costs, and available investment alternatives. For example, go to a savings institution and see what they are paying depositors on various accounts. To this add 2% for the cost of maintaining cash in the tills, office space, personnel, advertising, free gifts for depositors, deposit insurance, loan servicing, loan reserves for defaults and a ¼% profit margin. This will give you an idea of how much borrowers must be charged.

Life insurance companies, pension funds, and trust funds do not have to "pay" for their money like thrift institutions. Nonetheless, they do want to earn the highest possible yields, with safety, on the money in their custody. Thus, if a real estate buyer wants to borrow in order to buy a home, the buyer must compete successfully with the other investment opportunities available on the open market. To determine the rate for yourself, look at the yields on newly issued corporate bonds as shown in the financial section of your daily newspaper. Add ½ of 1% to this for the extra work in packaging and servicing mortgage loans and you will have the interest rate home borrowers must pay to attract lenders.

DUE-ON-SALE

From an investment risk standpoint, when a lender makes a loan with a fixed interest rate, the lender recognizes that during the life of the loan interest rates may rise or fall. When they rise, the lender remains locked into a lower rate. Most loans contain a **due-on-sale clause** (also called an **alienation clause** or a **call clause**). In the past, these were inserted by lenders so that if the borrower sold the property to someone considered uncreditworthy by the lender, the lender could call the loan balance due. When interest rates increase, though, lenders can use these clauses to increase the rate of interest on the loan when the property changes hands, by threatening to accelerate the balance of the loan unless the new owner will accept a higher rate of return.

PREPAYMENT

If loan rates drop it becomes worthwhile for a borrower to shop for a new loan and repay the existing one in full. To compensate, loan contracts sometimes call for a **prepayment penalty** in return for giving the borrower the right to repay the loan early. A typical prepayment penalty amounts to the equivalent of 6 months interest on the amount that is being paid early. However, the penalty varies from loan to loan and from state to state. Some loan contracts permit up to 20% of the unpaid balance to be paid in any one year without penalty. Other contracts make the penalty stiffest when the loan is young. In certain states, laws do not permit prepayment penalties on loans more than 5 years old. By federal law, prepayment penalties are not allowed on FHA and VA loans.

As we have already seen, a major problem for savings institutions is that they are locked into long-term loans while being dependent on short-term savings deposits. As a result, savings institutions now prefer to make mortgage loans that allow the interest rate to rise and fall during the life of the loan. To make this arrangement more attractive to borrowers, these loans are offered at a lower rate of interest than a fixed-rate loan of similar maturity.

ADJUSTABLE RATE MORTGAGES

  The first step toward mortgage loans with adjustable interest rates came in the late 1970s. The loan was called a **variable rate mortgage** and the interest rate could be adjusted up or down by the lender during the 30-year life of the loan to reflect the rise and fall in interest rates paid to savers by the lender. The Federal Home Loan Bank Board (FHLBB) limited adjustments to no more than ½ of 1% each 6 months and a maximum of 2½% over the life of the loan. Any changes in the interest rate on the loan were reflected each 6 months in the monthly payments on the loan. Then in 1980, the FHLBB approved the use of a **renegotiable rate mortgage** loan. This was a 30-year loan with a requirement that every 1, 3, or 5 years the interest rate be adjusted to reflect current market conditions. Monthly payments were then adjusted up or down accordingly.

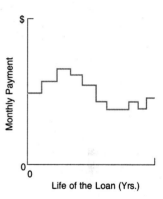

Figure 12:2. Adjustable Rate Mortgage

In 1981, the FHLBB authorized savings institutions to make the type of adjustable mortgage loan you are most likely to encounter in today's loan marketplace. This loan format is called an **adjustable rate mortgage (ARM)** or **adjustable mortgage loan (AML).** By 1988, the federal government enacted new regulations which standardized the ARM requirements in all of the federal agencies. The main requirement is that the interest rate on these loans be tied to some publicly available index that is mutually acceptable to the lender and the borrower. Basically, the

Current Format

concept is the same as the variable rate mortgage: as interest rates rise and fall in the open market, then the interest rate the lender is entitled to receive from the borrower rises and falls. The purpose is to more closely match what the savings institution receives from borrowers to what it must pay savers to attract funds.

The benefit of an ARM to a borrower is that ARMs carry an initial interest rate that is lower than the rate on a fixed-rate mortgage of similar maturity. This often makes the difference between being able to qualify for a desired home and not qualifying for it. Other advantages to the borrower are that if market interest rates fall, the borrower's monthly payments will fall. (This happens without incurring prepayment penalties or new loan origination costs, which could be the case with a fixed-rate loan.) Most ARMs allow assumption by a new buyer at the terms in the ARM, and most allow total prepayment without penalty, particularly if there has been an upward adjustment in the interest rate.

The disadvantage to the borrower of an ARM is that if interest rates rise the borrower is going to pay more. During periods of rising interest rates, property values and wages presumably will also rise. But the possibility of progressively larger monthly payments for the family home is still not attractive. As a result, various compromises have been worked out between lenders and borrowers whereby rates can rise on loans, but not by too much. In view of the fact that about one-half of all mortgage loans being originated by thrifts, banks, and mortgage companies are now adjustable, let's take a closer look at what a borrower gets with this loan format.

Interest Rate   The interest rate on an ARM is tied to an **index rate.** When the index rate moves up or down, so do the borrower's payments when adjustment time arrives. Lenders and borrowers alike want a rate that genuinely reflects current market conditions for interest rates and which can be easily verified. By far, the most popular index is the interest rate on 1-year U.S. Treasury securities. Next most popular is the cost of funds to thrift institutions as measured by the FHLBB. A few loans use 6-month Treasury bills as an index rate.

To the index rate is added the margin. The **margin** is for the lender's cost of doing business, risk of loss on the loan, and profit. Currently this runs from 2% to 3%, depending on the characteristics of the loan. The margin is a useful comparison device because if two lenders are offering the same loan terms and the same index, but one loan has a margin of 2% and the other 3%, then the one with the 2% margin will have lower loan payments. As a rule, the margin stays constant during the life of the loan. At each adjustment point in the loan's life, the lender takes the index rate and adds the margin. The total becomes the interest the borrower will pay until the next adjustment occurs.

Margin

The amount of time that elapses between adjustments is called the **adjustment period.** By far, the most common adjustment period is 1 year. Less commonly used are 6-month, 3-year, and 5-year adjustment periods. When market rates are rising, the longer adjustment periods benefit the borrower. When market rates are falling, the shorter periods benefit the borrower because index decreases will show up sooner in their monthly payments.

Adjustment Period

Lenders are now required by federal law to disclose an **interest rate cap** or ceiling on how much the interest rate can increase for any one adjustment period during the life of the loan. If the cap is very low, say ½% per year, the lender does not have much more flexibility than if holding a fixed-rate loan. Thus, there would be little reduction of initial rate on the loan compared to a fixed-rate loan. Compromises have prevailed, and the two most popular caps are 1% and 2% per year. In other words, the index rate may rise by 3%, but the cap limits the borrower's rate increase to 1% or 2%. Any unused difference may be added the next year, assuming the index rate has not fallen in the meantime. Since federal law now requires the ceiling, many lenders simply impose a very high ceiling (i.e., 18%) if they choose not to negotiate with the borrower.

Interest Rate Cap

What if a loan's index rate rises so fast that the annual rate cap is reached each year and the lifetime cap is reached soon in the life of the loan? A borrower might be able to handle a modest increase in payments each year, but not big jumps in quick succession. To counteract this possibility, a **payment cap** sets a

Payment Cap

limit on how much the borrower's monthly payment can increase in any one year. A popular figure now in use is 7½%. In other words, no matter how high a payment is called for by the index rate, the borrower's monthly payment can rise, at the most, 7½% per year. For example, given an initial rate of 10% on a 30-year ARM for $100,000, the monthly payment of interest and principal is $878 (see Table 11:1). If the index rate calls for a 2% upward adjustment at the end of 1 year, the payment on the loan would be $1,029. This is an increase of $151 or 17.2%. A 7½% payment cap would limit the increase to 107.5% × $878 = $943.85.

Negative Amortization

Although the 7½% payment cap in the above example protects the borrower's monthly payment from rising too fast, it does not make the difference between what's called for ($1,029) and what's paid ($943.85) go away. The difference ($85.15) is added to the balance owed on the loan and earns interest just like the original amount borrowed. This is called **negative amortization:** instead of the loan balance dropping each month as loan payments are made, the balance owed rises. This can bring concern to the lender who can visualize the day the loan balance exceeds the value of the property. A popular arrangement is to set a limit of 125% of the original loan balance. At that point, either the lender accrues no more negative amortization or the loan is reamortized depending on the wording of the loan contract. *Reamortized* in this situation means the monthly payments will be adjusted upward by enough to stop the negative amortization.

Disclosures

In response to consumers' concern over adjustable rate mortgages, an amendment to Regulation Z became effective October 1, 1988. It requires creditors to provide consumers with more extensive information about the variable rate feature of ARMs. The amendments apply only to closed-end credit transactions secured by the consumer's principal dwelling. Transactions secured by the consumer's principal dwelling with a term of one (1) year or less are exempt from the new disclosure. To comply with the amendment, lenders will have to provide consumers with a historical example that shows how actual changes in index values will have affected payments on a $10,000 loan, and also provide a statement of initial and maximum interest rates. Lenders must also provide prospective borrowers with an educational brochure about ARMs called "The Consumer Handbook on Adjustable Rate Mortgages" or a suitable substitute. All the information must be given to the consumer at the time the loan application form is provided to the consumer or before a nonrefundable fee is paid, whichever is earlier. The maximum interest rate must be stated as a specified amount or stated in a manner in which the consumer may easily ascertain the maximum interest rate at the time of entering the obligation.

Choosing Wisely

When a lender makes an ARM loan, the lender must explain to the borrower, in writing, the **worst-case scenario.** In other words, the lender must explain what will happen to the borrower's payments if the index rises the maximum amount each period up to the lifetime interest cap. If there is a payment cap, that and any possibility of negative amortization must also be explained. If the borrower is uneasy with these possibilities, then a fixed-rate loan should be considered. Most lenders offer fixed-rate loans as well as adjustable rate loans. VA loans are fixed-rate loans, but FHA now provides an adjustable rate loan program.

"**Teaser rate**" adjustables have been offered from time to time by a few lenders and are best avoided. This is an ARM with an enticingly attractive initial rate below the market. For example, the teaser rate may be offered at 2% below market. A borrower who cannot qualify at the market rate might be able to do so at the teaser rate. However, in a year the loan contract calls for a 2% jump followed by additional annual increases. This overwhelms the borrower who, unable to pay, allows foreclosure to take place.

GRADUATED PAYMENT MORTGAGE

The objective of a **graduated payment mortgage** is to help borrowers qualify for loans by basing repayment schedules on salary expectations. With this type of mortgage, the interest rate and maturity are fixed but the monthly payment gradually rises. For example, a 10%, $60,000, 30-year loan normally requires monthly payments of $527 for complete amortization. Under the graduated payment mortgage, payments could start out as low as $437 per month the first year, then gradually increase to $590 in the eleventh year and then remain at that level until the thirtieth year. Since the interest alone on this $60,000 loan is $500 per month, the amount owed on the loan actually increases during

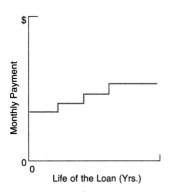

Figure 12:3. Graduated Payment Mortgage

its early years. Only when the monthly payment exceeds the monthly interest does the balance owed on the loan decrease.

The FHA insures graduated payment mortgages under Section 245 and offers five repayment plans. This program is designed to appeal to first-time home buyers in the $15,000 to $25,000 income range because it enables them to tailor their installment payments to their expanding incomes, and thus buy a home sooner than under regular mortgage financing. An **adjustable graduated payment mortgage** combines variable interest with graduated payment features.

A variation of the graduated payment mortgage is the **growing equity mortgage.** This is a 30-year fixed-rate mortgage with monthly payments that are increased 3% to 7% each year. This loan is designed to parallel the borrower's income and fully repay itself in 12 to 15 years.

SHARED APPRECIATION MORTGAGE

The basic concept of a **shared appreciation mortgage (SAM)** is that the borrower gives the lender a portion of the property's appreciation in return for a lower rate of interest. To illustrate, a lender who would otherwise charge 12% interest might agree to take 8% interest plus one-third of the appreciation of the property. The lender is accepting what amounts to a speculative investment in the property in return for a reduced interest rate. The borrower is able to buy and occupy a home that he or she might not otherwise be able to afford, but gives up part of any future price appreciation.

Despite the apparent advantages of the SAM, there are some major pitfalls. For example, at what point in the future is the gain recognized and the lender paid off? If the home is sold, the profits can be split in accordance with the agreement. However, what if the lender feels the home is being sold at too low a price? What if the home is not sold for cash? What if the borrower does not want to sell? One answer to the last situation is that the lender may set a time limit of 10 years on the loan. If the home has not been sold by that time, the home is appraised and the borrower pays the lender the lender's share of the appreciation. At a 10% appreciation rate, a $93,750 house would be worth $243,164 ten years later. If the lender was entitled to one-third of the $149,414 appreciation, the borrower would owe the lender $49,805 in appreciation plus the remaining $70,000 balance on the loan. Unless the borrower can pay cash, this would have to be refinanced at then current

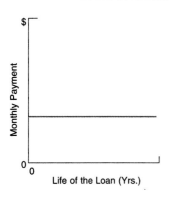

Figure 12:4. Shared Appreciation Mortgage

rates of interest. On the other hand, if the property experiences no appreciation in value, the borrower will have enjoyed a below-market-rate loan for 10 years and be responsible only for refinancing the remaining loan balance at that time.

EQUITY SHARING

Giving the party that provides the financing a "piece of the action in the deal" is not an innovation. Insurance companies financing shopping centers and office buildings have long used the idea of requiring part of the rental income and/or part of the profits plus interest on the loan itself. In other words, in return for providing financing the lender wants to share in some of the benefits normally reserved for the equity holder. The equity holder would agree to this either to get a lower rate of interest, such as in the SAM above, or to get financing when financing was scarce, or where the equity holder was not big enough to handle the deal alone. For example, on a $5 million project, the lender might agree to make a loan of $4 million at a very attractive rate if it can buy a half interest in the equity for $500,000.

Equity sharing is also found in residential financing. One variation is for an enterprising real estate person to find attractive income properties and sell a 50% equity interest to someone who wants to invest in real estate, but who has more money than time. The investor makes half of the down payment and signs for the loan. For this, the investor gets half of the income and profits and all of the tax deductions. The entrepreneur gets the other half in return for the remaining down payment and the effort of finding and managing the property.

"Rich Uncle" Financing

A second variation of equity sharing is often called "rich uncle" financing. The investor may be a parent helping a son or daughter buy a home or a son or daughter buying a parent's present home while giving the parent(s) the right to occupy it. A third variation is for an investor to provide most of the down payment for a home buyer, collect rent from the home buyer, pay the mortgage payments and property taxes, and claim depreciation. Each party has a right to a portion of any appreciation and the right to buy out the other. The FHLMC now recognizes the importance of equity sharing and will buy mortgage loans on shared-equity properties. The FHLMC requires that the owner-occupant contribute at least 5% of the equity, that the owner-occupant and the owner-investor sign the mortgage and note, that both be individuals, and that there be no agreement requiring sale or buy-out within 7 years of the loan date. Equity sharing can provide attractive tax benefits; however, you must seek competent tax advice before involving yourself or someone else in such a plan.

PACKAGE MORTGAGE

Normally, we think of real estate mortgage loans as being secured solely by real estate. However, it is possible to include items classed as personal property in a real estate mortgage, thus creating a **package mortgage.** In residential loans, such items as the refrigerator, clothes washer, and dryer can be pledged along with the house and land in a single mortgage. The purpose is to raise the value of the collateral in order to raise the amount a lender is willing to loan. For the borrower, it offers the opportunity of financing major appliances at the same rate of interest as the real estate itself. This rate is usually lower than if the borrower finances the appliances separately. Once an item of personal property is included in a package mortgage, selling it without the prior consent of the lender is a violation of the mortgage.

BLANKET MORTGAGE

A mortgage secured by two or more properties is called a **blanket mortgage.** Suppose you want to buy a house plus the vacant lot next door, financing the purchase with a single mortgage that covers both properties. The cost of preparing one mortgage instead of two is a savings. Also, by combining the house and lot, the lot can be financed on better terms than if it were financed separately, as lenders more readily loan on a house and land than on land alone. Note, however, that if the vacant lot is later sold separately from the house before the mortgage loan is fully repaid, it will be necessary to have it released from the blanket mortgage. This is usually accomplished by including a partial release clause in the original mortgage agreement that specifies how much of the loan must be repaid before the lot can be released.

REVERSE MORTGAGE

With a regular mortgage, the lender makes a lump sum payment to the borrower, who in turn repays it through monthly payments to the lender. With a **reverse mortgage,** also known as a reverse annuity mortgage or RAM, the lender makes a monthly payment to the homeowner who later repays in a lump sum. The reverse mortgage can be particularly valuable for an elderly homeowner who does not want to sell, but whose retirement income is not quite enough for comfortable living. The home-owner receives a monthly check, has full use of the property, and is not required to repay until he sells or dies. If he sells the home, money from the sale is taken to repay the loan. If he dies first, the property is sold through the estate and the loan repaid.

Under a **construction loan,** also called an interim loan, money is advanced as construction takes place. For example, a vacant lot owner arranges to borrow $60,000 to build a house. The lender does not advance all $60,000 at once because the value of the collateral is insufficient to warrant that amount until the house is finished. Instead, the lender will parcel out the loan as the building is being constructed, always holding a portion until the property is ready for occupancy, or in some cases actually occupied. Some lenders specialize only in construction loans and do not want to wait 20 or 30 years to be repaid. If so, it will be necessary to obtain a permanent long-term mortgage from another source for the purpose of repaying the construction loan. This is known as a permanent commitment or a **take-out loan,** since it takes the construction lender out of the financial picture when construction is completed and allows him to recycle his money into new construction projects.

CONSTRUCTION LOAN

Many real estate lenders still hold long-term loans that were made at interest rates below the current market. One way of raising the return on these loans is to offer borrowers who have them a **blended-rate loan.** Suppose you owe $50,000 on your home loan and the interest rate on it is 7%. Suppose further that the current rate on home loans is 12%. Your lender might offer to refinance your home for $70,000 at 9%, presuming the property will appraise high enough and you have the income to qualify. The $70,000 refinance offer would put $20,000 in your pocket (less loan fees), but would increase the interest you pay from 7% to 9% on the original $50,000. This makes the cost of the $20,000 14% per year. The arithmetic is as follows: you will now be paying 9% × $70,000 = $6,300 in interest. Before you paid 7% × $50,000 = $3,500 in interest. The difference, $2,800, is what you

BLENDED-RATE LOAN

pay to borrow the additional $20,000. This equates to $2,800 ÷ $20,000 = 14% interest. This is the figure you should use in comparing other sources of financing (such as a second mortgage) or deciding whether or not you even want to borrow.

A blended-rate loan can be very attractive in a situation where you want to sell your home and you do not want to help finance the buyer. Suppose your home is worth $87,500 and you have the above-described $50,000, 7% loan. A buyer would normally expect to make a down payment of $17,500 and pay 12% interest on a new $70,000 loan. But with a blended loan your lender could offer the buyer the needed $70,000 financing at 9%, a far more attractive rate and one that requires less income in order to qualify. Blended loans are available on FHA, VA, and conventional loans held by the FNMA. Other lenders also offer them on fixed-rate assumable loans they hold.

BUY-DOWNS

Buy-downs are used to reduce the rate of interest a buyer must pay on a new mortgage loan. For example, suppose a builder has a tract of homes for sale and the current interest rate on home loans is 12%. At that interest rate, there are few buyers. What the builder can do is to arrange with a lender to pay the lender discount points so that the lender can offer a loan at a lower interest to the buyer. This can be done for the life of the loan at the cost of about 8 discount points for every point of interest rate reduction. Or, it can be done for a shorter period, such as the first 3 years of the loan's life. For example, the builder could offer 9% interest for the first 3 years of the loan. Not only is 9% more attractive than 12%, but more buyers can qualify for loans at 9% than at 12%. Although the buy-down is costly to the builder, it will help sell homes that might otherwise go unsold. Moreover, a buy-down will usually boost sales more than a price reduction of like amount. The builder offering the buy-down will usually take a price reduction equal to the discount points if the buyer will forgo the buy-down. The disadvantage of a short-term buy-down is that market rates may not drop to allow refinancing and/or the buyer's income may not increase enough to accommodate the rising monthly payments.

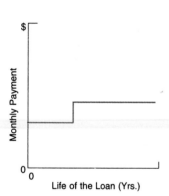

Figure 12:5. Buy-down Mortgage

EQUITY MORTGAGE

An **equity mortgage** is a loan arrangement wherein the lender agrees to extend a line of credit based on the amount of equity in a borrower's home. Since the Internal Revenue Code of 1986 limited interest deductions to home mortgages, these loans have become one of the fastest growing areas of real estate lending. The maximum amount of the loan is generally 70% to 80% of the appraised value of the home minus any first mortgage or other liens against the property. The borrower need not take all the credit available, but rather can draw against the mortgage as needed. Some lenders specify a minimum amount per withdrawal. The borrower pays interest only on the amount actually borrowed, not the maximum available. The borrower then has several years to repay the amount borrowed. The interest rate is adjustable and tends to be 1 to 3 percentage points above the "prime rate" paid by large corporations.

The equity mortgage will typically be a second mortgage that is used to tap the increase in equity resulting from rising home prices and first loan paydown. It's all done without having to refinance the first loan and uses the home as an asset against which the homeowner can borrow and repay as needed. Equity mortgages are very popular as a source of home improvement loans, money for college expenses, money to start a business, money for a major vacation and money to buy more real estate.

When a seller is willing to accept part of the property's purchase price in the form of the buyer's promissory note accompanied by a mortgage or deed of trust, it is called **seller financing.** This allows the buyer to substitute a promissory note for cash, and the seller is said to be "taking back paper." Seller financing is popular for land sales (where lenders rarely loan) on property where an existing mortgage is being assumed by the buyer, and on property where the seller prefers to receive his money spread out over a period of time with interest instead of lump-sum cash. For example, a retired couple sells a rental home they own. The home is worth $120,000, and they owe $20,000. If they need only $60,000 in cash, they might be more than happy to take $60,000 down, let the buyer assume the existing mortgage and accept the remaining $40,000 in monthly payments at current interest rates. Alternatively, the buyer and seller can agree to structure the $40,000 as an adjustable, graduated, partially amortized or interest-only loan.

SELLER FINANCING

If the seller receives the sales price spread out over two or more years, income taxes are calculated using the installment reporting method discussed in Chapter 13. Being able to spread out the taxes on a gain may be an incentive to use seller financing. The seller should be aware, however, that he may not be able to convert his "paper" to cash without a long wait or without having to sell it at a substantial discount to an investor. Additionally, the seller is responsible for servicing the loan and is subject to losses due to default and foreclosure.

Note that some real estate agents and lenders refer to a loan that is carried back by a seller as a **purchase money** loan. Others define a purchase money loan as any loan, carryback or institutional, that is used to finance the purchase of real property.

WRAPAROUND MORTGAGE

An alternative method of financing a real estate sale such as the one just reviewed is to use a **wraparound mortgage** or **wraparound deed of trust.** A "wraparound" encompasses existing mortgages and is subordinate (junior) to them. The existing mortgages stay on the property and the new mortgage wraps around them.

To illustrate, assume the existing $20,000 loan in the previous example carries an interest rate of 7% and that there are 10 years remaining on the loan. Assume further that current interest rates are 12%. With a wraparound it is possible for the buyer to pay less than 12% and at the same time for the seller to receive more than 12% on the money owed him. This is done by taking the buyer's $60,000 down payment and then creating a new junior mortgage that includes not only the $20,000 owed on the existing first mortgage but also the $40,000 the buyer owes the seller. In other words, the wraparound mortgage will be for $60,000, and the seller continues to remain liable for payment of the first mortgage. If the interest rate on the wraparound is set at 10%, the buyer saves by not having to pay 12% as he would on an entirely new loan. The advantage to the seller is that he is earning 10% not only on his $40,000 equity, but also on the $20,000 loan for which he is paying 7% interest. This gives the seller an actual yield of 11½% on his $40,000. (The calculation is as follows. The seller receives 10% on $60,000, which amounts to $6,000. He pays 7% on $20,000, which is $1,400. The difference, $4,600 is divided by $40,000 to get the seller's actual yield of 11½%.)

Wraparounds are not limited to seller financing. If the seller in the above example did not want to finance the sale, a third-party lender could provide the needed $40,000 and take a wraparound mortgage. The wraparound concept will not work when the mortgage debt to be "wrapped" contains an enforcement due-on-sale clause.

Another financing technique is **subordination.** For example, a person owns a $200,000 vacant lot suitable for building, and a builder wants to build an $800,000 building on the lot. The builder has only $100,000 cash and the largest construction loan available is $800,000. If the builder can convince the lot owner to take $100,000 in cash and $100,000 later, he would have the $1 million total. However, the lender making the $800,000 loan will want to be the first mortgagee to protect its position in the event of foreclosure. The lot owner must be willing to take a subordinate position, in this case a second mortgage. If the project is successful, the lot owner will receive $100,000, plus interest, either in cash after the building is built and sold or as monthly payments. If the project goes into foreclosure, the lot owner can be paid only if the $800,000 first mortgage claim is satisfied in full from the sale proceeds. As you can surmise here, the lot owner must be very careful that the money loaned by the lender actually goes into construction and that whatever is built is worth at least $800,000 in addition to the land.

SUBORDINATION

A **contract for deed,** also called an **installment contract** or **land contract,** enables the seller to finance a buyer by permitting him to make a down payment followed by monthly payments. However, title remains in the name of the seller. In addition to its wide use in financing land sales, it has also been a very effective financing tool in several states as a means of selling homes. For example, a homeowner owes $25,000 on his home and wants to sell it for $85,000. A buyer is found but does not have the $60,000 down payment necessary to assume the existing loan. The buyer does have $8,000, but for one reason or another cannot or chooses not to borrow from an institutional lender. If the seller is agreeable, the buyer can pay the seller $8,000 and enter into an installment contract with the seller for the remaining $77,000. The contract will call for monthly payments by the buyer to the seller that are large enough to allow the seller to meet the payments on the $25,000 loan plus repay the $52,000 owed to the seller, with interest. Unless property taxes and insurance are

CONTRACT FOR DEED

billed to the buyer, the seller will also collect for these and pay them. When the final payment is made to the seller (or the property refinanced through an institutional lender), title is conveyed to the buyer. Meanwhile, the seller continues to hold title and is responsible for paying the mortgage. In addition to wrapping around a mortgage, an installment contract can also be used to wrap around another installment contract, provided it does not contain an enforceable due-on-sale clause. (Please see Chapter 8 for more about the contractual side of installment contracts.)

OPTION

When viewed as a financing tool, an **option** provides a method by which the need to immediately finance the full price of a property can be postponed. For example, a developer is offered 100 acres of land for a house subdivision but is not sure that the market will absorb that many houses. The solution is to buy 25 acres outright and take three 25-acre options at present prices on the remainder. If the houses on the first 25 acres sell promptly, the builder can exercise the options to buy the remaining land. If sales are not good, the builder can let the remaining options expire and avoid being stuck with unwanted acreage.

A popular variation on the option idea is the **lease with option to buy** combination. Under it an owner leases to a tenant who, in addition to paying rent and using the property, also obtains the right to purchase it at a present price for a fixed period of time. Homes are often sold this way, particularly when the resale market is sluggish. (Please see Chapter 8 for more about a lease with option to buy.)

Options can provide speculative opportunities to persons with limited amounts of capital. If prices do not rise, the optionee loses only the cost of the option; if prices do rise, the optionee exercises the option and realizes a profit.

CREATIVE FINANCING

The decade of the 1980s started with a shortage of money for real estate loans and an abundance of financing ideas. Many of these involved seller-assisted financing. At one point in 1982 it was estimated that 80% of home mortgage financing was by way of assumptions and seller financing.

The wraparound mortgage and installment contract are considered forms of creative financing. Most were designed to pass along the benefits of a low-interest loan in a high-interest market. If interest rates fall, wrapping will be less attractive and new financing more attractive. Nonetheless, there is plenty of room for creative ideas to solve financing problems. For example, a $400,000 apartment building with a $200,000 first mortgage against it is for sale. The seller wants $120,000 in cash and will carry paper for the rest as long as the loan-to-value ratio does not exceed 80%. A buyer has $40,000 in cash plus a house worth $80,000 with a $20,000 loan against it. The solution is to refinance the apartment building with the lender for 70%. This is a standard L/V ratio for apartment buildings and creates $80,000 in cash. The buyer gives the seller $40,000 in cash, a $40,000 second mortgage against the apartment building, and a $40,000 second mortgage against the house.

In another example of creative financing, consider the builder with many unsold homes but plenty of buyers who would like to buy if they could finance buyers for their present homes. The builder offers to help finance the sale of a buyer's property in order to make his own sale. Two parties get the homes they want and the builder is relieved of unsold inventory.

One seller-financing arrangement that deserves special attention because of its traps for the unwary is the **overencumbered property.** Institutional lenders are closely regulated regarding the amount of money they can loan against the appraised value of the property. Individuals are not regulated. The following will illustrate the potential problem. Suppose a seller owns a house that is realistically worth $100,000 and the mortgage balance is $10,000. A buyer offers to purchase the property with the condition that he be allowed to obtain an $80,000 loan on the property from a lender. The $80,000 is used to pay off the existing $10,000 loan and to pay the broker's commission, loan fees, and closing costs. The remaining $62,000 is split $30,000 to the seller and $32,000 to the buyer. The buyer also gives the seller a note, secured by a second mortgage against the property, for $80,000. The seller may feel good about getting $30,000 in cash and an $80,000 mortgage, for this is more than the property is worth, or so it seems.

But the $80,000 second mortgage stands junior to the $80,000 first mortgage. That's $160,000 of debt against a $100,000 property. The buyer might be trying to resell the property for $160,000 or more, but the chances of this are slim. More likely

OVERLY CREATIVE FINANCING?

the buyer will wind up walking away from the property. This leaves the seller the choice of taking over the payments on the first mortgage or losing the property completely to the holder of the first.

Although such a scheme sounds crazy when viewed from a distance, the reason it can be performed is that the seller wants more for the property than it's worth. Someone then offers a deal showing that price, and the seller looks the other way from the possible consequences. Real estate agents who participate in such transactions are likely to find their licenses suspended. State licensing authorities take the position that a real estate agent is a professional who should know enough not to take part in a deal that leaves the seller holding a junior lien on an overencumbered property. This, too, seems logical when viewed from a distance. But when sales are slow and commissions thin, it is sometimes easy to put commission income ahead of fiduciary responsibility. If in doubt about the propriety of a transaction, the Golden Rule of doing unto others as you would have them do unto you still applies. (Or as some restate it: "What goes around, comes around.")

INVESTING IN MORTGAGES

Individuals can invest in mortgages in two ways. One is to invest in mortgage loan pools through certificates guaranteed by Ginnie Mae and Freddie Mac and available from stockbrokers. These yield about ½ of 1% below what FHA and VA borrowers are paying. In 1988, for example, this was approximately 10%, and the certificates are readily convertible to cash at current market prices on the open market if the investor does not want to hold them through maturity.

Individuals can also buy junior mortgages at yields above Ginnie Mae and Freddie Mac certificates. These junior mortgages are seconds, thirds, and fourths offered by mortgage brokers. They yield more because they are riskier as to repayment and much more difficult to convert to cash before maturity. "There is," as the wise old adage says, "no such thing as a free lunch." Thus, it is important to recognize that when an investment of any kind promises above-market returns, there is some kind of added risk attached. With junior mortgages, it is important to realize that when a borrower offers to pay a premium above the best loan rates available from banks and thrift institutions, it is because the borrower and/or the property does not qualify for the best rates.

Before buying a mortgage as an investment, one should have the title to the property searched. This is the only way to know for certain what priority the mortgage will have in the event of foreclosure. There have been cases where investors have purchased what they were told to be first and second mortgages only to find in foreclosure that they were actually holding third and fourth mortgages where the amount of debt exceeded the value of the property.

And how does one find the value of a property? By having it appraised by a professional appraiser who is independent of the party making or selling the mortgage investment. This value is compared to the existing and proposed debt against the property. The investor should also run a credit check on the borrower. The investor's final protection is, however, in making certain that the market value of the property is well in excess of the loans against it and that the property is well-constructed, well-located, and functional.

RENTAL

Even though tenants do not acquire fee ownership, **rentals** and **leases** are a means of financing real estate. Whether the tenant is a bachelor receiving the use of a $30,000 apartment for which he pays $350 rent per month or a large corporation leasing a warehouse for 20 years, leasing is an ideal method of financing when the tenant does not want to buy, cannot raise the funds to buy, or prefers to invest available funds elsewhere. Similarly, **farming leases** provide for the use of land without the need to purchase it. Some farm leases call for fixed rental payment. Other leases require the farmer to pay the landowner a share of the value of the crop that is actually produced—say 25%, and the landowner shares with the farmer the risks of weather, crop output, and prices.

Under a **sale and leaseback** arrangement, an owner-occupant sells the property and then remains as a tenant. Thus, the buyer acquires an investment and the seller obtains capital for other purposes while retaining the use of the property. A variation is for the tenant to construct a building, sell it to a prearranged buyer, and immediately lease it back.

LAND LEASES   Although **leased land** arrangements are common throughout the United States for both commercial and industrial users and for farmers, anything other than fee ownership of residential land is unthinkable in many areas. Yet in some parts of the United States (for example, Baltimore, Maryland; Orange County, California; throughout Hawaii; and parts of Florida) homes built on leased land are commonplace. Typically, these leases are at least 55 years in length and, barring an agreement to the contrary, the improvements to the land become the property of the fee owner at the end of the lease. Rents may be fixed in advance for the life of the lease, renegotiated at present points during the life of the lease, or a combination of both.

To hedge against inflation, when fixed rents are used in a long-term lease, it is common practice to use **step-up rentals.** For example, under a 55-year house-lot lease, the rent may be set at $400 per year for the first 15 years, $600 per year for the next 10 years, $800 for the next 10 years, and so forth. An alternative is to renegotiate the rent at various points during the life of a lease so that the effects of land value changes are more closely equalized between the lessor and the lessee. For example, a 60-year lease may contain renegotiation points at the fifteenth, thirtieth, and forty-fifth years. At those points the property would be reappraised and the lease rent adjusted to reflect any changes in the value of the property. Property taxes and any increases in property taxes are paid by the lessee.

FINANCING   If people always paid cash for real estate, the last four chapters
OVERVIEW   would not have been necessary. But 95% of the time they don't; so means have been devised to finance their purchases. This has been true since the beginning of recorded history and will continue into the future. The financing methods that evolve will depend on the problems to be solved. For example, long-term fixed-rate amortized loans were the solution to foreclosures in the 1930s, and they worked well as long as interest rates did not fluctuate greatly. Graduated payment loans were devised when housing prices rose faster than buyers' incomes. Adjustable rate loans were developed so that lenders could more closely align the interest they receive from borrowers with the interest they pay their savers. Extensive use of loan assumptions, wraparounds, and seller financing became necessary in the early

1980s because borrowers could not qualify for 16% and 18% loans and sellers were unwilling to drop prices.

With regard to the future, if mortgage money is expensive or in short supply, seller financing will play a large role. With the experience of rapidly fluctuating interest rates fresh in people's minds, loans with adjustable rates will continue to be widely offered. Fixed-rate loans will either have short maturities or carry a premium to compensate the lender for being locked into a fixed rate for a long period. When interest rates turn down again, borrowers with adjustable loans will benefit from lower monthly payments. If rates stay down long enough, fixed-rate loans will become more popular again.

REVIEW QUESTIONS

1. The place where a real estate borrower makes a loan application, receives a loan and makes loan payments describes the
   A. primary mortgage market.
   B. secondary mortgage market.
   C. first loan market.
   D. second loan market.

2. Historically, the foremost single source of funds for residential mortgage loans in this country has been
   A. commercial banks.
   B. insurance companies.
   C. mortgage companies.
   D. savings and loan associations.

3. When savings are removed from thrift institutions in large amounts for investment in Treasury securities,
   A. the real estate market enjoys an increase in activity.
   B. disintermediation occurs.
   C. Both A and B.
   D. Neither A nor B.

4. Reasons for the decline in residential loans made by the S&Ls include all but the following:
   A. Deregulation of the lending industry.
   B. Proliferation of savings and loan organizations.
   C. New laws which allowed higher risk loans.
   D. Placing the FSLIC under the FDIC.

5. A real estate loan which calls for the lender to receive interest plus a percentage of the rental income from a property is
   A. designed to protect the lender from inflation.
   B. known as a participation loan.
   C. Both A and B.
   D. Neither A nor B.

6. Mortgage companies
   A. originate loans.
   B. service loans which they have sold on the secondary mortgage market.
   C. Both A and B.
   D. Neither A nor B.

7. The secondary mortgage market provides
   A. a means for investors to acquire real estate loans with origination and servicing facilities.
   B. a way for a lender to sell real estate loans.
   C. Both A and B.
   D. Neither A nor B.

8. All of the following are true of the Federal National Mortgage Association EXCEPT that it is
   A. a privately owned corporation.
   B. managed by the federal government.
   C. active in buying FHA and VA mortgage loans.
   D. known as Fannie Mae.

9. FNMA will purchase
   A. first mortgage loans.   D. conventional loans.
   B. second mortgage loans.   E. All of the above.
   C. government-insured or guaranteed loans.

10. Participation certificates issued by Freddie Mac can be
    A. sold for cash.   C. Both A and B.
    B. used as collateral for loans.   D. Neither A nor B.

11. Collateralized mortgage obligations issued by the FHLMC provide an investor with investments of
    A. predictable maturity.   C. Both A and B.
    B. guaranteed yields.   D. Neither A nor B.

12. A large measure of the success of the secondary mortgage market is attributable to the advent of
    A. computers.
    B. electronic data transmission systems.
    C. Both A and B.
    D. Neither A nor B.

13. Which of the following forms of money represents unconsumed labor and materials?
    A. Real savings.   C. Both A and B.
    B. Fiat money.   D. Neither A nor B.

14. Enforcement of a due-on-sale clause can result from all of the situations below except
    A. an installment sale contract.
    B. a lease-option with option to buy.
    C. a lease of one year's duration.
    D. foreclosure of a junior lien.

15. In order to make adjustable rate mortgage loans more attractive to borrowers, lenders offer
   A. lower initial interest rates.
   B. gifts such as appliances, trips, etc.
   C. lower insurance rates.
   D. lower down payments.

16. Prior to the introduction of adjustable rate mortgages, the FHLBB approved the use of
   A. variable rate mortgages.
   B. renegotiable rate mortgages.
   C. Both A and B.
   D. Neither A nor B.

17. When considering an ARM loan, the lender must explain to the borrower, in writing, the
   A. worst-case scenario.
   B. best-case scenario.
   C. average case scenario.
   D. respective credit report.

18. Equity sharing is based on the concept of someone who has assets sharing those assets in exchange for
   A. a share of the ownership.
   B. tax benefits.
   C. Both A and B.
   D. Neither A nor B.

19. When an existing loan at a low interest rate is refinanced by a new loan at an interest rate between the current market rate and the rate on the old loan, the result is a
   A. combined loan.
   B. blended loan.
   C. wraparound loan.
   D. merged loan.

20. An individual who is contemplating the purchase of a mortgage as an investment should have
   A. the property appraised.
   B. a credit check made on the borrower.
   C. the title searched.
   D. All of the above.

Taxes and Assessments

OVERVIEW OF
CHAPTER 13

In this chapter we are primarily concerned with ad valorem taxes and various types of property assessments. Determining how much tax the property owner must pay involves these basic steps: appropriation, assessment, and tax rate calculation. The chapter also covers unpaid property taxes, assessment appeal, property tax exemptions and variations, tax limitation measures, and special assessments. In the latter half of the chapter, income taxes on the sale of a residence, including the lifetime exclusion, taxable gain, and installment sales, are covered. The chapter concludes with coverage of property tax and interest deductions and the agent's liability for tax advice.

LEARNING OBJECTIVES

After successful completion of this chapter, you should be able to:

1. Explain the purpose of property taxes and how they are determined.
2. Explain tax exemptions, variations, and limitation measures.
3. Define special assessments and explain the process for confirmation and apportionment.
4. Explain how to calculate income taxes on the sale of a residence.
5. Calculate the amount realized, taxable gain, and lifetime exclusion on the sale of a residence.
6. Describe property tax and interest deductions.
7. Explain what the agent's liability is for tax advice.
8. Describe the applicability of conveyance taxes.

KEY • TERMS

Adjusted sales price: the sales price of a property less commissions, fix-up, and closing costs

Ad valorem taxes: taxes charged according to the value of a property

Assessed value: a value placed on a property for the purpose of taxation

Assessment appeal board: local governmental body which hears and rules on property owner complaints of overassessment

Basis: the price paid for property; used in calculating income taxes

Installment sale: sale of real estate in which the proceeds of the sale are deferred beyond the year of sale

Documentary tax: a fee or tax on deeds and other documents payable at the time of recordation

Mill rate: property tax rate that is expressed in tenths of a cent per dollar of assessed valuation

Tax certificate: a document issued at a tax sale that entitles the purchaser to a deed at a later date if the property is not redeemed

Tax lien: a charge or hold by the government against property to insure the payment of taxes

PROPERTY TAXES

The largest single source of income in America for local government programs and services is the property tax. Schools (from kindergarten through two-year colleges), fire and police departments, local welfare programs, public libraries, street maintenance, parks, and public hospital facilities are mainly supported by property taxes. Some state governments also obtain a portion of their revenues from this source.

Property taxes are **ad valorem** taxes. This means that they are levied according to the value of one's property; the more valuable the property, the higher the tax, and vice versa. The underlying theory of ad valorem taxation is that those owning the more valuable properties are wealthier and hence able to pay more taxes.

How does a local government determine the amount of tax to collect each year from each property owner? Step 1 is local budget preparation and appropriation. Step 2 is the appraisal of all taxable property within the taxation district. Step 3 is to allocate the amount to be collected among the taxable properties in the district. Let's look more closely at this process.

Budget and Appropriation

Each taxing body with the authority to tax prepares its **budget** for the coming year. Taxing bodies include counties, cities, boroughs, towns and villages, and, in some states, school boards, sanitation districts, and county road departments. Each budget along with a list of sources from which the money will be derived is enacted into law. This is the **appropriation process.** Then estimated sales taxes, state and federal revenue sharing, business licenses, and city income taxes are subtracted from the budget. The balance must come from property taxes.

Appraisal and Assessment

Next, the valuation of the taxable property within each taxing body's district must be determined. A county or state assessor's office **appraises** each taxable parcel of land and the improvements thereon. In some states this job is contracted out to private appraisal companies. Appraisal procedures vary from state to state. In some, the appraised value is the estimated fair market cash value of the property. This is the cash price one would expect a buyer and a seller to agree upon in a normal open market transaction. Other states start with the fair market value of the land and add to it the cost of replacing the buildings and other improvements on it, minus an allowance for depreciation due to wear and tear and obsolescence.

The appraised value is converted into an assessed value upon which taxes are based. In some states, the **assessed value** is set equal to the appraised value; in others, it is a percentage of the appraised value. Mathematically, the percentage selected makes no difference as long as each property in a taxing district is treated equally. Consider two houses with appraised values of $60,000 and $120,000, respectively. Whether the assessed values are set equal to appraised values or at a percentage of appraised values, the second house will still bear twice the property tax burden of the first.

Tax Rate Calculation

The assessed values of all properties subject to property taxation are added together in order to calculate the tax rate. To explain this process, suppose that a building lies within the taxation districts of the Westside School District, the city of Rostin, and the county of Pearl River. The school district's budget for the coming year requires $800,000 from property taxes, and the assessed value of taxable property within the district is $20,000,000. By dividing $800,000 by $20,000,000, we see that the school district must collect a tax of 4 cents for every dollar of assessed valuation. This levy can be expressed three ways: (1) as a mill rate, (2) as dollars per hundred, or (3) as dollars per

	Mill Rate	Dollars per Hundred	Dollars per Thousand
School district	40 mills	$4.00	$40.00
City	30	3.00	30.00
County	10	1.00	10.00
Total	80 mills	$8.00	$80.00

Table 13:1. Expressing Property Tax Rates

thousand. All three rating methods are found in the United States.

As a **mill rate,** this tax rate is expressed as mills per dollar of assessed valuation. Since 1 mill equals one-tenth of a cent, a 4-cent tax rate is the same as 40 mills. Expressed as **dollars per hundred,** the same rate would be $4 per hundred of assessed valuation. As **dollars per thousand,** it would be $40 per thousand.

The city of Rostin also calculates its tax rate by dividing its property tax requirements by the assessed value of the property within its boundaries. Suppose that its needs are $300,000 and the city limits enclose property totaling $10,000,000 in assessed valuation. (In this example, the city covers a smaller geographical area than the school district.) Thus the city must collect 3 cents for each dollar of assessed valuation in order to balance its budget.

The county government's budget requires $2,000,000 from property taxes and the county contains $200,000,000 in assessed valuation. This makes the county tax rate 1 cent per dollar of assessed valuation. Table 13:1 shows the school district, city, and county tax rates expressed as mills, dollars per hundred, and dollars per thousand.

Applying the Rate

The final step is to apply the tax rate to each property. Applying the mill rate to a home with an assessed value of $20,000 is simply a matter of multiplying the 80 mills (the equivalent of 8 cents) by the assessed valuation to arrive at property taxes of $1,600 per year. On a dollars per hundred basis, divide the $20,000 assessed valuation by $100 and multiply by $8. The result is $1,600. To insure collection, a lien for this amount is placed against the property. It is removed when the tax is paid. Property tax liens are superior to other types of liens. A mortgage foreclosure does not clear property tax liens; they still must be paid.

To avoid duplicate tax bill mailings, it is a common practice for all taxing bodies in a given county to have the county collect for them at the same time that the county collects on its own behalf. Property tax years generally fall into two categories: January 1 through December 31, and July 1 through the following June 30. Some states require one payment per year; others collect in two installments. A few allow a small discount for early payment, and all charge penalties for late payments.

Because of the monumental volume of numbers and calculations necessary to budget, appropriate, appraise, assess, and calculate property taxes, computers are widely used in property tax offices. Computers also prepare property tax bills, account for property tax receipts, and mail computer-generated notices to those who have not paid.

UNPAID PROPERTY TAXES

If you own real estate and fail to pay the property taxes, you will lose the property. In some states, title to delinquent property is transferred to the county or state. A redemption period follows during which the owner, or any lienholder, can redeem the property by paying back taxes and penalties. If redemption does not occur, the property is sold at a publicly announced auction and the highest bidder receives a **tax deed.** In other states, the sale is held soon after the delinquency occurs and the redemption period follows. At the sale, a **tax certificate** or **certificate of sale** in the amount of the unpaid taxes is sold. The purchaser is entitled to a deed to the property provided the delinquent taxpayer, or anyone holding a lien on the property, does not step forward and redeem it during the redemption period that follows. If it is redeemed, the purchaser receives his money back plus interest. The reason that a lienholder (such as a mortgage lender) is allowed to redeem a property is that if the property taxes are not paid, the lienholder's creditor rights in the property are cut off due to the superiority of the tax lien.

The right of government to divorce a property owner from his land for nonpayment of property taxes is well established by law. However, if the sale procedure is not properly followed, the purchaser may later find the property's title successfully challenged in court. Thus, it behooves the purchaser to obtain a title search and title insurance and, if necessary, to conduct a quiet title suit.

By law, assessment procedures must be uniformly applied to all properties within a taxing jurisdiction. To this end, the assessed values of all lands and buildings are made available for public inspection. These are the **assessment rolls.** They permit a property owner to compare the assessed valuation on his property with assessed valuations on similar properties. If an owner feels overassessed, he can then file an appeal before an **assessment appeal board,** or before a board of review, board of equalization, or tribunal. Some states also provide further appeal channels or permit appeal to a court of law if the property owner remains dissatisfied with the assessment. Note that the appeal process deals only with the methods of assessment and taxation, not with the tax rate or the amount of tax.

ASSESSMENT APPEAL

    In some states, the **board of equalization** performs another assessment-related task: that of equalizing assessment procedures between counties. This is particularly important where county-collected property taxes are shared with the state or other counties. Without equalization, it would be to a county's financial advantage to underassess so as to lessen its contribution. At present, two equalization methods are in common usage: one requires that all counties use the same appraisal procedure and assessed valuation ratio, and the other allows each county to choose its own method and then applies a correction as determined by the board. For example, a state may contain counties that assess at 20%, 24%, and 30% of fair market value. These could be equalized by multiplying assessed values in the 20% counties by 1.50, in the 24% counties by 1.25, and in the 30% counties by 1.00.

More than half the land in many cities and counties is exempt from real property taxation. This is because governments and their agencies do not tax themselves or each other. Thus, government-owned offices of all types, public roads and parks, schools, military bases, and government-owned utilities are exempt from property taxes. Also exempted are most properties owned by religious and charitable organizations (so long as they are used for religious or charitable purposes), hospitals, and cemeteries. In rural areas of many states, large tracts of land are

PROPERTY TAX EXEMPTIONS

owned by federal and state governments, and these too are exempt from taxation.

Property tax exemptions are used to attract industries. For example, a local government agency buys industrial land and buildings and leases them to industries at a price lower than would be possible if they were privately owned and hence taxed. Alternatively, outright property tax reductions can be granted for a certain length of time to newly established or relocating firms. The rationale is that the cost to the public is outweighed by the economic boost that the new industry brings to the community. A number of states grant assessment reductions to homeowners. This increases the tax burden for households that rent and for commercial properties.

SPECIAL ASSESSMENTS

Often the need arises to make local municipal improvements that will benefit property owners within a limited area, such as the paving of a street, the installation of street lights, curbs, storm drains, and sanitary sewer lines, or the construction of irrigation and drainage ditches. Such improvements can be provided through **special assessments** on property.

The theory underlying special assessments is that the improvements must benefit the land against which the cost will be charged, and the value of the benefits must exceed the cost. The area receiving the benefit of an improvement is the **improvement district** or **assessment district**, and the property within that district bears the cost of the improvement. This is different from a **public improvement.** A public improvement, such as reconstruction of the city's sewage plant, benefits the general public and is financed through the general (ad valorem) property tax. A local improvement, such as extending a sewer line into a street of homes presently using septic tanks or cesspools, does not benefit the public at large and should properly be charged only to those who directly benefit. Similarly, when streets are widened, owners of homes lining a 20-foot-wide street in a strictly residential neighborhood would be expected to bear the cost of widening it to 30 or 40 feet and to donate the needed land from their front yards. But a street widening from two lanes to four to accommodate traffic not generated by the homes on the street is a different situation because the widening benefits the public at large. In this case the street widening is funded from public monies and the homeowners are paid for any land taken from them.

An improvement district can be formed by the action of a group of concerned citizens who want and are willing to pay for an improvement. Property owners desiring the improvement take their proposal to the local board of assessors or similar public body in charge of levying assessments. A public notice showing the proposed improvements, the extent of the improvement district, and the anticipated costs is prepared by the board. This notice is mailed to landowners in the proposed improvement district, posted conspicuously in the district, and published in a local newspaper. The notice also contains the date and place of public hearings on the matter at which property owners within the proposed district are invited to voice their comments and objections.

Forming an Improvement District

If the hearings result in a decision to proceed, then under the authority granted by state laws regarding special improvements, a local government ordinance is passed that describes the project and its costs and the improvement district boundaries. An assessment roll is also prepared that shows the cost to each parcel in the district. Hearings are held regarding the assessment roll. When everything is in order, the roll is **confirmed** (approved). Then the contract to construct the improvements is awarded and work is started.

Confirmation

The proposal to create an improvement district can also come from a city council, board of trustees, or board of supervisors. When this happens, notices are distributed and hearings held to hear objections from affected parties. Objections are ruled upon by a court of law and if found to have merit, the assessment plans must be revised or dropped. Once approved, assessment rolls are prepared, more hearings are held, the roll is confirmed, and the contract is awarded.

Upon completion of the improvement, each landowner receives a bill for his portion of the cost. If the cost to a landowner is less than $100, the landowner either pays the amount in full to the contractor directly or to a designated public official who, in turn, pays the contractor. If the assessment is larger, the landowner can immediately pay it in full or let it **go to bond.** If he lets it go to bond, local government officials prepare a bond issue that

Bond Issues

totals all the unpaid assessments in the improvement district. These bonds are either given to the contractor as payment for his work or sold to the public through a securities dealer and the proceeds are used to pay the contractor. The collateral for the bonds is the land in the district upon which assessments have not been paid.

The bonds spread the cost of the improvements over a period of 5 to 10 years and are payable in equal annual (or semi-annual) installments plus accumulated interest. Thus, a $2,000 sewer and street-widening assessment on a 10-year bond would be charged to a property owner at the rate of $200 per year (or $100 each 6 months) plus interest. As the bond is gradually retired, the amount of interest added to the regular principal payment declines.

Like property taxes, special assessments are a lien against the property. Consequently, if a property owner fails to pay his assessment, the assessed property can be sold in the same manner as when property taxes are delinquent.

Apportionment   Special assessments are apportioned according to benefits received rather than by the value of the land and buildings being assessed. In fact, the presence of buildings in an improvement district is not usually considered in preparing the assessment roll; the theory is that the land receives all the benefit of the improvement. Several illustrations can best explain how assessments are apportioned. In a residential neighborhood, the assessment for installation of storm drains, curbs, and gutters is made on a **front-foot basis.** A property owner is charged for each foot of his lot that abuts the street being improved.

In the case of a sanitary sewer line assessment, the charge per lot can either be based on front footage or on a simple count of the lots in the district. In the latter case, if there are 100 lots on the new sewer line, each would pay 1% of the cost. In the case of a park or playground, lots nearest the new facility are deemed to benefit more and thus are assessed more than lots located farther away. This form of allocation is very subjective, and usually results in spirited objections at public hearings from those who do not feel they will use the facility in proportion to the assessment that their lots will bear.

We now turn to the income taxes that are due if you sell your personal residence for more than you paid. Income taxes are levied by the federal government, by 44 states (the exceptions are Florida, Nevada, South Dakota, Texas, Washington, and Wyoming), and by 48 cities including New York City, Baltimore, Pittsburgh, Philadelphia, Cincinnati, Cleveland, and Detroit. The discussion here centers on the federal income tax and includes key provisions of the **Internal Revenue Code of 1986,** also known as the **Tax Reform Act of 1986,** as it applies to owner-occupied residences. Aspects of this Act that apply to real estate investments are located in Chapter 23. State and city income tax laws generally follow the pattern of federal tax laws.

INCOME TAXES ON THE SALE OF ONE'S RESIDENCE

The first step in determining the amount of taxable gain upon the sale of an owner-occupied residence is to calculate the home's **basis.** This is the price originally paid for the home plus any fees paid for closing services and legal counsel, and any fee or commission paid to help find the property. If the home was built rather than purchased, the basis is the cost of the land plus the cost of construction, such as the cost of materials and construction labor, architect's fees, building permit fees, planning and zoning commission approval costs, utility connection charges, and legal fees. The value of labor contributed by the homeowner and free labor from friends and relatives cannot be added. If the home was received as compensation, a gift, an inheritance, or in a trade, or if a portion of the home was depreciated for business purposes, special rules apply that will not be covered here and the seller should consult the Internal Revenue Service (IRS).

Calculating a Home's Basis

Assessments for local improvements and any improvements made by the seller are added to the original cost of the home. An improvement is a permanent betterment that materially adds to the value of a home, prolongs its life, or changes its use. For example, finishing an unfinished basement or upper floor, building a swimming pool, adding a bedroom or bathroom, installing new plumbing or wiring, installing a new roof, erecting a new fence, and paving a new driveway are classed as improvements and are added to the home's basis. Maintenance and repairs are not added as they merely maintain the property in ordinary operating condition. Fixing gutters, mending leaks in plumbing, replacing broken windowpanes, and painting the inside or outside of the home are considered maintenance and repair items. However, repairs made as part of an extensive remodeling or restoration job may be added to the basis.

Calculating the Amount Realized

The next step in determining taxable gain is to calculate the **amount realized** from the sale. This is the selling price of the home less selling expenses. Selling expenses include brokerage commissions, advertising, legal fees, title services, escrow or closing fees, and mortgage points paid by the seller. If the sale includes furnishings, the value of those furnishings is deducted from the selling price and reported separately as personal property. If the seller takes back a note and mortgage which are immediately sold at a discount, the discounted value of the note is used, not its face amount.

Calculating Gain on the Sale

The **gain on the sale** is the difference between the amount realized and the basis. Table 13:2 illustrates this with an example. Unless the seller qualifies for tax postponement or tax exclusion as discussed next, this is the amount to be reported as gain on the seller's annual income tax forms. To increase compliance with this rule, effective January 1, 1987, reporting of real estate transactions on IRS Form 1099 is required of persons in the following order: (1) the person responsible for the closing, (2) the mortgage lender, (3) the seller's broker, (4) the buyer's broker, and (5) any person designated by the IRS.

Income Tax Postponement

The income tax law of the United States provides that if a seller purchases another home, the gain on the sale of the first home is automatically postponed if the seller meets two conditions.

Buy home for $90,000; closing costs are $500	Basis is	$90,500
Add landscaping and fencing for $3,500	Basis is	$94,000
Add bedroom and bathroom for $15,000	Basis is	$109,000
Sell home for $125,000; sales commissions and closing costs are $8,000	Amount realized	$117,000
Calculation of gain:	Amount realized	$117,000
	Less basis	−109,000
	Equals gain	$ 8,000

Table 13:2. Calculation of Gain

Selling price of old home	$250,000
Less selling expenses	− 18,000
Less fix-up costs	− 7,000
Equals adjusted sales price	$225,000

Table 13:3. Adjusted Sales Price

The first condition is that another home must be purchased and occupied within the time period beginning 24 months before the closing date of the old home and ending 24 months after the closing date of the old home. A seller who decides to build has 24 months to finish and occupy the new home. These time limits must be strictly observed or the deferment is lost.

The second condition is that the next home must cost as much as or more than the adjusted sales price of the previous home. **Adjusted sales price** is the selling price of the old home less selling expenses and fix-up expenses. Fix-up expenses are for fix-up and repair work performed on the home to make it more salable. For fix-up and repair work to be deductible, the work must be performed during the 90-day period ending on the day the contract to sell is signed, and it must be paid for within another 30 days. Table 13:3 illustrates the method for calculating adjusted sales price.

If the new home costs less than the adjusted sales price of the old, there will be a taxable gain. For example, if the old home had a basis of $150,000 and an adjusted sales price of $225,000, and the new home cost $215,000, then there would be a taxable gain of $10,000 and a postponed gain of $65,000. The basis of the new home is $215,000 minus the postponed gain of $65,000, i.e., $150,000.

Postponement of gain is continued from one home to the next as long as the cost of each subsequent home exceeds the adjusted sales price of the previous home, and as long as the owner maintains residency at least 24 months between sales. (A shorter turnover period is usually allowed for work-related moves.) The basis of the first home is simply carried forward and included in the basis of the second home, which in turn is carried forward to the third home, and so on. Note that it is not the amount of cash one puts into a home, or the size of the mortgage that counts, but the sales price. Thus it is possible to move from a home with a small mortgage to a slightly more

1. Cost and improvements for first home	$ 50,000
2. Adjusted sales price of first home	80,000
3. Gain on sale of first home	30,000
4. Cost of second home	105,000
5. Basis in second home (line 4 minus line 3)	75,000
6. Adjusted sales price of second home	130,000
7. Gain on sale of second house (line 6 minus line 5)	55,000
8. Cost of third home	160,000
9. Basis in third home (line 8 minus line 7)	105,000

Table 13:4. Tax-deferred Residence Replacement

expensive home with a large mortgage, and finish the transaction with cash in the pocket and postponed taxes. Additionally, the law does not restrict the type of home one may own and occupy. Thus the seller of a single-family residence can buy another house, or a condominium, or a cooperative (or vice versa) and still qualify for postponement. Table 13:4 illustrates a progression of tax-deferred residence replacements.

LIFETIME EXCLUSION

The postponement of taxes on gains as one moves from one home to the next works well as long as consistently more expensive homes are purchased. However, there may come a time in the homeowner's life when a smaller and presumably less expensive home is needed. To soften the tax burden that such a move usually causes, Congress has enacted legislation that allows a once-in-a-lifetime election to avoid tax on up to $125,000 of gain on the sale of one's residence. To qualify for this, one must be 55 years of age or older on the date of sale and have owned and occupied the residence for at least 3 of the 5 years preceding the sale. Any profit over $125,000 is taxable, but may be postponed if another residence is purchased in accordance with the rules previously described. For example, a person owning a $225,000 home with a basis of $50,000 could sell and move to a $100,000 home with no taxable gain. A person owning a $175,000 home with a $50,000 basis could sell, rent an apartment rather than buy again, and have no taxable gain. By combining postponement with this $125,000 exclusion it is quite possible to eliminate the taxable gain from a lifetime of homeownership.

TAXABLE GAIN

Prior to January 1, 1987, any gain that could not be deferred was categorized as either a short-term or a long-term gain.

Short-term meant a holding period of 6 months or less, and long-term meant a holding period of more than 6 months. Tax treatment excluded 60% of long-term gains from one's income, thus lowering the income taxes due on the gain. As of January 1, 1987, the 60% exclusion was repealed and both long-term and short-term gain are now 100% taxable at ordinary income tax rates. Although ordinary rates are reduced in 1987 and 1988, the net effect is still a higher tax on gains. One aspect of the old rules appears to have remained: a loss on the sale of a personal residence cannot be used as a deduction against other income.

When a gain cannot be postponed or excluded, a popular method of deferring income taxes is to use the **installment method** of reporting the gain. This can be applied to homeowner gains that do not qualify for postponement or exclusion.

INSTALLMENT METHOD

Suppose that your property, which is free and clear of debt, is sold for $100,000. The real estate commission and closing costs are $7,500 and your basis is $40,000. As a result, the gain on this sale is $52,500. If you sell for all cash, you are required to pay all the income taxes due on that gain in the year of sale, a situation that may force you into a higher tax bracket. A solution is to sell to the buyer on terms rather than to send him to a lender to obtain a loan.

For example, if the buyer pays you $20,000 down and gives you a promissory note calling for a principal payment of $5,000, plus interest this year, and a principal payment of $25,000 plus interest in each of the next 3 years, your gain is calculated and reported as follows. Of each dollar of sales price received, 52.5¢ is reported as gain. Thus, $10,500 is reported this year and in each of the next 3 years. The interest you earn on the promissory note is reported and taxed separately as interest income.

If there is a $30,000 mortgage on the property that the buyer agrees to assume, the $100,000 sales price is reduced by $30,000 to $70,000 for tax-calculating purposes. The portion of each dollar paid to you by the buyer that must be reported as gain is $52,500 divided by $70,000, or 75%. If the down payment is $20,000 followed by $10,000 per year for 5 years, you would report 75% of $20,000, or $15,000 this year and $7,500 in each of the next 5 years. The gain is taxed at the income tax rates in effect at the time the installment is received.

If you sell by the installment method, that is, you sell property at a gain in one taxable year and receive one or more payments in later taxable years, the installment method of reporting is automatically applied. If this is not suitable, you can elect to pay all the taxes in the year of sale. The installment method is only available to those who are not "dealers" in real property. All dealers in real property are required to pay all the taxes in the year of sale.

PROPERTY TAX AND INTEREST DEDUCTIONS

The Internal Revenue Code of 1986 retains the deductibility of state and local real estate taxes. A homeowner can deduct real property taxes and personal property taxes from other income when calculating income taxes. This applies to single-family residences, condominiums, and cooperatives. The deduction does not extend to special assessment taxes for improvement districts.

The Internal Revenue Code of 1986 also retains the deductibility of interest, but subject to two limitations that will be discussed separately. However, the basic rule is that interest paid to finance the purchase of a home is deductible against a homeowner's other income. Also deductible are interest paid on improvement district bonds, loan prepayment penalties, and the deduction of points on new loans that are clearly distinguishable as interest and not service fees for making the loan. Loan points paid by a seller to help a buyer obtain an FHA or VA loan are not deductible as interest (it is not the seller's debt), but can be deducted from the home's selling price in computing a gain or loss on the sale. FHA mortgage insurance premiums are not deductible nor are those paid to private mortgage insurers.

INTEREST DEDUCTION LIMITATIONS

Previous tax laws allowed interest deductions on any number of personal residences owned by one taxpayer. The Internal Revenue Code of 1986 limits the interest deduction to two residential properties, and one must be the taxpayer's principal residence.

All of the interest is deductible on a loan to purchase a first or second home. However, if a home is refinanced and the amount borrowed exceeds the home's basis (original cost plus improvements, etc.), the interest on the excess amount is not deductible. This rule went into effect for loans made after

August 16, 1986, but it makes exceptions for loans made for medical and educational purposes. Thus, a homeowner will not only want to keep records of his or her home's basis for sale purposes but also as information for refinancing. Also, if refinancing above basis is for medical or educational purposes, then careful records of those expenses must be kept in order to justify the deduction. As the 1986 Code is written, if a home with a low basis and high market value is sold and another home bought, it appears that all the new mortgage loan interest would be deductible without qualification.

From an individual taxpayer's standpoint, the ability to deduct property taxes and mortgage interest on one's residence becomes more valuable in higher tax brackets. As viewed from a national standpoint, the deductibility of interest and property taxes encourages widespread ownership of the country's land and buildings.

BELOW-MARKET INTEREST

In 1984 and 1985, Congress enacted legislation requiring sellers to charge market rates of interest or be taxed as if they had. This legislation requires minimum rates tied to prevailing rates on federal securities, i.e., U.S. Treasury notes and bonds. Effective July 1, 1985, if the amount of seller financing in a transaction is $2.8 million or less, the seller must charge no less than 9% interest or a rate equal to the applicable federal rate (AFR). If the amount of seller financing in a transaction is greater than $2.8 million, the seller must charge a rate equal to or greater than the AFR. This rule applies to home sellers as well as investors. Investing in real estate and its tax implications are discussed in Chapter 23.

IMPACT ON REAL ESTATE

Because tax rules for real estate are continually changing, only the major rules have been reported and discussed here and in Chapter 23. As a real estate owner or agent you need a source of more frequent and more detailed information such as the annual income tax guide published by the Internal Revenue Service (free) or the privately published guides available in most bookstores. Additionally, you may wish to subscribe to a tax newsletter for up-to-the-minute tax information.

Please be aware that tax law changes have an impact on real estate values. In the past, tax laws have been very generous to real estate—particularly deductions for depreciation and interest as well as credits for the rehabilitation of old buildings. Many otherwise uneconomic real estate projects have become economically feasible because of tax laws. As tax laws have changed to reduce the incentive to buy real estate, it has had a dramatic effect on real estate investors, and, predictably, the sales price of parcels of real estate. The final impact of these changes is yet to be determined.

AGENT'S LIABILITY FOR TAX ADVICE

The real estate industry's desire for professional recognition, coupled with the results of several key court cases, strongly suggests that a real estate agent be reasonably knowledgeable about taxes. This does not mean the agent must have knowledge of tax laws at the level of an accountant or tax attorney. Neither does it mean an agent can plead ignorance of tax laws. Rather it means a real estate agent is now liable for tax advice (or lack of it) if the advice is material to the transaction, and to give such advice is common in the brokerage business. What this means is that an agent should have enough general knowledge of real estate tax laws to be able to answer basic questions accurately and to warn clients and recommend tax counsel if the questions posed by the transaction are beyond the agent's knowledge. Note that the obligation to inform exists even when a client fails to ask about tax consequences. This is to avoid situations in which, after the deed is recorded, the client says, "Gee, I didn't know I'd have to pay all these taxes, my agent should have warned me," and then sues the agent. Lastly, if the agent tries to fill the role of accountant or tax attorney for the client, then the agent will be held liable to the standards of an accountant or tax attorney.

To summarize, an agent must be aware of tax laws that affect the properties the agent is handling. An agent has a responsibility to alert clients to potential tax consequences, liabilities, and advantages whether they ask for it or not. Lastly, an agent is responsible for the quality and accuracy of tax information given out by the agent.

CONVEYANCE TAXES

Prior to 1968 the federal government required the purchase and placement of federal documentary tax stamps on deeds. The rate was 55¢ for each $500 or fraction thereof computed on the "new money" in the transaction. Thus, if a person bought a home for $75,000 and either paid cash or arranged for a new mortgage, the tax was based on the full $75,000. If the buyer assumed or took title subject to an existing $50,000 loan, then the tax was based on $25,000. Examples of federal documentary tax stamps, which look much like postage stamps, can still be seen on deeds recorded prior to 1968.

Effective January 1, 1968, the federal deed tax program ended and many states took the opportunity to begin charging a deed tax of their own. Some adopted fee schedules that are substantially the same as the federal government previously charged. Others base their fee on the purchase price without regard to any existing indebtedness left on the property by the seller. Forty-one states, the District of Columbia, and some counties and cities charge a transfer tax. The amount ranges from just a few dollars to as much as $4,500 on the sale of a $100,000 property. These fees are paid to the county recorder prior to recording and are in addition to the charge for recording the document itself. Some states also charge a separate tax on the value of any mortgage debt created by a transaction.

1. Local government programs and services are financed primarily through
   A. property taxes.
   B. federal income taxes.
   C. state income taxes.
   D. state sales taxes.

2. Taxes on real property are levied
   A. on an ad valorem basis.
   B. according to the value of the property.
   C. Both A and B.
   D. Neither A nor B.

3. The assessment ratio of real property in a community may be
   A. one hundred percent of its appraised value.
   B. more than its fair market value.
   C. more than its appraised value.
   D. All of the above.

4. Which of the following properties has the highest assessed value?
   A. Market value $75,000, assessed at 75% of value.
   B. Market value $50,000, assessed at 100% of value.
   C. Market value $90,000, assessed at 50% of value.
   D. Market value $130,000, assessed at 35% of value.

5. Tax rates may be expressed as
   A. a millage rate.
   B. dollars of tax per hundred dollars of valuation.
   C. dollars of tax per thousand dollars of valuation.
   D. All of the above.

REVIEW QUESTIONS

6. Which of the following would be the highest tax rate?
   A. 38 mills.
   C. $38/$1,000.
   B. $3.80/$100.
   D. No difference.

7. Jeff plans to bid on real estate being offered at a tax auction. Before bidding on a parcel he would be wise to
   A. conduct a title search.
   C. sign a contract.
   B. purchase title insurance.
   D. obtain a tax receipt.

8. Which of the following liens holds the highest degree of lien priority?
   A. Federal income tax liens.
   C. Ad valorem tax liens.
   B. Mechanics' liens.
   D. First mortgage liens.

9. Records of the assessed valuations of all properties within a jurisdiction are known as
   A. appraisal rolls.
   C. appropriation rolls.
   B. allocation rolls.
   D. assessment rolls.

10. Among the functions of the Board of Equalization are to
    A. equalize assessments between counties.
    B. equalize assessments between individual property owners.
    C. Both A and B.
    D. Neither A nor B.

11. Land and buildings may be exempted from property taxation
    A. as a means of attracting industry to a community.
    B. if they are used for religious or educational purposes.
    C. Both A and B.
    D. Neither A nor B.

12. All of the following types of property are usually exempt from taxation EXCEPT:
    A. government-owned utilities.
    B. residences owned by elderly homeowners.
    C. property owned by charitable organizations.
    D. hospitals.

13. Real property taxes are sometimes limited by laws which limit
    A. the amount of taxes that can be collected.
    B. how much a government can spend.
    C. Both A and B.
    D. Neither A nor B.

14. An improvement district may be created as a result of action originated by
    A. a group of concerned citizens.
    B. local governing bodies.
    C. Both A and B.
    D. Neither A nor B.

15. A property owner whose land is assessed for improvements in an improved district may pay his share by
    A. cash, directly to the contractor.
    B. letting it go to bond.
    C. Both A and B.
    D. Neither A nor B.

16. When a person sells land for more then he paid for it
   A. there is no federal tax applicable to the gain.
   B. the gain is taxed by all state governments.
   C. Both A and B.
   D. Neither A nor B.

17. Which of the following would NOT be considered an improvement to a home in determining its cost basis?
   A. Repairs to a leaky roof.
   B. Construction of a new fence.
   C. Repairs done as part of an extensive remodeling project.
   D. None of the above.

18. Deductions for a capital loss may NOT be taken on which of the following?
   A. A rented condominium unit held as an investment.
   B. A private home occupied by the owner.
   C. Both A and B.
   D. Neither A nor B.

19. Sources of information on income tax laws and rules include
   A. tax guides published by the Internal Revenue Service.
   B. privately published tax guides sold in bookstores.
   C. privately published tax newsletters.
   D. All of the above.

20. Conveyance taxes on the transfer of title to real property are levied by
   A. the federal government.
   B. some state governments.
   C. counties only.
   D. the Federal Housing Administration.

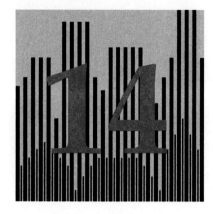

Title Closing and Escrow

OVERVIEW OF
CHAPTER 14

Once the title has been searched, a decision should have been made as to how to take title, prepare a deed, make loan arrangements, check property tax records, and begin the final steps in the process. In this chapter you will learn how the process evolves from the buyer's walk-through to the closing meeting or escrow. You will also become familiar with the calculations or at least the procedures to determine prorations and complete the final settlement statement. The various types of settlement statements, including the HUD statement are covered in detail.

LEARNING OBJECTIVES

After successful completion of this chapter, you should be able to:
1. Describe the buyers' walk-through and title closing.
2. Explain buyers' and sellers' responsibilities at the closing meeting.
3. Describe the transaction and relate the roles of the real estate agent and escrow agent.
4. Determine insurance, tax, interest, and other prorations at closing.
5. Explain what happens when there are delays or a failure to close.
6. Describe the residential and/or HUD closing or settlement statement(s).
7. Explain the restrictions and benefits of the Real Estate Settlement Procedures Act.

KEY • TERMS

Closing meeting: a meeting at which the buyer pays for the property and receives a deed to it and all other matters pertaining to the sale are concluded

Escrow agent: the person placed in charge of an escrow

Escrow closing: the deposit of documents and funds with a neutral third party along with instructions as to how to conduct the closing

Prorating: the division of ongoing expenses and income items between the buyer and the seller

Real Estate Settlement Procedures Act (RESPA): a federal law that deals with procedures to be followed in certain types of real estate closings

Settlement statement: an accounting of funds to the buyer and the seller at the completion of a real estate transaction

Title closing: the process of completing a real estate transaction

Walk-through: a final inspection of the property just prior to settlement

Numerous details must be handled between the time a buyer and seller sign a sales contract and the day title is conveyed to the buyer. Title must be searched (Chapter 6), a decision made as to how to take title (Chapter 4), a deed prepared (Chapter 5), loan arrangements made (Chapters 9 through 12), property tax records checked (Chapter 13), and so forth. In this chapter we will look at the final steps in the process, in particular, the buyer's walk-through, the closing meeting or escrow, prorations, and the settlement statement.

BUYERS' WALK-THROUGH

To protect both the buyer and the seller, it is good practice for a buyer to make a **walk-through.** This is a final inspection of the property just prior to the settlement date. It is quite possible the buyer has not been on the parcel or inside the structure since the initial offer and acceptance. Now, several weeks later, the buyer wants to make certain that the premises have been vacated, that no damage has occurred, that the seller has left behind personal property agreed upon, and that the seller has not removed and taken any real property. If the sales contract requires all mechanical items to be in normal working order, then the seller will want to test the heating and air-conditioning systems, dishwasher, disposer, stove, garage door opener, etc., and the refrigerator, washer, and dryer if included. The buyer will also want to test all of the plumbing to be certain the hot water heater works, faucets and showers run, toilets flush, and sinks drain. A final inspection of the structure is made, including walls, roof, gutters, driveway, decks, patios, etc., as well as the land and landscaping.

Note that a walk-through is not the time for the buyer to make the initial inspection of the property. That is done before the contract is signed, and if there are questions in the buyer's mind regarding the structural soundness of the property, a thorough inspection (possibly with the aid of a professional house inspector) should be conducted after signing the purchase contract, making the satisfactory inspection a condition to the buyer's obligation to purchase. The walk-through is for the purpose of giving the buyer the opportunity to make certain that agreements regarding the condition of the premises have been kept. If during the walk-through the buyer notes the walls were damaged when the seller moved out, or the furnace does not function, the buyer (or the buyer's agent) notes these items and asks that funds be withheld at the closing to pay for repairs.

TITLE CLOSING

Title closing refers to the completion of a real estate transaction. This is when the buyer pays for the property and the seller delivers the deed. The day on which this occurs is called the **closing date.** Depending on where one resides in the United States, the title closing process is referred to as a **closing, settlement,** or **escrow.** All accomplish the same basic goal, but the method of reaching that goal can follow one of two paths.

In some parts of the United States, particularly in the East, and to a certain extent in the Mountain states, the Midwest and the South, the title closing process is concluded at a meeting of all parties to the transaction or their representatives. Elsewhere, title closing is conducted by an escrow agent who is a neutral third party mutually selected by the buyer and seller to carry out the closing. With an escrow, there is no closing meeting; in fact, most of the closing process is conducted by mail. Let's look at the operation of each method.

CLOSING OR SETTLEMENT MEETING

When a meeting is used to close a real estate transaction, the seller meets in person with the buyer and delivers the deed. At the same time, the buyer pays the seller for the property. To ascertain that everything promised in the sales contract has been properly carried out, it is customary for the buyer and seller each to have an attorney present. The real estate agents who brought the buyer and seller together are also present, along with a representative of the firm that conducted the title search. If a new loan is being made or an existing one is being paid off at the closing, a representative of each lender will be present.

The location of the meeting and the selection of the person responsible for conducting the closing will depend on local custom and the nature of the closing. It is the custom in some states to conduct the closing at the real estate agent's office. In other localities it is conducted in the office of the seller's attorney. An alternative is to have the title company responsible for the title search and title policy conduct the closing at its office. If a new loan is involved, the lender may want to conduct the closing. If the seller is unable to attend the closing meeting, the seller appoints someone, such as his lawyer or real estate agent, to represent him at the meeting. Similarly, a buyer who is unable to attend can appoint a representative to be present at the meeting. Appointment of a representative is accomplished by preparing and signing a power of attorney.

To assure a smooth closing, each person attending is responsible for bringing certain documents. The seller and his attorney are responsible for preparing and bringing the deed together with the most recent property tax bill (and receipt if it has been paid). If required by the sales contract, they also bring the insurance policy for the property, the termite and wood-rot inspection report, deeds or documents showing the removal of unacceptable liens and encumbrances, a title insurance policy, a bill of sale for personal property, a survey map, and any needed offset statements or beneficiary statements. An **offset statement** is a statement by an owner or lienholder as to the balance due on an existing lien against the property. A **beneficiary statement** is a statement of the unpaid balance on a note secured by a trust deed. The loan payment booklet, keys to the property, garage door opener, and the like are also brought to the meeting. If the property is a condominium, cooperative, or planned unit development, the seller will bring to the closing such items as: the articles of incorporation; bylaws; conditions, covenants and restrictions (CC&Rs); annual budget; reserve fund status report; and management company's name. If the property produces

Seller's Responsibilities at Closing

income, existing leases, rent schedules, current expenditures, and letters advising the tenants of the new owner must also be furnished.

Buyer's Responsibilities at Closing

The buyer's responsibilities include having adequate settlement funds ready, having an attorney present if desired, and, if borrowing, obtaining the loan commitment and advising the lender of the meeting's time and place. The real estate agent is present because it is the custom in some localities that the agent be in charge of the closing and prepare the proration calculations. The agent also receives a commission check at that time and, as a matter of good business, will make certain that all goes well.

If a new loan is involved, the lender brings a check for the amount of the loan along with a note and mortgage for the borrower to sign. If an existing loan is to be paid off as part of the transaction, the lender is present to receive a check and release the mortgage held on the property. If a lender elects not to attend, the check and/or loan papers are given to the person in charge of the closing, along with instructions for their distribution and signing. A title insurance representative is also present to provide the latest status of title and the title insurance policy. If title insurance is not used, the seller is responsible for bringing an abstract or asking the abstracter to be present.

Agent's Duties

The seller and the seller's attorney may be unaware of all the things expected of them at the closing meeting. Therefore, it is the duty of the agent who listed the property to make certain that they are prepared for the meeting. Similarly, it is the duty of the agent who found the buyer to make certain that the buyer and the buyer's attorney are prepared for the closing meeting. If the agent both lists and sells the property, the agent assists both the buyer and seller. If more than one agent is involved in the transaction, each should keep the other(s) fully informed so the transaction will go as well as possible. At all times the buyer and seller are to be kept informed as to the status of the closing. An agent should give them a preview of what will take place, explain each payment or receipt, and in general prepare the parties for informed participation at the closing meeting.

The Transaction

When everyone concerned has arrived at the meeting place, the closing begins. Those present record each other's names as witnesses to the meeting. The various documents called for by the sales contract are exchanged for inspection. The buyer and his attorney inspect the deed the seller is offering, the title search and/or title policy, the mortgage papers, survey, leases, removals of encumbrances, and proration calculations. The lender also inspects the deed, survey, title search, and title policy. This continues until each party has a chance to inspect each document of interest.

A settlement statement (also called a closing statement) is given to the buyer and seller to summarize the financial aspects of their transaction. It is prepared by the person in charge of the closing either just prior to or at the meeting. It provides a clear picture of where the buyer's and seller's money is going at the closing by identifying each party to whom money is being paid. (An example of a closing statement is given later in this chapter.)

If everyone involved in the closing has done his or her homework and comes prepared to the meeting, the closing usually goes smoothly. When everything is in order, the seller hands a completed deed to the buyer. Simultaneously, the buyer gives the seller a check that combines the down payment and net result of the prorations. The lender has the buyer sign the mortgage and note and hands checks to the seller and the existing lender, if one is involved. The seller writes a check to his real estate broker, attorney, and the abstracter. The buyer writes a check to his attorney. This continues until every document is signed and everyone is paid. At the end, everyone stands, shakes hands, and departs. The deed, new mortgage, and release of the old mortgage are recorded and the transaction is complete.

Dry Closing

Occasionally an unavoidable circumstance can cause delays in a closing. Perhaps an important document, known to be in the mail, has not arrived. Yet it will be difficult to reschedule the meeting. In such a situation, the parties concerned may agree to a **dry closing**. In a dry closing, all parties sign their documents and entrust them to the person in charge of the closing for safekeeping. No money is disbursed and the deed is not delivered until the missing paperwork arrives. When it does, the closing attorney completes the transaction and delivers the money and documents by mail or messenger.

ESCROW

The use of an **escrow** to close a real estate transaction involves a neutral third party called an **escrow agent,** escrow holder, or escrowee who acts as a trusted stakeholder for all the parties to the transaction. Instead of delivering a deed directly to the buyer at the closing meeting, the seller gives the deed to the escrow agent with instructions that it be delivered only after the buyer has completed all of the buyer's promises in the sales contract. Similarly, the buyer hands the escrow agent the money for the purchase price plus instructions that it be given to the seller only after fulfillment of the seller's promises. Let's look closer at this arrangement.

A typical real estate escrow closing starts when a sales contract is signed by the buyer and seller. They select a neutral escrow agent to handle the closing. This may be the escrow department of a bank or savings and loan or other lending agency, an independent escrow company, an attorney, or the escrow department of a title insurance company. Sometimes real estate brokers offer escrow services. However, if the broker is earning a sales commission in the transaction, the broker cannot be classed as neutral and disinterested. Because escrow agents are entrusted with valuable documents and large sums of money, most states have licensing and bonding requirements that escrow agents must meet.

Escrow Agent's Duties

The escrow agent's task begins with the deposit of the buyer's earnest money in a special bank trust account and the preparation of a set of escrow instructions based on the signed sales contract. These must be promptly signed by the buyer and seller. The instructions establish an agency relationship between the escrow agent and the buyer, and the escrow agent and the seller. The instructions also detail in writing everything that each party to the sale must do before the deed is delivered to the buyer. In a typical transaction, the escrow instructions will tell the escrow agent to order a title search and obtain title insurance.

If an existing loan against the property is to be repaid as part of the sale, the escrow agent is asked to contact the lender to request a statement of the amount of money necessary to repay the loan and to request a mortgage release. The lender then enters into an agreement with the escrow agent wherein the lender is to give the completed release papers to the escrow agent; but the agent may not deliver them to the seller until the agent has remitted the amount demanded by the lender. If the existing loan is to be assumed, the escrow agent asks the lender for the current balance and any documents that the buyer must sign.

When the title search is completed, the escrow agent forwards it to the buyer or his attorney for approval. The property insurance and tax papers the seller would otherwise bring to the closing meeting are sent to the escrow agent for proration. Leases, service contracts, and notices to tenants are also sent to the escrow agent for proration and delivery to the buyer. The deed conveying title to the buyer is prepared by the seller's attorney (in some states by the escrow agent), signed by the seller, and given to the escrow agent. Once delivered into escrow, even if the seller dies, marries, or is declared legally incompetent before the close of escrow, the deed will still pass title to the buyer.

Reporting Requirements

The Internal Revenue code now provides that the seller's proceeds from all sales of real estate must now be reported to the Internal Revenue Service on their Form 1099. The responsibility for filing Form 1099 goes in the following order: the person responsible for the closing, the mortgage lender, the seller's broker, the buyer's broker, and any person designated by the U.S. Treasury. It is important to determine at the closing who needs to file the Form 1099. Since November 10, 1988, these forms must be filed at no charge to the taxpayer.

The Closing

As the closing date draws near, and provided all the instructions are otherwise complete, the escrow agent requests any additional money the buyer and lender must deposit in order to close. The day before closing the escrow agent calls the title company and orders a last minute check on the title. If no changes have occurred since the first (preliminary) title search, the deed, mortgage, mortgage release, and other documents to be recorded as part of the transaction are recorded first thing the following morning. As soon as the recording is confirmed, the escrow agent hands or mails a check to every party to whom funds are due from the escrow (usually the seller, real estate broker, and previous lender), along with any papers or documents that must be delivered through escrow (such as the fire insurance policy, copy of the property tax bill, and tenant leases). Several days later the buyer and lender will receive a title insurance policy in the mail from the title company. The public recorder's office also mails the documents it recorded to each party. The deed is sent to the buyer, the mortgage release to the seller, and the new mortgage to the lender.

Deed Delivery

In the escrow closing method, the closing, delivery of title, and recording usually take place all at the same moment. Technically, the seller does not physically hand a deed to the buyer on the closing day. However, once all the conditions of the escrow are met, the escrow agent becomes an agent of the seller in regard to the money in the transaction and an agent of the buyer in regard to the deed. Thus, the buyer, through an agent, receives the deed and the law regarding delivery is fulfilled.

It is not necessary for the buyer and seller to meet face-to-face during the escrow period or at the closing. This can eliminate personality conflicts that might be detrimental to an otherwise sound transaction. The escrow agent, having accumulated all the documents, approvals, deeds, and monies prior to the closing date, does the closing alone.

In a brokeraged transaction, the real estate agent may be the only person who actually meets the escrow agent. All communication can be handled through the broker, by mail, or by telephone. If a real estate agent is not involved, the buyer and/or seller can open the escrow, either in person or by mail. The use of an escrow agent does not eliminate the need for an attorney. Although there is no closing meeting for the attorneys to attend, they play a vital role in advising the buyer and seller on each document sent by the escrow agent for approval and signature.

DELAYS AND
FAILURE TO CLOSE

When a real estate purchase contract is written, a closing date is also negotiated and placed in the contract. The choice of closing date will depend on when the buyer wants possession, when the seller wants to move out, and how long it will take to obtain a loan, title search, and termite report and otherwise fulfill the contract requirements. In a typical residential sale this is 30 to 60 days with 45 days being a popular choice when new financing is involved.

Delays along the way are sometimes encountered and may cause a delay in the closing. This is usually not a problem as long as the buyer still intends to buy, the seller still intends to sell, and the delay is for a reasonable cause and a justifiable length of time. Many preprinted real estate purchase contracts include a statement that the broker may extend the time for performance including the closing date. Even if the contract contains a "time is of the essence" clause, unless there is supporting evidence in the contract that time really is of the essence, reasonable delays for reasonable causes are usually permitted by law.

Suppose the delay will be quite lengthy. For example, there may be a previously undisclosed title defect that will take months to clear or perhaps there are unusual problems in financing or there has been major damage to the premises. In such cases, relieving all parties from further obligations may be the wisest choice for all involved. If so, it is essential that the buyer and seller sign mutual release papers. These are necessary to rescind the purchase contract and cancel the escrow if one has been opened. The buyer's deposit is also returned. Without release papers the buyer still has a vaguely defined liability to buy and the seller can still be required to convey the property. A mutual release gives the buyer the freedom to choose another property and the seller the chance to fix the problem and remarket the property later.

A stickier problem occurs when one party wants out of the contract and attempts to use any delay in closing as grounds for contract termination. The buyer may have found a preferable property for less money and better terms. The seller may have received a higher offer since signing the purchase contract. Although the party wishing to cancel may threaten with a lawsuit, courts will rarely enforce cancellation of valuable contract rights because of reasonable delays that are not the fault of the other party. Moreover, courts will not go along with a reluctant buyer or seller who manufactures delays so as to delay the closing and then claim default and cancellation of the contract. If the reluctance continues and negotiations to end it fail, the performing party may choose to complete its requirements and then ask the courts to force the reluctant party to the closing table.

LOAN ESCROWS

Escrows can be used for purposes other than real estate sales transactions. For example, a homeowner who is refinancing his property could enter into an escrow with the lender. The conditions of the escrow would be that the homeowner deliver a properly executed note and mortgage to the escrow agent and that the lender deposit the loan money. Upon closing, the escrow agent delivers the documents to the lender and the money to the homeowner. Or, in reverse, an escrow could be used to pay off the balance of a loan. The conditions would be the borrower's deposit of the balance due and the lender's deposit of the mortgage release and note. Even the weekly office sports pool is an escrow—with the person holding the pool money acting as escrow agent for the participants.

PRORATING AT THE CLOSING

Ongoing expenses and income items must be prorated between the seller and buyer when property ownership changes hands. Items subject to proration include property insurance premiums, property taxes, accrued interest on assumed loans, and rents and operating expenses if the property produces income. If heating is done by oil and the oil tank is partially filled when title transfers, that oil can be prorated, as can utility bills when service is not shut off between owners. Several sample prorations common to most closings will help clarify the process.

Hazard Insurance

Hazard insurance policies for such things as fire, wind, storm, and flood damage are paid for in advance. At the beginning of each year of the policy's life, the premium for that year's coverage must be paid. When real estate is sold, the buyer may ask the seller to transfer the remaining coverage. The seller usually agrees if the buyer pays for the value of the remaining coverage on a prorated basis.

The first step in prorating hazard insurance is to find out how often the premium is paid, how much it is, and what period of time it covers. Suppose that the seller has a 1-year policy that cost $180 and started on January 1 of the current year. If the property is sold and the closing date is July 1, the policy is half used. Therefore, if the buyer wants the policy transferred, the buyer pays the seller $90 for the remaining 6 months of coverage.

Because closing dates do not always occur on neat, evenly divided portions of the year, nor do most items that need prorating, it is usually necessary to break the year into months and the months into days to make proration calculations. Suppose in the previous hazard insurance example that prorations are to be made on June 30 instead of July 1. This would give the buyer 6 months and 1 day of coverage. How much does the buyer owe the seller? The first step is to calculate the monthly and daily rates for the policy: $180 divided by 12 is $15 per month. Dividing the monthly rate of $15 by 30 days gives a daily rate of 50¢. The second step is to add 6 months at $15 and 1 day at 50¢. Thus, the buyer owes the seller $90.50 for the unused portion of the policy.

Loan Interest

When a buyer agrees to assume an existing loan from the seller, an interest proration is necessary. For example, a sales contract calls for the buyer to assume a 9% mortgage loan with a principal balance of $80,505 at the time of closing. Loan payments are due the tenth of each month, and the sales contract calls for a July 3 closing date, with interest on the loan to be prorated through July 2. How much is to be prorated and to whom?

First, we must recognize that interest is normally paid in arrears. On a loan that is payable monthly, the borrower pays interest for the use of the loan at the end of each month he has had the loan. Thus, the July 10 monthly loan payment includes the interest due for the use of $80,505 from June 10 through July 9. However, the seller owned the property through July 2, and from June 10 through July 2 is 23 days. At the closing the seller must give the buyer enough money to pay for 23 days interest on the $80,505. If the annual interest rate is 9%, one month's interest is $80,505 times 9% divided by 12, which is $603.79. Divide this by 30 days to get a daily interest rate of $20.126. Multiply the daily rate by 23 to obtain the interest for 23 days, $462.90.

30-Day Month

In many parts of the country it is the custom when prorating interest, property taxes, water bills, and insurance to use a 30-day month because it simplifies proration calculations. Naturally, using a 30-day month produces some inaccuracy when dealing with months that do not have 30 days. If this inaccuracy is significant to the buyer and seller, they can agree to prorate either by using the exact number of days in the closing month or by dividing the year rate by 365 to find a daily rate. Some states avoid this question altogether by requiring that the exact number of days be used in prorating.

Rents

It is the custom throughout the country to prorate rents on the basis of the actual number of days in the month. Using the July 3 closing date again, if the property is currently rented for $450 per month, paid in advance on the first of each month, what would the proration be? If the seller has already collected the rent for the month of July, he is obligated to hand over to the buyer that portion of the rent earned between July 3 and July 31, inclusive, a period of 29 days. To determine how many dollars this is, divide $450 by the number of days in July. This gives $14.516 as the rent per day. Then multiply the daily rate by 29 days to get $420.96, the portion of the July rent that the seller must hand over to the buyer. If the renter has not paid the July rent by the July 3 closing date, no proration is made. If the buyer later collects the July rent, he must return 2 days rent to the seller.

Property Taxes

Prorated property taxes are common to nearly all real estate transactions. The amount of proration depends on when the property taxes are due, what portion has already been paid, and what period of time they cover. Property taxes are levied on an annual basis, but depending on the locality they may be due at the beginning, middle, or end of the tax year. In some parts of the country, property owners are permitted to pay in two or more installments.

Suppose you live in a state where the property tax year runs from January 1 through December 31, property tax bills are mailed to property owners in late February, and taxes for the full year are due April 10. If a transaction calls for property taxes to be prorated through January 31, how is the calculation made? Since the new bill is not yet available, the old bill is often used as a guide. Suppose it was $1,200 for the year. The proration is from January 1 through January 31, a period of one month. One month's taxes are calculated as one-twelfth of $1,200 or $100. The seller owes the buyer $100 because the seller owned the property through January 31, yet the buyer will later receive and pay the property tax bill for the full year. If it is likely the new tax bill will be substantially different from the previous year's, the buyer and seller can agree to make another adjustment between themselves when the new bill is available. If property tax bills had been issued in January and taxes for the full year paid by the seller, the seller would be credited with 11 months × $100/month = $1,100 and the buyer charged $1,100.

Homeowners' Association

If the property being sold is a condominium unit or in a cooperative or a planned unit development, there will be a monthly homeowners' association payment to be prorated. Suppose the monthly fee is $120 and is paid in advance on the first of the month. If the closing takes place on the twentieth, then the buyer owes the seller $40 for the unused portion of the month.

Proration Date

Prorations need not be calculated as of the closing date. In the sales contract, the buyer and seller can mutually agree to a different proration date if they wish. If nothing is said, local law and custom will prevail. In some states it is customary to prorate as of the day before closing, the theory being that the buyer is the new owner beginning on the day the transaction closes. Other states prorate as of the day of closing. If the difference of 1 day is important to the buyer or seller, they should not rely on local custom, but agree in writing on a proration day of their own choosing.

Special assessments for such things as street improvements, water mains, and sewer lines are not usually prorated. As a rule, the selling price of the property reflects the added value of the improvements, and the seller pays any assessments in full before closing. This is not an ironclad rule; the buyer and seller in their sales contract can agree to do whatever they want about the assessment.

Proration Summary

Figure 14:1 summarizes the most common proration situations found in real estate closings. The figure also shows who is to be charged and who is to be credited and whether the proration is to be worked forward or backward from the closing date. As a rule, items that are paid in advance are prorated forward from the closing date—for example, prepaid fire insurance. Items that are paid in arrears, such as interest on an existing loan, are prorated backward from the closing date.

SAMPLE CLOSING

To illustrate the arithmetic involved, let us work through a residential closing situation. Note that this example is not particular to any region of the United States, but is rather a compos-

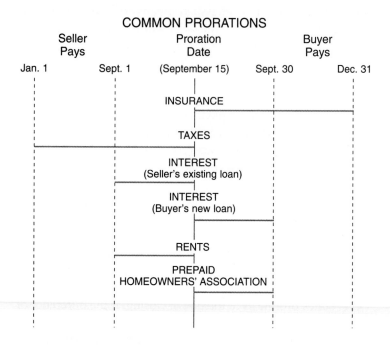

Figure 14:1. Common Prorations

ite that shows you how the most commonly encountered residential closing items are handled.

Homer Leavitt has listed his home for sale with List-Rite Realty for $125,000, and the sales commission is to be 6% of the selling price. A salesperson from Quick-Sale Realty learns about the property through the multiple listing service and produces a buyer willing to pay $123,000 with $33,000 down. The offer is conditioned on the seller paying off the existing $48,000, 12% interest mortgage loan and the buyer obtaining a new loan for $90,000. Property taxes, hazard insurance, and heating oil in the home's oil tank are to be prorated as of the closing date. The buyer also asks the seller to pay for a termite inspection and repairs if necessary, a title search, an owner's title insurance policy, conveyance taxes, and one-half of the closing fee. The seller accepts this offer on August 15, and they agree to close on September 15.

The property tax year for this home runs from January 1 through December 31. Mr. Leavitt has paid the taxes for last year, but not for the current year as yet. Newly issued tax bills show that $1,680 will be due on October 1 for the current year. The hazard insurance policy (fire, windstorm, etc.) that the buyer wishes to assume was purchased by the seller for $240 and covers the period June 15 through the following June 14. The Safety Title Insurance Company will charge the seller $400 for a combined title search, title examination, and owner's title policy package.

The buyer obtains a loan commitment from the Ajax National Bank for $90,000. To make this loan, the bank will charge a $900 loan origination fee, $100 for an appraisal, and $25 for a credit report on the buyer. The bank also requires a lender's title policy in the amount of $90,000 (added cost $90), 12 months of property tax reserves, and 4 months of hazard insurance reserves. The loan is to be repaid in equal monthly installments beginning November 1. The termite inspection by Dead-Bug Pest Company costs $39, and recording fees are $5 for deeds and mortgage releases and $10 for mortgages. The bank charges the buyer and the seller $110 each to conduct the closing plus $10 to prepare a deed for the seller and $2 to notarize it. The state levies a transfer tax on deeds of 50 cents per $500 of sales price, and the seller is leaving $130 worth of heating oil for the buyer.

The buyer and seller have each hired an attorney to advise them on legal matters in connection with the sales contract and closing. They are to be paid $150 and $120, respectively, out of the settlement. List-Rite Realty and Quick-Sale Realty have advised the closing agent that they are splitting the $7,380 sales commission equally.

Finally, the $3,000 earnest money deposit that the buyer made with the offer is to be credited toward the down payment. Using this information, which is summarized in Table 14:1 for your convenience, let us see how a settlement statement is prepared.

Figure 14:2 is the most widely used residential settlement form in the United States, and it is filled out to reflect the transaction outlined in Table 14:1. Let us work through this sample transaction in order to see where each item is placed on the settlement statement. (You will notice that the buyer is referred to as the borrower in Figure 14:2. This is not important for the moment and will be explained later.)

SETTLEMENT
STATEMENT

	Amount	Comments
Sale Price	$123,000	
Down Payment	$ 33,000	
Deposit (Earnest Money)	$ 3,000	Credit to buyer's down payment.
Existing Loan	$ 48,000	Seller to pay off through settlement. Interest rate is 12%.
New Loan	$ 90,000	Monthly payments begin Nov. 1. Interest rate is 9.6%.
Loan Origination Fee	$ 900	Paid by buyer in connection with obtaining $90,000 loan.
Appraisal Fee	$ 100	
Credit Report	$ 25	
Owner's Title Policy	$ 400	Seller pays Safety Title Co.
Lender's Title Policy	$ 90	Buyer pays Safety Title Co.
County Property Taxes	$ 1,680/yr	Due Oct. 15 for the period Jan. 1 through Dec. 31. Not yet paid.
Hazard Insurance	$ 240/yr	Existing policy with 9 months to run. Transfer to buyer.
Heating Oil	$ 130	Oil in tank. Transfer to buyer.
Pest Inspection	$ 39	Seller pays Dead-Bug Pest Co.
Property Tax Reserves	$ 1,680	12 months at $140 for lender.
Hazard Insurance Reserves	$ 80	4 months at $20 for lender.
Buyer's Attorney	$ 150	
Seller's Attorney	$ 120	
Closing Fee	$ 220	Ajax National Bank charge; buyer & seller each pay $110.
Deed Preparation	$ 10	Seller pays bank.
Notary	$ 4	Seller pays $2 for deed. Buyer pays $2 for mortgage.
Conveyance Tax	$ 123	Seller pays.
Record Deed	$ 5	Buyer pays.
Record Mortgage Release	$ 5	Seller pays.
Record Mortgage	$ 10	Buyer pays.
Brokerage Commission	$ 7,380	Seller pays; to be split equally between List-Rite Realty and Quick-Sale Realty.

Settlement and Proration date is September 15. All prorations are to be based on a 30-day banker's month.

Table 14:1. Transaction Summary

Lines 101 and 401 of the settlement statement show the price the buyer is paying and the seller is receiving for the property. Line 103 is the total of the buyer's settlement charges from the reverse side of the form. (The reverse side will be covered in a moment.) Lines 109 and 409 show the hazard insurance proration. The existing policy cost the seller $240 and has 9 months to run. For these 9 months the buyer is being charged $180 (line 109) and the seller is being credited the same amount (line 409). The heating oil remaining in the heating system tank is charged to the buyer (line 110) and credited to the seller (line 410). The gross amount due from the buyer is tallied on line 120.

On line 201 the buyer is credited with the earnest money paid at the time the purchase contract was written. On the next line the buyer is credited with the new $90,000 loan. Line 211 shows the property tax proration credit for the buyer; line 511 is the same proration as a charge to the seller. This is because $1,680 in property taxes are due on October 1 for the period January 1 through December 31. Not yet paid for the year, the buyer must pay these taxes on October 1. However, the seller owned the property from January 1 to September 15, a period of 8 months. At the rate of $140 a month, this means the seller must give the buyer $1,190 as part of the closing.

Line 220 lists the total of the buyer's credits. Line 301 is the total amount due from the buyer for this transaction. The difference, on line 303, is the amount of cash needed from the buyer to close the transaction.

Seller's Side

On the seller's side of the settlement statement, line 420 shows the total dollars due the seller from the sales price and proration credits. Line 502 is the total of the seller's settlement costs from the reverse side of the form. On line 504 the seller is charged for the existing mortgage loan that is being paid off as part of the closing. Accrued interest on that loan for the first half of September is charged the seller (line 506). Line 520 is a total of what must come out of the seller's funds at the closing. This is compared with the gross amount due the seller on line 601 and the difference (line 603) is the cash the seller will receive at the closing.

Settlement Charges

Continuing with Figure 14:2, the real estate commission is handled on lines 700, 701, and 702. Note that if the closing agent is to make a commission split such as shown here, the closing agent must have written instructions to do so from the real estate broker who is being paid by the seller. Otherwise, all the commission goes to the seller's broker, and the seller's broker pays the cooperating broker according to whatever agreement they have.

Figure 14:2

U.S. DEPARTMENT OF HOUSING AND URBAN DEVELOPMENT **SETTLEMENT STATEMENT**	**B. TYPE OF LOAN** 1. ☐ FHA 2. ☐ FmHA 3. ☐ CONV. UNINS. 4. ☐ VA 5. ☐ CONV. INS. 6. FILE NUMBER: 7. LOAN NUMBER: 8. MORTGAGE INSURANCE CASE NUMBER:

c. NOTE: *This form is furnished to give you a statement of actual settlement costs. Amounts paid to and by the settlement agent are shown. Items marked "(p.o.c.)" were paid outside the closing; they are shown here for informational purposes and are not included in the totals.*

D. NAME OF BORROWER:	E. NAME OF SELLER:	F. NAME OF LENDER:
Neidi Delone 2424 Newpaige Lane City, State 00000	Homer Leavitt 1654 West 12th Street City, State 00000	Acme National Bank 1111 West 1st Street City, State 00000

G. PROPERTY LOCATION:	H. SETTLEMENT AGENT: Acme National Bank PLACE OF SETTLEMENT: Acme National Bank	I. SETTLEMENT DATE:
1654 West 12th Street City, State 00000		Sept. 15, 19xx

J. SUMMARY OF BORROWER'S TRANSACTION		**K. SUMMARY OF SELLER'S TRANSACTION**	
100. GROSS AMOUNT DUE FROM BORROWER:		*400.* GROSS AMOUNT DUE TO SELLER:	
101. Contract sales price	$123,000	401. Contract sales price	$123,000
102. Personal property		402. Personal property	
103. Settlement charges to borrower *(line 1400)*	3,512	403.	
104.		404.	
105.		405.	
Adjustments for items paid by seller in advance		*Adjustments for items paid by seller in advance*	
106. City/town taxes to		406. City/town taxes to	
107. County taxes to		407. County taxes to	
108. Assessments to		408. Assessments to	
109. Hazard insurance 9/15 to 6/15	180	409. Hazard insurance 9/15 to 6/15	180
110. Heating oil	130	410. Heating oil	130
111.		411.	
112.		412.	
120. GROSS AMOUNT DUE FROM BORROWER	$126,822	*420.* GROSS AMOUNT DUE TO SELLER	$123,310
200. AMOUNTS PAID BY OR IN BEHALF OF BORROWER:		*500.* REDUCTIONS IN AMOUNT DUE TO SELLER:	
201. Deposit or earnest money	$ 3,000	501. Excess deposit *(see instructions)*	
202. Principal amount of new loan(s)	90,000	502. Settlement charges to seller *(line 1400)*	8,189
203. Existing loan(s) taken subject to		503. Existing loan(s) taken subject to	
204.		504. Payoff of first mortgage loan	48,000
205.		505. Payoff of second mortgage loan	
206.		506. Accrued interest 9/1 to 9/15	240
207.		507.	
208.		508.	
209.		509.	
Adjustments for items unpaid by seller		*Adjustments for items unpaid by seller*	
210. City/town taxes to		510. City/town taxes to	
211. County taxes 1/1 to 9/15	1,190	511. County taxes 1/1 to 9/15	1,190
212. Assessments to		512. Assessments to	
213.		513.	
214.		514.	
215.		515.	
216.		516.	
217.		517.	
218.		518.	
219.		519.	
220. TOTAL PAID BY/FOR BORROWER	$ 94,190	*520.* TOTAL REDUCTION AMOUNT DUE SELLER	$ 57,619
300. CASH AT SETTLEMENT FROM/TO BORROWER		*600.* CASH AT SETTLEMENT TO/FROM SELLER	
301. Gross amount due from borrower *(line 120)*	$126,822	601. Gross amount due to seller *(line 420)*	$123,310
302. Less amounts paid by/for borrower *(line 220)*	(94,190)	602. Less reductions in amount due seller *(line 520)*	(57,619)
303. CASH (☑ FROM) (☐ TO) BORROWER	$ 32,632	*603.* CASH (☑ TO) (☐ FROM) SELLER	$ 65,691

L. SETTLEMENT CHARGES		
700. *TOTAL SALES/BROKER'S COMMISSION* based on price $ 123,000 @ 6 % = $7380	**PAID FROM BORROWER'S FUNDS AT SETTLEMENT**	**PAID FROM SELLER'S FUNDS AT SETTLEMENT**
Division of Commission (line 700) as follows:		
701. $ 3,690 to List-Rite Realty		
702. $ 3,690 to Quick-Sale Realty		
703. Commission paid at Settlement		$7,380
704.		
800. ITEMS PAYABLE IN CONNECTION WITH LOAN		
801. Loan Origination Fee %	$ 900	
802. Loan Discount %		
803. Appraisal Fee to	100	
804. Credit Report to	25	
805. Lender's Inspection Fee		
806. Mortgage Insurance Application Fee to		
807. Assumption Fee		
808.		
809.		
810.		
811.		
900. ITEMS REQUIRED BY LENDER TO BE PAID IN ADVANCE		
901. Interest from Sept 15 to Sept 30 @ $ 24.00 /day	360	
902. Mortgage Insurance Premium for months to		
903. Hazard Insurance Premium for years to		
904. years to		
905.		
1000. RESERVES DEPOSITED WITH LENDER		
1001. Hazard insurance 4 months @ $ 20 per month	80	
1002. Mortgage insurance months @ $ per month		
1003. City property taxes months @ $ per month		
1004. County property taxes 12 months @ $ 140 per month	1,680	
1005. Annual assessments months @ $ per month		
1006. months @ $ per month		
1007. months @ $ per month		
1008. months @ $ per month		
1100. TITLE CHARGES		
1101. Settlement or closing fee to Acme National Bank	110	110
1102. Abstract or title search to		
1103. Title examination to		
1104. Title insurance binder to		
1105. Document preparation to Acme National Bank		10
1106. Notary fees to Acme National Bank	2	2
1107. Attorney's fees to		
(includes above items numbers;		
1108. Title insurance to Safety Title Insurance Company	90	400
(includes above items numbers;		
1109. Lender's coverage $ 90,000		
1110. Owner's coverage $ 123,000		
1111. Buyer's attorney	150	
1112. Seller's attorney		120
1113.		
1200. GOVERNMENT RECORDING AND TRANSFER CHARGES		
1201. Recording fees: Deed $ 5 ; Mortgage $ 10 ; Releases $ 5	15	5
1202. City/county tax/stamps: Deed $; Mortgage $		
1203. State tax/stamps: Deed $ 123 ; Mortgage $		123
1204.		
1205.		
1300. ADDITIONAL SETTLEMENT CHARGES		
1301. Survey to		
1302. Pest inspection to Dead-Bug Pest Company		39
1303.		
1304.		
1305.		
1400. *TOTAL SETTLEMENT CHARGES (enter on lines 103, Section J and 502, Section K)*	$3,512	$8,189

Lines 801, 803, and 804 indicate charges incurred by the buyer in connection with obtaining the new $90,000 loan. Line 901 shows the interest on the $90,000 loan calculated from the date of closing to the end of September. This brings the loan up to the first day of the next month and simplifies future bookkeeping for the monthly loan payments. At 9.6% the interest on $90,000 is $24.00 a day and the buyer is charged for 15 days.

As a condition for the loan the lender requires impound accounts for hazard insurance and property taxes. In order to have enough on hand to make the October 1 property tax payment, the lender requires (line 1004) an immediate reserve of $1,680. Beginning November 1, one-twelfth of the estimated taxes for next year will be added to the buyer's monthly payment so as to have money in the impound account from which to pay taxes next year. The same concept applies to the hazard insurance. It comes due in 8 months; therefore, the lender requires 4 months worth of reserves in advance (line 1001).

Lines 1101, 1105, and 1106 are the closing fee, deed preparation fee, and notary fees associated with this closing. Title insurance charges of $400 to the seller for the owner's policy and $90 to the buyer for the lender's policy are itemized on line 1108. Lines 1109 and 1110 show the coverage for each. The amounts paid from settlement funds to the attorneys of the buyer and seller are listed on lines 1111 and 1112. Note that the buyer and seller can choose to pay their attorneys outside of the closing. **Outside of the closing** or **outside of escrow** means a party to the closing has paid someone directly and not through the closing.

Government recording fees and conveyance taxes necessary to complete this transaction are itemized on lines 1201 and 1203 and charged to the buyer and seller as shown. On line 1302 the settlement agent pays the pest inspection company on behalf of the seller. This is another item that is sometimes paid outside of the closing, that is, the seller can write a check directly to the termite company once the inspection has been made. On line 1400 the totals for both the buyer and seller are entered. The same totals are transferred to lines 103 and 502.

Note that Figure 14:2 shows both the buyer's side of the transaction and the seller's side. In actual practice, the seller will receive this settlement statement with lines 100 through 303 blacked out, and the buyer will receive this statement with lines 400 through 603 blacked out.

In response to consumer complaints regarding real estate closing costs and procedures, Congress passed the **Real Estate Settlement Procedures Act (RESPA)** effective June 20, 1975, throughout the United States. The purpose of RESPA, which is administered by the U.S. Department of Housing and Urban Development (HUD), is to regulate and standardize real estate settlement practices when "federally related" first mortgage loans are made on one- to four-family residences, condominiums, and cooperatives. Federally related is defined to include FHA or VA or other government-backed or assisted loans, loans from lenders with federally insured deposits, loans that are to be purchased by FNMA, GNMA, FHLMC, or other federally controlled secondary mortgage market institutions, and loans made by lenders who make or invest more than $1 million per year in residential loans. As the bulk of all home loans now made fall into one of these categories, the impact of this law is far-reaching.

REAL ESTATE SETTLEMENT PROCEDURES ACT

RESPA prohibits kickbacks and fees for services not performed during the closing process. For example, in some regions of the United States prior to this Act, it was common practice for attorneys and closing agents to channel title business to certain title companies in return for a fee. This increased settlement costs without adding services. Now there must be a justifiable service rendered for each closing fee charge. The Act also prohibits the seller from requiring that the buyer purchase title insurance from a particular title company.

Restrictions

The Real Estate Settlement Procedures Act also contains restrictions on the amount of advance property tax and insurance payments a lender can collect and place in an impound or reserve account. The amount is limited to the property owner's share of taxes and insurance accrued prior to settlement, plus one-sixth of the estimated amount that will come due for these items in the 12-month period beginning at settlement. This requirement assures that the lender has an adequate but not excessive amount of money impounded when taxes and insurance payments fall due. If the amount in the reserve account is not sufficient to pay an item when it comes due, the lender must temporarily use its own funds to make up the difference. Then the lender bills the borrower or increases the monthly reserve payment. If there is a drop in the amount the lender must pay out, then the monthly reserve requirement can be reduced.

Considerable criticism and debate have raged over the topic of reserves. Traditionally, lenders have not paid interest to borrowers on money held as reserves, effectively creating an interest-free loan to themselves. This has tempted many lenders to require overly adequate reserves. RESPA sets a reasonable limit on reserve requirements and some states now require that interest be paid on reserves. Although not always required to do so, some lenders now voluntarily pay interest on reserves.

Benefits

Anyone applying for a RESPA-regulated loan will receive several benefits. First is a HUD information booklet explaining RESPA. Second is a good faith estimate of closing costs from the lender. Third, the lender will use the HUD Uniform Settlement Statement shown in Figure 14:2. Fourth, the borrower has the right to inspect the HUD Settlement Statement one business day before the day of closing.

The primary reason lenders are required to promptly give loan applicants an estimate of closing costs is to allow the loan applicant an opportunity to compare prices for the various services his transaction will require. Additionally, these estimates help the borrower estimate closing costs. Figure 14:3 illustrates a good faith estimate form.

RESPA does not require the lender to disclose estimates of escrow impounds for property taxes and insurance, although the lender can voluntarily add these items to the form. A new RESPA regulation does, however, require servicers of loans to disclose their calculation of escrow estimates for taxes and insurance. Note also that RESPA allows lenders to make estimates in terms of ranges. For example, escrow fees may be stated as $150 to $175 to reflect the range of rates being charged by local escrow companies for that service.

HUD Settlement
Statement

The HUD Settlement Statement used in Figure 14:2 is required of all federally related real estate lenders. Because it is actually a lender requirement, it uses the word *borrower* instead

Figure 14:3.

Good Faith Estimate of Closing Costs

The charges listed below are our Good Faith Estimate of some of the settlement charges you will need to pay at settlement of the loan for which you have applied. These charges will be paid to the title or escrow company that conducts the settlement. This form does not cover all items you will be required to pay in cash at settlement, for example, deposit in escrow for real estate taxes and insurance. You may wish to inquire as to the amounts of such other items. You may be required to pay other additional amounts at settlement. This is not a commitment to make a loan.

Services		Estimated Fees
801. Loan Origination Fee _____ % + $ _____		$
802. Loan Discount		$
803. Appraisal Fee		$
804. Credit Report		$
806. Mortgage Insurance Application Fee		$
807. Assumption Fee		$
808. Tax Service Fee		$
901. Interest		$
902. Mortgage Insurance Premium		$
1101. Settlement or Closing Fee		$
1106. Notary Fees		$
1109. Title Insurance, Lender's Coverage	List only those items borrower will pay	$
1109. Title Insurance, Owner's Coverage		$
1201. Recording Fees		$
1202. County Tax/Stamps		$
1203. City Tax/ Stamps		$
1302. Pest Inspection		$
1303. Building Inspection		$
		$
These numbers correspond to the HUD Settlement Statement	TOTAL	$

of buyer. However, if the loan is in connection with a sale, and most are, the buyer and the borrower are one and the same. The case where this is not true is when an owner is refinancing a property.

The HUD Settlement Statement has become so widely accepted that it is now used even when it is not required. Closing agents that handle high volumes of closings use computers with special HUD Settlement Statement programs to fill out these forms. The closing agent types the numbers onto a video screen and a tractor-fed printer with continuous-feed HUD forms takes care of the typing task.

REVIEW QUESTIONS

1. Details that must be handled between the time a purchase contract is signed and the closing typically include
   A. title search.
   B. deed preparation.
   C. loan arrangements.
   D. checking the property taxes.
   E. All of the above.

2. A buyer's walk-through is conducted for the purpose of
   A. appraising the property in order to get a loan on it.
   B. inspecting the property for major structural defects.
   C. meeting the seller and obtaining the keys to the property.
   D. making a final inspection just prior to closing.

3. At which of the following are the buyer and seller more likely to shake hands upon completing the real estate transaction?
   A. Escrow closing.
   B. Settlement meeting.

4. A settlement meeting may take place in the offices of
   A. the real estate agent.
   B. an attorney.
   C. a title company.
   D. a lender's office.
   E. All of the above.

5. When a real estate settlement is held in escrow,
   A. there is no closing meeting.
   B. the closing process may be conducted by mail.
   C. Both A and B.
   D. Neither A nor B.

6. The purpose of a settlement statement is to
   A. provide an accounting of all funds involved in the transaction.
   B. identify all parties who receive funds from the transaction.
   C. Both A and B.
   D. Neither A nor B.

7. Which of the following are disbursed at a "dry closing"?
   A. The deed to the buyer.
   B. The money due the seller.
   C. Both A and B.
   D. Neither A nor B.

8. Which of the following may serve as an escrow agent?
   A. A title company.
   B. A bank.
   C. An independent escrow company.
   D. All of the above.

9. Barnes sold his home to Hyatt through broker Quinn. The sale is to be settled through escrow. The escrow agent would be selected by
   A. Barnes.
   B. Hyatt.
   C. Quinn.
   D. Mutual agreement between Barnes and Hyatt.

10. In most states in which title transfers are handled in escrow, the escrow agent must be
    A. bonded.
    B. licensed.
    C. Both A and B.
    D. Neither A nor B.

11. In an escrow closing, funds are disbursed
    A. when all escrow papers have been signed.
    B. as soon as the buyer brings his money in.
    C. after necessary recordings take place.
    D. None of the above.

12. In an escrow closing, the escrow agent serves as agent for
    A. the buyer.
    B. the seller.
    C. Both A and B.
    D. Neither A nor B.

13. One advantage of the escrow closing method is that it can eliminate
    A. personal confrontation between buyer and seller.
    B. the need for an attorney.
    C. Both A and B.
    D. Neither A nor B.

14. In addition to the closing of sales of real property through standard purchase agreements, escrows can be used when a
    A. property is being refinanced.
    B. mortgage loan is being paid off.
    C. property is being sold under an installment contract.
    D. All of the above.

15. Martini sells her home to Rossi through broker Timms. The settlement date will be chosen by
    A. Martini.
    B. Rossi.
    C. Timms.
    D. Mutual agreement between Martini and Rossi.

16. When a home is sold and a new loan by an institutional lender is required to complete the transaction, the typical time between purchase contract signing and settlement will most likely be
    A. 0–29 days.
    B. 30–60 days.
    C. 61–120 days.
    D. over 120 days.

17. Among the items to be prorated at a settlement or escrow closing are
    A. taxes.
    B. rents from income-producing properties.
    C. Both A and B.
    D. Neither A nor B.

18. Prorations of items in a real estate closing are made usually as of the date of
   A.   signing of the sales contract.
   B.   title transfer.
   C.   buyers' walk-through.
   D.   the mortgage payment.

19. In a typical closing, insurance prorations will usually be
   A.   a credit to the seller and an expense to the buyer.
   B.   a credit to the buyer and an expense to the seller.
   C.   a credit to the seller and a credit to the buyer.
   D.   an expense to the buyer and an expense to the seller.

20. Under the provisions of RESPA,
   A.   the buyer must be given an estimate of closing charges and costs in advance of closing.
   B.   payments outside of escrow are prohibited.
   C.   Both A and B.
   D.   Neither A nor B.

Real Estate Leases

In this chapter you will look at leases from the standpoint of the tenant, owner, and property manager. First, we will cover some of the important terminology and explain a sample lease. Landlord-tenant laws, Statute of Frauds, setting rents, ground leases, lease termination, fair housing laws, and rent controls are also covered in this chapter. Specific terminology and concepts covered include assignment and subletting.

OVERVIEW OF CHAPTER 15

LEARNING OBJECTIVES

After successful completion of this chapter, you should be able to:

1. Define leasehold estate and explain how to create a valid lease.
2. Describe a lease document.
3. Explain landlord-tenant laws, Statute of Frauds, fair housing laws, and rent control in your state.
4. Define assignment, option clause, ground lease, economic rent, and contract rent.
5. Describe the eviction process.
6. Distinguish between subletting and assignment.
7. Explain the processes of setting rents and terminating leases.
8. Discuss the functions of on-site management including collection of rents and property maintenance.

KEY • TERMS

Assignment: the total transfer of the lessee's rights to another party

CPM, RPA: professional designations for property managers

Gross lease: tenant pays a fixed rent and the landlord pays all property expenses

Lessee: the tenant

Lessor: the landlord

Net lease: tenant pays a base rent plus maintenance, property taxes, and insurance

Option: the right at some future time to purchase or lease a property at a predetermined price

Quiet enjoyment: the right of possession and use of property without undue disturbance by others

Reversion: the right to retake possession at a future date

Sublessee: a lessee who rents from another lessee

Sublessor: a lessee who rents to another lessee

Sublet: to transfer only a portion of one's lease rights

Earlier chapters of this book discussed leases as estates in land (Chapter 3) and as a means of financing (Chapter 12). This chapter will look at leases from the standpoint of the tenant, the property owner, and the property manager. (During your lifetime you will be in one of these roles and perhaps all three.) Our discussion will begin with some important terminology. Then comes a sample lease document with explanation, plus information on locating, qualifying, and keeping tenants. The chapter concludes with information on job opportunities available in professional property management. Emphasis will be on residential property although a number of key points regarding commercial property leases will also be included.

THE LEASEHOLD ESTATE

A lease conveys to the **lessee** (tenant) the right to possess and use another's property for a period of time. During this time the **lessor** (the landlord or fee owner) possesses a **reversion** that entitles him to retake possession at the end of the lease period. Notice that a lease separates the right to use property from the property's ownership. The tenant gets the use of the property during the lease period and pays rent. The property owner is denied use of the property but receives rent in return. At the end of the lease the property owner gets the use of the property back but no more rent. The tenant no longer has the use of the property and no longer pays rent. This chapter describes how this very simple idea is carried out in practice.

A tenant's right to occupy land and/or buildings thereon is called a **leasehold estate.** The two most commonly found leasehold estates are the periodic estate and the estate for years. The **periodic estate** is one that continually renews itself for like periods of time until the tenant or landlord acts to terminate it. A month-to-month lease is an example of this. An **estate for years** is a lease with a specific starting date and a specific ending date. It can be for any length of time, and it does not automatically renew itself. A lease for one year is an example. There are two other leasehold categories: estate at will and tenancy at sufferance. An **estate at will,** rather seldom found, can be terminated by either tenant or landlord at any time. For example, the owner of a rental house decides to sell it upon expiration of the current lease. The owner and tenant agree that the tenant will be able to continue to rent until the house is sold. A **tenancy at sufferance** occurs when a tenant stays beyond his legal tenancy without the consent of the landlord. The tenant is commonly called a **holdover tenant** and no advance notice is required for eviction. He differs from a trespasser only in that his original entry onto the property was legal.

CREATING A VALID LEASE

A lease is both a conveyance and a contract. As a conveyance it conveys rights of possession to the tenant in the form of a leasehold estate. As a contract it contains provisions for the payment of rent and any other obligations the landlord and tenant have to each other.

For a valid lease to exist, it must meet the usual requirements of a contract as described in Chapter 7. That is to say, the parties involved must be legally competent, and there must be mutual agreement, lawful objective, and sufficient consideration. The main elements of a lease are (1) the names of the lessee and lessor, (2) a description of the premises, (3) an agreement to convey (let) the premises by the lessor and to accept possession by the lessee, (4) provisions for the payment of rent, (5) the starting date and duration of the lease, and (6) signatures of the parties to the lease.

In most states a lease for a term longer than one year must be in writing to be enforceable in court. A lease for one year or less or a month-to-month lease could be oral and still be valid, but as a matter of good business practice any lease should be put in writing and signed. This gives all parties involved a written reminder of their obligations under the lease and reduces chances for dispute.

THE LEASE DOCUMENT

Figure 15:1 illustrates a lease document that contains provisions typically found in a residential lease. These provisions are presented in simplified language to help you more easily grasp the rights and responsibilities created by a lease.

Conveyance

The first paragraph is the conveyance portion of the lease. At ① and ② the lessor and lessee are identified. At ③ the lessor conveys to the lessee and the lessee accepts the property. A description of the property follows at ④ and the **term** of the conveyance at ⑤. The property must be described so that there is no question as to the extent of the premises the lessee is renting. While a tenant, the lessee is entitled to **quiet enjoyment** of the property. This means uninterrupted use of the property without interference from the owner, the property manager, or any third party.

If the lease illustrated here was a month-to-month lease, the wording at ⑤ would be changed to read, "commencing April 15, 19xx and continuing on a month-to-month basis until terminated by either the lessee or the lessor." A month-to-month rental is a very flexible arrangement. It allows the owner to recover possession of the property on one-month notice and the tenant to leave on one-month notice with no further obligation to the owner. In rental agreements for longer periods of time, each party gives up some flexibility to gain commitment from the other. Under a one-year lease the owner commits the property to the tenant for a year. In return the tenant is committed to paying rent for a full year. In a like manner, the owner has the tenant's commitment to pay rent for a year but loses the flexibility of being able to regain possession of the property until the year is over.

Contract

The balance of the lease document is concerned with contract aspects of the lease. At ⑥ the amount of rent that the lessee will pay for the use of the property is set forth. In an estate for years the usual practice is to state the total rent for the entire lease period. This is the total number of dollars the lessee is obligated to pay to the lessor. The lessee can vacate the premises before

Figure 15:1.

LEASE

This lease agreement is entered into the __10th__ day of __April__ , 19 __xx__ between __John and Sally Landlord__ (hereinafter called the Lessor) and __Gary and Barbara Ten-__ ① ant ② (hereinafter called the Lessee). The Lessor hereby leases to the Lessee ③ and the Lessee hereby leases from the Lessor the premises known as __Apartment 24, 1234 Maple St., City, State__ ④ for the term of __one__ ⑤ year beginning 12:00 noon on __April 15, 19xx__ and ending 12:00 noon on __April 15, 19xx__ unless sooner terminated as herein set forth.

The rent for the term of this lease is __$ 6,000.00__ ⑥ payable in equal monthly installments of $ __500.00__⑦on the __15th__ day of each month beginning on __April 15, 19xx__. Receipt of the first monthly installment and __$ 500.00__ ⑧ as a security, damage, and clean-up deposit is hereby acknowledged. It is furthermore agreed that:

⑨ The use of the premises shall be as a residential dwelling for the above named Lessee only.

⑩ The Lessee may not assign this lease or sublet any portion of the premises without written permission from the Lessor.

⑪ The Lessee agrees to abide by the house rules as posted. A current copy is attached to this lease.

⑫ The Lessor shall furnish water, sewer, and heat as part of the rent. Electricity and telephone shall be paid for by the Lessee.

⑬ The Lessor agrees to keep the premises structure maintained and in habitable condition.

⑭ The Lessee agrees to maintain the interior of said premises and at the termination of this lease to return said premises to the Lessor in as good condition as it is now except for ordinary wear and tear.

⑮ The Lessee shall not make any alterations or improvements to the premises without the Lessor's prior written consent. Any alterations or improvements become the property of the Lessor at the end of this lease.

Figure 15:1. continued

㉖ *If the premises are not ready for occupancy on the date herein provided, the Lessee may cancel this agreement and the Lessor shall return in full all money paid by the Lessee.*

⑰ *If the Lessee defaults on this lease agreement, the Lessor may give the Lessee three days notice of intention to terminate the lease. At the end of those three days the lease shall terminate and the Lessee shall vacate and surrender the premises to the Lessor.*

⑱ *If the Lessee holds over after the expiration of this lease without the Lessor's consent, the tenancy shall be month to month at twice the monthly rate indicated herein.*

⑲ *If the premises are destroyed or rendered uninhabitable by fire or other cause, this lease shall terminate as of the date of the casualty.*

⑳ *The Lessor shall have access to the premises for the purpose of inspecting for damage, making repairs, and showing to prospective tenants or buyers.*

㉑ **John Landlord**
Lessor

Sally Landlord
Lessor

㉒ **Gary Tenant**
Lessee

Barbara Tenant
Lessee

the lease period expires but is still liable for the full amount of the contract. The method of payment of the obligation is shown at ⑦. Unless the contract calls for rent to be paid in advance, under common law it is not due until the end of the rental period. At ⑧ the lessor has taken a deposit in the form of the first monthly installment and acknowledges receipt of it. The lessor has also taken additional money as security against the possibility of uncollected rent or damage to the premises and for clean-up expenses. (The tenant is supposed to leave the premises clean.) The deposit is refunded, less legitimate charges, when the tenant leaves.

Items ⑨ through ⑳ summarize commonly found lease clauses. At ⑨ and ⑩ the lessor wants to maintain control over the use and occupancy of the premises. Without this he might find the premises used for an entirely different purpose or by people he did not rent to. At ⑪ the tenant agrees to abide by the house rules. These normally cover such things as use of laundry and trash facilities, swimming pool rules, noise rules, etc. Number ⑫ states the responsibility of the lessee and lessor with regard to the payment of utilities.

A strict legal interpretation of a lease as a conveyance means the tenant is responsible for upkeep and repairs unless the lessor promises to do so in the lease contract. The paragraph at ⑬ is that promise. Consumerism has had a profound influence on this matter. As a result courts and legislatures now take the position that the landlord is obligated to keep a residential property repaired and habitable even though this is not specifically stated in the contract. (Commercial property still goes by the strict interpretation, i.e., the landlord has to promise upkeep and repairs or the tenant doesn't get them.)

Number ⑭ is the tenant's promise to maintain the interior of the dwelling. If the tenant damages the property, the tenant must repair or pay for it. Normal wear and tear are considered to be part of the rent. At paragraph ⑮ the landlord protects himself against unauthorized alterations and improvements and then goes on to point out that anything the tenant affixes to the building becomes realty. As realty it remains a part of the building when the tenant leaves.

Paragraphs ⑯ through ⑲ deal with the rights of both parties if the premises are not ready for occupancy, if the lessee defaults after moving in, if the lessee holds over, or if the premises are destroyed. The lessor also retains the right (paragraph ⑳) to enter the leased premises from time to time for business purposes.

Finally, at ㉑ and ㉒, the lessor and lessee sign. It is not necessary to have these signatures notarized. That is done only if the lease is to be recorded and then only the lessor's signature is notarized. The purpose of recording is to give constructive notice that the lessee has an estate in the property. Recording is usually done only when the lessee's rights are not apparent from inspection of the property or where the lease is to run for more than three years. From the property owner's standpoint, the lease is an encumbrance on the property. If the owner should subsequently sell the property or mortgage it, the lessee's tenancy remains undisturbed. The buyer or lender must accept the property subject to the lease.

If one of the lessors dies, the lease is still binding on the remaining lessor(s) and upon the estate of the deceased lessor. Similarly, if one of the lessees dies, the lease is still binding on the remaining lessee(s) and upon the estate of the deceased lessee. This is based on common law doctrine that applies to contracts in general (see Chapter 7, "Deceased Party"). The lessee and lessor can, however, agree to do otherwise. The lessee could ask the lessor to **waive** (give up) the right to hold the lessee's estate to the lease in the event of the lessee's death. For example, an elderly tenant about to sign a lease might want to add wording to the lease whereby the tenant's death would allow his estate to terminate the lease early.

LANDLORD-TENANT LAWS

Traditionally, courts have been strict interpreters of lease agreements. This philosophy still prevails for leases on commercial property. However, with regard to residential rental property, the trend today is for state legislatures to establish special landlord-tenant laws. The intent is to strike a reasonable balance between the responsibilities of landlords to tenants and vice versa. Typically these laws limit the amount of security deposit a landlord can require, tell the tenant how many days notice he has to give before vacating a periodic tenancy, and require the landlord to deliver possession on the date agreed. The landlord must maintain the premises in a fit condition for living, and the tenant is to keep his unit clean and not damage it. The tenant is to obey the house rules, and the landlord must give advance notice before entering an apartment except in legitimate emergencies. Additionally, the laws set forth such things as the procedure for accounting for any deposit money not returned, the right of the tenant to make needed repairs and bill the landlord, the right of the landlord to file court actions for unpaid rent, and the proper procedure for evicting a tenant.

SETTING RENTS

There are several methods for setting rents. The most common is the **gross lease.** Under a gross lease the tenant pays a fixed rent, and the landlord pays all the operating expenses of the property. A tenant paying $450 per month on a month-to-month apartment lease or a person paying $12,000 per year for a one-year house lease are both examples of fixed rents.

A landlord will usually agree to a level rent for one year, but what if the tenant wants a longer lease term such as 2 years, or

5 years, or 10 years, or 25 years, or 99 years? For these situations the following rent setting methods are used in the real estate industry. The simplest is to have a **step-up** or **graduated rent.** For example, a 5-year office lease might call for monthly rents of 90¢ per square foot of floor space the first year, 95¢ the second year, $1.00 the third year, $1.05 the fourth year, and $1.10 the fifth. A residential tenant wishing a 2-year lease might find the landlord more receptive if the monthly rent is stepped up the second year.

Office and industrial leases of 5 or more years often include an **escalator** or **participation clause.** This allows the landlord to pass along to the tenant increases in such items as property taxes, utility charges, and maintenance. A variation is to have the tenant pay for all property taxes, insurance, repairs, utilities, etc. in addition to the base rent. This arrangement is called a **net lease** or a **triple net lease.** It is commonly used when an entire building is being leased and for long-term ground leases.

Another system for setting rents is the **percentage lease** wherein the owner receives a percentage of the tenant's gross receipts as rent. For example, a farmer who leases land may give the landowner 20% of the value of the crop when it is sold. The monthly rent for a small hardware store might be $600 plus 6% of gross sales above $10,000. A gasoline station may pay $1,000 plus 2¢ per gallon pumped. A supermarket may pay $7,500 plus 1½% of gross above $50,000 per month.

Still another way of setting rents on long-term leases is to **index** the rent to some economic indicator, such as an inflation index. If there is inflation, rents increase; if there is deflation, rents decrease. Arrangements such as step-ups, escalators, percentages, indexes, and net leases are all efforts by landlords to protect against rising costs of property operation and declining purchasing power, yet meet tenant's needs to have property committed to them for more than a year.

OPTION CLAUSES

Option clauses give the tenant the right at some future time to purchase or lease the property at a predetermined price. This gives a tenant flexibility. For example, suppose that a prospective tenant is starting a new business and is not certain how successful it will be. Therefore, in looking for space to rent, he will want a lease that allows an "out" if the new venture does not succeed, but will permit him to stay if the venture is successful. The solution is a lease with options. The landlord could offer a one-year lease, plus an option to stay for 2 more years at a higher rent plus a second option for an additional 5 years at a still higher rent. If the venture is not successful, the tenant is obligated for only one year. But if successful, he has the option of staying 2 more years, and if still successful, for 5 years after that.

Another option possibility is to offer the tenant a lease that also contains an option to buy the property for a fixed period of time at a preset price. This is called a **lease with option to buy** and is discussed in Chapter 8.

ASSIGNMENT AND SUBLETTING

Unless otherwise provided in the lease contract, a lessee may assign the lease or sublet. An **assignment** is the total transfer of the lessee's rights to another person. These parties are referred to as the **assignor** and the **assignee,** respectively. The assignee acquires all the right, title and interest of the assignor, no more and no less. However, the assignor remains liable for the performance of the contract unless released in writing by the landlord.

To **sublet** means to transfer only a portion of the rights held under a lease. The **sublease** thereby created may be for a portion of the premises, or part of the lease term. The party acquiring those rights is called the **sublessee.** The original lessee is the **sublessor** with respect to the sublessee. The sublessee pays rent to the lessee, who in turn remains liable to the landlord for rent on the entire premises.

LEASE TERMINATION

Most leases terminate because of the expiration of the term of the lease. The tenant has received the use of the premises and the landlord has received rent in return. However, a lease can be terminated if the landlord and the tenant mutually agree. The tenant surrenders the premises and the landlord releases him from the contract. This should, of course, be done in writing.

Eviction

If a tenant fails to live up to the terms of the lease agreement, the landlord has grounds for eviction. Usually this is for non-payment of rent, but it can also be for violation of some other aspect of the agreement such as holding over past the term of the lease, bringing animals into a "no pets" apartment, occupancy by more than the number of persons specified in the agreement, or operating in an illegal manner on the premises. Called **actual eviction,** the process usually begins with the landlord having a notice served on the tenant requiring the tenant to comply with the lease agreement or move out. If the tenant neither complies nor vacates, the landlord takes the matter to court. If the landlord wins the case, either by a preponderance of evidence or because the tenant does not appear to contest the eviction, then the court will terminate the tenant's lease rights and authorize a marshall or sheriff to go on the premises and force the tenant out.

A lease agreement may also be terminated through **constructive eviction.** This occurs when the landlord does not keep the premises fit for occupancy and the tenant is forced to move. For example, the landlord may be continually failing to repair broken plumbing lines or a leaking roof. The tenant's legal remedies are to claim wrongful eviction, move out, stop paying rent, and sue the landlord for breach of contract, either forcing the landlord to make repairs or to terminate the lease, possibly with money damages.

A **retaliatory eviction** is one whereby a landlord evicts a tenant because of a complaint made by the tenant. For example, a tenant may have complained to public health officials or building and safety authorities about conditions on the premises that are in violation of health laws or building codes. The landlord may retaliate or threaten to retaliate with an eviction (or a rent increase or a decrease in services); however, this is illegal.

The government, under its right of eminent domain, can also terminate a lease, but must provide just compensation. An example of this would be construction of a new highway that requires the demolition of a building rented to tenants. Both property owner and the tenants would be entitled to compensation.

Eminent Domain

A mortgage foreclosure can also bring about lease termination; it all depends on priority. If the mortgage was recorded before the lease was signed, then foreclosure of the mortgage also forecloses the lease. If the lease was recorded first, then the lease still stands. Because a lease can cloud a lender's title, wording is sometimes inserted in leases that makes them subordinate to any future financing of the property. This is highly technical, but nonetheless a very significant matter in long-term shopping center, office building, and industrial leases.

JOB OPPORTUNITIES

In reading this chapter you may have become interested in a career in real property management. The most successful apartment managers seem to be those who have had previous experience in managing people and money and who are handy with tools. Those with prior military experience or experience as owners or managers of small businesses are eagerly sought after. Least successful as on-site property managers are those who see it as a quiet, peaceful retirement job, those who are unable to work with and understand people, those who cannot organize or make decisions, those without a few handyman skills, and those strictly looking for an 8-to-5, Monday-to-Friday job. Commercial and industrial property management positions tend to be filled by persons who have had prior property management experience and who have a good understanding of how business and industry make use of real estate.

In a medium-to-large property management firm there will be job opportunities for building service personnel, purchasing agents, bookkeepers, clerks, secretaries, office managers, field supervisors, and executive managers. In a small office, one person plus a secretary will be responsible for all the off-site duties.

Training Programs

Finding experienced and capable property managers is not an easy task. Formal education in property management is not widely available in the United States. Instead, most managers learn their profession almost entirely by experience. An individual property owner can place an advertisement in a newspaper and attract a manager from another project, but most professional management firms have found it necessary to develop their own internal training programs. With such a program a management firm can start a person with no previous property management experience as an assistant manager on a large project. If a person learns the job and enjoys the work, there is a promotion to manager of a 50- or 60-unit building and an increase in salary. If this works well, there is a move to a larger complex with an assistant and another increase in salary. Each step brings more responsibility and more pay. This system provides a steady stream of qualified managers for the management firm. It is also a source of executive-level personnel for the off-site management office. In larger cities executive-level positions pay upward of $100,000 per year.

The dominant professional organization in the property management field is the **Institute of Real Estate Management (IREM)**. Established in 1933, the Institute is a division within the National Association of Realtors. Its primary purposes are to serve as an exchange medium for management ideas and to recognize specialists in the field. The Institute awards the designation **Certified Property Manager (CPM)** to members who successfully complete required educational courses in property management. The Institute also offers an educational program for resident managers of apartment buildings. The designation **Accredited Resident Manager (ARM)** is awarded upon successful completion. Forty-five percent of all property to be managed in the United States is managed by IREM members and there are in excess of 10,000 CPMs.

Second in size to IREM is the **Building Owners and Managers Institute (BOMI)**. Incorporated in 1970, BOMI provides educational programs aimed primarily at the commercial property management industry. Seven courses are offered ranging from design, operation, and maintenance of buildings to accounting, insurance, law, investments, and administration. Successful completion of the seven courses leads to the designation of **Real Property Administrator (RPA)**. BOMI also offers eight courses in heating, plumbing, refrigeration, air handling, electrical systems, control systems maintenance, energy management, and supervision as they apply to commercial buildings. Those who complete these courses receive the **Systems Maintenance Administrator (SMA)** designation.

1. A lease for a definite period of time, which terminates when that time has expired, is an estate
   A. for years.
   B. periodic estate.
   C. at will.
   D. at sufferance.

2. A lease of fixed length that continually renews itself for the like periods of time until the lessor or lessee acts to terminate it is
   A. a holdover estate.
   B. a periodic estate.
   C. an estate at will.
   D. an estate at sufferance.

3. A lease is a
   A. conveyance.
   B. contract.
   C. Both A and B.
   D. Neither A nor B.

4. To be valid, which of the following must be in writing and signed?
   A. A month-to-month lease.
   B. A 14-month lease.
   C. A three-month lease.
   D. All of the above.

5. The right of the lessee to uninterrupted use of the leased premises is called
   A. quiet possession.
   B. quiet enjoyment.
   C. quiet rights.
   D. tenant rights.

6. A written lease agreement is still legal even though it fails to include
   A. the terms of the lease.
   B. a property description.
   C. Both A and B.
   D. Neither A nor B.

7. As compared to a lease for years, a month-to-month lease gives flexibility to the
   A. landlord.
   B. tenant.
   C. Both A and B.
   D. Neither A nor B.

8. Bob Short and Bill Tall rent an apartment unit from owner Haf High. Bill dies during the lease term. The lease is still binding upon
   A. Bob.
   B. Haf.
   C. Bill's estate.
   D. All of the above.

9. The word "waive" means to
   A. say "goodbye."
   B. demand.
   C. relinquish.
   D. die naturally.

10. A lease which calls for specified rental increases at predetermined intervals is known as a
    A. step-up lease.
    B. graduated lease.
    C. Both A and B.
    D. Neither A nor B.

11. The clause in a lease which allows the landlord to pass along to the tenant certain increases in operating expenses is called
    A. an escalator clause.
    B. a participation clause.
    C. Both A and B.
    D. Neither A nor B.

12. When the tenant pays a base rent plus some or all of the operating expenses of a property, the result is a
    A. gross lease.
    B. net lease.
    C. percentage lease.
    D. graduated lease.

13. A lease in which the tenant pays a rent based upon the gross sales made from the rented premises is known as a
    A. percentage lease.
    B. participation lease.
    C. net lease.
    D. gross lease.

14. Which of the following is NOT specifically designed to protect against rising operating costs?
    A. A net lease.
    B. An escalator clause.
    C. An index clause.
    D. A gross lease.

15. A lease for years may be terminated by
    A. constructive eviction.
    B. eminent domain.
    C. mutual agreement.
    D. actual eviction.
    E. All of the above.

16. Experience with rent controls generally indicates that rent control
    A. solves more problems than it creates.
    B. creates more problems than it solves.

17. Property owners can attract tenants in a soft rental market by
    A. reductions in rent.
    B. rent concessions.
    C. Both A and B.
    D. Neither A nor B.

18. Generally, today's laws regarding eviction of a tenant for nonpayment of rents, as compared to those in the past, favor the
    A. tenant.
    B. landlord.

19. The best defense against losses from uncollected rent is
    A. a threat of legal action against the delinquent tenant.
    B. careful tenant selection, good service, and a businesslike policy on rent collections.

20. The Institute of Real Estate Management awards the designation
    A. REM.
    B. CPM.
    C. MAI.
    D. SREA.

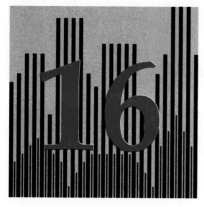

Real Estate Appraisal

OVERVIEW OF
CHAPTER 16

This chapter deals with the three approaches to estimating value—the market approach, the cost approach, and the income approach. The market approach is sometimes referred to as the market comparison approach, which provides an estimate of market or fair market value. The market approach is also used in estimating values of condominiums and townhouses. Other topics covered include competitive market analysis and gross rent multipliers. The cost and income approaches lead into a discussion of income forecasting, depreciation, construction costs, operating expense ratio, and capitalizing income. The chapter concludes with coverage of the appraisal report, principles of value, and the multiple meanings of the word "value."

LEARNING OBJECTIVES

After successful completion of this chapter, you should be able to:
1. Estimate value based on the market comparison approach.
2. Estimate the value of land and understand the need for competitive market analysis.
3. Understand how to use gross rent multipliers.
4. Apply the cost and income approaches to the determination of value.
5. Explain how the three approaches are used to come up with the appraiser's best estimate.
6. Describe the various types of appraiser reports.
7. Explain the characteristics and principles of value.
8. Understand the difference between a buyer's and seller's market.
9. Explain the many meanings of the word "value."
10. Identify professional appraisal societies and describe their roles.

KEY • TERMS

Appraise: to estimate the value of something

Capitalize: to convert future income to current value

Comparables: properties similar to the subject property that have sold recently

Cost approach: land value plus current construction costs minus depreciation

Depreciation: loss in value due to deterioration and obsolescence

FIRREA: the Financial Institution's Reform, Recovery, and Enforcement Act of 1989

Gross rent multiplier (GRM): a number that is multiplied by a property's gross rents to produce an estimate of the property's worth

Highest and best use: that use of a parcel of land which will produce the greatest current value

Income approach: a method of valuing a property based on the monetary returns it can be expected to produce

Market approach: a method of valuing property based on recent sales of similar properties

Market value: the cash price that a willing buyer and a willing seller would agree upon, given reasonable exposure of the property to the marketplace, full information as to the potential uses of the property, and no undue compulsion to act

Operating expenses: expenditures necessary to maintain the production of income

Scheduled gross, Projected gross: the estimated rent a fully occupied property can be expected to produce on an annual basis

To **appraise** real estate, in general terms, means to estimate its value. An **appraisal** is now defined under federal law as "a written statement used in connection with a federally related transaction that is independently and impartially prepared by a licensed or certified appraiser that states an opinion of the defined value of an adequately described property as of a specific date that is supported by the presentation and analysis of relevant market information." In more generic terms, an appraisal is defined in applying the Uniform Standard of Professional Appraisal Practice as "the act or process of estimating the value."

There are three approaches to making this estimate. The first is to locate similar properties that have sold recently and use them as bench marks in estimating the value of the property you are appraising. This is the **market approach,** also called the market-data approach or market comparison approach. The second approach is to add together the cost of the individual components that make up the property being appraised. This is the **cost approach;** it starts with the cost of a similar parcel of vacant land and adds the cost of the lumber, concrete, plumbing, wiring, labor, etc., necessary to build a similar building. Depreciation is then subtracted. The third approach is to consider only the amount of net income that the property can reasonably be expected to produce for its owner plus any anticipated price increase or decrease. This is the **income approach.** For the person who owns or plans to own real estate, knowing how much a property is worth is a crucial part of the buying or selling decision. For the real estate agent, being able to estimate the value of a property is an essential part of taking a listing and conducting negotiations.

MARKET VALUE

In this chapter you will see demonstrations of the market, cost, and income approaches and how they are used in determining market value. **Market value,** also called **fair market value,** is the highest price in terms of money that a property will bring if (1) payment is made in cash or its equivalent, (2) the property is exposed on the open market for a reasonable length of time, (3) the buyer and seller are fully informed as to market conditions and the uses to which the property may be put, (4) neither is under abnormal pressure to conclude a transaction, and (5) the seller is capable of conveying marketable title. Market value is at the heart of nearly all real estate transactions.

MARKET COMPARISON APPROACH

Let's begin by demonstrating the application of the **market comparison approach** to a single-family residence. The residence to be appraised is called the **subject property** and is described as follows:

> The subject property is a one-story, wood-frame house of 1,520 square feet containing three bedrooms, two bathrooms, a living room, dining room, kitchen, and utility room. There is a two-car garage with concrete driveway to the street, a 300-square-foot concrete patio in the backyard, and an average amount of landscaping. The house is located on a 10,200-square-foot, level lot that measures 85 by 120 feet. The house is 12 years old, in good repair, and located in a well-maintained neighborhood of houses of similar construction and age.

After becoming familiar with the physical features and amenities of the subject property, the next step in the market approach is to locate houses with similar physical features and amenities that have sold recently under market value conditions. These are known as **comparables** or "comps." The more similar they are to the subject property, the fewer and smaller the adjustments that must be made in the comparison process, and hence the less room for error. As a rule it is best to use comparable sales no more than 6 months old. During periods of relatively stable prices, this can be extended to 1 year. However, during periods of rapidly changing prices even a sale 6 months old may be out of date.

Comparables

To apply the market comparison approach, the following information must be collected for each comparable sale: date of sale, sales price, financing terms, location of the property, and a description of its physical characteristics and amenities. Recorded deeds at public records offices can provide dates and locations of recent sales. Although a deed seldom states the purchase price, nearly all states levy a deed transfer fee or conveyance tax, the amount of which is shown on the recorded deed. This tax can sometimes provide a clue as to the purchase price.

Sales Records

Records of past sales can often be obtained from title and abstract companies. Property tax assessors keep records on changes in ownership as well as property values. Where these records are kept up to date and are available to the public, they can provide information on what has sold recently and for how much. Assessors also keep detailed records of improvements made to land. This can be quite helpful in making adjustments between the subject property and the comparables. For real estate salespeople, locally operated multiple listing services provide asking prices and descriptions of properties currently offered for sale by member brokers along with descriptions, sales prices, and dates for properties that have been sold. In some cities, commercially operated financial services publish information on local real estate transactions and sell it on a subscription basis.

To produce the most accurate appraisal possible, each sale used as a comparable should be inspected and the price and terms verified. An agent who specializes in a given neighborhood will

Verification

have already visited the comparables when they were still for sale. The agent can verify price and terms with the selling broker or from multiple listing service sales records.

Number of Comparables

Three to five comparables usually provide enough basis for reliable comparison. To use more than five, the additional accuracy must be weighed against the extra effort involved. When the supply of comparable sales is more than adequate, one should choose the sales that require the fewest adjustments.

It is also important that the comparables selected represent current market conditions. Sales between relatives or close friends may result in an advantageous price to the buyer or seller, and sales prices that for some other reason appear to be out of line with the general market should not be used. Listings and offers to buy should not be used in place of actual sales. They do not represent a meeting of minds between a buyer and a seller. Listing prices do indicate the upper limit of prices, whereas offers to buy indicate lower limits. Thus, if a property is listed for sale at $80,000 and there have been offers as high as $76,000, it is reasonable to presume the market price lies somewhere between $76,000 and $80,000.

Adjustment Process

Let us now work through the example shown in Table 16:1 to demonstrate the application of the market comparison approach to a house. We begin at lines 1 and 2 by entering the address and sale price of each comparable property. For convenience, we shall refer to these as comparables A, B, and C. On lines 3 through 10, we make time adjustments to the sale price of each comparable to make it equivalent to the subject property today. **Adjustments** are made for price changes since each comparable was sold, as well as for differences in physical features, amenities, and financial terms. The result indicates the market value of the subject property.

Time Adjustments

Returning to line 3 in Table 16:1, let us assume that house prices in the neighborhood where the subject property and comparables are located have risen 5% during the 6 months that have elapsed since comparable A was sold. If it were for sale today, comparable A would bring 5% or $4,590 more. Therefore, we must add $4,590 to bring it up to the present. Comparable B

Table 16:1. Valuing a House by the Market Comparison Approach

Line	Item	Comparable Sale A		Comparable Sale B		Comparable Sale C	
1	**Address**	1702 Brookside Ave.		1912 Brookside Ave.		1501 18th Street	
2	**Sales price**		$91,800		$88,000		$89,000
3	**Time adjustment**	*sold 6 mos. ago, add 5%*	+4,590	*sold 3 mos. ago, add 2½%*	+2,200	*just sold*	0
4	**House size**	*160 sq ft larger at $40 per sq ft*	−6,400	*20 sq ft smaller at $40/sq ft*	+800	*same size*	0
5	**Garage/carport**	*carport*	+4,000	*3-car garage*	−2,000	*2-car garage*	0
6	**Other**	*larger patio*	−300	*no patio*	+600	*built-in bookcases*	−500
7	**Age, upkeep, & overall quality of house**	*superior*	−2,000	*inferior*	+400	*equal*	0
8	**Landscaping**	*inferior*	+1,000	*equal*	0	*superior*	−700
9	**Lot size, features, & location**	*superior*	−3,890	*inferior*	+900	*equal*	0
10	**Terms & conditions of sale**	*equal*	0	*special financing*	−1,500	*equal*	0
11	**Total adjustments**		−3,000		+1,400		−1,200
12	**ADJUSTED MARKET PRICE**		$88,800		$89,400		$87,800
13	**Correlation process:**						
	Comparable A $88,800 × 20% = $17,760						
	Comparable B $89,400 × 30% = $26,820						
	Comparable C $87,800 × 50% = $43,000						
14	**INDICATED VALUE**		$88,480				
	Round to		$88,500				

was sold 3 months ago, and to bring it up to the present we need to add 2½% or $2,200 to its sales price. Comparable C was just sold and needs no time correction as its price reflects today's market.

When using the market comparison approach, all adjustments are made to the comparable properties, not to the subject property. This is because we cannot adjust the value of something for which we do not yet know the value.

Because house A is 160 square feet larger than the subject house, it is logical to expect that the subject property would sell for less

House Size

money. Hence a deduction is made from the sales price of comparable A on line 4. The amount of this deduction is based on the difference in floor area and the current cost of similar construction, minus an allowance for depreciation. If we value the extra 160 square feet at $40 per square foot, we must subtract $6,400. For comparable B, the house is 20 square feet smaller than the subject house. At $40 per square foot, we add $800 to comparable B, as it is reasonable to expect that the subject property would sell for that much more because it is that much larger. Comparable C is the same-sized house as the subject property, so no adjustment is needed.

Garage and Patio Adjustments

Next, the parking facilities (line 5) are adjusted. We first look at the current cost of garage and carport construction and the condition of these structures. Assume that the value of a carport is $2,000; a one-car garage, $4,000; a two-car garage, $6,000; and a three-car garage, $8,000. Adjustments would be made as follows. The subject property has a two-car garage worth $6,000 and comparable A has a carport worth $2,000. Therefore, based on the difference in garage facilities, we can reasonably expect the subject property to command $4,000 more than comparable A. By adding $4,000 to comparable A, we effectively equalize this difference. Comparable B has a garage worth $2,000 more than the subject property's garage. Therefore, $2,000 must be subtracted from comparable B to equalize it with the subject property. For comparable C, no adjustment is required, as comparable C and the subject property have similar garage facilities.

At line 6, the subject property has a 300-square-foot patio in the backyard worth $600. Comparable A has a patio worth $900; therefore, $300 is deducted from comparable A's selling price. Comparable B has no patio. As it would have sold for $600 more if it had one, a +$600 adjustment is required. The patio at comparable C is the same as the subject property's. However, comparable C has $500 worth of custom built-in living room bookcases that the subject property does not have. Therefore, $500 is subtracted from comparable C's sales price. Any other differences between the comparables and the subject property such as swimming pools, fireplaces, carpeting, drapes, roofing materials, and kitchen appliances would be adjusted in a similar manner.

On line 7 we recognize differences in building age, wear and tear, construction quality, and design usefulness. Where the difference between the subject property and a comparable can be measured in terms of material and labor, the adjustment is the cost of that material and labor. For example, the $400 adjustment for comparable B reflects the cost of needed roof repair at the time B was sold. The adjustment of $2,000 for comparable A reflects the fact it has better-quality plumbing and electrical fixtures than the subject property. Differences that cannot be quantified in terms of labor and materials are usually dealt with as lump-sum judgments. Thus, one might allow $1,000 for each year of age difference between the subject and a comparable, or make a lump-sum adjustment of $2,000 for an inconvenient kitchen design.

Building Age, Condition, and Quality

Keep in mind that adjustments are made on the basis of what each comparable property was like on the day it was sold. Thus, if an extra bedroom was added or the house was painted after its sale date, these items are not included in the adjustment process.

Line 8 shows the landscaping at comparable A to be inferior to the subject property. A positive correction is necessary here to equalize it with the subject. The landscaping at comparable B is similar and requires no correction; that at comparable C is better and thus requires a negative adjustment. The dollar amount of each adjustment is based on the market value of lawn, bushes, trees, and the like.

Landscaping

Line 9 deals with any differences in lot size, slope, view, and neighborhood. In this example, all comparables are in the same neighborhood as the subject property, thus eliminating the need to judge, in dollar terms, the relative merit of one neighborhood over another. However, comparable A has a slightly larger lot and a better view than the subject property. Based on recent lot sales in the area, the difference is judged to be $890 for the larger lot and $3,000 for the better view. Comparable B has a slightly smaller lot judged to be worth $900 less, and comparable C is similar in all respects.

Lot Features and Location

Line 10 in Table 16:1 accounts for differences in financing. As a rule, the more accommodating the terms of the sale to the buyer, the

Terms and Conditions of Sale

higher the sales price, and vice versa. We are looking for the highest cash price the subject property may reasonably be expected to bring, given adequate exposure to the marketplace and a knowledgeable buyer and seller not under undue pressure. If the comparables were sold under these conditions, no corrections would be needed in this category. However, if it can be determined that a comparable was sold under different conditions, an adjustment is necessary. For example, if the going rate of interest on home mortgages is 12% per year and the seller offers to finance the buyer at 9% interest, it is reasonable to expect that the seller can charge a higher selling price. Similarly, the seller can get a higher price if he has a low-interest loan that can be assumed by the buyer. Favorable financing terms offered by the seller of comparable B enabled him to obtain an extra $1,500 in selling price. Therefore, we must subtract $1,500 from comparable B. Another situation that requires an adjustment on line 10 is if a comparable was sold on a rush basis. If a seller is in a hurry to sell, a lower selling price usually must be accepted than if the property can be given more time in the marketplace.

Adjusted Market Price

Adjustments for each comparable are totaled and either added or subtracted from its sale price. The result is the **adjusted market price** shown at line 12. This is the dollar value of each comparable sale after it has gone through an adjustment process to make it the same as the subject property. If it were possible to precisely evaluate every adjustment, and if the buyers of comparables A, B, and C had paid exactly what their properties were worth at the time they purchased them, the three prices shown on line 12 would be the same. However, buyers are not that precise, particularly in purchasing a home where amenity value influences price and varies considerably from one person to the next.

Correlation Process

While comparing the properties, it will usually become apparent that some comparables are more like the subject property than others. The **correlation** step gives the appraiser the opportunity to assign more weight to the more similar comparables and less to the others. At 13, comparable C is given a weight of 50% since it is more like the subject and required fewer adjustments. Moreover, this sameness is in areas where adjustments tend to be the hardest to estimate accurately: time, age, quality, location, view, and financial conditions. Of the remaining two comparables, comparable B is weighted slightly higher than comparable A because it is a more recent sale and required fewer adjustments overall.

In the correlation process, the adjusted market price of each comparable is multiplied by its weighting factor and totaled at line 14. The result is the **indicated value** of the subject property. It is customary to round off to the nearest $50 or $100 for properties under $10,000; to the nearest $250 or $500 for properties between $10,000 and $100,000; to the nearest $1,000 or $2,500 for properties between $100,000 and $250,000; and to the nearest $2,500 or $5,000 above that.

The process for estimating the market value of a condominium, townhouse, or cooperative living unit by the market approach is similar to the process for houses except that fewer steps are involved. For example, in a condominium complex with a large number of two-bedroom units of identical floor plan, data on a sufficient number of comparable sales may be available within the building. This would eliminate adjustments for differences in unit floor plan, neighborhood, lot size and features, age and upkeep of the building, and landscaping. The only corrections needed would be those that make one unit different from another. This would include the location of the individual unit within the building (end units and units with better views sell for more), the upkeep and interior decoration of the unit, a time adjustment, and an adjustment for terms and conditions of the sale.

When there are not enough comparable sales of the same floor plan within the same building and it is necessary to use different-sized units, an adjustment must be made for floor area. If the number of comparables is still inadequate and units in different condominium buildings must be used, adjustments will be necessary for neighborhood, lot features, management, upkeep, age, and overall condition of the building.

Subdivided lots zoned for commercial, industrial, or apartment buildings are usually appraised and sold on a square foot basis. Thus, if apartment land is currently selling for $3.00 per square foot, a 100,000-square-foot parcel of comparable zoning and usefulness would be appraised at $300,000. Another method is to value on a front-foot basis. For example, if a lot has 70 feet of

Unique Issues
Condominium, Townhouse, and Cooperative Appraisal

Market Approach to Vacant Land Valuation

street frontage and if similar lots are selling for $300 per front foot, that lot would be appraised at $21,000. Storefront land is often sold this way. House lots can be valued either by the square foot, front foot, or lot method. The lot method is useful when one is comparing lots of similar size and zoning in the same neighborhood. For example, recent sales of 100-foot by 100-foot house lots in the $18,000 to $20,000 range would establish the value of similar lots in the same neighborhood.

Rural land and large parcels that have not been subdivided are usually valued and sold by the acre. For example, how would you value 21 acres of vacant land when the only comparables available are 16-acre and 25-acre sales? The method is to establish a per acre value from comparables and apply it to the subject land. Thus, if 16- and 25-acre parcels sold for $32,000 and $50,000 respectively, and are similar in all other respects to the 21-acre subject property, it would be reasonable to conclude that land is selling for $2,000 per acre. Therefore, the subject property is worth $42,000.

4-3-2-1 Rule

The **4-3-2-1 rule** is a depth adjustment that appraisers sometimes use when valuing vacant lots. It states that the land at the back of the lot is worth less than the land at the front. To illustrate, consider a single-family residential lot that has 75 feet of frontage on a street and is 200 feet deep. Across the street and in an equally desirable location are two lots for sale that are each 75 feet on the street and 100 feet deep. Would you pay as much for the single 75′ × 200′ lot as you would for two 75′ × 100′ lots? Let us omit the arithmetic and just remember the principle: the land at the back of a lot is worth less than the land at the front.

Competitive Market Analysis

A variation of the market comparison approach and one that is very popular with agents who list and sell residential property is the **competitive market analysis (CMA).** This method is based on the principle that value can be estimated not only by looking at similar homes that have sold recently but also by taking into account homes presently on the market plus homes that were listed for sale but did not sell. The CMA is a listing tool that a sales agent prepares in order to show a seller what the home is likely to sell for, and the CMA helps the agent decide whether or not to accept the listing.

Figure 16:1 shows a competitive market analysis form published by the National Association of Realtors. The procedure in preparing a CMA is to select homes that are comparable to the

Figure 16:1. Competitive Market Analysis

Property Address _____ Date _____

For Sale Now: ①	Bed-rms.	Baths	Den	Sq. Ft.	1st Loan	List Price	Days on Market	Terms		

Sold Past 12 Mos. ②	Bed-rms.	Baths	Den	Sq. Ft.	1st Loan	List Price	Days on Market	Date Sold	Sale Price	Terms

Expired Past 12 Mos. ③	Bed-rms.	Baths	Den	Sq. Ft.	1st Loan	List Price	Days on Market	Terms		

④ F.H.A. — V.A. Appraisals

Address	Appraisal	Address	Appraisal

⑤ Buyer Appeal ⑥ Marketing Position

(Grade each item 0 to 20% on the basis of desirability or urgency)

⑤ Buyer Appeal	⑥ Marketing Position
1 Fine Location _____ %	1 Why Are They Selling _____ %
2 Exciting Extras _____ %	2 How Soon Must They Sell _____ %
3 Extra Special Financing _____ %	3 Will They Help Finance .... Yes ___ No ___ %
4 Exceptional Appeal _____ %	4 Will They List at Competitive Market Value .... Yes ___ No ___ %
5 Under Market Price ___ Yes ___ No ___ %	5 Will They Pay for Appraisal .... Yes ___ No ___ %
Rating Total _____ %	Rating Total _____ %

⑦
Assets _____
Drawbacks _____
Area Market Conditions _____

Recommended Terms _____

⑧ Selling Costs

Brokerage	$	Top Competitive Market Value	$ _____
Loan Payoff	$		
Prepayment Privilege	$		
FHA — VA Points	$	⑨	
Title and Escrow Fees: IRS Stamps Recons Recording	$	Probable Final Sales Price	$ _____
Termite Clearance	$		
Misc. Payoffs: 2nd T.D., Pool, Patio, Water Softener, Fence, Improvement Bond.	$		
	$	Total Selling Costs	$ _____
	$		
Total	$	Net Proceeds	$ _____ Plus or Minus $ _____

The statements and figures presented herein, while not guaranteed, are secured from sources we believe authoritative

Prepared by _____

subject property. The greater the similarity, the more accurate the appraisal will be and the more likely it is that the client will accept the agent's estimate of value and counsel. It is usually best to use only properties in the same neighborhood; this is easier for the seller to relate to and removes the need to compensate for neighborhood differences. The comparables should also be similar in size, age, and quality. Although a CMA does not require that individual adjustments be shown, it does depend on the agent's understanding of the process that takes place in that table. That is why Table 16:1 and its explanation are important. A residential agent may not be called upon to make a presentation as is done in Table 16:1; nonetheless, all those steps are considered and consolidated in the agent's mind before entering a probable final sales price on the CMA.

Homes for Sale   In section ① of the CMA shown in Figure 16:1, similar homes presently offered for sale are listed. This information is usually taken directly from the agent's multiple listing service (MLS) book, and ideally the agent will already have toured these properties and have first-hand knowledge of their condition. These are the homes the seller's property will compete against in the marketplace.

In section ② the agent lists similar properties that have sold in the past several months. Ideally, the agent will have toured the properties when they were for sale. Sale prices are usually available through MLS sales records. Section ③ is for listing homes that were offered for sale but did not sell. In other words, buyers were unwilling to take these homes at the prices offered.

In section ④ recent FHA and VA appraisals of comparable homes can be included if it is felt that they will be useful in determining the price at which to list. Two words of caution are in order here. First, using someone else's opinion of value is risky. It is better to determine your own opinion based on actual facts. Second, FHA and VA appraisals often tend to lag behind the market. This means in a rising market they will be too low; in a declining market they will be too high.

Buyer Appeal   In section ⑤ , buyer appeal, and in section ⑥, market position, the agent evaluates the subject property from the standpoint of whether or not it will sell if placed on the market. It is important to make the right decision to take or not to take a listing. Once taken, the agent knows that valuable time and money must be committed to get a property sold. Factors that make a property more appealing to a buyer include good location, extra features, small down payment, low interest, meticulous maintenance, and a price below market. Similarly, a property is more saleable if the sellers are motivated to sell, want to sell soon, will help with financing, and will list at or below market. A busy agent will want to avoid spending time on overpriced listings, listings for which no financing is available, and listings where the sellers have no motivation to sell. Under the rating systems in sections ⑤ and ⑥, the closer the total is to zero, the less desirable the listing; the closer to 100%, the more desirable the listing.

Section ⑦ provides space to list the property's high and low points, current market conditions, and recommended terms of sale. Section ⑧ shows the seller how much to expect in selling costs. Section ⑨ shows the seller what to expect in the way of a sales price and the amount of cash that can be expected from the sale.

The emphasis in CMA is on a visual inspection of the data on the form in order to arrive at market value directly. No pencil and paper adjustments are made. Instead, adjustments are made in a generalized fashion in the minds of the agent and the seller. In addition to its application to single-family houses, CMA can also be used on condominiums, cooperative apartments, town-houses, and vacant lots—provided sufficient comparables are available.

A popular market comparison method that is used when a property produces income is the **gross rent multiplier,** or **GRM.** The GRM is an economic comparison factor that relates the gross rent a property can produce to its purchase price. For apartment buildings and commercial and industrial properties, the GRM is computed by dividing the sales price of the property by its gross annual rent. For example, if an apartment building grosses $100,000 per year in rents and has just sold for $700,000, it is said to have a GRM of 7. The use of a GRM to value single-family houses is questionable since they are usually sold as owner-occupied residences rather than as income properties. Note that if you do work a GRM for a house, it is customary to use the monthly (not yearly) rent.

Gross Rent Multipliers

Building	Sales Price		Gross Annual Rents		Gross Rent Multiplier
No. 1	$245,000	÷	$ 34,900	=	7.02
No. 2	$160,000	÷	$ 22,988	=	6.96
No. 3	$204,000	÷	$ 29,352	=	6.95
No. 4	$196,000	÷	$ 27,762	=	7.06
As a Group:	$805,000	÷	$115,002	=	7.00

Table 16:2. Calculating Gross Rent Multipliers

Where comparable properties have been sold at fairly consistent gross rent multiples, the GRM technique presumes the subject property can be valued by multiplying its gross rent by that multiplier. To illustrate, suppose that apartment buildings were recently sold in your community as shown in Table 16:2. These sales indicate that the market is currently paying seven times gross. Therefore, to find the value of a similar apartment building grossing $24,000 per year, multiply by 7.00 to get an indicated value of $168,000.

The GRM method is popular because it is simple to apply. Having once established what multiplier the market is paying, one need only know the gross rents of a building to set a value. However, this simplicity is also the weakness of the GRM method because the GRM takes into account only the gross rent a property produces. Gross rent does not allow for variations in vacancies, uncollectible rents, property taxes, maintenance, management, insurance, utilities, or reserves for replacements.

Weakness of GRM   To illustrate the problem, suppose that two apartment buildings each gross $100,000 per year. However, the first has expenses amounting to $40,000 per year and the second, expenses of $50,000 per year. Using the same GRM, the buildings would be valued the same, yet the first produces $10,000 more in net income for its owner. The GRM also overlooks the expected economic life span of a property. For example, a building with an expected remaining life span of 30 years would be valued exactly the same as one expected to last 20 years, if both currently produce the same rents. One method of partially offsetting these errors is to use different GRMs under different circumstances. Thus, a property with low operating expenses

Table 16:3. Cost Approach to Value

Step 1:	Estimate land as vacant		$ 30,000
Step 2:	Estimate new construction cost of similar building	$120,000	
Step 3:	Less estimated depreciation	−12,000	
Step 4:	Indicated value of building		$108,000
Step 5:	Appraised property value by the cost approach		$138,000

and a long expected economic life span might call for a GRM of 7 or more, whereas a property with high operating expenses or a shorter expected life span would be valued using a GRM of 6 or 5 or even less.

COST APPROACH

There are times when the market approach is an inappropriate valuation tool. For example, the market approach is of limited usefulness in valuing a fire station, school building, courthouse, or highway bridge. These properties are rarely placed on the market and comparables are rarely found. Even with properties that are well-suited to the market approach, there may be times when it is valuable to apply another valuation approach. For example, a real estate agent may find that comparables indicate a certain style and size of house is selling in a particular neighborhood for $150,000. Yet the astute agent discovers through the cost approach that the same house can be built from scratch, including land, for $125,000. The agent builds and sells ten of these and concludes that, yes, there really is money to be made in real estate. Let us take a closer look at the cost approach.

Table 16:3 demonstrates the **cost approach.** Step 1 is to estimate the value of the land upon which the building is located. The land is valued as though vacant using the market comparison approach described earlier. In Step 2, the cost of constructing a similar building at today's costs is estimated. These costs include the current prices of building materials, construction wages, architect's fees, contractor's services, building permits, utility hookups, etc., plus the cost of financing during the construction stage and the cost of construction equipment used at the project site. Step 3 is the calculation of the amount of money that represents the subject building's wear and tear, lack of usefulness, and obsolescence when compared to the new building of Step 2. In Step 4, depreciation is subtracted from today's construction cost to give the current value of the subject building on a used basis. Step 5 is to add this amount to the land value. Let us work through these steps.

Estimating New Construction Costs

In order to choose a method of estimating construction costs, one must decide whether cost will be approached on a reproduction or on a replacement basis. **Reproduction cost** is the cost at today's prices of constructing an *exact replica* of the subject improvements using the same or very similar materials. **Replacement cost** is the cost, at today's prices and using today's methods of construction, for an improvement having the same or *equivalent usefulness* as the subject property. Replacement cost is the more practical choice of the two as it eliminates nonessential or obsolete features and takes full advantage of current construction materials and techniques. It is the approach that will be described here.

Square-Foot Method

The most widely used approach for estimating construction costs is the **square-foot method.** It provides reasonably accurate estimates that are fast and simple to prepare.

The square-foot method is based on finding a newly constructed building that is similar to the subject building in size, type of occupancy, design, materials, and construction quality. The cost of this building is converted to cost per square foot by dividing its current construction cost by the number of square feet in the building.

Cost Handbooks

Cost information is also available from construction cost handbooks. Using a **cost handbook** starts with selecting a handbook appropriate to the type of building being appraised. From photographs of houses included in the handbook along with brief descriptions of the buildings' features, the appraiser finds a house that most nearly fits the description of the subject house. Next to pictures of the house is the current cost per square foot to construct it. If the subject house has a better quality roof, floor covering, or heating system; greater or fewer built-in appliances, or plumbing fixtures; or a garage, basement, porch, or swimming pool, the handbook provides costs for each of these. Figure 16:2 illustrates the calculations involved in the square-foot method.

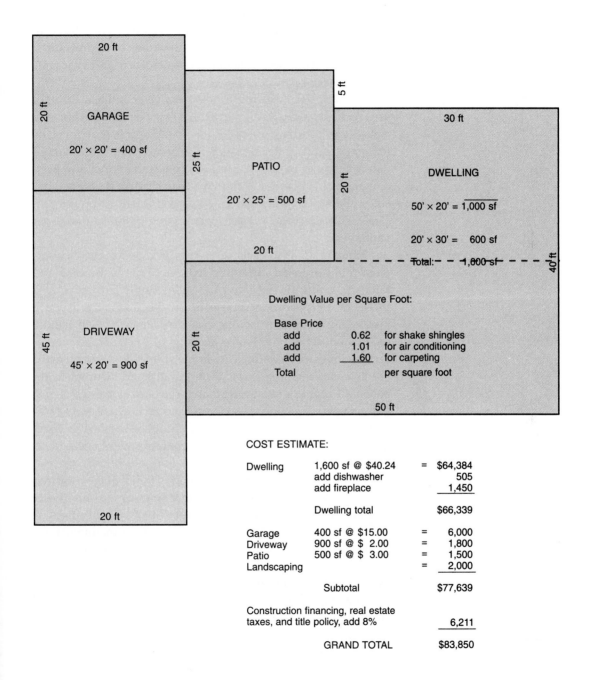

Figure 16:2. Square-foot Method of Cost Estimating

Estimating Depreciation   Having estimated the current cost of constructing the subject improvements, the next step in the cost approach is to estimate the loss in value due to depreciation since they were built. In making this estimate we look for three kinds of **depreciation:** physical deterioration, functional obsolescence, and economic obsolescence.

Physical deterioration results from wear and tear through use, such as wall-to-wall carpet that has been worn thin or a dishwasher, garbage disposal, or water heater that must be replaced. Physical deterioration also results from the action of nature in the form of sun, rain, heat, cold, and wind, and from damage due to plants and animal life such as tree roots breaking sidewalks and termites eating wood. Physical deterioration can also result from neglect (an overflowing bathtub) and from vandalism.

Functional obsolescence results from outmoded equipment (old-fashioned plumbing fixtures in the bathrooms and kitchen), faulty or outdated design (a single bathroom in a three- or four-bedroom house or an illogical room layout), inadequate structural facilities (inadequate wiring to handle today's household appliance loads), and overadequate structural facilities (high ceilings in a home). Functional and physical obsolescence can be separated into curable and incurable components. **Curable** is something that can be fixed at reasonable cost such as worn carpeting, a leaky roof, or outdated faucets in bathrooms. **Incurable** is something that cannot be reasonably fixed and must simply be lived with, for example, an illogical room layout.

Economic obsolescence is the loss of value due to external forces or events. For example, a once-popular neighborhood becomes undesirable because of air or noise pollution or because surrounding property owners fail to maintain their properties. Or, a city that is dependent on a military base finds the base closed and with it a big drop in demand for real estate. Or, the motel district in town loses customers because a new interstate highway has been built several miles away. Far more often, however, properties experience economic appreciation and not economic obsolescence. The appreciation can come from new industries moving into town, city growth in a new direction, a shortage of land in beach or waterfront areas, etc. Thus it is quite possible for the economic appreciation of a property to more than offset the depreciation it experiences. The result is a building that is physically and functionally depreciating and at the same time appreciating in value. Consequently, while the chronological age of a building is important to value, what is more important is the remaining economic life of the building and whether or not it is functionally adequate for use in the future. This is what real estate investors look for.

After calculating the current construction cost of the subject improvements and estimating the amount of depreciation, the next step is to subtract the amount of depreciation from the current construction cost to get the depreciated value of the improvements. This is added to the value of the land upon which the subject improvements rest. The total is the value of the property by the cost approach.

Final Steps in the Cost Approach

The market approach is very useful in connection with the sale or purchase of a home. The cost approach is very useful for someone planning to build. But what about someone planning to invest? For investors the income approach is the most popular method of valuing a property. The **income approach** considers the monetary returns a property can be expected to produce and converts that into a value the property should sell for if placed on the market today. This is called capitalizing the income stream. To **capitalize** means to convert future income to current value. To illustrate, suppose that an available apartment building is expected to return, after expenses, $18,000 per year. How much would you, as an investor, pay for the building? The answer depends on the return you require on each dollar you invest. Suppose you will accept a return of 9% per year. In that case you will pay $200,000 for this building. The calculation is as follows:

INCOME APPROACH

$$\frac{\text{Income}}{\text{Rate}} = \text{Value} \qquad \frac{\$18,000}{0.09} = \$200,000$$

This is the basic principle of capitalization. The appraisal work comes in estimating the net income a property will produce and looking at recent sales of similar properties to see what capitalization rates are currently acceptable to investors. Let us

Table 16:4. Projected Annual Operating Statement (Also called a Pro Forma Statement)

Scheduled gross annual income	$84,000	
Vacancy allowance and collection losses	4,200	
Effective Gross Income		$79,800
Operating Expenses		
Property taxes	9,600	
Hazard and liability insurance	1,240	
Property management	5,040	
Janitorial services	1,500	
Gardener	1,200	
Utilities	3,940	
Trash pickup	600	
Repairs and maintenance	5,000	
Other	1,330	
Reserves for replacement		
Furniture & furnishings	1,200	
Stoves & refrigerators	600	
Furnace &/or air-conditioning	700	
Plumbing & electrical	800	
Roof	750	
Exterior painting	900	
Total Operating Expenses		$34,400
Net Operating Income		$45,400
Operating Expense Ratio: $34,400 ÷ $79,800 = 43.1%		

look at the techniques one would use in estimating a property's income. Pay close attention because each $1 error in projected annual income or expenses can make a difference of from $8 to $15 in the market value of the property.

Income and Expense Forecasting The best starting point is to look at the actual record of income and expenses for the subject property over the past 3 to 5 years. Although the future will not be an exact repetition of the past, the past record of a property is usually the best guide to future performance. These historical data are blended with the current operating experience of similar buildings in order to estimate what the future will bring. The result is a projected operating statement, such as the one shown in Table 16:4, which begins with the estimated rents that the property can be expected to produce on an annual basis. This is the **projected gross,** or **scheduled gross,** and represents expected rentals from the subject property on a fully occupied basis. From this, vacancy and collection losses are subtracted. These are based partly on the building's past experience and partly on the operating experience of similar buildings.

The next step is to itemize anticipated **operating expenses** for the subject property. These are expenses necessary to maintain the production of income. For an apartment building without recreational facilities or an elevator, the list in Table 16:4 is typical. Again, we must consider both the property's past operating expenses and what we expect those expenses to be in the future. For example, even though a property is currently being managed by its owner and no management fee is being paid, a typical management fee, say 6% of the gross rents, is included.

Operating Expenses

Not included as operating expenses are outlays for capital improvements, such as the construction of a new swimming pool, the expansion of parking facilities, and assessments for street improvements. Improvements are not classified as expenses because they increase the usefulness of the property, which increases the rent the property will generate and therefore the property's value.

Reserves for replacement are established for items that do not require an expenditure of cash each year. To illustrate, lobby furniture (and furniture in apartments rented as "furnished") wears out a little each year, eventually requiring replacement. Suppose that these items cost $7,200 and are expected to last 6 years, at which time they must be replaced. An annual $1,200 reserve for replacement not only reflects wear and tear of the furniture during the year, but also reminds us that to avoid having to meet the entire furniture and furnishings replacement cost out of one year's income, money should be set aside for this purpose each year. In a similar manner, reserves are established for other items that must be replaced or repaired more than once during the life of the building, but not yearly.

Reserves

The operating expense total is then subtracted from the effective gross income. The balance that remains is the **net operating**

Net Operating Income

income. From the net operating income the property owner receives both a return *on* and a return *of* investment. The return *on* investment is the interest received for investing money in the property. The return *of* investment is compensation for the fact that the building is wearing out.

Operating Expense Ratio

At this point, the **operating expense ratio** can be calculated. It is obtained by dividing the total operating expenses by the effective gross income. The resulting ratio provides a handy yardstick against which similar properties can be compared. If the operating expense ratio is out of step compared to similar properties, it signals the need for further investigation. A range of 25% to 45% is typical for apartment buildings. The Institute of Real Estate Management of the National Association of Realtors publishes books and articles that give typical operating ratios for various types of income properties across the United States. Local inquiry to appraisers and brokers who specialize in income properties will also provide typical ratios for buildings in a community.

Capitalizing Income

The final step in the income approach is to capitalize the net operating income. In other words, what price should an investor offer to pay for a property that produces a given net income per year? The solution is: income ÷ rate = value. If the annual net operating income is $45,400 and if the investor intends to pay all cash, expects to receive a 10% return on his investment, and anticipates no change in the value of the property while he owns it, the solution is to divide $45,400 by 10%. However, most investors today borrow much of the purchase price and usually expect an increase in property value. Under these conditions, how much should the investor pay?

The best known method for solving this type of investment question involves using the Ellwood Tables, published in 1959 by L. W. Ellwood, MAI. However, for the person who does not use these tables regularly, the arithmetic involved can prove confusing. As a result **mortgage-equity tables** are now available from bookstores. These allow the user to look up a single number, called an **overall rate,** and divide it into the net operating income to find a value for the property.

For example, suppose an investor who is interested in buying the above property can obtain an 11%, fully amortized

**Table 16:5. Overall Rates—10-year Holding Period,
25-Year Loan for 75% of the Purchase Price,
18% Investor Return**

Appreciation,	Loan Interest Rate			
Depreciation	9%	10%	11%	12%
+100%	0.07251	0.07935	0.08631	0.09338
+ 50%	0.09376	0.10060	**0.10756**	0.11463
+ 25%	0.10439	0.11123	0.11819	0.12526
+ 15%	0.10864	0.11548	0.12244	0.12951
+ 10%	0.11077	0.11761	0.12457	0.13164
+ 5%	0.11289	0.11973	0.12669	0.13376
0	0.11502	0.12186	0.12882	0.13589
− 5%	0.11715	0.12399	0.13095	0.13802
− 10%	0.11927	0.12611	0.13307	0.14014
− 15%	0.12140	0.12824	0.13520	0.14227
− 25%	0.12565	0.13249	0.13945	0.14652
− 50%	0.13628	0.14312	0.15008	0.15715
− 100%	0.15753	0.16437	0.17133	0.17840

Source: *Financial Capitalization Rate Tables,* Financial Publishing Company, Boston, Mass. By permission.

25-year mortgage loan for 75% of the purchase price. He wants an 18% return on his equity in the property, plans to hold it 10 years, and expects it will increase 50% in value (after selling costs) during that time. How much should he offer to pay the seller? In Table 16:5, we look for an interest rate of 11% and for appreciation of 50%. This gives an overall rate of 0.10756 and the solution is:

$$\frac{\text{Income}}{\text{Overall rate}} = \text{Value} \qquad \frac{\$45,400}{0.10756} = \$422,090$$

Further exploration of the numbers in Table 16:5 shows that as loan money becomes more costly, the overall rate rises, and as interest rates fall, so does the overall rate. If the investor can anticipate appreciation in value, the overall rate drops; if he can't, the overall rate climbs. You can experiment by dividing some of the other overall rates in this table into $45,400 to see how the value of this property changes under different circumstances.

Depreciation

The pro forma in Table 16:4 provides reserves for replacement of such items as the roof, furnace, air conditioning, plumbing, electrical, exterior paint, and so forth. Nonetheless, as the building ages, the style of the building will become dated, the neighborhood will change, and the structure will experience physical deterioration. Allowance for this is usually accounted for in the selection of the capitalization rate. The less functional, economic, and physical obsolescence that is expected to take place, the lower the acceptable "cap" rate and vice versa.

Fictional Depreciation

In contrast to actual depreciation, there is the **fictional depreciation** that the U.S. Treasury allows income property owners to deduct as an expense when calculating income taxes. In late 1987, for example, the Treasury allowed the purchaser of an apartment building to completely depreciate the structure over a period of 27½ years regardless of the age or condition of the structure. This figure may be an understatement of the remaining life of the structure, but it was chosen by Congress to create an incentive to invest in real estate, not as an accurate gauge of a property's life. Thus it is quite common to see depreciation claimed on buildings that are in reality appreciating because of rising income from rents and/or falling capitalization rates.

CHOICE OF APPROACHES

For certain types of real property, some approaches are more suitable than others. This is especially true for single-family residences. Here you must rely almost entirely on the market and cost approaches as very few houses are sold on their ability to generate cash rent. Unless you can develop a measure of the "psychic income" in home ownership, relying heavily on rental value will lead to a property value below the market and cost approaches. Applying all three approaches to special-purpose buildings may also prove to be impractical. For example, in valuing a college or university campus or a state capitol building, the income and market approaches have only limited applicability.

When appraising a property that is bought for investment purposes such as an apartment building, shopping center, office building, or warehouse, the income approach is the primary method of valuation. As a cross-check on the income approach, an apartment building should be compared to other apartment buildings on a price per apartment unit basis or price per square foot basis. Similarly, an office, store, or warehouse can be compared to other recent office, store, or warehouse sales on a price per square foot basis. Additionally, the cost approach can be used to determine whether or not it would be cheaper to buy land and build rather than to buy an existing building.

APPRAISER'S BEST ESTIMATE

It is important to realize that the appraised value is the appraiser's best *estimate* of the subject property's worth. Thus, no matter how painstakingly it is done, property valuation requires the appraiser to make many subjective judgments. Because of this, it is not unusual for three highly qualified appraisers to look at the same property and produce three different appraised values. It is also important to recognize that an appraisal is made as of a specific date. It is not a certificate of value, good forever until used. If a property was valued at $115,000 on January 5th of this year, the more time that has elapsed since that date, the less accurate that value is as an indication of the property's current worth.

An appraisal does not take into consideration the financial condition of the owner, the owner's health, sentimental attachment, or any other personal matter. An appraisal does not guarantee that the property will sell for the appraised market value. (The buyer and the seller determine the actual selling price.) Nor does buying at the appraised market value guarantee a future profit for the purchaser. (The real estate market can change.) An appraisal is not a guarantee that the roof will not leak, that there are no termites, or that everything in the building works. An appraisal is not an offer to buy, although a buyer can order one made so as to know how much to offer. An appraisal is not a loan commitment, although a lender can order one made so as to apply a loan-to-value ratio when making a loan.

APPRAISAL REGULATION
The Appraisal Foundation

Due to harsh economic times in many areas of the country, standards of appraisals have come under extremely close scrutiny by many lenders. For instance, two appraisers may appraise the same property for significantly different values while using the same data, both acting in good faith. It is hard to draw a distinction, however, between an error in judgment and a fraudulent appraisal. The more difficult question is: How can a lender, in reviewing an appraisal, distinguish between good and bad appraisals? At least part of the answer is being addressed by an organization called the Appraisal Foundation. It is a private organization whose purpose is to establish and approve (1) uniform appraisal standards, (2) appropriate criteria for the certification and recertification of qualified appraisers, and (3) maintaining appropriate systems for the certification and recertification of qualified appraisers.

To effect this result, the Appraisal Foundation has established two subcommittees, the Appraiser Qualifications Board and the Appraisal Standards Board. The first establishes criteria for appraisers. The second is standards for the appraisal to be performed. The Foundation's aim is to disseminate such qualification criteria to the various states, governmental entities, and others to assist them in establishing and maintaining an appropriate system for the certification and recertification of qualified appraisers. They are the primary authors of the proposed Appraisal Reform Act currently pending before Congress.

Federal Regulation

Congress addressed the appraisal issue by recently enacting Title XI of the Financial Institution's Reform, Recovery, and Enforcement Act of 1989 (FIRREA). The Act, for the first time in history, establishes standards that will have a far-reaching impact on the appraisal industry.

Congress also created the Appraisal Subcommittee of the Federal Financial Institution's Examination Council to establish standards. The Subcommittee looks exclusively to the Appraisal Foundation for establishing standards under FIRREA for both appraiser qualifications as well as appraisal standards, and has proven to be an excellent effort by leaders in the appraisal industry, coupled with the governmental enforcement powers, to establish standards which ultimately benefits the lenders and public in general.

Developing the Appraisal

FIRREA creates mandatory requirements for real estate appraisals. These requirements are known as the **Uniform Standards of Professional Appraisal Practice,** commonly referred to as the **USPAP standards.**

In developing an appraisal, the Act requires that the appraiser must be aware of, understand, and correctly employ those recognized methods and techniques that are necessary to produce a credible appraisal. There are specific requirements for an appraiser's analysis, requiring consideration of current sales, options, or listings within certain time periods prior to the date of the appraisal. Specifically, this analysis of market data must consider all sales, options, or listings within: (1) one year for a one- to four-family residential property; and (2) within three years for all other property types. The Act further requires that the appraiser must consider and reconcile the quality and quantity of data available, and analyze, within the approaches used, the applicability or suitability of the approaches used as it pertains to the subject parcel of real estate.

The Appraisal Report

The new FIRREA legislation also established required regulations for the appraisal report. Each written appraisal report must also comply with the following specific reporting guidelines: (1) it must identify and describe the real estate being appraised; (2) it must identify the real property interest being appraised; (3) state the purpose of the appraisal; (4) define the value to be estimated; (5) set forth the effective date of the appraisal and the date of the report; (6) describe the scope of the appraisal; (7) set forth all the assumptions and limiting conditions that effect the analyses, opinions, and conclusions; (8) set forth the information considered in the appraisal procedures followed and the reasoning that supports the analyses, opinions, and conclusions; (9) set forth the appraiser's opinion of the highest and best use of real estate when such an opinion is necessary and appropriate; (10) explain and support the conclusion of any of the usual evaluation approaches; and (11) set forth any additional information that may be appropriate to show compliance with or clearly identify and explain permitted departures from any USPAP standards.

Each appraisal report must also: (1) clearly and accurately set forth the appraisal in a manner that will not be misleading; (2) contain sufficient information to enable the client or user of the report to understand it properly; and (3) clearly and accurately disclose any extraordinary assumption or limiting condition that directly affects the appraisal and indicates its impact on value.

FIRREA further requires that the appraisal report must include certification that, to the appraiser's best knowledge and belief: (1) the statement of facts contained in the report are true and correct; (2) the report analyses, opinions, and conclusions are limited only by the report assumptions and are personal and unbiased; (3) that the appraiser has no present prospective interest in the property that is the subject of the report; (4) that the appraiser's compensation is not contingent on an action or event resulting from the analyses, opinions, or conclusions used in the report; (5) that the analyses, opinions, and conclusions were developed and conform to the Act; (6) that the appraiser has (or has not) made personal inspections of the property; (7) that no one provided significant professional assistance to the person signing the report, who must be fully responsible for the contents of that report; and (8) that the appraiser's analyses, opinions, and conclusions were developed in conformity with the USPAP standards.

Review Appraisals

FIRREA also developed standards for reviewing appraisals and reporting their adequacy and appropriateness. In reviewing the appraisal, the appraiser must observe specific guidelines which identify the report being reviewed and the real property being appraised, the effective date of the report, and the date of the review. The review appraiser must also identify the scope of the review process to be conducted and form an opinion as to the adequacy and relevance of the data and propriety of any adjustments to the data. The opinion must also reflect the appropriateness of the appraisal and the methods and techniques used to develop the reasons for any disagreement with the appraiser.

Real Estate Analysis

At this time the Appraisal Subcommittee has not officially adopted the USPAP standards for developing appraisal analysis. However, it is anticipated that they will in the near future. It is important to remember that an analysis is not an appraisal. An **analysis** is the act or process of providing information, recommendations, and/or conclusions on diversified problems in real estate other than estimating the value, and can include a number of different forms of analysis, such as cash flow analysis, feasibility analysis, investment analysis, or market analysis. This differs from an **appraisal,** which under USPAP standards, is defined as the act or process of estimating value.

In developing the real estate analysis, the analyst must be aware of, understand, and correctly employ those recognized methods and techniques that are necessary to produce a credible analysis. The analyst must not commit a substantial error of omission or commission that significantly affects the analysis, nor render the analyst's services in a careless or negligent manner which, when considering the results of the analysis, would be misleading. The analyst must also observe the following specific guidelines: (1) clearly identify the client's objective; (2) define the problem to be considered and the purpose and intended use of the analysis, consider the scope of the assignment, adequately identify the real estate under consideration, and describe any special limiting condition; (3) collect, verify, and reconcile such data as may be required to complete the assignment and withhold no pertinent information; (4) apply the appropriate tools and techniques of analysis to data collected; and (5) base all projections of the analysis on a reasonably clear and appropriate evidence. There are additional requirements established, separate criteria for each type of analysis being utilized by the analyst.

In reporting the results of the real estate analysis, the analyst must communicate each analysis, opinion, and conclusions in a manner that is not misleading. Each written or oral analysis report must clearly and accurately set forth the analysis in a manner that will not be misleading, contain sufficient information to enable the persons who receive the report to understand it properly, and clearly and accurately disclose any extraordinary assumptions which would indicate an impact on the final conclusions or recommendation of the analysis.

Similar to the appraisal, the analysis report must contain a certification that is similar in content to that of the appraisal certification.

Appraiser Qualifications

To comply with new federal regulations established by the Appraisal Subcommittee, the Appraiser Qualifications Board of the Appraisal Foundation has established federal standards for certification and licensing of appraisers. Appraisers are now either licensed or certified as general or residential appraisers to be qualified to do appraisals for federal related institutions, and regulated loans. The appraisers are certified or licensed by their representative state based on the examination, education, and experience requirements. Examinations are administered by a state board in accordance with the Appraisal Foundation guidelines. Applicants for general real estate appraiser certification must have successfully completed 165 classroom hours in courses approved by the state licensing board. Applicants for residential real estate appraisers certification must have successfully completed 105 classroom hours in courses approved by the board. In either category of certification, the course work submitted must have included a minimum of 15 hours of coverage of the Uniform Standards of Professional Appraisal Practice. Applicants for a real estate appraiser license must have successfully completed 75 classroom hours in classes approved by the board, including the 15 hours of coverage of Uniform Standards of Professional Appraisal Practice.

In addition to the educational requirements, an applicant for general real estate appraiser certification must provide evidence satisfactory to the state licensing board that the applicant possesses the equivalent of 2,000 hours of appraisal experience over a minimum of 2 calendar years. At least 1,000 hours of experience must be in non-residential work. An applicant for a residential appraiser certification must provide evidence satisfactory to the board that the applicant possesses the equivalent of 2,000 hours of appraisal experience over a minimum of 2 calendar years. There is no requirement for non-residential work. An applicant for a state real estate appraiser license must provide evidence satisfactory to the state licensing board that the applicant possesses the equivalent of 2,000 hours of appraisal experience. There is no time requirement.

Appraisal License

Several states require that any person who appraises real estate for a fee must hold a license to do so. Depending on the state, this may be a regular real estate sales or broker license or a special appraiser's license. If you plan to make appraisals for a fee (apart from appraisal in connection with listing or selling a property as a licensed real estate salesperson or broker), make inquiry to your state's real estate licensing department as to appraisal licensing requirements.

CHARACTERISTICS OF VALUE

Up to this point we have been concerned primarily with value based on evidence found in the marketplace and how to report it. Before concluding this chapter, let us briefly touch on what creates value, the principles of real property valuation, and appraisal for purposes other than market value.

For a good or service to have value in the marketplace it must possess four characteristics: demand, utility, scarcity, and transferability. **Demand** is a need or desire coupled with the purchasing power to fill it, whereas **utility** is the ability of a good or service to fill that need. **Scarcity** means there must be a short supply relative to demand. Air, for example, has utility and is in demand, but it is not scarce. Finally, a good or service must be **transferable** to have value to anyone other than the person possessing it.

The **principle of anticipation** reflects the fact that what a person will pay for a property depends on the expected benefits from the property in the future. Thus, the buyer of a home anticipates receiving shelter plus the investment and psychic benefits of home ownership. The investor buys property in anticipation of future income.

PRINCIPLES OF VALUE

The **principle of substitution** states that the maximum value of a property in the marketplace tends to be set by the cost of purchasing an equally desirable substitute property provided no costly delay is encountered in making the substitution. In other words, substitution sets an upper limit on price. Thus, if there are two similar houses for sale, or two similar apartments for rent, the lower priced one will generally be purchased or rented first. In the same manner, the cost of buying land and constructing a new building sets a limit on the value of existing buildings.

The **highest and best use** of a property is that use which will give the property its greatest current value. This means you must be alert to the possibility that the present use of a parcel of land may not be the one that makes the land the most valuable. Consider a 30-year-old house located at a busy intersection in a shopping area. To place a value on that property based on its continued use as a residence would be misleading if the property would be worth more with the house removed and shopping or commercial facilities built on the land instead.

Highest and Best Use

The **principle of competition** recognizes that where substantial profits are being made, competition will be encouraged. For example, if apartment rents increase to the point where owners of existing apartment buildings are making substantial profits, builders and investors will be encouraged to build more apartment buildings.

Supply and Demand

Applied to real estate, the **principle of supply and demand** refers to the ability of people to pay for land coupled with the relative scarcity of land. This means that attention must be given to such matters on the demand side as population growth, personal income, and preferences of people. On the supply side, you must look at the available supply of land and its relative scarcity. When the supply of land is limited and demand is great, the result is rising land prices. Conversely, where land is abundant and there are relatively few buyers, supply and demand will be in balance at only a few cents per square foot.

The **principle of change** reminds us that real property uses are always in a state of change. Although it may be imperceptible on a day-to-day basis, change can easily be seen over longer periods of time. Because the present value of a property is related to its future uses, the more potential changes that can be identified, the more accurate the estimate of its present worth will be.

Diminishing Marginal Returns

The **principle of diminishing marginal returns,** also called the **principle of contribution,** refers to the relationship between added cost and the value it returns. It tells us that we should invest dollars whenever they will return to us more than $1 of value and we should stop when each dollar invested returns less than $1 in value.

The **principle of conformity** holds that maximum value is realized when there is a reasonable degree of homogeneity in a neighborhood. This is the basis for zoning laws across the country; certain tracts in a community are zoned for single-family houses, others for apartment buildings, stores, and industry. Within a tract there should also be a reasonable amount of homogeneity. For example, a $200,000 house would be out of place in a neighborhood of $90,000 houses.

MULTIPLE MEANINGS OF THE WORD "VALUE"

When we hear the word *value,* we tend to think of market value. However, at any given moment in time, a single property can have other values too. This is because value or worth is very much affected by the purpose for which the valuation was performed. For example, **assessed value** is the value given a property by the county tax assessor for purposes of property taxation. **Estate tax value** is the value that federal and state taxation authorities establish for a deceased person's property; it is used to calculate the amount of estate taxes that must be paid. **Insurance value** is concerned with the cost of replacing damaged property. It differs from market value in two major respects: (1) the value of the land is not included, as it is presumed only the structures are destructible, and (2) the amount of coverage is based on the replacement cost of the structures. **Loan value** is the value set on a property for the purpose of making a loan.

Plottage Value

When two or more adjoining parcels are combined into one large parcel it is called **assemblage.** The increased value of the large parcel over and above the sum of the smaller parcels is called **plottage value.** For example, local zoning laws may permit a six-unit apartment building on a single 10,000-square-foot lot. However, if two of these lots can be combined, zoning laws permit 15 units. This makes the lots more valuable if sold together.

Rental Value

Rental value is the value of a property expressed in terms of the right to its use for a specific period of time. The fee simple interest in a house may have a market value of $80,000, whereas the market value of one month's occupancy might be $600.

Replacement Value

Replacement value is value as measured by the current cost of building a structure of equivalent utility. **Salvage value** is what a structure is worth if it has to be removed and taken elsewhere, either in whole or dismantled for parts. Because salvage operations require much labor the salvage value of most buildings is usually very low.

This list of values is not exhaustive, but it points out that the word *value* has many meanings. When reading an appraisal report, always read the first paragraph to see why the appraisal was prepared. Before preparing an appraisal, make certain you know its purpose and then state it at the beginning of your report.

BUYER'S AND SELLER'S MARKETS

Whenever supply and demand are unbalanced because of excess supply, a **buyer's market** exists. This means a buyer can negotiate prices and terms more to his liking, and a seller who wants to sell must accept them. When the imbalance occurs because demand exceeds supply, it is a **seller's market;** sellers are able to negotiate prices and terms more to their liking as buyers compete for the available merchandise.

A **broad market** means that many buyers and sellers are in the market at the same time. This makes it relatively easy to establish the price of a property and for a seller to find a buyer quickly, and vice versa. A **thin market** is said to exist when there are only a few buyers and a few sellers in the market at the same time. It is oftentimes difficult to appraise a property in a thin market because there are so few sales to use as comparables.

PROFESSIONAL APPRAISAL SOCIETIES

During the 1930s, two well-known professional appraisal societies were organized: The **American Institute of Real Estate Appraisers (AIREA)** and the **Society of Real Estate Appraisers.** Although a person offering services as a real estate appraiser didn't need to be associated with either of these groups, there were advantages to membership. Both organizations developed designation systems to recognize appraisal education, experience, and competence. The Society and AIREA were unified in 1991, named the Appraisal Institute, and are considered to provide the most highly requested designations in the industry. Within the Appraisal Institute, the highest-level designation is the MAI (Member of the Appraisal Institute). To become an MAI requires a 4-year college degree or equivalent education, various Appraisal Institute courses, examinations, an income property demonstration appraisal, and at least 4,500 hours (with a maximum of 1,500 hours allowed in a 12-month period) of appraisal experience. There are about 6,000 MAIs in the United States. Also available is the SRA designation for residential appraisers that requires a 4-year college degree or acceptable alternative, appraisal course work, a passing appraisal examination score, a residential demonstration appraisal, and 3,000 hours of experience in residential real estate, with a maximum of 1,500 hours allowed in any 12-month period.

In addition to the institute and the society there are several other professional appraisal organizations in the United States. They are the National Association of Independent Fee Appraisers, the Farm Managers and Rural Appraisers, the National Society of Real Estate Appraisers, and the American Society of Appraisers. All exist to promote and maintain high standards of appraisal services and all offer a variety of appraisal education and designation programs.

1. Which of the following is NOT one of the three standard approaches to the appraisal of real property?
   A. Income approach.
   B. Cost approach.
   C. Assessment approach.
   D. Market approach.

2. To apply the market data approach, a real estate appraiser must collect all the following data on each comparable sale EXCEPT:
   A. date of sale.
   B. marketability of title.
   C. financing terms.
   D. sale price.

3. Adjustments for advantageous financing would be made in the
   A. market comparison approach to appraisal.
   B. cost approach to appraisal.
   C. income approach to appraisal.
   D. capitalization approach to appraisal.

4. After all adjustments are made to a comparable property, its comparative value for appraisal purposes is known as its
   A. adjusted market price.
   B. indicated market value.
   C. amended market price.
   D. Revised market price.

5. The value of vacant land is commonly stated in any of the following terms EXCEPT value per
   A. square foot.
   B. acre.
   C. front foot.
   D. square yard.

6. To evaluate a home in order to list it for sale, a real estate agent could use the
   A. standard market comparison method.
   B. competitive market analysis method.
   C. Both A and B.
   D. Neither A nor B.

7. Seller motivation is considered most in the
   A. income approach.
   B. cost approach.
   C. gross rent multiplier method.
   D. competitive market analysis method.

8. Which of the following approaches is most likely to provide only a rough estimate of the value of a rental property?
   A. Cost approach.
   B. Income approach.
   C. Market comparison approach.
   D. Gross rent multiplier.

9. In appraising an historically significant residence built in the Victorian era using the cost approach, an appraiser will probably appraise it on the basis of its
   A. reproduction cost.
   B. restoration cost.
   C. replacement cost.
   D. reconstruction cost.

10. Which of the following results from factors outside the property?
    A. Functional obsolescence.
    B. Physical deterioration.
    C. Economic obsolescence.
    D. None of the above.

11. The conversion of future income into present value is known as
    - A. capitalization.
    - B. amortization.
    - C. hypothecation.
    - D. appreciation.

12. The rents that a property can be expected to produce on an annual basis may be referred to as the
    - A. projected gross.
    - B. scheduled gross.
    - C. Both A and B.
    - D. Neither A nor B.

13. The operating expense ratio of a building is determined by dividing the total operating expenses by the
    - A. effective net income.
    - B. net operating income.
    - C. effective gross income.
    - D. actual gross income.

14. From the viewpoint of a qualified real estate appraiser, the value of the subject property is NOT affected by
    - A. demand.
    - B. scarcity.
    - C. highest and best use.
    - D. transferability.

15. The use of a property which will give it its greatest current value is its
    - A. highest use.
    - B. best use.
    - C. highest and best use.
    - D. maximum use.

16. The relationship between added cost and the value it returns is known as the principle of
    - A. diminishing marginal returns.
    - B. contribution.
    - C. Both A and B.
    - D. Neither A nor B.

17. The principle which holds that maximum value is realized when a reasonable degree of homogeneity is present in a neighborhood is known as the principle of
    - A. harmony.
    - B. homogeneity.
    - C. similarity.
    - D. conformity.

18. The process of combining two or more parcels of land into one larger parcel is called
    - A. assemblage.
    - B. plottage.
    - C. salvage.
    - D. reproduction.

19. A market where there is an excess of supply over demand is known as a
    - A. buyer's market.
    - B. broad market.
    - C. seller's market.
    - D. thin market.

20. The appraisal designation MAI stands for
    - A. Master Appraisal Instructor.
    - B. Master Appraisal Institute.
    - C. Member of the Appraisal Institute.
    - D. None of the above.

Licensing Laws and Professional Affiliation

In this chapter we will cover the various licensing law requirements, emphasizing the provisions of the state real estate license acts. A license act defines the licensees, explains the licensing procedure, and describes the obligations of the licensees with special emphasis on license suspension and revocation as applicable. A license act also covers the purpose and function of the real estate commission or department, bonds, and recovery funds, securities licensing, affiliating with a broker, franchise offices, and the independent contractor issue. The chapter concludes with coverage of professional real estate associations.

*OVERVIEW OF
CHAPTER 17*

LEARNING OBJECTIVES

After successful completion of this chapter, you should be able to:

1. Define a broker, salesman, franchise office, and real estate inspector.
2. Describe major licensing procedures and requirements in your state.
3. Explain the role of a state real estate commission or department.
4. Describe nonresident licensing, business firm licensing, and real estate inspector licensing.
5. List and explain those violations which could lead to license suspension or revocation.
6. Understand the purpose of a recovery fund, bonds, and a securities license.
7. Describe the affiliation one may have with a broker.
8. Discuss the independent contractor issue.
9. Explain the purpose and role of franchised offices.
10. Describe the role of the various professional real estate associations.

KEY • TERMS

Broker: a person or legal entity licensed to act independently in conducting a real estate brokerage business

Independent contractor: one who contracts to do work according to his own methods and is responsible to his employer only for the results of that work

License revocation: to recall and make void a license

License suspension: to temporarily make a license ineffective

Licensee: one who holds a license

Principal broker: the broker in charge of a real estate office

Real estate commission: a state board that advises and sets policies regarding real estate licensees and transaction procedures

Realtor: a registered trademark owned by the National Association of Realtors for use by its members

Recovery fund: a state-operated fund that can be tapped to pay for uncollectible judgments against real estate licensees

Sales associate: a salesperson or broker employed by a broker

Salesperson: a person employed by a broker to list, negotiate, sell, or lease real property for others

For most owners of real estate the decision to sell means hiring a broker to find a buyer. Although some owners choose to market their properties themselves, most find it advantageous to turn the job over to a real estate broker and pay a commission for the service of finding a buyer and carrying the deal through closing. The next three chapters are for the owner who plans to use a broker and for the person who plans to be a real estate salesperson or broker. We begin with a simplified real estate listing contract. Next we take a close look at the agency responsibilities a broker has toward a seller together with the seller's obligations toward the broker. Then we discuss seller and broker responsibilities toward persons who are interested in purchasing the listed property. Chapter 17 discusses examination and licensing requirements and an overview of how states regulate the real estate profession, including a section on how to choose a broker with whom to affiliate and professional real estate associations, in particular the National Association of Realtors.

RATIONALE FOR LICENSING

Does the public have a vested interest in seeing that real estate salespersons and brokers have the qualifications of honesty, truthfulness, good reputation, and real estate knowledge before they are allowed to negotiate real estate transactions on behalf of others? It was this concern that brought about real estate licensing laws as we know them today. Until 1917, no state required real estate agents to be licensed. Anyone who wanted to be an agent could simply hang up a sign stating that he was an agent. In larger cities there were persons and firms who specialized in bringing buyers and sellers together. In smaller towns, a local banker, attorney, or barber would know who had what for sale and be the person a buyer would ask for property information.

The first attempt to require that persons acting as real estate agents be licensed was made by the California legislature in 1917. That law was declared unconstitutional, with the main opposition being that the state was unreasonably interfering with the right of every citizen to engage in a useful and legitimate occupation. Two years later, in 1919, the California legislature passed a second real estate licensing act. This time it was upheld by the Supreme Court. That same year, Michigan, Oregon, and Tennessee also passed real estate licensing acts. Today, all 50 states and the District of Columbia require that persons who offer their services as real estate agents be licensed.

Loyalty, Honesty, and Truthfulness

The first license laws did not require examinations for competency nor did they require real estate education. Those came later. The first laws were aimed at weeding out persons who placed loyalty to themselves above loyalty to those who they were representing. By requiring persons to be licensed, the state had the power to refuse to issue a license to someone with a past record of dishonesty and untruthfulness. Additionally, the state could temporarily or permanently take away a license once it had been issued. To help make licensing laws work, the state refused to allow its courts to enforce claims for commissions by unlicensed persons.

That a real estate license applicant have a good reputation for honesty and truthfulness is still a very important part of real estate licensing today. If you apply for a license, you may be asked to provide a photograph, credit report, fingerprints, and/or personal character references. The state licensing agency will check for links to any past criminal convictions or other significant infractions of the law. Inquiry may be made of your character references to learn more about your reputation.

In the 1930s and 1940s states began adding the requirement of a license examination in an attempt to determine whether or not the license applicant also had some level of technical ability in real estate. Then, beginning in the 1950s, states began adding the requirement that a person take a certain number of hours of real estate education before being licensed. Thus, what we see today is that a person who plans to be a real estate agent must qualify both ethically and technically before being issued a license.

PERSONS REQUIRED TO BE LICENSED

In what situations does a person need a real estate license? A person who for compensation or the promise of compensation lists or offers to list, sells or offers to sell, buys or offers to buy, negotiates or offers to negotiate either directly or indirectly for the purpose of bringing about a sale, purchase, or option to purchase, exchange, auction, lease, or rental of real estate, or any interest in real estate, is required to hold a valid real estate license. Some states also require persons offering their services as real estate appraisers, property managers, mortgage bankers, or rent collectors to hold real estate licenses.

Property owners dealing with their own property and licensed attorneys conducting a real estate transaction as an incidental part of their duties as an attorney for a client are exempt from holding a license. Also exempt are trustees and receivers in bankruptcy, legal guardians, administrators and executors handling a deceased's estate, officers and employees of a government agency dealing in real estate, and persons holding power of attorney from an owner. However, the law does not permit a person to use the exemptions as a means of conducting a brokerage business without the proper license. That is, an unlicensed person cannot take a listing under the guise of a power of attorney and then act as a real estate broker.

BROKER

Before the advent of licensing laws, there was no differentiation between real estate brokers and real estate salespersons. People who brought about transactions were simply called real estate agents or whatever else they wanted to be called. With licensing laws came two classes of **licensee:** real estate broker and real estate salesperson (for many years called real estate salesman). A **real estate broker** is a person licensed to act independently in conducting a real estate brokerage business. A broker brings together those with real estate to be marketed and those seeking real estate and negotiates a transaction. For those services the broker receives a fee, usually in the form of a commission based on the selling price or lease rent. The broker may represent the buyer or the seller, or, upon full disclosure, both at the same time. The role is more than that of a middleman who puts two interested parties in contact with each other, for the broker usually takes an active role in negotiating price and terms acceptable to both the buyer and seller. A broker can be an actual person or a legal entity, i.e., a business firm. If a business firm, the person in charge must be a broker. The laws of all states permit a real estate broker to hire others for the purpose of bringing about real estate transactions. These persons may be other licensed real estate brokers or they may be licensed real estate salespersons.

A **real estate salesperson,** within the meaning of the license laws, is a person employed by a real estate broker to list and negotiate the sale, exchange, lease, or rental of real property for others for compensation, under the direction, guidance, and responsibility of the employing broker. Only an actual person can be licensed as a salesperson (a business firm cannot be licensed as a salesperson), and a salesperson must be employed by a broker; a salesperson cannot operate independently. Thus, a salesperson who takes a listing on a property does so in the name of his broker, and in some states the broker must sign along with the salesperson for the listing to be valid. In the event of a legal dispute caused by a salesperson, the dispute would be between the principal and the broker. Therefore, some brokers take considerable care to oversee the documents that their salespeople prepare and sign. Other brokers do not, relying instead on the knowledge and sensibility of their salespeople, and accepting a certain amount of risk in the process.

SALESPERSON

The salesperson is a means by which a broker can expand his sales force. Presumably, the more salespeople a broker employs, the more listings and sales generated, and thus the more commissions earned by the broker. Against this, the broker must pay enough to keep the sales force from leaving, provide sales facilities and personnel management, and take ultimate responsibility for any mistakes the salespersons make.

SALES ASSOCIATE   The term **sales associate** is not a license category. Rather it refers to anyone with a real estate license who is employed by a broker. Most often this will be a real estate salesperson. However, a person who holds a broker license can work for another broker. Such a person is a regular member of the employing broker's sales force just like someone with a sales-person license. The salespersons and brokers who work for a broker are known collectively as the broker's sales associates or sales force or sales staff. You will also hear the term real estate agent used in a general sense. Correctly speaking, the broker is a special agent of the property owner and the sales associate is a general agent of the broker. In common language today, real estate agent refers to anyone, broker or salesperson, who nego-tiates real estate transactions for others.

QUALIFICATIONS FOR LICENSING   Of the two license levels, the salesperson's license is regarded as the entry-level license and, as such, requires no previous real estate sales experience. The minimum age is 18 years. By comparison, the broker's license in nearly all states requires 1 to 5 years of experience (2 or 3 years is most common) as a real estate salesperson. Related real estate experience and college education in real estate can sometimes shorten the experience requirement. As a practical matter, however, a person is wise to gain plenty of experience as a salesperson before becoming a broker for the purpose of operating independently.

Examination   Examination of the license applicant's knowledge of real estate law and practices, mathematics, valuation, finance, and the like, is required for license granting in all states. Salesperson exams and broker exams typically contain 100 to 140 multiple-choice questions like those shown in Appendices B and C. Usually 3 to 4 hours are allowed to complete the exam. Salesperson exams cover the basic aspects of state license law, contracts and agency, real property ownership, transfer and use, subdivision map reading, fair housing laws, real estate mathematics, and the ability to follow written instructions. Broker exams cover the same topics in more depth and test the applicant's ability to prepare listings, offer and acceptance con-tracts, leasing contracts, and closing statements. The applicant's knowledge of real estate finance, appraisal, and office manage-ment are also tested.

Table 17:1. Real Estate Education and Experience Requirements

| STATE | SALESPERSON LICENSE | | BROKER LICENSE | | |
	Education Requirement	Continuing Education	Education Requirement	Experience Requirement	Continuing Education
Alabama	45 hours	Yes	60 hours	2 years	Yes
Alaska	None	No	None	2 years	No
Arizona	96 hours	Yes	180 hours	3 years	Yes
Arkansas	30 hours	Yes	None	2 years	Yes
California	135 hours	Yes	360 hours	2 years	Yes
Colorado	72 hours	Yes	120 hours	2 years	Yes
Connecticut	30 hours	Yes	90 hours	2 years	Yes
Delaware	93 hours	Yes	168 hours	5 years	Yes
Dist. of Col.	45 hours	Yes	135 hours	2 years	Yes
Florida	63 hours	Yes	135 hours	1 year	Yes
Georgia	60 hours	Yes	120 hours	3 years	Yes
Hawaii	40 hours	Yes	46 hours	2 years	Yes
Idaho	90 hours	Yes	180 hours	2 years	Yes
Illinois	30 hours	Yes	90 hours	1 year	Yes
Indiana	54 hours	No	108 hours	1 year	No
Iowa	30 hours	Yes	90 hours	2 years	Yes
Kansas	80 hours	Yes	24 hours	2 years	Yes
Kentucky	96 hours	No	336 hours	2 years	No
Louisiana	90 hours	Yes	150 hours	2 years	Yes
Maine	39 hours	Yes	129 hours	1 year	Yes
Maryland	45 hours	Yes	135 hours	3 years	Yes
Massachusetts	30 hours	No	31 hours	1 year	No
Michigan	40 hours	Yes	90 hours	3 years	Yes
Minnesota	90 hours	Yes	90 hours	2 years	Yes
Mississippi	60 hours	Yes	120 hours	1 year	Yes

Explanation: Hours are clock-hours in the classroom; experience requirement is experience as a licensed real estate salesperson; continuing education refers to education required for license renewal. Some states credit completed salesperson education toward the broker education requirement.

Education Requirements

Nearly all states require that license applicants take real estate education courses at private real estate schools, colleges, or through adult education programs at high schools. Table 17:1 shows the education and experience requirements in the United States at the time this book was written. The table is included to give you an overview of the emphasis currently being placed on education and experience by the various states. For up-to-the-minute information on education and experience requirements you should contact the real estate licensing department at your state capital.

Table 17:1. Real Estate Education and Experience Requirements   continued

STATE	SALESPERSON LICENSE Education Requirement	Continuing Education	BROKER LICENSE Education Requirement	Experience Requirement	Continuing Education
Missouri	60 hours	Yes	108 hours	1 year	Yes
Montana	60 hours	Yes	120 hours	2 years	Yes
Nebraska	60 hours	Yes	120 hours	2 years	Yes
Nevada	90 hours	Yes	960 hours	2 years	Yes
New Hampshire	None	Yes	None	1 year	Yes
New Jersey	75 hours	No	165 hours	2 years	No
New Mexico	60 hours	No	90 hours	2 years	No
New York	45 hours	Yes	90 hours	1 year	Yes
North Carolina	30 hours	No	120 hours	2 years	No
North Dakota	30 hours	Yes	90 hours	2 years	Yes
Ohio	120 hours	Yes	130 hours	2 years	Yes
Oklahoma	45 hours	Yes	90 hours	1 year	Yes
Oregon	90 hours	Yes	150 hours	3 years	No
Pennsylvania	60 hours	Yes	240 hours	3 years	Yes
Rhode Island	None	Yes	90 hours	1 year	Yes
South Carolina	60 hours	No	90 hours	3 years	No
South Dakota	30 hours	Yes	90 hours	2 years	Yes
Tennessee	60 hours	Yes	120 hours	3 years	No
Texas	180 hours	Yes	900 hours	2 years	Yes
Utah	90 hours	Yes	120 hours	3 years	Yes
Vermont	None	Yes	8 hours	1 year	Yes
Virginia	45 hours	Yes	180 hours	3 years	Yes
Washington	30 hours	Yes	90 hours	2 years	No
West Virginia	90 hours	Yes	180 hours	2 years	Yes
Wisconsin	72 hours	Yes	108 hours	None	Yes
Wyoming	30 hours	Yes	60 hours	2 years	Yes

Source: National Association of Real Estate License Law Officials, 563 West 500 South, Bountiful, Utah 84010. Check with your state for any subsequent changes.

Continuing Education

Licensing authorities in a growing number of states require additional course work each time a license is renewed. This is called **continuing education,** and its purpose is to force licensees to stay up to date in their field as a prerequisite to license renewal. States with continuing education requirements are also shown in Table 17:1.

LICENSING PROCEDURE

An application for a real estate salesperson or broker license can be obtained either in person or by mail from a state's real estate licensing department. The application is completed and returned to the department with the required fee. The character aspects of the applicant are checked and, if approved, an examination date is scheduled. (Some states reverse this and give the exam first and check the references second.) Most states offer their real estate exams monthly. A few offer testing bi-monthly or quarterly. Five states offer exams at least once a week.

The applicant is notified of the results in approximately 4 to 6 weeks. If passed, the fee for the license itself is now paid. Also, a salesperson applicant must name the broker he will be working for. This information is usually provided on a form signed by the employing broker. A broker applicant must give the address where he plans to operate his brokerage business. These forms are processed by the department and a license is mailed to the applicant in the case of a broker, or to the employing broker in the case of a salesperson. Upon receipt, the licensee can operate as a real estate salesperson or broker, as the case may be.

If the applicant fails the written examination, the usual procedure is to allow the applicant to repeat it until passed. A fee is charged to retake the exam and the applicant must wait until the next testing date.

Renewal

Once licensed, as long as a person remains active in real estate and meets any continuing education requirements, the license can be renewed by paying the required renewal fee. If a license is not renewed before it expires, most states allow a grace period and charge a late renewal fee. Once the grace period is passed, all license rights lapse and the individual must meet current application requirements and take the current written exam. If a licensee wishes to be temporarily inactive from the business but does not wish to let the license lapse, some states permit the license to be placed on inactive status. When the licensee wishes to reactivate the license, he pays a fee to the department. Then the license is moved from inactive to active status and he can start selling again.

EXAMINATION SERVICES

Real estate license examinations are administered by Applied Measurement Professionals (AMP) or Assessment Systems Incorporated (ASI). The remaining states write and grade their own exams.

As of this writing ASI examinations were being used in the following states: Alaska, Arizona, Arkansas, Colorado, Connecticut, Delaware, the District of Columbia, Hawaii, Idaho, Illinois, Indiana, Kansas, Kentucky, Louisiana, Maryland, Massachusetts, Montana, New Jersey, New Mexico, Pennsylvania, Rhode Island, South Dakota, Tennessee, Utah, Vermont, Washington, and Wyoming. AMP exams are being used in Alabama, Georgia, Michigan, Missouri, and Nebraska. The following states used their own exams, in some cases purchasing questions from one of the national services: California, Florida, Maine, Mississippi, North Carolina, Ohio, Oklahoma, Oregon, South Carolina, Texas, and West Virginia.

Exams written by the national testing services are divided into two parts. Part 1, called the **uniform test,** contains 80 to 100 questions that are relevant to the general principles and practices of real estate that are common or uniform across the country. Part 2, called the **state test,** contains 20 to 50 questions regarding the laws, rules, regulations, and practices of the jurisdiction where the examination is being given.

The tests are composed entirely of objective, multiple-choice questions which are constantly being revised and updated to keep them current with the changing practices and laws of real estate. There are many different versions of the tests, but all are equal in difficulty. More details regarding the contents of the AMP and ASI exams can be found in Appendices B and C. Sample exams are available from both AMP and ASI, and their addresses are in the same appendices. Like the national exam services, states that write their own tests have question banks of several thousand questions from which approximately 100 are chosen each time a test is given. Topic coverage and question styles will be substantially similar to the examples shown in Appendices B and C.

NONRESIDENT LICENSING

The general rule regarding license requirements is that a person must be licensed in the state within which he negotiates. Thus, if a broker or one of the broker's sales associates sells an out-of-state property, but conducts the negotiations entirely within the borders of his own state, a license is not needed in the state where the land is located. State laws also permit a broker in one state to split a commission with a broker in another state provided each conducts negotiations only within the state where he is licensed. Therefore, if Broker B, licensed in State B, takes a listing at his office on a parcel of land located in State B, and Broker C in State C sells it conducting the sale negotiations within State C, then Brokers B and C can split the commission. If, however, Broker C comes to State B to negotiate a contract, then a license in State B is necessary.

Many states will issue a **nonresident license** to out-of-state brokers. This is particularly helpful where a broker is located near a state border. In issuing a nonresident license, a state will usually require substantially the same examination and experience requirements as demanded of resident brokers. Some states will give the out-of-state broker credit for the uniform part of a license test already taken, requiring only passage of a test on local law, custom, and practice. Others require a complete examination. A few require no examination.

Notice of Consent

When a broker operates outside of his home state, he may be required to file a **notice of consent** in each state in which he intends to operate, usually with the secretary of state. This permits the secretary of state to receive legal summonses on behalf of the nonresident broker and provides a state resident an avenue by which he can sue a broker who is a resident of another state.

Moving to Another State

When a broker or salesperson moves his place of business from one state to another, a license is required in the new state. Many states will give credit for experience and part or all of the examination that was passed in the previous state. This can be particularly helpful for two-income families when one spouse is transferred to another state. Details of what a state will allow as credit are too complex and too changeable to include here. If negotiating across state lines or moving to another state as a real estate agent is of interest to you, you should contact that state's real estate licensing authority.

LICENSING THE BUSINESS FIRM

When a real estate broker wishes to establish a brokerage, the simplest method is a sole proprietorship under the broker's own name, such as David Lee, Real Estate Broker. Some states permit a broker to operate out of his residence. However, operating a business in a residential neighborhood can be bothersome to neighbors, and most states require brokers to maintain a place of business in a location that is zoned for businesses.

Fictitious Business Name

When a person operates under a name other than his own, he must register that name by filing a **fictitious business name statement** with the county clerk and the state real estate licensing authority. This statement must also be published in a local newspaper. Thus, if David Lee wishes to call his brokerage business Great Lakes Realty, his business certificate would show "David Lee, doing business as Great Lakes Realty." (Sometimes *doing business as* is shortened to dba or d/b/a.)

A real estate broker can operate as a sole proprietorship either under the broker's own name or a fictitious name. A broker can also operate in partnership with other brokers or as a corporation. Since a corporation is an artificial being (not an actual person), it cannot take a real estate examination. Therefore, its chief executive officer (usually the president) must be a licensed real estate broker and be responsible for the management of the firm. Other officers and stockholders may include brokers and salespersons and nonlicensed persons. However, only those actually licensed can represent the corporation in activities requiring a real estate license.

Branch Offices

If a broker expands by establishing branch offices that are geographically separate from the main or home office, each branch must have a branch office license and a licensed broker in charge. Often referred to as a **principal broker,** this person can be a partner, a corporate owner who is a broker, or a sales associate who has a broker's license. A few states allow a salesperson licensee to be in charge.

REAL ESTATE REGULATION

Thus far we have discussed why and when a real estate license is required and how to obtain one. The next question is, "Who makes these rules and how are they enforced?" The starting point is the state legislature. The legislature of each state has the authority to enact laws to promote the safety, health, morals, order, and general welfare of its population. This includes the licensing and regulation of real estate brokers and salespersons. The legislature establishes general requirements. For example, the legislature enacts laws requiring that real estate agents be licensed, that there will be two classes of licenses, that there will be a prelicense education requirement, that there will be a license examination, and that continuing education will be required. The legislature also establishes two bodies to carry out the requirements. One body deals primarily with working out the details of the legislature's intent, for example, how many questions should be on the license exam, what variety should be included, and how often the exam should be offered and where. This body or group is called a **real estate commission** in most states and has from 5 to 9 members. Some members are licensees from the real estate community while others are nonlicensed members of the general public. Commission members are volunteers selected by the governor to represent all geographical parts of the state. Meetings are usually held monthly at which members provide input to the state on such matters as the needs of real estate licensees, state policies regarding real estate, and the welfare of the general public in dealing with licensees.

The state's real estate **executive director,** or similar title, is appointed by the state to oversee real estate regulation. This person's responsibility is to carry out the wishes of the legislature and the real estate commission on a day-to-day basis. To assist in this, the legislature establishes a second body called a real estate department or real estate division.

Real Estate Department

Staffed by full-time civil service employees, the **real estate department** or **real estate division** answers correspondence, sends out application forms, arranges for examinations, collects fees, issues licenses, approves subdivision reports, and so forth. Staff is also available for the investigation of alleged malpractices and for audits of broker trust fund accounts. Additionally, the department publishes a periodic newsletter or magazine to keep licensees informed about changes in real estate law and prints books or leaflets describing the state's license and subdivision laws. In short, it is the real estate department with which licensees have the most contact, but it is the commission, the executive director, and the legislature that set license requirements and tell a licensee what he can and cannot do in real estate transactions. Figure 17:1 provides a visual summary of what has just been discussed.

LICENSE SUSPENSION AND REVOCATION

The most important control mechanism a state has over its real estate salespersons and brokers is that it can **suspend** (temporarily make ineffective) or **revoke** (recall and make void) a real estate license. Without one, it is unlawful for a person to engage in

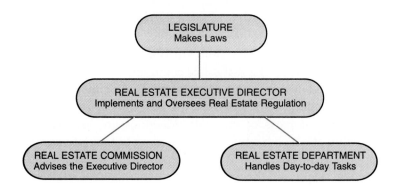

Figure 17:1. Real Estate Regulation

real estate activities for the purpose of earning a commission or fee. Unless an agent has a valid license, a court of law will not uphold his claim for a commission from a client.

Reasons for license suspension and revocation include any violation of the state's real estate act, misrepresentation or false promises, undisclosed dual agency, commingling, and acting as an undisclosed principal. Licenses can also be revoked or suspended for false advertising, obtaining a license by fraud, negligence, or incompetence, failure to supervise salespersons, failure to properly account for clients' funds, practicing law without a license, paying commissions to unlicensed persons, conviction of a felony or certain types of misdemeanors, dishonest conduct in general, and, in many states, failure to have a fixed termination date on an exclusive listing.

When the real estate commissioner or director receives a complaint from someone who feels he was wronged by a licensee, an investigation is conducted by the real estate department staff. Statements are received from witnesses. Title company records, public records, and the licensee's bank records are checked as necessary. The commissioner or director may call an informal conference and invite all parties involved to attend. If it appears that the complaint is serious enough and that a violation of the law has occurred, a formal hearing is held in the presence of the full commission. The licensee, the party bringing the complaint, and any necessary witnesses appear. Testimony is taken under oath and a written record is made of the proceedings. If the commissioner or director decides to suspend or revoke the respondent's license, the respondent has the right of appeal to the courts.

The potential of license loss for a wrongdoing strongly encourages licensees to operate within the law. However, suspension or revocation of a license does nothing to provide financial compensation for any losses suffered by a wronged party. This must be recovered from the broker either through a mutually agreed upon monetary settlement or a court judgment resulting from a civil lawsuit brought by the wronged party. But all too often court judgments turn out to be uncollectible because the defendant has no money.

BONDS AND RECOVERY FUNDS

There are two common solutions to the uncollectible judgment problem. Six states (Alabama, Alaska, Massachusetts, Montana, Tennessee, and West Virginia) require that a person post a bond with the state before a license will be issued. In the event of an otherwise uncollectible court judgment against a licensee, the bond money is used to provide payment. Bond requirements vary from $1,000 to $100,000 with $5,000 to $10,000 being the most popular range. Licensees can obtain these bonds from bonding companies for an annual fee or post the required amount of cash or securities with the state.

The second method of protecting the public is through a state-sponsored **recovery fund.** A portion of the money that each licensee pays for a real estate license is set aside in a fund which is made available for the payment of otherwise uncollectible judgments. Recovery funds offer coverage ranging from $2,000 to $100,000 per licensee with most states in the $25,000 to $50,000 range. The District of Columbia and 33 states use recovery funds. The states are Alabama, Alaska, Arizona, Arkansas, California, Colorado, Connecticut, Delaware, Florida, Georgia, Hawaii, Idaho, Illinois, Kansas, Kentucky, Louisiana, Maryland, Minnesota, Montana, Nevada, New Jersey, New Mexico, North Carolina, North Dakota, Ohio, Oklahoma, Pennsylvania, Rhode Island, South Dakota, Tennessee, Texas, Utah, Virginia and Wyoming.

The requirement for bonds and the establishment of recovery funds are not perfect solutions to the problem of uncollectible judgments because the wronged party must expend considerable effort to recover his loss, and it is quite possible that the maximum amount available per transaction or licensee will not fully compensate for the losses suffered. However, either system is better than none at all.

SECURITIES LICENSE

Be aware that there may be times when a real estate salesperson or broker also needs a securities license. This occurs when the property being sold is an investment contract in real estate rather than real estate itself. This investment contract is classified as a **security.** Examples of securities include real estate limited partnerships, rental pools where condominium owners put their units into a pool for a percentage of the pool's income, and some timeshares. Securities licenses are issued by the National Association of Securities Dealers based on successful completion of their examination. Legal counsel is advised if there is the possibility you may be selling securities. Counsel will also advise on state and federal laws requiring the registration of real estate securities before they are sold.

AFFILIATING WITH A BROKER

If you plan to enter real estate sales, selecting a broker to work for is one of the most important decisions you must make. The best way to approach it is to carefully consider what you have to offer the real estate business and what you expect in return. And look at it in that order! It is easy to become captivated by the big commission income you visualize coming your way. But if that is your only perspective, you will meet with disappointment. The reason people will pay you money is to receive some product or service in return. Your clients are not concerned with your income goal; it is only incidental to their goals. If you help them attain their goals, you will reach yours.

Before applying for a real estate license, ask yourself whether or not the working hours and conditions of a real estate agent are suitable to you. Specifically, are you prepared to work on a commission-only basis? Evenings and weekends? On your own? With people you've never met before? If you can comfortably answer yes to these questions, then start looking for a broker to sponsor you. (Salesperson license educational requirements can be completed and the examination taken without broker sponsorship, but a salesperson must have a broker to work for before the actual license is issued.)

Your next step is to look for those features and qualities in a broker that will complement, enhance, and encourage your personal development in real estate. If you are new to the industry, training and education will most likely be at the top of your list. Therefore, in looking for a broker you will want to find one that will offer you some on-the-job training. (What you have learned to date from books, classes, and license examination preparation will be helpful, but you will need additional specific training.) Real estate franchise operations and large brokerage offices usually offer extensive training. In smaller offices, the broker in charge is usually responsible for seeing that newcomers receive training. An office that offers no training to a newcomer should be avoided.

Training

Another question high on your list will be compensation. Very few offices provide a newcomer with a guaranteed minimum wage or even a draw against future commissions. Most brokers feel that one must produce to be paid and the hungrier the salesperson, the quicker the production. A broker who pays salespersons regardless of sales produced simply must siphon the money from those who are producing. The old saying, "There's no such thing as a free lunch" applies to sales commissions.

Compensation

Compensation for salespersons is usually a percentage of the commissions they earn for the broker. How much each receives is open to negotiation between the broker and each salesperson working for him. A broker who provides office space, extensive secretarial help, a large advertising budget, a mailing program, and generous long-distance telephone privileges might take 40% to 50% of each incoming commission dollar for office overhead. A broker who provides fewer services might take 25% or 30%.

Salespersons with proven sales records can usually reduce the portion of each commission dollar that must go to the broker. This is because the broker knows that with an outstanding sales performer, a high volume of sales will offset a smaller percentage for overhead. Conversely, a new and untried salesperson, or one with a mediocre past sales record, may have to give up a larger portion of each dollar for the broker's overhead.

When one brokerage agency lists a property and another locates the buyer, the commission is split according to any agreement the two brokers wish to make. The most common arrangement is a fifty-fifty split. After splitting, each broker pays a portion of the money he receives to the salesperson involved in accordance with their commission agreement.

While investigating commission arrangements, one should also inquire about incentive and bonus plans, automobile expense reimbursement, health insurance, life insurance, errors and omission insurance, and retirement plans.

An alternative commission arrangement is the **100% commission** wherein the salesperson does not share his commission with the broker. Instead the salesperson is charged a fee for office space, advertising, telephone, multiple listing, and any other expenses the broker incurs on behalf of the salesperson. Generally speaking, 100% arrangements are more popular with proven performers than with newcomers.

Broker Support   Broker support will have an impact on success. Specifically: Does each salesperson have a desk to work from? Are office facilities efficient and modern? Does the broker provide secretarial services? What is the broker's advertising policy and who pays for ads? Who pays for signs, business cards, franchise fees, and realty board dues? Does the broker have sources of financing for clients? Does the broker allow his salespersons to invest in real estate? Does the broker have a good reputation in the community?

Finding a Broker   Many licensees associate with a particular broker as a result of friendship or word-of-mouth information. However, there are other ways to find a suitable position. An excellent way to start your search is to decide what geographical area you want to work in. If you choose the same community or neighborhood in which you live, you will already possess a valuable sense and feel for that area.

Having selected a geographical area, look in the Sunday newspaper real estate advertisements section and the telephone book Yellow Pages for names of brokers. Hold interviews with several brokers and as you do, remember that you are interviewing them just as intensively as they are interviewing you. At your visits with brokers be particularly alert to your feelings. Intuition can be as valuable a guide to a sound working relationship as a list of questions and answers regarding the job.

As you narrow your choices, revisit the offices of brokers who particularly impressed you. Talk with some of the salespersons who have worked or are working there. They can be very candid and valuable sources of information. Be wary of individuals who are extreme in their opinions: rely instead on the consensus of opinion. Locate clients who have used the firm's services and ask them their opinions of the firm. You might also talk to local appraisers, lenders, and escrow agents for candid opinions. If you do all this advance work, the benefits to you will be greater enjoyment of your work, more money in your pocket, and less likelihood of wanting to quit or move to another office.

Having selected a broker with whom to associate, your next step is to make an employment contract. An **employment contract** formalizes the working arrangement between the broker and his salespersons. An oral contract may be satisfactory, but a written one is preferred because it sets forth the relationship with a higher degree of precision and is a written record of the agreement. This greatly reduces the potential for future controversy and litigation.

Employment Contract

The employment contract will cover such matters as compensation (how much and under what circumstances), training (how often and if required), hours of work (including assigned office hours and open houses), company identification (distinctive articles of clothing and name tags), fees and dues (license and realty board), expenses (automobile, advertising, telephone), fringe benefits (health and life insurance, pension, and profit-sharing plans), withholding (income taxes and social security), territory (assigned area of the community), termination of employment (quitting and firing), and general office policies and procedures (office manual).

Is the real estate sales associate an employee of the broker or an independent contractor? The answer is both. On one hand, the sales associate acts like an **employee** because the associate

INDEPENDENT CONTRACTOR STATUS

works for the broker, usually at the broker's place of business, prepares listings and sales documents on forms specified by the broker, and upon closing, receives payment from the broker. On the other hand, the sales associate acts like an **independent contractor** because the associate is paid only if the associate brings about a sale that produces a commission. An important distinction between the two is whether or not the broker must withhold income taxes and social security from the associate's commission checks. If the sales associate is considered by the Internal Revenue Service (IRS) to be an employee for tax purposes, the broker must withhold. If classed as an independent contractor for tax purposes, the sales associate is responsible for his own income taxes and social security. The IRS prefers employee status because it is easier to collect taxes from an employer than from an employee.

The IRS will treat real estate sales associates as independent contractors if they meet all of the following three requirements. First, the associate must be a licensed real estate agent. Second, a large percentage of the associate's payment for services as a real estate agent must be directly related to sales and not to hours worked. Third, a written agreement must exist between the associate and the broker stating that the associate will be treated as an independent contractor for tax purposes. If an agent and his sponsoring broker do not comply with this statute, they run the risk of losing their independent contractor status. If this occurs the sponsoring broker becomes subject to the same filing requirements as any other employer in the normal course of business.

These are highlights of the issue. If you plan to work for a broker, you may find it valuable to have this matter as well as your entire employment contract reviewed by an attorney before you sign it.

FRANCHISED OFFICES

Prior to the early 1970s, real estate brokerage was a small business industry. Most brokerages were one-office firms. A large brokerage was one having four or five offices and selling 200 properties a year. Then real estate franchise organizations entered the real estate business in a big way. **Franchisers** such as Century-21, Red Carpet, REMAX, and Gallery of Homes offered brokerage firms national identification, large-scale advertising, sales staff training programs, management advice, customer referrals, financing help for buyers, and guaranteed sales plans. In return, the brokerage firm (the franchisee) paid a fee of from 3% to 8% of gross commission income. The idea became popular and by the mid-1980s approximately half of the real estate licensees affiliated with the National Association of Realtors were working in franchised offices, and their numbers are continuing to grow through the late 1980s. Meanwhile, the number of franchisers grew to over 60 including such names as Realty World, ERA, International Real Estate Network, Better Homes and Gardens Realty, and Mayflower Realty.

Statistics show that franchising appeals mostly to firms with 10 to 50 sales associates. Larger firms are more capable of providing the advantages of a franchise for themselves. Smaller firms tend to occupy market niches and often consist of one or two licensees who do not bring in additional sales associates. For a newly licensed salesperson wishing to affiliate with a firm, a franchised firm offers immediate public recognition, extensive training opportunities, established office routines, regular sales meetings, and access to a nationwide referral system. Franchise affiliation is not magic however; success still depends on the individual to make sales calls, value property, get listings, advertise, show property, qualify, negotiate, and close transactions.

During the late 1970s a large real estate firm in California—Coldwell Banker, began an expansion program by purchasing multibranch real estate firms in other states. Today, the Coldwell Banker chain has over one thousand offices across the United States. Merrill Lynch, the Wall Street stock brokerage firm, has also entered the real estate brokerage business. It, too, has bought existing real estate brokerage firms to accomplish this and now has more real estate agents than stockbrokers. Other Wall Street firms are looking into the real estate brokerage business, as are several large corporations such as Sears, Roebuck, which has purchased Coldwell Banker. Other large national and regional firms include Cushman and Wakefield, REMAX, Grubb & Ellis, Long and Foster, Shannon and Luchs, Marcus and Millichap, and Rubloff, Inc.

For a newcomer, affiliating with a national or regional real estate firm offers benefits like those of a franchised firm (recognition, training, routines, etc.). The main difference is who owns

National Real Estate Firms

the firm. A franchised firm will be locally owned and managed, i.e., an independent firm. Regional and national firms are locally managed, but the sales associate will only occasionally, if ever, meet the owner(s).

PROFESSIONAL REAL ESTATE ASSOCIATIONS

Even before laws required real estate agents to have licenses, there were professional real estate organizations. Called real estate boards, they joined together agents within a city or county on a voluntary basis. The push to organize came from real estate people who saw the need for some sort of controlling organization that could supervise the activities of individual agents and elevate the profession's status in the public's mind. Next came the gradual grouping of local boards into state associations, and finally, in 1908, the National Association of Real Estate Boards (NAREB) was formed. In 1914, NAREB developed a model license law that became the basis for real estate license laws in many states.

Today the local boards are still the fundamental units of the National Association of Realtors (NAR; the name was changed from NAREB in 1974). Local board membership is open to anyone holding a real estate license. Called boards of REALTORS®, real estate boards, and realty boards, or Associations of REALTORS®, they promote fair dealing among their members and with the public and protect members from dishonest and irresponsible licensees. They also promote legislation that protects property rights, offer short seminars to keep members up to date with current laws and practices and, in general, do whatever is necessary to build the dignity, stability, and professionalization of the industry. Local boards often operate the local multiple listing service, although in some communities it is a privately owned and operated business.

State associations are composed of the members of local boards plus sales associates and brokers who live in areas where no local board exists. The purposes of the state associations are to unite members statewide, to encourage legislation that benefits and protects the real estate industry and safeguards the public in their real estate transactions, and to promote economic growth and development in the state. Also, state associations hold conventions to educate members and foster contacts among them.

The NAR is made up of local boards and state associations in the United States. The term *Realtor* is a registered trade name that belongs to NAR. Realtor is not synonymous with real estate agent. It is reserved for the exclusive use of members of the National Association of Realtors, who as part of their membership pledge themselves to abide by the association's Code of Ethics. The term *Realtor* cannot be used by non-members and in some states the unauthorized use of the term is a violation of the real estate law. Prior to 1974, the use of the term *Realtor* was primarily reserved for principal brokers. Then, by a national membership vote, the decision was made to create an additional membership class, the **Realtor-Associate,** for salespersons and broker licensees working for members.

Realtor

One of the most important features of the National Association of Realtors is its **Code of Ethics.** First adopted in 1913, the Realtor Code of Ethics has been revised several times since then and now contains 23 articles that pertain to the Realtor's relation to his clients, to other real estate agents, and to the public as a whole. The full code is reproduced in Figure 17:2.

CODE OF ETHICS

Although a complete review of each article is beyond the scope of this chapter, it can be seen that some articles parallel existing laws. For example, Article 10 speaks against racial discrimination and Article 12 speaks for full disclosure. However, the bulk of the code addresses itself to the obligations of a Realtor that are beyond the written law. For example, in Article 2, the Realtor agrees to stay informed regarding laws and regulations, proposed legislation, and current market conditions in order to advise clients properly. In Article 5, the Realtor agrees to willingly share with other Realtors the lessons of experience. In other words, to be recognized as a Realtor, one must not only comply with the letter of the law, but also observe the ethical standards by which the industry operates.

In some states, ethical standards such as those in the NAR Code of Ethics have been legislated into law. Called **canons** or **standards of conduct,** their intent is to promote ethical practices by all real estate licensees, not just by those who join the National Association of Realtors. Additionally, the National Association of Realtors publishes 34 **Standards of Practice.** These interpret various articles in the Code of Ethics.

Figure 17:2. Code of Ethics

Code of Ethics and Standards of Practice
of the
NATIONAL ASSOCIATION OF REALTORS®

Where the word REALTORS® is used in this Code and Preamble, it shall be deemed to include REALTOR-ASSOCIATE®s.

While the Code of Ethics establishes obligations that may be higher than those mandated by law, in any instance where the Code of Ethics and the law conflict, the obligations of the law must take precedence.

Preamble...
Under all is the land. Upon its wise utilization and widely allocated ownership depend the survival and growth of free institutions and of our civilization. REALTORS® should recognize that the interests of the nation and its citizens require the highest and best use of the land and the widest distribution of land ownership. They require the creation of adequate housing, the building of functioning cities, the development of productive industries and farms, and the preservation of a healthful environment.

Such interests impose obligations beyond those of ordinary commerce. They impose grave social responsibility and a patriotic duty to which REALTORS® should dedicate themselves, and for which they should be diligent in preparing themselves. REALTORS®, therefore, are zealous to maintain and improve the standards of their calling and share with their fellow REALTORS® a common responsibility for its integrity and honor. The term REALTOR® has come to connote competency, fairness, and high integrity resulting from adherence to a lofty ideal of moral conduct in business relations. No inducement of profit and no instruction from clients ever can justify departure from this ideal.

In the interpretation of this obligation, REALTORS® can take no safer guide than that which has been handed down through the centuries, embodied in the Golden Rule, "Whatsoever ye would that others should do to you, do ye even so to them."

Accepting this standard as their own, REALTORS® pledge to observe its spirit in all of their activities and to conduct their business in accordance with the tenets set forth below.

Articles 1 through 5 are aspirational and establish ideals REALTORS® should strive to attain.

ARTICLE 1
REALTORS® should become and remain informed on matters affecting real estate in their community, the state, and nation so that they may be able to contribute responsibly to public thinking on such matters.

NATIONAL ASSOCIATION OF REALTORS®

The Voice for Real Estate®

ARTICLE 2
In justice to those who place their interests in a real estate professional's care, REALTORS® should endeavor always to be informed regarding laws, proposed legislation, governmental regulations, public policies, and current market conditions in order to be in a position to advise their clients properly.

ARTICLE 3
REALTORS® should endeavor to eliminate in their communities any practices which could be damaging to the public or bring discredit to the real estate profession. REALTORS® should assist the governmental agency charged with regulating the practices of brokers and sales licensees in their states. (Amended 11/87)

ARTICLE 4
To prevent dissension and misunderstanding and to assure better service to the owner, REALTORS® should urge the exclusive listing of property unless contrary to the best interest of the owner. (Amended 11/87)

ARTICLE 5
In the best interests of society, of their associates, and their own businesses, REALTORS® should willingly share with other REALTORS® the lessons of their experience and study for the benefit of the public, and should be loyal to the Board of REALTORS® of their community and active in its work.

Articles 6 through 23 establish specific obligations. Failure to observe these requirements subject REALTORS® to disciplinary action.

ARTICLE 6
REALTORS® shall seek no unfair advantage over other REALTORS® and shall conduct their business so as to avoid controversies with other REALTORS®. (Amended 11/87)

• **Standard of Practice 6-1**
REALTORS® shall not misrepresent the availability of access to show or inspect a listed property. (Cross-reference Article 22.) (Amended 11/87)

ARTICLE 7
In accepting employment as an agent, REALTORS® pledge themselves to protect and promote the interests of the client. This obligation of absolute fidelity to the client's interests is primary, but it does not relieve REALTORS® of the obligation to treat fairly all parties to the transaction.

• **Standard of Practice 7-1**
Unless agreed otherwise in writing, REALTORS® shall submit to the seller all offers until closing. Unless the REALTOR® and the seller agree otherwise, REALTORS® shall not be obligated to continue to market the property after an offer has been accepted. Unless the subsequent offer is contingent upon the termination of an existing contract, REALTORS® shall recommend that the seller obtain the advise of legal counsel prior to acceptance. (Cross-reference Article 17.) (Amended 5/87)

• **Standard of Practice 7-2**
REALTORS®, acting as listing brokers, shall submit all offers to the seller as quickly as possible.

- **Standard of Practice 7-3**
  REALTORS®, in attempting to secure a listing, shall not deliberately mislead the owner as to market value.

- **Standard of Practice 7-4**
  (Refer to Standard of Practice 22- 1, which also relates to Article 7, Code of Ethics.)

- **Standard of Practice 7-5**
  (Refer to Standard of Practice 22- 2, which also relates to Article 7, Code of Ethics.)

- **Standard of Practice 7-6**
  REALTORS®, when acting as principals in a real estate transaction, cannot avoid their responsibilities under the Code of Ethics.

ARTICLE 8
REALTORS® shall not accept compensation from more than one party, even if permitted by law, without the full knowledge of all parties to the transaction.

ARTICLE 9
REALTORS® shall avoid exaggeration, misrepresentation, or concealment of pertinent facts relating to the property or the transaction. REALTORS® shall not, however, be obligated to discover latent defects in the property or to advise on matters outside the scope of their real estate license. (Amended 11/86)

- **Standard of Practice 9-1**
  REALTORS® shall not be parties to the naming of a false consideration in any document, unless it be the naming of an obviously nominal consideration.

- **Standard of Practice 9-2**
  (Refer to Standard of Practice 21- 3, which also relates to Article 9, Code of Ethics.)

- **Standard of Practice 9-3**
  (Refer to Standard of Practice 7-3, which also relates to Article 9, Code of Ethics.)

- **Standard of Practice 9-4**
  REALTORS® shall not offer a service described as "free of charge" when the rendering of a service is contingent on the obtaining of a benefit such as a listing or commission.

- **Standard of Practice 9-5**
  REALTORS® shall, with respect to the subagency of another REALTOR®, timely communicate any change of compensation for subagency services to the other REALTOR® prior to the time such REALTOR® produces a prospective buyer who has signed an offer to purchase the property for which the subagency has been offered through MLS or otherwise by the listing agency.

- **Standard of Practice 9-6**
  REALTORS® shall disclose their REALTOR® status when seeking information from another REALTOR® concerning real property for which the other REALTOR® is an agent or subagent.

- **Standard of Practice 9-7**
  The offering of premiums, prizes, merchandise discounts or other inducements to list to sell is not, in itself, unethical even if receipt of the benefit is contingent on listing or purchasing through the REALTOR® making the offer. However, REALTORS® must exercise care and candor in any such advertising or other public or private representations so that any party interested in receiving or otherwise benefiting from the REALTOR®'s offer will have clear, thorough, advance understanding of all the terms and conditions of the offer. The offering of any inducements to do business is subject to the limitations and restrictions of state law and the ethical obligations established by Article 9, as interpreted by any applicable Standard of Practice. (Adopted 11/84)

- **Standard of Practice 9-8**
  REALTORS® shall be obligated to discover and disclose adverse factors reasonably apparent to someone with expertise in only those areas required by their real estate licensing authority. Article 9 does not impose upon the REALTOR® the obligation of expertise in other professional or technical disciplines. (Cross- reference Article 11.) (Amended 11/86)

ARTICLE 10
REALTORS® shall not deny equal professional services to any person for reasons of race, color, religion, sex, handicap, familial status, or national origin. REALTORS® shall not be parties to any plan or agreement to discriminate against a person or persons on the basis of race, color, religion, sex, handicap, familial status, or national origin. (Amended 11/89)

ARTICLE 11
REALTORS® are expected to provide a level of competent service in keeping with the standards of practice in those fields in which the REALTOR® customarily engages.

REALTORS® shall not undertake to provide specialized professional services concerning a type of property or service that is outside their field of competence unless they engage the assistance of one who is competent on such types of property or service, or unless the facts are fully disclosed to the client. Any persons engaged to provide such assistance shall be so identified to the client and their contribution to the assignment should be set forth.

REALTORS® shall refer to the Standards of Practice of the National Association as to the degree of competence that a client has a right to expect the REALTOR® to possess, taking into consideration the complexity of the problem, the availability of expert assistance, and the opportunities for experience available to the REALTOR®.

- **Standard of Practice 11-1**
  Whenever REALTORS® submit an oral or written opinion of the value of real property for a fee, their opinion shall be supported by a memorandum in the file or an appraisal report, either of which shall include as a minimum the following:

  1. Limiting conditions
  2. Any existing or contemplated interest
  3. Defined value
  4. Date applicable
  5. The estate appraised
  6. A description of the property
  7. The basis of the reasoning including applicable market data and/or capitalization computation

  This report or memorandum shall be available to the Professional Standards Committee for a period of at least two years (beginning subsequent to final determination of the court if the appraisal is involved in litigation) to ensure compliance with Article 11 of the Code of Ethics of the NATIONAL ASSOCIATION OF REALTORS®.

- **Standard of Practice 11-2**
  REALTORS® shall not undertake to make an appraisal when their employment or fee is contingent upon the amount of appraisal.

Figure 17:2. continued

- **Standard of Practice 11-3**
  REALTORS® engaged in real estate securities and syndications transactions are engaged in an activity subject to regulations beyond those governing real estate transactions generally, and therefore have the affirmative obligation to be informed of applicable federal and state laws, and rules and regulations regarding these types of transactions.

ARTICLE 12
REALTORS® shall not undertake to provide professional services concerning a property or its value where they have a present or contemplated interest unless such interest is specifically disclosed to all affected parties.

- **Standard of Practice 12-1**
  (Refer to Standards of Practice 9-4 and 16-1, which also relate to Article 12, Code of Ethics.) (Amended 5/84)

ARTICLE 13
REALTORS® shall not acquire an interest in or buy or present offers from themselves, any member of their immediate families, their firms or any member thereof, or any entities in which they have any ownership interest, any real property without making their true position known to the owner or the owner's agent. In selling property they own, or in which they have any interest, REALTORS® shall reveal their ownership or interest in writing to the purchaser or the purchaser's representative. (Amended 11/90)

- **Standard of Practice 13-1**
  For the protection of all parties, the disclosures required by Article 13 shall be in writing and provided by REALTORS® prior to the signing of any contract. (Adopted 2/86)

ARTICLE 14
In the event of a controversy between REALTORS® associated with different firms, arising out of their relationship as REALTORS®, the REALTORS® shall submit the dispute to arbitration in accordance with the regulations of their Board or Boards rather than litigate the matter.

- **Standard of Practice 14-1**
  The filing of litigation and refusal to withdraw from it by REALTORS® in an arbitrable matter constitutes a refusal to arbitrate. (Adopted 2/86)

- **Standard of Practice 14-2**
  The obligation to arbitrate mandated by Article 14 includes arbitration requests initiated by REALTORS®' clients. (Adopted 5/87)

- **Standard of Practice 14-3**
  Article 14 does not require REALTORS® to arbitrate in those circumstances when all parties to the dispute advise the Board in writing that they choose not to arbitrate before the Board. (Adopted 5/88)

ARTICLE 15
If charged with unethical practice or asked to present evidence or to cooperate in any other way, in any disciplinary proceeding or investigation, REALTORS® shall place all pertinent facts before the proper tribunals of the Member Board or affiliated institute, society, or council in which membership is held and shall take no action to disrupt or obstruct such processes. (Amended 11/89)

- **Standard of Practice 15-1**
  REALTORS® shall not be subject to disciplinary proceedings in more than one Board of REALTORS® with respect to alleged violations of the Code of Ethics relating to the same transaction.

- **Standard of Practice 15-2**
  REALTORS® shall not make any unauthorized disclosure or dissemination of the allegations, findings, or decision developed in connection with an ethics hearing or appeal. (Adopted 5/84)

- **Standard of Practice 15-3**
  REALTORS® shall not obstruct the Board's investigative or disciplinary proceedings by instituting or threatening to institute actions for libel, slander or defamation against any party to a professional standards proceeding or their witnesses. (Adopted 11/87)

- **Standard of Practice 15-4**
  REALTORS® shall not intentionally impede the Board's investigative or disciplinary proceedings by filing multiple ethics complaints based on the same event or transaction. (Adopted 11/88)

ARTICLE 16
When acting as agents, REALTORS® shall not accept any commission, rebate, or profit on expenditures made for their principal-owner, without the principal's knowledge and consent.

- **Standard of Practice 16-1**
  REALTORS® shall not recommend or suggest to a client or a customer the use of services of another organization or business entity in which they have a direct interest without disclosing such interest at the time of the recommendation or suggestion. (Amended 5/88)

- **Standard of Practice 16-2**
  When acting as agents or subagents, REALTORS® shall disclose to a client or customer if there is any financial benefit or fee the REALTOR® or the REALTOR®'s firm may receive as a direct result of having recommended real estate products or services (e.g., homeowner's insurance, warranty programs, mortgage financing, title insurance, etc.) other than real estate referral fees. (Adopted 5/88)

ARTICLE 17
REALTORS® shall not engage in activities that constitute the unauthorized practice of law and shall recommend that legal counsel be obtained when the interest of any party to the transaction requires it.

ARTICLE 18
REALTORS® shall keep in a special account in an appropriate financial institution, separated from their own funds, monies coming into their possession in trust for other persons, such as escrows, trust funds, clients' monies, and other like items.

ARTICLE 19
REALTORS® shall be careful at all times to present a true picture in their advertising and representations to the public. REALTORS® shall also ensure that their status as brokers or REALTORS® is clearly identifiable in any such advertising. (Amended 11/86)

- **Standard of Practice 19-1**
  REALTORS® shall not submit or advertise property without authority, and in any offering, the price quoted shall not be other than that agreed upon with the owners.

- **Standard of Practice 19-2**
(Refer to Standard of Practice 9-4, which also relates to Article 19, Code of Ethics.)

- **Standard of Practice 19-3**
REALTORS®, when advertising unlisted real property for sale in which they have an ownership interest, shall disclose their status as both owners and as REALTORS® or real estate licensees. (Adopted 5/85)

- **Standard of Practice 19-4**
REALTORS® shall not advertise nor permit any person employed by or affiliated with them to advertise listed property without disclosing the name of the firm. (Adopted 11/86)

- **Standard of Practice 19-5**
Only REALTORS® as listing brokers, may claim to have "sold" the property, even when the sale resulted through the cooperative efforts of another broker. However, after transactions have closed, listing brokers may not prohibit successful cooperating brokers from advertising their "cooperation," "participation," or "assistance" in the transaction, or from making similar representations.

Only listing brokers are entitled to use the term "sold" on signs, in advertisements, and in other public representations. (Amended 11/89)

ARTICLE 20
REALTORS®, for the protection of all parties, shall see that financial obligations and commitments regarding real estate transactions are in writing, expressing the exact agreement of the parties. A copy of each agreement shall be furnished to each party upon their signing such agreement.

- **Standard of Practice 20-1**
At the time of signing or initialing, REALTORS® shall furnish to each party a copy of any document signed or initialed. (Adopted 5/86)

- **Standard of Practice 20-2**
For the protection of all parties, REALTORS® shall use reasonable care to ensure that documents pertaining to the purchase and sale of real estate are kept current through the use of written extensions or amendments. (Adopted 5/86)

ARTICLE 21
REALTORS® shall not engage in any practice or take any action inconsistent with the agency of other REALTORS®.

- **Standard of Practice 21-1**
Signs giving notice of property for sale, rent, lease, or exchange shall not be placed on property without the consent of the owner.

- **Standard of Practice 21-2**
REALTORS® obtaining information from a listing broker about a specific property shall not convey this information to, nor invite the cooperation of a third party broker without the consent of the listing broker.

- **Standard of Practice 21-3**
REALTORS® shall not solicit a listing which is currently listed exclusively with another broker. However, if the listing broker, when asked by the REALTOR®, refuses to disclose the expiration date and nature of such listing; i.e., an exclusive right to sell, an exclusive agency, open listing, or other form of

contractual agreement between the listing broker and the client, the REALTOR® may contact the owner to secure such information and may discuss the terms upon which the REALTOR® might take a future listing or, alternatively, may take a listing to become effective upon expiration of any existing exclusive listing. (Amended 11/86)

- **Standard of Practice 21-4**
REALTORS® shall not use information obtained by them from the listing broker, through offers to cooperate received through Multiple Listing Services or other sources authorized by the listing broker, for the purpose of creating a referral prospect to a third broker, or for creating a buyer prospect unless such use is authorized by the listing broker.

- **Standard of Practice 21-5**
The fact that a property has been listed exclusively with a REALTOR® shall not preclude or inhibit any other REALTOR® from soliciting such listing after its expiration.

- **Standard of Practice 21-6**
The fact that a property owner has retained a REALTOR® as an exclusive agent in respect of one or more past transactions creates no interest or agency which precludes or inhibits other REALTORS® from seeking such owner's future business.

- **Standard of Practice 21-7**
REALTORS® shall be free to list property which is "open listed" at any time, but shall not knowingly obligate the seller to pay more than one commission except with the seller's knowledgeable consent. (Cross-reference Article 7.) (Amended 5/88)

- **Standard of Practice 21-8**
When REALTORS® are contacted by owners regarding the sale of property that is exclusively listed with another broker, and REALTORS® have not directly or indirectly initiated the discussion, REALTORS® may discuss the terms upon which they might take a future listing or, alternatively, may take a listing to become effective upon expiration of any existing exclusive listing. (Amended 11/86)

- **Standard of Practice 21-9**
In cooperative transactions REALTORS® shall compensate cooperating REALTORS® (principal brokers) and shall not compensate nor offer to compensate, directly or indirectly, any of the sales licensees employed by or affiliated with other REALTORS® without the prior express knowledge and consent of the cooperating broker.

- **Standard of Practice 21-10**
Article 21 does not preclude REALTORS® from making general announcements to property owners describing their services and the terms of their availability even though some recipients may have exclusively listed their property for sale or lease with another REALTOR®. A general telephone canvass, general mailing or distribution addressed to all property owners in a given geographical area or in a given profession, business, club, or organization, or other classification or group is deemed "general" for purposes of this standard.

Article 21 is intended to recognize as unethical two basic types of solicitations:

First, telephone or personal solicitations of property owners who have been identified by a real estate sign, multiple listing compilation, or other information service as having exclusively listed their property with another REALTOR®; and

Figure 17:2. continued

Second, mail or other forms of written solicitations of property owners whose properties are exclusively listed with another REALTOR® when such solicitations are not part of a general mailing but are directed specifically to property owners identified through compilations of current listings, "for sale" signs, or other sources of information required by Article 22 and Multiple Listing Service rules to be made available to other REALTORS® under offers of subagency or cooperation. (Adopted 11/83)

- **Standard of Practice 21-11**
  REALTORS®, prior to accepting a listing, have an affirmative obligation to make reasonable efforts to determine whether the property is subject to a current, valid exclusive listing agreement. (Adopted 11/83)

- **Standard of Practice 21-12**
  REALTORS®, acting as agents of buyers, shall disclose that relationship to the seller's agent at first contact. (Cross-reference Article 7.) (Adopted 5/88)

- **Standard of Practice 21-13**
  On unlisted property, REALTORS®, acting as agents of buyers, shall disclose that relationship to the seller at first contact. (Cross-reference Article 7.) (Adopted 5/88)

- **Standard of Practice 21-14**
  REALTORS®, acting as agents of the seller or as subagents of the listing broker, shall disclose that relationship to buyers as soon as practicable. (Adopted 5/88)

- **Standard of Practice 21-15**
  Article 21 does not preclude REALTORS® from contacting the client of another broker for the purpose of offering to provide, or entering into a contract to provide, a different type of real estate service unrelated to the type of service currently being provided (e.g., property management as opposed to brokerage). However, information received through a Multiple Listing Service or any other offer of cooperation may not be used to target the property owners to whom such offers to provide services are made. (Adopted 2/89)

- **Standard of Practice 21-16**
  REALTORS®, acting as subagents or buyer's agents, shall not use the terms of an offer to purchase to attempt to modify the listing broker's offer of compensation to subagents or buyer's agents nor make the submission of an executed offer to purchase contingent on the listing broker's agreement to modify the offer of compensation. (Adopted 2/89)

ARTICLE 22

In the sale of property which is exclusively listed with a REALTOR®, REALTORS® shall utilize the services of other brokers upon mutually agreed upon terms when it is in the best interests of the client.

Negotiations concerning property which is listed exclusively shall be carried on with the listing broker, not with the owner, except with the consent of the listing broker.

- **Standard of Practice 22-1**
  It is the obligation of the selling broker as subagent of the listing broker to disclose immediately all pertinent facts to the listing broker prior to as well as after the contract is executed.

- **Standard of Practice 22-2**
  REALTORS®, when submitting offers to the seller, shall present each in an objective and unbiased manner.

- **Standard of Practice 22-3**
  REALTORS® shall disclose the existence of an accepted offer to any broker seeking cooperation. (Adopted 5/86)

- **Standard of Practice 22-4**
  REALTORS®, acting as exclusive agents of sellers, establish the terms and conditions of offers to cooperate. Unless expressly indicated in offers to cooperate made through MLS or otherwise, a cooperating broker may not assume that the offer of cooperation includes an offer of compensation. Entitlement to compensation in a cooperative transaction must be agreed upon between a listing and cooperating broker prior to the time an offer to purchase the property is produced. (Adopted 11/88)

ARTICLE 23

REALTORS® shall not publicly disparage the business practice of a competitor nor volunteer an opinion of a competitor's transaction. If their opinion is sought and if the REALTOR® deems it appropriate to respond, such opinion shall be rendered with strict professional integrity and courtesy.

The Code of Ethics was adopted in 1913. Amended at the Annual Convention in 1924, 1928, 1950, 1951, 1952, 1955, 1956, 1961, 1962, 1974, 1982, 1986, 1987, 1989, and 1990.

EXPLANATORY NOTES (Revised 11/88)

The reader should be aware of the following policies which have been approved by the Board of Directors of the National Association:

In filing a charge of an alleged violation of the Code of Ethics by a REALTOR®, the charge shall read as an alleged violation of one or more Articles of the Code. A Standard of Practice may only be cited in support of the charge.

The Standards of Practice are not an integral part of the Code but rather serve to clarify the ethical obligations imposed by the various Articles. The Standards of Practice supplement, and do not substitute for, the Case Interpretations in *Interpretations of the Code of Ethics*.

Modifications to existing Standards of Practice and additional new Standards of Practice are approved from time to time. The reader is cautioned to ensure that the most recent publications are utilized.

Articles 1 through 5 are aspirational and establish ideals that a REALTOR® should strive to attain. Recognizing their subjective nature, these Articles shall not be used as the bases for charges of alleged unethical conduct or as the bases for disciplinary action.

NOTE: The Delegate Body at the 1990 Annual Convention approved numerous amendments to the Code of Ethics and Standards of Practice to ensure gender neutrality. However, only areas with content change reflect a revision date.

NATIONAL ASSOCIATION
OF REALTORS®
430 North Michigan Avenue
Chicago, Illinois 60611-4087

EQUAL HOUSING
OPPORTUNITY

Form No. 166-288-2 (12/90)

In addition to its emphasis on real estate brokerage, the National Association of Realtors also contains a number of specialized professional groups within itself. These include the American Institute of Real Estate Appraisers, the Farm and Land Institute, the Institute of Real Estate Management, the Realtors National Marketing Institute, the Society of Industrial Realtors, the Real Estate Securities and Syndication Institute, the American Society of Real Estate Counselors, the American Chapter of the International Real Estate Federation, and the Women's Council of Realtors. Membership is open to Realtors interested in these specialties.

Realtist

The National Association of Real Estate Brokers (NAREB) is a national trade association representing minority real estate professionals actively engaged in the industry. Founded in 1947, its 5,000 members use the trade name **Realtist.** The organization extends through 14 regions across the country with more than 60 active local boards. NAREB education and certification programs include the Real Estate Management Brokers Institute, National Society of Real Estate Appraisers, Real Estate Brokerage Institute, and United Developers Council. The organization's purposes are to promote high standards of service and conduct and to protect the public against unethical, improper, or fraudulent real estate practices.

GRI Designation

To help encourage and recognize professionalism in the real estate industry, state Boards of Realtors sponsor education courses leading to the GRI designation. Course offerings typically include real estate law, finance, appraisal, investments, office management, and salesmanship. Upon completion of the prescribed curriculum, the designation Graduate Realtor's Institute is awarded.

REVIEW QUESTIONS

1. Which of the following may conduct a real estate brokerage business without a proper license?
   A. Members of the state bar.
   B. Attorneys-in-fact.
   C. Both A and B.
   D. Neither A nor B.

2. A person who sells real estate for others
   A. must be licensed in order to collect compensation.
   B. need not be licensed if no compensation is involved.
   C. Both A and B.
   D. Neither A nor B.

3. Which of the following could be licensed as a real estate broker?
   A. A corporation.
   B. A partnership.
   C. An actual person.
   D. A sole proprietorship.
   E. All of the above.

4. Which of the following is NOT a real estate license category?
   A. Salesperson.
   B. Broker.
   C. Attorney-in-fact.
   D. Both A and C.

5. A real estate listing is a contract between
   A. the owner, and the listing broker.
   B. the owner, the broker and the listing salesperson.
   C. the owner and the listing salesperson.
   D. the broker and the listing salesperson.

6. The ultimate responsibility for a mistake in a document prepared by a real estate salesperson rests
   A. equally upon the salesperson and the employing broker.
   B. upon the employing broker.
   C. Both A and B.
   D. Neither A nor B.

7. Continuing education requirements exist for the purpose of
   A. assuring that only competent license applicants are granted real estate licenses.
   B. requiring licensees to stay up to date in their field.
   C. Both A and B.
   D. Neither A nor B.

8. Before being granted an original salesperson's license, an applicant must
   A. pass the examination for salesperson licensure.
   B. name the broker with whom the applicant will be associated.
   C. complete any state-mandated education requirements.
   D. All of the above.

9. A broker who wishes to operate outside his home state will usually be required to file a notice of consent with the Secretary of State in
   A. his home state.
   B. each state in which he wishes to operate.
   C. Washington, D.C.
   D. Any state.

10. A real estate broker may operate his business as a sole proprietorship under
   A. his own name.
   B. a fictitious name.
   C. Both A and B.
   D. Neither A nor B.

11. For a corporation to be granted a license as a real estate broker,
   A. all officers must be licensed as real estate brokers.
   B. all stockholders must be licensees.
   C. the chief executive officer must be a licensed broker.
   D. salespersons may NOT hold office in the corporation.

12. In most states, a branch office maintained by a licensed brokerage firm must
   A. secure a branch office license in the firm's name.
   B. be managed by a licensed real estate broker.
   C. Both A and B.
   D. Neither A nor B.

13. The requirement that a real estate agent hold a real estate license is set by the
   A. real estate commission.
   B. legislature.
   C. real estate director or commissioner.
   D. governor.

14. In most states, members of the real estate commission are
   A. full-time employees appointed by the governor.
   B. all licensed real estate agents.
   C. Both A and B.
   D. Neither A nor B.

15. A real estate salesperson may reasonably expect to work
   A. for a salary.   D. Both A and B.
   B. on his own.   E. Both B and C.
   C. with people.

16. The term "Realtor" applies to any
   A. licensed real estate salesperson.
   B. licensed real estate broker.
   C. member of a state real estate commission.
   D. member of the National Association of Realtors.

17. Any person who earns a real estate commission and is not licensed is guilty of
   A. duress.   C. breaking the law.
   B. an unethical act.   D. negligence.

18. Which of the following persons are specifically exempt from holding a real estate license?
   A. War veterans.   C. Part-time salespersons.
   B. Executors of estates. D. Listers of real estate.

19. A license may be revoked upon proof of
   A. dispute between broker and salesperson as to a commission.
   B. violation of fair housing law.
   C. refusal to accept an overpriced listing.
   D. not selling enough real estate.

20. A property owner who wants to sell his home is interested in
   A. how much he can get for it.
   B. how much it will cost to sell.
   C. how much the listing salesperson will earn.
   D. Both A and B.

The Principal-Broker Relationship – Employment

OVERVIEW OF
CHAPTER 18

This chapter covers the employment relationship between a broker and his principal. The main topics of the chapter include the listing agreement, exclusive right to sell listing, the exclusive agency listing, open listing, net listing, and the listing period. The chapter also covers the multiple listing service and broker compensation. A discussion of procuring cause, listing contract termination, and bargain brokers is also included.

LEARNING OBJECTIVES

After successful completion of this chapter, you should be able to:
1. Distinguish among the various kinds of listings.
2. Explain the purpose behind the exclusive authority to purchase.
3. Describe the multiple listing service, the listing period, and agent's authority.
4. Explain the principle of earning commission.
5. Define procuring cause.
6. Explain how to terminate a listing contract.
7. Discuss "bargain" and "flat fee" brokers.

KEY • TERMS

Advance fee listing: listing in which a broker gets paid in advance and charges an hourly rate

Broker: one who, for a fee, acts as an agent for others in negotiating contracts or sales

Exclusive authority to purchase: listing utilized by buyer's brokers

Exclusive right to sell: a listing that gives the broker the right to collect a commission no matter who sells the property during the listing period

Listing: a contract wherein a broker is employed to find a buyer or tenant

Multiple Listing Service: organization of member brokers agreeing to share listing information and share commissions

Net listing: a listing agreement that pays the broker an uncertain amount of commission, generating the principal net proceeds from the sale

Ready, willing, and able buyer: a buyer who is ready to buy at the seller's price and terms and who has the financial capability to do so

Chapter 17 discussed licensure requirements and professional affiliations. This chapter will discuss the principal-broker relationship as it relates to employment, listing agreements, and compensation of real estate brokers. Chapter 19 will then expand into theories of agency relationships and duties of care that result from the laws of agency. Note that the formalities of employment are not necessarily required to establish an agency relationship, so the licensee may be responsible as an agent without the benefits of formal employment!

A **real estate listing** is an *employment contract* between a property owner and a real estate broker. Through it the property owner appoints the broker as the owner's agent for the specific purpose of finding a buyer or tenant who is willing to meet the conditions set forth in the listing. It does not authorize the broker to sell or convey title to the property or to sign contracts.

LISTING AGREEMENT

Although persons licensed as real estate salespersons perform listing and sales functions, they are actually extensions of the broker. A seller may conduct all aspects of a listing and sale through a salesperson licensee, but it is the broker behind the salesperson with whom the seller has the listing contract and who is legally liable for its proper execution. If you plan to be a salesperson for a broker, be aware of what is legally and ethically required of a broker because you are the broker's eyes, ears, hands, and mouth. If your interest is in listing your property with a broker, know that it is the broker with whom you have the listing contract even though your day-to-day contact is with the broker's sales associates. **Sales associates** are the licensed salespersons or brokers who work for a broker.

When a property owner signs a listing, all the essential elements of a valid contract must be present. The owner and broker must be legally capable of contracting, there must be mutual assent, and the agreement must be for a lawful purpose. Nearly all states require that a listing be in writing and signed to be valid and thereby enforceable in a court of law.

Figure 18:1 illustrates a simplified **exclusive right to sell listing** agreement. Actual listing contracts tend to be longer and more complex and vary in detail from one contract to the next. The listing in Figure 18:1 is an educational introduction to listings that provides in plain English commonly found listing contract provisions. Beginning at ①, there is a description of the property plus the price and terms at which the broker is instructed to find a buyer. At ②, the broker promises to make a reasonable effort to find a buyer. The period of time that the listing is to be in effect is shown at ③. It is usually to the broker's advantage to make the listing period for as long as possible as this provides more time to find a buyer. Sometimes even an overpriced property will become saleable if the listing period is long enough and prices rise fast enough. However, most owners want a balance between their flexibility and the amount of time necessary for a broker to conduct a sales campaign. In residential sales, 3 to 4 months is a popular compromise; farm, ranch, commercial, and industrial listings are usually made for 6 months to 1 year.

At ④, the owner agrees not to list the property with any other brokers, permit other brokers to have a sign on the property, or advertise it during the listing period. Also, the owner agrees not to revoke the broker's exclusive right to find a buyer as set forth by this contract.

The broker recognizes that the owner may later accept price and terms that are different from those in the listing. The wording at ⑤ states that the broker will earn a commission no matter what price and terms the owner ultimately accepts.

Figure 18:1.

EXCLUSIVE RIGHT TO SELL
LISTING CONTRACT

Property Description: A single-family house at 2424 E. Main Street, City, State. Legally described as Lot 17, Tract 191, County, State.

Price: $105,000

Terms: Cash

② *In consideration of the services of* ABC Realty Company *(herein called the "Broker"), to be rendered to* Roger Leeving and Mary Leeving *(herein called the "Owner"), and the promise of said Broker to make reasonable efforts to obtain a purchaser, therefore, the Owner hereby grants to the Broker*

③ *for the period of time from noon on* April 1, 19xx *to noon on* July 1, 19xx *(herein called the "listing period")*

④ *the exclusive and irrevocable right to advertise and find a purchaser for the above described property at the price and terms shown*

⑤ *or for such sum and terms or exchange as the owner later agrees to accept.*

⑥ *The Owner hereby agrees to pay Broker a cash fee of* 6% *of the selling or exchange price:*

⑦ *(A) in case of any sale or exchange of the above property within the listing period either by the Broker, the Owner, or any other person, or*

⑧ *(B) upon the Broker finding a purchaser who is ready, willing, and able to complete the purchase as proposed by the owner, or*

⑨ *(C) in the event of a sale or exchange within 60 days of the expiration of the listing period to any party shown the above property during the listing period by the Broker or his representative and where the name was disclosed to the Owner.*

⑩ *The Owner agrees to give the Broker access to the buildings on the property for the purposes of showing them at reasonable hours, and allows the Broker to post a "For Sale" sign on the premises.*

Figure 18:1. continued

⑪ *The Owner agrees to allow the Broker to place this listing information in any multiple listing organization of which he is a member and to engage the cooperation of other brokers as subagents to bring about a sale.*

⑫ *The Owner agrees to refer to the Broker all inquiries regarding this property during the listing period.*

⑬ *Accepted:*

  ABC Realty Company

By: Kurt Kwiklister   *Owner:* Roger Leeving

                             Owner: Mary Leeving

Date: April 1, 19xx

Brokerage Commission

At ⑥, the amount of compensation the owner agrees to pay the broker is established. The usual arrangement is to express the amount as a percentage of the sale or exchange price, although a stated dollar amount could be used if the owner and broker agreed. In any event, the amount of the fee is negotiable between the owner and the broker. An owner who feels the fee is too high can list with someone who charges less or sell the property himself. The broker recognizes that if the fee is too low it will not be worthwhile spending time and effort finding a buyer. The typical commission fee in the United States at present is 5% to 7% of the selling price for houses, condominiums, and small apartment buildings, and 6% to 10% on farms, ranches, and vacant land. On multimillion-dollar improved properties, commissions usually drop to the 1% to 4% range. Brokerage commissions are not set by a state regulatory agency or by local real estate boards. In fact, any effort by brokers to set commission rates among themselves is a violation of federal and state anti-trust laws. The penalty can be as much as triple damages and criminal liability.

The conditions under which a commission must be paid by the owner to the broker appear next. At ⑦, a commission is deemed to be earned if the owner agrees to a sale or exchange of the property no matter who finds the buyer. In other words, even if the owner finds a buyer, or a friend of the owner finds a buyer, the broker is entitled to a full commission fee. If the owner disregards the promise at ④ and lists with another broker who then sells the property, the owner is liable for two full commissions.

The wording at ⑧ is included to protect the broker against the possibility that the owner may refuse to sell after the broker has expended time and effort to find a buyer at the price and terms of the listing contract. The listing itself is not an offer to sell property. It is strictly a contract whereby the owner employs the broker to find a buyer. Thus, even though a buyer offers to pay the exact price and terms shown in the listing, the buyer does not have a binding sales contract until the offer is accepted in writing by the owner. However, if the owner refuses to sell at the listed price and terms, the broker is still entitled to a commission. If the owner does not pay the broker voluntarily, the broker can file a lawsuit against the owner to collect.

Protecting the Broker

At ⑨, the broker is protected against the possibility that the listing period will expire while still working with a prospective purchaser. In fairness to the owner, however, two limitations are placed on the broker. First, a sales contract must be concluded within a reasonable time after the listing expires, and second, the name of the purchaser must have been given to the owner before the listing period expires.

Protecting the Owner

Continuing at ⑩, the owner agrees to let the broker enter the property at reasonable hours to show it and put a "For Sale" sign on the property. At ⑪, the property owner gives the broker specific permission to enter the property into a multiple listing service and to engage the cooperation of other brokers as sub-agents to bring about a sale.

At ⑫, the owner agrees to refer all inquiries regarding the availability of the property to the broker. The purpose is to discourage the owner from thinking that he might be able to save a commission by personally selling it during the listing period, and to provide sales leads for the broker. Finally, at ⑬, the owner and the broker (or the broker's sales associate if authorized to do so) sign and date the agreement.

The listing illustrated in Figure 18:1 is called an **exclusive right to sell or exclusive authorization to sell** listing. Its distinguishing characteristic is that no matter who sells the property during the listing period, the listing broker is entitled to a

EXCLUSIVE RIGHT TO SELL LISTING

commission. This is the most widely used type of listing in the United States. Once signed by the owner and accepted by the broker, the primary advantage to the broker is that the money and effort the broker expends on advertising and showing the property will be to the broker's benefit. The advantage to the owner is that the broker will usually put more effort into selling a property if the broker holds an exclusive right to sell than if the broker has an exclusive agency or an open listing.

EXCLUSIVE AGENCY LISTING

The **exclusive agency listing** is similar to the listing shown in Figure 18:1, except that the owner may sell the property himself during the listing period and not owe a commission to the broker. The broker, however, is the only broker who can act as an agent during the listing period; hence the term *exclusive agency*. For an owner, this type of listing may seem like the best of two worlds: the owner has a broker looking for a buyer, but if the owner finds a buyer first, the owner can save a commission fee. The broker is less enthusiastic because the broker's efforts can too easily be undermined by the owner. Consequently, the broker may not expend as much effort on advertising and showing the property as with an exclusive right to sell.

OPEN LISTING

Open listings carry no exclusive rights. An owner can give an open listing to any number of brokers at the same time, and the owner can still find a buyer and avoid a commission. This gives the owner the greatest freedom of any listing form, but there is little incentive for the broker to expend time and money showing the property as the broker has little control over who will be compensated if the property is sold. The broker's only protection is that if the broker does find a buyer at the listing price and terms, the broker is entitled to a commission. This reluctance to develop a sales effort usually means that few, if any, offers will be received and the result may be no sale or a sale below market price. Yet, if a broker does find a buyer, the commission earned may be the same as with an exclusive right to sell.

NET LISTING

A **net listing** is created when an owner states the price he wants for his property and then agrees to pay the broker anything above that price as the commission. It can be written in the form of an exclusive right to sell, an exclusive agency, or an open listing. If a homeowner asks for a "net $60,000" and the broker sells the home for $65,000, the commission would be $5,000. By using the net listing method, many owners feel that they are forcing the broker to look to the buyer for the commission by marking up the price of the property. In reality though, would a buyer pay $65,000 for a home that is worth $60,000? Because of widespread misunderstanding regarding net listings, some states prohibit them outright, and most brokers strenuously avoid them even when requested by property owners. There is no law that says a broker must accept a listing; a broker is free to accept only those listings for which the broker can perform a valuable service and earn an honest profit.

Traditionally, real estate brokers charge a fee for their services based on a percentage of the sales price. Out of this percentage the broker (1) pays all out-of-pocket costs of marketing the property such as advertising and office overhead, (2) pays those who negotiate the transaction, and (3) earns a profit for the firm. If a buyer is not found, the broker receives no money. This means commissions earned from sold properties must also pay for costs incurred by nonsales. Sellers who have marketable property that is priced to sell subsidize sellers whose property is either unattractive or overpriced. As a solution to this inequity, attention is now being given by the real estate industry to the concept of advance fee listings and advance cost listings.

ADVANCE FEE LISTING

An **advance fee listing** is a listing wherein a broker charges a seller much like an attorney charges a client. In other words, the broker asks for an advance deposit from the seller. Against this the broker charges an hourly fee for time spent selling the property plus out-of-pocket expenses. With the seller paying for services as consumed, the seller becomes much more realistic about marketability and listed price. There is less inclination to price above market in hopes that if the broker works long enough, a buyer might be found who will pay above market or that the market will eventually rise to the asking price.

An **advance cost listing** covers only out-of-pocket costs incurred by the broker such as advertising, multiple listing fees, flyers, mailings, toll calls, survey, soil report, title report, travel

Advance Cost Listing

expenses, and food served during open houses. With either the advance fee or advance cost arrangement the broker can still charge a commission based on sales price. In this case costs and hourly fees are deducted from the commission at the closing. With the broker receiving payment for costs (and effort) up front, the sales commission can be lowered.

The mechanics of advance fee and advance cost listings must be very clearly explained to the seller before the listing is signed. There must be an accurate accounting of where the seller's money is being spent. (This is an ideal task for a computer.) Moreover, state real estate regulators may have specific rules and prohibitions that must be followed. Watch the advance fee trend in the 1990s. If it takes hold, it will be an important factor in changing real estate agents from commissioned sales people to professionals who can command an hourly fee for their time.

EXCLUSIVE
AUTHORITY
TO PURCHASE

Previous portions of this chapter have presumed the general rule that the real estate broker represents the seller. Historically, it has been the seller who has hired brokers to assist in marketing property. There are circumstances, however, in which a buyer may want to employ a broker's services to help them to locate property, or to assist them in negotiating the acquisition of a specified property. In such cases, the broker's primary responsibility is to the purchaser rather than to the seller. In this circumstance, the purchaser can reveal confidential information to the broker and rely on the broker's expertise and competence. This may be particularly helpful in situations where a real estate transaction is complex, or there are peculiar concerns unique to certain regions of the country (termites in Houston, radon in Maine, soil conditions in California) about which a buyer wants to be adequately advised before buying real estate in that area. In some cases, a purchaser simply feels he needs expert advise on making real estate acquisitions anywhere.

In these situations, the principal needs to be assured as to the scope of employment of the broker (i.e., locating the property) and, similar to a listing contract, the broker needs to be assured that he is protected, and that the buyer does not "go around" the broker and cut the broker out of a commission once the property has been identified. Figure 18:2 shows a simplified version of an Exclusive Authority to Purchase contract. Note at ① the parties

Figure 18:2. EXCLUSIVE BUYER AGENCY AGREEMENT

This Agreement is made in _____ on this _____ day of _____, 19___, whereby _____ (hereinafter referred to as ("Buyer") hereby appoints Buyer's Broker (hereinafter referred to as "Broker") as Buyer's exclusive agent for the purposes set forth in Section 2 hereof and under the terms specified herein.

Section 1. Buyer agrees to conduct all negotiations for property of the type described in Section 2 hereof through Broker, and to refer to Broker all inquiries received in any form from real estate brokers, salespersons, prospective sellers, or any other source, during the time this Agreement is in effect.

Section 2. Buyer desires to purchase or lease real property (which may include items of personal property) described as follows:

Type: (_) Residential   (_) Residential Income   (_) Other
       (_) Commercial   (_) Industrial   (_) Vacant Land

General
Description:_____

Approximate price range: $_____ to $_____, or any other amount which Buyer ultimately decides to spend.

Preferred Terms:_____

Section 3. Broker's authority as Buyer's exclusive agent shall begin upon Buyer's signing this Agreement, and shall continue until _____, 19____ . unless sooner terminated or by completion of the purpose(s) of the agency as set forth in Section 2 hereof.

Section 4. Broker represents that Broker is duly licensed as a real estate broker, and agrees that Broker will use Broker's best efforts as Buyer's agent to locate property as described in Section 2 hereof, and to negotiate acceptance of any offer to purchase or lease such property. Broker shall submit to Buyer for the Buyer's consideration, properties appearing to Broker to substantially meet the criteria set forth in Section 2.

Section 5. In consideration of the services to be performed by Broker, Buyer agrees to pay Broker an amount equal to the greater of:

      (a)   (_) <u>Retainer Fee</u>. Buyer will pay Broker a non refundable retainer fee of $_____ due and payable upon signing of this Agreement. (_) Retainer Fee shall be credited against commission, IF ANY as set forth in Sub Section 5(c) herein or Retainer Fee shall be retained by Broker in addition to commission; or

      (b)   (_) <u>Hourly Fee</u>. Buyer will pay Broker at the rate of $_____ per hour for the time spent by Broker pursuant to this Agreement, to be paid to Broker when billed to Buyer. (_) Fee shall be credited against commission, IF ANY or (_) Fee shall be considered full payment of Broker's compensation; or

      (c)   (_) <u>Commission</u>. Parties hereby agree that Broker shall first seek compensation out of the transaction. Should the fee so obtained be greater than that listed in subsection (c) (1) or (2) below, Broker shall pay Buyer the difference at closing. Should the fee so obtained by less than that listed in subsection (1) or (2) hereof, Buyer shall pay Broker the difference at closing.

Section 6. If a seller in an agreement made on behalf of Buyer fails to close such agreement, with no fault on the part of Buyer, the commission provided in Section 5, subsection (c), shall be waived. If such transaction fails to close because of any fault on the part of Buyer, such commission will not be waived, but will be due and payable immediately in an amount no less than that referred to in Paragraph 6, said amount to be agreed upon by the parties to be liquidated damages. In no case shall Broker be obligated to advance funds for the benefit of Buyer in order to complete a closing.

Section 7. (_) Broker does (_) does not have Buyer's permission to disclose Buyer's identity to third parties without prior written consent of Buyer.

Section 8. Buyer understands that other potential buyers may consider, make offers on, or purchase through, Broker the same or similar properties as Buyer is seeking to acquire. Buyer consents to Broker's representation of such other potential buyers before, during and after the expiration of this Agreement.

Section 9. The parties agree not to discriminate against any prospective seller or lessor because of the race, creed, color, sex, marital status, national origin, familial or handicapped status of such person.

Accepted:

_____   _____
(Buyer's Broker)   (Buyer)

By: _____   _____
       (Title)   (Buyer)

are named. The real difference in this contract, versus the Listing Agreement, occurs at ②, designating the property to be required in general terms, so that the broker has guidance as to what type of property to be looking for. Compensation is different also. Most buyer's brokers would anticipate being able to access commission splits through the traditional MLS system. If, however, a seller or listing broker refuses to split a commission, there must be an alternative for compensation at ③ for that buyer's broker. Note at ④, there is an expiration date for the term of the agreement, at ⑤ a requirement by the owner to referral inquiries to the broker, and at ⑥ a signature provision for both the buyer's broker and the purchaser.

MULTIPLE LISTING SERVICE

Multiple listing service (MLS) organizations enable a broker with a listing to make a blanket offering of subagency and/or compensation to other member brokers, thus broadening the market exposure for a given property. Member brokers are authorized to show each other's properties to their prospects. If a sale results, the commission is divided between the broker who found the buyer and the broker who obtained the listing, less a small deduction for the cost of operating the multiple listing service.

Market Exposure

A property listed with a broker who is a multiple listing service member receives the advantage of greater sales exposure which, in turn, means a better price and a quicker sale. For the buyer it means learning about what is for sale at many offices without having to visit each individually. For a broker or salesperson with a prospect but not a suitable property listed in that office, the opportunity to make a sale is not lost because the prospect can be shown the listings of other brokers.

To give a property the widest possible market exposure and to maintain fairness among its members, most multiple listing organizations obligate each member broker to provide information to the organization on each new listing within three to seven days after the listing is taken. To facilitate the exchange of information, multiple listing organizations have developed customized listing forms. These forms are a combination of an exclusive right-to-sell listing agreement (with authority to place the listing into multiple) plus a data sheet on the property.

The data sheet, which describes all the physical and financial characteristics of the property, and a photograph of the property are published weekly in a multiple listing book that is distributed to MLS members. Then, if Broker B has a prospect interested in a property listed by Broker A, Broker B telephones Broker A and arranges to show the property. If Broker B's prospect makes an offer on the property, Broker B contacts Broker A and together they call on the seller with the offer.

MLS has recently amended their by-laws to allow for buyer brokerage. The MLS profile sheets provide the listing broker the opportunity to make an offer to compensate the buyer's brokers through a new feature of MLS called **MLS Plus.** It allows the buyer's broker, who is a member of MLS, to access all the benefits of MLS, but to reject the automatic offer of sub-agency. In effect, the buyer's broker can access the commission split, but maintain his fiduciary duty to the purchaser, rather than to the seller of the property.

MLS organizations have been taken to court for being open only to members of local real estate boards. The role that multiple listing services play directly or indirectly in commission splitting is also being tested in the courts. Another idea that has been tested in courts is that an MLS be open to anyone who wants to list a property, broker or owner. It is generally held, though, that owners lacking real estate sophistication would place much inaccurate information in the MLS and this would do considerable harm to MLS members who must rely on that information when describing and showing properties. It is also important to note that the sharing of MLS information to non-members violates federal copyright laws.

Computerized MLS

In addition to publishing MLS books, a number of multiple listing services store their listing information in computers. A salesperson with a briefcase-sized MLS terminal can use any telephone, dial the MLS computer, place the hand piece on the terminal, and request up-to-the minute information for any property in the computer. This is a popular system with sales people who are constantly in the field showing property or in their cars (where they can link up by cellular telephone). It is also quicker than waiting for updated printed MLS information.

Video Disc Electronic advances now make it possible to give a prospective buyer a visual tour through a neighborhood without leaving the broker's office. A single video disc can store over 100,000 still photographs of individual properties, neighborhoods, schools, shopping centers, recreation facilities, etc. The discs are professionally shot and duplicated and made available to real estate offices for a fee. So large is the storage capacity of a disc that every property in a community can be photographed and placed on the disc. In the real estate office a salesperson can play back any image on the disc onto a television screen. With an MLS book in hand, the salesperson can show a prospect a color picture of each property for sale along with pictures of the street and neighborhood, plus nearby schools and shopping facilities. Realty offices with computerized access to MLS files can interface the video disc with the MLS computer.

BROKER COMPENSATION The broker earns a commission at whatever point in the transaction he and the owner agree upon. In nearly all listing contracts this point occurs when the broker produces a **"ready, willing, and able buyer" at price and terms acceptable to the owner.** (See ⑧ in Figure 18:1.) "Ready and willing" means a buyer who is ready to buy at the seller's price and terms. "Able" means financially capable of completing the transaction. An alternative arrangement is for the broker and owner to agree to a "no sale, no commission" arrangement whereby the broker is not entitled to a commission until the transaction is closed.

The difference between the two arrangements becomes important when a buyer is found at price and terms acceptable to the owner, but no sale results. The "ready, willing, and able" contract provides more protection for the broker since the commission does not depend on the deal reaching settlement. The "no sale, no commission" approach is to the owner's advantage, for commission payment is not required unless there is a completed sale. Court decisions have tended to blur the clear-cut distinction between the two. For example, if the owner has a "no sale, no commission" agreement, it would appear that if the broker found a ready, willing, and able buyer at the listing price and terms and the owner refused to sell, the owner would owe no commission for there was no sale. However, a court of law would find in favor of the broker for the full amount of the commission if the refusal to sell was arbitrary and without reasonable cause or in bad faith.

Another change that is taking place is that traditionally it was up to the owner to decide if the buyer was, in fact, financially able to buy. The legal thinking today is that the broker should be responsible because he is in a much better position to analyze the buyer's financial ability than the owner.

A broker under an open listing or an exclusive agency listing is entitled to a commission if the broker was the procuring cause of the sale and can prove it. Procuring cause means that it was the broker's efforts that originated the sale. Suppose that a broker shows an open-listed property to a prospective buyer and during the listing period or an extension the prospect goes directly to the owner and concludes a deal. Even though the owner negotiates his own transaction and prepares his own sales contract, the broker is entitled to a full commission for finding the buyer. This would also be true if the owner and the buyer used a subterfuge or strawman to purchase the property to avoid paying a commission. State laws protect the broker who in good faith has produced a buyer at the request of an owner.

Procuring Cause

When an open listing is given to two or more brokers, the first one who produces a buyer is entitled to the commission. For example, Broker 1 shows a property to Prospect P, but no sale is made. Later P goes to Broker 2 and makes an offer which is accepted by the owner. Although two brokers have attempted to sell the property, only one has succeeded, and that one is entitled to the commission. The fact that Broker 1 receives nothing, even though he may have expended considerable effort, is an important reason why brokers dislike open listings.

The usual situation in a listing contract is that the broker finds a buyer acceptable to the owner. Thus, in most listing contracts the agency terminates because the objective of the contract has been completed. In the bulk of the listings for which a buyer is not found, the agency is terminated because the listing period expires. If no listing period is specified, the listing is considered to be effective for a "reasonable" length of time. A court might consider 3 months to be reasonable for a listing on a home and 6 months reasonable for an apartment building or commercial property.

TERMINATING THE EMPLOYMENT CONTRACT

Listing contracts without termination dates are revocable by the principal at any time, provided the purpose of the revocation is not to deprive the broker of an earned commission. A major disadvantage of listings without termination dates is that all too often they evolve into expensive and time-consuming legal hassles.

Even when a listing has a specific termination date, it is still possible for the owner to tell the broker to stop showing the property and not to bring any offers. However, liability for breach of the employment aspect of the contract remains and the broker can demand compensation for effort expended on behalf of the owner to that point. This can be as much as a full commission if the broker has already found a ready, willing, and able buyer at the owner's price and terms.

Mutual Agreement

A listing can be terminated by mutual agreement of both the owner and broker without money damages. Because listings are the stock in trade of the brokerage business, brokers do not like to lose listings, but sometimes this is the only logical alternative open since the time and effort in setting and collecting damages can be very expensive. Suppose, however, that a broker has an exclusive right-to-sell listing and suspects that the owner's request to cancel is because he has found a buyer and wants to avoid paying a commission. The broker can stop showing the property, but the owner is still obligated to pay a commission if the property is sold before the listing period expires. Whatever the broker and seller decide, they should put it in writing and sign it.

With an open listing, once the property is sold by anyone, broker or owner, all listing agreements pertaining to the property automatically terminate. Similarly, with an exclusive agency listing, if the owner sells the property the broker's listing automatically terminates.

Abandonment, etc.

A listing can be terminated by improper performance or abandonment by the broker. Thus, if a broker acts counter to the owner's best financial interests, the listing is terminated, no commission is payable, and the broker may be subject to a lawsuit for any damages suffered by the owner. If a broker takes a listing and then does nothing to promote it, the owner can assume that the broker abandoned it and thereby has grounds for revocation. The owner should keep written documentation in the event the matter ever goes to court.

A listing is automatically terminated by the death of either the owner or the broker, or if either is judged legally incompetent by virtue of insanity.

BARGAIN BROKERS

The full-service real estate broker who takes a listing and places it in the Multiple Listing Service, places and pays for advertising, holds open house, qualifies prospects, shows property, obtains offers, negotiates, opens escrow, and follows through until closing is the mainstay of the real estate selling industry. The vast majority of open-market sales are handled that way. The remainder are sold by owners, some handling everything themselves and some using flat-fee brokers who oversee the transaction but do not do the actual showing and selling.

Flat-Fee Brokers

For a fee that typically ranges from $400 to $1,500, a **flat-fee broker** will list a property, suggest a market price, write advertising, assist with negotiations, draw up a sales contract, and turn the signed papers over to an escrow company for closing. The homeowner is responsible for paying for advertising, answering inquiries, setting appointments with prospects, showing the property, and applying whatever salesmanship is necessary to induce the prospect to make an offer. Under the flat-fee arrangement, also called self-help brokerage, the homeowner is effectively buying real estate services on an a la carte basis. Some brokerage firms have been very successful offering sellers a choice between a la carte and full service.

Discount Broker

A **discount broker** is a full-service broker who charges less than the prevailing commission rates in his community. The discount broker attracts sellers by offering to do the job for less money, for example, 3% or 4% instead of 5% to 7%. Charging less means a discount broker must sell more properties to be successful. Consequently, most discount brokers are careful to take listings only on property that will sell quickly.

PERCEIVED VALUE

Before leaving the topic of listings, it will be valuable to spend a moment on the perceived value of real estate sales services. Several studies have been conducted that show home-sellers feel the fee charged by brokers is too high in relation to time spent selling the property. Those in the real estate business know that the amount of time and effort to market a property is extensive and that often it is all for nothing if the property does not sell. However the public does not see this, and believes that very little effort is involved, especially if the home sells at market value in 2 or 3 weeks after being shown only a handful of times. Ironically, a market value sale within a month and without the inconvenience of dozens of showings is what the seller is actually seeking. Once it is achieved, however, the fee seems too expensive for the time involved. This leads some sellers to think in terms of selling their property themselves, perhaps with the aid of a self-help brokerage service. For example, if a person is selling a $100,000 house with an $80,000 loan against it, there is but $20,000 in equity to work with. If the broker's commission is 6% of the sales price ($6,000), the seller is actually paying 30% of his equity to the broker.

What stops more people from do-it-yourself selling is that they need a broker to evaluate the property, describe current market and financing conditions, estimate the most probable selling price, write the sales contract, and handle the closing. To a considerable degree, a real estate licensee's success will come from providing the services homeowners feel they need, listing property at or near market, emphasizing the value of services rendered, and operating in a professional manner to bring about a smooth and speedy sale.

REVIEW QUESTIONS

1. Sales associate Lee secured a written listing on a property for sale, signed by the owner and the employing broker. Is this an enforceable listing contract?
   A. Yes, because the broker is a licensed agent.
   B. Yes, if all essential elements of a listing contract are present.
   C. No, because no contract exists until the property is sold.
   D. No, because no consideration will be paid until the property is sold.

2. A real estate listing
   A. is an employment contract between a property owner and a real estate broker.
   B. authorizes a real estate broker to sell and convey title to an owner's real property.
   C. Both A and B.
   D. Neither A nor B.

3. A listing to find a buyer for each of the following types of properties will usually be for a period of time ranging from six months to one year EXCEPT:
   A. farms.
   B. commercial properties.
   C. residential properties.
   D. industrial properties.

4. A typical exclusive right to sell listing requires the owner to
   A. exclude other brokers from advertising or placing a sign on the property.
   B. pay a commission if a purchaser is found who agrees to buy at the price and terms stipulated in the listing.
   C. Both A and B.
   D. Neither A nor B.

5. The amount of commission to be paid the broker for selling a property is
   A. set by state law.
   B. negotiated at the time a buyer is found.
   C. set forth in the rules of the state real estate commission.
   D. stated in the listing contract.

6. Under the terms of an exclusive right to sell listing, a commission is due the listing broker if a buyer is found by
   A. the listing broker.
   B. a sales associate employed by the listing broker.
   C. the owner, through his own efforts.
   D. another broker.
   E. All of the above.

7. Which of the following is NOT true of an exclusive right to sell listing?
   A. Brokers will usually exert their maximum sales effort under this type of listing.
   B. The broker will receive a commission regardless of whether the property is sold.
   C. The owner may not sell of his own efforts without liability for a commission to the broker.
   D. The property may not be listed with another broker during the listing period.

8. An exclusive agency listing
   A. permits the owner to sell of his own efforts without liability to pay a commission to the listing broker.
   B. allows the owner to list concurrently with other brokers.
   C. Both A and B.
   D. Neither A nor B.

9. All of the following are true of net listings EXCEPT:
   A. many states prohibit a broker from accepting a net listing.
   B. most brokers are reluctant to accept them, even when permitted to do so.
   C. all net listings are open listings.
   D. the commission is the excess above the seller's net price.

10. Under the terms of an advance fee listing, the listing broker receives
    A. an hourly fee for time spent in selling the property.
    B. compensation for out-of-pocket expenses.
    C. Both A and B.
    D. Neither A nor B.

11. An advance cost listing differs from an advance fee listing in that
    A. the broker receives compensation for out-of-pocket expenses, but no hourly fee.
    B. the commission will not be based on the sales price.
    C. Both A and B.
    D. Neither A nor B.

12. Under the terms of a multiple listing agreement, if a broker other than the listing broker sells the property, the owner
    A. may be liable for two commissions on the sale.
    B. may sell of his own efforts without any obligation to pay a commission.
    C. Both A and B.
    D. Neither A nor B.

13. The advantages of a multiple listing arrangement include
    A. greater market exposure of the property.
    B. the possibility of a higher sales price.
    C. quicker sale.
    D. All of the above.

14. Recent innovations for marketing properties through multiple listing services include
    A. computerized listings.   C. Both A and B.
    B. video disc display of listings. D. Neither A nor B.

15. When a property under an open listing is shown to a prospect by two different brokers and a sale results, the commission is
    A. payable to the broker who first showed the property to the buyer.
    B. divided between the two brokers.
    C. payable to the broker who made the sale.
    D. payable in full to each broker.

16. An exclusive listing contract with a definite termination date is NOT terminable by
    A. sale of the property.
    B. death of the listing salesperson.

17. An open listing may be terminated by which of the following means?
    A. Sale of the property.
    B. Abandonment by the broker.
    C. Destruction of the property by casualty.
    D. Death of the owner.
    E. All of the above.

18. If a purchaser arbitrarily defaults on a purchase contract, any earnest money previously paid, in the absence of an agreement to the contrary, will be
   A. paid to the broker as compensation for his efforts.
   B. divided between the broker and the owner/seller.
   C. returned to the purchaser.
   D. paid to the owner/seller.

19. Which of the following is most likely to accept only listings that he thinks will sell quickly?
   A. Flat-fee brokers.   C. Discount brokers.
   B. Full-service brokers.   D. Self-help brokers.

20. All of the following statements are true EXCEPT:
   A. the statute of frauds requires all agency agreements to be made in writing in order to be enforceable.
   B. a real estate listing is an agency contract.
   C. in a real estate listing, the property owner is the principal.
   D. a real estate broker is the agent under a real estate listing.

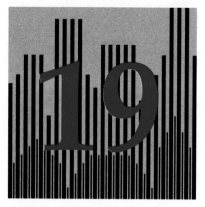

The Principal-Broker Relationship – Agency

OVERVIEW OF CHAPTER 19

This chapter covers the principal and agent relationship, and the law of agency in general. Creation of the agency relationship and obligations of the broker to his principal and to third parties are discussed. The new concepts of owner disclosure statements and buyer agency are also discussed. The final portions of the chapter deal with dual agency and anti-trust laws.

LEARNING OBJECTIVES

After successful completion of this chapter, you should be able to:
1. Discuss how an agency relationship can be created.
2. Define the different types of agency authority.
3. List the duties of care of a licensee to his principal.
4. List the duties of a licensee to third parties.
5. Discuss the pitfalls of dual agency.
6. Explain the concept of buyer agency.
7. Explain the risks of federal anti-trust laws.

KEY • TERMS

Agent: the person empowered to act by and on behalf of the principal

Boycotting: two or more people conspiring to restrain competition

Commingling: the mixing of clients' or customers' funds with an agent's personal funds

Dual agency: representation of two or more principals in a transaction by the same agent

Middleman: a person who brings two or more parties together but does not represent either party

Ostensible authority: an agency relationship created by the conduct of the principal

Price fixing: two or more people conspiring to charge a fixed fee, having an anti-competitive effect

Principal: a person who authorizes another to act

Puffing: statements a reasonable person would recognize as non-factual or extravagant

Third parties: persons who are not parties to a contract but who may be affected by it

The previous chapter has stressed the mechanics of real estate listings. Let us now take a close look at the agency aspects of the principal-broker relationship, i.e., the legal responsibilities of the broker toward the principal and vice versa.

AGENCY

An **agency** is created when one person (called the **principal**) delegates to another person (called the **agent**) the right to act on the principal's behalf. There are three levels of agency: universal, general, and specific. In a **universal agency** the principal gives the agent legal power to transact matters of all types on the principal's behalf. An example is an unlimited power of attorney. Universal agencies are rarely encountered in practice, and courts generally frown on them because they are so broad. In a **general agency** the agent is given the power to bind the principal in a particular trade or business. For example, a salesperson is a general agent of his or her employing broker. Another example is that of a property manager for a property owner. In a **special agency** the principal empowers the agent to perform a particular act or transaction. One example is a real estate listing. Another is a power of attorney to sign a deed on behalf of someone who will be out of the country.

The principal in an agency relationship can be either a natural person or a legal person such as a corporation. Likewise, an agent can be either a natural person or a corporation such as a real estate brokerage company. The persons and firms with whom the principal and agent negotiate are called **third parties.** You will also hear these third parties referred to as the broker's **customers** and the principal referred to as the broker's **client.** Sometimes you will see the phrase principals only in real estate advertisements where property is offered for sale by its owner without the aid of a broker. This means the owner wants to be contacted by persons who want to buy and not by real estate agents who want to list the property.

Establishing the Agent's Authority

A written listing agreement outlines the agent's (broker's) authority to act on behalf of the principal (owner) and the principal's obligations to the agent. A written agreement is the preferred method of creating an agency because it provides a document to evidence the existence of the agency relationship.

Agency authority may also arise from custom in the industry, common usage, and conduct of the parties involved. For example, the right of an agent to post a "For Sale" sign on the listed property may not be expressly stated in the listing. However, if it is the custom in the industry to do so, and presuming there are no deed restrictions or city ordinances to the contrary, the agent has **implied authority** to post the sign. A similar situation exists with regard to showing a listed property to prospects. The seller of a home can expect to have it shown on weekends and evenings whereas a commercial property owner would expect showings only during business hours.

Ostensible authority is conferred when a principal gives a third party reason to believe that another person is his agent even though that person is unaware of the appointment. If the third party accepts this as true, the principal may well be bound by the acts of his agent. For example, you give your house key to a plumber with instructions that when he has finished un-stopping the waste lines he is to lock the house and give the key to your next door neighbor. Even though you do not call and expressly appoint your neighbor as your agent to receive your key, once the plumber gives the key to your neighbor, your neighbor becomes your agent with regard to that key. Since you told the plumber to leave the key there, he has every reason to believe that you appointed your neighbor as your agent to receive the key.

An **agency by ratification** is one established after the fact. For example, if an agent secures a contract on behalf of a principal and the principal subsequently ratifies or agrees to it, a court may hold that an agency was created at the time the initial negotiations started. An **agency by estoppel** can result when a principal fails to maintain due diligence over his agent and the agent exercises powers not granted to him. If this causes a third party to believe the agent has these powers, an agency by estoppel has been created. An **agency coupled with an interest** is said to exist when an agent holds an interest in the property he is representing. For example, a broker is a part-owner in a property he has listed for sale.

Anytime an agency is created, such as an attorney for a client, a property manager for an owner, or a broker for a seller, a **fiduciary relationship** is created. The agent (called the **fiduciary**) must be faithful to the principal, exhibit trust and honesty, and exercise good business judgment. In other words, the agent owes fidelity to the principal. For a real estate broker this means the broker must faithfully perform the agency agreement, be loyal to the principal, exercise competence, and account for all funds handled in performing the agency. Let's look at these various requirements more closely.

BROKER'S OBLIGATIONS TO HIS PRINCIPAL

Faithful performance (also referred to as **obedience**) means that the agent is to obey all legal instructions given by the principal, and to apply best efforts and diligence to carry out the objectives of the agency. For a real estate broker this means performance as promised in the listing contract. A broker who promises to make a "reasonable effort" or apply "diligence" in finding a buyer and then does nothing to promote the listing gives the owner legal grounds for terminating the listing. Faithful performance also means not departing from the principal's instructions. If the agent does so (except in extreme emergencies not foreseen by the principal), it is at the agent's own risk. If the principal thereby suffers a loss, the agent is responsible for that loss. For example, a broker accepts a personal note from a buyer as an earnest money deposit, but fails to tell the seller that the deposit is not in cash. If the seller accepts the offer and the note is later found to be worthless, the broker is liable for the amount of the note.

Faithful Performance

Another aspect of faithful performance is that the agent must personally perform the tasks delegated to him. This protects the principal who has selected an agent on the basis of trust and confidence from finding that the agent has delegated that responsibility to another person. However, a major question arises on this point in real estate brokerage, as a large part of the success in finding a buyer for a property results from the cooperative efforts of other brokers and their salespeople. Therefore, listing agreements usually include a statement that the listing broker is authorized to secure the cooperation of other brokers and pay them part of the commission from the sale.

Loyalty to Principal

Once an agency is created, the agent must be loyal to the principal. The law is clear in all states that in a listing agreement the broker (and the broker's sales staff) occupy a position of trust, confidence, and responsibility. As such, the broker is legally bound to keep the property owner fully informed as to all matters that might affect the sale of the listed property and to promote and protect the owner's interests.

Unfortunately, greed and expediency sometimes get in the way. As a result, numerous laws have been enacted for the purpose of protecting the principal and threatening the agent with court action for misplaced loyalty. For example, an out-of-town landowner who is not fully up to date on the value of his land visits a local broker and wants to list it for $30,000. The broker is much more knowledgeable of local land prices and is aware of a recent city council decision to extend roads and utilities to the area of this property. As a result, the broker knows the land is now worth $50,000. The broker remains silent on the matter, and the property is listed for sale at $30,000. At this price the broker can find a buyer before the day is over and have a commission on the sale. However, the opportunity for a quick $20,000 is too tempting to let pass. He buys the property (or to cover up, buys in the name of his wife or a friend) and shortly thereafter resells it for $50,000. Whether he sold the property to a buyer for $30,000 or bought it and resold it for $50,000, the broker did not exhibit loyalty to the principal. Laws and penalties for breach of loyalty are stiff: the broker can be sued for recovery of the price difference and the commission paid, his real estate license can be suspended or revoked, and he may be required to pay additional fines and money damages.

If a licensee intends to purchase a property listed for sale by his agency or through a cooperating broker, he is under both a moral and a legal obligation to make certain that the price paid is the fair market value and that the seller knows who the buyer is, and that the buyer is a licensee.

Loyalty to the principal also means that when seeking a buyer or negotiating a sale, the broker must continue to protect the owner's financial interests. Suppose that an owner lists his home at $82,000 but confides in the broker, "If I cannot get $82,000, anything over $79,000 will be fine." The broker shows the home to a prospect who says, "Eighty-two thousand is too much. What will the owner really take?" or "Will he take seventy-nine thousand?" Loyalty to the principal requires the broker to say that the owner will take $82,000, for that is the price in the listing agreement. If the buyer balks, the broker can suggest that the buyer submit an offer for the seller's consideration. State laws require that all offers be submitted to the owner, no matter what the offering price and terms. This prevents the agent from rejecting an offer that the owner might have accepted if he had known about it. If the seller really intends for the broker to quote $79,000 as an acceptable price, the listing price should be changed; then the broker can say, "The property was previously listed for $82,000, but is now priced at $79,000."

Protecting the Owner's Interest

A broker's loyalty to his principal includes keeping the principal informed of changes in market conditions during the listing period. If after a listing is taken an adjacent landowner is successful in rezoning his land to a higher use and the listed property becomes more valuable, the broker's responsibility is to inform the seller. Similarly, if a buyer is looking at a property priced at $30,000 and tells the broker, "I'll offer $27,000 and come up if need be," it is the duty of the broker to report this to the owner. The owner can then decide if he wants to accept the $27,000 offer or try for more. If the broker does not keep the owner fully informed, he is not properly fulfilling his duties as the owner's agent.

The duty of **reasonable care** implies competence and expertise on the part of the broker. It is the broker's responsibility to disclose

Reasonable Care

all knowledge and material facts concerning a property to his principal. Also, the broker must not become a party to any fraud or misrepresentation likely to affect the sound judgment of the principal.

Although the broker has a duty to disclose all material facts of a transaction, legal interpretations are to be avoided. Giving legal interpretations of documents involved in a transaction can be construed as practicing law without a license, an act specifically prohibited by real estate licensing acts. Moreover, the broker can be held financially responsible for any wrong legal information he gives to a client.

The duty of reasonable care also requires an agent to take proper care of property entrusted to him by his principal. For example, if a broker is entrusted with a key to an owner's building to show it to prospects, it is the broker's responsibility to see that it is used for only that purpose and that the building is locked upon leaving. Similarly, if a broker receives a check as an earnest money deposit, he must properly deposit it in a bank and not carry it around for several weeks.

Accounting for Funds Received

The earnest money that accompanies an offer on a property does not belong to the broker, even though the broker's name is on the check. For the purpose of holding clients' and customers' money, laws in nearly all states require a broker to maintain a **trust account.** All monies received by a broker as agent for his principal are to be promptly deposited in this account or in the trust account of the attorney, escrow, or title company handling the transaction. Most states require that a trust account be a demand deposit (checking account) at a bank or a trust account at a trust company. Some states allow brokers to deposit trust funds in bank accounts that earn interest. The broker's trust account must be separate from his personal bank account and the broker is required by law to accurately account for all funds received into and paid out of the trust account. As a rule, a broker will have one trust account for properties listed for sale and another trust account for rental properties managed by the broker. State-conducted surprise audits are made on broker's trust accounts to ensure compliance with the law. Failure to comply with trust fund requirements can result in the loss of one's real estate license.

Commingling

If a broker places money belonging to a client or customer in his own personal account, it is called **commingling** and is grounds for suspension or revocation of the broker's real estate license. The reason for such severe action is that from commingling it is a very short step to **conversion,** i.e., the agent's personal use of money belonging to others. Also, clients' and customers' money placed in a personal bank account can be attached by a court of law to pay personal claims against the broker.

If a broker receives a check as an earnest money deposit, along with instructions from the buyer that it remain uncashed, the broker may comply with the buyer's request as long as the seller is informed of this fact when the offer is presented. Similarly, the broker can accept a promissory note if he informs the seller. The objective is to disclose all material facts to the seller that might influence the decision to accept or reject the offer. The fact that the deposit accompanying the offer is not cash is a material fact. If the broker withholds this information, there is a violation of agency.

*BROKER'S
OBLIGATIONS
TO THIRD PARTIES*

A broker's fiduciary obligations are to the principal who has employed him. State laws nonetheless make certain demands on the broker in relation to the third parties the broker deals with on behalf of the principal. Foremost among these are honesty, integrity, and fair business dealing. This includes the proper care of deposit money and offers as well as responsibility for written or verbal statements. Misrepresenting a property by omitting vital information is as wrong as giving false information. Disclosure of such misconduct usually results in a broker losing the right to a commission. Also possible are loss of the broker's real estate license and a lawsuit by any party to the transaction who suffered a financial loss because of the misrepresentation.

In guarding against misrepresentation, a broker must be careful not to make statements not known to be true. For example, a prospect looks at a house listed for sale and asks if it is connected to the city sewer system. The broker does not know the answer, but sensing it is important to making a sale, says, yes. If the prospect relies on this statement, purchases the house and finds out that there is no sewer connection, the broker may be at the center of litigation regarding sale cancellation, commission loss, money damages, and state license discipline. The answer should be, "I don't know, but I will find out for you."

Suppose the seller has told the broker that the house is connected to the city sewer system, and the broker, having no reason to doubt the statement, accepts it in good faith and gives that information to prospective buyers. If this statement is not true, the owner is at fault, owes the broker a commission, and both the owner *and* the broker may be subject to legal action for sale cancellation and money damages. When a broker must rely on information supplied by the seller, it is best to have it in writing and verify its accuracy. However, relying on the seller for information does not completely relieve the broker's responsibility to third parties. If a seller says his house is connected to the city sewer system and the broker knows that is impossible because there is no sewer line on that street, it is the broker's responsibility to correct the erroneous statement.

Most people have a good sense of what constitutes intentional fraud and vigorously avoid it. Not quite so obvious, and yet equally dangerous from the standpoint of dissatisfaction and legal liability, is the area of ignorance. Ignorance results from not knowing all the pertinent facts about a property. This may result from the broker not taking time to check the facts or from not knowing what to look for in the first place. This is called "what the agent should have known" and there has been some far-reaching litigation that is forcing real estate brokers and their salespeople to know more about the product they are selling. The 1984 *Easton vs. Strassburger* case (152 C.A. 3d 90) is explained next to illustrate what is expected of those in the real estate industry.

COURT CASE EXAMPLES

The *Easton* case involved the sale of a house built on filled land that was not properly engineered and compacted. The sellers did not disclose to the listing broker, to the broker who found the buyer, or to the buyer that there had been landslide activity on the property and what corrective measures had been taken. The listing broker's sales associates were aware that (1) the house was built on fill land, (2) there was netting on a slope that had slid and was repaired, and (3) the floor of the guest house was uneven. None of these "red flags" were further investigated or brought to the attention of the buyer. After the buyer closed and took possession, the land problems got worse, virtually destroying the property's value. The buyer sued the seller and the listing broker. The jury awarded the buyer $197,000 and held the seller, listing broker, and selling broker liable.

In the *Easton* case, the judge stated that a real estate broker has a "...duty to conduct a reasonably competent and diligent inspection of the residential property listed for sale and to disclose to prospective purchasers all facts materially affecting the value or desirability of the property that such an investigation would reveal." For the real estate agent, this means a careful inspection of the property to determine obvious defects or red flags. A **red flag** is something that would warn a reasonably observant agent that there may be an underlying problem. The agent is then responsible for disclosing this to the seller and any prospective buyers. The agent is not responsible for knowing the underlying problem that produces the red flag. (In other words, in the *Easton* case the judge did not require the real estate agent to be a soils engineer.) But the case does strongly suggest that a broker recommend to the seller and/or buyer that a specialist be hired to determine whether or not there is an underlying problem causing the red flag.

Red Flags

Although the *Easton* case dealt with soil problems, the careful agent will also want to inspect such things as kitchen appliances, water heater, water supply, swimming pool, sewer hookup, heating and air conditioning systems, electrical capacity, plumbing, roof, walls, ceiling, fireplace, foundation, garage, fences, sidewalks, sprinklers, etc. The broker may also want to have the seller purchase a home warranty for the buyer as a means of reducing legal liability for all involved. What we see in the Easton case is the legal system pushing the real estate industry further toward professionalism. When instructing the jury in the Easton case the judge said, "A real estate broker is a licensed person or entity who holds himself out to the public as having particular skills and knowledge in the real estate field." In the future you may expect to see more court cases on this issue as well as legislation that defines the standard of care owed by a broker to a prospective purchaser.

If you, as an agent, hire someone to look into a question that was raised by a seller, prospect, or red flag, make certain you hire someone who is professionally qualified. In the following

Choosing Your Helpers

case the broker listed a house and in due course found a buyer for it. The sale was contingent on getting an inspection and approval of the plumbing, furnace, air conditioning, and roof. The buyer asked the broker for someone who could do this, and the broker hired someone who had been used occasionally to make minor inspections. The inspection was made, the items were reported to be in good order, and the closing took place. Upon moving in, the buyer found the house lacked water pressure because the pipes were corroded. This was confirmed by the city water department. The buyer had the pipes replaced and sent the broker the bill for $2,200. The broker felt no liability and did not pay. The buyer then sued the broker. At the trial, the buyer introduced evidence that the broker had assured the buyer that the broker would have a man check the plumbing and other items. At the trial the man who made the inspection stated he inspected the house but did not check the water pressure. The court found the broker to be negligent: the broker should have known enough to hire a competent plumber, not a handyman. In deciding for the buyer, the judge expressed the opinion that a real estate agent, like a doctor or lawyer, holds himself out to be an expert in his field.

As Is   After reading about the two cases above you may begin to think that selling a property "as is" is a safe way to avoid the liability to disclose. This is not necessarily so. In another case that found its way to the courts, a property had been condemned by local government authorities for building code violations. The broker listed and sold it, making it very clear and in writing to the buyer that the property was being sold "as is." Although "as is" means the seller is not going to make repairs, a court found this statement did not excuse the broker from informing the buyer that the building was condemned.

Masking   An agent must be on guard for a principal who wants to do something illegal or unethical. For example, a seller wants to mask a sale so as not to trigger a due-on-sale clause. The broker should advise against this and have no part of it. Otherwise the seller and broker may find themselves defending an expensive lawsuit brought by an innocent buyer when the lender learns about the transfer and calls the loan due. Moreover, the broker may also be sued by the seller on the grounds that the broker did not discourage the seller from doing this act.

Seller disclosure statements are a detailed disclosure of house defects (or lack thereof) on a form often produced by a real estate trade association. As a general rule, the seller needs to fill out the forms, which are then presented to the buyer as a representation of the seller's statement of condition of the property. The seller is the most likely person to fill out the disclosure because the seller simply knows more about the property than anybody else. To date only two states (Maine and California) have mandated Seller Disclosure Statements. Both have had excellent results and very few consumer complaints. Twenty four states recommend them but do not require them. Seven states require owner disclosures about health hazards, and 19 states are considering mandatory disclosures. The risks of using the form are nominal and the benefits are great.

OWNER DISCLOSURE STATEMENT

In the last ten years there has been extensive litigation on the sales of real property based on misrepresentations and material omissions. When the buyer sues, the broker has often found himself as a defendant, because the seller is gone, and the broker marketed the property. This creates an unfair burden on a broker who may have no knowledge of the defect, nor the expertise to investigate the potential for defects.

For the seller's benefit, the seller disclosure form gives the opportunity for the seller to reinvestigate the house. Very few of us have perfect homes. Many sellers simply overlook the defects (we all learn to live with them or forget about them, particularly when it's our house). This failure to disclose, however, results in misrepresentation on the part of seller because of negligence or perhaps because he innocently overlooked it. In the worst case scenario, he may intentionally misrepresent, or intentionally fail to mention, a defect in order to induce the buyer to purchase. In all circumstances, the seller's disclosure form yields these benefits: (1) it informs the buyer as to which defects exist, (2) it provides a basis from which the buyer can conduct further investigation on the property, (3) it allows the buyer to make an informed decision as to whether or not to purchase, and (4) it may provide a more concrete basis for litigation if the buyer can determine that the seller filled out the disclosure statement incorrectly or failed to disclose a defect which the seller knew was material.

Similarly, brokers can find the disclosure statement beneficial because they now have written proof as to what disclosures were made to them (which should be compared with their listing agreement and the MLS disclosures) to assure consistency in marketing their product. In addition, knowing that there is a defect allows the broker to effectively market the property "as is," disclosing the defects and therefore limiting liability for both the seller (they sometimes overlook potential liability in their eagerness to sell) and the broker.

BUYER AGENCY

As stated in the previous chapter, most agency relationships presume that the real estate broker represents the seller. In those situations where the broker represents the buyer, however, it is important to note that the same fiduciary duties (performance, accounting, reasonable care, and loyalty) apply between the real estate broker and the buyer, and the seller, in turn, becomes the third party. This creates a situation where the seller is represented by the listing broker, but the buyer is represented by the buyer's broker. There are two areas of genuine concern: (1) the seller may take the cooperating broker into confidence because the seller thinks the cooperating broker represents him instead of the buyer; and (2) the listing broker may take the cooperating broker into confidence because of his reliance on the presumption of sub-agency under the MLS system. In either case, this could result in a detrimental reliance. Therefore, it is critically important that the broker representing the buyer disclose to the listing broker and seller immediately, if not sooner, that he represents the buyer in order to eliminate the potential for that detrimental reliance. This should be in the form of a written disclosure to the listing broker and seller, as well as a written rejection of the MLS sub-agency. It would also be prudent to insert the buyer representation in the earnest money contract.

ERRORS AND OMISSION INSURANCE

Because of the trend in recent years to a more consumer-oriented and more litigious society, the possibility of a broker being sued has risen to the point that **errors and omission insurance (E&O)** has become very popular. The broker pays an annual fee to an insurance company that in turn will defend the broker and pay legal costs and judgments. E&O, as it is sometimes called, does not cover intentional acts of a broker to deceive, does not cover punitive damages, and does not cover negligence or misrepresentation when buying or selling for one's own account. Other than that, E&O offers quite broad coverage. This includes defending so-called "nuisance cases" in which the broker may not be at fault but must defend anyway. Moreover, E&O covers not only courtroom costs and judgments, but pre-trial conferences and negotiations and out-of-court settlements. Today E&O is simply a cost of the real estate business just like rent, telephone, and automobile expenses.

Sometimes it is hard for a broker to know just what will result in an unhappy buyer and a lawsuit. For example, a broker showed a large house that was listed in the multiple listing service. The MLS card said the house contained 5,400 square feet of living space. The broker told the prospect that 5,400 was an estimate he had not checked and the prospect did not seem concerned or measure the house. The prospect made an offer with a $5,000 deposit and it was accepted by the seller. Several days later, in a conversation with the local tax assessor, the buyer learned that the tax records listed the house at 4,600 square feet. On the grounds of the square footage discrepancy, the buyer wanted to rescind the contract and retrieve the deposit. The seller rescinded the contract but would not return the deposit. The house was placed back on the market and sold for the original asking price a short time later. A year later the broker who had listed the property, the broker who had found the unhappy buyer, and the seller were sued by the unhappy buyer for return of the $5,000 deposit plus $10,000 in exemplary and punitive damages. In part because the case was not clear-cut, it dragged on for well over a year. In the end, legal expenses amounted to more than anyone gained.

Another case that a broker had to defend seemed hardly the fault of the broker. An out-of-town lot owner wrote the broker with the lot and tract number and an authorization to find a buyer. The lot was in a mountain subdivision of vacant wooded land. The broker located the boundary stakes, put a sign on the lot, and sold it. A year later the problem surfaced: It seems the lot numbers were all marked on the outside of the boundary stakes rather than the inside as was customary. Although the

Boundary Stake Case

correct lot was very little different, the buyer would not accept it. The buyer wanted his money back plus 25%. In the negotiations that followed, the broker's error and omission insurance company bought the lot and listed it with the broker who resold it.

PUFFING

Puffing refers to nonfactual or extravagant statements that a reasonable person would recognize as exaggeration. Thus, a buyer may have no legal complaint against a broker who told him that a certain hillside lot had the most beautiful view in the world or that a listed property had the finest landscaping in the county. Usually a reasonable buyer can see these things and make up his own mind. However, if a broker in showing a rural property says it has the world's purest well water, there had better be plenty of good water when the buyer moves in. If a consumer believes the broker and relies on the representation, the broker may have a potential liability. The line between puffing and misrepresentation is subjective. It is best to simply avoid puffing.

PRINCIPAL'S OBLIGATIONS

The principal also has certain obligations to the agent. Although these do not receive much statutory attention in most states, they are important when the principal fails to live up to those obligations. The principal's primary obligation is **compensation.** Additionally, the agent is eligible for **reimbursement** for expenses not related to the sale itself. For example, if an agent had to pay a plumber to fix a broken pipe for the owner, the agent could expect reimbursement from the owner over and above the sales commission.

The other two obligations of the principal are indemnification and performance. An agent is entitled to **indemnification** upon suffering a loss through no fault of his own, such as when a misrepresentation by the principal to the agent was passed on in good faith to the buyer. The duty of **performance** means the principal is expected to do whatever he reasonably can to accomplish the purpose of the agency such as referring inquiries by prospective buyers to the broker.

BROKER'S SALES STAFF

A broker's sales associates are general agents of the broker. A sales associate owes the broker the duties of competence, obedience, accounting, loyalty, and full disclosure. The broker's

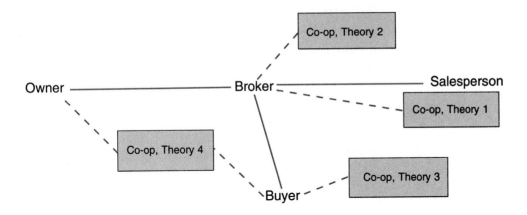

Figure 19:1. Theories of Agency

obligations to the sales associate are compensation, reimburse-ment, indemnification, and performance. In addition, the bro-ker will authorize the extent to which the sales associate can bind the broker. For example, is the sales associate's signature by itself sufficient to bind the broker to a listing or must the broker also sign it? With regard to third parties, the sales associate owes them honesty, integrity, and fair business dealings. Because a sales associate is an agent of the broker and the broker is an agent of the principal, the sales associate is called a **subagent** of the principal.

The fiduciary obligations of the cooperating broker is one of the most difficult legal problems of real estate brokerage. In ap-proximately 70% of all sales made through multiple listing services, the broker who locates the buyer is not the same broker that listed the property. This results in a dilemma: Is the broker who located the buyer (the **cooperating broker**) an agent of the buyer or the seller? There are four theories as to how this agency should work, illustrated in Figure 19:1.

 The traditional view (Theory 1) is that everyone is an agent (or subagent) of the seller because the seller has an employment contract with the listing broker and the cooperating broker has his rights through that employment contract and the MLS subagency presumption. Theory 2 is that since the cooperating broker has no contract with the seller (only an agreement to share with the listing broker) and none with the buyer, he is the agent of

COOPERATING BROKER

neither. Theory 3 is that the cooperating broker represents the buyer by virtue of the fact that the cooperating broker is trying to locate a suitable property for the buyer. Theory 4 is that the real estate broker can represent both parties, often referred to as being a dual agent.

The Complicating Issues

You will recall that the real estate broker has a fiduciary duty to the seller in our traditional listing relationship. Part of that duty is that he must make full disclosure of every item he knows concerning the real estate and his agency relationship. What then is an agent to do if a buyer gives him confidential information? If the agent pretends to be a dual agent, can he represent both parties and disclose all information to both without violating confidential relationships? In many cases it is not what the agent intends, but what the consumer perceives as the agent's duty of care. That is, does the buyer think that the cooperating broker represents him?

A recent Federal Trade Commission study found that 71% of buyers surveyed believe this to be the case. And buyers come to believe this because it is the cooperating broker who is spending time with them *and* is taking them to see properties *and* will write and present the offer *and*, if needed, come back with a counteroffer. Moreover, the cooperating broker hopes to make a good enough impression that a sale will be made and the buyer in the future will return to that broker for more real estate dealings.

Possible Alternatives

To better understand each of the legal theories involving the cooperating brokers duty of agency, each theory will be discussed individually. Simply stated, the theory is that the fiduciary duty of care runs to the party who has employed the broker; who pays the commission, by itself, is *not* a controlling issue.

Seller Representation, the Traditional View

One should assume that all real estate brokers represent the seller. The rules of agency are very simple. There is a fiduciary duty to the seller to disclose everything the agent knows and to achieve for that seller the highest price the market will bear. As previously discussed, the broker owes a high duty of care and honesty and integrity to the purchaser and must disclose those items which may harm or result in damage to the purchaser. The broker does not represent the purchaser, however, and there is no fiduciary duty to the purchaser of full disclosure and loyalty. Although overly simplistic, a simple analogy is to clothing salesmen. In this situation, the clothing salesman represents the store owner. His job is to sell the clothing for the highest price or marked price to consumers to generate a profit for the store owner. The salesman, however, is accommodating, helpful, informative, and wants the customer to be happy and return for subsequent purchases. There is no fiduciary duty, however, to that purchaser. Under some traditional lines of thinking, a real estate broker works in a similar capacity. He is a salesman working on behalf of the seller and owes his sole fiduciary duty to that party whom he represents, although he should always be accommodating and helpful to the purchaser.

Under the second legal theory, the broker operates as a middleman who represents neither party. He simply brings the parties together and neither party expects the middleman's loyalty. This middleman principle can work in some sophisticated real estate transactions. The problem with this theory though is that if either party thinks that the broker represents him, an agency relationship could be created and fiduciary duties established, resulting in potential liability for the broker. It is very difficult, in most situations, to represent neither party, yet still be an effective agent.

Middleman Principle

The third theory simply provides that the buyer hire a broker to represent him. In this case, it should be very clear that the buyer's broker is loyal to the buyer and is working to get the best deal for the buyer. Another benefit of buyer representation is that with the present system, buyers are shown only listed properties. The buyer's broker can investigate properties offered for sale by owners and can approach owners who have not put their properties on the market. As stated previously, the buyer's broker can be paid by the seller, he can split the commission with the listing broker, or he can be paid directly by the buyer.

Buyer's Broker

There are two basic drawbacks to buyer's brokerage. The first is that the average consumer is accustomed to a system where the seller pays the full cost of marketing the property and the public expects the broker to represent the seller. Certainly in most cases the buyer does not want to pay the broker out of his own pocket. The second and more serious issue is the situation in which the buyer represents or hires the broker and then decides that he wants to make an offer on one of the broker's listings. In this situation the broker has a fiduciary duty to his listing seller. He also has a fiduciary duty to the buyer that employed him to locate property. When this happens it results in the classic dual agency situation in which a broker has fiduciary duties to both parties. Many brokers, feeling a market niche representing buyers, have decided to take no listings to avoid the potential for conflict.

Dual Agency   If a broker represents a seller, it is the broker's duty to obtain the highest price and the best terms possible for the seller. If a broker represents a buyer, the broker's duty is to obtain the lowest price and best terms for the buyer. When the same broker represents two or more principals in the same transaction, it is a **dual** or **divided agency** and a conflict of interest results. If the broker represents both principals in the same transaction, to whom is the broker loyal? Does he work equally hard for each principal? This is an unanswerable question; therefore, the law requires that each principal be told not to expect the broker's full allegiance and thus each principal is responsible for looking after his own interest. If a broker represents more than one principal and does not obtain their consent, the broker cannot claim a commission and the defrauded principal(s) may be able to rescind the transaction. Moreover, the broker's real estate license may be suspended or revoked. This is true even though the broker does his best to be equally fair to each principal.

A dual agency also develops when a buyer agrees to pay a broker a fee for finding a property and the broker finds one, lists it, and earns a fee from the seller as well as the buyer. Again, both the buyer and seller must be informed of the dual agency in advance of negotiations. If either principal does not approve of the dual agency, he can refuse to participate.

Disclosure   One can easily see that the problem of agency representation particularly with the complication of the cooperating broker, can be a difficult subject. Agency relationships can be created without written agreements (ostensible authority), consumers can misunderstand the broker's role in a transaction, and there are very few rules under the traditional laws of agency that give the agent or the consumer an easy understanding of how the agency relationships work in the real world.

The simplest solution to this complicated problem is education, both for the real estate licensees and for the consumer. In many cases the brokers do not really understand which party they represent. For instance, if a broker's best friend requests some help in acquiring property and he wants to buy one of the broker's listings, it is easy to see the problem of divided loyalty a broker can encounter. The buyer on the other hand has requested the broker's help, and, as previously discussed, often thinks the broker represents him in these situations. The solutions have been developed through the National Association of Realtors, the National Association of Real Estate License Law Officials, and various state real estate commissions. That solution is merely disclosure to the extent that all parties to the transaction understand who the real estate licensee represents. Many states now have required disclosure forms which every licensee is required to use. A sample of a simplified version of these forms is shown as Figure 19:2. This form discloses to the buyer that the broker represents the seller in all transactions unless the buyer chooses to hire that broker to represent him. One should also note that the disclosure must be made very early in the transaction. Usually at the point of first significant contact with the buyer (i.e., obtaining specific information from the buyer as to his financial capacity, as to the property he wants to purchase, or other information which may be deemed to be confidential).

Another complication develops when the buyer decides that he wants the broker to represent him. Many states now provide that if you are going to be a buyer's broker, you must give a similar disclosure to the seller early in the transaction. A simplified version of this form is shown as Figure 19:3. Most state regulations provide that this form be given to the seller prior to submitting any written offers or prior to any personal contact with the seller. In both of these situations the purpose is to inform the opposing principal not to confide in the other party's agent.

Perhaps the most difficult problem is when you represent the buyer and the buyer requests that the broker submit an offer on one of his own listings. This clearly establishes a conflict of dual agency where the licensee represents the buyer and also represents the seller. There is simply no way you can disclose to both parties all the confidences that the broker knows without breaching his fiduciary duty. No state has outlawed dual agency, but this theory is still difficult to deal with in everyday

Figure 19-2. Agency Disclosure to Buyer

INFORMATION FOR A PROSPECTIVE REAL ESTATE BUYER OR TENANT

When working with a real estate broker in buying or leasing real estate, Texas law requires that you be informed of whom the broker is representing in the transaction.

As a prospective buyer or tenant, you should know that:

- Both the broker who lists property for sale or lease (the listing broker) and the broker who deals with a buyer or tenant (the "co-broker" or "selling" broker) are usually paid by the owner and are the owner's agents.

- Their duties, loyalties and faithfulness are owed to the owner, and they must inform the owner of all important information they know which might affect the owner's decision concerning the sale or lease of the property.

- While neither broker is your agent, the brokers can provide you with information about available properties and sources of financing and aid you in analyzing and comparing the physical and economic features of different properties, as well as showing you the properties and assisting you in making an offer to purchase or lease.

Both brokers are obligated by law to treat you honestly and fairly. They must:

- Present all written offers to the owner promptly.

- Disclose material facts about the property known to the broker.

- Offer the property without regard to race, creed, sex, religion or national origin.

If you choose to have a real estate broker represent you as your agent, you should enter into a written contract that:

- Clearly establishes the obligations of both parties; and,

- Sets out how your agent will be paid and by whom.

If you have any questions regarding the roles and responsibilities of real estate brokers, please ask.

I certify that I have provided _____

the Prospective Buyer or Tenant with a copy of this information.

_____
Broker or Sales Associate

_____
Date

I have received, read and understand this information.

_____
Prospective Buyer/Tenant or its representative

_____
Prospective Buyer/Tenant or its representative

Figure 19.3. Agency Disclosure to Seller

INFORMATION FOR A PROSPECTIVE REAL ESTATE SELLER OR LANDLORD

When working with a real estate broker in selling or leasing real estate, Texas law requires that you be informed of whom the broker is representing in the transaction.

As a prospective seller or landlord, you should know that:

- Broker is the agent of buyer or tenant.

- The duties, loyalties and faithfulness of a broker representing a buyer or tenant are owed to the buyer or tenant, and he must inform the buyer or tenant of all important information he knows which might affect the buyer or tenant's decision concerning the purchase or lease of the property.

Brokers are obligated by law to treat you honestly and fairly. They must:

- Present all written offers to the owner promptly.

- Disclose to the buyer or tenant material facts about the property known to the broker.

- Present or show property without regard to race, creed, sex, religion or national origin.

If you currently do not have a real estate broker representing you, and want to have one, you should enter into a written contract that:

- Clearly establishes the obligations of both parties; and,

- Sets out how your agent will be paid and by whom.

If you have any questions regarding the roles and responsibilities of real estate brokers, please ask.

I certify that I have provided the Prospective Seller or Landlord or its representative with a copy of this information.

_____
Brokerage Company Name

_____
Broker or Sales Associate

_____
Date

I have received, read and understand this information.

_____
Prospective Seller/Landlord or its representative

_____
Prospective Seller/Landlord or its representative

practice. A licensee is better advised to disclose his conflict of interest to both parties and offer to withdraw from the transaction if either party complains of his conflict.

There are two key factors in this disclosure of dual agency. The first is that it is the principal's decision to make, not the broker's. It is the principal that stands to lose on a breach of confidential information and has the most at risk. The second key factor in this disclosure is that the principals must understand how serious the conflict of interest is. A broker that says "here is a disclosure you have to sign—it's a required standard form" may not be making an effective disclosure. The broker must be sure that the parties understand who that broker represents and the nature of that confidential relationship. This should eliminate misplaced confidences.

PROPERTY DISCLOSURE STATEMENTS

The federal government through the Department of Housing and Urban Development (HUD) has enacted legislation aimed at protecting purchasers of property in new subdivisions from misrepresentation, fraud, and deceit. The HUD requirements, administered by the Office of Interstate Land Sales Registration, apply primarily to subdivision lots located in one state and sold to residents of another state. The purpose of this law, which took effect in 1969 and was amended in 1979, is to require that developers give prospective purchasers extensive disclosures regarding the lots in the form of a **property report.**

The requirement that a property report be prepared according to HUD specifications was the response of Congress to the concern that all too often buyers were receiving inaccurate or inadequate information. A color brochure might be handed to prospects picturing an artificial lake and boat marina within the subdivision, yet the developer has not obtained the necessary permits to build either and may never do so. Or, a developer implies that the lots being offered for sale are ready for building when in fact there is no sewer system and the soil cannot handle septic tanks. Or prospects are not told that many roads in the subdivision will not be built for several years, and when they are lot owners will face a hefty paving assessment followed by annual maintenance fees because the county has no intention of maintaining them as public roads.

In addition to addressing the above issues, the property report also discloses payment terms, what happens if there is a default, any soil problems, distance to school and stores, any additional costs to expect, availability of utilities, restrictive covenants, oil and mineral rights, etc. The property report must be given to each purchaser before a contract to purchase is signed. Failure to do so gives the purchaser the right to cancel any contract or agreement.

Property Report

The property report is *not* a government approval of the subdivision. It is strictly a disclosure of pertinent facts that the prospective purchaser is strongly encouraged to read before buying. A number of states also have enacted their own disclosure laws. Typically these apply to developers of housing subdivisions, condominiums, cooperatives, and vacant lots. In these reports the developer is required to make a number of pertinent disclosures about the lot, structure, owners' association, neighborhood, financing terms, etc., and this must be given to the prospective purchaser before a purchase contract can be signed. Once signed, HUD and most states allow the buyer a "cooling-off" period of from 3 to 7 days during which the buyer can cancel the contract and receive all his money back. Like the HUD property report, a state-required property report does not mean the state has approved or disapproved the subdivision. The property report is strictly a disclosure statement designed to help the prospective purchaser make an informed decision about buying.

Not an Approval

Federal antitrust laws, particularly the Sherman Antitrust Act, have made a major impact on the real estate brokerage industry. The purpose of federal antitrust laws is to promote competition in an open marketplace. To some people not familiar with the real estate business, it could appear that all real estate brokers charge the same fee (*i.e.*, 6%). In fact and in practice, nothing is further from the truth. Real estate brokers establish their fees from a complex integration of market factors, and all real estate brokerage fees are a result of a negotiated agreement between the owner and the broker. In tougher markets a broker may charge a much higher fee (10% to 12% of the gross sales price). Very expensive property, in a good market, may be listed by a

ANTITRUST LAWS

broker for an amount that is substantially less (2% to 5% of the gross sales price).

Price Fixing

Price fixing in any industry is so grossly anti-competitive and contrary to the free enterprise form of government that price fixing is construed to be "per se" illegal. This means that the conduct of price fixing is, in itself, so illegal that no series of mitigating circumstances can correct it. While a brokerage company can establish a policy on fees, they should be acutely aware that any hint, or any perceived hint, of price fixing between brokers can result in both civil and criminal penalties. That is, if the court determines that a broker has engaged in price fixing with another broker or group of brokers, the licensee could serve time in the federal penitentiary in addition to paying a substantial fine. Consequently, brokers are well advised *never* to discuss their fees, under *any* circumstances, except with the owner of the property.

Boycotting

Another aspect of antitrust laws which have affected brokers has been boycotting of other brokers in the marketplace. This, too, is a violation of the Sherman Antitrust Act. In some circumstances, realtor trade associations have established rules for membership which has resulted in some brokers being unfairly excluded (unreasonably high fees, part-time employment, "discount" brokers, etc.). Standards for membership are usually an attempt to upgrade the professionalism of the industry and maintain high standards. The difficulty that is encountered, however, is that high quality real estate brokers who are excluded from competing with members of broker trade associations results in an unfair market advantage. Antitrust cases involving boycotting have tended to recognize the procompetitive efforts of Boards of Realtors, MLS systems, and other similar trade associations, however. Therefore, Boards of Realtors and other trade associations can establish reasonable fees, residency requirements, and other, pertinent, requirements for membership. However no membership requirements can be established which may arbitrarily exclude licensed real estate brokers from participation.

1. When an agent is given the right to transact all types of matters on behalf of the principal, he serves as a
   A. notary public.
   B. third party.
   C. universal agent.
   D. special agent.

2. An agent who is authorized to bind his employer in a trade or business is
   A. a special agent.
   B. a general agent.
   C. an exclusive agent.
   D. a principal agent.

3. The relationship of a real estate broker to the owner of property listed for sale with the broker is that of a
   A. general agent.
   B. universal agent.
   C. limited agent.
   D. special agent.

4. An agent's authority may be granted by
   A. written agreement.
   B. custom in the industry.
   C. Both A and B.
   D. Neither A nor B.

5. When an agent's authority arises from custom in the industry, it is identified as
   A. implied authority.
   B. ostensible authority.
   C. customary authority.
   D. conventional authority.

6. An agency may be created by
   A. ratification.
   B. estoppel.
   C. Both A and B.
   D. Neither A nor B.

7. Broker Gomez was part owner of an apartment building along with two co-owners. When they decided to sell the building, broker Gomez was named as the agent in the listing agreement. Broker Gomez thus held an agency
   A. by ratification.
   B. coupled with an interest.
   C. by estoppel.
   D. by implication.

8. A broker has fiduciary responsibilities to
   A. the owner of property listed by him.
   B. third parties with whom he deals.
   C. Both A and B.
   D. Neither A nor B.

9. Fiduciary responsibilities of an agent to his principal include all of the following EXCEPT:
   A. faithful performance.
   B. loyalty.
   C. accounting for funds or property received.
   D. provision of legal advice.

10. A broker may act as an agent for both parties in a transaction only with the permission of
    A. the property owner.
    B. the real estate commission.
    C. both parties.
    D. the purchaser.

11. Isaacs introduced owner DiVita to prospect Park. DiVita and Park conducted negotiations among themselves without assistance from Isaacs. The role of Isaacs was that of a
    A. dual agent.
    B. middleman.
    C. single agent.
    D. cooperating broker.

12. Any earnest money deposits paid by the purchaser
    A. belong to the broker.
    B. must be placed in a proper trust account.
    C. Both A and B.
    D. Neither A nor B.

13. The placing of funds belonging to others in a broker's personal bank account constitutes
    A. commingling.
    B. grounds for revocation of the broker's license.
    C. Both A and B.
    D. Neither A nor B.

14. A broker who misrepresents a property to a prospect may be subject to all of the following EXCEPT:
    A. loss of his rights to a commission.
    B. revocation of his broker's license.
    C. criminal prosecution.
    D. civil action for damages.

15. An owner who gives false information regarding the listed property may be liable for
    A. a commission to the broker.   D. All of the above.
    B. cancellation of the sale.   E. None of the above.
    C. money damages to the purchaser.

16. A broker who intentionally misleads a prospect by making an incorrect statement which he knows is not true is
    A. guilty of fraud.   D. All of the above.
    B. subject to license revocation. E. None of the above.
    C. subject to litigation.

17. An agent who fails to investigate the cause of an apparent underlying defect in a property which he is selling may be found
    A. criminally liable.   C. guilty of a felony.
    B. liable for civil damages.   D. Both A and C.

18. A broker can indemnify himself against legal actions by those with whom he deals by purchasing
    A. errors and omissions insurance.
    B. middleman insurance.

19. The obligations of a principal to an agent include
    A. compensation.   D. performance.
    B. reimbursement.   E. All of the above.
    C. indemnification.

20. The relationship of a sales associate to the employing broker is
    A. that of a special agent.
    B. subject to all laws and rules of agency.
    C. an employer-employee relationship.
    D. that of a universal agent.

Fair Housing, Equal Credit, and Community Reinvestment

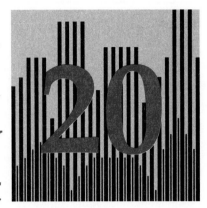

This chapter concentrates on federal legislation which has had a strong impact on expanding the ability of individuals to own real estate. The concept of fair housing prohibits discrimination in the purchase of real property. Equal credit has made lending sources available for thousands who could not previously qualify for loans. The Community Reinvestment Act encourages lenders to make loans in disadvantaged areas.

OVERVIEW OF
CHAPTER 20

LEARNING OBJECTIVES

After successful completion of this chapter, you should be able to:
1. Discuss the various types of fair housing violations.
2. Explain the applicability of the different fair housing statutes.
3. Describe the newest amendments to the Fair Housing Act.
4. Explain the prohibited requests of the ECOA.
5. Explain how credit applications are evaluated under the ECOA.
6. Describe the FHLBB guidelines of the CRA.

KEY • TERMS

Blockbusting: The illegal practice inducing panic selling in a neighborhood for financial gain

Community Reinvestment Act: Federal statute encouraging federally-regulated lenders to encourage their participation in low-income areas

Equal Credit Opportunity Act: Federal law that provides equal credit to borrowers

Fair Credit Reporting Act: Federal law giving an individual the right to inspect his or her file with the credit bureau and correct any errors

Familial status: One or more individuals under the age of eighteen who are domiciled with a parent or other person having custody

Handicapped: Having a physical or mental impairment which substantially limits one or more life activities, or having a record of such impairment.

Protected class: A class of people which by law are protected from discrimination

Steering: Practice of directing home seekers to particular neighborhoods based on race, color, religion, sex, national origin, or handicapped or adults-only status

Tester: An individual or organization that responds to or test for compliance with fair housing laws

It is almost impossible to fully explain the effects of federal legislation on real estate over the last 30 years. The scope and effect of the changes resulting from federal legislation is felt daily and has touched virtually every aspect of the real estate business. The federal government's emphasis on protection of individual rights was imposed because many states found this goal politically difficult to pursue, and in many cases a long history of prejudice was an overwhelming obstacle.

FAIR HOUSING

The federal legislation has been liberally applied to virtually all areas of discrimination—race, color, creed, national origin, alienage, sex, marital status, age, familial status, and handicapped status. The theories supporting these federal laws are applied differently though, depending on the source of the law and enforcement of the applicable statute. Let's review these theories in greater detail.

CONSTITUTIONAL IMPACT ON OWNERSHIP OF REAL PROPERTY

The most fundamental rights in real property are obtained in the U.S. Constitution. These rights are so firmly established and so broadly affect real estate that they deserve discussion at the outset. The Declaration of Independence declared that all men are created equal and set the stage for an attitude of the government which we enjoy in the United States. It was with this forethought that our founders wrote the United States Constitution which instilled in all citizens certain inalienable rights of which they can never be deprived. As far as real property ownership is concerned, the most significant of these rights are stated in the Fifth, Fourteenth, and Thirteenth Amendments to the Constitution.

The Fifth Amendment clearly states that no person shall "... be deprived of life, liberty, or property without due process of law, ..." It was from this fundamental statement that we have developed the inherent right that nobody can have their property taken from them without court proceedings. This concept has been expanded over the last 25 years or so to include the prohibition of certain types of discrimination, creating certain "protected classes" of people who may not be discriminated against.

To date, the types of discrimination which have been deemed "suspect" by the United States Supreme Court have included discrimination on the basis of race, color, religion, national origin, and alienage. This is logical in that a citizen of the United States cannot alter his race, color, national origin, or alienage, and is entitled to practice the religion of his choice. Therefore, very strict constitutional prohibitions have been established by the courts to eliminate this type of discrimination for any other citizen in the United States. It should be emphasized that there is no *constitutional* prohibition of discrimination on the basis of sex, age, or marital status.

One of the most significant areas of litigation has been based on racial discrimination. This has been applied to all federal activity through the Fifth Amendment, and to state and individual actions through enforcement of interpretation of the Thirteenth and Fourteenth Amendments to the Constitution.

The Fourteenth Amendment prohibits any state (as distinguished from the federal government) from depriving a person of life, liberty, or property without due process of law, and prohibits any state from denying any person within its jurisdiction the equal protection of the laws. The significant case in interpreting the Fourteenth Amendment as it applies to the states was *Shelley v. Kraemer.* In this Supreme Court case, some white property owners were attempting to enforce a deed restriction which required that all property owners must be Caucasian. The state courts granted the relief sought. The

Supreme Court, however, reversed the case, stating that the action of state courts in imposing penalties deprive parties of other substantive rights without providing adequate notice. The opportunity to defend has long been regarded as a denial of due process of law as guaranteed by the Fourteenth Amendment. The court stated that equality and the enjoyment of property rights was regarded by the framers of the Fourteenth Amendment as an essential precondition to realization of other basic civil rights and liberties which the Fourteenth Amendment was intended to guaranty. Therefore, it was concluded that the "equal protection" clause of the Fourteenth Amendment should prohibit the judicial enforcement by state courts of restrictive covenants based on race or color.

The Thirteenth Amendment to the United States Constitution prohibits slavery and involuntary servitude. This amendment formed the basis for the most significant landmark case on discrimination, *Jones v. Alfred H. Mayer Company.* That case basically held that any form of discrimination, even by individuals, creates a "badge of slavery" which in turn results in the violation of the Thirteenth Amendment. The Supreme Court stated that in enforcing the Civil Rights Act of 1866, Congress is empowered under the Thirteenth Amendment to secure to all citizens the right to buy whatever a white man can buy and the right to live wherever a white man can live. The court further stated, "If Congress cannot say that being a free man means at least this much, then the Thirteenth Amendment has a promise the Nation cannot keep." This case effectively prohibits discrimination of all types and is applicable to real estate transactions.

FAIR HOUSING LAWS   In addition to the constitutional issues, there are two major federal laws that prohibit discrimination in housing. The first is the Civil Rights Act of 1866. It states that, "All citizens of the United States shall have the same right in every State and Territory, as is enjoyed by the white citizens thereof to inherit, purchase, lease, sell, hold, and convey real and personal property." In 1968, the Supreme Court affirmed that the 1866 act prohibits "all racial discrimination, private as well as public, in the sale of real property." The second is the **Fair Housing Law,** officially known as Title VIII of the Civil Rights Act of 1968, as amended. This law makes it illegal to discriminate on the basis of race, color, religion, sex, national origin, physical handicap, or familial status in connection with the sale or rental of housing and any vacant land offered for residential construction or use.

In 1988, the president signed a new amendment to the Civil *New Amendments* Rights Act of 1968 which became effective on March 12, 1989. It expands the Civil Rights Act of 1968 to provide for housing for the handicapped as well as people with children under the age of 18. The Civil Rights Act now provides protection for any form of discrimination based on race, color, religion, national origin, sex, *familial status,* or *handicapped status.* The new law's application may be very broad, and needs to be discussed in more detail.

The new amendment defines *handicapped* as: Handicapped

1. having a physical or mental impairment which substantially limits one or more major life activities; or
2. having a record of having such an impairment; or
3. being regarded as having such an impairment.

The act apparently includes recovered mental patients as well as those who are presently suffering from a mental handicap.

The full extent of how the discrimination against handicapped will affect us is really not known. It is surely going to change our attitude about certain restrictions. It is assumed, for instance, that a blind person could live with a guide dog in a housing project that prohibits pets. The handicapped are also allowed to make reasonable modifications to existing units, as long as it is at the handicapped's expense. The handicapped renter must also restore the unit to its original use upon termination of occupancy. The law also makes it unlawful for a landlord or owner to refuse to make reasonable accommodations, rules, policies, practices, or services when it is necessary to afford a handicapped person an equal opportunity to use and enjoy the dwelling. In addition, all new multifamily dwellings with four or more units must be constructed to allow access and use by handicapped persons. If the building has no elevators, only first floor units are covered by this provision. Doors and hallways in the buildings must be wide enough to accommodate wheelchairs. Light switches and other controls must be in convenient locations. Most rooms and spaces must be on an accessible route, and special accommodations such as grab bars in the bathrooms must be provided.

There are some exceptions under the handicapped person provision. The term *handicapped* for instance, does not include current illegal use of or addiction to a controlled substance. Nor does handicapped status include any person whose tenancy imposes a direct threat to the health, safety, and property of others. *However, there are no guidelines as to how a licensee, apartment manager, or homeowner's association can determine either of these two exceptions.* Since there are no clear guidelines, all licensees are advised to treat all people they perceive to have a mental or physical handicap as members of a protected class of individuals which may not under any circumstances be discriminated against.

Familial Status

Familial status is defined as one or more individuals (who have not obtained the age of 18 years) being domiciled with a parent or another person having legal custody of such individual or individuals or the designee of such parent or other person having such custody, with the written permission of such parent or other person. These protections also apply to any person who is pregnant or is in the process of securing legal custody of any individual who has not obtained the age of 18 years.

The most significant effect of this amendment is that all homeowner association property, apartment projects, and condominiums now have to have facilities adapted for children and cannot discriminate against anyone on the basis of familial status when leasing, selling, or renting property.

There are specific exemptions to this portion of the act also. A building can qualify for an exemption if: 1) it provides housing under the state or federal program that the Secretary of Housing and Urban Development determines is specifically designed and operated to assist elderly persons; or 2) it provides housing intended for, and is generally occupied only by, persons 62 years of age or older; or 3) it provides housing generally intended and operated for at least one person 55 years of age or older per unit and meets certain regulations which will be adopted by the Secretary of Housing and Urban Development.

The penalties for violation of the act are severe. The first violation of the act results in a fine of not more than $50,000, and for subsequent violations, a fine of not more than $100,000. The fines are in addition to other civil damages, potential injunctions, reasonable attorney's fees, and costs.

These new amendments to the Fair Housing Law have a significant impact for all licensees attempting to sell, list, lease, or rent real estate. It is now going to be unlawful to refuse to sell or rent or to refuse to negotiate the sale or rental of any property based on familial status or handicapped status. Any printing and advertising cannot make any reference to preference based on handicapped or familial status. As stated previously, the landlord cannot deny the right of a handicapped tenant to make any changes in the physical structure of the building provided that the tenant agrees to reinstate the building back to its original form when he leaves.

It is safe to say that there are a lot of fact situations and circumstances which will occur that have not been specifically addressed by the statute. It is critically important that licensees recognize these two new prohibitions against discrimination and deem them just as serious violations of an individual's civil rights as are more traditional theories of race, color, religion, national origin, and sex.

Specifically, what do these two federal statutes prohibit, and what do they allow? The 1968 Fair Housing Law provides protection against the following acts if they discriminate against one or more of the protected classes:

1. Refusing to sell or rent to, deal or negotiate with any person;
2. Discriminating in the terms or conditions for buying or renting housing;
3. Discriminating by advertising that housing is available only to persons of a certain race, color, religion, sex, or national origin, those who are not handicapped, or adults only;
4. Denying that housing is available for inspection, sale, or rent when it really is available;
5. Denying or making different terms or conditions for home loans by commercial lenders;
6. Denying to anyone the use of or participation in any real estate services, such as brokers' organizations, multiple listing services, or other facilities related to the selling or renting of housing;
7. Steering or blockbusting

Steering

Steering is the practice of directing home seekers to particular neighborhoods based on race, color, religion, sex, national origin, non handicapped, or adult only housing. Steering includes efforts to exclude minority members from one area of a city as well as to direct them to minority or changing areas. Examples include showing only certain neighborhoods, slanting property descriptions, and downgrading neighborhoods. Steering is often subtle, sometimes no more than a word, phrase, or facial expression. Nonetheless, steering accounts for the bulk of the complaints filed against real estate licensees under the Fair Housing Act.

Blockbusting

Blockbusting is the illegal practice of inducing panic selling in a neighborhood for financial gain. Blockbusting typically starts when one person induces another to sell his property cheaply by stating that an impending change in the racial or religious composition of the neighborhood will cause property values to fall, school quality to decline, and crime to increase. The first home thus acquired is sold (at a mark-up) to a minority member. This event is used to reinforce fears that the neighborhood is indeed changing. The process quickly snowballs as residents panic and sell at progressively lower prices. The homes are then resold at higher prices to incoming residents.

Note that blockbusting is not limited to fears over people moving into a neighborhood. In a Virginia case, a real estate firm attempted to gain listings in a certain neighborhood by playing upon residents' fears regarding an upcoming expressway project.

Housing Covered by the 1968 Fair Housing Law

The 1968 Fair Housing Law applies to the following types of housing:

1. Single-family houses owned by private individuals when (1) a real estate broker or other person in the business of selling or renting dwellings is used and/or (2) discriminatory advertising is used;
2. Single-family houses not owned by private individuals;
3. Single-family houses owned by a private individual who owns more than three such houses or who, in any two-year period, sells more than one in which the individual was not the most recent resident;
4. Multi-family dwellings of five or more units;

5. Multi-family dwellings containing four or fewer units, if the owner does not reside in one of the units.

Not covered by the 1968 Fair Housing Law are the sale or rental of single-family houses owned by a private individual who owns three or fewer such single-family houses if (1) a broker is not used, (2) discriminatory advertising is not used, and (3) no more than one house in which the owner was not the most recent resident is sold during any two-year period. Not covered by the 1968 Act are rentals of rooms or units in owner-occupied multidwellings for two to four families, if discriminatory advertising is not used. The act also does not cover the sale, rental, or occupancy of dwellings which a religious organization owns or operates for other than a commercial purpose to persons of the same religion, if membership in that religion is not restricted on account of race, color, or national origin. It also does not cover the rental or occupancy of lodgings which a private club owns or operates for its members for other than a commercial purpose. Housing for the elderly may also allow discrimination in not permitting children or young adult occupants in the development or building, provided that the housing is primarily intended for the elderly, has minimum age requirements (55 or 62), and meets certain HUD guidelines.

Acts Not Prohibited by the 1968 Fair Housing Law

Note, however, that the above listed acts *not* prohibited by the 1968 Fair Housing Law *are* prohibited by the 1866 Civil Rights Act when discrimination based on race occurs in connection with such acts.

There are three ways that adherence to the 1968 act can be enforced by someone who feels discriminated against. The first is to file a written complaint with the Department of Housing and Urban Development in Washington, D.C. The second is to file court action directly in a U.S. District Court or state or local court. The third is to file a complaint with the U.S. Attorney General. If a complaint is filed with HUD, HUD may investigate to see if the law has been broken, may attempt to resolve the problem by conference, conciliation, or persuasion, may refer the matter to a state or local fair housing authority, or may recommend that the complaint be filed in court. A person seeking enforcement of the 1866 act must file a suit in a Federal court.

Fair Housing Enforcement

No matter which route is taken, the burden of proving illegal discrimination under the 1968 act is the responsibility of the person filing the complaint. If successful, the following remedies are available: (1) an injunction to stop the sale or rental of the property to someone else making it available to the complainant, (2) money for actual damages caused by the discrimination, (3) punitive damages, and (4) court costs. There are also criminal penalties for those who coerce, intimidate, threaten, or interfere with a person's buying, renting, or selling of housing.

Agent's Duties

A real estate agent's duties are to uphold the 1968 Fair Housing Law and the 1866 Civil Rights Act. If a property owner asks an agent to discriminate, the agent must refuse to accept the listing. An agent is in violation of fair housing laws by giving a minority buyer or seller less than favorable treatment or by ignoring him or referring him to an agent of the same minority. Violation also occurs when an agent fails to use best efforts, does not submit an offer because of race, color, religion, sex, national origin, physical handicap, or occupancy by children.

Testers

From time to time a licensee may be approached by fair housing testers. These are individuals or organizations that respond to advertising and visit real estate offices to test for compliance with fair housing laws. The tester does not announce himself or herself as such or ask if the office follows fair housing practices. Rather, the tester plays the role of a person looking for housing to buy or rent and observes whether or not fair housing laws are being followed. If not followed, the tester lodges a complaint with the appropriate fair housing agency.

State Laws

What has been said so far has to do with federal housing laws. In addition, many states, counties, and cities have enacted their own fair housing laws. You will need to contact local fair housing authorities as these laws often go beyond the federal laws. For example, within some states it is illegal to discriminate on the basis of age, marital status, presence of children, physical handicap, sexual orientation, and welfare status. Within other states, an owner-occupant may discriminate only in his own single-family or two-family home, not the four-family building allowed in the 1968 act.

The Equal Credit Opportunity Act was originally passed to provide for equal credit for borrowers by making it unlawful to discriminate against an applicant for credit based on sex or marital status. In 1976 the act was amended to prohibit discrimination in any credit transaction based on race, color, religion, national origin, age (not including minors), receipt of income from a public assistance program, and the good faith exercise of rights under the Consumer Credit Protection Act.

EQUAL CREDIT OPPORTUNITY ACT

To effect this prohibition on discrimination, a creditor is prohibited from requiring certain information from the borrower:

Prohibited Requests

1. Information concerning a spouse or former spouse, except when that spouse will be contractually obligated for repayment or if the spouse resides in a community property state;
2. Information regarding the applicant's marital status unless the credit requested is for an individual's unsecured account, or unless the applicant resides in a community property state and the community property is to be relied upon to repay the credit. Inquiries as to the applicant's marital status are limited, however, to categories of "married," "unmarried," and "separated." "Unmarried" includes single, divorced, and widowed persons and may be specified in the application.
3. Information concerning the source of an applicant's income without disclosing that information regarding alimony, child support, or separate maintenance is to be furnished only at the option of the applicant. The big exception to the rule is when the applicant expects to use any of those sources of income for repayment. If so, the lender may request this information.
4. Information regarding an applicant's birth control practices or any intentions concerning the bearing or rearing of children, although a lender still has the right to ask an applicant about the number and ages of any dependents or about dependent-related financial obligations.
5. Questions regarding race, color, religion, or national origin of the applicant.

There are minor exceptions when a real estate loan is involved. These exceptions are allowed in order to provide certain information that may be used by the federal government for the purposes of monitoring conformance with the Equal Credit Opportunity Act. When the information is requested, the lender is required to advise the applicants that the furnishing of the specific information is for purposes of monitoring the lender's compliance and is requested on a voluntary basis only. If the applicant does not wish to answer the questions, the lender simply notes the refusal on the application form. The refusal to give the information requested cannot be used in any way in considering whether or not credit is granted to the applicant. If the applicant agrees to provide the information on a voluntary basis, the following information can be furnished:

1. Race or national origin;
2. Sex, relating to gender only (not sexual preference);
3. Marital status (using the categories of married, unmarried, or separated);

When considering race and national origin only the following categories can be used: American Indian or Alaskan Native, Asian or Pacific Islander, Black, White, Hispanic, or "other."

Evaluating Credit Applications

As previously stated, the lender cannot use information obtained from an applicant which might be considered to be discriminatory. Each applicant has to be evaluated on the same basic information as any other individual person. Lenders can't refuse credit based on individual category, such as newlyweds, recent divorcees, etc. The lender's rules must be applied uniformly to all applicants. The areas in which there can be no discrimination have already been discussed (sex, marital status, race, color, religion, national origin, age, public assistance) but some of these areas need to be discussed in greater detail.

Age

A lender is prohibited from taking an applicant's age into account in determining their ability to repay. The only exception to this prohibition is minors, who lack contractual capacity and cannot enter into real estate transactions.

Children

As discussed in the previous sections on fair housing, the Equal Credit Opportunity Act has always provided that there can be no assumptions or statistics relating to the likelihood that a group of persons may bear children. In prior years, lenders required non pregnancy affidavits and other indications that a young newly married couple would not endanger the income-producing capacity of the wife.

Income from part-time employment or retirement income cannot be discounted because of the basis of its source. However, the creditor may still consider the amount and probability of continuance of such income.

Part-time Income

Alimony and child support and separate maintenance cannot be considered in evaluating a loan application unless the creditor determines that such payments are not likely to be made consistently. In such cases the lender has the right to determine whether or not the applicant has the ability to compel payment and the credit worthiness of the party who is obligated to make such payments.

Alimony and Child Support

The Equal Credit Opportunity Act requires a creditor to consider the separate record of the applicant. This prohibits the lender from tying the applicant's credit history to the past record of the spouse or former spouse.

Credit History

A creditor may consider an applicant's immigration status and whether or not he or she is a permanent resident of the United States.

Immigration Residency

If an applicant is denied credit the lender must give notice to the applicant and advise the rejected applicant of the federal agency that administers compliance with the Equal Credit Opportunity Act for that particular loan transaction. The statement of specific reasons must give the precise reason or reasons for the denial of credit. There are suggested guidelines for giving reasons for credit denial including:

Credit Denial

1. unable to verify credit references;
2. temporary or irregular employment;
3. insufficient length of employment;
4. insufficient income;
5. excessive obligations;
6. inadequate collateral;
7. too short a period of residency;
8. delinquent credit obligation.

Failure to comply with the Equal Credit Opportunity Act or the accompanying federal regulations makes a creditor subject to a civil liability for damages limited to $10,000 in individual actions

Penalties

and the lesser of $500,000 or 1% of the creditor's net worth in class actions. The court may also award court costs and reasonable attorney's fees to an aggrieved applicant.

COMMUNITY REINVESTMENT ACT

The Housing and Community Redevelopment Act of 1977 took effect on November 6, 1978. The Community Reinvestment Act (CRA) expands the concept that regulated financial institutions must serve the needs of their communities. Whenever a financing institution regulated by the federal government applies for a charter, branch facility, office relocation, or acquisition of another financing institution, the record of the institution's help in meeting local credit needs must be one of the factors considered by the Federal Home Loan Bank Board.

The basic requirements of the Community Reinvestment Act for any institution applying for recognition are the following:

1. The institution must define its community by drawing a map that shows the areas served by the lender. This is essentially the area in which it does business and may overlap the area of another institution.
2. The institution must submit a list of types of credit it offers in that community. This list must also be made available to the public. The decision as to what types of loans an institution makes is still left to the institution, but the information must be made available to the public.
3. The lender must provide notice in its lobby that its performance is being evaluated by federal regulators. The notice must advise that a CRA statement and a File of Public Comments are available.

CRA Statement

The CRA Statement, which must be made available to the public as well as the federal regulators, calls for mandatory information and some optional information which the statement should contain. The mandatory information consists of the following:

1. A map of the lender's definition of its community;
2. A list of credit services it offers;
3. Copy of the public notice; and
4. A File of Public Comments received in the past two years that relate to the CRA Statement.

The optional information which should be contained in the CRA Statement consists of:

1. A description of how current efforts help meet community needs and standards;
2. A periodic report of the institution's record in helping to meet community credit needs; and
3. A description of efforts made to ascertain credit needs of the community.

Part of the enforcement procedure of the Community Reinvestment Act calls for open hearings to be held on an application for a branch or any other internal expansions should a protest be lodged against that expansion. Anyone may be asked to be placed on the list for notification of all pending applications. The federal regulating authority must determine whether or not a protest is "substantial" and could therefore justify a hearing within ten days of the protest filing.

The Federal Home Loan Bank Board (FHLBB) has listed the following guidelines that various federal examiners look for when assessing CRA performances. Three major areas that require examination fall under Section 563e.7 of the Insurance of Accounts Regulations and are numbered (b), (h), and (j) of the Community Reinvestment Act.

FHLBB Guidelines

   Subsection (b) concerns the extent of the institution's marketing and special credit-related programs to make members of the community aware of the credit services offered by the institution, such as public seminars, direct mailings or media campaigns, foreign language advertising, financial counseling, cooperative efforts with local governments or community groups seeking code compliance, technical assistance for revitalization of their neighborhoods. Subsection (h) deals with the institution's participation including investments, and local community development or redevelopment projects or programs. This includes HUD programs, economic development strategies, neighborhood reinvestment corporations, and neighborhood preservation projects.

   Subsection (j) relates to the institution's participation in government insured, guaranteed, or subsidized loan programs for housing, small businesses, or small farms. This includes the lending institution's participation in government HUD programs, Veterans Administration programs, Department of Agriculture programs for rural housing loans guaranteed by the Farmer's Home Administration, or Small Business Administration loans. Other participation which can help to satisfy in both Subsections (h) and (j) involve community development block grants established by HUD. Housing finance agency development, rehabilitation, or home improvement programs for lower and moderate income residents are local development company loan programs.

Minorities
Most statutes and constitutions prohibit discrimination against **minorities.** Minorities are defined as any group, or any member of a group that can be identified either: 1) by race, color, religion, sex, or national origin; or 2) by any other characteristic on the basis of which discrimination is prohibited by federal, state, or local fair housing law. It is not always a small group; it refers to any group that can be distinguished in a particular situation from some other group on a basis of race, sex, national origin, or so forth. It has nothing to do with numbers or size of the group. Whenever whites are discriminated against, they too are a minority group.

It is very difficult to ascertain what impact the Community Reinvestment Act will have on lending institutions and practices of lenders generally. Many areas of the statute are vague, and it is difficult for the federal regulators to establish hard and fast rules because of the variety of different needs the lending institutions generally serve in different communities. As with a lot of other federal legislation, it may take some time before the full impact of this act is felt.

REVIEW QUESTIONS

1. Discrimination in the availability of housing on the basis of race is prohibited by the
   A. Civil Rights Act of 1866.
   B. Fair Housing Act of 1968.
   C. Both A and B.
   D. Neither A nor B.

2. Vera, a real estate broker, was offered a rental listing by a homeowner who stated that he would not rent the property to a person of certain religious beliefs. Vera should
   A. refuse to accept the listing on these terms.
   B. accept the listing and leave it up to the owner to refuse any offers received from persons of that religion.
   C. accept the listing and steer persons of that religion to other properties.
   D. file a complaint of discrimination against the owner.

3. Under federal law, the owner of one single-family dwelling in which he has resided for ten years, who does not employ an agent and does not use discriminatory advertising, may discriminate in the sale or rental of the property on any of the following bases EXCEPT:
   A. religion.
   B. race.
   C. color.
   D. national origin.

4. State and local laws which restrict or prohibit discrimination in the availability of rental housing may
   A. be more restrictive than federal statutes.
   B. prohibit additional forms of discrimination.
   C. Both A and B.
   D. Neither A nor B.

5. The Civil Rights Act of 1866 prohibits
   A. racial discrimination.
   B. steering.
   C. blockbusting.
   D. discrimination for any reason.

6. All of the following are prohibited by the Fair Housing Act of 1968, as amended, EXCEPT:
   A. discrimination in advertising.
   B. denial of availability of housing on the basis of religion.
   C. discrimination in terms or conditions for sale or rent.
   D. discrimination on the basis of age.

7. An amendment to the Fair Housing Act of 1968, signed by the President in 1988 prohibits:
   A. discrimination on the basis of physical handicap.
   B. the offering of different loan terms by commercial lenders based on race or religion of the loan applicant.
   C. refusal to sell, rent, or negotiate with any person.
   D. steering and blockbusting.

8. The practice of directing homeseekers to particular neighborhoods based on race, color, religion, sex, or national origin
   A. is known as steering.
   B. is prohibited by the Civil Rights Act of 1866.
   C. constitutes blockbusting.
   D. None of the above.
   E. All of the above.

9. All of the following are true for the inducement of panic selling in a neighborhood for financial gain EXCEPT:
   A. it is prohibited by the Fair Housing Act of 1968.
   B. it is limited to fear of loss of value because of the changing of the racial composition of a neighborhood.
   C. it is known as blockbusting.
   D. the prohibition applies to licensed real estate agents.

10. The Fair Housing Act of 1968 applies to
    A. single-family housing.
    B. multiple dwellings.
    C. Both A and B.
    D. Neither A nor B.

11. A church which operates housing for the elderly may restrict occupancy to members of the church if
   A.   membership in the church is open to all persons.
   B.   the units are to be rented, but not if they are being offered for sale.
   C.   Both A and B.
   D.   Neither A nor B.

12. A victim of discrimination in housing may seek enforcement of the 1968 Fair Housing Act by any of the following means EXCEPT:
   A.   filing a complaint with the Department of Housing and Urban Development.
   B.   filing action in federal court.
   C.   filing a complaint with the U.S. Attorney General.
   D.   filing a complaint with the state real estate department.

13. A person seeking enforcement of the Civil Rights Act of 1866 may do so by filing
   A.   an action in federal court.
   B.   a complaint with the U.S. Attorney General.
   C.   an action in county court.
   D.   a complaint with HUD.

14. A licensed real estate agent is offered a listing by an owner who stipulates that he will not sell to any person of a certain national origin. The agent should
   A.   accept the listing and leave it up to the owner to reject offers from these persons.
   B.   refuse to accept the listing.
   C.   report the owner to the real estate department.
   D.   file a complain against the owner with HUD.

15. The Sunset Hills Country Club has several guest bedrooms which are made available to members and guests for a nominal charge, but are not available to the general public. Does this constitute a violation of the federal fair housing laws?
   A.   Yes, because rental housing of this nature must be open to the public.
   B.   Yes, because the charging of a fee constitutes a commercial purpose.
   C.   No, because the club is exempt under the provisions of the Fair Housing Act of 1968.
   D.   No, because this does not constitute steering or blockbusting.

Condominiums, Cooperatives, PUDs, and Timeshares

This chapter covers the history of condominiums, U.S. housing laws, and methods of dividing the land. The condominium declaration is covered in some detail. Other topics include management, maintenance fees, taxes, insurance, and financing. The advantages and disadvantages of condominium living are listed along with a list of things to check before buying. Other condo topics include a discussion of legislation, condo conversions, and physical appearance. Cooperative apartments, PUDs, and Timesharing are also covered.

LEARNING OBJECTIVES

After successful completion of this chapter, you should be able to:

1. Explain the concepts of dividing the land and land-use efficiency.
2. Describe the features of the condominium declaration.
3. Explain the advantages and disadvantages of condo living.
4. Describe condo financing and conversions.
5. Explain the features of both timesharing and cooperative apartments.
6. Define the PUD and explain its purpose.
7. Describe the key features of resort timesharing.
8. Describe the unique character of condominium financing.
9. List what to inspect prior to buying.

KEY • TERMS

Bylaws: rules that govern how an owners' association will be run

CC&Rs: covenants, conditions, and restrictions by which a property owner agrees to abide

Common elements: those parts of a condominium which are owned by all the unit owners

Condominium: individual ownership of a space of air plus undivided ownership of the common elements

Cooperative: land and building owned or leased by a corporation which, in turn, leases space to its shareholders

Limited common elements: common elements whose use is limited to certain owners

Planned Unit Development: individually owned lots and houses with community ownership of common areas

Proprietary lease: a lease issued by a cooperative corporation to its shareholders

Reserves: money set aside for expenses that do not occur every month

Timesharing: the exclusive use of a property for a specified number of days each year

HISTORY   The idea of combining community living with community ownership is not new. Two thousand years ago the Roman Senate passed condominium laws that permitted Roman citizens to own individual dwelling units in multiunit buildings. This form of ownership resulted because land was scarce and expensive in Rome. After the fall of the Roman Empire, condominium ownership was used in the walled cities of the Middle Ages. Here it was primarily a defensive measure since residing outside the walls was dangerous because of roving bands of raiders. With the stabilization of governments after the Middle Ages, the condominium concept became dormant. Then in the early twentieth century, in response to land scarcity in cities, the idea was revived in Western Europe. From there the concept spread to several Latin American countries and, in 1951, to Puerto Rico. Puerto Rican laws and experience in turn became the basis for passage by Congress in 1961 of Section 234 of the National Housing Act. Designed as a legal model that condominium developers could follow in order to obtain FHA loan insurance, Section 234 also served as a model for state condominium laws now in effect across the United States.

In this chapter we'll begin with a discussion of condominiums, in particular an overview of their organization, operation, benefits, and drawbacks. Then we'll turn our attention to cooperatives, planned unit developments, and time-sharing.

The first step in creating a **condominium** is for the state to pass laws that create the legal framework for condominium ownership. All states have passed them, and they are variously known as a state's horizontal property act, strata titles act, **condominium act**, or a similar name. They all follow the FHA model plus each state's particular refinements. As the names suggest, these laws address the problem of subdividing the airspace over a given parcel of land. Prior to these acts, the legal framework that made it possible for people to own a cubicle of airspace plus an undivided interest in the shell of the building and the land under and around the building did not exist. Moreover, condominium acts had to be designed to be acceptable to lenders who would be asked to loan on condominiums, property tax authorities who would have to assess them, and income tax authorities who would allow owners to deduct loan interest and property taxes. The lawmakers were successful, and today millions of people live in condominiums.

CONDOMINIUM

Physically, a condominium can take the shape of a 2-story garden apartment building, a 40-story tower with several living units on each floor, row houses, clustered houses, or even detached houses sharing a single parcel of land. Condominiums are not restricted to residential uses. In recent years, a number of developers across the nation have built office buildings and sold individual suites to doctors, dentists, and lawyers. The same idea has been applied to shopping centers and industrial space. A condominium does not have to be a new building: many existing apartment houses have been converted from rental status to condominium ownership with only a few physical changes to the building.

The distinguishing features of a condominium are its separate and common elements and its system of self-government. The separate elements, called **separate property,** are those areas in the condominium that are exclusively owned and used by the individual condominium owners. These are the individual dwelling units in the building. More precisely, the separate property is the airspace occupied by a unit. This is the space lying between the interior surfaces of the unit walls and between the floor and the ceiling. Everything else is a common element

Separate and Common Elements

in which each unit owner holds an undivided interest. Thus the land and the shell of the building are **common elements** owned by all. Common elements include, for example, the manager's apartment, lobby, hallways, stairways, elevators, recreation areas, landscaping, and parking lot. Sometimes you will hear the term **limited common element.** This is a common element the use of which is restricted to a specific unit owner. Examples are assigned parking stalls and individual storage units.

Owners' Association

When a developer wants to create a condominium (either built from the ground up or the conversion of an existing building to condominium ownership), the developer prepares and records with the public recorder what is variously known as an enabling declaration, master deed, plan of condominium ownership, or **condominium subdivision.** This document, usually 50 to 150 pages long, converts a parcel of land held under a single deed into a number of individual separate property estates (the condominium units) and an estate composed of all the common elements. Survey maps are included to show the location of each condominium unit plus all the common elements.

The developer also creates a legal framework so that the unit owners can govern themselves. This is the condominium **owners' association** of which each unit purchaser automatically becomes a member. Although the association can be organized as a trust or unincorporated association, most often it will be organized as a corporation in order to provide the legal protections normally afforded by a corporation to its owners. Additionally, it will be organized as not-for-profit so as to avoid income taxes on money collected from members. The main purpose of the owners' association is to control, regulate, and maintain the common elements for the overall welfare and benefit of its members. The owners' association is a mini-government by and for the condominium owners.

Bylaws

The rules by which an owners' association operates are called its **bylaws.** They are prepared by the developer's attorney and recorded with the master deed. The bylaws provide the rules by which the association's board of directors is elected and set the standards by which the board must rule. The bylaws set forth how association dues (maintenance fees) will be established and collected, how contracts will be let for maintenance, management, and repair work, and how personnel will be hired.

Finally, the developer must file a list of regulations by which anyone purchasing a unit in the condominium must abide. These are known as **covenants, conditions, and restrictions (CC&Rs).** They tell a unit owner such things as not to store personal items on balconies or driveways, what color the exterior of the living room drapes should be, to what extent an owner can alter the exterior of his unit, and whether or not an owner can install a satellite television dish on the roof. Additional regulations may be embodied in a set of **house rules.** Typically, these govern such things as when the swimming pool and other recreation facilities will be open for use and when quiet hours will be observed in the building.

CC&Rs

Each purchaser of a condominium unit receives a deed from the developer. The deed describes the location of the unit, both in terms of the unit number in the building and its surveyed airspace. The deed will also describe the common elements and state the percentage interest in the common elements that the grantee is receiving. The deed is recorded upon closing just like a deed to a house.

Deed

Upon selling, the owner has a new deed prepared that describes the unit and the common element interest and delivers it to the purchaser at closing. If the condominium is on leased land, the developer will deliver a lease (or sublease) to the unit buyer. Upon resale, that lease is assigned to the buyer.

Once the units in the building have been sold and the association turned over to the unit owners, the unit owners can change the rules. Generally, the bylaws require a three-fourths vote and the CC&Rs require a two-thirds vote from the association members for a change. House rules can be changed with a simple majority or, in some cases, by the board of directors without a vote of the association.

Voting Rules

Condominium bylaws provide that a **board of directors** be elected by the association members. The board is authorized to administer the affairs of the condominium including purchasing

Board of Directors

of hazard and liability insurance for the common elements, arranging for maintenance and repair of common elements, enforcing CC&Rs and house rules, assessing and collecting a sufficient amount of monthly homeowner fees and special assessments, and listening to complaints and suggestions from unit owners as to how the condominium should be run.

Board members are usually elected at the annual meeting of the association, are unit owners, and serve for one year. Typically there will be 5 to 7 members on the board, and one will be elected as president, one as vice-president, one as secretary, and one as treasurer. Meetings are held monthly unless added business requires more frequent meetings. Board meetings are usually open to all association members who can then watch the proceedings and provide input. To help spread the work, the board will appoint committees on which owners are asked to serve. Examples are landscaping, architectural, security, clubhouse, and social committees. Directors and committee members are not usually paid for their time.

Annual Meetings

Once a year the owners' association as a whole will meet for an **annual meeting.** Besides the election of board members for the following year, this is an opportunity for association members to vote on major issues such as changes in the CC&Rs and bylaws, monthly maintenance fee increases, special assessments, and any other matters the board feels should be put to a general ownership vote rather than handled at a board meeting. Owners also receive an annual report of the fiscal health of the association and other information pertinent to their ownership.

Condominium Management

Most condominium associations will employ a condominium **management company** to advise the board and take care of day-to-day tasks. The management company is usually responsible for finding, hiring, and paying gardeners, trash haulers, janitors, repair personnel, and a pool maintenance firm. The management company collects maintenance fees and special assessments from unit owners, accounts for condominium expenses, handles the payroll, and pays for contracted services.

If the association chooses to hire an on-site manager, that person is usually responsible for enforcing the house rules, handling complaints or problems regarding maintenance, making daily security checks, and supervising the swimming pool and recreation areas. The extent of his or her duties and responsibilities is set by the owners' association. The association should also retain the right to fire the resident manager and the management firm if their services are not satisfactory.

The costs of maintaining the common elements in a condominium are allocated among the unit owners in accordance with percentages set forth in the master deed. These are called **maintenance fees** or **association dues** and are collected monthly. Failure to pay creates a lien against the delinquent owner's unit. The amount collected is based on the association's budget for the coming year. This is based on the board of directors' estimate of the cost of month-to-month maintenance, insurance, legal and management services, plus reserves for expenses that do not occur monthly.

Maintenance Fees

The importance of setting aside **reserves** each month is illustrated by the following example. Suppose it is estimated that the exterior of a 100-unit building will have to be painted every 7 years and that the cost is expected to be $25,200. To avoid a special painting assessment of $252 per unit, the association instead collects $3 per month from each unit owner for 84 months. If the reserves are kept in an interest-bearing savings account as they should be, less than $3 per month would need to be collected.

Reserves

Since condominium law recognizes each condominium dwelling unit as a separate legal ownership, property taxes are assessed on each unit separately. Property taxes are based on the assessed value of the unit which is based on its market value. As a rule, it is not necessary for the taxing authority to assess and tax the common elements separately. The reason is that the market value of each unit reflects not only the value of the unit itself, but also the value of the fractional ownership in the common elements that accompanies the unit.

Property Taxes and Insurance

The association is responsible for purchasing hazard and liability insurance covering the common elements. Each dwelling unit owner is responsible for purchasing hazard and liability insurance for the interior of his dwelling.

Thus, if a visitor slips on a banana peel in the lobby or a hallway of the building, the association is responsible. If the accident occurs in an individual's unit, the unit owner is responsible. In a high-rise condominium, if the roof breaks during a heavy rainstorm and floods several apartments below, the association is responsible. If an apartment owner's dishwasher overflows and soaks the apartments below him, he is responsible. If patio furniture is stolen from the swimming pool area, the association is responsible. If patio furniture (or any personal property for that matter) is stolen from an individual's unit, that is the unit owner's responsibility. Policies designed for associations and policies for condominium owners are readily available from insurance companies.

If a condominium unit is being rented, the owner will want to have landlord insurance, and the tenant, for his own protection, will want a tenant's hazard and liability policy.

Condominium Financing

Because each condominium unit can be separately owned, each can be separately financed. Thus, a condominium purchaser can choose whether or not to borrow against his unit. If he borrows, he can choose a large or small down payment and a long or short amortization period. If he wants to repay early or refinance, that is his option too. Upon resale, the buyer can elect to assume the loan, pay it off, or obtain new financing. In other words, while association bylaws, restrictions, and house rules may regulate the use of a unit, in no way does the association control how a unit may be financed.

Since each unit is a separate ownership, if a lender needs to foreclose against a delinquent borrower in the building, the remaining unit owners are not involved. They are neither responsible for the delinquent borrower's mortgage debt nor are they parties to the foreclosure.

Loan Terms

Loan terms offered condominium buyers are quite similar to those offered on houses. Typically, lenders will make conventional, uninsured loans for up to 80% of value. With private mortgage insurance, this can be raised to 90% or 95%. On FHA-approved buildings, the FHA offers insurance terms similar to those for detached dwellings. Financing can also be in the form of an installment contract or a seller carryback.

Deposit Practices

If a project is not already completed and ready for occupancy when it is offered for sale, it is common for the developer to require a substantial deposit. The best practice is to place this in an escrow account payable to the developer upon completion. Without this precaution, some developers will use deposits to help pay the expenses of construction while the building is being built. Unfortunately, if the deposits are spent by a developer who goes bankrupt before the project is completed, the buyer receives neither a finished unit nor the return of his deposit. If the deposits are held in escrow, the buyers do not receive a unit but they do get their deposits back.

During the late 1970s the idea of condominium ownership became very popular in the United States. Builders constructed new condominiums at a rapid pace, but there were not enough to fill demand. Soon enterprising developers found that existing apartment buildings could be converted to condominiums and sold to the waiting public. Compared to new construction, a condominium conversion is often simpler, faster, and more profitable for the developer. The procedure involves finding an attractively built existing building that is well-located and has good floor plans. The developer does a face-lift on the outside, adds more landscaping, paints the interior, and replaces carpets and appliances. The developer also files the necessary legal paperwork to convert the building and land into condominium units and common elements.

Condominium Conversions

A potential problem area with condominium conversions, and one that a prospective buyer should be aware of, is that converted buildings are used buildings that were not intended as condominiums when built. As used buildings, there may be considerable deferred maintenance, and the building may have thermal insulation suitable to a time when energy costs were lower. If the building was originally built for rental purposes, sound-deadening insulation in the walls, floors, and ceilings may be inadequate. Fire protection between units may also be less than satisfactory. In contrast, newly built condominiums must meet current building code requirements regarding thermal and sound insulation, fire-wall construction, and so forth.

It is worth noting that not all condominium conversions are carried out by developers. Enterprising tenants have successfully converted their own buildings and saved considerable sums of money. It is not uncommon for the value of a building to double when it is converted to a condominium. Tenants who are willing to hire the legal, architectural, and construction help they need can create valuable condominium homes for themselves in the same building where they were previously renters.

*Advantages
of Condominium Living*

Compared to detached dwellings, condominium living offers a number of advantages and some disadvantages. On the advantage side, instead of four or five detached dwellings on an acre of land, a condominium builder can place 25 or even 100 living units. This spreads the cost of the site among more dwellings, and the builder does not have the miles of streets, sewers, or utility lines that would be necessary to reach every house in a spread-out subdivision. Furthermore, the use of shared walls and foundations,that one dwelling unit's ceiling is another's floor, and that one roof can cover many vertically stacked units can produce savings in construction materials and labor. In central city districts where a single square foot of vacant land can cost $100 or more, only a high-rise condominium can make housing units possible. In the suburbs where land is cheaper, a condominium is often the difference between buying and renting for some people.

Other advantages are the lure of "carefree living" wherein such chores as lawn mowing, watering, weeding, snow removal, and building maintenance are provided. For some people, it is the security often associated with clustered dwellings and nearby neighbors. Other advantages are extensive recreational and social facilities that are not economically feasible on a single-dwelling basis. It is commonplace to find swimming pools, recreation halls, tennis and volleyball courts, gymnasiums, and even social directors at condominiums.

Lastly, we cannot overlook the psychological and financial advantages of ownership. Many large rental apartment projects produce the same economies of scale and amenities just described. Nonetheless, most Americans prefer to own rather than rent their dwellings. Part of this is the pride of owning something. Part comes from a desire for a savings program, the potential for capital appreciation, and income tax laws that favor owners over renters.

*Disadvantages
of Condominium Living*

A major disadvantage of condominium living is the close proximity of one's neighbors and the extra level of government. In other words, buying into a condominium means buying into a group of people whose lifestyles may differ from yours and whose opinions as to how to run the association will differ from yours. By way of contrast, if you buy a single-family detached house on a lot, you will have (subject to zoning and legal restrictions) sole control over the use of it. You can choose to remodel or add on. You can choose what color to paint your house and garage, how many people and animals will live there, what type of landscaping to have, from whom to purchase property insurance, whether to rent it out or live in it, and so on. Your next-door neighbor will have the same rights over his land. You cannot dictate to him what color to paint his house, what kind of shrubs to grow, or from whom to buy hazard insurance if he buys it at all.

In a condominium, the owners have a considerable degree of control over each other in matters that affect the common good of the association. Moreover, certain decisions must be made as a group, such as what kinds of common element hazard and liability insurance to carry, how much to carry, and from whom to purchase it. If there is an outdoor swimming pool, a decision must be made as to what months it should be heated and how warm it should be kept. The group as a whole must decide on how the landscaping is to be maintained, who will do it, and how much should be spent. If there is to be security service, again there must be a group decision as to how much, when, and who should be hired. If a large truck runs into a unit on the other end of the building, it's an association problem because each owner has an undivided interest in the whole building.

All matters affecting the condominium must be brought to the attention of the board of directors, often by way of a committee. All committee and board positions are filled by volunteers from the association. Thus, owning a condominium is not entirely carefree, and there will be times when the board of directors will do things differently from what an individual owner would like. Another possibility is that there may be a lack of interested and talented people to serve as directors and on committees. Consequently, things that need to be done may be left undone, possibly posing a hazard to the association. Individual unit owners may be unaware of the management and maintenance requirements for a multimillion-dollar building and may have hired a management firm that knows (or does) even less.

If you are considering the purchase of a condominium unit, consider the above points with care. Also look closely at the

Before Buying

association's finances. The association may not have adequate reserves for upcoming maintenance work such as painting the building and putting on a new roof. If so, existing owners and new buyers will be in for a rude surprise in the form of a special assessment. Check the budget to see if it covers everything adequately and ask about lawsuits against the association that might drain its finances.

Although articles of incorporation, CC&Rs, and bylaws make boring reading, if you offer to buy a condominium unit, you should make the offer contingent on your reading and approving them. These are the rules you agree to live by, and it's better to read them before committing to buy than after. You may find prohibitions against your pet cat or dog or against renting your unit while you are temporarily transferred overseas. (At the closing the seller must give you a current set of these documents along with the deed and keys to the unit. When you sell, you must give a current set to your buyer.)

Before buying, pay special attention to construction quality. Will ongoing maintenance be expensive? Is there deferred maintenance? Ask if the clubhouse and recreation facilities are owned by the association or by the developer who will continue to charge you for their use year after year. Is soundproofing between units adequate or will you hear your neighbor's piano, drums, and arguments? What is the owner-tenant mix? The most successful condominiums are predominantly owner occupied rather than renter occupied. This is because owners usually take more interest and care in their properties, and this in turn boosts resale values. The list of things to look for and ask about when buying into a condominium is longer than there is space here, and bookstores have good books that will help you. But before moving on, the following two thoughts apply to any purchase of a condominium, cooperative, planned unit development, or timeshare. First, keep a balance between your heart and your head. It is easy to be enchanted to the point that no further investigation is made, perhaps knowing in advance it would sour the deal. Second, ask those who have already bought if they would buy again.

COOPERATIVE APARTMENTS

Now that you have just read about condominiums, take yourself back to the year 1900 in New York City. You've been renting an apartment unit on Manhattan for several years and would like to own it. Your neighbors in the building have expressed the same desire, but condominium legislation is more than half a century in the future. How would you and your neighbors accomplish this, given existing legal frameworks? Your answer is the corporate form of ownership, a form of multiperson ownership well established in America by that time. To carry out your collective desires, you form a not-for-profit corporation. Shares in the corporation are sold to the building's tenants and the money used as a down payment to buy the building. Title to the building is placed in the name of the corporation, and each shareholder receives from the corporation a lease to his apartment. Thus, the shareholders own the corporation, the corporation owns the building, and the corporation gives its shareholders leases to their apartments. Each month each shareholder makes a payment to the corporation to enable it to make the required monthly payment on the debt against the building and to pay for maintenance and repairs. Government of the building is handled by a board of directors that meets monthly and at an annual meeting of all the shareholders.

This form of residential ownership, which can be found in significant numbers in New York City, Miami, Chicago, San Francisco, and Honolulu is called a **cooperative apartment.** The individual shareholders are called **cooperators,** and the lease that the corporation gives to a shareholder is called a **proprietary lease.**

When a cooperator wishes to sell, the cooperator does not sell his apartment but rather the shares of stock that carry with it a proprietary lease on that apartment. Although for all practical purposes the transaction looks like a sale of real estate, from a legal standpoint it is a sale of corporate stock. As such, the listing and selling forms that are used for houses and condominiums are not suitable and special cooperative forms must be used.

Financing a cooperative is different from financing a house or condominium. When a cooperative apartment building is first organized, the entire property is in the name of the cooperative corporation, and there is one mortgage loan on all of it. To illustrate, suppose a 10-unit building will cost the cooperators $1,000,000 and all the units are considered equal in desirability. A lender will finance 70% of the purchase if the cooperators raise

Financing

the remaining 30%. This requires the cooperators to sell 10 shares of stock, each share for $30,000 and good for one apartment unit in the building. The lender provides the remaining $700,000 to complete the purchase, and the corporation gives the lender a note for $700,000 secured by a mortgage against the building. Suppose the monthly payments on this loan are $7,000; this means each month each cooperator must contribute $700 toward the mortgage plus money to maintain and operate the building, pay the property taxes on it, and keep it insured.

Default   What happens if one of the cooperators fails to make his monthly payment to the cooperative? For the cooperative to send the lender anything less than the required $7,000 per month puts the loan in default. This means the remaining cooperators must make up the difference. Meanwhile, they can seek voluntary reimbursement by the tardy cooperator, or, if that does not work, terminate him as a shareholder and resell the share to someone who will make the payments.

Resale   What happens if a shareholder in good standing wants to sell his unit? Since the underlying mortgage is against the entire building, it is impossible to refinance a portion of the building. Only the whole building can be refinanced and that requires approval by the cooperators as a whole. Traditionally, this has forced the cooperator to sell his share for all cash or on an installment sale plan. This is a handicap where the value of the share has increased substantially due to property value increase and reduction of the building's mortgage loan. As a solution, at least two states, New York and California, have enacted legislation allowing state-regulated lenders to make loans using cooperative stock as collateral.

Government   A cooperative apartment is governed by its articles of incorporation, bylaws, CC&Rs, and house rules. The governing body is a board of directors elected by the cooperators. The board hires the services needed to maintain and operate the building just as in a condominium. Annual meetings are also held, just as in a condominium.

Differences   Now that the condominium format is available, relatively few cooperatives are being organized. This is largely because in a condominium the individual apartment unit can be financed separately from the remainder of the building. Moreover, if one condominium unit owner fails to make loan payments, the remaining owners in the building are not responsible for that loan. The condominium unit owner also has the personal choice of whether to have no debt, a little debt, or a lot of debt against his unit. Unpaid property taxes are another potential difference. In a condominium each unit is taxed separately, and nonpayment brings a property tax foreclosure sale against just the delinquent unit, not the entire building.

A similarity exists between condominiums and cooperatives with respect to the money collected each month for the general maintenance and upkeep of the building. In either case, nonpayment will bring action against the tardy owner by the association that can result in foreclosure of that owner. Income tax rules effectively allow the same homeowner deductions on cooperatives as on condominiums and houses. However, a strict set of rules must be followed because technically a cooperator does not own real estate, but shares of stock.

Similarity

Due to the financing difficulty and mutual liability potential associated with cooperatives, several states have enacted legislation that allows new cooperatives to be financed entirely by the sale of stock that in turn is pledged to a lender. This way the failure of one cooperator to make mortgage loan payments does not jeopardize the other cooperators. Also, a county assessor can assess each cooperator individually for property tax purposes if the board of directors so requests. This avoids joint liability. If you are considering the purchase of a cooperative, read the articles of incorporation, bylaws, CC&Rs, and house rules before buying. Some operate under old rules, some under new rules, some will have rules you will be comfortable with, and some will not.

New Legislation

Although the opening example in this section on cooperatives was one of tenants banding together to buy their building, cooperatives are also organized and sold by real estate developers. These can be existing buildings converted by developers to cooperative ownership and new buildings built by developers from the ground up. In either case, a prospective purchaser will find it worthwhile to reread earlier paragraphs in this chapter on deposit practices, conversions, advantages, disadvantages, and before buying.

PLANNED UNIT DEVELOPMENT

If you buy into a condominium, you get a dwelling unit as separate property plus an undivided interest in the land and other common elements. If you buy into a cooperative, you get stock in the corporation that owns the building and a lease on a particular apartment. If you buy into a **planned unit development (PUD),** you get a house and lot as separate property plus ownership in a community association that owns the common areas. Common areas may be as minimal as a few green spaces in open areas between houses or as extensive as to also include parks, pools, clubhouse facilities, jogging trails, boat docks, horse trails, and a golf course.

Although you own your lot and house as separate property in a PUD, there will be CC&Rs to follow. The PUD developer will establish an initial set of CC&Rs, then turn them over to the association for enforcement. Thus, your lot and home are not quite all yours to do with as you please because your association can dictate what color you can paint the exterior of your home, what you can and cannot plant in your front yard, and how many people and pets can reside with you. As with condominiums and cooperatives, PUD CC&Rs are not meant to be burdensome for the sake of being burdensome, but rather to maintain the attractiveness and tranquillity of the development and in doing so keep home values up.

The dwellings in a planned unit development typically take the form of detached houses and houses that share a common wall,such as row houses, townhouses, and cluster houses. Because each owner owns his land, vertical stacking of homes is limited to one owner and housing densities to 8 or 10 units per acre. Even though this is twice the density of a typical detached house subdivision, by careful planning a developer can give each owner the feeling of more spaciousness. One way is by taking advantage of uneven terrain. If a parcel contains some flat land, some hilly land, some land covered with trees and a running stream, the dwellings can be clustered on the land best suited for building and thus preserve the stream, woods, and steep slopes in their natural state. With a standard subdivision layout the developer would have to remove the groves of trees, fill in the stream, and terrace the slopes, and would still be able to provide homes for only half the number of families.

Resort timesharing is a method of dividing up and selling a living unit at a vacation facility for specified lengths of time each year. The idea started in Europe in the 1960s when groups of individuals would jointly purchase ski resort lodgings and summer vacation villas with each owner taking a week or two of exclusive occupancy. Resort developers quickly recognized the market potential of the idea, and in 1969 the first resort timeshare opened in the United States. Since then hotels, motels, condominiums, townhouses, lodges, villas, recreational vehicle parks, campgrounds, houseboats, and even a cruise ship have been timeshared.

RESORT TIMESHARING

Nearly all timeshares fall into one of two legal formats. The first is the **right-to-use** format. This gives the buyer a contractual right to occupy a living unit at a resort property for one week a year for a specific term of 20 to 40 years. The cost for the entire period is paid in advance. At the end of the contract term all of the buyer's possessory rights terminate unless the contract contains a renewal clause or a right to buy. The developer creates these contracts by either buying or leasing a resort property and then selling 50 one-week-a-year right-to-use contracts on each living unit. (The other two weeks of the year are reserved for maintenance.) Approximately 30% of the timeshare market is right-to-use.

Right-to-Use

The second format is **fee simple** ownership. Here the timeshare purchaser obtains a fee ownership in the unit purchased. The purchaser owns the property for one week a year in perpetuity, and the sale is handled like a sale of real estate. There will be a formal closing, a title policy, execution of a mortgage and note, and delivery of a recordable deed that conveys the timeshare interest. A developer offers fee timeshares by either building or buying a resort property and then selling 50 one-week-a-year fee simple slices in each unit, with the remaining two weeks for maintenance. Approximately 70% of the timeshare market is fee simple.

Fee Simple

Costs   The initial cost of a timeshare week at a resort in the United States is typically $6,000 to $10,000, depending on the quality and location of the resort, the time of year (low season or high season), and form of ownership (right-to-use is usually less expensive). Additionally, there will be an annual maintenance fee of $140 to $280 per timeshare week. Buyers can purchase two or more timeshare weeks if they want a longer vacation. Some buyers purchase one week in the summer and one week in the winter.

Benefits   The appeal of time-sharing to developers is that a resort or condominium complex that can be bought and furnished for $100,000 per unit can be resold in 50 timeshare slices at $6,000 each, i.e., $300,000 a unit. The primary appeal of time-sharing to consumers is having a resort to go to every year at a prepaid price. This is particularly appealing during inflationary times although the annual maintenance fee can change. There may be certain tax benefits if the timeshare is financed and for property taxes paid on fee simple timeshares. There may also be appreciation of the timeshare unit if it is in a particularly popular and well-run resort.

Then again, some or all of these benefits may not materialize. First, the lump sum paid for a timeshare week does look cheaper than hotel bills year after year. However, the timeshare must be paid for in full in advance (or financed at interest) whereas the hotel is paid as it is used each year. Also, there is a timeshare maintenance fee of $20 to $40 per day that goes for clerk and maid service, linen laundry and replacement, structural maintenance and repairs, swimming pool service, hazard and liability insurance, reservations, collections and accounting services, general management, etc.

Second, going to the same resort for the same week every year for the next 40 years may become wearisome. Yet that is what a timeshare buyer is agreeing to do. And, if the week goes vacant, the maintenance fee must still be paid. To offset this, two large resort exchange services and several smaller ones exist, and some of the larger timeshare developers allow their buyers to exchange weeks among their various projects. There is a cost, however, to exchanging. There may be as many as three fees to pay: an initiation fee, an annual membership fee, and a fee when an exchange is made. These can amount to $100 or more for an exchange. Moreover, someone else with a timeshare week they don't want that you do want at the right time of the year must also be in the exchange bank. Satisfaction is usually achieved in exchanging by being flexible in accepting an exchange. Note too, if you own an off-season week at one resort, do not count on exchanging it for a peak-season vacation somewhere else. Exchange banks require members to accept periods of equal or lesser popularity.

Third, tax laws through 1985 allowed deductions for interest expense on timeshares that are financed and for property taxes on fee timeshares. At the time this book went to press, there were federal tax reform proposals to limit those deductions. Timeshares have occasionally been touted as tax shelter vehicles; however, that has already met the ire of the Internal Revenue Service.

Fourth, although there have been several reported instances of timeshare appreciation, it is generally agreed in the timeshare industry and by consumer groups that the primary reason to purchase a resort timeshare is to obtain a vacation, not appreciation. In fact, a timeshare industry rule-of-thumb is that one-third of the retail price of a timeshare unit goes to marketing costs. This acts as a damper on timeshare resale prices and even suggests that a buyer may be able to purchase a timeshare on the resale market for less than from a developer.

Commitment

Against the comfort of knowing that as a timeshare owner one has a long-term commitment to use a resort, one also has a long-term commitment to its maintenance, repair, refurbishing, and management. This is similar to ownership in a condominium, except with ownership split among as many as 50 owners for each unit, will any owner have a large enough stake to want to take an active part in overseeing the management? As a result, management falls to the developer who, having once sold out the project, may no longer have as much incentive to oversee things as carefully as it did during the sales period. The developer can turn the job over to a management firm, but who oversees them to make certain the timeshare owners get good service at a fair price?

State Regulation

Approximately 25 states have adopted timeshare regulations. Many of these follow the Model Timeshare Act designed by the

National Association of Real Estate License Law Officials and the National Timesharing Council and endorsed by the National Association of Realtors. Much timeshare legislation is in the form of consumer protection and disclosure (prospectus) requirements. Other legislation deals with how timeshares should be assessed for property taxation and what type of license a person employed to sell timeshares should hold, if any. Due to high-pressure sales techniques observed at some timeshare sales offices, a number of states have enacted mandatory "cooling-off" periods of five days during which a buyer can rescind his contract. Because of multimillion-dollar consumer losses due to uncompleted timeshare projects, the sale of the same timeshare to more than one party, and money collected with deeds never sent, surety bonds and escrows are now required by some states. Meanwhile, any prospective timeshare purchaser or salesperson would do well to take plenty of time in deciding, have all paperwork reviewed by their attorney before signing, and spend time talking to existing purchasers to ask if they would buy again.

REVIEW QUESTIONS

1. State laws which provide the legal framework for condominium ownership may be identified by any the following terms EXCEPT:
   A. strata titles act.　　　　　C. condominium act.
   B. cooperative housing act.　 D. horizontal property act.

2. Condominium developments are restricted to
   A. residential dwelling units.　C. Noth A and B.
   B. multiple unit buildings.　　 D. Neither A nor B.

3. In order to create a condominium development, a developer may
   A. construct a new building.　 C. Both A and B.
   B. convert an existing building. D. Neither A nor B.

4. Individual units in a condominium development are classed as
   A. separate property.　　　　 C. cooperative elements.
   B. common elements.　　　　 D. limited common elements.

5. Within a condominium development, common elements are owned by
   A. the owners' association.
   B. all unit owners, who hold undivided interests in the elements.
   C. the condominium developer.
   D. individual unit owners as community property.

6. Which of the following would be classified as limited common elements in a condominium development?
   A. Elevators.　　　　　　　　C. Assigned parking spaces.
   B. Hallways.　　　　　　　　 D. The manager's apartment.

7. The plan for a condominium development which converts a single parcel of land into individual separate property estates and an estate composed of all common elements may be referred to as
   A. an enabling declaration.
   B. a master deed.
   C. Both A and B.
   D. Neither A nor B.

8. The rules by which an owners' association operates are known as
   A. bylaws.
   B. covenants, conditions, and restrictions.
   C. house rules.
   D. ordinances.

9. The purchaser of a condominium unit is obligated to abide by the development's
   A. covenants, conditions, and restrictions.
   B. house rules.
   C. Both A and B.
   D. Neither A nor B.

10. In a condominium, the authority to raise homeowner fees (association dues) rests with the
   A. board of directors.
   B. management company.
   C. condominium act.
   D. city and county.

11. The guest of a unit owner was injured by stepping on broken glass in the swimming pool at the Sunset Hills condominium. Liability for this injury would probably initially fall upon
   A. the unit owner.
   B. the condominium association.
   C. management company.
   D. developers.

12. The purchaser of a condominium unit
   A. surrenders personal freedoms to community rule.
   B. exchanges freedom of choice for freedom from responsibility.
   C. Both A and B.
   D. Neither A nor B.

13. Ownership of the interior space of your home and garage and an undivided interest in the building structures, common areas, and land area of the entire project describes a
   A. condominium.
   B. cooperative.
   C. PUD.
   D. corporate form of ownership

14. Traditionally, the resale of cooperative shares have been financed by means of
   A. installment sales agreements.
   B. second mortgages on the seller's unit.
   C. bonds.
   D. government securities.

15. The governing body of a cooperative is called a
   A. cooperation.
   B. corporation.
   C. CC&R.
   D. board of directors.

16. The owner of a unit in a planned unit development holds title to all of the following EXCEPT:
    A. the air above his unit.
    B. the land beneath his unit.
    C. a share of the common area.
    D. fee simple title to his unit.

17. In a planned unit development, the owners' association can dictate all of the following EXCEPT:
    A. exterior paint colors.
    B. exterior landscaping.
    C. use of common areas.
    D. interior paint colors.

18. Of the two principal forms of timeshare formats, which comprises the larger percentage of the market?
    A. Right-to-use.
    B. Fee simple.
    C. Each holds an approximately equal market share.
    D. Statistics are not available.

19. Under the right-to-use plan of timesharing, the purchaser
    A. holds title to real property.
    B. is a tenant in common with other users of the unit.
    C. Both A and B.
    D. Neither A nor B.

20. The sale of timeshares is regulated in about twenty-five states by
    A. the National Association of License Law Officials.
    B. the National Timesharing Council.
    C. the National Association of Realtors.
    D. state legislation.

Land-Use Control

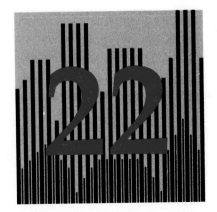

Land-use control describes any legal restriction that controls how a parcel of land may be used. There are both public controls and private controls. Public controls include zoning, building codes, subdivision regulations, and master plans. Private controls come in the form of deed restrictions. This chapter covers all those topics and concludes with a brief discussion of environmental impact statements.

OVERVIEW OF
CHAPTER 22

LEARNING OBJECTIVES

After successful completion of this chapter, you should be able to:

1. Describe the many aspects and results of zoning, changes, and downzoning.
2. Understand and discuss the application of subdivision regulations and building codes.
3. Explain the use of deed restrictions.
4. Describe the environmental impact statement.
5. Explain the purpose of planning ahead and the need for master plans.
6. Define transferable development rights.

KEY • TERMS

Building codes: local and state laws that set minimum construction standards

Certificate of occupancy: a government-issued document that states a structure meets local zoning and building code requirements and is ready for use

Downzoning: rezoning of land from a higher-density use to a lower-density use

Environmental impact statement: a report that contains information regarding the effect of a proposed project on the environment of an area

Land-use control: a broad term that describes any legal restriction that controls how a parcel of land may be used

Master plan: a comprehensive guide for the physical growth of a community

Nonconforming use: an improvement that is inconsistent with current zoning regulations

Restrictive covenants: clauses placed in deeds and leases to control how future owners and lessees may or may not use the property

Variance: allows an individual landowner to vary from zoning requirements

Zoning: public regulations that control the specific use of land

Land-use control is a broad term that describes any legal restriction that controls how a parcel of land may be used. Land-use controls can be divided into two broad categories: public controls and private controls. Examples of public controls are zoning, building codes, subdivision regulations, and master plans. Private controls come in the form of deed restrictions. Let us explore further.

ZONING   Rudimentary forms of zoning can be traced back as far as medieval times when regulations prohibited certain activities from taking place within the town wall. In Colonial America, cities and towns regulated the location of foul-smelling industries such as tallow rendering and leather tanning. In the late 1880s Boston limited the heights of buildings as did Baltimore, Indianapolis, and Washington, D.C. Between 1909 and 1915, Los Angeles adopted a complex series of land-use laws. However, credit for the first truly comprehensive and systematic zoning law goes to New York City in 1916. Three years in the making, it went beyond anything up to that time and set a basic pattern that has been followed and refined by American cities, towns, and counties ever since.

Zoning laws divide land into zones (districts) and within each zone regulate the purpose for which buildings may be constructed, the height and bulk of the buildings, the area of the lot that they may occupy, and the number of persons that they can accommodate. Through zoning a community can protect existing land users from encroachment by undesirable uses and ensure that future land uses in the community will be compatible with one another. Zoning also can control development so that each parcel of land will be adequately serviced by streets, sanitary and storm sewers, schools, parks, and utilities.

The authority to control land use is derived from the basic police power of each state to protect the public health, safety, morals, and general welfare of its citizens. Through an enabling act passed by the state legislature, the authority to control land use is also given to individual towns, cities, and counties. These local government units then pass zoning ordinances that establish the boundaries of the various land-use zones and determine the type of development that will be permitted in each of them. By going to your local zoning office, you can learn how a parcel of land is zoned. By then consulting the zoning ordinance, you can see the permitted uses for the parcel.

Zoning Symbols

For convenience, zones are identified by code abbreviations such as R (residential), C (commercial), I or M (industrial-manufacturing) and A (agriculture). Within general categories are subcategories, for example, single-family residences, two-family residences, low-rise apartments, and high-rise apartments. Similarly, there will usually be several subcategories of commercial ranging from small stores to shopping centers and several subcategories of manufacturing ranging from light, smoke-free to heavy industry.

Additionally, there can be found overlay zoning categories such as RPD (residential planned development) and PUD (planned unit development). These are designed to permit a mixture of land uses within a given parcel. For example, a 640-acre parcel may contain open spaces plus clusters of houses, townhouses, and apartments, and perhaps a neighborhood shopping center. Another combination zone is RO (residential-office) that allows apartment buildings alongside or on top of office buildings.

Note that there is no uniformity to zoning classifications in the United States. A city may use *A* to designate apartments while the county uses *A* to designate agriculture. Similarly, one city may use *I* for industrial and another city use *I* for institutional (hospitals and universities, for example).

Land-Use Restrictions

Besides telling a landowner the use to which he may put his land, the zoning ordinance imposes additional rules. For example, land zoned for low-density apartments may require 1,500 square feet of land per living unit, a minimum of 600 square feet of living space per unit for one bedroom, 800 square feet for two bedrooms, and 1,000 square feet for three bedrooms. The zoning ordinance may also contain a set-back requirement that states that a building must be placed at least 25 feet back from the street, 10 feet from the sides of the lot, and 15 feet from the rear lot line. The ordinance may also limit the building's height to 2½ stories and require two parking spaces for each dwelling unit. As can be seen, zoning encourages uniformity.

Enforcement

Zoning laws are enforced by virtue of the fact that in order to build a person must obtain a building permit from his city or county government. Before a permit is issued, the proposed structure must conform with government-imposed structural standards and comply with the zoning on the land. If a landowner builds without a permit, he can be forced to tear down his building.

Nonconforming Use

When an existing structure does not conform with a new zoning law, it is "grandfathered-in" as a **nonconforming use.** Thus, the owner can continue to use the structure even though it does not conform to the new zoning. However, the owner is not permitted to enlarge or remodel the structure, or to extend its life. When the structure is ultimately demolished, any new use of the land must be in accordance with the zoning law. If you are driving through a residential neighborhood and see an old store or service station that looks very much out of place, it is probably a nonconforming use that was allowed to stay because it was built before the current zoning on the property went into effect.

Once a zoning ordinance has been passed, it can be changed by **amendment.** Thus, land previously zoned for agriculture may be changed to residential. Land along a city street that has become a major thoroughfare may change from residential to commercial. An amendment can be initiated by a property owner in the area to be rezoned or by local government. Either way, notice of the proposed change must be given to all property owners in and around the affected area, and a public hearing must be held so that property owners and the public at large may voice their opinions on the matter.

Amendment

A **variance** allows an individual landowner to deviate from current zoning requirements for his parcel. For example, a variance might be granted to the owner of an odd-shaped lot to reduce the setback requirements slightly so that he can fit a building on it. Variances usually are granted where strict compliance with the zoning ordinance or code would cause undue hardship. A variance can also be used to change the permitted use of a parcel. However the variance must not change the basic character of the neighborhood, and it must be consistent with the general objectives of zoning as they apply to that neighborhood.

Variance

A **conditional use permit** allows a land use that does not conform with existing zoning provided the use is within the limitations imposed by the permit. A conditional use permit is usually quite restrictive, and if the conditions of the permit are violated the permit is no longer valid. For example, a neighborhood grocery store operating under a conditional use permit can only be a neighborhood grocery. The structure cannot be used as an auto parts store.

Conditional Use Permit

Spot zoning refers to the rezoning of a small area of land in an existing neighborhood. For example, a neighborhood convenience center (grocery, laundry, barbershop) might be allowed in a residential neighborhood provided it serves a useful purpose for neighborhood residents and is not a nuisance.

Spot Zoning

Downzoning means that land previously zoned for higher-density uses (or more active uses) is rezoned for lower-density uses (or less active uses). Examples are downzoning from high-

Downzoning

rise commercial to low-rise commercial, apartment zoning to single-family, and single-family to agriculture. Although a landowner's property value may fall as a result of downzoning, there is no compensation to the landowner as there is no taking of land as with eminent domain.

Buffer Zone

A **buffer zone** is a strip of land that separates one land use from another. Thus, between a large shopping center and a neighborhood of single-family homes, there may be a row of garden apartments. Alternatively, between an industrial park and a residential subdivision, a developer may leave a strip of land in grass and trees rather than build homes immediately adjacent to the industrial buildings. Note that *buffer zone* is a generic term and not necessarily a zoning law category.

Legality, Value

A zoning law can be changed or struck down if it can be proved in court that it is unclear, discriminatory, unreasonable, not for the protection of the public health, safety, and general welfare, or not applied to all property in a similar manner. A topical, but difficult, legal issue involves "taking." When property is zoned so that it destroys or severely limits its use, it becomes condemnation, not zoning, because the property has been effectively "taken."

Zoning alone does not create land value. For example, zoning a hundred square miles of lonely desert or mountain land for stores and offices would not appreciably change its value. Value is created by the number of people who want to use a particular parcel of land for a specific purpose. To the extent that zoning channels that demand to certain parcels of land and away from others, zoning does have a powerful impact on property value.

SUBDIVISION REGULATIONS

Before a building lot can be sold, a subdivider must comply with government regulations concerning street construction, curbs, sidewalks, street lighting, fire hydrants, storm and sanitary sewers, grading and compacting of soil, water and utility lines, minimum lot size, and so on. In addition, the subdivider may be required to either set aside land for schools and parks or provide money so that land for that purpose may be purchased nearby. These are often referred to as **mapping requirements** and until the subdivider has complied with all state and local regulations, the subdivision will not be approved. Without approval the plan cannot be recorded which, in turn, means that the lots cannot be sold to the public. If the subdivider tries to sell lots without approval, he can be stopped by a government court order and in some states fined. Moreover, permits to build will be refused to lot owners and anyone who bought from the subdivider is entitled to a refund.

BUILDING CODES

Recognizing the need to protect public health and safety against slipshod construction practices, state and local governments have enacted **building codes.** These establish minimum acceptable material and construction standards for such things as structural load and stress, windows and ventilation, size and location of rooms, fire protection, exits, electrical installation, plumbing, heating, lighting, and so forth.

Before a building permit is granted, the design of a proposed structure must meet the building-code requirements. During construction, local building department inspectors visit the construction site to make certain that the codes are being observed. Finally, when the building is completed, a **certificate of occupancy** is issued to the building owner to show that the structure meets the code. Without this certificate, the building cannot be legally occupied.

Traditionally, the establishment of building codes has been given by states to individual counties, cities, and towns. The result has been a lack of uniformity from one local government to the next, oftimes adding unnecessary construction costs and occasionally leaving gaps in consumer protection. The trend today is toward statewide building codes that overcome these weaknesses and at the same time improve the uniformity of mortgage collateral for the secondary mortgage market.

DEED RESTRICTIONS

Although property owners tend to think of land-use controls as being strictly a product of government, it is possible to achieve land-use control through private means. In fact, Houston, Texas operates without zoning and relies almost entirely upon private land-use controls to achieve a similar effect.

Private land-use controls take the form of **deed** and **lease restrictions.** In the United States it has long been recognized that the ownership of land includes the right to sell or lease it on whatever legally acceptable conditions the owner wishes, including the right to dictate to the buyer or lessee how he shall or shall not use it. For example, a developer can sell the lots in his subdivision subject to a restriction written into each deed that the land cannot be used for anything but a single-family residence containing at least 1,200 square feet of living area. The legal theory is that if the buyer or lessee agrees to the restrictions, he is bound by them. If they are not obeyed, any lot owner in the subdivision can obtain a court order to enforce compliance. The only limit to the number of restrictions that an owner may place on his land is economic. If there are too many restrictions, the landowner may find that no one wants the land.

Deed restrictions, also known as restrictive covenants, can be used to dictate such matters as the purpose of the structure to be built, architectural requirements, setbacks, size of the structure, and aesthetics. In neighborhoods with view lots, they are often used to limit the height to which trees may be permitted to grow. Deed restrictions cannot be used to discriminate on the basis of race, color, religion, sex, or national origin; if they do, they are unenforceable by the courts.

PLANNING AHEAD FOR DEVELOPMENT

When a community first adopts a zoning ordinance, the usual procedure is to recognize existing land uses by zoning according to what already exists. Thus, a neighborhood that is already developed with houses is zoned for houses. Undeveloped land may be zoned for agriculture or simply left unzoned. As a community expands, undeveloped land is zoned for urban uses and a pattern that typically follows is the availability of new roads, the aggressiveness of developers, and the willingness of landowners to sell. All too often this results in a hodgepodge of land-use districts, all conforming internally because of tightly enforced zoning, but with little or no relationship among them. This happens because they were created over a period of years without the aid of a long-range land-use plan that took a comprehensive view of the entire growth pattern of the city. Since uncoordinated land use can have a negative impact on both the quality of life and the economic vitality of a community, more attention is now being directed toward land-use master plans to guide the development of towns and cities, districts, coastlines, and even whole states.

To prepare a **master plan** (or **general plan** or **comprehensive plan**), a city or regional planning commission is usually created. The first step is a physical and economic survey of the area to be planned. The physical survey involves mapping existing roads, utility lines, developed land, and undeveloped land. The economic survey looks at the present and anticipated economic base of the region, its population, and its retail trade facilities. Together the two surveys provide the information upon which a master plan is built. The key is to view the region as a unified entity that provides its residents with jobs and housing as well as social, recreational, and cultural opportunities. In doing so, the master plan uses existing patterns of transportation and land use and directs future growth so as to achieve balanced development. For example, if agriculture is important to the area's economy, special attention is given to retaining the best soils for farming. Waterfront property may also receive special planning protection. Similarly, if houses in an older residential area of town are being converted to rooming houses and apartments, that transition can be encouraged by planning apartment usage for the area. In doing this, the master plan guides those who must make day-to-day decisions regarding zoning changes and gives the individual property owner a long-range idea of what his property may be used for in the future.

Master Plan

To assure long-run continuity, a master plan should look at least 15 years into the future and preferably 25 years or more. It must also include provisions for flexibility in the event that the city or region does not develop as expected, such as when population grows faster or slower than anticipated. Most importantly, the plan must provide for a balance between the economic and social functions of the community. For example, to emphasize culture and recreation at the expense of adequate housing and the area's economic base will result in the slow decay of the community because people must leave to find housing and jobs.

Long-Run Continuity

The purpose of an **environmental impact statement (EIS),** also called an environmental impact report (EIR), is to gather into one document enough information about the effect of a

ENVIRONMENTAL IMPACT STATEMENTS

proposed project on the total environment so that a neutral decision maker can judge the environmental benefits and costs of the project. For example, a city zoning commission considering a zone change can request an EIS that will show the expected impact of the change on such things as population density, automobile traffic, noise, air quality, water and sewage facilities, drainage, energy consumption, school enrollments, employment, public health and safety, recreation facilities, wildlife, and vegetation. The idea is that with this information at hand, better decisions regarding land uses can be made. When problems can be anticipated in advance, it is easier to make modifications or explore alternatives.

At the city and county level, where the EIS requirement has the greatest effect on private development, the EIS usually accompanies the development application that is submitted to the planning or zoning commission. Where applicable, copies are also sent to affected school districts, water and sanitation districts, and highway and flood control departments. The EIS is then made available for public inspection as part of the hearing process on the development application. This gives concerned civic groups and the public at large an opportunity to voice their opinions regarding the anticipated benefits and costs of the proposed development. If the proposed development is partially or wholly funded by state or federal funds, then state or federal hearings are also held.

PRECAUTIONS

Because zoning can greatly influence the value of a property, it is absolutely essential that when you purchase real estate you be aware of the zoning for the parcel. You will need to know what the zoning will allow and what it won't; whether the parcel is operating under a restrictive or temporary permit; and what the zoning and planning departments might allow on the property in the future. Where there is any uncertainty or where a zone change or variance will be necessary in order to use the property the way you want to, a conservative approach is to make the offer to buy contingent on obtaining planning and zoning approval before going to settlement.

If you are a real estate agent, you must stay abreast of zoning and planning and building matters regarding the properties you list and sell. A particularly sensitive issue that occurs regularly is a property listed for sale that does not meet zoning and/or building code requirements. For example, suppose the current (or previous) owner of a house has converted the garage to a den or bedroom without obtaining building permits and without providing space for parking elsewhere on the parcel. Legally, this makes the property unmarketable. If you, as agent, sell this property without telling the buyer about the lack of permits, you've given the buyer grounds to sue you for misrepresentation and the seller for rescission. When faced with a situation like this, you should ask the seller to obtain the necessary permits. If the seller refuses, and the buyer still wants to buy, make the problem very clear to the buyer and have the buyer sign a statement indicating acceptance of title under these conditions. You can also refuse to accept the listing if it looks as though it will create more trouble than it's worth.

Professionals

The point here is that the public has a right to expect real estate agents to be professionals in their field. Thus the agent is expected to be fully aware of the permitted uses for a property and whether or not current uses comply. This is necessary to properly value the property for listing and to provide accurate information to prospective buyers. Even if the seller in the above example was unaware of his zoning and building violations, it is the agent's responsibility to recognize the problem and inform the seller. An agent cannot take the position that if the seller didn't mention it, then the agent needn't worry about it and if the buyer later complains, it's the seller's problem, not the agent's. Recent court decisions clearly indicate that the agent has a responsibility to inform the seller of a problem so that the seller cannot later complain to the agent, "You should have told me about that when I listed the property with you and certainly before I accepted the buyer's offer."

REVIEW QUESTIONS

1. Through zoning, a community can protect existing land users from all of the following, EXCEPT:
   A. encroachment by undesirable uses.
   B. uncontrolled development.
   C. incompatible uses of land.
   D. competitive business establishments.

2. Historically, early forms of land zoning can be traced to
   A. medieval towns and cities.
   B. colonial America.
   C. Boston, Baltimore, and Indianapolis in the late 1800s.
   D. All of the above.

3. Land-use controls may be imposed by
   A. state governments.   C. subdivision developers.
   B. local governments.   D. All of the above.

4. Zoning laws may NOT be used to regulate which of the following?
   A. The purpose for which a building may be constructed.
   B. The number of persons a building may accommodate.
   C. The placement of interior partitions.
   D. The height and bulk of a building.

5. The basic authority for zoning laws is derived from a state's
   A. powers of eminent domain.
   B. right of taxation.
   C. Both A and B.
   D. Neither A nor B.

6. Zoning laws
   A. tell a landowner the use to which he may put his land.
   B. compensate an owner for loss of property value due to zoning.
   C. Both A and B.
   D. Neither A nor B.

7. Applied to land use, zoning laws may do all of the following EXCEPT:
   A. encourage uniformity in land usage.
   B. set minimum square footage requirements for buildings.
   C. determine the location of a building on a lot.
   D. dictate construction standards for buildings.

8. A use of property which is not in agreement with present zoning laws
   A. is called a nonconforming use.
   B. may be permitted under a so-called "grandfather clause."
   C. Both A and B.
   D. Neither A nor B.

9. Permission to use a building for a nonconforming use may be accomplished by
   A. amendment of the zoning ordinance.
   B. obtaining a zoning variance.
   C. Both A and B.
   D. Neither A nor B.

10. A zoning variance
    A. allows an owner to deviate from existing zoning law.
    B. involves a change in the zoning law.
    C. Both A and B.
    D. Neither A nor B.

11. When a small area of land in an existing neighborhood is rezoned, this is known as
A. downzoning.
B. spot zoning.
C. conditional zoning.
D. a zoning variance.

12. A garden apartment development is situated between an office park and a subdivision of single-family residences. These apartments are in a
A. buffer zone.
B. downzone.
C. spot zone.
D. commercial zone.

13. Minimum standards for materials and construction of buildings are set by
A. zoning laws.
B. building codes.
C. deed restrictions.
D. subdivision regulations.

14. Before a newly constructed building may be utilized by tenants, the owner must secure a certificate of
A. inspection.
B. utilization.
C. approval.
D. occupancy.

15. Building codes may be enacted
A. by local governments.
B. at the state level of government.
C. Both A and B.
D. Neither A nor B.

16. A subdivider wants to limit the height to which trees can grow so as to preserve views. He would most likely do this with a
A. zoning amendment.
B. conditional use permit.
C. buffer zone.
D. deed restriction.

17. The effect of a proposed development on a community is determined by the preparation of
A. a property disclosure report.
B. an environmental impact statement.
C. a prospectus.
D. the community's master plan.

18. An environmental impact statement will NOT reveal the effect of a planned development on
A. air quality.
B. automobile traffic.
C. property values.
D. school enrollments.

19. Windfalls and wipeouts in land value which are brought about by land-use controls may sometimes be eliminated by creating
A. an environmental impact statement.
B. transferable development rights.
C. Both A and B.
D. Neither A nor B.

20. To date, transferable development rights have been used to protect
A. historical buildings.
B. agricultural land.
C. environmentally sensitive land.
D. All of the above.

Investing in Real Estate

OVERVIEW OF
CHAPTER 23

The real estate investor basically takes two risks: he may never obtain a return on his investment and he may never recover his investment. This chapter introduces you to the benefits and dangers of investing. Cash flow, tax shelters, loss limitations, capital gain, tax law changes, equity buildup, and leverage are just a few of the topics covered. The chapter also deals with property selection, investment timing, developing a personal investment strategy, valuing an investment, limited partnership, and disclosure laws. The chapter concludes with a brief discussion on the effort and courage it takes to be an investor.

LEARNING OBJECTIVES

After successful completion of this chapter, you should be able to:

1. List and explain the benefits of real estate investing.
2. Define cash flow, tax shelter, loss limitation, capital gain, leverage, and equity build-up.
3. Describe the applicable tax rules and tax law changes.
4. Explain the effect of age distribution.
5. Discuss the concepts of property selection and investment timing.
6. Explain how to develop a personal investment strategy and how to value an investment.
7. Describe the facets of limited partnerships.
8. Explain the disclosure and blue-sky laws.

KEY • TERMS

Active investor: as defined by tax law, an investor who takes an active role in property management.

Cash flow: the number of dollars remaining each year after collecting rents and paying operating expenses and mortgage payments

Downside risk: the possibility that an investor will lose his money in an investment

Equity build-up: the increase of one's equity in a property due to mortgage balance reduction and price appreciation

Investment strategy: a plan that balances returns available with risks that must be taken in order to enhance the investor's overall welfare

Leverage: the impact that borrowed funds have on investment return

Negative cash flow: a condition wherein the cash paid out exceeds the cash received

Passive investor: as defined by tax law, an investor who does not materially participate in property management.

Prospectus: a disclosure statement that describes an investment opportunity

Straight-line depreciation: depreciation in equal amounts each year over the life of the asset

Tax shelter: the income tax savings that an investment can produce for its owner

There are more millionaires in the United States as a result of real estate investing than from any other source, including oil wells and computers. Moreover, real estate success and wealth have been and are available to people from all walks of life and all income levels. For most people thinking of making it big financially, real estate is at the top of the list. Considering that real estate provides 240 million people in the United States a place to sleep at night as well as approximately half that number a place to work during the day plus all the other uses we make of real estate, you can begin to see why there are so many opportunities in real estate investing.

The keys to your personal success are time and your intelligence. There are some who say that luck plays the main role in real estate success and that it's all a matter of waiting for the right deal to come along. In reality, however, success results when opportunity and preparedness meet. As you become more knowledgeable as to what makes a good real estate investment and you apply your time looking for real estate opportunities, you will experience success.

It is impossible to do full justice to the topic of real estate investing in one chapter. There are, however, dozens of books entirely on the subject, many of which you can find at your local library and bookstore. What this chapter will do is introduce you to some highlights of real estate investing. We'll begin with the investment benefits of real estate and then look at risks and rewards of various types of real estate, investment timing, investment strategies, and limited partnerships.

BENEFITS OF REAL ESTATE INVESTING

The monetary benefits of investing in real estate come from cash flow, tax shelter, mortgage reduction, and appreciation. **Appreciation** is the increase in property value that you as the owner hope will occur while you own the property. Enough appreciation can offset underestimated expenses, overestimated rents, and a rising adjustable rate loan. Without appreciation, a property must produce enough rental income to pay the operating expenses and loan interest, cover wear and obsolescence, and give the investor a decent return. **Mortgage reduction** occurs when, as an investor, you use a portion of a property's rental income to reduce the balance owed on the mortgage. At first the reduction is quite small because most of the loan payments are applied to interest. But eventually the balance owed begins to fall at a more rapid rate. Let's now look at cash flow, tax shelter, depreciation, and taxation of gains.

Cash Flow

Cash flow refers to the number of dollars remaining each year after collecting rents and paying operating expenses and mortgage payments. For example, suppose you own a small apartment building that generates $30,500 per year in rents. The operating expenses (including reserves) are $10,000 per year and mortgage payments are $20,000 per year. Given these facts, your cash flow picture would be as shown in Figure 23:1.

The purpose of calculating cash flow is to show the cash-in-the-pocket effect of owning a particular property. In Figure 23:1, $500 per year is going into your pocket. When money is flowing into your pocket, it is called a **positive cash flow.** If you must dip into your pocketbook to keep a property

Rent receipts for the year	$ 30,500
Less operating expenses	10,000
Less mortgage loan payments	20,000
Equals cash flow	$ 500

Figure 23:1.

going, you have a **negative cash flow,** also called an "alligator." For example, if in Figure 23:1, the mortgage payments were $21,000 per year, there would be a negative cash flow. A negative cash flow does not automatically mean a property is a poor investment. There may be tax benefits and appreciation that more than off-set this.

Two additional terms you should know are *net spendable* and *cash-on-cash.* **Net spendable** is the same thing as cash flow. **Cash-on-cash** is the cash flow that a property produces in a given year divided by the amount of cash required to buy the property. For example, if a property has a cash flow of $5,000 per year and can be purchased with a $50,000 down payment (including closing costs), the cash-on-cash figure for that property is 10%. For many real estate investors, this is the heart of the investment decision, namely, "How much do I have to put down and how much will I have in my pocket at the end of each year?"

TAX SHELTER

Broadly defined, **tax shelter** describes any tax-deductible expense generated by an investment property. Real estate examples are interest, maintenance, insurance, property taxes, and depreciation. Narrowly defined, **tax shelter** refers only to depreciation that a taxpayer can report as a taxable deduction against other income.

The United States Congress has a decades-long history of tinkering with depreciation rules for income tax calculation. During the 1960s and 1970s, to encourage investment in real estate, especially residential real estate, Congress wrote income tax rules that allowed very generous treatment of depreciation expenses. The laws thus enacted made it possible to deduct depreciation on property that was, in fact, appreciating in value. Moreover, tax laws made it possible to take a larger portion of depreciation early in the life of a building and less later. This produced paper losses for tax purposes that could offset income from one's job or from other investments. The tax benefits became so attractive that they were often a compelling force in choosing a property. In other words, an investor looked forward to not only the rents a property could produce, but also the tax savings it would produce as well as mortgage reduction and anticipated appreciation. This, plus favorable tax status upon trade or sale, made real estate the hottest investment around.

The height of quick write-off came with a 1981 federal tax law that permitted a building to be entirely depreciated in 15 years, no matter how old or how new it was. Moreover, this depreciation method, called the **Accelerated Cost Recovery System (ACRS),** allowed most of the depreciation to be taken in the early years of ownership—when it is usually most valuable to an investor. Then the tide started to change. Congress was concerned that real estate had become an immense tax loophole that needed tightening. In 1984 the depreciation period was lengthened to 18 years. In 1985 it went to 19 years, and rules were added regarding below-market interest rates on seller carryback financing (see Chapter 13). Then in the fall of 1986, major tax reforms were passed by Congress that took away nearly all the extra tax benefits previously given to real estate. Now, Congress said, real estate investments would have to stand more on their economic merits, not on favorable tax treatment. Let us look at some of the important changes regarding the taxation of real estate investments as brought by this bill.

1987-1988 TAX RULES

One of the important changes in real estate investors' income tax calculations for 1987, 1988, and beyond has to do with depreciation. Under the new tax rules that took effect on January 1, 1987, the minimum depreciation period for real estate changes from 19 years to 27½ years for residential, and from 19 years to 31½ years for commercial. (Property already owned and depreciated before that date continues to follow whatever rules were in effect when its depreciation began; i.e., they were **"grandfathered-in."**) Also, as of January 1, 1987,

Rent receipts for the year	$ 30,500
Less operating expenses	10,000
Less interest on loan	19,500
Less depreciation	8,000
Equals taxable income	**($ 7,000)***

*In accounting language, parentheses indicate a negative or minus amount.

Figure 23:2.

accelerated depreciation for real estate is repealed and only straight-line depreciation can be used. (Again, existing investments continue to use whatever depreciation method they started with.)

Another aspect of the new tax rules is that there are now stricter limits on how much loss can be deducted from a person's other income. This is true whether the property was purchased before or after January 1, 1987. Let's take a closer look, as this is a major consideration in whether to buy, sell, or hold real estate as an investment, and is important in choosing what types of real estate to own. Using our investment example, suppose that the $20,000 mortgage payment consists of $19,500 in interest (which is an expense for tax purposes) and $500 in loan reduction (which is not an expense for tax purposes). Suppose also that tax law allows $8,000 in depreciation on the property for the year. The result is a taxable loss as shown in Figure 23:2.

Loss Limitations

Under the old (pre-1987) tax rules, all of the operating expenses, the interest, and the depreciation was deductible against other income, with relatively little restriction. Under the new rules—i.e., those in effect beginning January 1, 1987, there are substantial restrictions, and a distinction is made between "passive investors" and "active investors." If you are a **passive investor,** you can deduct your loss only against income from other passive investments. A passive investor is one who does not materially participate on a "regular, substantial and continuous basis," for example, a limited partner. For passive investments made before 1987, this rule is being phased in over four years, from 1987 through 1990.

If you are an **active investor** (for example, you manage the rentals you own), it is possible to use as much as $25,000 of your losses to offset your other income (such as your job income). However, this applies only to taxpayers with up to $100,000 of adjusted gross income (as defined on one's annual IRS Form 1040). For those with higher adjusted gross incomes, the loss deduction is gradually reduced, and is eliminated at $150,000 of adjusted gross income. This aspect of the tax law change will have little effect on the middle-income person who owns a rental house or two, or a small apartment building, and has a hand in managing them. But you can expect to see people affected by the tax reform law restructure some of their investments and participate more in them. For example, investors with passive losses will look for properties with passive income, such as parking lots. Those who do not actively manage their real estate holdings will take a more active role in order to qualify as an active investor. Loss-producing partnerships will be attractive acquisitions for income-producing corporations.

CALCULATING DEPRECIATION

As noted earlier, under tax rules effective January 1, 1987, depreciation is to be straight-line (so-called because it is a straight line on a graph; see Figure 23:3). **Straight-line depreciation** is calculated by taking the total amount of anticipated depreciation and dividing by the number of years. For example, a building valued at $275,000 for depreciation purposes and depreciated over 27½ years using the straight-line method will have $10,000 in depreciation each year. (Note that only improvements are depreciable; land is not. Therefore, when buying investment real estate, it is necessary to subtract the value of the land from the purchase price before calculating depreciation.)

In contrast to straight-line depreciation, **accelerated depreciation** is any method of depreciation that allows depreciation at a rate faster than straight-line during the first several years of

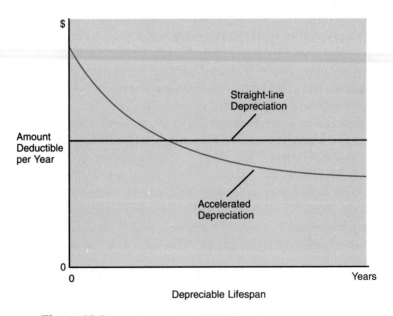

Figure 23:3.

ownership. Although this is not allowed for real property placed in service starting January 1, 1987, it is retained for certain types of personal property used in business (such as a real estate agent's automobile) and for real property started on accelerated depreciation before 1987. Figure 23:3 illustrates both straight-line and accelerated depreciation. Neither method allows a taxpayer to depreciate more than the cost of the asset.

Passive losses (including depreciation) that are unusable in any given year can be carried forward from year to year and used later. Any losses carried forward into the year of sale can be deducted in full at that time. Depreciation recapture, a tax rule used in some past years to counterbalance the benefits of accelerated depreciation, phases out during 1987 and is repealed in 1988.

GAIN ON SALE

A major tax law change that went into effect starting January 1, 1987, is the repeal of the long-term capital gain exclusion. Sixty percent of the gain from real and personal property sold before that date, provided it was owned for more than six months, was excluded from income. Under the new rule, all gains are included and taxed as ordinary income, regardless of how long the property has been owned. While ordinary income tax rates have been reduced, the net effect is a higher tax on gains.

WATCH LIST

Tax law changes have been made in the past decade with increasing frequency and impact. In fact, since the mid-1980s one of the biggest risks in real estate has been and continues to be tax law changes. The values of land and buildings can, and do, go up and down with changes in tax rules. (This is in addition to the marketplace risks that an investor must take.) Therefore, it is of great importance that you stay abreast of tax law changes, impending tax law changes, and even swings in the mood of Congress toward real estate. As noted earlier in this chapter, the 1960s and 1970s saw exceptionally favorable treatment of real estate by the tax laws. In the 1990s, real estate will have to stand on its own as an economic investment, although the capital gains exclusion may be reinstated. Keep this in mind as you continue to read this chapter. Also keep in mind that because approximately two out of three households in the United States own their homes, home ownership is likely to

Equity at Time of Purchase		Equity 5 Years Later		Equity Build-up	
Purchase price	$200,000	Market value	$220,000	Current equity	$100,000
Mortgage loan	- 140,000	Less loan balance	- 120,000	Less beginning equity	- 60,000
Down payment (equity)	$ 60,000	Equals current equity	$100,000	Equals equity build-up	$ 40,000

Figure 23:4. Calculating Equity Build-up

continue its favored tax status. Thus, as reported in Chapter 13, the new tax rules have pretty much left intact the personal deduction for home loan interest and property taxes, the 2-year rollover privilege, and the $125,000 gain exclusion for persons over 55.

EQUITY BUILD-UP

An owner's **equity** in a property is defined as the market value of the property less all liens or other charges against the property. Thus, if you own a property worth $125,000 and owe $75,000, your equity is $50,000. If you own that property with your brother or sister, each with a one-half interest, your equity is $25,000 and his/her equity is $25,000.

Equity build-up is the change in your equity over a period of time. Suppose you purchase a small apartment building for $200,000, placing $60,000 down and borrowing the balance. Your beginning equity is your down payment of $60,000. If after 5 years you have paid the loan down to $120,000 and you can sell the property for $220,000, your equity is now $100,000. Since you started with $60,000, your equity build-up is $40,000. Figure 23:4 recaps this calculation.

LEVERAGE

Leverage is the impact that borrowed funds have on investment return. The purpose of borrowing is to earn more on the borrowed funds than the funds cost. For example, suppose you are an investor and you have $250,000 to invest in an apartment building. If you use all your money to buy a $250,000 building, there is zero leverage. If you use your $250,000 to buy a $500,000 building, there is 50% leverage. If you use your $250,000 to buy a $2,500,000 building there is 90% leverage.

Whether or not to leverage depends on whether the property can reasonably be expected to produce cash flow, tax benefits, mortgage reduction, and appreciation in excess of the cost of the borrowed funds. The decision also depends on your willingness to take risk. For example, the $250,000 building would have to fall to zero value before you lost all of your money. Moreover, the building could experience a vacancy rate on the order of 60%, and there would still be enough cash to meet out-of-pocket operating expenses. In other words, with zero leverage there is very little likelihood of a total financial wipe-out.

In contrast, if you buy the $2,500,000 apartment building, a 10% drop in the property's value to $2,250,000 wipes out your entire equity. Moreover, even the slightest drop-off in occupancy from 95% down to 85% will cause great strain on your ability to meet mortgage loan payments and out-of-pocket operating expenses.

But, suppose apartment building values increase by 10%. If you bought the $250,000 building, it will now be worth $275,000, an increase of $25,000 on your investment of $250,000. If you bought the $2,500,000 building, it will now be worth $2,750,000, an increase of $250,000 on your investment of $250,000. As you can see, leverage can work both against you and for you. If the benefits from borrowing exceed the costs of borrowing, it is called **positive leverage**. If the borrowed funds cost more than they are producing, it is called **negative leverage.**

INVESTMENT TIMING

Investment timing refers to the fact that the risks and rewards available from owning improved real estate depend to a great extent on the point in the life of a property at which an investment is made. The riskiest point to invest is when a project is in the idea stage. Although the project may look feasible on paper, major unknowns exist such as the ability to obtain proper zoning, building permits, and a loan commitment; the actual cost of construction, the ability to find tenants, the actual rent they will pay, and the actual operating costs of the property. As each of these hurdles is cleared, the risk of the investor diminishes.

The least risky point to invest is when the building is finished and filled with tenants. At this point actual rents and actual operating expenses are known, and for the first ten years of the building's life major repairs are not expected. However, an investor entering at this point can expect to receive smaller return on his investment than if he had invested earlier when the risks were greater. After the tenth year, risks and expenses increase somewhat and so should the returns. Poor construction quality may become apparent and result in costly repairs. By the time the building is 20 years old, the building will need paint plus new appliances, water heaters, and air conditioners.

During the third and fourth decade, major expense items such as a new roof, replacement of plumbing fixtures, repair of parking areas, and general renovation become necessary. Also, maintenance costs climb as a building becomes older and decisions will be necessary regarding whether or not major remodeling should be undertaken. Meanwhile, the character of the neighborhood around the property may be changing—houses converted to apartments, apartments to shopping centers and offices, and so forth. There may be a population shift into the area or out of the area. The investor must consider the effect of these changes on the probable remaining economic life of a structure before offering to buy it. If he buys with the intention of removing the structure, then he is returning to the first stage of the development cycle.

LIMITED PARTNERSHIPS

The vast majority of investors in the United States do not have the capital to buy a multi-million dollar project single-handedly. Moreover, many persons who would like to own real estate for its yield and tax benefits do not do so because they wish to avoid the work and responsibilities of property management. As a result the use of limited partnerships for real estate investment has become widespread in the United States in the last 30 years.

A limited partnership is composed of general and limited partners. The **general partners** organize and operate the partnership, contribute some capital, and agree to accept the full financial liability of the partnership. The **limited partners** provide the bulk of the investment capital, have little say in the day-to-day management of the partnership, share in the profits and losses, and contract with their general partners to limit the financial liability of each limited partner to the amount he or she invests.

The advantages of limited liability, minimum management responsibility, and direct pass-through of profits and losses for taxation purposes have made this form of ownership popular. However, being free of management responsibility is only advantageous to the investors if the general partners are capable and honest. If they are not, the only control open to the limited partners is to vote to replace the general partners.

Before investing in a limited partnership, one should carefully read the **prospectus** that describes the investment. One should also investigate the past record of the general partners, for this is usually a good indication of how the new partnership will be managed. The investigation should include their previous investments, talking to past investors, and checking court records for any legal complaints brought against them. Additionally, the prospective partner should be prepared to stay in for the duration of the partnership as the resale market for limited partnership interests is small.

EFFORT AND COURAGE

As the opening paragraph of this chapter suggested, you can become rich in real estate, very, very rich. But success won't drop in your lap; it takes effort and courage. Good properties and good opportunities are always available, but you will look at 50 properties to find one. And then you will need to know which are the 49 you don't want. That is the part that takes effort. To know what a good opportunity looks like, you need to learn. This book is a step in that direction. From here, start reading articles and books on real estate investing from libraries and bookstores and take course work in real estate investing. But most important, now is the time to get out and start looking at properties if you have not already done so. Begin to get a sense in the field for what you are learning from your books and classes. Ask questions as you go along. After you've viewed several dozen properties and talked to appraisers, lenders, brokers, property managers, etc., you will begin to get a feel for the market—what's for sale, what a property can earn, how much mortgage money costs, etc. As you do this you will see everything you've learned in this book come to life.

As you continue, you will recognize what a good investment property looks like. At this point, your next big step is to muster the courage to acquire it. All the real estate investment education you've received will not translate into money in your pocket until you make an offer—until you put your money, reputation, and good judgment on the line. But once you get the feel of it, it becomes easier and if you stick with it for ten years, you'll probably find it harder not to be a millionaire than it is to be one.

1. ABZ Realty offers you a four-unit residential building in which each unit rents for $500 per month. Given a 5 percent vacancy rate, operating expenses of $700 per month, and mortgage payments of $1,500 per month, you can anticipate a monthly
   A. net spendable of $200.   C. negative cash flow of $200.
   B. net spendable of $300.   D. negative cash flow of $300.

2. Monetary benefits of investing in real estate come from
   A. cash flow.   C. mortgage reduction.
   B. tax shelter.   D. All of the above.

3. A negative cash flow may be offset by
   A. tax shelter.   C. Both A and B.
   B. appreciation.   D. Neither A nor B.

4. Mortgage balance reduction
   A. is an out-of-pocket expense.
   B. is a deduction for tax purposes.
   C. is tax exempted.
   D. is quite large at the beginning of the loan period.

5. The value of depreciation on an investment property is
   A. inversely proportional to the investor's tax bracket.
   B. the same to all investors, regardless of their tax bracket.
   C. directly proportional to the investor's tax bracket.
   D. not a factor in the investment decision.

6. Tax laws allow depreciation on a building to be
   A. started over each time the property is sold.
   B. more than its value.
   C. Both A and B.
   D. Neither A nor B.

7. Equity build-up in a property can be the result of
   A. mortgage reduction.   C. Both A and B.
   B. appreciation.   D. Neither A nor B.

8. Negative leverage occurs when
   A. borrowed funds cost more than they produce in benefits.
   B. an investment property depreciates in value.
   C. Both A and B.
   D. Neither A nor B.

9. What is the cash-on-cash ratio for a property which has a cash flow of $16,900 and could be purchased with a down payment of $130,000?
   A. 7.69%.   C. 0.12.
   B. 0.219.   D. 0.13.

10. To be considered a good investment, when a property which generates a negative cash flow is sold,
   A. there must be a substantial increase in property value.
   B. there need be little increase in property value.
   C. the investor is best off if the property has decreased in value.

11. Which of the following would expect to receive a higher return per investment dollar? An investor who purchased during the
    A. first decade of building life.
    B. second decade of building life.
    C. third or fourth decade of building life.
    D. All would expect the same return.

12. For most people, when is the best time in life to undertake high-risk investments?
    A. Under age 25.
    B. Age 25 to 45.
    C. Age 55 to 65.
    D. Over age 65.

13. In a typical limited partnership, the
    A. organizers are the limited partners.
    B. investors are the general partners.
    C. Both A and B.
    D. Neither A nor B.

14. In a limited partnership, which cannot lose more than the amount they have invested?
    A. General partners.
    B. Limited partners.
    C. Organizers.
    D. Managers.

15. A disclosure statement given to prospective investors in a limited partnership, outlining the plans and prospects for the parthership, is called a
    A. Prospectus
    B. Forecast statement
    C. Cash flow
    D. Binder

APPENDIX A

Construction Illustrations and Terminology

Figure A:1.   **Combined Slab and Foundation (thickened edge slab)**

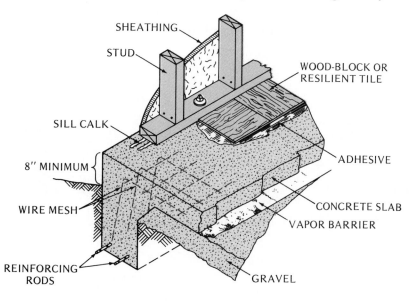

SHEATHING

STUD

WOOD-BLOCK OR RESILIENT TILE

SILL CALK

8″ MINIMUM

ADHESIVE

WIRE MESH

CONCRETE SLAB

VAPOR BARRIER

REINFORCING RODS

GRAVEL

Basement Details

Figure A:2.

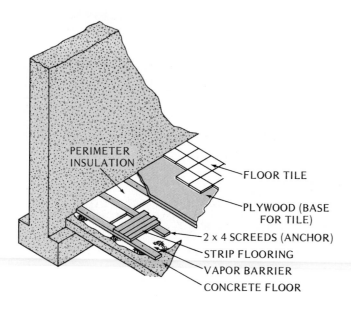

PERIMETER INSULATION

FLOOR TILE

PLYWOOD (BASE FOR TILE)

2 x 4 SCREEDS (ANCHOR)

STRIP FLOORING

VAPOR BARRIER

CONCRETE FLOOR

Floor Framing

Figure A:3.

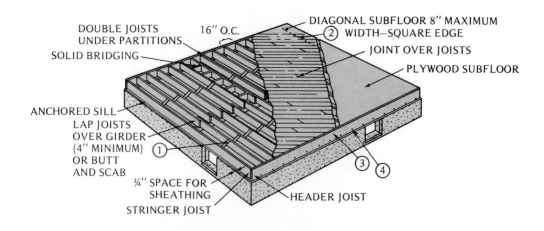

DOUBLE JOISTS UNDER PARTITIONS

16" O.C.

DIAGONAL SUBFLOOR 8" MAXIMUM
② WIDTH—SQUARE EDGE

JOINT OVER JOISTS

SOLID BRIDGING

PLYWOOD SUBFLOOR

ANCHORED SILL

LAP JOISTS OVER GIRDER (4" MINIMUM) ① OR BUTT AND SCAB

¾" SPACE FOR SHEATHING

STRINGER JOIST

③ ④

HEADER JOIST

Figure A:4.   **Wall Framing Used with Platform Construction**

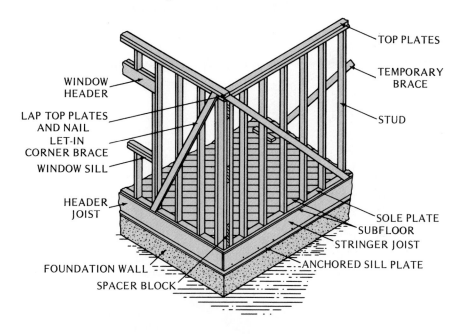

Figure A:5.   **Headers for Windows and Door Openings**

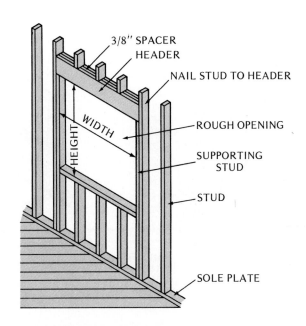

Vertical Application of Plywood or Structural Insulating Board Sheathing

Figure A:6.

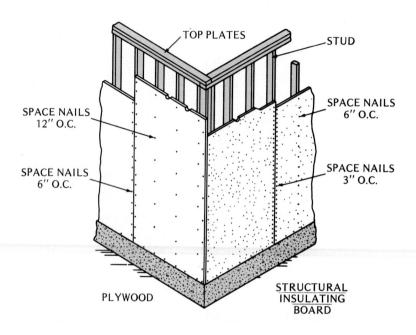

TOP PLATES

STUD

SPACE NAILS
6″ O.C.

SPACE NAILS
12″ O.C.

SPACE NAILS
3″ O.C.

SPACE NAILS
6″ O.C.

PLYWOOD

STRUCTURAL
INSULATING
BOARD

Exterior Siding

Figure A:7.

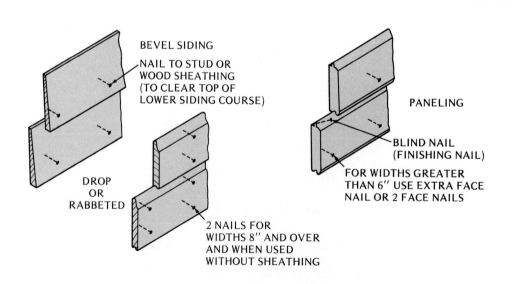

BEVEL SIDING

NAIL TO STUD OR
WOOD SHEATHING
(TO CLEAR TOP OF
LOWER SIDING COURSE)

PANELING

DROP
OR
RABBETED

BLIND NAIL
(FINISHING NAIL)

FOR WIDTHS GREATER
THAN 6″ USE EXTRA FACE
NAIL OR 2 FACE NAILS

2 NAILS FOR
WIDTHS 8″ AND OVER
AND WHEN USED
WITHOUT SHEATHING

Figure A:8.   **Vertical Board Siding**

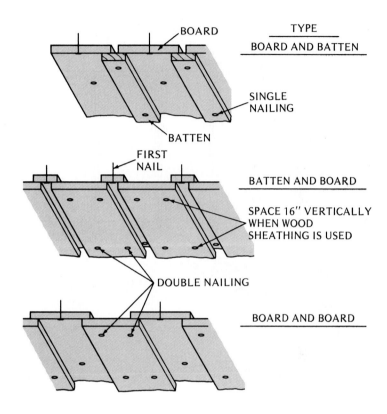

TYPE

BOARD

BOARD AND BATTEN

SINGLE
NAILING

BATTEN

FIRST
NAIL

BATTEN AND BOARD

SPACE 16" VERTICALLY
WHEN WOOD
SHEATHING IS USED

DOUBLE NAILING

BOARD AND BOARD

Application of Gypsum Board Finish

Figure A:9.

A: vertical application; B: horizontal application

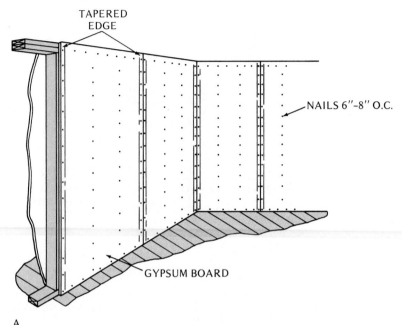

TAPERED EDGE

NAILS 6″–8″ O.C.

GYPSUM BOARD

A

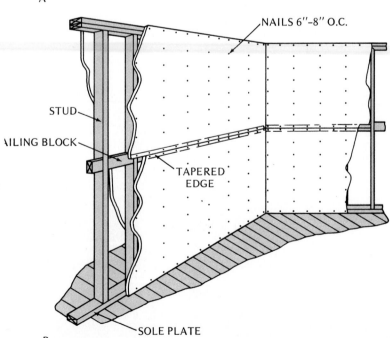

NAILS 6″–8″ O.C.

STUD

\ILING BLOCK

TAPERED EDGE

SOLE PLATE

B

Figure A:10.   **Application of Insulation**

A: wall section with blanket type; B: wall section with "press-fit" insulation; C: ceiling with full insulation

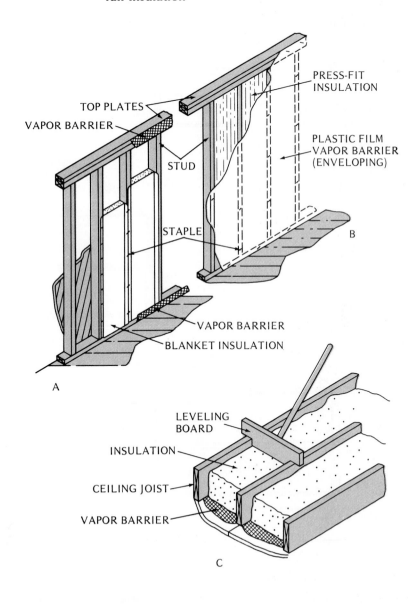

Placement of Insulation   **Figure A:11.**

A: in walls, floor and ceiling; B: in 1½ story house; C: at attic door; D: in flat roof

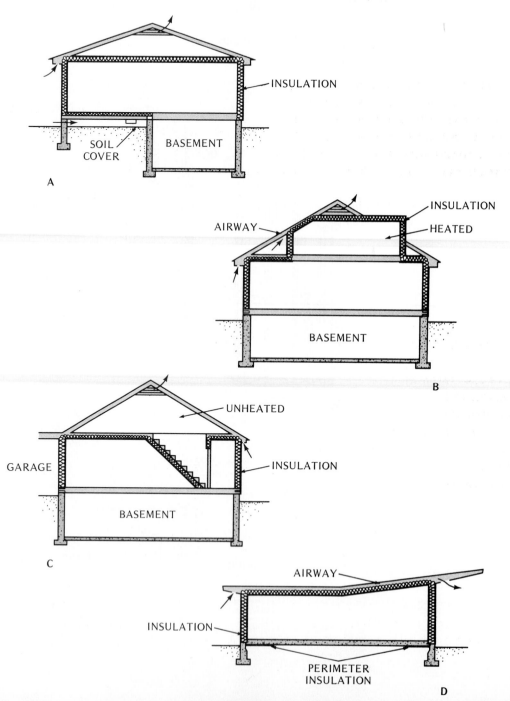

Figure A:12.

Masonry Fireplace

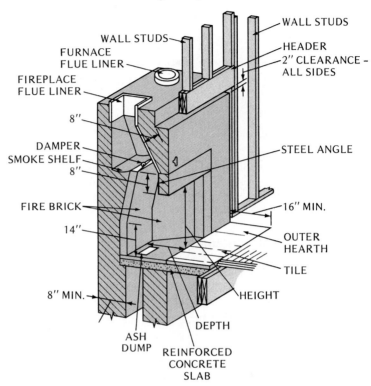

Figure A:13.

Stairway Details

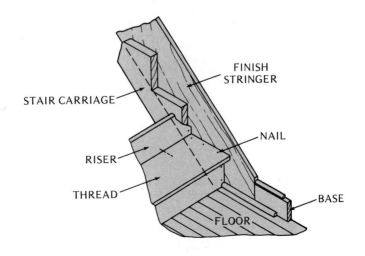

Door Details

Figure A:14.

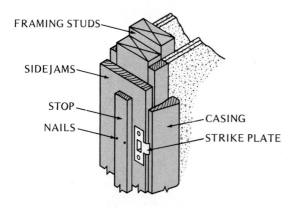

FRAMING STUDS

SIDEJAMS

STOP

NAILS

CASING

STRIKE PLATE

Sound Insulation

Figure A:15.

Wall Detail	Description	STC Rating
├──16″──┤ 2 x 4	½" Gypsum Wallboard	32
	⅝" Gypsum Wallboard	37
2 x 4	⅝" Gypsum Wallboard (Double Layer Each Side)	45
2 x 4 BETWEEN OR "WOVEN"	½" Gypsum Wallboard 1½" Fibrous Insulation	49
├──16″──┤ 2 x 4	Resilient Clips to ⅜" Gypsum Backer Board ½" Fiberboard (Laminated) (Each Side)	52

Figure A:16.   **Ceiling and Roof Framing**

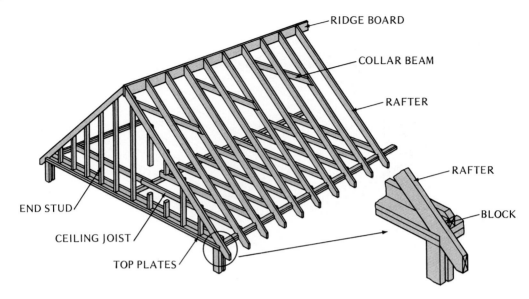

Figure A:17.   **Installation of Board Roof Sheathing,
Showing Both Closed and Spaced Types**

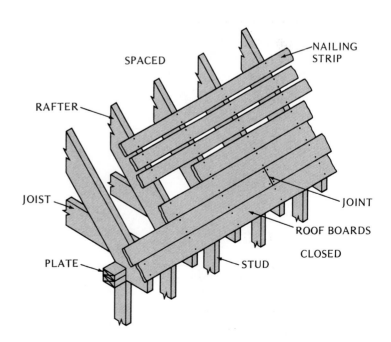

Built-up Roof

Figure A:18.

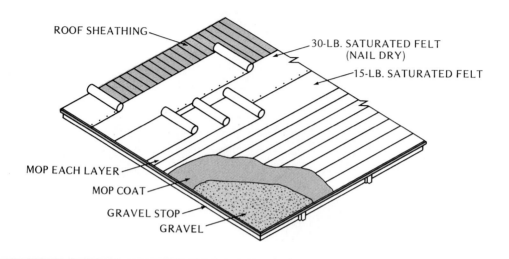

Application of Asphalt Shingles

Figure A:19.

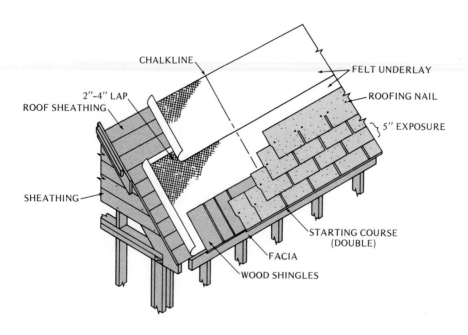

Figure A:20.   **Roofs Using Single Roof Construction**

A: flat roof; B: low-pitched roof

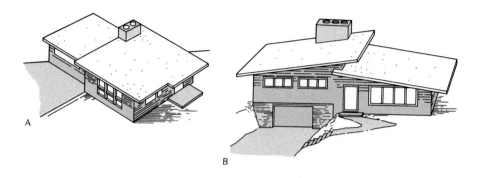

Figure A:21.   **Types of Pitched Roofs**

A: gable; B: gable with dormers; C: hip

A: gable; B: gable with dormers; C: hip

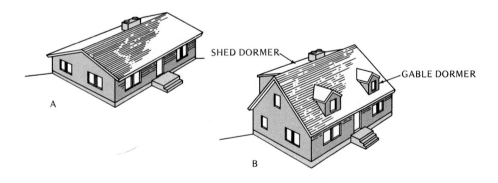

APPENDIX B
Real Estate Math Review

Percent (%) means part per hundred. For example, 25% means 25 parts per hundred; 10% means 10 parts per hundred. Percentages are related to common and decimal fractions as follows:

5%	= 0.05	=	$\frac{1}{20}$
10%	= 0.10	=	$\frac{1}{10}$
25%	= 0.25	=	$\frac{1}{4}$
75%	= 0.75	=	$\frac{3}{4}$
99%	= 0.99	=	$\frac{99}{100}$

A percentage greater than 100% is greater than 1. For example:

110%	= 1.10	=	$1\text{-}\frac{1}{10}$
150%	= 1.50	=	$1\text{-}\frac{1}{2}$
200%	= 2.00	=	2
1,100%	=11.00	=	11

To change a decimal fraction to a percentage, move the decimal point two places to the right and add the % sign. For example:

0.001	=	0.1%
0.01	=	1%
0.06	=	6%
0.35	=	35%
0.356	=	35.6%

A percentage can be changed to a common fraction by writing it as hundredths and then reducing it to its lowest common denominator. For example:

20%	=	$\frac{20}{100}$	=	$\frac{1}{5}$
90%	=	$\frac{90}{100}$	=	$\frac{9}{10}$
225%	=	$\frac{225}{100}$	=	$2\frac{1}{4}$

To add decimals, place the decimal points directly over one another. Then place the decimal point for the solutions in the same column and add. For example:

$$\begin{array}{r} 6.25 \\ 1.10 \\ \underline{10.277} \\ 17.627 \end{array}$$

If you are working with percentages, there is no need to convert to decimal fractions; just line up the decimal points and add. For example:

$$\begin{array}{r} 68.8\% \\ 6.0\% \\ \underline{25.2\%} \\ 100.0\% \end{array}$$

When subtracting, the same methods apply. For example:

$$\begin{array}{rr} 1.00 & 100\% \\ \underline{-0.80} & \underline{-80\%} \\ 0.20 & 20\% \end{array}$$

When there is a mixture of decimal fractions and percentages, first convert them all either to percentage or to decimal fractions.

Multiplying decimals is like multiplying whole numbers except that the decimal point must be correctly placed. This is done by counting the total number of places to the right of the decimal point in the numbers to be multiplied. Then count off the same number of places in the answer. The following examples illustrate this:

$$\begin{array}{cccccc} 0.6 & 0.2 & 1.01 & 6 & 6 & 0.03 \\ \underline{\times 0.3} & \underline{\times 0.2} & \underline{\times 2} & \underline{\times 0.1} & \underline{\times 0.11} & \underline{\times 0.02} \\ 0.18 & 0.04 & 2.02 & 0.6 & 0.66 & 0.0006 \end{array}$$

When dividing, the process starts with properly placing the decimal point. A normal division then follows. When a decimal number is divided by a whole number, place the decimal point in the answer directly above the decimal point in the problem. For example:

$$\begin{array}{cc} 1.03 & 0.033 \\ 3\overline{)3.09} & 3\overline{)0.099} \end{array}$$

To divide by a decimal number, you must first change the divisor to a whole number. Then you must make a corresponding change in the dividend. This is done by simply moving both decimal points the same number of places to the right. For example, to divide 0.06 by 0.02, move the decimal point of each to the right two places.

$0.02\overline{)0.06}$ becomes $2\overline{)6}$

$0.5\overline{)3}$ becomes $5\overline{)30}$

$0.05\overline{)30}$ becomes $5\overline{)3,000}$

When multiplying or dividing with percentages, first convert them to decimal form. Thus 6% of 200 is

$$\begin{array}{r} 200 \\ \times\ \underline{0.06} \\ 12.00 \end{array}$$

PROBLEMS INVOLVING RATES

A simple way to solve rate problems is to think of
the word **is** as = (an equal sign).
the word **of** as × (a multiplication sign).
the word **per** as ÷ (a division sign).

for example:
"7% of $50,000 is $3,500"
translates:
"7% × $50,000 = $3,500"

Problem 1
Beverly Broker sells a house for $60,000. Her share of the commission is to be 2.5% of the sales price. How much does she earn?
Her commission is 2.5% of $60,000
Her commission = 0.025 × $60,000
Her commission = $1,500

Problem 2
Sam Salesman works in an office which will pay him 70% of the commission on each home he lists and sells. With a 6% commission, how much would he earn on a $50,000 sale?
His commission is 70% of 6% of $50,000
His commission = 0.70 × 0.06 × $50,000
His commission = $2,100

Problem 3
Newt Newcomer wants to earn $21,000 during his first 12 months as a salesman. He feels he can average 3% on each sale. How much property must he sell?

3% of sales is $21,000

0.03 × sales = $21,000

sales = $21,000 ÷ 0.03

sales = $700,000

Note: An equation will remain an equation as long as you make the same change on both sides of the equal sign. If you add the same number to both sides, it is still an equation. If you subtract the same amount from each side, it is still equal. If you multiply both sides by the same thing, it remains equal. If you divide both sides by the same thing, it remains equal.

Problem 4

An apartment building nets the owners $12,000 per year on their investment of $100,000. What percent return are they receiving on their investment?

$12,000 is ____% of $100,000

$12,000 = ____% × $100,000

$$\frac{\$12,000}{\$100,000} = 12\%$$

Problem 5

Smith wants to sell his property and have $47,000 after paying a 6% brokerage commission on the sales price. What price must Smith get?

$47,000 is 94% of selling price

$47,000 = 0.94 × selling price

$$\frac{\$47,000}{0.94} = \text{selling price}$$

$50,000 = selling price

Problem 6

Miller sold his home for $75,000, paid off an existing loan of $35,000, and paid closing cost of $500. The brokerage commission was 6% of the sales price. How much money did Miller receive? The amount he received is 94% of $75,000 less $35,500.

amount = 0.94 × $75,000 − $35,000

amount = $70,500 − $35,500

amount = $35,000

Problem 7

The assessed valuation of the Kelly home is $10,000. If the property tax rate is $12.50 per $100 of assessed valuation, what is the tax?

The tax is $\dfrac{\$12.50}{\$100}$ of $10,000

$$\text{tax} = \frac{\$12.50}{\$100} \times \$10,000$$
$$\text{tax} = \$1,250$$

Problem 8
Property in Clark County is assessed at 75% of market value. What should the assessed valuation of a $40,000 property be?
Assessed valuation is 75% of market value
Assessed valuation = 0.75 × $40,000
Assessed valuation = $30,000

Problem 9
An insurance company charges $0.24 per $100 of coverage for a one-year fire insurance policy. How much would a $40,000 policy cost?

Cost is $\dfrac{\$0.24}{\$100}$ of $40,000

$\text{Cost} = \dfrac{\$0.24}{\$100} \times \$40,000$

Cost = $96

AREA MEASUREMENT

The measurement of the distance from one point to another is called *linear* measurement. Usually this is along a straight line, but it can also be along a curved line. Distance is measured in inches, feet, yards, and miles. Less commonly used are chains (66 feet) and rods (16 and a half feet). Surface areas are measured in square feet, square yards, acres (43,560 square feet), and square miles. In the metric system, the standard unit of linear measurement is the meter (39.37 inches). Land area is measured in square meters and hectares. A hectare contains 10,000 square meters or 2.471 acres.

To determine the area of a square or rectangle, multiply its length times its width. The formula is:
Area = Length × Width
A = L × W

Problem 10
A parcel of land measures 660 feet by 330 feet. How many square feet is this?
Area = 660 feet × 330 feet
Area = 217,800 square feet

How many acres does this parcel contain?
Acres = 217,800 ÷ 43,560
Acres = 5

If a buyer offers $42,500 for this parcel, how much is the offering per acre?

$42,500 ÷ 5 = $8,500

To determine the area of a right triangle, multiply one-half of the base times the height:

A = ½ × B × H
A = ½ × 25 × 50
A = 625 square feet

A = ½ × B × H
A = ½ × 40 × 20
A = 400 square feet

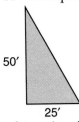

To determine the area of a circle, multiply 3.14 (π) times the square of the radius:

$A = \pi \times r^2$
$A = 3.14 \times 40^2$
A = 3.14 × 1,600
A = 5,024 sq ft

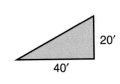

Note: Where the diameter of a circle is given, divide by two to get the radius.

To determine the area of composite figures, separate them into their various components. Thus:

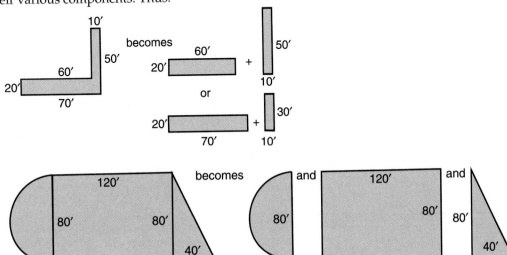

VOLUME
MEASUREMENT

Volume is measured in cubic units. The formula is:
Volume = Length × Width × Height
$$V = L \times W \times H$$

For example, what is the volume of a room that is 10 ft by 15 ft with an 8 ft ceiling?
$$V = 10' \times 15' \times 8'$$
$$V = 1,200 \text{ cu ft}$$

> **Caution:** When solving area and volume problems, make certain that all the units are the same. For example, if a parcel of land is one-half mile long and 200 ft wide, convert one measurement so that both are expressed in the same unit; thus the answer will be either in square feet or in square miles. There is no such area measurement as a mile-foot. If a building is 100 yards long by 100 feet wide by 16' 6" high, convert to 300 ft by 100 ft by 16.5 before multiplying.

RATIOS
AND PROPORTIONS

If the label on a five-gallon can of paint says it will cover 2,000 square feet, how many gallons are necessary to cover 3,600 sq ft?

A problem like this can be solved two ways:
One way is to find out what area one gallon will cover. In this case 2,000 sq ft ÷ 5 gallons = 400 sq ft per gallon. Then divide 400 sq ft/gal into 3,600 sq ft and the result is 9 gallons.
The other method is to set up a proportion:

$$\frac{5 \text{ gal}}{2,000 \text{ sq ft}} = \frac{Y \text{ gal}}{3,600 \text{ sq ft}}$$

This reads, "5 gallons is to 2,000 sq ft as 'Y' gallons is to 3,600 sq ft." To solve for "Y," multiply both sides of the proportion by 3,600 sq ft. Thus:

$$\frac{5 \text{ gal} \times 3,600 \text{ sq ft}}{2,000 \text{ sq ft}} = Y \text{ gal}$$

Divide 2,000 sq ft into 3,600 sq ft and multiply the result by 5 gallons to get the answer.

FRONT-FOOT
CALCULATIONS

When land is sold on a front-foot basis, the price is the number of feet fronting on the street times the price per front foot.

Price = front footage × rate per front foot

Thus a 50 ft × 150 ft lot priced at $1,000 per front foot would sell for $50,000. Note that in giving the dimensions of a lot, the first dimension given is the street frontage. The second dimension is the depth of the lot.

APPENDIX C _____

Measurement Conversion Table

Mile =
    5,280 feet
    1,760 yards
      320 rods
       80 chains
         = 1.609 kilometers

Square mile =
      640 acres
         = 2.590 sq kilometers

Acre =
    43,560 sq ft
     4,840 sq yds
      160 sq rods
         = 4,047 sq meters

Rod =
    16.5 feet
         = 5.029 meters

Chain =
     66 feet
      4 rods
   100 links
         = 20.117 meters

Meter =
   39.37 inches
         = 1,000 millimeters
    3.281 feet
         = 100 centimeters
    1.094 yards
         = 10 decimeters

Kilometer =
    0.6214 miles
    3,281 feet
    1,094 yards
         = 1,000 meters

Square meter =
    10,765 sq ft
    1.196 sq yds
         = 10,000 sq centimeters

Hectare =
    2.47 acres
    107,600 sq ft
    11,960 sq yds
         = 10,000 sq meters

Square kilometer =
    0.3861 sq miles
    247 acres
         = 1,000,000 sq meters

Kilogram =
    2.205 pounds
         = 1,000 grams

Liter =
    1.052 quarts
    0.263 quarts
         = 1,000 milliliters

Metric ton =
    2,205 pounds
    1.102 tons
         = 1,000 kilograms

APPENDIX D

Answers to Chapter Questions and Problems

CHAPTER 2	**1.** B	**2.** E	**3.** E	**4.** A	**5.** B	**6.** B
	7. A	**8.** D	**9.** B	**10.** C	**11.** D	**12.** A
	13. A	**14.** A	**15.** A	**16.** B	**17.** D	**18.** D
	19. A	**20.** B				

CHAPTER 3	**1.** B	**2.** E	**3.** B	**4.** D	**5.** C	**6.** D
	7. B	**8.** A	**9.** C	**10.** C	**11.** B	**12.** D
	13. C	**14.** E	**15.** D	**16.** D	**17.** C	**18.** E
	19. B	**20.** A				

CHAPTER 4	**1.** C	**2.** A	**3.** B	**4.** B	**5.** A	**6.** C
	7. A	**8.** A	**9.** C	**10.** D	**11.** D	**12.** B
	13. C	**14.** C	**15.** D	**16.** A	**17.** C	**18.** A
	19. A	**20.** B				

CHAPTER 5	**1.** D	**2.** C	**3.** A	**4.** D	**5.** B	**6.** C
	7. B	**8.** B	**9.** A	**10.** C	**11.** A	**12.** D
	13. C	**14.** D	**15.** C	**16.** D	**17.** B	**18.** C
	19. C	**20.** C				

CHAPTER 6	**1.** D	**2.** C	**3.** A	**4.** D	**5.** D	**6.** C
	7. C	**8.** C	**9.** B	**10.** B	**11.** C	**12.** B
	13. C	**14.** B	**15.** D	**16.** B	**17.** D	**18.** B
	19. C	**20.** D				

1. E	2. D	3. C	4. C	5. D	6. C	CHAPTER 7
7. D	8. B	9. C	10. D	11. D	12. D	
13. D	14. C	15. C	16. A	17. D	18. B	
19. B	20. B					

1. B	2. E	3. A	4. C	5. C	6. C	CHAPTER 8
7. D	8. B	9. A	10. D	11. C	12. C	
13. E	14. A	15. B	16. E	17. A	18. A	
19. D	20. B					

1. B	2. C	3. C	4. C	5. E	6. C	CHAPTER 9
7. C	8. C	9. C	10. C	11. C	12. A	
13. C	14. D	15. B	16. C	17. C	18. C	
19. C	20. A					

1. D	2. C	3. C	4. D	5. A	6. B	CHAPTER 10
7. C	8. E	9. B	10. D			

1. A	2. B	3. A	4. E	5. C	6. B	CHAPTER 11
7. D	8. B	9. B	10. A	11. C	12. C	
13. D	14. B	15. D	16. A	17. C	18. C	
19. D	20. B					

1. A	2. D	3. B	4. D	5. C	6. C	CHAPTER 12
7. C	8. B	9. E	10. C	11. C	12. C	
13. A	14. C	15. A	16. C	17. A	18. C	
19. B	20. D					

1. A	2. C	3. A	4. A	5. D	6. D	CHAPTER 13
7. A	8. C	9. D	10. C	11. C	12. B	
13. C	14. C	15. C	16. D	17. A	18. B	
19. D	20. B					

1. E	2. D	3. B	4. E	5. C	6. C	CHAPTER 14
7. D	8. D	9. D	10. C	11. C	12. C	
13. A	14. D	15. D	16. B	17. C	18. B	
19. A	20. A					

1. A	2. B	3. C	4. B	5. B	6. D	CHAPTER 15
7. C	8. D	9. C	10. C	11. C	12. B	
13. A	14. D	15. E	16. B	17. C	18. A	
19. B	20. B					

CHAPTER 16	1. C	2. B	3. A	4. A	5. D	6. C
	7. D	8. D	9. A	10. C	11. A	12. C
	13. C	14. C	15. C	16. C	17. D	18. A
	19. A	20. C				

CHAPTER 17	1. D	2. C	3. E	4. C	5. A	6. B
	7. B	8. D	9. B	10. C	11. C	12. C
	13. B	14. D	15. E	16. D	17. C	18. B
	19. B	20. D				

CHAPTER 18	1. B	2. A	3. C	4. C	5. D	6. E
	7. B	8. A	9. C	10. C	11. A	12. D
	13. D	14. C	15. C	16. B	17. E	18. D
	19. C	20. A				

CHAPTER 19	1. C	2. B	3. D	4. C	5. A	6. C
	7. B	8. A	9. D	10. C	11. B	12. B
	13. C	14. C	15. D	16. D	17. B	18. A
	19. E	20. B				

CHAPTER 20	1. C	2. A	3. B	4. C	5. A	6. D
	7. A	8. A	9. B	10. C	11. A	12. D
	13. A	14. B	15. D			

CHAPTER 21	1. B	2. D	3. C	4. A	5. B	6. C
	7. C	8. A	9. C	10. A	11. B	12. C
	13. A	14. A	15. D	16. C	17. D	18. B
	19. D	20. D				

CHAPTER 22	1. D	2. D	3. D	4. C	5. D	6. A
	7. D	8. C	9. D	10. A	11. B	12. A
	13. B	14. D	15. C	16. D	17. B	18. C
	19. B	20. D				

CHAPTER 23	1. D	2. D	3. C	4. A	5. C	6. A
	7. C	8. A	9. D	10. A	11. C	12. D
	13. C	14. B	15. A			

Index and Glossary

unlimited liability for its debts 536

General plan: a comprehensive guide for land development 521

General warranty deed 81; sample document 81

Gift deed: a deed that states "love and affection" as the consideration 88

Ginnie Mae: a real estate nickname for the Government National Mortgage Association 268

Good consideration: consideration without monetary value such as love and affection 132

Good faith estimate of closing costs 338

Good repair, covenant of 177

Government National Mortgage Association (GNMA): a government agency that sponsors a mortgage-backed securities program and provides low-income housing subsidies 268

Government rights in land 38; eminent domain 39; escheat 40; police power 40; property taxes 38

Government survey: a system for surveying land that uses latitude and longitude lines as references 23

Graduated payment mortgage: a fixed interest rate loan wherein the monthly payment starts low and then increases 279

Grant: the act of conveying ownership 77

Grant deed: a deed that is somewhat narrower than a warranty deed in terms of covenants and warranties 84; sample deed 85

Grantee: the person named in a deed who acquires ownership 77

Grantee index 106

Granting clause in a deed 82

Grantor: the person named in a deed who conveys ownership 77

Grantor-Grantee indexes: alphabetical lists used to locate documents in the public records 106

GRI (Graduate, Realtors Institute): a designation awarded to Realtors who complete a prescribed course of real estate study 423

Grid system: state-sponsored survey points to which metes and bounds surveys can be referenced 32

Gross lease: the tenant pays a fixed rent and the landlord pays all property expenses 350

Gross rent multiplier (GRM): a number that is multiplied by a property's gross rent to produce an estimate of the property's worth 371

Groundwater level: the upper limit of percolating water below the earth's surface 18

Growing equity mortgage: a fixed-rate loan with increasing monthly payments that pays off early 280

Guardian's deed: used to convey property of a minor or legally incompetent person 88

Guide meridians: survey lines running north and south that correct for the earth's curvature 24

H

Habendum clause: the "To have and to hold" clause found in deeds, part of the words of conveyance 83

Heirs: those designated by law to receive the property of the deceased when there is no will 89

Highest and best use: that use of a parcel of land which will produce the greatest current value 389

Holdover tenant: a tenant who stays beyond his lease period and who can be evicted or given a new lease 55, 345

Holographic will: one that is entirely handwritten and signed by the testator but not witnessed 91

Homeowner's association: condominium 494; prorating at closing 329

Homeownership: For coverage, *see* the specific topic for which you are interested, such as appraisal, condominiums, deeds, forms of ownership, insurance, listings, mortgages, offer and acceptance, taxation, title closing, title insurance, zoning, etc.

Home seller program: a plan whereby the FNMA will buy mortgages from home sellers 267

Homestead Act: allows persons to acquire fee title to federal lands 95

Homestead protection: state laws that protect against the forced sale of a person's home 52

House: construction *illustrated,* Appendix A; *See also Homeownership*

House rules: rules regarding day-to-day use of the premises; condominium 495; rentals 349

Housing: Equal Credit Opportunity Act 245

How to read this book 2

HUD: Department of Housing and Urban Development, GNMA 268; OILSR 468; RESPA 337; settlement statement 337

Hundred percent commission: an arrangement whereby the sales-person pays for office overhead directly rather than splitting commission income with his broker 412

Hypothecate: to use property to secure a debt without giving up possession of it 175

I

Illiquid asset: an asset that may be difficult to sell on short notice 246

Illiquidity: the possibility that it may be difficult to sell on short notice 290

Implied authority: agency authority arising from industry custom, common usage, and conduct of the parties involved 448

Implied contract: a contract created by the actions of the parties involved 123

Implied obligations 138

Impound or Reserved account: an account into which the lender places monthly tax and insurance payments 213; RESPA requirements 337

Improvement district: a geographical area which will be assessed for a local improvement 302

Improvements: any form of land development, such as buildings, roads, fences, pipelines, etc. 14

Income approach: a method of valuing property based on the monetary returns that a property can be expected to produce 360, 377

Income taxes: residence 305

Incurable depreciation: depreciation that cannot be fixed and simply must be lived with 376

Indemnification 460

Indenture: an agreement or contract 82

Independent contractor: one who contracts to do work according to his own methods and is responsible to his employer only for the results of that work 414; employee 414

Index lease: rent is tied to some economic indicator such as inflation 351

Index rate: the interest rate to which an adjustable mortgage is tied 276, 351

Indicated value: the worth of the subject property as shown by recent sales of comparable properties 367

Individuals as lenders 262, 285

Industrial brokerage 7

Informal reference: to identify a parcel of land by its street address or common name 19

Wall Street as a source of mortgage money 263

Warranty: an assurance or guarantee that something is true as stated 79

Warranty deed 147; a deed which usually contains the covenants of seizin, quiet enjoyment, encumbrances, further assurance, and warranty forever 81; sample document 80

Warranty forever: the grantor's guarantee that he will bear the expense of defending the grantee's title 79

Waste: abuse or destructive use of property 51

Water right: the right to use water on or below or bordering a parcel of land 18

Water table: the upper limit of percolating water below the earth's surface 18

Wills 89; "poor man's will" 67

Witnessing documents 104; wills 91

Wood rot 149

Words of conveyance: the grantor's statement that he is making a grant to the grantee 77

Wraparound deed of trust 286

Wraparound mortgage: a mortgage that encompasses existing mortgages and is subordinate to them 286

Writ of execution: a court document directing the county sheriff to seize and sell a debtor's property 49

Written contracts: when required 132

Z

Zoning laws 515